Lecture Notes in Computer Science

Lecture Notes in Artificial Intelligence   14734

Founding Editor

Jörg Siekmann

Series Editors

Randy Goebel, *University of Alberta, Edmonton, Canada*
Wolfgang Wahlster, *DFKI, Berlin, Germany*
Zhi-Hua Zhou, *Nanjing University, Nanjing, China*

The series Lecture Notes in Artificial Intelligence (LNAI) was established in 1988 as a topical subseries of LNCS devoted to artificial intelligence.

The series publishes state-of-the-art research results at a high level. As with the LNCS mother series, the mission of the series is to serve the international R & D community by providing an invaluable service, mainly focused on the publication of conference and workshop proceedings and postproceedings.

Helmut Degen · Stavroula Ntoa
Editors

Artificial Intelligence in HCI

5th International Conference, AI-HCI 2024
Held as Part of the 26th HCI International Conference, HCII 2024
Washington, DC, USA, June 29 – July 4, 2024
Proceedings, Part I

 Springer

Editors
Helmut Degen
Siemens Corporation
Princeton, NJ, USA

Stavroula Ntoa
Foundation for Research
and Technology – Hellas (FORTH)
Heraklion, Crete, Greece

ISSN 0302-9743   ISSN 1611-3349 (electronic)
Lecture Notes in Artificial Intelligence
ISBN 978-3-031-60605-2   ISBN 978-3-031-60606-9 (eBook)
https://doi.org/10.1007/978-3-031-60606-9

LNCS Sublibrary: SL7 – Artificial Intelligence

This Springer imprint is published by the registered company Springer Nature Switzerland AG
The registered company address is: Gewerbestrasse 11, 6330 Cham, Switzerland

If disposing of this product, please recycle the paper.

Foreword

This year we celebrate 40 years since the establishment of the HCI International (HCII) Conference, which has been a hub for presenting groundbreaking research and novel ideas and collaboration for people from all over the world.

The HCII conference was founded in 1984 by Prof. Gavriel Salvendy (Purdue University, USA, Tsinghua University, P.R. China, and University of Central Florida, USA) and the first event of the series, "1st USA-Japan Conference on Human-Computer Interaction", was held in Honolulu, Hawaii, USA, 18–20 August. Since then, HCI International is held jointly with several Thematic Areas and Affiliated Conferences, with each one under the auspices of a distinguished international Program Board and under one management and one registration. Twenty-six HCI International Conferences have been organized so far (every two years until 2013, and annually thereafter).

Over the years, this conference has served as a platform for scholars, researchers, industry experts and students to exchange ideas, connect, and address challenges in the ever-evolving HCI field. Throughout these 40 years, the conference has evolved itself, adapting to new technologies and emerging trends, while staying committed to its core mission of advancing knowledge and driving change.

As we celebrate this milestone anniversary, we reflect on the contributions of its founding members and appreciate the commitment of its current and past Affiliated Conference Program Board Chairs and members. We are also thankful to all past conference attendees who have shaped this community into what it is today.

The 26th International Conference on Human-Computer Interaction, HCI International 2024 (HCII 2024), was held as a 'hybrid' event at the Washington Hilton Hotel, Washington, DC, USA, during 29 June – 4 July 2024. It incorporated the 21 thematic areas and affiliated conferences listed below.

A total of 5108 individuals from academia, research institutes, industry, and government agencies from 85 countries submitted contributions, and 1271 papers and 309 posters were included in the volumes of the proceedings that were published just before the start of the conference, these are listed below. The contributions thoroughly cover the entire field of human-computer interaction, addressing major advances in knowledge and effective use of computers in a variety of application areas. These papers provide academics, researchers, engineers, scientists, practitioners and students with state-of-the-art information on the most recent advances in HCI.

The HCI International (HCII) conference also offers the option of presenting 'Late Breaking Work', and this applies both for papers and posters, with corresponding volumes of proceedings that will be published after the conference. Full papers will be included in the 'HCII 2024 - Late Breaking Papers' volumes of the proceedings to be published in the Springer LNCS series, while 'Poster Extended Abstracts' will be included as short research papers in the 'HCII 2024 - Late Breaking Posters' volumes to be published in the Springer CCIS series.

I would like to thank the Program Board Chairs and the members of the Program Boards of all thematic areas and affiliated conferences for their contribution towards the high scientific quality and overall success of the HCI International 2024 conference. Their manifold support in terms of paper reviewing (single-blind review process, with a minimum of two reviews per submission), session organization and their willingness to act as goodwill ambassadors for the conference is most highly appreciated.

This conference would not have been possible without the continuous and unwavering support and advice of Gavriel Salvendy, founder, General Chair Emeritus, and Scientific Advisor. For his outstanding efforts, I would like to express my sincere appreciation to Abbas Moallem, Communications Chair and Editor of HCI International News.

July 2024   Constantine Stephanidis

HCI International 2024 Thematic Areas and Affiliated Conferences

- HCI: Human-Computer Interaction Thematic Area
- HIMI: Human Interface and the Management of Information Thematic Area
- EPCE: 21st International Conference on Engineering Psychology and Cognitive Ergonomics
- AC: 18th International Conference on Augmented Cognition
- UAHCI: 18th International Conference on Universal Access in Human-Computer Interaction
- CCD: 16th International Conference on Cross-Cultural Design
- SCSM: 16th International Conference on Social Computing and Social Media
- VAMR: 16th International Conference on Virtual, Augmented and Mixed Reality
- DHM: 15th International Conference on Digital Human Modeling & Applications in Health, Safety, Ergonomics & Risk Management
- DUXU: 13th International Conference on Design, User Experience and Usability
- C&C: 12th International Conference on Culture and Computing
- DAPI: 12th International Conference on Distributed, Ambient and Pervasive Interactions
- HCIBGO: 11th International Conference on HCI in Business, Government and Organizations
- LCT: 11th International Conference on Learning and Collaboration Technologies
- ITAP: 10th International Conference on Human Aspects of IT for the Aged Population
- AIS: 6th International Conference on Adaptive Instructional Systems
- HCI-CPT: 6th International Conference on HCI for Cybersecurity, Privacy and Trust
- HCI-Games: 6th International Conference on HCI in Games
- MobiTAS: 6th International Conference on HCI in Mobility, Transport and Automotive Systems
- AI-HCI: 5th International Conference on Artificial Intelligence in HCI
- MOBILE: 5th International Conference on Human-Centered Design, Operation and Evaluation of Mobile Communications

List of Conference Proceedings Volumes Appearing Before the Conference

1. LNCS 14684, Human-Computer Interaction: Part I, edited by Masaaki Kurosu and Ayako Hashizume
2. LNCS 14685, Human-Computer Interaction: Part II, edited by Masaaki Kurosu and Ayako Hashizume
3. LNCS 14686, Human-Computer Interaction: Part III, edited by Masaaki Kurosu and Ayako Hashizume
4. LNCS 14687, Human-Computer Interaction: Part IV, edited by Masaaki Kurosu and Ayako Hashizume
5. LNCS 14688, Human-Computer Interaction: Part V, edited by Masaaki Kurosu and Ayako Hashizume
6. LNCS 14689, Human Interface and the Management of Information: Part I, edited by Hirohiko Mori and Yumi Asahi
7. LNCS 14690, Human Interface and the Management of Information: Part II, edited by Hirohiko Mori and Yumi Asahi
8. LNCS 14691, Human Interface and the Management of Information: Part III, edited by Hirohiko Mori and Yumi Asahi
9. LNAI 14692, Engineering Psychology and Cognitive Ergonomics: Part I, edited by Don Harris and Wen-Chin Li
10. LNAI 14693, Engineering Psychology and Cognitive Ergonomics: Part II, edited by Don Harris and Wen-Chin Li
11. LNAI 14694, Augmented Cognition, Part I, edited by Dylan D. Schmorrow and Cali M. Fidopiastis
12. LNAI 14695, Augmented Cognition, Part II, edited by Dylan D. Schmorrow and Cali M. Fidopiastis
13. LNCS 14696, Universal Access in Human-Computer Interaction: Part I, edited by Margherita Antona and Constantine Stephanidis
14. LNCS 14697, Universal Access in Human-Computer Interaction: Part II, edited by Margherita Antona and Constantine Stephanidis
15. LNCS 14698, Universal Access in Human-Computer Interaction: Part III, edited by Margherita Antona and Constantine Stephanidis
16. LNCS 14699, Cross-Cultural Design: Part I, edited by Pei-Luen Patrick Rau
17. LNCS 14700, Cross-Cultural Design: Part II, edited by Pei-Luen Patrick Rau
18. LNCS 14701, Cross-Cultural Design: Part III, edited by Pei-Luen Patrick Rau
19. LNCS 14702, Cross-Cultural Design: Part IV, edited by Pei-Luen Patrick Rau
20. LNCS 14703, Social Computing and Social Media: Part I, edited by Adela Coman and Simona Vasilache
21. LNCS 14704, Social Computing and Social Media: Part II, edited by Adela Coman and Simona Vasilache
22. LNCS 14705, Social Computing and Social Media: Part III, edited by Adela Coman and Simona Vasilache

47. LNCS 14730, HCI in Games: Part I, edited by Xiaowen Fang
48. LNCS 14731, HCI in Games: Part II, edited by Xiaowen Fang
49. LNCS 14732, HCI in Mobility, Transport and Automotive Systems: Part I, edited by Heidi Krömker
50. LNCS 14733, HCI in Mobility, Transport and Automotive Systems: Part II, edited by Heidi Krömker
51. LNAI 14734, Artificial Intelligence in HCI: Part I, edited by Helmut Degen and Stavroula Ntoa
52. LNAI 14735, Artificial Intelligence in HCI: Part II, edited by Helmut Degen and Stavroula Ntoa
53. LNAI 14736, Artificial Intelligence in HCI: Part III, edited by Helmut Degen and Stavroula Ntoa
54. LNCS 14737, Design, Operation and Evaluation of Mobile Communications: Part I, edited by June Wei and George Margetis
55. LNCS 14738, Design, Operation and Evaluation of Mobile Communications: Part II, edited by June Wei and George Margetis
56. CCIS 2114, HCI International 2024 Posters - Part I, edited by Constantine Stephanidis, Margherita Antona, Stavroula Ntoa and Gavriel Salvendy
57. CCIS 2115, HCI International 2024 Posters - Part II, edited by Constantine Stephanidis, Margherita Antona, Stavroula Ntoa and Gavriel Salvendy
58. CCIS 2116, HCI International 2024 Posters - Part III, edited by Constantine Stephanidis, Margherita Antona, Stavroula Ntoa and Gavriel Salvendy
59. CCIS 2117, HCI International 2024 Posters - Part IV, edited by Constantine Stephanidis, Margherita Antona, Stavroula Ntoa and Gavriel Salvendy
60. CCIS 2118, HCI International 2024 Posters - Part V, edited by Constantine Stephanidis, Margherita Antona, Stavroula Ntoa and Gavriel Salvendy
61. CCIS 2119, HCI International 2024 Posters - Part VI, edited by Constantine Stephanidis, Margherita Antona, Stavroula Ntoa and Gavriel Salvendy
62. CCIS 2120, HCI International 2024 Posters - Part VII, edited by Constantine Stephanidis, Margherita Antona, Stavroula Ntoa and Gavriel Salvendy

https://2024.hci.international/proceedings

Preface

The 5th International Conference on Artificial Intelligence in HCI (AI-HCI 2024), an affiliated conference of the HCI International conference, aimed to bring together academics, practitioners, and students to exchange results from academic and industrial research, as well as industrial experiences, on the use of artificial intelligence (AI) technologies to enhance human-computer interaction (HCI).

The rapid progress of AI, witnessing advancements across numerous domains, has transformed it from a research and academic field to a service available to the wide public, a landmark which has been recently achieved. In this rapidly evolving context, Human-Centered Artificial Intelligence has garnered the interest of researchers and scholars, emphasizing the seamless integration of AI technologies into human activities through well-planned design and development, and the prioritization of human values and well-being. Submissions explored user requirements and perceptions of AI systems, discussed evaluation aspects, and proposed frameworks to foster user participation in AI decision-making. Furthermore, papers delved into issues related to explainability and transparency, encompassing user studies, design principles, frameworks for explainable AI, and approaches to explanations of neural networks. Trust in AI and ethical considerations have constituted inspiring avenues of research, with contributions investigating issues related to fair representations, bias identification, responsible AI and the role of designers, ethical constraints, as well as trust formation and repair. Further, contributions included in the proceedings also addressed the role of AI systems in HCI. From methods to design AI systems to the use of AI tools in design, authors have illuminated the interplay between these two fields offering rich insights into aspects such as co-creation, interaction design, evaluation, but also information uncertainty, human annotation, emotion recognition, and gamification. Finally, numerous papers have explored application domains within the realm of AI in HCI across various contexts, such as immersive environments, industrial AI, e-Commerce, cultural heritage and learning. As editors of the proceedings of AI-HCI 2024, we are proud to present this outstanding collection of research contributions, which demonstrate the intricate interplay between AI and HCI and how they are shaping our future technological environments.

Three volumes of the HCII 2024 proceedings are dedicated to this year's edition of the AI-HCI conference. The first focuses on topics related to Human-Centered Artificial Intelligence, Explainability and Transparency, and AI Systems and Frameworks in HCI. The second focuses on topics related to Ethical Considerations and Trust in AI, Enhancing User Experience Through AI-Driven Technologies, and AI in Industry and Operations. Finally, the third focuses on topics related to Large Language Models for Enhanced Interaction, Advancing Human-Robot Interaction Through AI, and AI Applications for Social Impact and Human Wellbeing.

The papers in the AI-HCI 2024 volumes were accepted for publication after a minimum of two single-blind reviews from the members of the AI-HCI Program Board or, in some cases, from members of the Program Boards of other affiliated conferences. We would like to thank all of them for their invaluable contribution, support, and efforts.

July 2024

Helmut Degen
Stavroula Ntoa

5th International Conference on Artificial Intelligence in HCI (AI-HCI 2024)

The full list with the Program Board Chairs and the members of the Program Boards of all thematic areas and affiliated conferences of HCII 2024 is available online at:

http://www.hci.international/board-members-2024.php

HCI International 2025 Conference

The 27th International Conference on Human-Computer Interaction, HCI International 2025, will be held jointly with the affiliated conferences at the Swedish Exhibition & Congress Centre and Gothia Towers Hotel, Gothenburg, Sweden, June 22–27, 2025. It will cover a broad spectrum of themes related to Human-Computer Interaction, including theoretical issues, methods, tools, processes, and case studies in HCI design, as well as novel interaction techniques, interfaces, and applications. The proceedings will be published by Springer. More information will become available on the conference website: https://2025.hci.international/.

General Chair
Prof. Constantine Stephanidis
University of Crete and ICS-FORTH
Heraklion, Crete, Greece
Email: general_chair@2025.hci.international

https://2025.hci.international/

Contents – Part I

Explainability and Transparency

AI Systems and Frameworks in HCI

Contents – Part II

Enhancing User Experience Through AI-Driven Technologies

AI in Industry and Operations

Contents – Part III

Human-Centered Artificial Intelligence

Qualitative User-Centered Requirements Analysis for a Recommender System for a Project Portfolio Platform in Higher Education Institutions

Giulio Behringer[(✉)], Svenja Rößler[(✉)], and Mahsa Fischer[(✉)] [iD]

Heilbronn University, Max-Planck-Street 39, 74081 Heilbronn, Germany
{giulio.behringer,svenja.roessler,mahsa.fischer}@hs-heilbronn.de

Abstract. The integration of digital technologies in education has led to major changes, including the rise of project-based work. However, learners often face challenges in navigating through the abundance of available resources. To tackle this issue, a recommender system is being designed to support a digital project portfolio platform. The system aims to improve transparency, networking, collaboration, and cooperation among educational stakeholders. Personalised recommendations are crucial to match resources to individual learners' needs, improve their experience and foster potential collaborations and entrepreneurial ideas. To achieve this goal, understanding the learner's requirements is essential. This study aims to investigate the needs of students in the development of a recommendation system for a project portfolio platform in education through an extensive literature review and qualitative semi-structured interviews. The study involved interviews with seven students from different study programs and educational departments using pre-designed mockups and presentation slides. The results showed that students considered the use of a user-centred recommendation system for a project portfolio platform in educational institutions to be important and valuable. Further research could include other study programs in the qualitative survey. The representativeness of the overall findings can then be evaluated using quantitative methods.

Keywords: Recommender Systems · Human-Computer Interaction · Education

1 Introduction and Motivation

The advance of information and communication technologies has had a major impact on education. Online education, in particular, is widely promoted and appreciated by most learners [59, 62]. By combining traditional teaching methods with Internet technology, online education overcomes the limitations of time, space and environment of traditional education. It also enables the sharing and

Supported by Stiftung Innovation in der Hochschullehre.

H. Degen and S. Ntoa (Eds.): HCII 2024, LNAI 14734, pp. 3–19, 2024.
https://doi.org/10.1007/978-3-031-60606-9_1

reuse of educational resources. [20,69]. Particular attention is paid to project-based work at educational institutions. Every semester, numerous innovative ideas and projects emerge at educational institutions, many of which remain unexplored. Furthermore, disciplinary boundaries are becoming blurred as research questions can be addressed through the collaborative interaction of multiple disciplines [26,47]. As a result, learners are faced with difficulties such as information overload and learning loss. It can be challenging for them to filter out the information they need from the vast amount of learning resources [50]. For this reason, the focus of personalised learning is on offering suitable learning resources that meet the individual needs and requirements of different learners [8].

The research project IdeaLize is funded by Stiftung Innovation in der Hochschullehre and tackles this issue for project based work in education by developing a digital platform to present projects, ideas, and skills in a transparent manner, while also fostering networking and collaboration among educational institution stakeholders. Projects can be managed in a more sustainable way, and the resulting knowledge can be shared and easily viewed through a project portfolio. This fosters inspiration for collaborative projects as well as initiating startups, and provides opportunities for students and faculty to connect and exchange ideas across locations and academic disciplines [25].

In this context, recommender systems play an important role by providing learners with relevant resources and information. Nowadays, recommender systems have become an integral part of a person's everyday life and support keeping the focus on the huge amount of information [40]. Aside from common applications such as online stores or streaming services, recommender systems can also be used in education to provide value to users [55,64]. The primary aim of recommender systems is to automatically provide a precise recommendation that could be particularly useful for the user. In this context, collaborative, content-based or context-based filters are often used to generate recommendations. In addition, the generation of recommendations can be personalised or non-personalised [71]. This can lead to new opportunities such as potential collaborations, the identification of interesting inspirations, and entrepreneurial ideas [25]. As the relevance of recommender systems increases, so does the need for research into user-centred design and development. Furthermore, recommendations need to be provided to the user in a way that gives them the best experience [10,18,36,45]. As a result, user feedback plays an important role in the design and development process of the recommender system. Studies show that it is important for the success of a project to record and understand the project requirements right from the start [15,44]. Moreover, the satisfaction of users is an important indicator to evaluate the acceptance of a recommendation system, in addition to the effectiveness of algorithms [41,66].

The study focuses on the qualitative requirements analysis of a recommendation system in the educational context for project-based work, through semi-structured interviews. Derived from this, the following research question arises:

– What student needs are important to consider when designing a recommendation system?

In detail, the following sub-questions will be answered:

- What project information is valuable to students in a condensed overview and in a detailed view?
- What are important reasons for students, to connect with projects and individuals?
- Which interaction possibilities with projects are particularly relevant to students?
- How do students perceive the ability to customize the recommendation algorithm according to their needs?
- What criteria related to project-based recommendations are particularly important to students?

2 Related Work

In many academic degree programs, students are assessed on their knowledge and skills through **projects**. This provides students with development and management experience similar to that gained in industry. Despite their common focus on assessing student learning outcomes, the projects are diverse and can be categorised according to different aspects. When selecting a project, it is important to consider factors such as potential industry players and the interaction between students, the teacher, and potential companies. Additionally, the project description is a crucial aspect [51]. The project description is one of the most important sources of information, especially in the early stages of project development. These are often unproven technologies, unfinished products or services that can be better understood with the help of the project description [49,70].The timeliness of project data is another important concern. Old project data loses relevance and predictive power for newly created projects [70].

Research on **project-based teaching** [31,33,42,46,48,61,63] highlights the benefits for both students and teachers, such as increasing teachers' teaching skills [42]. [33] showed the improvement of students' reading skills with the help of project-based teaching. There is also research on mechanisms and influencing factors in the context of project-based teaching. [21] explain important factors for collaboration, such as the willingness to collaborate, the benefits, the collaboration mechanism and the system itself. For the latter, [43] refer to specially developed software applications, so-called **learning management systems**, which play an important role in achieving goals in educational institutions. On the one hand, learning management systems offer the opportunity to exchange ideas and information on projects and provide feedback. On the other hand, the system is ideal for collaboration [34,43]. In addition, a high degree of **personalisation** is an important component for a successful platform in the education sector. Personalisation is essential, especially in the context of e-learning structures, as the backgrounds and needs, goals and interests, as well as the abilities and personalities of the large number of learners differ [35,38]. One potential method for achieving a high level of personalisation is through the use of recommendation systems.

[52]. Especially in the context of increasing variety, **recommendation systems** become indispensable to help users navigate through the millions or billions of content available on platforms [17]. In practice, learners may find themselves in an interactive environment that offers a wide range of actions to take, but they often do not have a clear view of which of these are more relevant to their own needs. Here, we can utilise the well-established research on recommender systems. Specifically, recommender systems can guide users in a personalised manner, thereby reducing information overload [14,56]. These systems are designed to meet users' information needs by predicting their future interests [39,57].

Recommender systems help the user to identify objects that are of particular interest to the user from an unmanageable number of objects [71]. In general, the use of **recommender systems in education** are becoming more and more popular [9]. Fields of application are e.g. the recommendation of the appropriate student learning group [55] or of specific learning content [65]. Furthermore, recommender systems are used to support students in the subject enrollment decision [24] and for personalized learning path [54]. Overall, the research literature on recommender systems in education dealing with technology-enhanced learning is diverse and extensive [54].

The main categories of recommender systems include collaborative, content-based, and hybrid **recommendation methods** [60]. Collaborative filtering generates recommendations based on similar users [3,4,6,58]. Content-based filtering is created based on content analysis [7]. Furthermore, knowledge-based filtering here focuses on domain-specific knowledge and trade-offs [3]. Hybrid filtering can be used to minimise the weaknesses of individual recommendation methods. In this case, two or more recommendation methods are combined with each other [7]. Contextual filters and demographic filters have been identified in the literature but do not apply to the research project.

A promising approach comes from the area of social media platforms. When creating content, the focus of social media platforms is on the individual user. Success depends largely on the constant involvement and participation of users [12,13]. Therefore, interest-based discovery has become the key factor in the creation and distribution of new content [67]. Collaborative filtering and supervised learning methods for predicting users' immediate reactions to recommendations, such as clicks, dwell time, likes, have been very successful [16,19,68].

Open areas of research concern the use of artificial intelligence in recommender system algorithms to enhance the personalisation of academic choices, and the need to account for diversity in learner profiles and characteristics [53]. Recently, there has been a trend towards **interactive recommender systems**. This allows users to interact with the generated recommendation and provide feedback that can influence the outcome in real time [2]. This approach supports a variety of system actions, such as providing endorsements to students and preference elicitation, as well as user responses, including indirect and direct feedback. By enabling richer forms of mixed-mode interactions, interactive recommender systems can be applied to enhance the user experience [27]. Nevertheless, the user should not be overwhelmed with interaction options and information. Therefore, [11] defines five triggers to control the cognitive load of users.

3 Gaps in Literature

Significant challenges arise in the context of project work at educational institutions. In particular, the interaction of all stakeholders involved: students, teaching staff and possibly industry partners must be managed. In addition, a suitable project description and ultimately also an evaluation of the project are required [51].

In addition to the opportunities presented by content discovery through user interactions on platforms, there are also challenges. One such challenge is cognitive overload experienced by users [11,67]. This problem has been present since the 1990s, but its significance is increasing with the growing number of users and content being produced [22,28,37]. The heterogeneity of media content presents an additional challenge. In addition to textual content, large amounts of data can also be presented in the form of images, videos, or other online user traffic data [29]. An outcome of information overload is stress, which ultimately leads to disengagement [23].

Some platforms have implemented various interaction options, such as Facebook's 'Like' function, filter options using 'hashtags', or star ratings for products on Amazon. These approaches have improved the recommendation system, but they are increasingly reaching their limits. The recommendation systems' focus on short-term reactions, such as clicks, means that they do not take the long-term effects into account. Additionally, the lack of exploration causes these systems to increasingly focus on known user interests, creating a satisfaction effect. It is important to consider the long-term impact of recommendations and to explore new user interests to avoid creating a biased user experience [1,17].

In addition to recommendation accuracy, other factors now play a significant role in the quality of a recommendation, contributing to the user's overall experience on the platform [17]. [32] used various metrics to measure recommendation quality, including reach, novelty, and serendipity. Diversity is also an important aspect that has already been analysed by [5,30].

4 Methodology

The goal of this study is to identify the requirements for a recommendation system in an educational environment for a project based, digital platform. To align development and the needs of users, interviews were conducted with individuals from the target group. For these qualitative semi-structured Interviews, students from different study programs and backgrounds have participated in this study.

The Table 1 below presents the background information of the interviewees. The semi-structured interviews were conducted at three locations of the univesity of Heilbronn: Heilbronn Bildungscmapus (four participants), Heilbronn Sontheim (two participants), and Künzelsau (one particiapant). In total seven participants took part in the study and shared their experiences and ideas for a recommendation system in an educational environement.

Table 1. General background information on the interviewed students.

Student	Bachelor's Degree	Master's Degree	Study program	Location
1	X	–	Computer Science	Bildungscampus
2	X	–	Computer Science	Bildungscampus
3	X	–	Industrial Eng	Künzelsau
4	X	–	Business Eng. Logistics	Sontheim
5	–	X	Digital Transformation	Bildungscampus
6	–	X	Business Management	Bildungscampus
2	X	–	Software Eng	Sontheim

Although five students were at bachelor's level, the rest of the students belong to master's degree. All the participants have experience in project work in education at different levels of intensity.

The interview questions were based on mockups and presentation slides prepared in advance. The scenarios presented required the students to put themselves in a particular situation in order to answer the questions. The students were introduced to the concept of the project portfolio platform to be developed and were shown mockups of the platform's login process as an introduction to the interview. During the test scenarios they were asked about the topics of:

1. Project information in preview and detailed view
2. Connecting with people and projects
3. Interactions
4. Personal recommendations

The first area regarding the project information consisted of two steps. Firstly, open-ended questions were asked without any pre-given examples. Secondly, the interviewer presented brainstormed information from the development team, which was openly discussed with the interviewees. The remaining areas of the interview consisted of an initial scenario combined with the question the students needed to answer along with their experiences and expectations. The interviews were transcribed, paraphrased, and then categorized and evaluated using an inductive approach.

5   Object of Investigation

The focus of the research was the development of an open innovation university platform for students, lecturers, and employees. This platform has the aim to connect the members of different locations and study programs to enhance interdisciplinary work and make projects more visible. Project work is an essential part of universities of applied sciences and is often limited to the period of one semester.

6   Results

6.1   Project Overview and Detailed Information

The first goal of the interviews was to identify the needed project information for the project overview and the detailed page that is needed to give more insight to the students. If the platform provides relevant information to the students, the platform could be used as an overview of existing projects. The students were asked about the needed information to catch their interests.

Title of the Project. All interviewees considered the project title to be a standard feature, and some even didn't mention it. They confirmed that this information is so normal to them that they couldn't think of a project without knowing the title. Two of them who came up with this by themselves put focus on the importance of a good chosen title. They pointed out the relevance of a title that is short and meaningful to catch the interest for the project.

Project Image. The statements of the interviewees for visual representation of the projects were ambivalent. Although the relevance of an image for drawing attention to the projects was mentioned, there were doubts as to whether there would be enough interesting visual material available for the type of student and research projects, which are often technically related. The fear was also expressed that similar images of computers and software code would always be used for similar projects, e.g. in computer science.

Categorization. Based on the responses of the students interviewed, thematic allocation is one of the most important factors. This could be done, for instance, by assigning overarching subject areas, e.g. technology, economics, computer science, ... or, more specifically, by specifying the individual study programs and their overlapping subject areas, e.g. business informatics in combination with computer science and business administration. The assignment must be easy to understand, e.g. by using clear symbols, so as not to distract from the actual topic. It is particularly important for the project creator to assign the project to students who have specialist knowledge in the field and can therefore provide qualified help and constructive feedback better than someone not specialized in the field.

Status and Progress. Additionally, there were several requests to display an overview of the project's progress. The importance of this information was explained as follows: when considering joining a project, the project's status is a decisive factor. It is not sufficient to only seek support in the early stages; it is necessary to know which phase the project is in, to better assess both motivation and effort. Furthermore, for more advanced projects, they can serve as inspiration, while for projects at a similar stage, exchanging experiences with like-minded individuals was mentioned as an advantage. In conclusion, the emphasis appears to be on the status information rather than a particular development phase.

Others. Some Elements that are known from other platforms were mentioned by single persons and could be interesting for specific use cases. For example, the amount of time that needs to be spent to read the full amount of information. This feature could be known mostly from newspaper, blog or article websites and apps. Another single mentioned information is the number of team members that are participating in the project. There were differing opinions regarding the rating, the advantage was mentioned that a rating by professors is suitable as an indicator of the quality of the project. Chapter 6.3 summarizes additional findings on the topic of interaction. In general, the students agreed that the presentation should be well-structured and concise. The preview is meant to generate interest based on thematic connections rather than the number of interactions.

Additional Information on the Detailed Project View. All interviewees agreed that a **project description** is particularly important when a user decides to open a project for more details after showing initial interest from the overview page. After visiting the homepage, users expressed curiosity about various aspects of the project, such as its problem statement, purpose, and intended outcomes. It was agreed that the project description should provide a clear and concise summary that introduces the user to the topic without concealing the complexity of the issue. If the project owners intend to seek assistance from others, it is important to clearly define the necessary skills and experience required for the helper. The familiar forms of a project flyer or abstract were mentioned here. Two interviewees drew a comparison with the information that would typically be included in project documentation, such as the **project period, semester, supervising lecturer, and team members** involved. Additionally, two interviewees expressed the desire for a **project or milestone plan** as supplementary information. They believe that the viewer should be able to understand the current status and get access to new updates. The interest in a project status already mentioned in the first part is mentioned again here. To make it easier for interested individuals to engage with the topic without having to read the entire project documentation, it was suggested by one interviewee to include **relevant literature**.

6.2   Connecting People and Projects

The second objective was to find out what opportunities arise from linking people and projects. In particular, the focus was on the additional information that students need to see the benefits of such connections. During the interviews, a distinction was made between networking with other people and networking with other projects.

People to People. Various points were mentioned for connecting with other people. With regard to the platform presented in the context of the university, the opportunity to find out about the skills and knowledge of other students was mentioned, among other things. As motivation, the interviewees stated, for example, that this would give them an impression of their own abilities in relation to job hunting or to find out about skills learned in related degree programs. These statements can be summarized under the interest in assessing one's own competitiveness. In addition, visiting another user's profile was motivated by an interest in the projects created by this person. Overall, the interest in matching and finding other projects was rated higher than matching with people. One reason for this was the existence of other platforms such as LinkedIn that fulfill this need. However, contact with other people on the platform was considered important when it came to collaborating on a project. When collaborating with others, easy and quick networking and contact with other project members was mentioned as a crucial point.

People to Projects. The statements made in relation to projects can be broadly categorised into three areas. Some mentions relate to the thematic connection between the projects and the user's own study and project interests. The following points were listed as relevant here. The interest in the literature used in similar projects, the opportunity to gain new perspectives on the topic dealt with, and the exchange between these projects to learn something for one's project or approach. The main motivation for networking with other projects was mainly due to the added value for their work or learning new skills. Even if the interviewees considered collaboration on other projects to be rather unrealistic due to a lack of time, they named the following points as particularly relevant in the event of collaboration. Get to know the team before starting the content-related collaboration and the possibility to contact them easily and quickly during the collaboration.

6.3   Interaction

The aim of the Interaction category was to determine the advantages and disadvantages associated with different types of interaction, as well as identifying any existing preferences. In general, the Inteviewpartners mentioned that the interviewees stated that their interest in a project would not be affected by the amount of interaction, regardless of whether the project topic was relevant to them or not.

Rating. Various aspects were evaluated using a star rating system. Students find this method familiar and easy to understand. However, doubts were raised about the assumption that the person awarding the stars had thoroughly reviewed the project. Project ratings are often criticised for being subjective and lacking in detail. They provide little information about the quality of the project and are typically limited to either very good or very bad ratings. To improve differentiation, evaluations could be separated by groups such as professors and students, or people from within and outside the department.

Comments. The students saw a particular advantage in the combination of ratings and comments. By giving reasons for the evaluation, it is significantly more relevant than without reasons. Comments were seen as irrelevant to connecting with projects. To provide truly relevant feedback on the projects, students face the issue that the projects are only presented as an overview, lacking the necessary details for meaningful feedback.

Likes. In contrast to star ratings, likes are considered to be a personal opinion rather than an assessment of the quality of the projects. Awarding likes is simple and corresponds to common patterns in social media. The use of different emojis as ratings was perceived as simple but not essential.

Views. Showing the amount of views, was not important at all.

6.4 Personal Recommendation

The final section addresses two main topics: the students' preferred recommendation metrics and their individual influence on the recommendation algorithm. Prioritising the relevance and diversity of recommendations for students is an essential factor. It is important to have a balanced mix of relevant projects based on individual interests and abilities, as well as diverse projects in related areas of interest. Additionally, it should be possible to remove unwanted recommendations. This leads to the second aspect of influencing the recommendation algorithm. In general, students should be able to customise the recommendation algorithm according to their preferences and ideas. The option for students to provide positive feedback for interesting projects via a 'Like' function is considered very useful. It is important to distinguish clearly between the 'Like' and comment functions, which should relate to the respective project and not to the recommendation algorithm. If a student is consistently given uninteresting assignments, they should have the option to provide feedback through a Like/Dislike button. This action should permanently remove the project from the recommendations.

7 Discussion and Critical Appraisal

All interviewees had a positive attitude towards the use of a recommendation system for the project portfolio platform in order to avoid losing track of the mass of projects in the university environment.

The results of the study highlight the importance of providing a **project overview and detailed information** to students when presenting projects on educational platforms. The findings suggest that students value key elements such as project title, categorization, as well as the status and progress updates, and additional information in the project overview. The respondents' statements on the visual presentation of the projects were ambiguous and were critically analysed. One key aspect identified in the study is the significance of a well-chosen project title. Students emphasized the importance of a title that is short and meaningful to capture their interest in a project. In line with the statements from the literature [49,51,70] on project description, students want in the detail project view a clear and concise description. This is crucial for users who want more detailed information after the initial expression of interest, such as the problem, the purpose and the results. Furthermore, the project period, semester, etc. were occasionally mentioned by students, which according to [70] are also important.

Moreover, **networking with other students** can be useful for them for a number of reasons. One significant reason is to evaluate their own competitiveness by learning about the skills and knowledge of other students. Additionally, networking allows students to discover the projects of others and potentially collaborate on them. When it comes to collaboration, students value the convenience and speed of getting in touch with project members. When it comes to **networking among students and projects**, other aspects play an important role. One important reason is to establish thematic connections between their own study and project interests. This allows them to explore the literature used in similar projects and gain new perspectives on the topic at hand. Networking with other projects also provides an opportunity for students to exchange ideas and learn from each other, ultimately adding value to their own work and facilitating the acquisition of new skills. Although collaboration on other projects may be difficult due to time constraints, students appreciate the opportunity to become acquainted with project teams before collaborating and to maintain open communication throughout the collaborative process. The findings identified from networking from person to person and from person to project lead to the conclusion that the use of an learning management systems is suitable for the exchange of ideas and information. It also offers the ideal conditions for collaboration [34, 43].

Furthermore, the results also revealed preferred **interaction** options that are most relevant for students. Students consider interaction opportunities with projects to be particularly important for receiving feedback and evaluations. While star ratings are familiar [1], there are concerns about their depth of review and subjectivity. To enhance feedback quality, combining ratings with comments is seen as advantageous. The Like function is an integral part of many social media platforms [17]. From the findings of the study, it is clear that likes are not a desirable way for students to interact with a portfolio platform. Likes are seen by students as less informative for evaluating project quality than comments. Students appreciate receiving detailed feedback mechanisms that go beyond superficial ratings or views when interacting with projects.

The study also provided insightful findings with regard to **personalized recommendations**. Students perceive the ability to customize the recommendation algorithm to their needs as crucial for receiving relevant and diverse project recommendations. They prioritize the relevance and diversity of recommendations, seeking a balanced mix of projects aligned with their interests and abilities, as well as exposure to diverse projects in related areas. In contrast to traditional evaluation methods, such as the Accuracy Score, students prefer other factors, such as diversity [5, 17, 30]. The option to remove unwanted recommendations is essential for refining the selection process. Criteria related to project-based recommendations that are particularly important to students include the ability to provide feedback through like/dislike buttons, ensuring that they can influence the algorithm based on their preferences and interests. In comparison with current research, the trend can be confirmed that a high degree of personalization is desired and required [35, 38].

Fundamentally, some critical aspects must be outlined in the context of this scientific work. Most interviewees were from the technology-oriented courses and based at the two university campuses in Heilbronn. To ensure the study's significance, it is important to provide all students from different study programs with an opportunity to express their opinions. Furthermore, a follow-up study must significantly increase the number of respondents to make a representative statement on the requirements for a recommendation system for a project portfolio platform.

8   Conclusion and Outlook

This article investigates students' requirements for a recommendation system for a project portfolio platform in the education sector. The goal is to identify the needs of students, as these form the foundation for the development of a recommendation system. The data was collected through semi-structured interviews with seven students from the University of Heilbronn. All participants had experience with project work at universities with different approaches due to the different degree programs and the different locations of the university.

The results showed that all interviewees consider the use of a recommendation system for a project portfolio platform at educational institutions to be important and valuable. A meaningful title and categorisation are essential for arousing interest in the project overview. In the detailed view, the main focus should be on the project description. Furthermore, the results provide important insights into the reasons why students consider networking with projects and people important. In addition to a high degree of personalisation, the results showed that a combination of rating and comments is desired in terms of the preferred interaction option.

This study focuses on student needs regarding a recommender system for a poject portfolio platform in an educational environement. It would be beneficial to extend the study to other study programs and universities and to explore how the results can be transferred to a recommendation system for a project portfolio platform.

The interviews covered the perspective of the students and collected their experiences and learnings. The next steps will be to quantitatively evaluate the findings from the interviews. In addition, it would be useful to gather information from the perspective of teachers and cooperating companies to get a more comprehensive picture.

References

1. Aggarwal, C.C.: An Introduction to Recommender Systems, pp. 1–28. Springer International Publishing, Cham (2016)
2. Alkan, O., Daly, E.M., Botea, A.: An evaluation framework for interactive recommender systems. In: Adjunct Publication of the 27th Conference on User Modeling, Adaptation and Personalization, UMAP 2019 Adjunct, pp. 217–218. Association for Computing Machinery, New York (2019). https://doi.org/10.1145/3314183.3323680
3. Almonte, L., Guerra, E., Cantador, I., Lara, J.: Recommender systems in model-driven engineering. Softw. Syst. Modeling, 1–32 (2021)
4. Alshammari, M.: An explainable recommender system based on semantically-aware matrix factorization. Ph.D. thesis, University of Louisville, August 2019. https://doi.org/10.18297/etd/3273
5. Anderson, A., Maystre, L., Anderson, I., Mehrotra, R., Lalmas, M.: Algorithmic effects on the diversity of consumption on spotify. In: Proceedings of The Web Conference 2020, WWW 2020, pp. 2155–2165. Association for Computing Machinery, New York (2020). https://doi.org/10.1145/3366423.3380281
6. André, E., Dybkjær, L., Minker, W., Neumann, H., Pieraccini, R., Weber, M. (eds.): PIT 2008. LNCS (LNAI), vol. 5078. Springer, Heidelberg (2008). https://doi.org/10.1007/978-3-540-69369-7
7. Ardissono, L., Kuflik, T. (eds.): UMAP 2011. LNCS, vol. 7138. Springer, Heidelberg (2012). https://doi.org/10.1007/978-3-642-28509-7
8. Baral, R., Li, T.: Exploiting the roles of aspects in personalized poi recommender systems. Data Min. Knowl. Disc. **32**, 320–343 (2018)
9. Barria-Pineda, J.: Exploring the need for transparency in educational recommender systems. In: Proceedings of the 28th ACM Conference on User Modeling, Adaptation and Personalization, UMAP 2020, pp. 376–379. Association for Computing Machinery, New York (2020). https://doi.org/10.1145/3340631.3398676
10. Beel, J., Dixon, H.: The 'unreasonable' effectiveness of graphical user interfaces for recommender systems. In: Adjunct Proceedings of the 29th ACM Conference on User Modeling, Adaptation and Personalization, pp. 22–28 (2021)
11. Belabbes, M.A., Ruthven, I., Moshfeghi, Y., Rasmussen Pennington, D.: Information overload: a concept analysis. J. Documentation **79**(1), 144–159 (2023)
12. Beyer, Y., Enli, G.S., Maasø, A.J., Ytreberg, E.: Small talk makes a big difference: recent developments in interactive, sms-based television. Telev. New Media **8**(3), 213–234 (2007)
13. Boyd, D.M., Ellison, N.B.: Social network sites: definition, history, and scholarship. J. Comput.-Mediat. Commun. **13**(1), 210–230 (2007)
14. Burke, R.: Hybrid recommender systems: survey and experiments. User Model. User-Adapted Interact. **12** (2002). https://doi.org/10.1023/A:1021240730564
15. Chen, L., de Gemmis, M., Felfernig, A., Lops, P., Ricci, F., Semeraro, G.: Human decision making and recommender systems. ACM Trans. Interact. Intell. Syst. **3**(3) (2013). https://doi.org/10.1145/2533670.2533675
16. Chen, M., et al.: Values of user exploration in recommender systems. In: Proceedings of the 15th ACM Conference on Recommender Systems, RecSys 2021, pp. 85–95, Association for Computing Machinery, New York (2021). https://doi.org/10.1145/3460231.3474236

17. Chen, M., et al.: Values of user exploration in recommender systems. In: Proceedings of the 15th ACM Conference on Recommender Systems, RecSys 2021, pp. 85–95. Association for Computing Machinery, New York (2021). https://doi.org/10.1145/3460231.3474236

18. Cosley, D., Lam, S.K., Albert, I., Konstan, J.A., Riedl, J.: Is seeing believing? how recommender system interfaces affect users' opinions. In: Proceedings of the SIGCHI Conference on Human Factors in Computing Systems, pp. 585–592 (2003)

19. Covington, P., Adams, J., Sargin, E.: Deep neural networks for youtube recommendations. In: Proceedings of the 10th ACM Conference on Recommender Systems, RecSys 2016, pp. 191–198. Association for Computing Machinery, New York (2016). https://doi.org/10.1145/2959100.2959190

20. Cui, L.Z., Guo, F.L., Liang, Y.j.: Research overview of educational recommender systems. In: Proceedings of the 2nd International Conference on Computer Science and Application Engineering, CSAE 2018. Association for Computing Machinery, New York (2018). https://doi.org/10.1145/3207677.3278071

21. Cui, X., Xing, L.: Research on my country's industry-university-research cooperation model and restricting factors–based on the perspective of the government, enterprises, and universities. Sci. Technol. Manag. Res. **6** (2010)

22. Edmunds, A., Morris, A.: The problem of information overload in business organisations: a review of the literature. Int. J. Inf. Manage. **20**(1), 17–28 (2000)

23. Eppler, M.J., Mengis, J.: The Concept of Information Overload - A Review of Literature from Organization Science, Accounting, Marketing, MIS, and Related Disciplines (2004), pp. 271–305. Gabler, Wiesbaden (2008)

24. Fernández-García, A.J., Rodríguez-Echeverría, R., Preciado, J.C., Manzano, J.M.C., Sánchez-Figueroa, F.: Creating a recommender system to support higher education students in the subject enrollment decision. IEEE Access **8**, 189069–189088 (2020)

25. Fischer, M.: Idealize (2023). https://www.hs-heilbronn.de/de/idealize (Accessed: 10 Jan 2024)

26. Fischer, M., Rößler, S., Szafarski, D.: Enhancing reusability in computer science project work: a qualitative exploration in Germany and Finland. In: ICERI2023 Proceedings, 16th annual International Conference of Education, Research and Innovation, IATED, pp. 2783–2792. 13-15 November (2023). https://doi.org/10.21125/iceri.2023.0729

27. Fotopoulou, E., Zafeiropoulos, A., Feidakis, M., Metafas, D., Papavassiliou, S.: An interactive recommender system based on reinforcement learning for improving emotional competences in educational groups. In: Kumar, V., Troussas, C. (eds.) Intelligent Tutoring Systems, pp. 248–258. Springer International Publishing, Cham (2020). https://doi.org/10.1007/978-3-030-49663-0_29

28. Fu, S., Li, H., Liu, Y., Pirkkalainen, H., Salo, M.: Social media overload, exhaustion, and use discontinuance: examining the effects of information overload, system feature overload, and social overload. Inform. Proc. Manag. **57**(6), 102307 (2020)

29. Gantz, J., Reinsel, D.: The digital universe in 2020: Big data, bigger digital shadows, and biggest growth in the far east. In: IDC iView: IDC Analyze the Future, pp. 1–16. IDC (2012)

30. Gediminas, A., Kwon, Y.O.: Maximizing aggregate recommendation diversity: A graph-theoretic approach. CEUR Workshop Proceedings **816**, 3–10 (2011), workshop on Novelty and Diversity in Recommender Systems, DiveRS 2011 - At the 5th ACM International Conference on Recommender Systems, RecSys 2011 ; Conference date: 23-10-2011 Through 23-10-2011

31. Gratchev, I.: Replacing exams with project-based assessment: analysis of students' performance and experience. Education Sciences **13**(4) (2023). https://doi.org/10.3390/educsci13040408, https://www.mdpi.com/2227-7102/13/4/408
32. Herlocker, J.L., Konstan, J.A., Terveen, L.G., Riedl, J.T.: Evaluating collaborative filtering recommender systems. ACM Trans. Inf. Syst. **22**(1), 5–53 (2004). https://doi.org/10.1145/963770.963772
33. Imbaquingo, A., Cárdenas, J.: Project-based learning as a methodology to improve reading and comprehension skills in the english language. Educ. Sci. **13**(6) (2023). https://doi.org/10.3390/educsci13060587, https://www.mdpi.com/2227-7102/13/6/587
34. Janossy, J.: Proposed model for evaluating c/lms faculty usage in higher education institutions. In: Proceedings of Society for Information Technology & Teacher Education International Conference 2008, pp. 2979–2986. Association for the Advancement of Computing in Education (AACE) (March 2008)
35. Klašnja-Milićević, A., Ivanović, M., Nanopoulos, A.: Recommender systems in e-learning environments: a survey of the state-of-the-art and possible extensions. Artif. Intell. Rev. **44**(4), 571–604 (2015)
36. Knijnenburg, B.P., Willemsen, M.C., Kobsa, A.: A pragmatic procedure to support the user-centric evaluation of recommender systems. In: Proceedings of the Fifth ACM Conference on Recommender Systems, pp. 321–324 (2011)
37. Koltay, T.: Information Overload in a Data-Intensive World, pp. 197–217. Springer International Publishing, Cham (2017). https://doi.org/10.1007/978-3-319-59090-5_10
38. Koper, R., Olivier, B.: Representing the learning design of units of learning. Educ. Technol. Soc. **7**, 97–111 (2004)
39. Koren, Y., Bell, R., Volinsky, C.: Matrix factorization techniques for recommender systems. Computer **42**(8), 30–37 (2009). https://doi.org/10.1109/MC.2009.263
40. Kouki, P., Schaffer, J., Pujara, J., O'Donovan, J., Getoor, L.: Personalized explanations for hybrid recommender systems. In: Proceedings of the 24th International Conference on Intelligent User Interfaces, IUI 2019, pp. 379–390. Association for Computing Machinery, New York (2019). https://doi.org/10.1145/3301275.3302306
41. Libreros, J.A., Mayas, C., Hirth, M.: Recommender systems in continuing professional education for public transport: Challenges of a human-centered design. In: Adjunct Proceedings of the 31st ACM Conference on User Modeling, Adaptation and Personalization, UMAP 2023 Adjunct, pp. 331–336. Association for Computing Machinery, New York (2023). https://doi.org/10.1145/3563359.3596995
42. Liu, H.H., Wang, Q., Su, Y.S., Zhou, L.: Effects of project-based learning on teachers' information teaching sustainability and ability. Sustainability **11**(20) (2019). https://doi.org/10.3390/su11205795, https://www.mdpi.com/2071-1050/11/20/5795
43. Machado, M., Tao, E.: Blackboard vs. moodle: comparing user experience of learning management systems. In: 2007 37th Annual Frontiers In Education Conference - Global Engineering: Knowledge Without Borders, Opportunities Without Passports, pp. S4J–7–S4J–12 (2007). https://doi.org/10.1109/FIE.2007.4417910
44. Mahmood, A., Asghar, F., Naoreen, B.: Success factors on research projects at university" an exploratory study. Procedia. Soc. Behav. Sci. **116**, 2779–2783 (2014)
45. Margetis, G., Ntoa, S., Antona, M., Stephanidis, C.: Human-centered Design Of Artificial Intelligence, chap. 42, pp. 1085–1106. John Wiley & Sons, Ltd. (2021). https://doi.org/10.1002/9781119636113.ch42, https://onlinelibrary.wiley.com/doi/abs/10.1002/9781119636113.ch42

46. Martinez, C.: Developing 21st century teaching skills: A case study of teaching and learning through project-based curriculum. Cogent Education **9**(1), 2024936 (2022). https://doi.org/10.1080/2331186X.2021.2024936
47. Nowotny, H., Scott, P., Gibbons, M.: Re-thinking science: Mode 2 in societal context*. In: Carayannis, E.G., Campbell, D.F.J. (eds.) Knowledge creation, diffusion, and use in innovation networks and knowledge clusters: a comparative systems approach across the United States, Europe, and Asia, pp. 39–51. Praeger Publishers, Westport, CT (2006)
48. Ortega-Gras, J.J., Gómez-Gómez, M.V., Bueno-Delgado, M.V., Garrido-Lova, J., Cañavate-Cruzado, G.: Designing a technological pathway to empower vocational education and training in the circular wood and furniture sector through extended reality. Electronics **12**(10) (2023).https://doi.org/10.3390/electronics12102328, https://www.mdpi.com/2079-9292/12/10/2328
49. Parhankangas, A., Ehrlich, M.: How entrepreneurs seduce business angels: an impression management approach. J. Bus. Ventur. **29**(4), 543–564 (2014)
50. Qing, S., Sizhao, C., Weimin, W., Xiaomei, L., Tiankuan, H.: Personalized recommendation model based on collaborative filtering algorithm of learning situation. Data Analy. Knowl. Dis. **4**(5), 105–117 (2020)
51. Raibulet, C., Lago, P.: Industrial project-based course on service oriented design -experience sharing. In: 2022 IEEE/ACM First International Workshop on Designing and Running Project-Based Courses in Software Engineering Education (DREE), pp. 20–24 (2022). https://doi.org/10.1145/3524487.3527360
52. Resnick, P., Varian, H.R.: Recommender systems. Commun. ACM **40**(3), 56–58 (1997). https://doi.org/10.1145/245108.245121
53. Rivera, A.C., Tapia-Leon, M., Lujan-Mora, S.: Recommendation systems in education: a systematic mapping study. In: Rocha, Á., Guarda, T. (eds.) ICITS 2018. AISC, vol. 721, pp. 937–947. Springer, Cham (2018). https://doi.org/10.1007/978-3-319-73450-7_89
54. Rodriguez Medina, A.E., Ramirez Martinell, A.: Recommender system in higher education: a preliminary study of state of the art. In: 2019 XIV Latin American Conference on Learning Technologies (LACLO), pp. 231–236 (2019). https://doi.org/10.1109/LACLO49268.2019.00047
55. Rosaci, D., Sarné, G.M.L.: An agent-based architecture to recommend educational video. In: WOA (2014)
56. Santos, O.C., Boticario, J.G.: Practical guidelines for designing and evaluating educationally oriented recommendations. Comput. Educ. **81**, 354–374 (2015)
57. Sarwar, B., Karypis, G., Konstan, J., Riedl, J.: Item-based collaborative filtering recommendation algorithms. In: Proceedings of the 10th International Conference on World Wide Web, WWW 2001, pp. 285–295. Association for Computing Machinery (2001). https://doi.org/10.1145/371920.372071, https://doi.org/10.1145/371920.372071
58. Schmidt, J.H., Sørensen, J.K., Dreyer, S., Hasebrink, U.: Wie können empfehlungssysteme zur vielfalt von medieninhalten beitragen. Perspektiven für öffentlich-rechtliche Rundfunkanstalten. Media Perspektiven **11**, 522–531 (2018)
59. Shi, H., Chen, L., Xu, Z., Lyu, D.: Personalized location recommendation using mobile phone usage information. Appl. Intell. **49**(10), 3694–3707 (2019)
60. Thorat, P.B., Goudar, R.M., Barve, S.: Survey on collaborative filtering, content-based filtering and hybrid recommendation system. Inter. J. Comput. Appli. **110**(4), 31–36 (2015)
61. Tong, Y., Wei, X.: Teaching design and practice of a project-based blended learning model. Int. J. Mob. Blended Learn. (IJMBL) **12**, 33–50 (2020)

62. Urdaneta-Ponte, M.C., Mendez-Zorrilla, A., Oleagordia-Ruiz, I.: Recommendation systems for education: systematic review. Electronics **10**(14) (2021). https://doi.org/10.3390/electronics10141611, https://www.mdpi.com/2079-9292/10/14/1611

63. Wang, X., Lee, C.F., Li, Y., Zhu, X.: Digital transformation of education: Design of a "project-based teaching" service platform to promote the integration of production and education. Sustainability **15**(16) (2023). https://doi.org/10.3390/su151612658, https://www.mdpi.com/2071-1050/15/16/12658

64. Westrup, D.: Empfehlungssysteme für wissensgemeinschaften: ein social recommender für eine community of practice. In: Rohland, H., Kienle, A., Friedrich, S. (eds.) DeLFI 2011 - Die 9. e-Learning Fachtagung Informatik, pp. 43–54. Gesellschaft für Informatik e.V., Bonn (2011)

65. Westrup, D.: Empfehlungssysteme für wissensgemeinschaften: ein social recommender für eine community of practice. DeLFI 2011-Die 9. e-Learning Fachtagung Informatik (2011)

66. Zameer, G., Fatima, A.J.A., Fathima, A.: Integrating external factors and technology acceptance model to understand scholar intention and use of recommendation system for course selection (Aug 2022). https://doi.org/10.21203/rs.3.rs-2126671/v1

67. Zelenkauskaite, A., Simões, B.: Big data through cross-platform interest-based interactivity. In: 2014 International Conference on Big Data and Smart Computing (BIGCOMP), pp. 191–196 (2014). https://doi.org/10.1109/BIGCOMP.2014.6741435

68. Zhang, S., Yao, L., Sun, A., Tay, Y.: Deep learning based recommender system: a survey and new perspectives. ACM Comput. Surv. **52**(1) (2019). https://doi.org/10.1145/3285029

69. Zhang, X., Luo, H., Chen, B., Guo, G.: Multi-view visual bayesian personalized ranking for restaurant recommendation. Appl. Intell. **50**(9), 2901–2915 (2020)

70. Zhou, M., Lu, B., Fan, W., Wang, G.A.: Project description and crowdfunding success: an exploratory study. Inf. Syst. Front. **20**(2), 259–274 (2018)

71. Ziegler, J., Loepp, B.: Empfehlungssysteme. In: Handbuch Digitale Wirtschaft, pp. 717–741. Springer Gabler, Wiesbaden (2020)

Examining User Perceptions to Vocal Interaction with AI Bots in Virtual Reality and Mobile Environments: A Focus on Foreign Language Learning and Communication Dynamics

Antonella Cavallaro, Marco Romano(✉), and Rossana Laccone

Department of International Humanities and Social Sciences at the University of International Studies of Rome – UNINT, Rome, Italy
marco.romano@unint.eu

Abstract. The integration of artificial intelligence (AI) into daily life, particularly in the form of generative and conversational AI, has become a reality accessible to everyone. This article evaluates the use of voicebots, which are chatbots with vocal interfaces, as educational tools to enhance conversational skills in adult education. The assessment considers their impact on the learning experience and their effects on conversation-related anxiety. Two interfaces of interaction with AI voice bots are tested: immersive virtual reality avatars and voice bots integrated in ChatGPT. The results indicate that both AI-integrated voicebots are effective for language learning without dedicated tools due to their adaptability and AI features. Users demonstrate a willingness for self-directed learning and confidence in technology's efficacy. Particularly combining voicebots with immersive virtual reality shows promising results, even if further longitudinal studies are needed.

Keywords: Education · Artificial Intelligence · Conversational skills · Foreign Languages skills

1 Introduction

Last year's technology revolution was characterized by the introduction of artificial intelligence (AI) into everyday life [1]. This technology simulates human intelligence in machines and encompasses a broad range of approaches and tools, such as neural networking, natural language processing, and computer vision. Two main types of AI are being developed: narrow AI and general AI [2]. While the narrow AI is designed to perform specific task and it is coming of everyday use as for example as voice assistance such as "Siri"or like image recognition AI such as those used in security systems to track individuals, General AI (also known as Artificial General Intelligence - AGI) is jet in developing. AGI refers to systems that can understand, learn, and apply knowledge to various tasks in machine learning, cognitive science, neuroscience, and philosophy. GPT is a tool developed by OpenAI that enables the understanding and generation of human-like conversations and is probably one of the most well-known forms of AI narrow.

H. Degen and S. Ntoa (Eds.): HCII 2024, LNAI 14734, pp. 20–30, 2024.
https://doi.org/10.1007/978-3-031-60606-9_2

Since becoming available to the public, ChatGPT has demonstrated its applicability to the field of education. The authors in [3] conducted research investigating the potential advantages of ChatGPT in improving student learning and facilitating teaching tasks. In the context of language teaching and learning, several studies such as [4] and [5] investigated the potential applications of ChatGPT. Furthermore, Firat in [6] emphasizes that voice-bot chat, equipped with artificial intelligence like that in ChatGPT, can also enhance auto-didactic learning due to its accessibility and affordability. The aim of our pilot study is to investigate people's perception of the usefulness of this technology in their self-directed foreign language learning. Our main focus is on two aspects:

- Perception of usability and usefulness of the use of ChatGPT in adult language learning;
- The different perceptions of usefulness and usability based on different ways of interacting with the voice bot (smartphone and immersive virtual reality)

To achieve our objectives, we will conduct a study in two phases. The first phase consists of a scenario in which subjects are exposed to a simulation of a conversation in English (a foreign language for the participants) with the ChatGPT voice bot. Two types of modalities of the voice bot are tested: in the first group, the experience takes place in an immersive virtual reality application and the interaction with ChatGPT is mediated by an avatar. In the second group, the interaction with the voice bot is mediated by the ChatGPT application on the smartphone, and the interaction is only vocal and doesn't involve other senses besides the visual. The second phase consists of the administration of a questionnaire to obtain the subject's opinion on the experience with the voice bot. A large sample design is projected on the basis of our first exploration.

2 Related Works

In last the years numerous evidence showed the potential of the application of Virtual Reality (VR) and AI in educational filed [3; 7; 8; 9; 20]. The researchers in [10] have provided insights into the acceptability of VR for educational purposes among high school teachers in Italy, suggesting its potential as a powerful tool for student development. This technology has also significantly transformed the way individuals learn foreign languages. In [11], the researchers conducted a study on the effectiveness of a generative model-based conversational agent in supporting students learning English as a second language (ESL). They found that the agent was able to understand students' questions and provide appropriate and relevant responses, leading to improved language proficiency. The AI-driven technology behind voice-bots enables people to provide instant feedback on pronunciation, grammar, and vocabulary usage and helping learners to improve their language skills in real time. One of the key advantages of using voice-bots for language learning is the ability to customize the experience to the learner's level and their pace. This personalized approach can enhance motivation and engagement, making the language learning process more enjoyable and effective [12-14]. AI voice-bots can offer a wide range of language learning resources, including vocabulary drills, cultural insights, and interactive scenarios that simulate real-life conversations. Baidoo-Anu and Ansah in [15] summarized the characteristics of ChatGPT and other AI tools in relation to their application in education as follows:

Personalized Tutoring: ChatGPT can be used to provide personalized tutoring and feedback to students based on their individual learning needs and progresses;

- *Automated Essay Grading*: ChatGPT can be trained to grade student essays;
- *Language Translation:* ChatGPT can be used to translate educational materials into different languages, making them more accessible to a wider audience;
- *Interactive Learning*: ChatGPT can be used to create interactive learning experiences where students can interact with a virtual tutor in a conversational manner;
- *Adaptive Learning:* ChatGPT can be used to create adaptive learning systems that adjust their teaching methods based on a student's progress and performance.

Engaging in conversations with a voice-bot, language learners can practice speaking and listening in a more natural and interactive way [16].

3 Methods

In this section we present: the scenario designed for our study, the design and the tools used for interaction of participants with AI and the questionnaire acquiring the subjects' opinion used to.

3.1 Participants

A total of 25 people aged between 23 and 50 are recruited for the study. One participant is excluded from the sample because he doesn't complete the questionnaire. Three are excluded from the first sample because their English is too poor to support a conversation with the AI. In total, 21 subjects meet all the criteria. The sample is divided into two groups: Group 1 (G1) consists of 11 subjects, 5 males and 5 females, with a mean age of 31 (ranging from 23 to 42 years old). Group 2 (G2) is composed of 10 subjects, 3 males and 7 females, with an average age of 31.8 (ranging from 25 to 50 years old). The study adhered to ethical standards for research involving human participants as required by the institution Table 1.

Table 1. Characteristics of the participants in the sample.

	N	M	F	MA	SD
G1	11	5	5	31	5,8
G2	10	3	7	31,8	7,3

Inclusion Criteria. The inclusion criteria are as follows: A) Possessing a minimum level of english-speaking competency (A2 or higher); B) being between the ages of 20 and 50.

Exclusion Criteria. To adhere to the standards of our research, we excluded individuals who do not speak english or have low speaking competencies, those with evident cognitive or psychiatric illness, and those lacking effective communication skills or the ability to engage in basic interactions. This decision is based on the study's assessment methods, which require a specific level of fundamental communication.

3.2 Experimental Design

A scenario is designed and implemented in order to experienced subjects with AI. Both groups are exposed to two different phases: the phase 1 is the experience with AI and the second one consists of the self-administration of questionnaire. Particularly G1 follow "Immersive VR experience with AI" while G2 follow the condition "AI App on a Smartphone". The following sub-sections describe the tools, scenario, and questionnaire used, while the 'Procedures' subsection describes the entire process and conditions.

3.3 Tools

For our aims we used two applications Virtual Speech and ChatGPT respectively download on a Meta Oculus Quest 2 and iPhone XR. Finally, a questionnaire is developed starting from [10] and Google Forms is used for the administration. All the tools are described below:

Virtual Speech[1]. This software application utilizes virtual reality (VR) technologies to simulate public speaking scenarios for users. Virtual Speech is designed to help individuals practice and improve their communication and public speaking skills in a virtual environment. Among the spaces and the training of the app, we use the section "Role-play with AI".

ChatGPT[2]. ChatGPT is a free-to-use AI system developed by Open AI. We use it for engaging conversations, gain insights, Automate tasks. Several modalities to interact with the AI is available on ChatGPT, in our study we use the voice-bot. Trought Voice the user can get in conversation with the AI with own Smartphone, and the AI get back vocal response to user.

Meta Oculus Quest 2[3]. The Quest 2 is a virtual reality (VR) head-mounted device designed to offer virtual reality experiences to the subject. Meta Quest 2 is equipped with a stereoscopic display, delivering separate images to each eye, stereo sound, and sensors like accelerometers and gyroscopes. These sensors track the user's head movements, aligning the virtual camera's orientation with the user's eye positions in the real world.

Smartphone iPhone XR. The iPhone XR is a smartphone developed by Apple Inc. The device runs on Apple's iOS operating system. Among the phone features the audio ones are stereo speakers with wider stereo sound.

Questionnaire. We used a modified version of the TAM questionnaire based on [10]. We have further modified the questionnaire to evaluate the user's experience when interacting with the AI. The questionnaire consists of 24 items rated on a 5-point Likert scale.

---

[1] https://virtualspeech.com/

[2] https://chat.openai.com/

[3] https://www.meta.com/it/en/quest/products/quest-2/tech-specs/

According to [17], using a 5-point Likert scale can improve response rates and quality while reducing respondent frustration. The data was reorganized into five scales: the intention of technology use (IU), perceived usefulness (PU), perceived ease of use (EU), engagement in technology use (EN). Comfort in Interaction (CI) was added to carry out the study. The questionnaire items are shown in Table 2. The Perceived Ease of Use (EU) subscale consists of 4 items and measures the degree to which a person believes that using a particular system would be effortless [18]. The PU subscale, consisting of 7 items, measures the subject's perception of the usefulness of the voice-bot in improving their English skills. The EN subscale comprises six items that assess the subject's engagement with the technology. The IU subscale, on the other hand, assesses the subject's intention to use the technology and the potential to promote it to other customers, and is composed of two items. A 4-item CI Scale has been added to investigate the level of comfort experienced during interactions with technology. An open-ended question has been added to gather opinions on advice and limitations. All Likert-scale questions require a response, while the open-ended question is optional.

3.4 Procedures

After recruitment, participants are invited to read and accept the conditions of the experiment. They are required to participate in an initial training session with one of two technologies: ChatGPT or immersive VR. Following this, they will be asked to anonymously complete a questionnaire. The study is conducted in a psychological office.

- *Phase one*: participants are invited to interact with AI voice-bot. The time for interaction lasts 10 min and consists of a conversation with AI following a scenario set in a restaurant.

Before beginning the conversation trial, participants are given explanations on the use of the technology, including the VR headset and ChatGPT. They are then given ten minutes to interact with the technologies and ask any questions to the experimenters. Following this, they are instructed to begin the conversation according to the provided description. Once the conversation begins, the experimenter leaves the room, and the participants interact with the AI alone.

Participants in group 1 (G1) are instructed to wear a virtual reality (VR) headset and practice using it. The training covers how to move within the virtual space and interact with virtual objects. Following this, participants are invited to enter the 'Roleplay with AI' section of the Virtual Speech program. They are then instructed to begin the interaction by selecting the 'Café Roleplay' option. As type of input is chosen "Auto Audio", in this way the conversational turn is similar to ChatGPT ones. At the end "Free-flowing conversation" modalities guide the style of conversation between subject and AI Avatar. At the end, the participant is instructed to say *"Hello [Name of the Avatar as shown in the scenario], can we simulate a conversation at a restaurant, where I am the customer, and you are the host?"* If the AI responds positively to the participants, the experimenter leaves the room, and the participants are left alone. The AI avatar simulation lasts an average of 8.75 min.

Table 2. Item modified Questionnaire.

Cod	Description	N	G1	G2
EU1	Communicating with the voice-bot is easy	21	11	10
CI1	Even if I feel confident when speaking a foreign language, I feel anxious about it	21	11	10
PU1	Using the voice-bot helps to practice my English more quickly than before	21	11	10
EN1	The application makes learning and practice more interesting	21	11	10
IU1	I would like to practice a foreign language with the AI-empowered voice-bot	21	11	10
EU2	Focusing attention on the didactic task is easy	21	11	10
CI2	I get nervous and confused when I am speaking to AI	21	11	10
EN2	The voice-bot increases my attention to specific words in the given context than before	21	11	10
EN3	I like interacting with the voice-bot to practice English	21	11	10
IU2	I would recommend colleagues try AI-empowered voice-bot technology to practice a foreign language	21	11	10
EU3	Interacting with the voice-bot interface is easy	21	11	10
CI3	I feel quite sure of myself when I am speaking in foreign languages	21	11	10
PU2	After using the voice-bot, I believe that I could get better results in a test than before	21	11	10
EU4	Overall, I find it easy to use the voice-bot	21	11	10
PU3	After using the voice-bot, I have learned more words on the given topic than before	21	11	10
EN4	Overall, I enjoy using the voice-bot	21	11	10
PU4	The application helped me to speak more fluently on the given topic than before	21	11	10
EN5	Overall, I think that the voice-bot is exciting	21	11	10
CI4	I am confortable when I use VR technology to interact with voice-bot	21	11	10
PU5	The application makes English learning easier than before	21	11	10
CI5	I am not so worried when I don't understand what AI is saying in foreign language	21	11	10
PU6	Overall, I find the application useful for practice and learning English	21	11	10
EN6	Performing the exercises is captivating	21	11	10
PU7	How useful do you think the experience you just had can be in improving your level of English?	21	11	10

G2 participants are invited to open the application on their smartphone and activate the voice-bot. They can interact with the app for 10 min and ask questions to the experimenters if needed. At the end of this time, the experimenter instructs the subject to say to ChatGPT, 'Hello, can we simulate a conversation at a restaurant where I am the customer, and you are the host?' When the AI responds positively to participants, the experimenter leaves the room and the participants remain alone Table 3.

Table 3. Conversational Scenario durations means.

	Scenario 1	Mean of Duration
G1	Restaurant	8,75
G2	Restaurant	7.09

- *Phase 2:* Following the conversation with the AI voice-bot, participants from both groups are invited to respond to a questionnaire. Once they have completed the simulation with the application, they can contact an experimenter who will provide them with a QR code that grants access to the Google modules link. The experimenter will then leave the room until the participant submits the questionnaire.

4 Results

All participants completed the Likert-scale questions of the questionnaire, resulting in a total of 504 responses. Additionally, 7 participants responded to open-ended questions. The results of the questionnaires are presented in Table 4, which shows the mean (M), standard deviations (SD), and coefficients of variation (CVs). The first column of the table displays an alphanumeric code used to identify the items. The second column provides a description of each item, while the third column shows the mean. The last column reports the coefficients of variation. Upon initial analysis of the data, the results indicate a positive impact of technology on the majority of participants. For the commentary on the results, we have separately analyzed the scales related to the Technology Acceptance Model [19] and the scale related to the feeling of interaction with AI. In this first part, we present the results of groups G1 and G2 on the scales of EU, PU, EN, and IU, and then we discuss the CI scale. The scores of all items related to the intention of use have a mean of more than 4.00 in both groups, indicating that all participants agree on the availability of using AI voice-bots to improve their English skills. The mean scores of Group 1 indicate a positive impact on ease of use (EU), perceived usefulness (PU), and engagement (EN). The low coefficients of variation in all items on these scales demonstrate good agreement among participants of G1. As for example the item PU2 *After using the voice-bot, I believe that I could get better results in a test than before* has a mean score of 4,09 with a CV of 0,07 or EN1 *The application makes learning and practice more interesting* where the mean is of 4,64 on 5.00 and a CV of 0,11. The main degree of discordance in group 2 registered is on item EN2 *The voice-bot increases my attention to specific words in the given context than before* (M = 3,64; CV = 0,28). Regarding G2 scores, there is more deviation among participants, although the scores of the items related to the four TAM scales are mostly above 4.00 for Engagement, indicating that participants in Group 2 also enjoy interacting with AI through ChatGPT and find it interesting. However, unlike G1, a coefficient of variation greater than 0.30 is recorded for items EN1, EN2, PU2, PU3, PU4, PU7, indicating more disagreement among participants Except for item EN1, all items where the correlation is weaker (from 0.31 to 0.37) have an average score between 3.60 and 4.00. The most accordance in G2 is registred in item EN6 *Performing the exercises is captivating* with a mean of 4.30 and a CV of 0.16.

At the end the CI scale includes several items that measure the feeling of confidence and comfort in interaction with AI. The scale also investigated the participants' level of anxiety in speaking foreign language interacting with AI. The scores on this scale show the higher degree of discordance between participants in both group, indicating that individual psychological factor have a greater impact on these items than the structure of technology itself. Particularly an high disagreement is registered for both group on items C1 Even if I feel confident when speaking a foreign language, I feel anxious about it, C2 I get nervous and confused when I am speaking to AI and C3 I feel quite sure of myself when I am speaking in foreign languages. Regarding item C1, individual variables could lead to subjective anxiety, whereas C3 may be more associated with the participants' levels of proficiency in English.

Only item CI4 registers a good coefficient of variation in both groups (0.17 for G1 and 0.23 for G2), indicating a comfortable feeling when using AI technology, whether interacting with a VR Avatar (M = 4.09) or ChatGPT (M = 3.60).

Qualitative analysis of responses to open-ended questions suggests that AI voicebots have a positive impact on the participants. Participants viewed their interaction with AI voice-bots as a valuable and enriching experience.

I think it is a very useful tool for improving my English, I have never think to use ChatGPT in this way!

This underlines the importance of regular training and highlights how voice bots make it possible. As a criticism, participants found the same difficulties in fluency of conversation when something starts to be misunderstood, both in immersive VR and ChatGPT.

When I didn't understand the question, Ai doesn't reformulate it for me using simpler vocabulary and I have no way of knowing the meaning of unknown vocabulary.

Suddenly, he started speaking to me in Italian on his own initiative. I asked him to speak in English.

Open-ended questions also raise the importance of receiving feedback from voice bots about errors or corrections in grammar or pronunciation, as well as dual audio and visual output.

It might be useful for you to show me the question in writing and highlight any unfamiliar vocabulary so that I can learn it. I would also like you to help me with my pronunciation by correcting me and possibly rephrasing my sentence in a more grammatically correct or friendly language.

Table 4. Results.

Cod		G1			G2	
	M	**SD**	**CVs**	**M**	**SD**	**CVs**
EU1	3,91	0,70	0,18	3,60	0,84	0,23
EU2	4,18	0,60	0,14	3,80	1,03	0,27
EU3	3,91	0,94	0,24	3,70	0,95	0,26
EU4	4,36	0,81	0,19	4,10	1,20	0,29
EN1	4,64	0,50	0,11	4,00	1,25	0,31
EN2	3,64	1,03	0,28	3,60	1,26	0,35
EN3	4,27	0,79	0,18	4,20	0,92	0,22
EN4	4,27	0,65	0,15	4,00	1,05	0,26
EN5	4,09	1,04	0,26	3,80	1,03	0,27
EN6	4,27	0,79	0,18	4,30	0,67	0,16
IU1	4,18	0,75	0,18	4,20	0,92	0,22
IU2	4,55	0,52	0,11	4,00	1,05	0,26
PU1	4,18	0,60	0,14	4,20	0,92	0,22
PU2	4,09	0,30	0,07	3,80	1,23	0,32
PU3	3,64	0,92	0,25	3,70	1,25	0,34
PU4	4,00	0,63	0,16	3,70	1,16	0,31
PU5	4,00	0,77	0,19	3,70	0,82	0,22
PU6	4,64	0,50	0,11	4,10	0,88	0,21
PU7	4,18	0,60	0,14	3,80	1,40	0,37
CI1	2,91	1,38	0,47	3,50	1,18	0,34
CI2	2,00	1,26	0,63	2,60	1,58	0,61
CI3	3,27	1,01	0,31	2,90	1,37	0,47
CI4	4,09	0,70	0,17	3,60	0,84	0,23
CI5	3,73	1,49	0,40	3,80	0,63	0,17

5   Conclusions

The study indicates that voice-bots integrated with artificial intelligence can be effective tools for improving foreign language skills, even without specific learning tools. The versatility of voice-bots in providing interactive and engaging conversational experiences highlights their potential to enhance language acquisition. Although not reliant on dedicated learning tools, the adaptability and AI capabilities of these tools contribute to a positive perception of their effectiveness in supporting language learning efforts. Future research should investigate AI voice-bots equipped with specific learning tools for foreign languages, as individuals have demonstrated a willingness to adopt this technology as a valuable aid for self-directed learning. The use of technological tools demonstrates an increasing awareness of their potential to aid self-directed learning. The user's trust in the efficacy of the technology is evident in their independent use of these resources. This study investigates the perceived effectiveness of improving conversational skills in individuals with intermediate-level English proficiency, in terms of improvement in basic grammar and syntax to those aiming to enhance conversational fluency or engage in technical language conversations. It would be interesting to expand this investigation to students with different levels of proficiency. The study found that using an AI voice bot and immersive virtual reality together resulted in slightly better outcomes. This improvement may be due to the more interactive nature of the avatar compared to the voice-bot on a smartphone. However, this is only a pilot study, and due to the small sample size, a significant comparison of the data between the two groups could not be made. Therefore, only descriptive analysis can be conducted. Further research, including controlled trials, is required to validate these findings and provide more comprehensive insights into the observed trends. The data suggests that subjects who have undergone immersive virtual reality experiences may have a heightened perception of experience. However, due to the limited sample size, statistical comparison of the data was not possible. Future applications will be speculated upon with larger sample sizes to achieve greater statistical stability of the data and to analyze any potential differences more thoroughly.

Acknowledgments. We extend our heartfelt gratitude to Toinette van der Walt for her invaluable support and guidance as a language teacher for foreigners. Her expertise and dedication have greatly enriched our research endeavors.

References

1. Poola, I.: How artificial intelligence in impacting real life everyday. Int. J. Adv. Res. Dev. **2**(10), 96–100 (2017)
2. Bundy, A.: Preparing for the future of artificial intelligence (2017)
3. Kasneci, E., et al.: ChatGPT for good? on opportunities and challenges of large language models for education. Learn. Individ. Differ.Individ. Differ. **103**, 102274 (2023)
4. Kostka, I., & Toncelli, R. (2023). Exploring applications of ChatGPT to English language teaching: Opportunities, challenges, and recommendations. *TESL-EJ*, *27*(3).https://doi.org/10.55593/ej.27107int
5. Huang, J., Li, S.: Opportunities and challenges in the application of ChatGPT in foreign language teaching. Int. J. Educ. Soc. Sci. Res. **6**(04), 75–89 (2023)
6. Firat, M.: How ChatGPT can transform autodidactic experiences and open education. Open Education Faculty, Anadolu Unive, Department of Distance Education (2023)
7. Kavanagh, S., Luxton-Reilly, A., Wuensche, B., Plimmer, B.: A systematic review of virtual reality in education. Themes Sci. Technol. Educ. **10**(2), 85–119 (2017)
8. Chen, L., Chen, P., Lin, Z.: Artificial intelligence in education: a review. Ieee Access **8**, 75264–75278 (2020)
9. Romano, M., Laccone, R. P., Frolli, A. Designing a VR educational application to enhance resilience and community awareness through cultural exploration. *In ICERI2023 Proceedings* (pp. 9258–9267). IATED (2023).

10. Romano, M., et al.: Exploring the potential of immersive virtual reality in Italian schools: a practical workshop with high school teachers. Multimodal Technol. Interact. **7**(12), 111 (2023)

11. Peng, Z.E., Wang, L.M.: Listening effort by native and nonnative listeners due to noise, reverberation, and talker foreign accent during English speech perception. J. Speech Lang. Hear. Res. **62**(4), 1068–1081 (2019)

12. Wei, L.: Artificial intelligence in language instruction: impact on English learning achievement, L2 motivation, and self-regulated learning. Front. Psychol. **14**, 1261955 (2023)

13. Kim, N. Y., Cha, Y., Kim, H. S.: Future english learning: chatbots and artificial intelligence. Multimedia-Assisted Language Learning, **22**(3) (2019)

14. Bisogni, F., Laccone, R. P., Esposito, C., Frolli, A., Romano, M.: Virtual reality and foreign language learning. In: ICERI 2023 Proceedings (pp. 9201–9207). IATED (2023).

15. Baidoo-Anu, D., Ansah, L.O.: Education in the era of generative artificial intelligence (AI): Understanding the potential benefits of ChatGPT in promoting teaching and learning. J. AI **7**(1), 52–62 (2023)

16. Topsakal, O., Topsakal, E.: Framework for a foreign language teaching software for children utilizing AR, voicebots and ChatGPT (Large Language Models). J. Cogn. Syst. **7**(2), 33–38 (2022)

17. Samuels, P.: Advice on reliability analysis with small samples. Birmingham City University, Birmingham, UK (2015)

18. Venkatesh, V., Davis, F.D.: A theoretical extension of the technology acceptance model: four longitudinal field studies. Manage. Sci. **46**(2), 186–204 (2000)

19. Davis, F. D.: User acceptance of information systems: the technology acceptance model (TAM) (1987).

20. Cantone, A. A., Ercolino, M., Romano, M., Vitiello, G.: Designing virtual interactive objects to enhance visitors' experience in cultural exhibits. In: Proceedings of the 2nd International Conference of the ACM Greek SIGCHI Chapter, pp. 1–5 (2023)

Evaluation of Generative AI-Assisted Software Design and Engineering: A User-Centered Approach

Mahsa Fischer$^{(\boxtimes)}$ ⓘ and Carsten Lanquillon ⓘ

Heilbronn University of Applied Sciences, Heilbronn, Germany
`mahsa.fischer@hs-heilbronn.de`

Abstract. This paper evaluates the impact of generative artificial intelligence (AI) on software design and engineering through a user-centered approach. The integration of generative AI tools in software development processes is scrutinized across various phases, from ideation to deployment. By conducting a literature review and a preliminary evaluation with 18 students, this study identifies critical tasks within the software development life cycle where generative AI tools can enhance productivity and creativity. The paper outlines the potential of generative AI to expedite tasks like code completion, prototype design, requirements validation, and documentation, thereby potentially transforming software engineering practices. It emphasizes a user-centered perspective, assessing tools based on criteria such as usability, effectiveness, and integration within existing workflows. Furthermore, the study highlights the importance of human-AI collaboration, suggesting that while generative AI can significantly support software development tasks, human oversight and critical evaluation of AI-generated outputs remain essential. This research contributes to understanding how generative AI tools can be effectively integrated into software development processes, offering insights into the benefits and challenges of these emerging technologies from a user-centric viewpoint.

Keywords: Generative Artificial Intelligence · Software Engineering · User-Centered Artificial Intelligence · Design Thinking

1   Introduction

The recent progress in generative artificial intelligence (AI) tools has motivated researchers to investigate the productivity of these tools among different disciplines and question how they would affect how people will accomplish future tasks [26]. The capacity of these tools to generate human-like content, such as text, images, and code, has been a driving force behind their integration in various sectors, including software design and engineering. Notably, a McKinsey study [8] has demonstrated that the task of completing code can be done twice as fast by software developers, using generative AI and enabling tremendous

H. Degen and S. Ntoa (Eds.): HCII 2024, LNAI 14734, pp. 31–47, 2024.
https://doi.org/10.1007/978-3-031-60606-9_3

productivity gains in four key areas: expediting manual and repetitive work, avoiding writer's block for starting a new code, accelerating updates to existing code, and increasing developers' ability to tackle new challenges, e.g., while synthesizing unfamiliar code or framework.

The true potential of generative AI goes beyond automating specific tasks to transforming the entire software design and engineering process. Therefore, our investigation extends beyond the confines of code completion and delves into the whole software development life cycle, from the inception of an idea to the delivery of a fully functional software product. Our scientific contribution is twofold: First, we list and briefly describe high-level software development tasks and sub-tasks as a foundation for our evaluation. Second, we conduct a preliminary classroom evaluation with students as potential future software development experts on how well current AI-based tools can support these tasks.

2   Methodology

First, state-of-the-art research in the field of generative AI supportive tools for various software development phases and activities is screened based on a systematic literature review. Then, a preliminary evaluation of selected generative AI tools is conducted with 18 business information systems students as possible future software development experts in a classroom setting to study their capabilities and suitability. To do so, different evaluation criteria have been identified for each phase. This approach emphasizes on the user experience of the impacted people while using generative AI tools. In this context, the users are the software designers and developers using generative AI tools to enhance productivity. Using these tools aims not to replace humans with intelligent systems but to enhance their capabilities, allowing them to tackle complex tasks more effectively and efficiently.

3   Background

This section briefly introduces the software development cycle from a design thinking perspective. It explains the associated tasks and phases that are key to identifying generative AI application opportunities. We introduce a human-centric AI perspective to reflect better and evaluate the interaction between AI and humans in software development.

3.1   Software Development

Developing software does not start with coding. According to [37], there are two types of software engineering approaches: *project-based* and *product-based*.

Project-Based Software Engineering starts with a problem that a client has identified and requests a software engineering team to solve. The software engineers try to understand the situation and determine the requirements for the software to be coded as a solution to the client's problem.

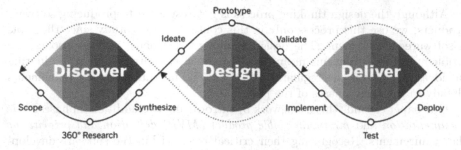

Fig. 1. The design thinking approach at SAP according to [15].

In contrast, *product-based software engineering* starts with an idea that developers have identified. Any idea that they have noticed could be of market interest. This process has no client; it is only an opportunity developers have identified. The software developers map this opportunity to possible product features.

In both cases, it is crucial to understand the current problem, research existing solutions in the market, and try to understand the situation from the target group's perspective, i. e., the potential future users of the system.

3.2 Software Development Cycle and Design Thinking Process

Our study is based on the design thinking process used at SAP [15]. As shown in Fig. 1, the process consists of several phases grouped into higher-level phases, which we refer to as *stages*. In the following, we briefly outline the rationale for the main stages first. Then, we provide an extended list of detailed phases that form the basis of our evaluation.

The *discovery stage* includes kicking off the project and understanding the problem at hand by conducting research using different methods such as interviews, literature reviews, and surveys. The key idea is to put the software developers in the shoes of the target group. Finally, they synthesize all the collected data and define personas, fictitious individuals owning the target groups' typical characteristics, pain points, and responsibilities. Yet, at the end of this stage, how do we know that we are ready for the following design stage? How might we help identify personas with these pain points to solve their problems?

The *design stage* starts with generating ideas for this problem, deciding on the best ideas as a team, and prototyping the selected ideas to make them more tangible. This helps to communicate the concept much more quickly to the stakeholders and potential users. This allows us to better evaluate the idea according to the requirements identified. As the prototype and, accordingly, the idea gets more detailed and refined after a couple of iterations, it is ready to bring to the next phase.

Finally, in the *delivery stage*, the design mockups and prototypes generated in the design stage will get life. They will be implemented in productive solutions that need to be tested, iteratively improved, released, and deployed in the natural environment for real users.

Although the design thinking process is not restricted to producing software products, we use this process only in this context for our study since the topic is software development. The design thinking cycle helps us to approach the problem and find solutions in an iterative and user-centric manner, evaluating the ideas and prototypes regularly with users and making necessary refinements already in the early phases of the project.

Our paper extends this framework by introducing two additional phases: *code documentation* and *minimum viable product (MVP) definition and prioritizing* the requirements. Recognizing their critical roles within the software development process, both of which stand to benefit significantly from generative AI support. This leads to the following ten phases within the software development cycle: 1. explore and scope, 2. research 360 and synthesize, 3. ideate, 4. prototype, 5. validate, 6. define MVP/prioritize requirements, 7. implement, 8. document code, 9. test, and 10. deploy, including continuous integration and continuous delivery (CI/CD).

The *MVP definition* is positioned between the validation phase of the design prototype and the implementation. This phase translates the validated ideas of the prototype to technical requirements and prioritizes these according to their business value for the end users. This exercise leads to the definition of the MVP, which refers to "version of a new product, which allows a team to collect the maximum amount of validated learning about customers with the least effort" as a fundamental concept of the lean startup methodology [33].

Code documentation is conducted concurrently with the implementation phase, focusing on the often overlooked yet crucial task of comprehensive code documentation. Effective documentation is critical to software engineering, ensuring the sustainability and maintenance of code and the dissemination of knowledge within development teams and beyond. The integration of generative AI in this phase holds the promise of automating and enhancing the process of code documentation, reducing human effort and errors while improving the overall documentation quality.

In the following evaluation, we focus on phases 3 to 10, starting with the ideation phase of the design thinking process.

3.3   Generative Artificial Intelligence

AI aims to create systems that mimic or even surpass human intelligence, covering computation methodologies for perception, reasoning, and action [43] as well as learning. In doing so, tackling tasks easily solved by humans but difficult to formalize and code is considered the crucial challenge [14].

Generative AI, a subset of AI systems, is designed to produce novel content such as text, images, audio, and video, mirroring human creativity. These systems are trained on extensive datasets, enabling them to discern patterns, styles, or features within the data. As a result, they can create new data instances that resemble or even replicate the characteristics of the original dataset [12].

In contrast, traditional or discriminative AI primarily analyzes input data, recognizes patterns, and makes predictions. This differentiation highlights AI's broad capabilities and applications, from interpreting and categorizing existing information to generating innovative content.

The concept of *prompting* in generative AI involves providing texts or other data forms to an AI system, which then generates contextually relevant content. This approach enables an AI system to address tasks it was not explicitly trained to solve and, thus, to exhibit so-called *emergent capabilities* that often yield valuable solutions in various scenarios.

Applying this generative capability in software development facilitates the creation of diverse artifacts throughout the development cycle. A critical step in this process involves identifying and formulating different tasks, specifying their inputs and outputs, and defining criteria for evaluating the quality of the solutions. This study aims to illustrate the potential of generative AI to enhance and streamline the software development process significantly.

4   Evaluation of Generative AI Tools

In this study, we focus on the software development phases 3 to 10, starting with the ideation phase of the design thinking process. 18 business information systems undergraduates evaluated generative AI tools to gain more insight into their experiences as future young professionals while exploring the usage of generative AI tools in each phase of software development.

To evaluate generative AI tools, defining criteria for comparing them is essential. The capabilities of the tools, such as the number of features and included modalities (e.g., text-only input versus images or videos), are important factors to consider. Furthermore, the generated results' quantity, quality, and validity are important. For example, [7] defined criteria such as comprehensiveness, accuracy, and clarity in the use case of generated medical information by ChatGPT.

The criteria identified for using generative AI in the overall software development process can be divided into three main dimensions: user experience, IT strategy, and quality of the results. The *user experience* dimension relates to the usability, user satisfaction, effectiveness, and efficiency of using the generative AI tool. The *IT strategy* dimension includes the security aspects of using generative AI and organization, which refers to how well the corresponding AI can be implemented in the existing workflow and scalability. IT strategy as a dimension is particularly important in the corporate context because companies should view the acquisition of generative AI as an investment, like purchasing operating software or machines. Consequently, this acquisition must pay off in the long term and, thus, be compatible with the IT strategy. Hinderberger [17] describes that the scalability of use cases that apply generative AI is important. While data scientists concentrate on the mathematical evaluation of data, the focus with increasing maturity and scaling is on software developers, who drive integration into the system landscape and manage the industrialization and professionalization of IT processes. The *quality of the results* dimension refers to the correctness, validity, comprehensiveness, and accuracy of the generated results by the generative AI tool. Since the results are AI-generated, the question is if the results are correct and understandable for users. Finally, the learning ability of the tools is crucial, i.e., how well can an AI system learn from new data and human feedback and adapt its strategies?

In addition to criteria for the entire development process discussed above, Table 1 lists more specific criteria associated with common tasks for the phases considered in our study.

4.1 Ideate

Ideation, the process of generating and developing new ideas, is a crucial aspect of innovation and scientific progress [6]. This includes disrupting habitual thought patterns and encouraging creative thinking [25]. Incentives can significantly improve the quality and quantity of ideas generated [40]. Scientific thinking, which includes thinking about scientific content, is closely related to idea generation and involves various cognitive processes [10]. The evaluation criteria for this phase are shown in Table 1. Another interesting aspect is whether the tools combine ideas to develop new ones [30].

The evaluation results indicated that tools such as ChatGPT, Google Bart, or Microsoft Bing can be used to generate ideas. These tools are helpful and a good starting point for inspiration. They provide context information to clarify their results, enhancing the user's transparency.

4.2 Prototype

Prototyping is a crucial aspect of product development with a significant impact on design performance [3]. The use of prototypes in the early stages of design is widespread, and it is important to understand the key objectives and techniques [4]. The prototyping process, including its types, best practices, and limitations, is also discussed, focusing on its application in education and science in [22]. Automatic generation of design mockups is more complex than just generating ideas. Design mockups are not standalone results but are related to each other and have a defined interaction flow. Different generative AI tools, such as Uizard AI, are available for generating designs. This tool generates several related design mockups using text prompts, screenshots, and hand-drawn wireframes as input. The designers can edit the generated mockup, zoom in/out, and test the mockup by clicking on the preview. Other tools in this area are Prototype AI and Figma AI plugins. The current tools have a high potential to make the design process more efficient but are not enough to make this process completely automatic. Further developments are necessary for the tools to better match the results to complex use cases.

4.3 Validate

This phase includes the validation of the defined software requirements. The idea is to review the software requirements using generative AI tools and let the tool

Table 1. Common tasks and evaluation criteria for using generative AI tools in selected software design and development cycle phases.

Phase	Tasks	Evaluation Criteria
Ideate	generate ideas for new products or new features for existing products, prioritize ideas, combine ideas, and develop new ideas	number of generated ideas, quality of ideas (validity, correctness, comprehensiveness, accuracy, and transparency)
Prototype	generate design wireframe, sketches, or high-fidelity mockups, produce design variations with different interaction flows or visual designs	coherency among generated design screens, quality of the mockups (validity, correctness, comprehensiveness, accuracy, and transparency)
Validate	validate requirements and suggest new and more precise formulations for functional and non-functional software requirements, validate visual design mockups against defined criteria, generate usability tests, analyze feedback data	ISO Standards, INVEST, SMART
Define MVP	prioritize software requirements, recognize dependencies among defined user stories	business strategy, stakeholder priority, complexity, development cost-benefit, added usability
Implement	generate and complete code, suggest code alternatives, improve code quality based on clean code and architecture criteria	automation, reliability, code correctness, code time complexity, productivity
Document Code	generate in-code documentation, design and architecture specifications, and user manuals	communicate important design decisions, understandable, correctness, comprehensiveness
Test	debug code and suggest solutions, generate test cases and automatic unit and system tests	quality of the generated test cases (accuracy, comprehensibility, completeness/ test coverage, reliability, and efficiency)
Deploy	create predictive models, automate decision-making processes	accuracy, error detection rate, reliability, efficiency

suggest improvements according to the provided criteria. The criteria include ISO standards, INVEST, and SMART. Doran [9] has introduced the SMART criteria (Specific, Measurable, Achievable, Relevant, and Time-Bound)to write management objectives and goals. INVEST framework stands for Independent, Negotiable, Valuable, Estimable, Small, and Testable and is used in the context of agile software management to improve the measurability of user stories [2]. ISO standards, e.g., ISO 9126, define functionality, usability, reliability, performance, and supportability as acceptance criteria for the requirements. ISO/IEC 25010 introduces a product quality model to define comprehensive requirements [27] and define eight criteria of usability, security, compatibility, maintainability, portability, security, traceability, and compatibility. According to ISO/IEC 12207 [18], criteria such as traceability, consistency with stakeholder requirements, testability, feasibility of system architectural design, feasibility of operation, and maintenance can be used to evaluate the requirements. The prompt can include these criteria to ensure that the generative AI tools consider these aspects in the evaluation and improvement suggestions.

Singh et al. [36] state that AI is already used in requirements engineering in requirements elicitation, analysis, and prioritization. AI systems can recognize ambiguous, contradictory, and inconsistent requirements in requirements analysis. Technologies used for this include artificial neural networks, machine learning, genetic algorithms, and deep learning models. Ebert [11] suggests that generative AI can be helpful to automatically categorize and tag the requirements, making them easily searchable and tracked. Carvallo et al. [5] have introduced ChatGPT to their classroom and observed how well the students could use it for requirements engineering tasks. There, ChatGPT answered the students' questions.

In our study, students tested generative AI tools such as ChatGPT (versions 3.5 and 4), Google Bart, and GitHub Copilot. They provided the tools with three different requirements and asked them to evaluate the requirements based on the above criteria and give a new, improved version. The tools explain the context and elaborate on the criteria, then argue which criteria are not implemented in formulating the requirement and propose a new version. According to the students' experience, using generative AI tools to evaluate the requirements list can be very useful. The tools addressed the issues, for example, where the terminology was unclear. One example of the response of ChatGPT 4 was: "Unambiguous and consistent: The current wording is relatively vague. What exactly does *safe and simple* mean?". Especially for beginners, these instructions can be handy and remind them about essential criteria for high-quality software. These results also confirm the findings of [11] that generative AI can identify conflicts and ambiguity in the requirements documentation.

4.4   Define MVP

Defining the MVP is an essential but challenging task in software development. It focuses on prioritizing the requirements according to the market needs. It helps to use the available resources efficiently and bring the software cycles to the market as early as possible. The goal is to avoid producing software that no one requires and desires. Proper decision-making around the priorities for the product MVP is even more crucial for startups due to the limited time and budget. The first requirements implemented as MVP are the ones that are specifically important and relevant for the stakeholders and have high technical feasibility [13]. Wu [45] has investigated integrating ChatGPT in the MVP development process to improve the quality and efficiency of the design and foster innovation. They suggest a framework and discuss the benefits of using ChatGPT in this process. Wohlin et al. [44] conducted an industry survey with two companies to identify the criteria of requirement prioritization and how these can bring value to the product. Thirteen criteria have been defined to be evaluated by survey participants. Based on this study, the following nine criteria are selected: business strategy, stakeholder priority, complexity, development cost-benefit, and added usability.

In our evaluation study, the requirements of an example product were first prioritized using the analytical hierarchy process (AHP). This was selected as promising in a comparative analysis of prioritization techniques by Khan et al. [19]. Then, the students used three generative AI tools, ChatGPT 4, Chatsonic by Writesonic, and Google Bard, and let the tools suggest a priority for the given requirements. The result showed that the tools were able to provide the priorities. The best result was achieved by Google Bard, which provided identical priorities as to the AHP approach.

4.5 Implement

Using different supporting tools for the implementation phase of software development is very common. Developers are used to getting help from their IDE (integrated development environment) for code completion suggestions and debugging tasks. Usage of Q&A platforms with human-created content, such as Stack Overflow, has belonged to the daily working experience of the developers. Integrating generative AI functionalities into this process can increase the developers' productivity and take over some routine and time-consuming tasks. Ebert [11] lists the use cases where generative AI tools such as GitHub Copilot, ChatGPT, Tabnine, and Hugging Face can be used for developing software. From code generation and completion to reverse engineering or answering questions based on code documentation, these tools can increase the efficiency and productivity of their users and reduce human effort in debugging the code. Additional generative AI tools that support developers in the implementation phase are Mutable.ai, and Amazon CodeWhisperer. [39] conducted an empirical study about using ChatGPT for code generation, repair, and summarizing. To evaluate their results, they have defined criteria such as code correctness, code time complexity, and repair rate. Their results indicated that ChatGPT has problems when solving new or more complex tasks. It was highlighted that ChatGPT has a limited amount of attention span in code repair tasks. In a controlled experiment with software developers, Peng et al. [29] observed 55.8% faster task completion using GitHub Copilot compared to the control group.

Quality is the most important criterion for using generative AI in programming [11,23,24,28,29,39]. Reliability and the increase in productivity are by far the most frequently mentioned in the literature.

The literature review in this field showed that generative AI tools have great potential to increase efficiency and productivity in software development, particularly by automating routine tasks and facilitating complex programming processes. However, they also pose challenges, such as the need for precise verification of the generated codes and integration into existing workflows. From today's perspective, applying generative AI tools for software development can be helpful, but with caution and considering the challenges mentioned above. Careful implementation and constant monitoring are crucial to maximize their benefits and minimize potential risks. These tools are valuable resources that, if used correctly, can revolutionize software development.

4.6   Document Code

Although the phase of code documentation was not directly addressed in the design thinking process, this activity is vital for the communication between the developers, the code's maintenance, and the software's scalability. Source code documentation is a time-consuming activity that developers need to accomplish while programming the software. Automating this activity would increase the developers' productivity and free up resources for more important and complex tasks. Khan et al. [20] have automatically applied Codex to generate code documentation. Codex is based on GPT-3 and is pre-trained by natural language input and programming language content from GitHub. Their study has compared the results of the generated documentation with other existing approaches and observed a 11.2% improvement. Good documentation should be understandable by third-party experts [21]. The rationale behind the design decisions should be communicated through the documentation so that new developers or external stakeholders can understand the reason behind the important decisions made throughout the development [16,21]. The automatically generated documentation should be correct, comprehensive, and precise. Like other phases of software development, the user experience of the generative AI tool plays an important role in integrating the tool into the process developers. The students used Chat-GPT (versions 3.5 and 4), and Google Bart with two different code samples. Although all three tools could support the code documentation, ChatGPT provided more details in the code documentation in comparison to Google Bard.

4.7   Test

The testing phase plays a crucial role in ensuring the quality and functionality of the software. The advances in AI technologies have opened up new opportunities to optimize and automate this process. AI tools promise to increase testing efficiency while delivering more precise results. The criteria for evaluating generative AI tools for the testing phase are:

- *Accuracy:* How accurately do the tools generate relevant test cases based on the specifications and requirements?
- *Comprehensibility:* Are the generated test cases understandable and comprehensible for developers?
- *Completeness and reliability:* Can the developer rely on the tool to create comprehensive test coverage and cover all relevant aspects?
- *Efficiency:* How quickly does the tool generate test cases?
- *Usability:* Is the tool easy to use and understand, even for people who may not be experts in the field of AI?

Ricca et al. [32] provide a taxonomy for the typical problems in software testing that AI can tackle. According to their findings, AI and machine learning can help developers to generate test cases and run automatic tests. However, the generated test cases are still simple and need to reach further to be more effective.

In our study, students have tested generative AI tools such as TestIM.io, Mabl, GitHub Copilot, ChatGPT, Applitools to generate test cases for an open-source code on GitHub. The students liked the user experience of GitHub Copilot, as it works directly in the editor and automatically completes code passages. Users can describe their test cases with simple comments, where GitHub Copilot generates the corresponding code. This seamless integration into the development environment and intuitive handling make it a user-friendly tool. According to the students' experience, the main difference between Applitools and other tools tested is its ability to extend Selenium tests through the Applitools Eyes technology. This technology makes it possible to take snapshots of relevant parts of the application during the testing process. This unique feature made the students rate this tool as highly reliable, as the tool consistently recognized differences in the layout and made no mistakes. Furthermore, Applitools got high scores from students in learnability. It learns through frequent testing and user feedback, ensuring adaptive and user-oriented functionality. The results indicate that the tools have their strengths and weaknesses, and using multiple tools together can be helpful to get better results. For example, the students noted that combining Applitools with ChatGPT or GitHub Copilot has a synergistic effect. The precise but more complex functionalities of Applitools, in combination with the user-friendly code generation of ChatGPT or GitHub Copilot, help to overcome challenges such as more complicated setup and code generation efficiently. The students recommended using generative AI tools for testing, especially for developers with less experience. However, the coverage of the cases is still not enough to be able to rely only on these tools. This confirmed the findings of [32] that the current AI tools are more facilitators for testing in collaboration with humans and can not generate robust test scripts to run fully automated.

4.8 Deploy

AI is increasingly important in the software's continuous integration (CI) and deployment (CD). It can help manage the resources to maximize the system's speed and efficiency in data transfer, server configurations, or service management. [31] The evaluation criteria for generative AI tools used in the deployment phase are similar to the test phase. Accuracy, error detection rate, reliability, and efficiency are important factors to be considered.

The following scenarios are examples of AI support in the deployment process [31,35]:

1. Create predictive models: AI algorithms can analyze data and identify trends to predict future resource requirements or system utilization. This helps select the best deployment plans and identify potential problems.
2. Automate decision-making processes: AI can help determine the right deployment model or the number of system instances based on various factors such as user needs, system performance, and costs.
3. Improve maintainability: the system can be configured faster and more effectively in terms of bug fixes configured, which increases the system's stability.
4. Increase user experience: AI can help optimize the software to meet the user's needs and requirements and ensure a positive user experience.
5. Promote scalability: AI techniques can help adapt the software to respond to possible expansions or requirements and continue functioning effectively.

According to the study of [41] with students using ChatGPT as a support tool in different software development phases, The students got significant help from ChatGPT. It reduced deployment issues, optimized deployment processes, and resulted in smoother and more reliable deployments.

Although our students did not have the chance to try different generative AI tools for the deployment phase, the results of the literature review show that it can increase productivity and accuracy. This should be investigated more in future research.

5   Related Work

Software engineers have historically relied on human-powered Q&A platforms like Stack Overflow to support coding. With the rise of generative AI, developers have incorporated AI chatbots like ChatGPT and GitHub Copilot into their software development process. Recognizing the potential parallels between human-powered Q&A platforms and AI-driven, question-based chatbots, Li et al. [23] have explored how developers integrate these supporting tools into their real-world coding experiences. Their study compared Stack Overflow with ChatGPT, finding that while ChatGPT provides fast, clear, and respectful responses, concerns exist regarding its reliability and lack of validation mechanisms, such as Stack Overflow's voting system [23].

Waseem et al. [41] have conducted a study with seven undergraduate students while using ChatGPT in their project in different phases of software development. Their result showed that using ChatGPT in the process of software development was helpful for students to be more productive. Still, the participants had challenges ensuring the quality of the automatically generated code and integrating it seamlessly into the whole system. ChatGPT positively affected productivity, accuracy, efficiency, and collaboration in all the phases that the students evaluated.

York [46] has investigated evaluating ChatGPT 3.5 and former versions in the brainstorming, UX design, and web development used for undergraduates and junior designers. According to his results, ChatGPT 3.5 performed only satisfactorily, and for generating code, it might be critical to utilize it for a real product in organizations. It generates personas that lead to repetitive versions with too many similarities.

Bilgram and Laarmann [1] have investigated using ChatGPT for brainstorming and idea generation, persona creation, generating interview questions, outlining a user journey, and prototyping a web-based App. Their results indicate that generating ideas works well, but the ideas generated in the first iteration might be superficial. A suggested improvement was to give the methodology that ChatGPT should use to make the concepts more concrete. In their example, ChatGPT uses *SCAMPER* (Substitute, Combine, Adapt, Modify, Put, Eliminate, and Reverse) creativity technique. The code generated with ChatGPT was a website based on HTML and CSS with a basic design version of the App.

Tholander and Jonsson [38] have used ChatGPT 3 in the creative design process for ideation, early prototypes, and sketches. Their study shows that generative AI tools can also be useful for creating supportive material, such as personas and scenarios, in the design process.

Ebert [11] showed the high potential of generative AI tools such as GitHub Copilot, ChatGPT, and Google Bart and their advantage of increasing the productivity of software developers. Besides addressing the advantages and possible use cases of these tools, the paper also warns about the new risks related to cybersecurity and aspects that get back to the non-deterministic and non-explainable characteristics of these tools. Rodriguez et al. [34] emphasize the importance of carefully designed prompts for using large language models in automated software traceability. Integrating generative AI tools offers promising opportunities but requires technical improvements.

Ma et al. [24] investigated ChatGPT's ability to understand code syntax and semantic structures that include abstract syntax trees (AST), control flow graphs (CFG), and call graphs (CG). They evaluated the performance of ChatGPT on tasks in C, Java, Python, and Solidity programming languages. Their results showed that while ChatGPT performs well in understanding code syntax, it faces problems with understanding code semantics, especially dynamic semantics. Furthermore, their study identified hallucinations of ChatGPT in interpreting semantic structures of code and fabricating nonexistent facts.

6   Discussion

Generative AI tools are helpful in different phases of software development. They are a good starting point to develop the initial results quickly and iterate more using concrete prompts to get closer to the intended results. Although the generated results are astonishing, it is essential that human experts evaluate them and fine-tune them with iterative collaboration with the tools or continue without them to improve and complement the results. Prompt engineering is essential in achieving better and more relevant results from the large language models. According to [42], prompts with built-in motivation, structure, or provided examples and consequences positively influence the outcome.

Modern generative AI tools like ChatGPT have the potential to revolutionize software engineering. They support the tasks mentioned above for all software development cycle phases, from idea generation and design prototyping to coding and document generation, testing, and deployment. However, software development's high reliability and risk control requirements raise concerns about the lack of interpretability [24] and cybersecurity concerns. Since the output of these tools is non-deterministic and not explainable [11], this affects the reliability of these systems and user trust. Integrating the generative AI tool as part of companies' software development toolchain comes with a risk of data privacy. Companies own sensitive customer data and credential information about their innovation roadmap.

Ozkaya [28] addresses the concerns of using large language models in software engineering, such as data quality and bias, privacy and content ownership, environmental concerns, explainability, and unintended consequences. More research work is required to find solutions for these risks.

7   Conclusion and Outlook

This study has investigated integrating generative AI tools in different phases of the software development process, from idea generation to implementation, testing, and software deployment. In addition to a literature review, 18 business information system students have evaluated generative AI tools in these phases. For each phase, evaluation criteria for the tools were identified, and tasks that generative AI tools can support were described, yielding several insights: First, using generative AI tools in the process of software development can be helpful for beginners. The tools' results can be a useful starting point by providing first sketches for a new design or code snippets in an unfamiliar programming language. Furthermore, the tools can also be used to validate and test the developer's results. For example, they help validate the formulated requirements to identify ambiguity, lack of clarity, or bugs in the code. Finally, the tools can accelerate and take on time-consuming tasks such as code documentation, which is usually not the developers' favorite task but is vital to accomplish.

As mentioned in the discussion, some risks have to be considered when integrating these tools into the toolchain of organizations regarding data privacy. Furthermore, it is important to validate the automatically generated output by generative AI and ensure the results are correct and relevant.

This study is limited to a literature review and a preliminary evaluation study conducted by business information system students. In future research, we plan to extend the evaluation to professional software designers and developers in the industry. Many companies have already started by integrating tools such as GitHub Copilot and are gathering experience about the productivity of their teams using these tools. It would be interesting to collect the first experiences and approaches these companies have taken in this new era of software development.

This study can help the community in two ways. First, it provides current gaps and pain points of designers and developers in the software development life cycle. The gaps identified may guide the research community in improving and enhancing current tools. Second, it provides a good overview of the user experience of the current generative AI tools. By employing a structured and user-centric evaluation framework, we have explored the transformative potential of these tools while emphasizing the importance of preserving and strengthening human-AI collaboration.

References

1. Bilgram, V., Laarmann, F.: Accelerating innovation with generative AI: AI-augmented digital prototyping and innovation methods. IEEE Eng. Manage. Rev. **51**(2), 18–25 (2023). https://doi.org/10.1109/EMR.2023.3272799
2. Buglione, L., Abran, A.: Improving the user story agile technique using the INVEST criteria. In: 2013 Joint Conference of the 23rd International Workshop on Software Measurement and the 8th International Conference on Software Process and Product Measurement, pp. 49–53 (2013). https://doi.org/10.1109/IWSM-Mensura.2013.18
3. Camburn, B.: A systematic method for design prototyping. J. Mech. Des. **137**(8), 081102 (2015). https://doi.org/10.1115/1.4030331
4. Camburn, B.: Design prototyping methods: State of the art in strategies, techniques, and guidelines. Des. Sci. **3**, e13 (2017). https://doi.org/10.1017/dsj.2017.10
5. Carvallo, J.P., Erazo-Garzón, L.: On the use of ChatGPT to support requirements engineering teaching and learning process. In: Berrezueta, S. (ed.) Proceedings of the 18th Latin American Conference on Learning Technologies (LACLO 2023), pp. 328–342. Springer Nature Singapore, Singapore (2023)
6. Cash, P., Štorga, M.: Multifaceted assessment of ideation: Using networks to link ideation and design activity. J. Eng. Des. **26**(10–12), 391–415 (2015). https://doi.org/10.1080/09544828.2015.1070813
7. Cocci, A.: Quality of information and appropriateness of ChatGPT outputs for urology patients. Prostate Cancer Prostatic Dis. **27**(1), 103–108 (2023).https://doi.org/10.1038/s41391-023-00705-y, https://doi.org/10.1038/s41391-023-00705-y
8. Deniz, B.K., Gnanasambandam, C., Harrysson, M., Hussin, A., Srivastava, S.: Unleashing developer productivity with generative AI. https://www.mckinsey.com/capabilities/mckinsey-digital/our-insights/unleashing-developer-productivity-with-generative-ai (2013) Accessed 30 Jan 2024
9. Doran, G.: There's a S.M.A.R.T. way to write management's goals and objectives. Manag. Rev. **70**(11), 35–36 (1981)
10. Dunbar, K.N., Klahr, D.: Scientific thinking and reasoning. In: The Oxford Handbook of Thinking and Reasoning. Oxford University Press (2012).https://doi.org/10.1093/oxfordhb/9780199734689.013.0035
11. Ebert, C., Louridas, P.: Generative AI for software practitioners. IEEE Softw. **40**(4), 30–38 (2023). https://doi.org/10.1109/MS.2023.3265877

12. Epstein, Z., et al.: The investigators of human creativity, art and the science of generative AI. Science **380**(6650), 1110–1111 (2023).https://doi.org/10.1126/science.adh4451
13. Felfernig, A.: AI Techniques for software requirements prioritization. World Sci. Publishing Company, pp. 29–47 (2021).https://doi.org/10.1142/9789811239922_0002
14. Goodfellow, I., Bengio, Y., Courville, A.: Deep learning. MIT Press (2016). http://www.deeplearningbook.org
15. Hauser, A.: Unleash your innovation power: Combining design thinking, agile and lean. https://medium.com/@HauserAndreas/unleash-your-innovation-power-combining-design-thinking-agile-and-lean-part-1-cb7a3360c2af (2019) Accessed 30 Jan 2024
16. Hind, M., et al.: Experiences with improving the transparency of AI models and services (2019)
17. Hinderberger, F.: Vom Proof-of-Concept zum Full-Scale-Product. Springer Fachmedien Wiesbaden, Wiesbaden, pp. 125–147 (2021)
18. ISO12207-2008: ISO/IEC/IEEE International Standard - Systems and software engineering – Software life cycle processes. IEEE STD 12207-2008, pp. 1–138 (2008). https://doi.org/10.1109/IEEESTD.2008.4475826
19. Khan, J., Rehman, I., Khan, Y., Khan, I., Rashid, S.: Comparison of requirement prioritization techniques to find best prioritization technique. Int. J. Mod. Edu. Comput. Sci. **7**(11), 53–59 (2015). https://doi.org/10.5815/ijmecs.2015.11.06
20. Khan, J.Y., Uddin, G.: Automatic code documentation generation using GPT-3. In: Proceedings of the 37th IEEE/ACM International Conference on Automated Software Engineering. ASE '22, Association for Computing Machinery, New York, NY, USA (2023). https://doi.org/10.1145/3551349.3559548
21. Königstorfer, F., Thalmann, S.: Software documentation is not enough! Requirements for the documentation of AI. Digit. Policy Regul. Gov. **23**(5), 475–488 (2021). https://doi.org/10.1108/DPRG-03-2021-0047
22. Kunicina, N., Zabasta, A., Patlins, A., Bilic, I., Peksa, J.: Prototyping process in education and science. In: 2020 IEEE 61th International Scientific Conference on Power and Electrical Engineering of Riga Technical University (RTUCON), pp. 1–6 (2020). https://doi.org/10.1109/RTUCON51174.2020.9316550
23. Li, J., Mynatt, E., Mishra, V., Bell, J.: Always Nice and Confident. Developer's Experiences Engaging Generative AI Chatbots Versus Human-Powered Q&A Platforms, Sometimes Wrong (2023)
24. Ma, W., et al.: ChatGPT: Understanding code syntax and semantics (2023)
25. Ness, R.B.: Promoting innovative thinking. Am. J. Pub. Health **105**(S1), S114–S118 (2015). https://doi.org/10.2105/AJPH.2014.302365, PMID: 25706005
26. Noy, S., Zhang, W.: Experimental evidence on the productivity effects of generative artificial intelligence. Science **381**(6654), 187–192 (2023). https://doi.org/10.1126/science.adh2586
27. Nuzula, M.I.F., Rochimah, S.: Evaluation of service quality in human resource information systems using the ISO/IEC 25010. In: 2023 International Seminar on Application for Technology of Information and Communication: Smart Technology Based on Industry 4.0: A New Way of Recovery from Global Pandemic and Global Economic Crisis, iSemantic 2023. Institute of Electrical and Electronics Engineers Inc, pp. 215–220 (2023).https://doi.org/10.1109/iSemantic59612.2023.10295365
28. Ozkaya, I.: Application of large language models to software engineering tasks: Opportunities, risks, and implications. IEEE Softw. **40**(3), 4–8 (2023). https://doi.org/10.1109/MS.2023.3248401

29. Peng, S., Kalliamvakou, E., Cihon, P., Demirer, M.: The Impact of AI on Developer Productivity: Evidence from GitHub Copilot (2023)
30. Pennefather, P.P.: Creative prototyping with generative AI: Augmenting creative workflows with generative AI. Apress (2023). https://doi.org/10.1007/978-1-4842-9579-3
31. Pothukuchi, A.S., Kota, L.V., Mallikarjunaradhya, V.: Impact of generative AI on the software development lifecycle (sdlc). Int. J. Creative Res. Thoughts **11**(8) (2023), available at SSRN: https://ssrn.com/abstract=4536700
32. Ricca, F., Marchetto, A., Stocco, A.: AI-based test automation: A grey literature analysis. In: 2021 IEEE International Conference on Software Testing, Verification and Validation Workshops (ICSTW), pp. 263–270 (2021). https://doi.org/10.1109/ICSTW52544.2021.00051
33. Ries, E.: The lean startup: How today's entrepreneurs use continuous innovation to create radically successful businesses. Crown (2011)
34. Rodriguez, A.D., Dearstyne, K.R., Cleland-Huang, J.: Prompts matter: Insights and strategies for prompt engineering in automated software traceability (2023)
35. Romero, J., Medina-Bulo, I., Chicano, F.: Optimising the software development process with artificial intelligence. Springer Nature (2023). https://books.google.de/books?id=KAU50AEACAAJ
36. Singh, V., Asari, V., Kumar, S., Patel, R.: Computational methods and data engineering: Proceedings of ICMDE 2020, Volume 2. Springer Singapore, Imprint: Springer (2021). https://books.google.de/books?id=Gfd9zwEACAAJ
37. Sommerville, I.: Engineering software products: An introduction to modern software engineering. Pearson Education, Incorporated (2020). https://books.google.de/books?id=yFAkzgEACAAJ
38. Tholander, J., Jonsson, M.: Design ideation with AI - sketching, thinking and talking with generative machine learning models. In: Proceedings of the 2023 ACM Designing Interactive Systems Conference. DIS'23, Association for Computing Machinery, New York, NY, USA, pp. 1930–1940 (2023).https://doi.org/10.1145/3563657.3596014
39. Tian, H., et al.: Is ChatGPT the ultimate programming assistant – how far is it? (2023)
40. Toubia, O.: Idea generation, creativity, and incentives. Mark. Sci. **25**(5), 411–425 (2006). https://doi.org/10.1287/mksc.1050.0166
41. Waseem, M., Das, T., Ahmad, A., Fehmideh, M., Liang, P., Mikkonen, T.: Using ChatGPT throughout the software development life cycle by novice developers (2023)
42. White, J., et al.: A prompt pattern catalog to enhance prompt engineering with ChatGPT (2023)
43. Winston, P.H.: Artificial Intelligence. Addison-Wesley, 3 edn (1992)
44. Wohlin, C., Aurum, A.: Criteria for selecting software requirements to create product value: An industrial empirical study. In: Biffl, S., Aurum, A., Boehm, B., Erdogmus, H., Grünbacher, P. (eds.) Value-Based Software Engineering, pp. 179–200. Springer, Heidelberg (2006). https://doi.org/10.1007/3-540-29263-2_9
45. Wu, L.: Agile design and AI integration: revolutionizing MVP development for superior product design. Int. J. Edu. Humanit. **9**(1), 226–230 (2023)https://doi.org/10.54097/ijeh.v9i1.9417
46. York, E.: Evaluating ChatGPT: Generative AI in UX design and web development pedagogy. In: Proceedings of the 41st ACM International Conference on Design of Communication. SIGDOC'23, Association for Computing Machinery, New York, NY, USA, pp. 197–201 (2023). https://doi.org/10.1145/3615335.3623035

A Three-Year Analysis of Human Preferences in Delegating Tasks to AI

Huiying Jin and Masato Uchida$^{(\boxtimes)}$ 🆔

Waseda University, Tokyo 169-8555, Japan
hy.k3399@fuji.waseda.jp m.uchida@waseda.jp

Abstract. For the practical application and development of future artificial intelligence (AI) technologies, analyzing human preferences when delegating tasks to AI has become crucial. Additionally, the advancement of technology will impact human perceptions. Therefore, to assess how AI advancement has affected human perceptions, we compared changes in human preferences before and after the widespread adoption of generative AI. This assessment was approached from two distinct perspectives: task categories and delegation factors. Task category clustering was conducted with the input from survey respondents to reassign categories based on their perceptions, enabling the analysis of preferred tasks, and determining whether they have changed. To understand the factors that affect human decision-making regarding delegation, we conducted structural equation modeling (SEM). This analysis allowed us to examine whether the data fit the hypothesized delegation framework and analyze the changes. Furthermore, it enabled us to estimate the magnitudes of the effects of latent factors. Through these two statistical analyses, we discovered that people have become more and more risk-conscious with the development of technology. The introduction of AI services has heightened public awareness regarding the capabilities and limitations of AI, leading to increased consciousness of potential risks associated with this technology. Furthermore, we found that achieving machine capability is still important. Delegability to AI is expected to increase as technology advances. Moreover, the results of analysis shows that careful consideration of motivation is essential. Tasks for which individuals lack motivation are more likely to be delegated to AI, highlighting their suitability for practical implementation in real-world applications.

Keywords: Human-AI Interaction · Task Delegation · Survey Analysis

1 Introduction

Recently, artificial intelligence (AI) particularly generative AI, has undergone rapid evolution, demonstrating practical applications in real-world scenarios.

This work was supported in part by the Japan Society for the Promotion of Science through Grants-in-Aid for Scientific Research (C) (23K11111).

Advances in AI technology further accelerated the release of various services: large language models (LLMs) services such as ChatGPT [4] and image generation systems such as Midjourney [16] and DALL-E 2 [7]. There were some unexpected updates. A work written by an AI sentence generation service won the literary award of Japan [18] and a painting drawn by the image generation AI, Midjourney, won first place at an art competition [15]. Nevertheless, there are many challenges involving implementing AI in real-world applications, such as ethical and legal concerns [10], AI bias [2,14], or copyright issues [22]. Although systems have been developed, some of them have not been widely used due to doubts regarding their use by certain individuals. Therefore, development efforts should prioritize meeting the needs of the people. The analysis of human preferences in delegating tasks to AI is crucial for the development and practical implementation of future AI technologies in human-AI interaction. Furthermore, the advancement of technology is expected to influence human perception. Studying the types of tasks that humans prefer to delegate to AI and investigating the specific factors influencing delegability is important to research.

Lubars and Tan proposed a framework for AI task delegability [13]. They surveyed in the United States in 2019 to gain an empirical understanding of human preferences in different tasks and claimed that delegation decisions are influenced by four key factors: difficulty, motivation, risk, and trust. We conducted the same surveys in Japan on two separate occasions, first in 2020 and then again in 2023 based on Lubars' framework. To assess how AI advancements have impacted human perceptions, we compared changes in human preference before and after the widespread adoption of generative AI from two perspectives: task categories and delegation factors. This enabled us to analyze the changes in human perceptions toward AI over these three years.

The analysis was conducted from two perspectives. The first perspective is task category clustering, which involves reassigning categories based on respondents' perceptions to analyze preferred tasks and determine if they have changed. In contrast to prior studies that subjectively determined task categories, we adopted a novel approach by clustering tasks based on survey responses to explore new categories. This approach aimed to uncover the underlying aspects of human task recognition, shedding light on human unconsciousness in the process, and enabling us to gain deeper insights into the delegability of AI. The second perspective involves structural equation modeling (SEM), which can be used to investigate whether the data fit the hypothesized delegation framework and analyze the changes. It also allows us to estimate the magnitudes of the postulated factor effects.

Our analysis revealed that with the development of AI technology, people have become more conscious of the risks in tasks. This finding suggests that, with the release of AI services, people are now more cognizant of the capabilities and limitations of AI. There is an increased awareness of the potential risks associated with AI. Additionally, we found that the high machine ability is still important for human. Therefore, even for tasks that are currently not highly delegated, it is expected that as technology continues to advance, the level of delegation may increase as machine ability improves. Simultaneously, we have observed that tasks that people are more reluctant to carry out are more likely to be delegated to AI. Consequently, AI capable of performing tasks that people are unwilling to do can be expected to be put into practical use earlier.

The remainder of this paper is organized as follows. First, we outline the related research relevant to our works in Sect. 2. Section 3 provides detailed information about the survey and analysis methods employed in this study. Subsequently, the results of the analysis are presented in Sect. 4. Discussion of the survey result and limitation of our research are covered in Sect. 5. Finally, Sect. 5 concludes the study and discusses the direction for future works.

2   Related Work

2.1   Ethical Issues Regarding AI

With the practical application of AI technology in our everyday lives, new societal issues such as ethics, privacy, and AI bias have emerged. Consequently, the ethics of AI is currently a subject of significant debate in academic and policy circles.

Ethical concerns regarding AI have been discussed by Mittelstadt [17]. It is pointed out that, given the current lack of common goals and robust legal and professional liability systems in AI development, it is advisable to formally recognize AI development as a profession, akin to other high-risk occupations. Additionally, it is suggested that ethical considerations in AI should not be treated as an individual problem but as part of the ethics of AI for businesses and organizations. This emphasizes the notion that ethics is a continual process rather than a fixed destination.

Responsibility for risks or failures related to AI is also a widely debated issue. Oronzo et al. conducted an experiment in which participants were asked to consider a scenario where either a human or AI made a mistake in judgment regarding offenses punishable by a fine or years in prison [19]. They found that individuals who delegated tasks to AI were blamed less than individuals acting independently.

The issue of AI discrimination has been extensively discussed, and research is also progressing to explore methods to investigate potential solutions. AI algorithmic bias results in discriminatory hiring practices based on gender, race, color, and personal characteristics. Chen et al. revealed that algorithmic bias stems from limited raw datasets and biased algorithm designers [5]. To minimize this issue, they suggest employing technical measures such as bias-free dataset frameworks and improved algorithm transparency, as well as management measures such as ethical governance within firms and external oversight.

2.2   Human-AI Collaboration

Several studies have been proposed to address how AI and humans can collaborate effectively, with some focusing on the complementarity of abilities and others on human involvement. Patrick et al. investigated the effects of AI delegation on human task performance and task satisfaction on image classification tasks [9]. By intentionally introducing noise to the image data to enhance labeling difficulty, the study observed that collaborative efforts between AI and humans result in improved performance and task satisfaction compared to individuals working alone.

However, some research has revealed negative results involving human-AI collaboration. When humans collaborate with AI, they may delegate tasks without proper consideration. Thus, Marc et al. suggested that improving AI delegation could be achieved by providing humans with knowledge about AI [20]. They found that AI knowledge limits the use of AI, suggesting that AI knowledge is not necessarily positive for human-AI collaboration.

A recent study by Bondi et al. introduced a collaboration model. For tasks in which AI systems are more prone to making incorrect predictions than humans, they recommend deferring the decision for those tasks to humans [3]. In addition, when deferring tasks to humans, they stressed the importance of considering the manner and extent to which information regarding the results of AI prediction should be shared with humans. Bondi et al. also has reported that withholding the prediction results of AI and informing humans about delayed predictions can enhance human performance. Furthermore, they suggests that it is crucial to consider how to inform humans about the AI's decision of deferring predictions.

2.3 AI Task Delegation

To address societal issues and promote effective research on AI technology, we need to understand how humans perceive AI and how they feel about it. Therefore, we must study delegation factors through fact-finding surveys.

Lubars and Tan introduced a task delegability framework in 2019, as Fig. 1 and Table 1 shown they stating that delegation decisions in various tasks are influenced by four key factors: difficulty, motivation, risk, and trust [13]. They compiled 100 tasks from various sources to explore human preferences. The survey comprised two versions: one assessing if participants would delegate a task to AI when they perform it (personal survey), and the other assessing if they would delegate when someone else performs it (expert survey). The results indicated a preference for machine-in-the-loop designs over full AI control, with trust being the most closely related factor to human preferences in AI task delegation. However, these findings are based on a 2019 dataset, and the evolving environment and technologies raise questions about shifts in people's perceptions, given advancements in AI technologies such as generative AI. Moreover, although categories were subjectively assigned to each task by Lubars and Tan, the analysis regarding task categories was not discussed in the literature. Therefore, a study about task categories is required to analyze preferred tasks that humans prefer to delegate to AI.

In 2022 empirical research regarding Lubars' frameworks for task delegation was conducted by Cvetkovic et al. [6]. They showed that frameworks adapted with fewer factors better fit the data, and the factor of trust was shown to be the

Fig. 1. Framework introduced by Lubars and Tan [13].

Table 1. Overview of the factors in Lubars' AI task delegability framework.

Factors	Components
Motivation	Intrinsic motivation, goals, utility
Difficulty	Social skills, creativity, effort required, expertise required, human ability
Risk	Accountability, uncertainty, impact
Trust	Machine ability, interpretability, value alignment

most predictive of delegability. The result consistent with Lubars' study indicates that trust contributes the most to AI task delegation. However, the target group of this previous research was limited to students with postgraduate educational levels, and only 93 responses were used for analysis. A more widely targeted and large sample survey is required to accurately analyze the overall trends. Therefore, we analyzed data from two-time points and investigated whether human preferences have changed or not.

3   Survey Design

We conducted empirical research in Japan to analyze human preferences in delegating tasks to AI. The survey used the same 100 tasks from diverse domains and the same delegation factors as the survey conducted by Lubars and Tan, and it was translated from English to Japanese. To analyze shifts in people's perceptions due to technological advancements, the same survey was conducted twice over three years. The first survey was conducted in November 2020, and the second survey was conducted in May 2023.

The tasks in the survey include tasks such as medical diagnosis, which can only be performed by experts. When delegating tasks to AI, there are two scenarios to consider: one where the task is performed by oneself, and another where it is executed by a third party, such as an expert. Therefore, similar to Lubars' survey, we have conducted two types of surveys to investigate these scenarios. The Personal Survey includes all four delegation factors in Table 1, which

Table 2. Age of participants.

Personal Survey			Expert Survey		
Age	Number	Percentage	Age	Number	Percentage
18–25	135	14.8%	18–25	76	12.0%
26–35	220	24.1%	26–35	220	34.8%
36–45	208	22.8%	35–45	150	23.7%
46–55	204	22.4%	46–55	100	15.8%
56–65	120	13.2%	56–65	67	10.6%
66–75	17	1.9%	66–76	14	2.2%
76–	7	0.8%	76–	6	1.9%
Total	911		Total	633	

Table 3. Gender of participants.

2020			2023		
Age	Number	Percentage	Age	Number	Percentage
Male	784	50.8%	Male	872	56.5%
Female	748	48.4%	Female	672	43.5%
Other	12	0.8%	Other	0	0.0%

assess whether participants would delegate a task to AI when they perform it themselves. In the Expert Survey, as motivation for the delegation factor was not deemed operative, questions were directed toward factors other than motivation. Additionally, to explore changes in people's perceptions of AI with the development of LLM, questions related to ChatGPT were included in the 2023 survey.

For each year, we used different survey designs. The survey in 2020 consisted of three sections: 1) informed consent and general explanation 2) demographic questions 3) questions about task delegation (personal survey or expert survey). In 2023, we surveyed with five sections: 1) informed consent and general explanation, 2) demographic question, 3) personal survey, 4) expert survey, and 5) question about experience with generative AI service. Participants first provided informed consent, including details about the survey's purpose, a brief explanation of the task, information on compensation, and assurances of confidentiality.

To ensure the reliability of the analysis, the display order of tasks in each section was randomized. For each task, we utilized a 5-point Likert scale to measure participants' agreement levels regarding the factors for delegating tasks to AI (refer to Table 1). Participants were asked to indicate their preferences regarding the level of delegability of AI in different tasks, with four options: full AI automation, AI leading with human assistance (human-in-the-loop), humans leading with AI assistance (machine-in-the-loop), and no AI assistance.

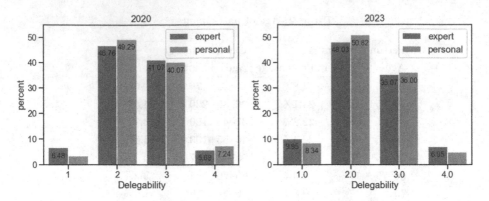

Fig. 2. Percentage of delegability.

Table 4. Change of average delegability. The p-values are represented as follows: * for $p < 0.001$ and NS (Not Significant) for $p >= 0.05$.

	Personal Survey	Expert Survey
2020	2.512	2.460
2023	2.373	2.390
Difference	0.139 (*)	0.07 (NS)

We created the survey using Qualtrics [21] and gathered experiment participants using crowd-sourcing services Lancers [12]. To enhance the quality of the survey, participants had to answer two attention tests correctly. In 2020, we collected 2042 responses for our survey, including 1322 from the personal survey and 720 from the expert survey. Although for the survey in 2023, each participant answered both the personal and expert surveys, we obtained 1005 responses. After excluding invalid answers where participants answered the attention checks incorrectly, these data were adjusted on age group by sampling the larger number according to the smaller number to ensure accurate analysis. However, this distribution does not represent the entire population of Japan. Participant details are summarized in Tables 2 and 3.

4   Analysis Results

4.1   Comparison of Delegability

This section shows the results of a comparison of AI task delegability between 2020 and 2023, which reveals overall trends of delegability. Figure 2 illustrates a decline in AI delegability for 2023. We found a significant difference between 2020 and 2023 in the personal survey ($p < 0.001$), as shown in Table 4. This decline in AI delegability suggests that people may have had higher expectations of

Table 5. Kruskal-Wallis test based on age groups.

	Kruskal-Wallis result	p-value
18–25	1.900	0.593
26–35	4.154	0.245
36–45	4.650	0.199
46–55	11.801	0.008
56–65	5.977	0.113
66–75	0.618	0.892
76–	1.795	0.616

Table 6. Steel-Dwass test result of age 46–55. The p-values are represented as follows: * for $p < 0.05$ and NS (Not Significant) for $p >= 0.05$.

	2020 Personal Survey	2020 Expert Survey
2023 Personal Survey	0.038 (*)	0.332
2023 Expert Survey	0.020 (*)	0.241

AI three years ago. However, as technology progressed and practical applications expanded, people have become more aware of the current limitations of AI technology.

Additionally, to investigate where this decrease in delegability is occurring, we conducted a comparison based on age groups. Kruskal-Wallis test [11] was used to assess the presence of any difference between the four groups (2020 personal survey, 2020 expert survey, 2023 personal survey, and 2023 expert survey). Using the Kruskal-Wallis test, Table 5 shows participants between the ages 46–55 were found to be significant ($p < 0.01$) for group differences. Steel-Dwass test [8,24] of multiple groups were applied following the Kruskal-Wallis test, and as Table 6 we found a significant difference between the 2020 personal survey and 2023 expert survey among the 46–55 age group participants. The discussion regarding these results is presented in Sect. 5.

4.2   Task Category Clustering

In contrast to prior subjective categorizations, this study employed an objective approach by clustering tasks based on respondents' perceptions. We analyzed 1544 data points including 911 personal survey and 633 expert survey as in Table 2 collected in 2020 to calculate the average scores for 14 questions related to task delegation factors. Tasks were then grouped into multiple categories applying the k-means clustering method based on these scores, with the number of clusters set to eight, which was consistent with the previous study. These categories were also applied to the 2023 dataset for comparisons.

Figure 3 shows the average delegability of each cluster (category), and details of the tasks for each cluster are stated in Appendix. The cluster numbers are

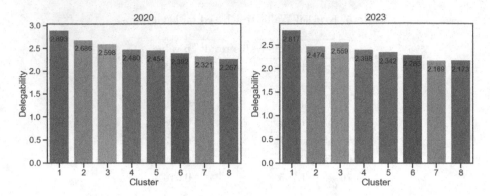

Fig. 3. Average preference for each cluster.

Table 7. The variations in the average task delegation factor for each cluster.

Factors \ Clusters	2 2020/2023	7 2020/2023	5 2020/2023	6 2020/2023	8 2020/2023	4 2020/2023	1 2020/2023	3 2020/2023
Social Skills	3.584/3.685	4.034/4.107	3.750/3.896	3.628/3.511	3.364/3.379	3.055/3.006	2.801/3.187	3.703/3.867
Creativity	3.099/3.119	3.462/3.254	3.543/3.379	4.148/4.210	3.554/3.544	3.186/3.200	2.420/2.659	3.317/3.309
Expertise required	3.534/3.482	4.261/4.106	3.836/3.778	3.586/3.638	2.890/2.798	2.723/2.578	3.228/3.387	4.151/4.077
Human ability	3.305/3.306	2.854/3.045	2.966/3.060	2.707/2.935	3.069/3.217	3.257/3.290	3.304/3.228	2.739/2.879
Uncertainty	3.708/3.638	3.918/4.006	3.857/3.813	3.559/3.433	3.377/3.445	3.213/3.048	3.584/3.678	4.022/3.971
Accountability	3.656/3.623	3.795/3.842	3.412/3.629	2.782/2.813	2.533/2.550	2.424/2.455	3.956/3.925	3.876/3.900
Impact of failure	3.360/3.430	4.203/4.081	3.639/3.560	2.598/2.732	2.771/2.662	2.160/2.265	3.436/3.311	3.957/4.027
Intrinsic motivation	2.919/2.687	2.204/2.239	3.063/2.606	3.075/3.089	3.292/3.144	3.367/3.252	2.262/2.605	2.257/2.304
Machine ability	3.383/3.430	2.678/2.757	2.841/2.984	3.188/3.392	2.750/3.152	3.497/3.503	3.946/3.803	3.433/3.312

assigned based on the descending order of average delegability using data from 2020, and the same numbers are used for 2023. From this figure, it is evident that, between 2020 and 2023, the ranking of delegability was generally maintained, with some variations. Table 7 provides a detailed analysis of these variations, showing the changes in the average value of the task delegation factor for each cluster, in order of magnitude. In this table, the top three numbers are highlighted in red, and the bottom three are filled in blue.

The most significant delegability drop occurred in Cluster 2 ($p < 0.01$). These tasks require a high level of human ability, but less creativity. It suggests a rise in human leading with AI assistance in the past three years, shifting this cluster from the second to the third highest in 2023.

Following Cluster 2, Cluster 7 also showed a significant decrease ($p < 0.05$) in delegability. These clusters involve tasks with a high level of social skills and expertise that are considered unsolvable by AI. Risks such as uncertainty, accountability and failure in these tasks can have a significant impact. Moreover, it is difficult for AI to complete and there is low intrinsic motivation for humans.

Conversely, Clusters 1 and 3 maintained high delegability. The tasks within these clusters humans do not prefer to do and seem achievable by AI. Additionally, both clusters exhibit high accountability, demonstrating that people consistently prioritize risk components, specifically accountability, and this per-

Table 8. Latent variables and observed variables for SEM. The one in parentheses is the observed factor which has two latent factors and has the lower path coefficient.

Latent variables (Factors)	Observed variables (Components)
Motivation	Intrinsic motivation, (human ability)
Difficulty	Social skills, effort required, expertise required, human ability
Risk	Accountability, uncertainty, impact, (social skills), (value alignment)
Trust	Machine ability, value alignment

ception has not changed despite technological advancements. Cluster 1 tasks do not require creativity or social skills, while Cluster 3 tasks involve potential risks such as high unvertainty, accountability and impact of failures. Therefore, despite differing reasons, this high delegability persists in 2023.

4.3 Structural Equation Modeling

Model Fit and Selection. Identifying the factors that contribute to AI task delegation could gain insight into task delegation. This study conducted investigations into task delegation in 2020 and 2023. The research purpose is to examine the change in awareness regarding task delegation in technological advancements by comparing the results between these years. Since the expert survey lacks responses for motivation, for each year, only the 911 responses from the personal survey and answers regarding task delegation factors were utilized to create a covariance matrix of survey results.

Obtained covariance matrix were used to construct a structural equation model (SEM) for AI delegation [25]. SEM is a statistical method for analyzing the relationships among various factors behind observed data. Data obtained by observation are called observed variables, while factors that cannot be directly observed numerically are called latent variables. During the construction of SEM, we referred to the results of previously conducted exploratory factor analysis [23] and Lubars' framework to establish latent variables and observed factors. As Table 8 shown, for the latent variables, we adopted four variables: motivation, difficulty, risk, and trust which are same as Lubars' framework in Table 1. The observed variables used for these latent variables were intrinsic motivation and human ability as motivation, human abilities, effort, expertise and social skills as difficulty, social skills, uncertainty, impact, accountability, values alignment as risk, and values alignment and machine ability as trust. Apart with Lubars' framework we did not used goals, and utility as factor motivation, creativity as factor difficulty, interpretability as trust. Moreover, human ability, social skills, and values alignment are considered to be related to the two latent variables, such that they are observed variables for both two latent variables.

Table 9. Results from the measurement invariance analysis.

Model	Name	χ^2 (df)	CFI	RMSEA	AIC
1	Configural Invariance	327.6 (70)	.951	.045	495.875
2	Metric Invariance	360.216 (83)	.947	.043	504.114
3	Scalar Invariance	442.924 (92)	.933	.046	566.924
4	Residual Invariance	454.654 (103)	.933	.043	558.017
5	Factor Variance Invariance	468.354 (108)	.931	.043	561.583
6	Factor Covariance Invariance	470.962 (109)	.931	.043	562.165

Next, to compare people's perceptions toward AI task delegation in 2020 and 2023, a sample group comparison was conducted using a multi-group analysis model. Since this research compares results between two surveys that were constructed at different time points, we need to know whether our survey measured the same thing across different years. Thus, such comparisons require measurement invariance to ensure that the survey scale is measuring the same construct across different groups. Configural invariance reveals the equivalence of basic constructs across groups. Metric invariance shows the equivalence of factor loadings across various groups. Scalar invariance implies the equivalence of variable intercepts across groups. Residual invariance determines the equivalence of residual variances across the groups.

Model fit results quantify how well the model based on hypothesis fits the data. The fit results of the models are shown in Table 9. As shown in Table 9, the model fit for the configural invariance was acceptable. Moreover, the model fit of the metric invariance, scalar invariance and residual invariance models is not significantly worse than the configural invariance model. Since the configural, metric, scalar, and residual invariance steps have been passed, we can compare group means between the survey in 2020 and the survey in 2023 with the latent variables.

The model with configural invariance has the lowest Akaike information criteria (AIC) and Comparative fit index (CFI) >.95. Therefore, we chose Model 1 as the subject of the analysis. All SEM analyses above were conducted using IBM SPSS Amos [1].

Analysis Results. The results of SEM are depicted in Figs. 4 and 5, and the meaning of each observed variable is listed in the sub-caption under the figures.

Path coefficients are the parameter of the model, which determines how the dependent variable reacts to a unit change in an explanatory variable if other variables in the model are maintained constant. Standardized path coefficients are used to measure how much a causal variable has influence on an endogenous or outcome variable in the model. The estimated standardized path coefficients

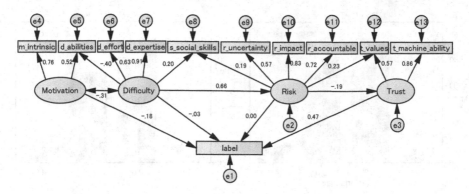

Fig. 4. SEM result for survey of 2020.

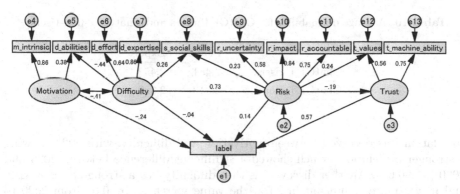

Fig. 5. SEM result for survey of 2023 (Note: m_intrinsic, intrinsic motivation; d_abilities, human ability; d_effort, effort required; d_expertise, expertise required; s_social_skills, social skills; r_uncertainty, uncertainty; r_impact, impact; r_accountable, accountability; t_values, value alignment; t_machine_ability, machine ability)

from the latent factors to the observed variables, except for the label (delegation level), were all statistically significant. Additionally, the estimated path coefficients from the latent factors to the label were significant for motivation and trust.

Firstly, in 2023, the path coefficient from motivation to intrinsic increased by 0.1 compared to 2020. In 2020, the path coefficient from motivation to abilities was greater than the path coefficient from difficulty, but in 2023, the path coefficient from difficulty became greater than that from abilities. In other words, while people used to assess whether their confidence in completing a task was influenced by motivational factors, they now consider ability as a measure of task difficulty. For factor trust, the path coefficient to machine ability decreased by 0.11 in 2023 compared to 2020, which implies that the effect of factor trust on machine ability has decreased.

Evaluating the relationship between common factors, it is apparent that there is a considerable difference in values. Similar to Lubars et al.'s framework, a

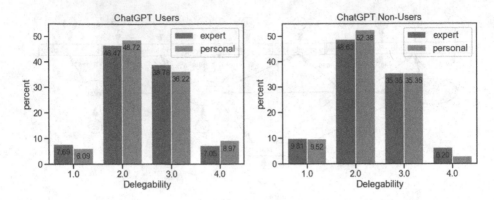

Fig. 6. Percentage of delegability for ChatGPT Users and ChatGPT non-users.

Table 10. Average delegability for ChatGPT users and ChatGPT non-Users.

	Personal	Expert
ChatGPT Users	2.481	2.452
ChatGPT Non-Users	2.313	2.380

correlation was observed between motivation and difficulty, with 2023 showing a stronger correlation, which showed a significant difference between 2023 and 2020 ($p < 0.05$). Another discovery is that difficulty has a strong effect on risk, and it was more significant in 2023, the value increased by 0.07 from 2020 to 2023. However, this result has not previously been described by Lubars and Tan. This intriguing finding might be explained by the fact that difficult tasks could be more risky such as tasks that require expert knowledge. In addition, the effect of the factor risk to trust did not change over the three years.

To consider the effect of four factors on the label (delegability), trust has the most influence on the delegability. Path coefficient from trust to delegability increased by 0.1 in 2023 compared to 2020 which has shown significant differences ($p < 0.05$), which implies that when people decide whether to delegate tasks to AI, trust of AI is the most important factor to consider. The effect of factor risk on delegability also had some changes. In 2020, the path coefficient from risk to delegability was 0, but by 2023, it had increased to 0.14, exerting more influence on delegability.

5 Discussion

This study aimed to evaluate the shifts in human preferences for AI task delegation and the factors that influence these preferences. We conducted the same survey on two separate occasions in 2020 and 2023, allowing us to analyze changes in attitudes toward AI over three years. We investigated how advancements in AI technology have shaped human perspectives on AI.

The factor of trust had the most significant impact on the decision of whether to delegate a task to AI or not, aligning with the results of Lubars' survey. Since the trust factor involves machine ability and value alignment, we can conclude that technological development is important for increasing task delegability to AI and the application of AI in daily life. Individuals, particularly those with an extensive understanding of AI or prior experience with AI services, are aware of AI's capabilities. As demonstrated in Fig. 6 and Table 10, participants who have used ChatGPT show a stronger preference for "AI only" and "machine-in-the-loop" assistance compared to those who have not used ChatGPT. From the importance of machine ability, we can expect that those tasks that currently have a low level of delegation also could increase in the future as technological advances.

However, motivation is a factor that also should be carefully considered. People tend to delegate tasks to AI when they do not feel motivated to perform those tasks. These motivations harmed task delegability. Therefore, we should consider the types of tasks that people dislike, as they are more likely to be easily put into practical use.

Furthermore, individuals have started to more carefully consider the risks associated with task failure. When confronted with tasks involving high uncertainty or risk, and where it is perceived that AI cannot still complete them, people tend not to delegate to AI. This shift originates from advancements in technology, enabling individuals to better understand what AI is more capable of, what it cannot do, and where it is more prone to errors compared to the past. The decrease in delegation in the age group of 46–55 years might be related to these factors. Individuals in this age group often hold positions where they have responsibilities in both their professional and personal lives. Due to increased sensitivity to risks, delegation has significantly decreased in this age group.

6   Limitation

Our study has several limitations. First, our survey participants are individuals who use Lancers, and it was not conducted randomly among selected individuals. Additionally, the respondents in 2020 and 2023 were not necessarily the same individuals, and there is a possibility that the user base on Lancers has changed over time. Therefore, there might be some bias in the sample. Furthermore, due to differences in our survey methodologies between 2020 and 2023, the comparison conditions are not perfectly matched. The potential impact of the differing survey methods might exist or might not, but in this paper, we have not assessed the implications of that impact. If there is an impact, it might be present in the clustering analysis. However, since individuals may perceive personal survey and expert survey differently, we cannot definitively claim the presence of bias. Another limitation of our implementation is that our survey was conducted in Japan. There might be some perceptual differences in other countries due to the environment and cultural differences of people. Future studies should more carefully define survey designs and consider the bias of the dataset. Additionally, this study was conducted both before and after the release of generative AI services, and changes in delegability were observed against this backdrop. While this analysis reflects the current scenario, further investigation, and in-depth analysis are needed to understand how delegability may change in the future.

7 Conclusion

A common result from clustering analysis and SEM is that people have become more risk-conscious as technology has developed. Risky tasks were more carefully considered before deciding whether to delegate them to AI. In addition, motivation needs to be carefully considered. Tasks that individuals lacked motivation, were unwilling to perform, or did not possess the ability to complete were more likely to be delegated to the AI. Motivation harms task delegation, and in 2023, compared to 2020, people exhibited a stronger tendency not to delegate tasks to AI but to perform tasks they want to do themselves and tasks they believe they can accomplish. AI that can perform tasks that people do not want to do can be expected to be put into practical use sooner. The high machine ability is still important. Even for tasks that are not highly delegated at present, it is expected that the level of delegation might increase as technology develops.

A Task Category Clustering Result

See Table 11.

Table 11. Task category clustering result.

Cluster	Tasks
1	Moving & packing merchandise in a warehouse for shipping to customers
1	Writing reports and publishing Olympic (or other sports) results, standings, and stats (sports news coverage)
1	Assembling automobiles in a factory
1	Filling out and submitting your federal tax return paperwork
2	Diagnosing whether a person has the flu
2	Setting tariffs on goods imported from China
2	Inferring damage for insurance purposes after a car accident
2	Monitoring your health and alerting when you should go to the doctor
2	Detecting and removing fake/deceptive online reviews (e.g., for hotels or products)
2	Picking jobs to apply to
2	Advising people on nutrition/their diet to help improve their health, similar to what a nutritionist might do
2	Taking photos of a planned event, such as a wedding or graduation, similar to what a professional photographer might do
2	Responding to emails at work
2	Scheduling an important business meeting with several co-workers

continued

Table 11. continued

Cluster	Tasks
2	Describing images or scenes for visually impaired people
2	Translating an article you'd like to read from a foreign language to English
2	Driving to work
2	Driving a truck delivering goods/cargo between cities
2	Serving food to customers at a restaurant
2	Assisting an elderly person with showering or bathing
3	Diagnosing whether a person has cancer
3	Predicting the sale value of a real estate property
3	Monitoring a person's driving and intervening when they're distracted/in danger of making a mistake (e.g., emergency braking)
3	Detecting/recognizing abnormal or suspicious activities of people in crowds in public places for the purposes of security and safety (similar to part of what a police officer might do)
3	Cleaning up toxic waste, e.g., after a chemical spill
3	Establishing compensation/wage/salary level for an employee
3	Identifying people who attended a political rally
3	In court, determining a defendant's risk (e.g., in committing another crime or missing the court date), to help judges make decisions about bail, sentencing, or parole
3	Helping stroke patients with physical rehabilitation, by guiding or assisting with exercise motions when needed (similar to what a physical therapist might do as part of their job)
3	Analyzing and controlling the flow of traffic in a city
3	Analyzing and sorting legal documents for important information, e.g., to find legal precedents for arguing a case in court (similar to some of what a paralegal might do)
3	Analyzing financial market conditions and executing market orders for a large company (e.g. buy/sell stocks)
3	Conducting a risk prognosis assessment for deciding which patients to transfer to the ICU given limited resources (intensive care)
4	Writing a birthday card to your mother
4	Writing a blog post
4	Playing a board game (e.g., Monopoly, Scrabble)
4	Guiding and explaining exhibits in a museum (similar to what a museum tour guide might do)
4	Thinking of conversation topics while hanging out with friends
4	Picking a movie to watch with a group of friends
4	Cooking dinner
4	Choosing and ordering food to eat for dinner
4	Cleaning your house
4	Playing a competitive game (e.g., poker, Starcraft, Dota2)
4	Brushing your teeth
4	Helping elderly individuals to increase their mobility by guiding them through crowded public spaces (e.g., walking to the grocery store)
4	Picking out and buying a birthday present for an acquaintance
4	Picking songs to listen to
4	Picking a movie to watch
4	Buying groceries

continued

Table 11. continued

Cluster	Tasks
5	Explaining the diagnosis and treatment options for the flu to a patient
5	Identifying and flagging fake/deceptive news articles
5	Identifying the social relationship between two people (e.g., are they friends, a couple, strangers, siblings)
5	Predicting the sexual orientation of a person
5	Managing your personal finances/investments (similar to what a financial advisor might do)
5	Helping to locate a missing child by searching public spaces
5	Finding and rescuing survivors after earthquakes
5	Coordinating and oversee construction of a building, e.g., consulting with engineers, surveyors, specialists, and construction workers – similar to some of what an architect might do
5	Walking your dog
5	Deciding which applicants to hire as new employees for an open position at work
5	Monitoring farm animals' (e.g., cows) behavior, predicting health issues, and alerting the farmer
5	Voting in federal elections
5	Writing reports and publishing updates on House/Senate/gubernatorial races during election day (election news coverage)
5	Tracking important moments and information and creating memory aids for elderly people
5	Assisting your elderly parent
5	Cutting, drying, and styling hair, similar to what a barber or hairstylist might do
6	Picking which advertisements to show to people on social media websites
6	Finding people who might like to meet for a date
6	Analyzing and critiquing aesthetic qualities of photographs or other forms of art
6	Writing a novel or a short story (creative writing)
6	Designing new clothing to manufacture and sell (similar to what a fashion designer might do)
6	Picking a topic to write a short story about
6	Choreographing dance moves for a person to perform
6	Planning menus and developing recipes at a restaurant
7	Responding to 911-police incident reports, similar to what a patrol officer might do
7	Babysitting your child
7	Diagnosing whether a person has depression
7	Explaining the diagnosis and treatment options of depression to a patient
7	Devising treatment plans for patients with depression
7	Devising treatment plans for patients with cancer
7	Devising treatment plans for patients sick with the flu
7	Identifying and flagging online hate speech
7	Teaching a religion's doctrine and practices to followers, similar to some of the responsibilities of clergy/religious leaders
7	Arguing your case when you're a defendant in a criminal court
7	Providing and coordinating patient care in a health facility, similar to a small part of what a Registered Nurse might do

continued

Table 11. continued

Cluster	Tasks
7	Explaining the diagnosis and treatment options of cancer to a patient
7	Interviewing job applicants and rating candidates
7	Deciding military actions such as whether to launch airstrikes
7	Deciding which applicants receive a loan from a bank (loan assessment)
7	Serving on jury duty: deciding if a defendant is innocent or guilty
8	Teaching your child elementary school math (e.g., multiplication, fractions)
8	Finding products you might be interested in while you're shopping
8	Telling a joke
8	Picking which news stories to show to people on social media websites
8	Asking a person out on a date
8	Editing an internet forum comment before you post it (e.g., for maximum popularity)
8	Deciding on an outfit for you to wear
8	Drawing or painting something (making art)
8	Reading bedtime stories to your child
8	Breaking up with your romantic partner
8	Reviewing a book or a movie

References

1. IBM SPSS Amos. https://www.ibm.com/products/structural-equation-modeling-sem
2. Bogen, M., Rieke, A.: Help Wanted: An Examination of Hiring Algorithms, Equity, and Bias (2018). https://apo.org.au/node/210071
3. Bondi, E., et al.: Role of human-AI interaction in selective prediction. In: Proceedings of the 36th AAAI Conference on Artificial Intelligence (2022)
4. ChatGPT. https://chat.openai.com
5. Chen, Z.: Ethics and discrimination in artificial intelligence-enabled recruitment practices. Human. Soc. Sci. Commun. **10**, 1–12 (2023)
6. Cvetkovic, I., Bittner, E.A.C.: Task delegability to AI: evaluation of a framework in a knowledge work context. In: Proceedings of Hawaii International Conference on System Sciences (2022)
7. DALL-E 2. https://openai.com/dall-e-2
8. Dunn, O.J.: Multiple comparisons using rank sums. Technometrics **6**, 241–252 (1964)
9. Hemmer, P., Westphal, M., Schemmer, M., Vetter, S.T., Vossing, M., Satzger, G.: Human-AI collaboration: the effect of AI delegation on human task performance and task satisfaction. In: Proceedings of the 28th International Conference on Intelligent User Interfaces (2023)
10. Jobin, A., Ienca, M., Vayena, E.: The global landscape of AI ethics guidelines. Nat. Mach. Intell. **1**, 389–399 (2019)
11. Kruskal, W.H., Wallis, W.A.: Use of ranks in one-criterion variance analysis. J. Am. Stat. Assoc. **47**, 583–621 (1952)
12. Lancers. https://www.lancers.jp
13. Lubars, B., Tan, C.: Ask not what AI can do, but what AI should do: towards a framework of task delegability. In: Proceedings of the 33rd International Conference on Neural Information Processing Systems (2019)

14. Mehrabi, N., Morstatter, F., Saxena, N., Lerman, K., Galstyan, A.: A survey on bias and fairness in machine learning. ACM Comput. Surv. **54**(6), 1–35 (2021)
15. Metz, R.: AI won an art contest, and artists are furious (2022). https://edition.cnn.com/2022/09/03/tech/ai-art-fair-winner-controversy/index.html
16. Midjourney. https://www.midjourney.com
17. Mittelstadt, B.D.: Principles alone cannot guarantee ethical AI. Nat. Mach. Intell. **1**, 501–507 (2019)
18. Nikkei Inc. https://www.nikkei.com/article/DGXZQOUE16CMP0W2A210C-2000000. (in Japanese)
19. Parlangeli, O., Francesco Curro, P.P., Guidi, S.: Moral judgements of errors by AI systems and humans in civil and criminal law. Behav. Inf. Technol. 1–11 (2023)
20. Pinski, M., Adam, M., Benlian, A.: AI knowledge: improving AI delegation through human enablement. In: Proceedings of the 2023 CHI Conference on Human Factors in Computing Systems (2023)
21. Qualtrics. https://www.qualtrics.com
22. Small, Z.: As Fight Over A.I. Artwork Unfolds, Judge Rejects Copyright Claim (2023). https://www.nytimes.com/2023/08/21/arts/design/copyright-ai-artwork.html
23. Spearman, C.E.: General intelligence objectively determined and measured. Am. J. Psychol. **15**, 201–293 (1904)
24. Steel, R.G.D.: 163 query: error rates in multiple comparisons. Biometrics **17**, 326–328 (1961)
25. Thakkar, J.J.: Structural Equation Modelling Application for Research and Practice (with AMOS and R). Springer, Singapore (2020). https://doi.org/10.1007/978-981-15-3793-6

Evaluating the Effectiveness of the Peer Data Labelling System (PDLS)

Graham Parsonage[1]([✉]), Matthew Horton[2], and Janet Read[2]

[1] University of the West of Scotland, Paisley, UK
`graham.parsonage@uws.ac.uk`
[2] University of Central Lancashire, Preston, UK
`{mplhorton,jcread}@uclan.ac.uk`
`https://chici.org/`

Abstract. The Peer Data Labelling System (PDLS) is a novel and extensible approach to generating labelled data suitable for training supervised machine learning (ML) algorithms for use in Child Computer Interaction (CCI) research and development. For a supervised ML model to make accurate predictions it requires accurate data on which to train. Poor quality input data to systems results in poor quality outputs often referred to as garbage in, garbage out (GIGO) systems.

PDLS is an alternative system to commonly employed approaches to facial and emotion recognition such as the Facial Action Coding System (FACS) or algorithmic approaches such as AFFDEX or FACET.

This paper presents the approaches taken to evaluate the effectiveness of PDLS. Algorithmic approaches did not produce consistent classifications and major amendments to the PDLS would be required if that validation route was pursued. The human review process found that the pupil observers and reviewers reached consensus in classifying most of the data as engaged. Recognising disengagement is more challenging, and further work is required to ensure that there is more consistency in what the participants recognise as engagement and disengagement.

Keywords: Data labelling · Engagement · Machine Learning

1 Introduction

The Peer Data Labelling System (PDLS) [18] is a novel and extensible approach to generating labelled data suitable for training supervised machine learning (ML) algorithms for use in Child Computer Interaction (CCI) research and development. For a supervised ML model to make accurate predictions it requires accurate data on which to train. Poor quality input data to systems results in poor quality outputs often referred to as garbage in, garbage out (GIGO) systems.

PDLS is an alternative system to commonly employed approaches to facial and emotion recognition such as the Facial Action Coding System (FACS) [8] or algorithmic approaches such as AFFDEX [1,16] or FACET [14]. This paper describes the methods used to evaluate the effectiveness of PDLS.

H. Degen and S. Ntoa (Eds.): HCII 2024, LNAI 14734, pp. 67–83, 2024.
https://doi.org/10.1007/978-3-031-60606-9_5

1.1   The Peer Data Labelling System (PDLS)

The PDLS uses peer observation to synchronously capture and label video data. In the original studies [18] pupils worked in pairs as a learner and an observer. The learner was recorded completing a computerised task while the observer logged their ongoing engagement with the task as a binary value, engaged or disengaged. The logged values were used to split the video into clips labelled either engaged or disengaged. On completion of the task the pupils swapped roles and repeated the process. The pupils also completed a questionnaire to assess their feelings on the PDLS. The PDLS was evaluated against the usability metrics effectiveness, efficiency and satisfaction and was judged to be both efficient and satisfactory. Further work was required to validate the effectiveness of the PDLS and this paper describes that process.

1.2   Engagement

Pupil engagement is widely considered a positive factor and an important driver of pupil attainment [3]. Definitions of engagement range from a focus on interaction with a specific learning activity to a multidimensional approach requiring the pupil to engage at behavioural, affective and cognitive levels [10]. The PDLS study considered engagement on task, namely a pupil's interaction with a computerised learning activity completed within a school classroom. Furthermore, while some scholars conceptualise engagement and disengagement as related but separate phenomena [9], within this context, engagement and disengagement are treated as opposing ends of a single scale.

1.3   Methods of Emotion Recognition

A popular and established system for emotion recognition is the Facial Action Coding System (FACS) [8]. Originally developed in the 1970s, but still used today, FACS breaks down facial expressions into combinations of muscle movements called Action Units (AU) [4]. One drawback to FACS is the considerable training required, which at the time of writing is estimated by the Paul Ekman Group to be between 50 and 100 h [7]. Additionally, for the large corpus of videos or images required to train a ML model, the time required for a group of trained practitioners to retrospectively label the data is likely to render such an approach impractical.

An alternative approach commonly used both in academia and commercially is to automate the emotion classification process using algorithms such as AFFDEX [1,16] or FACET [14]. There are several studies [6,19] that attempt to validate the comparative effectiveness and performance of the algorithms. Software such as iMotions [11] can combine facial expression analysis with other sensors such as eye tracking or an electroencephalography (EEG) to combine a range of insights into the human emotional state [13]. Although the algorithmic approach clearly has the potential to save considerable time compared to the retrospective analysis by human experts outlined above and can be used to perform real-time analysis, there is concern that current emotion recognition systems are less accurate than their human counterparts when employed on children [2]. Here it is argued that a real-time evaluation and classification at point of capture performed by child observers has the potential to offer significant benefits over either approach.

1.4 Existing Data Sets for Machine Learning that Include Children

A search for existing data sets featuring children, that are suitable for use in behavioural studies, indicates that specialised child-centred data sets are relatively scarce. Princeton University Library have curated a directory of databases containing face stimulus sets available for use in behavioural studies of which just four are specific to children [20]. The most substantial database The Child Affective Facial Expressions Set (CAFE) [15] features around 1200 pictures of children aged 2 to 8. There are three other databases listed [12,17,21] all of which are relatively specialised and small, particularly compared to more generalised image data sets such as ImageNet [5]. This lack of material restricts the options for CCI researchers looking for data as a starting point on which to train their models.

2 Assessing Accuracy Using iMotions

The iMotions software was used to perform post hoc verification of the labels generated by PDLS. The video data from the first study was input into iMotions, which was configured to perform emotion analysis using the Affectiva AFFDEX algorithm [1] which reports on a range of emotions including engagement.

Before analysis by the software, the video data was standardised at 25 frames per second and further broken down into 3 s clips for ease of processing. Attempts to process the full-length videos caused the software to fail. The software was unable to perform an engagement classification on many of the frames indicated by 0 in the report. In other cases, it generated percentage scores that fluctuate from one end of the scale (0 to 100) to the other over very short timescales (Table 1).

In the given example, which covers a period of just over half a second (553 ms) the software reported results ranging from no classification to engagement levels ranging from <1% to >98%. The most likely cause of the fluctuations are noise in the data but these scores clearly differ from the children's judgements which were more consistent and longer in duration. This may also reflect, at least in part, the preservation of the context in which the original judgments were made.

It should be noted that iMotions allows the user to calibrate the software where analysis is performed at the point of capture, but the retrospective validation used did not allow for this, which may have affected the results. The iMotions software also supports a multimodal approach to classification, offering additional tools such as electroencephalogram (EEG), electromyography (EMG),

Table 1. Segment of the iMotions Engagement Report using Affectiva AFFDEX

Timestamp (*ms*)	Engagement Rating %
14252	0.13487616181373596
14298	0.098771192133426666
14344	0
14390	0.23590019345283508
14436	0
14482	0.85175901651382446
14528	60.243587493896484
14575	98.717597961425781
14621	0
14667	0
14713	0
14759	98.322868347167969
14805	13.619963645935059

and electrocardiogram (ECG) which extend its analytical capabilities beyond facial coding. However, such features require a range of different sensors to capture the data, which also makes such an approach unfeasible for capturing and labelling the data on the scale required in a classroom.

Using iMotions to validate this data set was not considered viable due to both the fluctuations in the data and the large number of instances where the software was not able to make a classification. The second approach to classifying the data employed expert reviewers who viewed the same video footage.

3   Assessing Accuracy Using Reviewers

3.1   Participants

Two reviewers, Reviewer 1 (R1) and Reviewer 2 (R2) watched the videos recorded during the PDLS studies. During the original study, a pupil observer watched another pupil, the pupil learner complete a computerised task and used a simple web interface to record their engagement status as either engaged or disengaged. Using the same interface, the reviewers judged the level of engagement of the pupil learner using the same binary classification. Once both reviewers had independently reviewed the footage the first author reviewed the results to establish where there were differences between the reviewers' and the pupils' judgments.

Both reviewers are qualified educators currently working in Higher Education with significant experience of working with children of this age group. R1 was a secondary school teacher in the UK (children aged 11–16 years) before moving to higher education. The author is also an experienced educator who has also previously worked as a secondary school teacher.

The reviewers were familiar with the project and the notion of engagement on task utilised in this work. The reviewers received no additional training to support them in identifying engagement or disengagement.

3.2 Apparatus

A web interface was developed that presented the reviewers with a list of videos generated by the original studies. On selecting a video from the list, a page loaded, showing the video recording from the study and the logging interface. The reviewers selected their ID from the Validator drop-down list and the Study ID was prepopulated. On selecting the Play Video button, the video started, and the reviewers used the Record Engagement drop-down list to select the pupil's engagement status as either engaged or disengaged. This is the same method that the pupils used to generate the statuses when they observed the original study (Fig. 1).

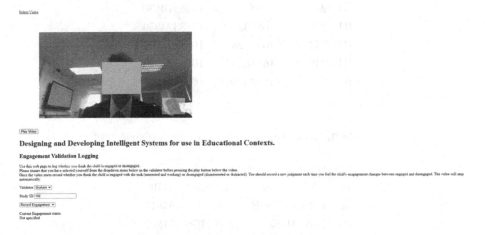

Fig. 1. Interface for Validating a Study

On selecting Play Video, a timestamp was generated capturing the video start time and written to a database. When the video ended, a timestamp was automatically generated representing the end of the video (Table 2).

When the reviewers logged a change in engagement status a timestamp was generated and written to the database along with the engagement status. Table 3 shows this for Study ID 166.

From this, the start and end times for each observed engagement status were derived (Table 4).

Finally, the offset into the video was calculated, and the starting point and duration of each period were calculated. This process is shown for Study id 166

Table 2. Video Start and End Times - Reviewer 1

uid	study_id	start_time	end_time
uid	study_id	start_time	end_time
R1	166	1686554794	1686555222
R1	171	1686555249	1686556345
R1	172	1686562958	1686563733
R1	173	1686563761	1686564978
R1	196	1688315013	1688315310
R1	212	1688315329	1688316061
R1	213	1688316199	1688316743
R1	219	1688316760	1688317003
R1	231	1688317025	1688317203
R1	237	1688317224	1688317642
R1	238	1688317662	1688318123
R1	239	1688318138	1688319151
R1	242	1688319186	1688319480
R1	243	1688322608	1688323050
R1	244	1688323067	1688323763
R1	245	1688323779	1688323926
R1	246	1688323942	1688324251

Table 3. Generating Engagement Timestamps

uid	status	id	time
R1	ENGAGED	166	1686554798
R1	DISENGAGED	166	1686554814
R1	ENGAGED	166	1686554820
R1	DISENGAGED	166	1686554876
R1	ENGAGED	166	1686554879
R1	DISENGAGED	166	1686554919
R1	ENGAGED	166	1686554921
R1	DISENGAGED	166	1686555046
R1	ENGAGED	166	1686555049
R1	DISENGAGED	166	1686555124
R1	ENGAGED	166	1686555126
R1	DISENGAGED	166	1686555200
R1	ENGAGED	166	1686555203

Table 4. Engagement Statuses - Study 166

Start	End	Study ID	Status
1686554798	1686554813	166	ENGAGED
1686554814	1686554819	166	DISENGAGED
1686554820	1686554875	166	ENGAGED
1686554876	1686554878	166	DISENGAGED
1686554879	1686554918	166	ENGAGED
1686554919	1686554920	166	DISENGAGED
1686554921	1686555045	166	ENGAGED
1686555046	1686555048	166	DISENGAGED
1686555049	1686555123	166	ENGAGED
1686555124	1686555125	166	DISENGAGED
1686555126	1686555199	166	ENGAGED
1686555200	1686555202	166	DISENGAGED
1686555203	1686555222	166	ENGAGED

for R1. It shows that R1 logged the first engaged status at 4 s. R1 did not see a change in status for 16 s, at which point a disengaged status was recorded for a period of 6 s, and so forth (Table 5).

This process was repeated for both the reviewers and the original pupil observations for all studies.

3.3   Results

To understand how the reviewers and pupils perceived disengagement over time, the frequency of the period of recorded disengagement for all the studies was derived. Table 6 summarises the time span of the disengagement observations, ranging between one and twenty seconds, grouped by the observers, and Fig. 2 plots the data.

R1 has recorded 14 instances of disengagement with a duration of 2 s and 26 instances of disengagement with a duration of 3 s. In the original studies, the pupil observers only recorded a single instance with a duration of 2 s and 6 instances of disengagement lasting 3 s. R2 recorded six instances for both periods.

Table 5. Completed Validation Timings (Study 166)

Start:	4	Duration:	16	Status:	ENGAGED
Start:	20	Duration:	6	Status:	DISENGAGED
Start:	26	Duration:	56	Status:	ENGAGED
Start:	82	Duration:	3	Status:	DISENGAGED
Start:	85	Duration:	40	Status:	ENGAGED
Start:	125	Duration:	2	Status:	DISENGAGED
Start:	127	Duration:	125	Status:	ENGAGED
Start:	252	Duration:	3	Status:	DISENGAGED
Start:	255	Duration:	75	Status:	ENGAGED
Start:	330	Duration:	2	Status:	DISENGAGED
Start:	332	Duration:	74	Status:	ENGAGED
Start:	406	Duration:	3	Status:	DISENGAGED
Start:	409	Duration:	19	Status:	ENGAGED

Table 6. Comparative Observation of Disengagement by Duration over all Videos

	Frequency of Observation		
Duration (secs)	R1	R2	Pupil Observer
1	0	1	0
2	14	6	1
3	26	6	6
4	8	4	9
5	3	0	5
6	8	2	2
7	5	1	5
8	6	6	2
9	2	1	2
10	1	1	2
11	0	1	3
12	0	1	2
13	1	2	1
14	0	1	1
15	1	0	0
16	1	0	1
17	0	1	0
18	0	0	0
19	0	1	0
20	0	0	0

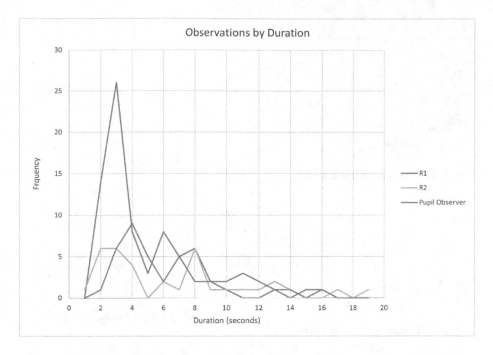

Fig. 2. Comparative Observations of Disengagement by Duration over all Videos

Figure 3 shows the distribution for all the videos. Two outliers from the Pupil Observer data for Study 173 with durations of 334 and 198 s have been omitted to aid in visualising the data shown on graph 3f. Box plots indicate the distribution of the data around the median with the box bounding 50% of the data lying between the 1st and 3rd quartile, also known as the interquartile range. In all three plots, the mean value is higher than the median and the data is said to be positively skewed. Data points falling outside the whiskers are referred to as outliers and, indicate logged periods of disengagement that are not in line with the other observations. In this case, they are all much greater than the other observed durations.

The median values logged for the duration of disengagement are 3 s for R1, 6 s for R2, and 7 s for the pupil observer. The mean values are 4.68 s for R1, 6.63 s for R2, and 20 s for the pupil observers.

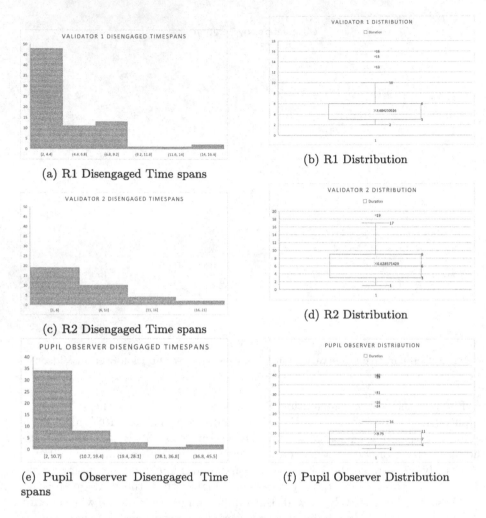

(a) R1 Disengaged Time spans

(b) R1 Distribution

(c) R2 Disengaged Time spans

(d) R2 Distribution

(e) Pupil Observer Disengaged Time spans

(f) Pupil Observer Distribution

Fig. 3. Observed Disengagement by Duration

3.4 Normalised Results

The comparative observations of disengagement shown in Fig. 2 suggest that R1 was more inclined to record short periods of disengagement lasting two or three seconds, which were not observed in the original study or by R2. On reviewing the data, the author identified that often the subject appeared temporarily distracted and immediately returned to the task, and as such did not disengage. To remove these anomalies from the data set, all the logged values with duration $\leq$ 3 s were discarded.

The author also reviewed the other instances of recorded disengagement that fell outside the interquartile ranges in the data. In Study 173, the Pupil Observer recorded periods of disengagement lasting 469 and 198 s, which deviate signifi-

Table 7. Normalised Comparative Observation by Duration

Duration (secs)	Revised Frequency of Observation		
	R1	R2	Pupil Observer
1	0	0	0
2	0	0	0
3	0	0	0
4	6	3	9
5	3	0	4
6	7	2	3
7	3	0	2
8	4	5	2
9	2	1	1
10	1	1	1
11	0	1	1
12	0	1	0
13	1	2	1
14	0	1	1
15	1	0	0
16	1	0	1
17	0	1	0
18	0	0	0
19	0	1	1
20	0	0	0

cantly from the other instances recorded, so this study was discarded. Likewise in Study 213 the Pupil Observer recorded periods of 26 s and 40 s of disengagement that were not validated by R1 or R2. Other than some minor distraction, the author could not discern disengagement lasting for these time spans. Study 213 was discarded.

Studies 237 and 239 also have long periods of disengagement recorded by the Pupil Observer of 39 s and 31 s, respectively, which were not supported by the reviewers. In Study 237 the subject has a brief conversation with the teacher but continues to work, and in Study 239 the subject appears confused by the task and says "I don't get it" but continues to work. Both studies are discarded.

Table 7 summarises the revised time span of the disengagement observations that range between 1 and 20 s after removing the anomalies and Fig. 4 plots the data.

Table 8 and Table 9 summarise the data normalisation process. Eighty-six instances of logged disengaged statuses have been discarded, reducing the count from 161 to 86 occurrences. Most of these come from the validation exercise,

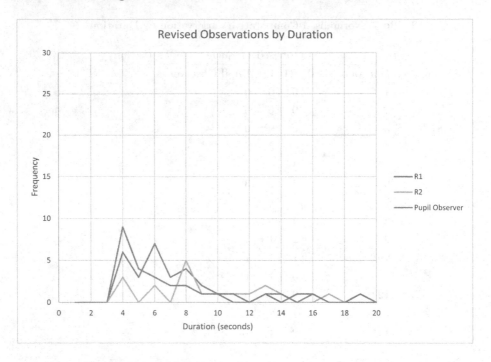

Fig. 4. Normalised Comparative Observations by Duration

Table 8. Summarised Disengagement by Duration

	R1	R2	Pupil Observer
Count	76	35	50
Average	4.68	6.63	20
STD	2.93	4.60	52.76
Median	3	6	7

Table 9. Normalised Summarised Disengagement by Duration

	R1	R2	Pupil Observer
Count	29	19	27
Average	7.10	9.58	7.26
STD	3.08	4.15	4.03
Median	6	8	6

with 47 instances discarded from R1 and 16 from R2. From the original study, 23 instances of disengagement were discarded, 7 of which had a short duration of 2 or 3 s.

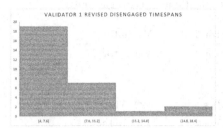

(a) R1 Revised Disengaged Time spans

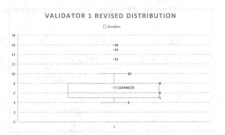

(b) R1 Revised Distribution

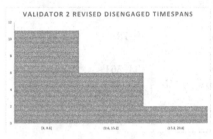

(c) R2 Normalised Disengaged Time spans

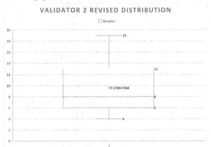

(d) R2 Normalised Distribution

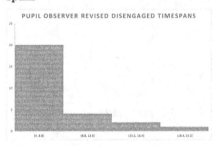

(e) Pupil Observer Normalised Disengaged Time spans

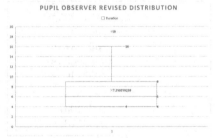

(f) Pupil Observer Normalised Distribution

Fig. 5. Normalised Observed Disengagement by Duration

The removal of the outliers from the study data has reduced the mean duration from 20 s to 7.26 s, while discarding the observations with a short duration has decreased the median value from 7 to 6 s.

Figure 5 shows the normalised distribution for the entire data set.

3.5 Data Validation

Table 10 summarises the normalised observation of disengagement for all the included studies.

Study 212 appears to be different from the other studies in terms of the frequency of the observations. On review, there was little evidence to support

Table 10. Normalised Instances of Observations of Disengagement

Study ID	Pupil Observer	Validator 1	Validator 2
Study ID	Pupil Observer	Validator 1	Validator 2
166	No Disengaged Status		
171	526–530 s	525–538 s	529–537 s
172	150–154 s 313–319 s 345–350 s 405–409 s	150–159 s 312–316 s 400–404 s	150–154 s 397–408 s
196	75–79 s 114–118 s	74–80 s 115–121 s	69–79 s
212	24–31 s 37–46 s 72–77 secondsv 85–90 s 133–147 s 158–163 s 185–192 s 211–217 s 231–235 s 301–311 s 357–373 s 399–403 s 457–468 s	20–35 s 160–166 s 355–363 s 398–403 s	353–361 s
219	24–31 s 93–105 s 133–138 s 172–180 s	21–37 s 105–112 s	19–38 s 104–112 s
238, 242, 243	No Disengaged Status		
244	627–631 s 681–694 s		
245	No Disengaged Status		
246	297–305 s		294–307 s

the Pupil Observer's observations of disengagement. During the instance logged starting at 37 s, the learner looks amused and may be slightly distracted, but appears to continue working on the task. The Pupil Observer logs two instances of disengagement between 72 and 90 s each lasting 5 s where the learner continues to work. Likewise with the other observations it appears that the pupil may be amused by some external event which may be generated by the observer but does not appear to disengage from the task.

Discarding the observations from Study 212 leaves 11 studies and yields 14 instances of disengagement logged with 9 validated or 64% and a duration of 80 s. During the same period, the pupil observer recorded 3530 s of engagement, indicating that the learners were disengaged for just over 2% of the time while performing the task set. Table 11 summarises the validated disengagement data and indicates that the pupils were disengaged for just 53 s during the study.

Table 11. Validated Disengagement

Study ID	Validated Disengagement
171	4 s
172	4 s 6 s 4 s
196	4 s 4 s
219	7 s 12 s
246	8 s

4 PDLS Effectiveness

What then does this say about the effectiveness of the PDLS process? First, the majority of the data labelled during the process is verified by the reviewers. That is to say, in this study the default state of the learners is engaged and the process is accurate and effective in identifying engagement.

Identifying disengagement is more problematic, and the review process identified weaknesses in the process. Reviewers were divided on what constitutes disengagement in this context. R1 recorded a high number of instances of 2 or 3 s that R2 and the pupils did not log as disengagement.

R1 appears to have recorded a status when the pupil is temporarily distracted and the challenge here is that because the process is conducted in real time there is no way of knowing how long the distraction will last. The approach taken here was to discard the data, but an alternative approach could be to ignore small durations of disengagement and change the label to engaged. The latter approach would clearly help the efficiency of the PDLS process. Either way, training for the observers to aid consistency in drawing the distinction between temporary distraction and disengagement from task before they participate may create more consistent observations and improve the effectiveness of the process.

The reviewers indicated that the interface to record the engagement status was difficult to use and that the feedback from the software was not clear enough.

The current system used a drop-down box to toggle between classifications, and this can be replaced by a clicker, which would facilitate recording statuses without having to concentrate on the screen. The textual on-screen feedback as to the current engagement level can be replaced with a larger graphic to help participants quickly identify the current recorded status.

5 Conclusion and Further Work

The PDLS [18] is intended as a system for generating labelled data using peer observation. This paper evaluates the effectiveness of the process using both the iMotions software and human reviewers. The iMotions software did not produce consistent classifications and major amendments to the PDLS would be required if that validation route was pursued. The human review process found that the pupil observers and reviewers reached consensus in classifying most of the data as engaged. Recognising disengagement is more challenging, and further work is required to ensure that there is more consistency in what the participants recognise as engagement. Several changes are proposed for the software interface prior to further studies to support more efficient recordings.

Further work will concentrate on the development of the PDLS process. In particular the accuracy of the data labelling process which should be supported with better briefing for participants and an improved interface for logging. It is intended that a library of tasks will be developed to better support data collection. In doing so it is hoped that a corpus of data will be built to support other researchers who wish to carry out ML based tasks with children.

References

1. Bishay, M., Preston, K., Strafuss, M., Page, G., Turcot, J., Mavadati, M.: Affdex 2.0: a real-time facial expression analysis toolkit. arXiv preprint arXiv:2202.12059 (2022)
2. Bryant, D., Howard, A.: A comparative analysis of emotion-detecting AI systems with respect to algorithm performance and dataset diversity. In: Proceedings of the 2019 AAAI/ACM Conference on AI, Ethics, and Society, pp. 377–382 (2019)
3. Christenson, S., Reschly, A.L., Wylie, C., et al.: Handbook of Research on Student Engagement, vol. 840. Springer, Heidelberg (2012). https://doi.org/10.1007/978-1-4614-2018-7
4. Cohn, J.F., Ambadar, Z., Ekman, P.: Observer-based measurement of facial expression with the facial action coding system. In: The Handbook of Emotion Elicitation and Assessment, vol. 1, no. 3, pp. 203–221 (2007)
5. Deng, J., Dong, W., Socher, R., Li, L.J., Li, K., Fei-Fei, L.: Imagenet: a large-scale hierarchical image database. In: 2009 IEEE Conference on Computer Vision and Pattern Recognition, pp. 248–255. IEEE (2009)
6. Dupré, D., Krumhuber, E.G., Küster, D., McKeown, G.J.: A performance comparison of eight commercially available automatic classifiers for facial affect recognition. PLoS ONE 15(4), e0231968 (2020)
7. Ekman, P.: Facial action coding system, January 2020. https://www.paulekman.com/facial-action-coding-system/

8. Ekman, P., Friesen, W.V.: Facial action coding system. Environ. Psychol. Nonverbal Behav. (1978)
9. Fredricks, J.A., Blumenfeld, P.C., Paris, A.H.: School engagement: potential of the concept, state of the evidence. Rev. Educ. Res. **74**(1), 59–109 (2004)
10. Groccia, J.E.: What is student engagement? New Dir. Teach. Learn. **2018**(154), 11–20 (2018)
11. iMotions: Unpack human behavior, November 2022. https://imotions.com/
12. Khan, R.A., Crenn, A., Meyer, A., Bouakaz, S.: A novel database of children's spontaneous facial expressions (LIRIS-CSE). Image Vis. Comput. **83**, 61–69 (2019)
13. Kulke, L., Feyerabend, D., Schacht, A.: A comparison of the Affectiva Imotions facial expression analysis software with EMG for identifying facial expressions of emotion. Front. Psychol. **11**, 329 (2020)
14. Littlewort, G., et al.: The computer expression recognition toolbox (CERT). In: 2011 IEEE International Conference on Automatic Face and Gesture Recognition (FG), pp. 298–305. IEEE (2011)
15. LoBue, V., Thrasher, C.: The child affective facial expression (CAFE) set: validity and reliability from untrained adults. Front. Psychol. **5**, 1532 (2015)
16. McDuff, D., Mahmoud, A., Mavadati, M., Amr, M., Turcot, J., Kaliouby, R.E.: Affdex SDK: a cross-platform real-time multi-face expression recognition toolkit. In: Proceedings of the 2016 CHI Conference Extended Abstracts on Human Factors in Computing Systems, pp. 3723–3726 (2016)
17. Negrão, J.G., et al.: The child emotion facial expression set: a database for emotion recognition in children. Front. Psychol. **12**, 666245 (2021)
18. Parsonage, G., Horton, M., Read, J.: The peer data labelling system (PDLS). A participatory approach to classifying engagement in the classroom. In: Abdelnour Nocera, J., Kristın Lárusdóttir, M., Petrie, H., Piccinno, A., Winckler, M. (eds.) INTERACT 2023. LNCS, vol. 14143, pp. 224–233. Springer, Cham (2023). https://doi.org/10.1007/978-3-031-42283-6_13
19. Stöckli, S., Schulte-Mecklenbeck, M., Borer, S., Samson, A.C.: Facial expression analysis with affdex and facet: a validation study. Behav. Res. Methods **50**(4), 1446–1460 (2018)
20. Testerman, M.: Databases (a-z) - face image databases - research guides at Princeton university, January 2022. https://libguides.princeton.edu/facedatabases. Accessed 22 Feb 2024
21. Webb, R., Ayers, S., Endress, A.: The city infant faces database: a validated set of infant facial expressions. Behav. Res. Methods **50**(1), 151 159 (2018)

Enhancing Historical Understanding in School Students: Designing a VR Application with AI-Animated Characters

Francesca Perillo[1]([✉])[iD], Marco Romano[2][iD], and Giuliana Vitiello[1][iD]

[1] Department of Computer Science, University of Salerno, Via Giovanni Paolo II, 132, 84084 Fisciano, SA, Italy
fperillo@unisa.it

[2] Dipartimento di Scienze Umanistiche e Sociali Internazionali, Università degli Studi Internazionali di Roma, 00147, Rome, Italy

Abstract. Virtual reality technologies are being integrated into professional training and school education. Applications for practice and learning in both formal and informal settings are becoming more prevalent as the cost of headsets decreases, making these technologies more accessible to students and schools alike. Furthermore, the emergence of Large Language Models, such as the one supporting ChatGPT, which is widely available, opens up new possibilities for enhancing immersive learning experiences through interactive characters. This paper presents the design process of an immersive VR system for school students, where VR avatars assist students in critically engaging with historical topics. In a reconstructed historical scenario, avatars represent historical figures and are trained to advocate for a given thesis. Students can interact with these virtual characters through voice interaction and ask questions to better understand a historical situation. Additionally, students can immerse themselves in the app in small groups, interact with multiple avatars simultaneously, listen to different theses, and avatars can engage in dialogue with each other while the student observes.

Keywords: immersive virtual reality · learning experience · interactive system design

1 Introduction

Over the last few decades, Virtual Reality (VR) have become increasingly important in various aspects of our daily lives [10,32]. They have radically changed our experience of interacting with the digital world and introduced new possibilities in various fields. Among the many applications, the use of headset has proven to be particularly promising in the field of education [14]. They have been transformed from simple entertainment devices into powerful and multifunctional educational tools [25]. The use of headset in education has evolved

H. Degen and S. Ntoa (Eds.): HCII 2024, LNAI 14734, pp. 84–93, 2024.
https://doi.org/10.1007/978-3-031-60606-9_6

from engaging graphical simulations to fully immersive and interactive educational experiences. These devices enable students to observe and actively participate in lessons and activities, fostering deeper engagement and learning [7]. For instance, in scientific and medical fields, headset enable students to explore the human body in detail, simulate laboratory experiments, or even assist in virtual medical procedures [11, 15, 23].

Another important aspect is the ability to adapt to learning contexts [8]. This technology allows educators to create personalised learning experiences that meet the specific needs of students [26, 28]. By developing customised learning scenarios, headset facilitate different learning styles, ensuring each student learns in a suitable environment [4, 16]. The use of virtual learning environments significantly extends educational opportunities beyond the limitations of traditional classrooms. Moreover, The potential of VR became even more evident during the lockdown imposed by the COVID-19 pandemic in 2020. Indeed, in VR students can engage in remote lessons from any location, explore virtual museums, and collaborate with peers on educational projects without the need for physical proximity [3, 13]. Before the pandemic period, the use of VR devices was mainly driven by students, while institutions were cautious and slow to embrace and integrate VR into teaching-learning processes. According to a study by Mario A. Rojas-Sánchez et al. [24] the pancemic period has transformed this perception. In this period, artificial intelligence has also begun to find increasingly relevant applications in people's daily lives. For example, robots equipped with Artificial Intelligence (AI) for more naturally perceived multimodal interaction are now being experimented with as domestic support, particularly for the elderly [5, 9].

Exploring the fusion of VR and AI, researchers such as M. Luck and R. Aylett [17] start to investigate the integration of these two technologies to establish Intelligent VR Environments. The addition of AI added a new dimension of intelligence and adaptability to virtual environments, enabling more personalised and interactive experiences. Users can now interact with intelligent virtual agents, receive contextual responses and experience virtual environments that dynamically respond to their actions and choices. Shaunak K Bakshi et al. [2] emphasize the promising prospects of combining AI and VR specifically in the realm of medical training. When discussing the interaction between AI and humans, it is important to consider the collaborative aspect of this interaction. Dafoe et al. in [12] introduce the collaborative method as a new perspective. They argue that machines must learn to agree with human expectations and collaborate effectively with them. The authors list four key components of cooperative intelligence: Understanding, Communication, Engagement, and Norms. These components are similar to human collaborative activities. We also need to consider the Human-Centred Design (HCD) factor. Battistoni et al. [6] explain how to adapt the HCD process to give the AI as the user a central role, to further empower the interactive system, and to adapt the interaction design to the actual capabilities, limitations and potential of the AI. The authors emphasise the importance of interaction simplicity for AI's continuous learning, promoting improvement through engagement and contextual understanding. Clarity of user input promotes accurate interpretation and reduces repetition of learning. Context awareness is also essential, allowing AI to adapt interaction methods and feedback mechanisms. Patton et al. [20] emphasise that television and video games are common sources of distraction for children.

This paper outlines the development journey of an immersive VR system tailored for school students, aiming to enhance their critical engagement with historical subjects. Within a reconstructed historical setting, VR avatars take on the roles of significant historical figures, adeptly advocating for specific theses. Students are empowered to interact with these virtual characters via voice commands, probing them with questions to deepen their comprehension of historical contexts. Moreover, students have the opportunity to immerse themselves in the application within small group settings, engaging simultaneously with multiple avatars presenting various theses. Notably, "avatars engage in dialogue amongst themselves, providing students with an insightful observational experience."

2 Literature Review

According to AlGerafi et al. [1], VR and Augmented Reality (AR) offer a personalized educational experience. It is important to promote immersive and interactive learning environments and demonstrate how these technologies promote active learning, collaboration and critical thinking through interactive simulations and experiences. The study of AlGerafi et al. emphasises the importance of providing equal opportunities for all students to access AR and VR tools, to ensure that all learners can benefit from these innovative technologies. The study by Makransky G. et al. [18] examines the impact of VR on science education, with a particular emphasis on its effects on virtual science learning. The study findings suggest that the integration of VR technology enhances the study experience, particularly in terms of presence and motivation. Marougkas et al. [19] found that integrating VR applications with some types of learning is considered more effective. Infact, Li Ying at al. [31] found that VR can enhance the effectiveness of the curriculum by providing an immersive environment. This allows students to intuitively understand abstract concepts that are often difficult to describe. Pherson-Geyse et al. [22] also point out that experiences outside the classroom help students connect theory to real-life situations.

Peixoto et al. [21] argue that the use of VR has a positive relationship with student and foreign language learning, especially when compared to conventional pedagogical practices. The use of VR has a positive relationship with student motivation and satisfaction. Cantone et al. [10] developed a VR world for foreign language learning. The study focused on the effectiveness of this approach and the importance of using virtual objects in the scene. Also Scavarelli et al. [29] suggest that considering the accessibility and interaction between physical and virtual environments is crucial in the context of learning. Moreover, VR in education enhances students' understanding of topics, performance, grades, and educational experience [30]. Romano et al. [27] conducted a usability experiment suggesting that recreational activities should be included in VR systems. This study points us to a probable problem with regard to the loss of interest and attention during long periods of interaction with the system. The inclusion of recreational activities can help to prevent this situation.

3   Contextual Analysis

A recent investigation in two high schools in south of Italy has revealed a discrepancy between the widespread talk about new technologies, especially VR headsets, and their actual use in learning. Despite the growing discussion and promises associated with the integration of these technologies in the educational context, the outcomes of the investigation indicate a low effective adoption rate by high schools. Many students feel unmotivated and bored with traditional learning methods. However, most students do not believe that these methods should be completely replaced. Instead, they suggest integrating them with playful and entertaining activities. These activities can help make the concepts learned in class more memorable by providing a more dynamic and engaging approach to learning. This finding highlights the significance of implementing a balanced approach that considers both conventional methods and modern technologies in education. These findings are in line with the experiences of teachers and researchers working in the field of education. To enhance the effectiveness of teaching, it is important to integrate recreational and entertainment activities. This overlap of perspectives underlines the need for innovative approaches, taking into account students' preferences and needs, to promote more engaging and meaningful learning.

3.1   Current Situation: Students Real-Life After School Scenario

According to teachers, researchers and students' feedback, a representative picture of the current situation has been outlined in Fig. 1, highlights a growing sense of loss of interest and motivation in traditional learning methods. This scenario illustrates an increasing lack of motivation and disinterest among students towards traditional learning methods. Students report feeling bored during class and believe that these methodologies are not engaging or stimulating enough. This scenario highlights the importance of reviewing and adapting educational practices to match the needs and preferences of today's students.

Given the current situation, we propose focusing on two distinct learning moments: classroom instruction and autonomous learning at home. Specifically, we believe it is crucial to modify the latter to prevent students from becoming bored or disinterested while studying independently. Students may lose interest when studying alone, especially if the material is not engaging or stimulating. To prevent boredom and keep them motivated to continue their own learning, autonomous learning can be modified to make it more interesting. The aim of this study is to investigate how to enhance the enjoyment of studying for students, with a focus on independent study in humanities, specifically history. To

Fig. 1. Student real-life after school scenario (AS IS scenario)

achieve this, we propose developing innovative approaches that involve interactive, engaging, and personalized activities to make studying a more stimulating and rewarding experience.

According to the students' feedback, we carried out a representative real-life after school scenario. Figure 1 presents a student real-life after school scenario, which will be explained in the following.

Scenario

Student real-life after school scenario (AS IS scenario)
The student is following a history lesson about the political factions of the Guelphs and Ghibellines in Italian history `1 of 6`. He is interested in the subject matter taught during the frontal lesson. He wants to continue studying it independently at home `2 of 6`. The boy starts to study at 15:30 (3.30pm) `3 of 6` but is quickly distracted by other more engaging activities `4 of 6`. At 18:30 (6.30pm), he found himself forced to study quickly `5 of 6`, relying on less reliable sources before dinner `6 of 6`.

3.2 Potential Requirements Throw Intelligence Centred Design Approach

To help students learn independently, we have designed a solution that combines AI and VR. After attending a lecture on a particular topic, students can reinforce what they have learned in the classroom through an engaging learning approach. Wearing a VR headset, students can be transported directly into the historical context being studied, creating an immersive and participatory experience. The aim is to make students feel an integral part of the historical period they are studying, allowing them to listen to the speeches of the characters of the time. Moreover, the ability to actively interact with the VR environment and characters allows students to ask questions and receive direct answers from virtual characters.

Based on lesson learned of previous studies [4,6,16] and on current situation scenario, we define some possible requirements in Table 1.

3.3   Transformation Scenario

Based on the requirements outlined in the previous section, the system we propose is centered around an Immersive Virtual Reality (IVR) app, where various historical settings are reconstructed. Within each setting, one or more historical characters endowed with AI capabilities are present. Through verbal communication or an alternative message-based communication system, which can be accessed through a panel appearing when the user approaches, users can engage in conversation with these characters. The AI can be based on OpenAI's APIs but trained on one or more specific theses, enabling the character to respond as one would expect from the real historical figure. The app can be configured for single-user or multi-user use, allowing students to interact independently or in the presence of a teacher and classmates. A particular case is when two characters can engage in dialogue with each other based on user input.

The visionary scenario in Fig. 2 allows us to describe the complete future system in detail, based on our analysis.

Scenario

Visionary scenario based on our analysis.

The student is attending a history lesson on the political factions of the Guelphs and Ghibellines in Italian history ▇ 1 of 6 ▇. He is interested in the subject matter taught during the lesson and wish to continue studying it independently at home using the new methodology ▇ 2 of 6 ▇. After school, he quickly went home, anxious to learn more. He is very lucky because his school is using a new VR methodology to teach some subjects such as art, history and literature. Upon arriving home, the student puts on his VR headset; the immersive experience allowed him to take part in historical landscape of old Italy. He walks through the old Italian streets until they encounter two of the characters that their teacher explained during the lesson ▇ 4 of 6 ▇. Two representatives of the Guelphs and Ghibellines factions are engaged in a conversation. The student interrupts them to ask some questions. The discussion continues between the two virtual AI characters and the guy, until one of the characters informs him that he has covered all the knowledge that his teachers presented in the frontal lesson. Despite this, the guy still the need to ask further questions of the two AI characters ▇ 5 of 6 ▇. When he took off his VR headset, he was amazed at how the technology made history lessons an interactive experience. The guy has gained enough knowledge, but he is still fascinated and would like to read the PDF of the course as well. ▇ 6 of 6 ▇

Table 1. The table displays potential requirements for designing a virtual reality application for educational purposes.

Requirements	Rationale
Functional requirements	
Based on image recognition and localisation, the system provides VR functionality to visitors.	VR techniques should be implemented taking into account different indoor or outdoor settings.
The system provides relevant responses to end users based on their input.	In order to provide personalised responses, the AI included in VR should be implemented by taking into account the specific input from the student.
Environmental and contextual requirements	
The system must be designed to create the optimum environment.	Students interacting with the VR environment need to feel as if they are in the same environment as the content they are studying.
Environment must be adaptable	Students interacting with the system must pay attention to the content they are learning in the classroom. Therefore, the environment must change according to the user's knowledge.
The visit can be outdoor and/or indoor	An environment can have both outdoor and indoor areas. Our scenarios are set in an outdoor area, but some indoor areas must be present (e.g. a virtual museum for art lessons).
The system should not allow the student to use the VR technology for any other purpose.	The visit should continue for the duration of the interaction between the student and the AI avatar. Other uses of the system that are not relevant to the study must be excluded.
The system must be a self-control system.	We have defined this system for personal use by students. The end users may have a lot of skills with the system or no skills at all. For this reason, if there is a problem with the system, it should be able to fix it automatically without any intervention from the users.
Natural and responsible interaction with users.	Interact naturally and responsibly with users, allowing them to ask questions, receive answers and actively participate in the conversation
Data requirements	
Data must be accurate and updated frequently	The data must change according to the user's current knowledge.
Usability requirements	
The user interface should provide a simple management of users mistakes	Students should focus only on the learning experience without worrying about the technology. It is essential to reduce the number of possible inadvertent user errors.
The system should be easy to use and should require little training effort.	Ensuring that students have access to an intuitive and user-friendly learning system is critical to supporting their academic success and overall well-being throughout their learning journey.
The object must support mobility.	As described by the scenarios, the visitors walk into VR to explore the site and interact with the AI characters. Therefore, if visitors choose to move using the room scale modality, also the mobility could be an important component to consider in the interaction design.
Ensure empathy and emotional engagement with users.	Show empathy and emotional engagement with users helps to create an emotional connection and improving the overall experience.
AI requirements	
Interaction must be easily interpretable by AI.	It's crucial to set the language in which users will communicate and advise them against using other languages or dialects.
Facilitate collaborative decision-making, where both the AI and the user actively participate in reaching a common decision.	Our idea is to avoid fully automated decision-making, where the AI is the only decision maker, or user-dependent decision-making, where the user makes decisions independently. Instead, a hybrid approach that combines elements of the two options above might be used.
Interaction must have a clear context.	If there is noise, privacy concerns, or other distractions, the system should provide multimodal or alternative communication methods that are clear and immediate for the AI. For example, text input via physical or virtual keyboards, reactions to the user's position in virtual space, pre-set message panels, etc.
The interaction must be appropriately tailored to support single or multiple users.	AI should engage with different users within the same space, ensuring each user is easily distinguishable to enable the AI to make informed decisions effectively.

Fig. 2. The diagram illustrates the functionality of the prototype.

4 Conclusions and Future Works

In conclusion, this work has explored the design process of an immersive learning app featuring AI-animated characters to enhance historical understanding among school students. The design approach employed, known as the Intelligence-Centered Design Process, extends the traditional user-centered design process, allowing for the identification of AI requirements that enable AI characters to interact more effectively in virtual space. Moving forward, we intend to collaborate closely with high school institutions to conduct longitudinal studies and gather feedback on usability, learning experience, and student learning outcomes, thereby advancing our understanding of the app's effectiveness in educational settings.

References

1. AlGerafi, M.A.M., Zhou, Y., Oubibi, M., Wijaya, T.T.: Unlocking the potential: a comprehensive evaluation of augmented reality and virtual reality in education. Electronics **12**(18) (2023). https://doi.org/10.3390/electronics12183953, https://www.mdpi.com/2079-9292/12/18/3953
2. Bakshi, S.K., Lin, S.R., Ting, D.S.W., Chiang, M.F., Chodosh, J.: The era of artificial intelligence and virtual reality: transforming surgical education in ophthalmology. Br. J. Ophthalmol. (2020)
3. Barra, P., et al.: Metacux-a multi-user, multi-scenario environment for a cooperative workspace. In: Proceedings of the 15th Biannual Conference of the Italian SIGCHI Chapter, pp. 1–3 (2023)
4. Barra, P., et al.: Metacux: social interaction and collaboration in the metaverse. In: Abdelnour Nocera, J., Kristín Lárusdóttir, M., Petrie, H., Piccinno, A., Winckler, M. (eds.) INTERACT 2023. LNCS, vol. 14145, pp. 528–532. Springer, Cham (2023). https://doi.org/10.1007/978-3-031-42293-5_67

5. Battistoni, P., et al.: Using artificial intelligence and companion robots to improve home healthcare for the elderly. In: Gao, Q., Zhou, J., Duffy, V.G., Antona, M., Stephanidis, C. (eds.) HCII 2023. LNCS, vol. 14055, pp. 3–17. Springer, Cham (2023). https://doi.org/10.1007/978-3-031-48041-6_1

6. Battistoni, P., Di Gregorio, M., Romano, M., Sebillo, M., Vitiello, G.: Can AI-oriented requirements enhance human-centered design of intelligent interactive systems? Results from a workshop with young HCI designers. Multimodal Technol. Interact. **7**(3) (2023). https://doi.org/10.3390/mti7030024, https://www.mdpi.com/2414-4088/7/3/24

7. Bisogni, F., Laccone, R., Esposito, C., Frolli, A., Romano, M.: Virtual reality and foreign language learning. In: ICERI2023 Proceedings, pp. 9201–9207. IATED (2023)

8. Cantone, A.A., Ercolino, M., Romano, M., Vitiello, G.: Designing virtual interactive objects to enhance visitors' experience in cultural exhibits. In: Proceedings of the 2nd International Conference of the ACM Greek SIGCHI Chapter, pp. 1–5 (2023)

9. Cantone, A.A., Esposito, M., Perillo, F.P., Romano, M., Sebillo, M., Vitiello, G.: Enhancing elderly health monitoring: achieving autonomous and secure living through the integration of artificial intelligence, autonomous robots, and sensors. Electronics **12**(18), 3918 (2023)

10. Cantone, A.A., et al.: Contextualized experiential language learning in the metaverse. In: Proceedings of the 15th Biannual Conference of the Italian SIGCHI Chapter, pp. 1–7 (2023)

11. Chen, F.Q., et al.: Effectiveness of virtual reality in nursing education: meta-analysis. J. Med. Internet Res. **22**(9), e18290 (2020)

12. Dafoe, A., Bachrach, Y., Hadfield, G., Horvitz, E., Larson, K., Graepel, T.: Cooperative AI: machines must learn to find common ground. Nature **593**(7857), 33–36 (2021)

13. Faggiano, M.P., Fasanella, A.: Lessons for a digital future from the school of the pandemic: from distance learning to virtual reality. Front. Sociol. **7**, 1101124 (2022)

14. Freina, L., Ott, M.: A literature review on immersive virtual reality in education: state of the art and perspectives. In: The International Scientific Conference Elearning and Software for Education, vol. 1, pp. 10–1007 (2015)

15. Izard, S.G., Juanes Méndez, J.A., Palomera, P.R.: Virtual reality educational tool for human anatomy. J. Med. Syst. **41**, 1–6 (2017)

16. Katsionis, G., Virvou, M.: Personalised e-learning through an educational virtual reality game using web services. Multimedia Tools Appl. **39**, 47–71 (2008)

17. Luck, M., Aylett, R.: Applying artificial intelligence to virtual reality: intelligent virtual environments. Appl. Artif. Intell. **14**(1), 3–32 (2000)

18. Makransky, G., Lilleholt, L.: A structural equation modeling investigation of the emotional value of immersive virtual reality in education. Educ. Technol. Res. Dev. **66**(5), 1141–1164 (2018)

19. Marougkas, A., Troussas, C., Krouska, A., Sgouropoulou, C.: Virtual reality in education: a review of learning theories, approaches and methodologies for the last decade. Electronics **12**(13), 2832 (2023)

20. Patton, J.E., Stinard, T.A., Routh, D.K.: Where do children study? J. Educ. Res. **76**(5), 280–286 (1983)

21. Peixoto, B., Pinto, R., Melo, M., Cabral, L., Bessa, M.: Immersive virtual reality for foreign language education: a Prisma systematic review. IEEE Access **9**, 48952–48962 (2021)

22. Pherson-Geyser, M., de Villiers, R., Kavai, P., et al.: The use of experiential learning as a teaching strategy in life sciences. Int. J. Instr. **13**(3), 877–894 (2020)
23. Pottle, J.: Virtual reality and the transformation of medical education. Future Healthc. J. **6**(3), 181 (2019)
24. Rojas-Sánchez, M.A., Palos-Sánchez, P.R., Folgado-Fernández, J.A.: Systematic literature review and bibliometric analysis on virtual reality and education. Educ. Inf. Technol. **28**(1), 155–192 (2023)
25. Romano, M., Laccone, R., Frolli, A.: Designing a VR educational application to enhance resilience and community awareness through cultural exploration. In: ICERI2023 Proceedings, pp. 9258–9267. IATED (2023)
26. Romano, M., Díaz, P., Aedo, I.: Empowering teachers to create augmented reality experiences: the effects on the educational experience. Interact. Learn. Environ. **31**(3), 1546–1563 (2023)
27. Romano, M., Díaz, P., Ignacio, A., D'Agostino, P.: Augmenting smart objects for cultural heritage: a usability experiment. In: De Paolis, L.T., Mongelli, A. (eds.) AVR 2016. LNCS, vol. 9769, pp. 186–204. Springer, Cham (2016). https://doi.org/10.1007/978-3-319-40651-0_15
28. Romano, M., et al.: Exploring the potential of immersive virtual reality in Italian schools: a practical workshop with high school teachers. Multimodal Technol. Interact. **7**(12), 111 (2023)
29. Scavarelli, A., Arya, A., Teather, R.J.: Virtual reality and augmented reality in social learning spaces: a literature review. Virtual Reality **25**, 257–277 (2021)
30. Soliman, M., Pesyridis, A., Dalaymani-Zad, D., Gronfula, M., Kourmpetis, M.: The application of virtual reality in engineering education. Appl. Sci. **11**(6), 2879 (2021)
31. Ying, L., Jiong, Z., Wei, S., Jingchun, W., Xiaopeng, G.: Vrex: virtual reality education expansion could help to improve the class experience (vrex platform and community for VR based education). In: 2017 IEEE Frontiers in Education Conference (FIE), pp. 1–5. IEEE (2017)
32. Zheng, J., Chan, K., Gibson, I.: Virtual reality. IEEE Potentials **17**(2), 20–23 (1998)

A Multidisciplinary Heuristic Evaluation of AI-Enhanced Web Tools: Insights and Implications for Legal Contract Management Systems

Ruan Rocha Américo de Souza(iD), Camille N. Santiago Caminha(iD), and Marcelo C. Ferreira$^{(\boxtimes)}$(iD)

Centro de Estudos e Sistemas Avançados do Rrecife - CESAR, Recife, Brazil
{rras,cnsc,mcf}@cesar.org.br

Abstract. This study investigates the efficacy of the Heuristic Evaluation Method with a mix of expert and non-expert participants in assessing AI suggestion features in web systems. The methodology comprised three stages: an initial Heuristic Evaluation employing the 18 Guidelines for Human-AI Interaction, a Participant Survey to gauge perceptions using a demographic question, nine Likert statements, and two open-ended questions, and finally, Analysis and Triangulation to interpret and integrate the findings. Significant differences emerged between expert and non-expert perspectives. Non-experts identified more violations, predominantly of a less severe nature, compared to the more balanced severity spread among experts. Both groups focused on similar areas of violation but with different proportions of violations number, indicating a nuanced understanding of functionality by experts. Non-experts reported greater personal growth, though they valued their contributions less. The study underscored the consolidation process's importance in heuristic evaluations, reducing the total number of identified violations and refining the problem list. This research indicates that heuristic evaluation as a tool can be used for early usability assessment of AI features in web systems, supporting the utility of the Guidelines for Human-AI Interaction in scenarios as the described in this paper. The approach proved effective, especially in scenarios where direct user testing is impractical. The diverse participant profiles enriched the evaluation, with non-experts bringing unique insights, albeit facing challenges indicating a need for enhanced training and support. The study contributes to the field by confirming the value of incorporating a variety of perspectives in heuristic evaluations for AI-enhanced web functionalities.

Keywords: Artificial Intelligence and IoT · Design Methods and Techniques · Evaluation Methods and Techniques · HCI Theories and Methods · Heuristics and Guidelines for Design

H. Degen and S. Ntoa (Eds.): HCII 2024, LNAI 14734, pp. 94–109, 2024.
https://doi.org/10.1007/978-3-031-60606-9_7

1   Introduction

In recent years, artificial intelligence (AI) has experienced growth, driven by technological advances and the increasing demand for automated solutions in various sectors such as healthcare, the legal, and technology. Besides that, the launch of Chat GPT® and other AI tools has generated a "hype" [1] in the AI field, being widely discussed in reliable news sources such as The New York Times and The Guardian [2].

With this increasing demand, Human Computer Interaction (HCI) field and workers face challenges such as: (i) the lack of protocols for effectively planning and evaluating the interaction between people and AIs through standardized validations [3]; and (ii) the need for Methods and Techniques for evaluation during the initial phase of using the solution, especially when targeted at individuals in higher hierarchical positions within organizations with limited available time.

Recognizing these challenges, the purpose of this paper is to present a digital interface evaluation strategy for a real world AI feature - for a Contract Approval Management tool - applied by an innovation institute (CESAR) in a web application during the first phase of its use. The strategy involves the use of the heuristic evaluation technique [7], based on the Guidelines for Human-AI Interaction [5], through a multidisciplinary approach where the selected inspectors were 2 design experts, 1 developer, 1 quality engineer, and a data scientist.

The research also included additional objectives, namely: (i) evaluating the significance of differences in evaluators' perspectives, given the potential for varied interpretations and viewpoints resulting from multidisciplinary; and (ii) comprehending the unique contributions of each domain to the evaluation.

The next sections will discuss theories and concepts related to methods and challenges for evaluating AI in HCI field, including the Heuristic Evaluation. Next, will be presented the context of the Tool and AI Feature that was evaluated to further describe the methodology of evaluation and results. Finally, the discussion will show insights and lessons learned.

2   Methods and Challenges of HCI When Evaluating AI Tools

The HCI community has discussed the use of different methods and techniques with the purpose of designing and evaluating AI tools. [3] presents 20 research studies (third-party, preliminary, and empirical) in which methods and techniques were used at various stages of the design process, such as the use of interviews and surveys, qualitative and quantitative research, as well as interactive design, ethnographic observations, user evaluation, and contextual analysis. However, even though different methods are used, the application of these methodologies in the real-world remains intricate, particularly due to AI's intrinsic complexities and the absence of robust methods and techniques, especially when there is little or no access for user testing.

Moreover, AI high risk of variability in responses and learning from these tools [4] and the need for user trust bring the need for (i) robust methodologies and protocols for evaluating AI tools [3]; (ii) understand how these tools can be used in the real world [3]; and (iii) use quantitative and qualitative evidence to verify that tools add value [3,5].

3 Heuristic Evaluation and Human-AI Interaction Guidelines

A tradition of development and implementation of design rules or heuristics marks the history of the Human-Computer Interaction (HCI) field to enhance both usability and the overall User experience (UX) in different contexts such as Web [6,7], Mobile Interfaces [8,9] and Games [10,11]. In the context of the AI field, case studies show the use of evaluation methods in AI Tools [12,13] and companies such as Google and Microsoft have published materials and guidelines evaluating interactions between people and AI [5,14].

The debate over guidelines for AI is not recent and has been discussed for over 20 years. Illustrations of principles and guidelines include: (i) regulating the degree of autonomy in intelligent systems to avert unintended adaptations or actions [15]; (ii) orchestrating user expectations to avoid misinformation or user dissatisfaction during engagement [16]; (iii) facilitating the user-driven request of intelligent services; (iv) tailoring actions to align with deduced objectives and associated confidence levels; and (v) determining the optimal course of action balancing costs, benefits, and uncertainties [17].

The 18 guidelines published by Microsoft [5] (Table 1) are the most relevant in terms of evidence and validation. They are described in an article with a high index conference titled "Guidelines for Human-AI Interaction". In this work, the authors highlight the evidence of the study and classify them as relevant to be applied in Usability inspection Methods such as Heuristic Evaluation [7] - even though they recommend future work to examine the uses and values of guidelines. Additionally, recent academic work has evaluated the impact of the Human-AI Interaction guidelines. Their results suggest that they have a positive effect on UX but are not always successful in translating user preferences [18].

Table 1. 18 Guidelines for Human-AI Interaction

Guidelines for Human AI Interaction	Description
1: Make clear what the system can do	Help the user understand what the AI system is capable of doing
2. Make clear how well the system can do what it can do	Help the user understand how often the AI system may make mistakes
3. Time services based on context	Time when to act or interrupt based on the user's current task and environment

continued

Table 1. continued

Guidelines for Human AI Interaction	Description
4. Show contextually relevant information	Display information relevant to the user's current task and environment
5. Match relevant social norms	Ensure the experience is delivered in a way that users would expect, given their social and cultural context
6. Mitigate social biases	Ensure the AI system's language and behaviors do not reinforce undesirable and unfair stereotypes and biases
7. Support efficient invocation	Make it easy to invoke or request the AI system's services when needed
8. Support efficient dismissal	Make it easy to dismiss or ignore undesired AI system services
9. Support efficient correction	Make it easy to edit, refine, or recover when the AI system is wrong
10. Scope services when in doubt	Engage in disambiguation or gracefully degrade the AI system's services when uncertain about a user's goals
11. Make clear why the system did what it did	Enable the user to access an explanation of why the AI system behaved as it did
12. Remember recent interactions	Maintain short term memory and allow the user to make efficient references to that memory
13. Learn from user behavior	Personalize the user's experience by learning from their actions over time
14. Update and adapt cautiously	Limit disruptive changes when updating and adapting the AI system's behaviors
15. Encourage granular feedback	Enable the user to provide feedback indicating their preferences during regular interaction with the AI system
16. Convey the consequences of user actions	Immediately update or convey how user actions will impact future behaviors of the AI system
17. Provide global controls	Allow the user to globally customize what the AI system monitors and how it behaves
18. Notify users about changes	Inform the user when the AI system adds or updates its capabilities

4 The Evaluated Tool

The tool to be evaluated is a web application designed for the management of contractual approvals, specifically developed to optimize and enhance the contract review and approval process within the legal departments of large corporations. Essential in the lifecycle of legal contracts, this tool plays a fundamental role, ensuring that all clauses and terms undergo a detailed examination and are approved by experts before the contracts are finalized.

At its core, the tool allows managers and members of legal teams to make annotations and markings on contract documents. These markings are crucial for indicating clauses that require specialized review. After marking, these clauses go through a rigorous approval process, ensuring accuracy and legal compliance before the contract is finalized.

Among various other features, the tool has two ways to identify clauses that require review. The first is the standard/manual identification, where users select the desired clause by searching in a list of clauses after having marked specific sections of the contract that require attention. Figure 1 contains a low-fidelity prototype that illustrates the screen where default identification occurs. As can be seen, a user who already knows the desired clause can perform a textual search, and if the user is unsure, it is possible to search for a clause using a series of dropdowns. The second is facilitated identification by AI suggestions, which is the feature being studied in this article. This AI feature suggests potential clauses for the user to choose. Figure 2 contains a low-fidelity prototype that illustrates the screen where identification facilitated by AI occurs, showing a list of clause suggestions from which the user can choose. Additionally, the toggle available to activate and deactivate the suggestion feature can be observed. For the user to reach the part of the process where clause identification is made, they must have previously created a marking on the contract and selected one of the existing markings. It is after selecting one of these markings that the system shows them the onboarding modal, which aims to introduce the suggestion feature. Figure 3 illustrates this modal.

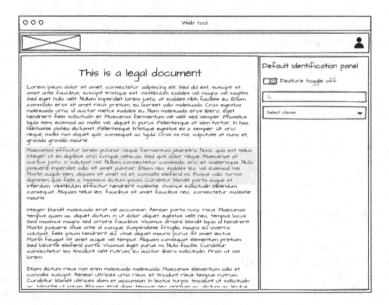

Fig. 1. Low fidelity prototype illustrating the default identification panel.

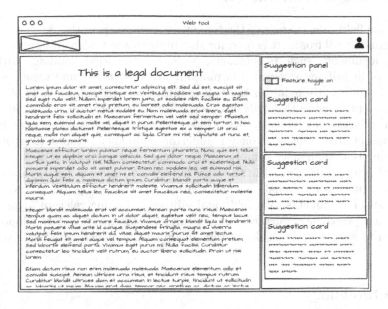

Fig. 2. Low fidelity prototype illustrating the AI feature making suggestions.

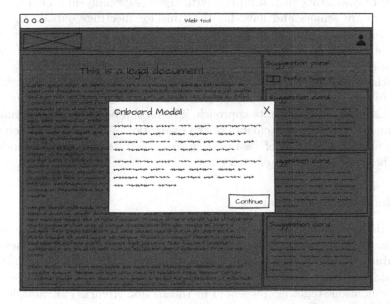

Fig. 3. Low fidelity prototype illustrating the AI feature onboard modal.

5   The Legal Field and AI

In the legal field - the context of the tool evaluated in this work - AI plays a crucial role on several fronts. It is used for the analysis and review of large volumes of legal documents, such as contracts, petitions, and legal opinions, with the purpose of identifying relevant information, inconsistencies, and errors, saving time and significantly reducing the risk of human errors. Additionally, AI algorithms are employed in the analysis of historical data from court cases, allowing predictions based on various factors. AI also plays an important role in detecting suspicious activities, such as money laundering, in financial transactions, as well as ensuring that companies comply with current legal regulations [2, 3].

Another application of AI in the legal field is assistance in legal research. AI platforms, such as legal chatbots and search engines specialized in law, assist lawyers and law students in quickly and efficiently finding relevant legal information and precedents. Furthermore, virtual assistants are widely adopted by law firms to answer basic legal questions from clients quickly and effectively [2, 3].

6   Methodology

The methodology of this research focuses on the heuristic evaluation of digital tools that have embedded AI features through a multidisciplinary approach. The decision to use heuristic evaluation for the study was based on: (i) the difficulty of evaluating such solutions with users, especially in scenarios where these users are seniors and have limited time for meetings outside the scope of their professional duties. (ii) the limited number of expert designers in the context of real-life projects. (iii) the challenges related to the scarcity of studies on the application of this method in digital tools with embedded AI.

To achieve this objective, it was understood that the methodology should be divided in 3 stages. The first being the execution of the heuristic evaluation using a multidisciplinary participants approach. The second being the application of a questionnaire with the participants of the evaluation. And, the third being the analysis and triangulation of results. Figure 4 illustrate the used methodology listing the goals and details of each stages.

6.1   Heuristic Evaluation

The heuristic evaluation presented here followed both Nielsen's execution recommendations [7,19] and the Guidelines for Human-AI Interaction [5]. They were chosen due to their focus on digital tools with incorporated AI and the fact that these guidelines were developed through a rigorous methodological process over several validation stages, as presented in the section "Heuristic Evaluation and Human-AI Interaction Guidelines". Its process occurred in 3 stages:

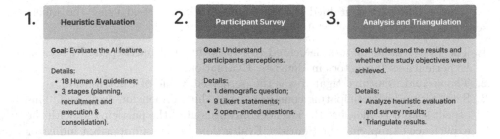

Fig. 4. Used Methodology

1. The first stage was focused on planning, in which the support material used by the inspectors was prepared by using Google Sheets as the platform. The support material consisted of a spreadsheet with 3 pages. The first page contained the description of the evaluation process, which included: (i) the definition of heuristics; (ii) a brief presentation of the Human-AI interaction guidelines [5]; (iii) how to carry out the inspection; (iv) the severity scales; and (v) the list of the system's screens that needed to be inspected. The second page presented in detail the 18 Guidelines for Human-AI guidelines, with examples of contemporary systems that made good use of the recommendations for each guideline. Finally, the third page contained the template to be used for noting found violations.
2. In the second stage, participant recruitment took place, selecting five people, 2 experts and 3 non-experts. The following criteria were used: (i) having participated in the development of the AI feature; (ii) having at least one representative of each professional profile involved in the development (Designer, Developer, QA, and Data Scientist); and (iii) availability.
3. The third and last stage was marked by the execution of the inspection and the consolidation of findings. The execution began with a synchronous and remote meeting, where the evaluation was presented along with the support material, and participants could clarify their doubts about the process. This was followed by an asynchronous and remote phase over two weeks where each participant conducted their inspection. Finally, the consolidation of the results was carried out synchronously and remotely, using Google Meet.

6.2 Participant Experience Survey

A survey was applied to the inspectors to understand their perceptions of the experience of conducting the heuristic evaluation with AI heuristics. The completion was asynchronous, and Google Forms was used to collect the responses. This survey was divided into 3 parts. The first was for the mapping of the participant's profile. Second had statements to be analyzed using a 1 to 5 Likert scale. And the last with Open-ended questions.

The first part was intended to map the profiles of the participants and divide them between experts and non-experts.

The second part contained the statements to be assessed using the Likert scale, the objective of each statement is listed below:

1. The first statement was dedicated to evaluating the participants' Previous Experience as Inspectors in Heuristic Evaluation.
2. The second item investigated was the perceived Value of Contribution.
3. Satisfaction in Participating constituted the third dimension evaluated. This aspect sought to measure the level of contentment of the participants with the experience of applying the Heuristic Evaluation, being an important indicator of engagement and receptivity to the method.
4. Next, the questionnaire addressed the Understanding Difficulties faced by participants. This section aimed to identify barriers or challenges in understanding the process and the heuristics used.
5. Clarity of Expectations was the fifth aspect evaluated, investigating how participants perceived the communication and clarification of the objectives and procedures of the Heuristic Evaluation.
6. Access to relevant Resources for conducting the evaluation was also measured, aiming to understand whether participants felt they had sufficient tools and information to perform their tasks.
7. Personal or Professional Development provided by the experience constituted another important dimension of the research. This item sought to capture the participants' perceptions of the impact of the activity on their skills and knowledge.
8. Willingness to Participate Again was measured next, providing insights into the likelihood of participants engaging in similar activities in the future.
9. And the propensity to Recommend the Experience was evaluated at the end, providing insights into the likelihood of the participants recommending the experience to others.

Finally, in the third part, the questionnaire included open-ended questions to gather qualitative insights. This part consisted of two questions, one focused on mapping challenges encountered by participants during the heuristic evaluation process and another focused on mapping suggestions for improvement.

After the execution of the heuristic evaluation and the survey, the analysis of results took place. The data from the heuristic evaluation and the survey were systematized and analyzed, making correlations when applicable. The tool used for this was Google Docs.

7   Results

7.1   Heuristic Evaluation Results

Inspection Results Before Consolidation. Table 2 shows the results of the inspections carried out by each of the participants, column 1 presents the participant who owns the results shown in the other columns.

Through an analysis of the results obtained before the consolidation, it is possible to notice that for non-experts:

Table 2. Inspection Results before Consolidation

Participant	Number of violations	Affected places	Violated guidelines
Non-expert 1	18 violations (1 cosmetic, 7 minor, 9 major, 1 catastrophic)	Suggestions Panel (4 times); Onboarding Modal (2 times); Suggestion Card (3 times); Toggle (2 times); Other (7 times)	1, 2, 2, 2, 3, 3, 7, 8, 9, 9, 11, 12, 13, 14, 15, 16, 17, 18
Non-expert 2	10 violations (2 cosmetic, 6 minor, 2 major)	Suggestions Panel (4 times); Onboarding Modal (1 time); Suggestion Card (3 times); Toggle (1 time); Other (1 time)	2, 4, 9, 11, 12, 13, 15, 16, 17, 18
Non-expert 3	4 violations (2 minor, 2 major)	Suggestions Panel (4 times)	12, 13, 16, 18
Expert 1	12 violations (6 minor, 5 major, 1 catastrophic)	Suggestions Panel (6 times); Onboarding Modal (1 time); Standard Identification Panel (1 time); Other (4 times)	1, 2, 4, 5, 10, 11, 12, 13, 14, 15, 16, 17
Expert 2	12 violations (1 cosmetic, 5 minor, 6 major)	Suggestions Panel (5 times); Onboarding Modal (2 times); Suggestion Card (1 time); Other (4 times)	1, 2, 3, 4, 8, 10, 11, 13, 15, 16, 17, 18

1. The total number of violations found was 32;
2. The average number of violations found per participant was 11;
3. The distribution of violations by severity was: 3 cosmetic, 15 minor, 13 major, and 1 catastrophic.
4. The distribution of the most affected locations was: Suggestions Panel (12 times), Onboarding Modal (3 times), Suggestion Card (6 times), Toggle (3 times), Other (8 times).
5. The distribution of the most violated heuristics was: 1 (1 time), 2 (4 times), 3 (2 times), 4 (1 time), 7 (1 time), 8 (1 time), 9 (3 times), 11 (2 times), 12 (3 times), 13 (3 times), 14 (1 time), 15 (2 times), 16 (3 times), 17 (2 times), and 18 (3 times).

As for experts:

1. The total number of violations found was 24;
2. The average number of violations found per participant was 12;
3. The distribution of violations by severity was 1 cosmetic, 11 minor, 11 major, and 1 catastrophic;
4. The distribution of the most affected locations was: Suggestions Panel (11 times), Onboarding Modal (3 times), Standard Identification Panel (1 time), Suggestion Card (1 time), Other (8 times).
5. The distribution of the most violated heuristics was: 1 (2 times), 2 (2 times), 3 (1 time), 4 (2 times), 5 (1 time), 8 (1 time), 10 (2 times), 11 (2 times), 12 (1 time), 13 (2 times), 14 (1 time), 15 (2 times), 16 (2 times), 17 (2 times), and 18 (1 time).

Heuristic Evaluation Results After Consolidation. Table 2 shows the consolidated results for the heuristic evaluations. After the consolidation, we can observe the following:

1. The total number of violations found was 20;
2. The distribution of violations by severity was 11 minor, 9 major;
3. The distribution of the most affected locations was: Suggestions Panel (8 times), Onboarding Modal (1 time), Standard Identification Panel (1 time), Toggle (1 time), Other (9 times).
4. The distribution of the most violated heuristics was: 1 (2 times), 2 (2 times), 3 (1 time), 4 (1 time), 7 (1 time), 8 (1 time), 9 (2 times), 10 (1 time), 11 (1 time), 12 (2 times), 13 (1 time), 14 (1 time), 15 (1 time), 16 (1 time), 17 (1 time), and 18 (1 time).

Table 3. Heuristic Evaluation Results - After Consolidation

Number of violations	Affected places	Violated guidelines
20 violations (11 minor, 9 major)	Suggestions Panel (8 times); Onboarding Modal (1 time); Standard Identification Panel (1 time); Toggle (1 time); Other (9 times)	1, 1, 2, 2, 3, 4, 7, 8, 9, 9, 10, 11, 12, 12, 13, 14, 15, 16, 17, 18

Out of the 20 violations in the consolidated results, 7 of them were found exclusively by non-expert inspectors. Table 3 presents the severity, the affected places and the violated guidelines of them (Table 4).

Table 4. Violations found exclusively by non-expert

Number of violations	Affected places	Violated guidelines
7 violations (5 minor, 2 major)	Suggestions Panel (2 times); Toggle (1 time); Other (4 times)	1, 2, 7, 9, 9, 12, 14

7.2 Survey Results

The survey applied to the participant group provided valuable insights into their experience with the Heuristic Evaluation technique. This investigation employed a mixed methodology, using both a 1 to 5 Likert scale to assess nine distinct statements and open-ended questions to gather qualitative insights.

Initially, Previous Experience as an Inspector was analyzed. Experts consistently showed high prior experience, with an average of 5.0, in contrast to non-experts, who indicated lesser familiarity, with an average of 2.33. Regarding the Value of Contribution, experts perceived their contributions as valuable, achieving an average of 4.5. Non-experts also rated their contributions positively, albeit to a lesser degree, with an average of 3.67.

Satisfaction in Participating was high among both groups, with experts recording an average of 4.0 and non-experts an average of 5.0. As for Understanding Difficulties, experts reported few difficulties, with an average of 1.5, while non-experts faced more challenges, with an average of 2.67. Clarity of Expectations was rated positively by experts, with an average of 4.5, and moderately by non-experts, with an average of 3.67.

In terms of Access to Resources, both groups felt they had sufficient access, with experts indicating an average of 5.0 and non-experts, an average of 4.67. Personal or Professional Development had mixed perceptions among experts, with an average of 2.5, while non-experts felt a good level of development, with an average of 4.0.

Willingness to Participate Again was strong in both groups, with averages of 5.0 for both experts and non-experts. In Recommending the Experience, both experts and non-experts were inclined to recommend the experience, with averages of 4.0 and 4.33, respectively.

In the open-ended question responses, experts mentioned initial challenges in understanding the guidelines and familiarizing themselves with the heuristics, but considered the overall process generally adequate. For instance, Expert 1 said that it was "time consuming to get used with the AI guideline" but complemented saying that it was the "only difficulty faced". Participant Expert 2 said that the only challenge was "getting used to the 18 AI heuristics". On the other hand, Non-experts reported challenges related to the practical application of the heuristics and clarity of expectations. Participant Non-expert 3, for example, said that "the true understanding of what was expected as the final deliverable" was challenging and that "using examples of heuristic evaluations of features within the application itself might possibly make it even easier". Participant Non-expert 1 additionally said that "the first challenge was drawing parallels between the examples provided and the actual functionality being presented", continued saying "distancing myself from how the functionality was implemented to evaluate it more impartially wasn't that easy" and finished saying that "assessing severity" was hard. Participant Non-expert 2 declared no issues, in contrast to what had been mentioned by the other two.

8   Discussion

From the analysis of the results presented in the previous section, a significant difference is noted between the perspectives of experts and non-experts. Non-expert participants identified a larger number of violations (34), including a higher number of less severe violations (3 cosmetic, 15 minor), whereas the experts had more balanced numbers (1 cosmetic, 11 minor, 11 major, and 1 catastrophic). This finding suggests that the difference in profile influences the detection of problems.

Regarding the influence of the profile on the identification of the locations where the violations occurred, it was observed that in the results of the experts there was a greater concentration of violations in specific areas, whereas, in the results of non-experts, this concentration was somewhat lower. However, the locations with the highest concentration were the same for both profiles ("Suggestions Panel" and "Other"). This may indicate a more precise approach and a deeper understanding of feature on the part of the experts, as the concentration of violations in the consolidated results followed a similar proportion to that of the experts.

In terms of professional development and perception of value, non-experts reported greater personal and professional growth (4.0) and valued their contributions less positively compared to experts. This observation may indicate that participation in heuristic evaluations is particularly beneficial for individuals with non-expert profiles, offering an opportunity for learning and increased self-appreciation.

The impact of the consolidation process was notable, with a decrease in the total number of violations after consolidation (from 56 to 20), suggesting that group discussion is efficient in filtering out less relevant or duplicated violations, resulting in a more concise and focused list of problems to be addressed. This finding highlights the importance of the consolidation process in heuristic evaluations to refine and validate the results.

The diversity of perspectives, stemming from the inclusion of both experts and non-experts, enriched the evaluation process. While the experts provided technical and detailed insights, the non-experts brought a broader view, essential for identifying problems potentially overlooked by a homogeneous group. This was evidenced by the fact that 7 of the 20 violations recorded in the consolidation were reported exclusively by non-experts.

The difficulties reported by non-experts highlight the need for more training and support in applying the heuristic evaluation process. Strategies such as creating more detailed training materials and conducting orientation sessions or practical workshops might be beneficial. The radical difference in the number of violations found by each non-expert may be another indication of the impact caused by a lack of full understanding of the support material used.

9   Conclusion

This research aimed to understand if conducting a heuristic evaluation with both expert and non-expert participants yields effective results in the context of evaluating AI features in a web system. The methodology comprised three stages: heuristic evaluation, participant survey, and analysis and triangulation. The results highlighted significant differences in the perspectives of experts and non-experts, with non-experts identifying a larger number of less severe violations and experts showing a more balanced identification across violation severity.

A noteworthy observation from the study is the impact of the participant's profile on the identification of violation locations. Experts concentrated on specific areas, indicating a deeper understanding of functionality, while non-experts showed a broader, though less concentrated, focus. This suggests that both groups contribute uniquely, with experts providing technical and detailed insights and non-experts offering a broader view, essential for identifying issues potentially overlooked by a homogeneous group of experts. In fact, the inclusion of both profiles enriched the evaluation process, as evidenced by the fact that 7 of the 20 violations recorded post-consolidation were reported exclusively by non-experts.

Furthermore, the study underscores the importance of the consolidation process in heuristic evaluations. The significant decrease in the total number of violations after consolidation (from 56 to 20) demonstrates the efficiency of group discussions in filtering out less relevant or duplicated violations, thus refining the list of problems.

From a professional development standpoint, non-experts reported greater personal and professional growth, suggesting that participation in heuristic evaluations offers valuable learning opportunities, particularly for those with non-expert profiles. However, the reported difficulties by non-experts in applying the heuristic evaluation process highlight the need for more training and support. This could be addressed through strategies such as detailed training materials, orientation sessions, and practical workshops.

This research indicates that the heuristic evaluation can be used for assessing the usability of AI features in early stages of web system in contexts like the ones described. It also validates the Human-AI Interaction Guidelines as a robust set of guidelines for heuristic evaluations in this context. In conclusion, employing heuristic evaluation with a mix of expert and non-expert participants proves to be a promising approach in scenarios where AI functionalities are in early usage stages, and direct usability testing with users is challenging. This approach not only offers a diverse range of insights but also fosters an environment conducive to professional growth and learning, particularly for non-expert participants.

However, it is important to acknowledge that heuristic evaluations have a tendency to disregard more serious usability problems, and the lack of expert inspectors in the execution in general tends to reduce the number of identified issues [20]. In addition to these considerations, it is noteworthy that this study employed heuristic evaluation in a highly specific context, focusing on the assessment of an AI feature designed to suggest clauses in legal contracts. Furthermore, this evaluation took place within the organizational framework of a collaborative project at an innovation center, in partnership with a multinational corporation. This unique organizational and contextual setup has its particular characteristics. Other contexts may or may not translate into different results. Finally, it is important to acknowledge that the data acquired through this methodology, although providing valuable insights, should not be regarded as an infallible verity, and it does not serve as a substitute for evaluation techniques that necessitate direct user involvement. Anticipating future evaluation cycles, we aim to incorporate additional insights obtained from methods such as focus groups, user surveys, and usability testing.

References

1. Lingo, R.: The Role of ChatGPT in Democratizing Data Science: An Exploration of AI-facilitated Data Analysis in Telematics. arXiv preprint (2023). https://doi.org/10.48550/arXiv.2308.02045
2. Nick Clegg defends release of open-source AI model by Meta | Artificial intelligence (AI) | The Guardian. https://www.theguardian.com/technology/2023/jul/19/nick-clegg-defends-release-open-source-ai-model-meta-facebooks. Accessed 30 Jan 2024
3. Tulk Jesso, S., Kelliher, A., Sanghavi, H., Martin, T., Henrickson Parker, S.: Inclusion of clinicians in the development and evaluation of clinical artificial intelligence tools: a systematic literature review. Front. Psychol. **13** (2022). https://doi.org/10.3389/fpsyg.2022.830345
4. Doshi-Velez, F., Kim, B.: Towards a rigorous science of interpretable machine learning. arXiv e-prints (2017). https://doi.org/10.48550/arXiv.1702.08608
5. Amershi, S., et al.: Guidelines for Human-AI interaction. In: Proceedings of the 2019 CHI Conference on Human Factors in Computing Systems, pp. 1–13. Association for Computing Machinery, Glasgow, Scotland Uk (2019). https://doi.org/10.1145/3290605.3300233
6. Leventhal, L, Barnes, J.: Usability Engineering: Process, Products, and Examples. Pearson/Prentice Hall (2008)
7. Nielsen, J., Molich, R.: Heuristic evaluation of user interfaces. In: Proceedings of the SIGCHI Conference on Human Factors in Computing Systems, pp. 249–256. Association for Computing Machinery. Seattle, Washington, USA (1990). https://doi.org/10.1145/97243.97281
8. Bertini, E., Gabrielli, S., Kimani, S., Catarci, T., Santucci, G.: Appropriating and assessing heuristics for mobile computing. In: Proceedings of the Working Conference on Advanced Visual Interfaces, pp. 119–126. Association for Computing Machinery. Venezia, Italy (2006). https://doi.org/10.1145/1133265.1133291
9. Machado Neto, O., Pimentel, M.: Heuristics for the assessment of interfaces of mobile devices. In: Proceedings of the 19th Brazilian Symposium on Multimedia and the Web, pp. 93–96. Association for Computing Machinery. Salvador, Brazil (2013). https://doi.org/10.1145/2526188.2526237
10. Pinelle, D., Wong, N., Stach, T., Gutwin, C.: Usability heuristics for networked multiplayer games. In: Proceedings of the 2009 ACM International Conference on Supporting Group Work, pp. 169–178. Association for Computing Machinery. Sanibel Island, Florida, USA (2009). https://doi.org/10.1145/1531674.1531700
11. Desurvire, H., Wiberg, C.: Game Usability Heuristics (PLAY) for evaluating and designing better games: the next iteration. In: Ozok, A.A., Zaphiris, P. (eds.) OCSC 2009. LNCS, vol. 5621, pp. 557–566. Springer, Heidelberg (2009). https://doi.org/10.1007/978-3-642-02774-1_60
12. Nazar, M., Alam, M., Yafi, E., Su'ud, M.: A systematic review of human-computer interaction and explainable artificial intelligence in healthcare with artificial intelligence techniques. IEEE Access **9**, 153316–153348 (2021). https://doi.org/10.1109/ACCESS.2021.3127881
13. Šumak, B., Brdnik, S., Pušnik, M.: Sensors and artificial intelligence methods and algorithms for human-computer intelligent interaction: a systematic mapping study. Sensors **22**, 20 (2022). https://doi.org/10.3390/s22010020
14. People+AI Guidebook. https://pair.withgoogle.com/guidebook/. Accessed 30 Jan 2024

15. Norman, D.: How might people interact with agents. Commun. ACM **37**(7), 68–71 (1994). https://doi.org/10.1145/176789.176796
16. Höök, K.: Steps to take before intelligent user interfaces become real. Interacting Comput.**12**, 409–426 (2000). https://doi.org/10.1016/S0953-5438(99)00006-5
17. Horvitz, E.: Principles of mixed-initiative user interfaces. In: Proceedings of the SIGCHI Conference on Human Factors in Computing Systems, pp. 159–166. Association for Computing Machinery. Pittsburgh, Pennsylvania, USA (1999) https://doi.org/10.1145/302979.303030
18. Li, T., Vorvoreanu, M., Debellis, D., Amershi, S.: Assessing Human-AI interaction early through factorial surveys: a study on the guidelines for human-AI interaction. ACM Trans. Comput.-Hum. Interact. **30**(5) (2023). https://doi.org/10.1145/3511605
19. How to Conduct a Heuristic Evaluation. https://www.nngroup.com/articles/how-to-conduct-a-heuristic-evaluation/. Accessed 30 Oct 2024
20. Hollingsed, T., Novick, D.: Usability inspection methods after 15 years of research and practice. In: Proceedings of the 25th Annual ACM International Conference on Design of Communication, pp. 249–255. Association for Computing Machinery. El Paso, Texas, USA (2007). https://doi.org/10.1145/3511605

PyFlowML: A Visual Language Framework to Foster Participation in ML-Based Decision Making

Serena Versino[1]([envelope]) [ID], Tommaso Turchi[1] [ID], and Alessio Malizia[1,2] [ID]

[1] Department of Computer Science, University of Pisa, Pisa, Italy
`serena.versino@phd.unipi.it`, {`tommaso.turchi,alessio.malizia`}`@unipi.it`
[2] Molde University College, Molde, Norway
`alessio.malizia@himolde.no`

Abstract. Nowadays, Artificial Intelligence (AI) has become ubiquitous, with machine learning (ML) systems – rooted in algorithms and statistical models – playing a pivotal role in societal advancement. Nevertheless, given their complexity, less-experienced computing practitioners depend on skilled professionals. This paper addresses the challenge of democratizing AI, emphasizing the need for inclusivity in ML-based system design. We introduce the PyFlowML prototype, which extends the PyFlow framework, to investigate how Visual Programming Languages (VPLs) and no-code platforms can enhance user engagement in ML. PyFlowML tailors visual scripting capabilities to meet the specific needs and complexities inherent in ML analysis. This preliminary study is based on a heuristic evaluation of PyFlowML's usability: we analyzed expert interactions with the tool, exploring its features to design trustworthy ML-based prototypes using Explainable AI (XAI) techniques. We employed the cognitive walk-through method, wherein experts engaged in a series of activities with PyFlowML while sharing their thoughts in real time during the session. While initial findings are promising, they also indicate that to effectively lower the entry barrier to ML-based system design and encourage broader participation, it is crucial to implement strategies that reduce the inherent complexity of ML analysis. This research sets the groundwork for future exploration into how VPL-based tools can transform the design of ML-based systems, aiming for more inclusive and collaborative AI development.

Keywords: visual programming language · participation · AI democratization · machine learning

1 Introduction

Artificial Intelligence (AI) has become ubiquitous in modern society, significantly impacting various socio-cultural aspects of daily life. We encounter AI in diverse applications, ranging from language translation and email spam filtering to virtual personal assistants organizing our work schedules or even smartphone recommendations for dining options. With its pervasive influence across numerous industries, AI is reshaping business practices by aiding organizations in improving their products, processes, and decision-making capabilities [1,2]. In academia, AI's role is equally transformative, prompting institutions to reevaluate and adapt their teaching and learning methodologies to incorporate this technology effectively [3]. Therefore, AI-based systems can transform how we live, interact with one another, and perceive ourselves. Recommender systems, for instance, use algorithms to manipulate search engine results based on user queries, thereby influencing our consumption choices [4], public opinion, and perceptions of social reality [5]. These systems filter and rank information based on hidden factors such as search history and demographic information [6].

We are witnessing a rapid development of AI, which is accelerating the shift towards a more algorithmic-driven society [7]. Nevertheless, technological advancements have resulted in a concentration of the knowledge required for developing and managing AI-based systems within a small group of specialists [8]. The increasing algorithms complexity has limited the control over these systems to skilled computing practitioners, leading to a growing reliance on their expertise by both individuals and societies. While not every end-user is equipped or inclined to acquire the skills necessary for the design and development of AI-based systems, these experienced practitioners may not have a thorough understanding of the societal and domain-specific consequences of the solutions they develop [9]. This gap is concerning in sectors where responsible and trustworthy AI-based systems are essential for decision-making processes [10].

Participating in designing and developing algorithmic solutions benefits both experienced and inexperienced users. It enhances understanding and trust in AI-based systems, supporting individuals from various backgrounds to thrive in our technology-driven society. Participation can be facilitated through the democratization of AI, where socio-technical conditions are established to enable users to actively contribute to the evolution of AI-based systems [11]. By bridging the gap between domain experts and computing professionals, this approach can ensure these systems align with their application domains' specific needs and ethical considerations.

Recent literature highlights the need for cultural transformation, achievable through End-User Development (EUD). EUD provides individuals with the means to transition from passive roles as consumers of artefacts and systems to active problem solvers [11,12]. For instance, it can enable inexperienced users to customize smart environments [13,14] and personal devices [15]. This shift towards active engagement aligns with the concept of cultures of participation, promoting collaboration among multi-disciplinary practitioners in socio-technical environments. Such collaborative efforts are key to achieving common goals within these environments [16,17].

Within AI, ML-based systems are grounded in complex algorithms and statistical models. Active participation in designing ML-based systems can foster effective appropriation of such systems across diverse user domains [18,19]. In the field of Human-centered AI (HCAI), ongoing research presents new approaches to engage inexperienced users through visual user interfaces [20]. For instance, in educational settings, Visual Programming Languages (VPLs) and no-code platforms, such as Scratch [21], provide user-friendly experiences by avoiding complex computational operations. Thus, the present study is guided by the following research question: "Can VPL-based frameworks foster the participation of both experienced and inexperienced practitioners in the design of ML-based systems?" Our research conducts a qualitative evaluation of the challenges and opportunities associated with using VPL-based tools, as exemplified through the assessment of the PyFlowML prototype. Given the novelty of the domain, we adopt a heuristic strategy that focuses on the processes and activities associated with user interactions rather than on the final product. This approach allows us to evaluate the overall user experience through the Cognitive Dimensions (CDs) Framework [22]. We employed a focused approach in a small-scale usability test of the prototype, which serves as a foundational step for future work. This paper is structured into seven sections: (1) Introduction; (2) Related Works, discussing VPL definitions and their applications in the ML domain; (3) PyFlowML prototype, introducing the design and features of our prototype; (4) Expert Evaluation, describing the cognitive walk-through and heuristic approaches; (5) Results, where we articulate the findings from our experiment; (6) Post-Hoc Analysis and Lessons Learned, reflecting on the insights gained and potential implications; and (7) Conclusion and future works.

2   Related Works

Empirical studies support the claim that VPL-based tools exhibit enhanced user-friendliness compared to traditional text-based programming languages such as Javascript and Python [23]. The low-code or no-code programming approach can be a valuable asset for beginners, especially those with limited or no prior coding experience. This section introduces definitions of VPLs and provides examples of ML-based systems developed using these languages.

2.1   Visual Programming Languages

Programming languages are defined by two key components: their syntax, which refers to the language's form, and their semantics, which convey the language's meaning. In VPLs, the syntax that carries semantic significance incorporates visual elements [24]. VPL is a key component of EUD, and provides non-programmers with the means to create, modify, and enhance software applications using two-dimensional graphical interfaces. VPL-based approaches employ graphical representations of programming constructs and rules, enabling a more intuitive software development process [25].

As highlighted in the recent review by Kuhail et al. [26], the merge of two well-established taxonomies, that is Myers [27] and Burnett and Baker [28], provides four distinct categories of VPLs. They include block-based, form-based, diagram-based and icon-based languages.

Block-based languages are programming imperative, and they adopt drag-and-drop code blocks from a predefined list of commands into a script area [23]. This approach minimizes syntax errors and eases the mental effort, focusing on conceptual understanding over coding activities. Prominent examples in education and research include Scratch [21] and Tapas [29]. The primary users of Scratch are children with limited or no prior coding experience. Through programming and sharing interactive projects, users acquire computer science skills and develop their ability to think creatively, reason methodically, and collaborate. Tapas is a programming environment designed to enhance computational thinking skills through a combination of a blocks programming environment and a tangible user interface [30]. It utilizes physical objects whose interactions with the real world correspond to digital operations executed within the system.

In Icon-based Languages, graphical symbols, or icons, represent objects and actions, enabling the construction of applications through a system of triggers and actions. Platforms employing them are suitable at aggregating content from various heterogeneous sources, thereby facilitating the creation of Personal Information Spaces that can satisfy specific information needs. The composition method abstracts from underlying technical complexities, rendering it accessible to non-experts in computing. [31].

Form-based Languages such as Forms/3 [32] allow developers to configure forms with triggers and actions. These can be added either through textual or visual elements. These components facilitate the creation and configuration of computational cells, as well as the definition of their interdependencies.

Diagram-based or flow-based languages utilize a data flow computational paradigm, which is represented as a directed graph [33]. In this representation, the nodes symbolize various functions. Each node performs a specific function or operation on data and represents individual processing modules. Nodes are often depicted as graphical icons, and they are connected by arcs or links that represent the pathways along which data flows between nodes. Incoming arcs to a node signify the input data for a function, whereas outgoing arcs indicate the output data, essentially representing the outcomes of the function. The arcs connect the output of one node to the input of another, indicating the direction of data flow. The input/output ports or pins correspond to the data that the nodes receive and produce. Ports are used to connect nodes together, and they define the types of data that can be transmitted between nodes. Flow-based languages have gained widespread adoption across various domains. For example RoboFlow [34], specifically designed for robot programming. It allows for the intuitive creation and manipulation of robotic workflows, facilitating a more accessible approach to complex robotic systems programming. Similarly, Grasshopper [35] and Dynamo[1] have extensive application in architecture and design. Their node-based interface empowers users to generate intricate 3D geometrical forms and data-driven models, thus bridging the gap between computational design and physical realization. Instead, Ryven [36], based on a flexible platform equipped with built-in nodes that can be customized for developing

---

[1] https://dynamobim.org.

new algorithms, is utilized in academic research and can be applied across various domains. However, directly integrating ML techniques can be challenging for inexperienced users.

2.2   End-User Development for Machine Learning

Recent literature and market developments have introduced a variety of software and platforms that leverage VPLs for data mining, ML, and data analytics. For instance, block-based languages like Blockly[2] and ML Blocks [37] have gained prominence in academic research. BlocklyML, a no-code derivative of Google's Blockly, is specifically designed for Python and ML implementations. ML Blocks, on the other hand, enables users to assemble datasets, apply ML classifiers, and export models, offering an accessible gateway for beginners into ML and data science. In the realm of flow-based languages, platforms like Dataiku[3] and SAS Viya[4] provide collaboration features suitable for users with varying levels of computing expertise. However, the non-open-source nature and limited customizability of these platforms pose a constraint, as they lack integrated Explainable AI techniques, which can enable inexperienced users to interpret and understand the decision-making processes. Conversely, open-source platforms such as ENSO[5], RIVET[6], KNIME[7], Orange [38], and Rapid Miner Studio[8] offer more flexibility. ENSO and RIVET, while highly customizable, lack extensive support for specialized ML components, with RIVET requiring additional extensions for more models. KNIME and Rapid Miner Studio, despite their comprehensive features, can be complex due to their numerous in-built components and may require expertise for adding new operators. Orange strikes a balance, catering to experienced users and beginners alike, although advanced customization necessitates coding skills and in-depth ML knowledge. Finally, LabVIEW[9], a non-open-source tool, and TeachableMachine[10], an open-source but non-customizable platform, represent two other popular VPL-based tools appealing to non expert users. However, both of these platforms lack integrated Explainable AI techniques.

In summary, the literature concerning VPL-based tools reveals a common trend: many are either non-customizable, lack integrated interpretability techniques, or are overly complex for customization. This points to a research gap in developing simplified ML-based systems that are accessible to experts across various domains with limited computing experience. Integrating such simplification and Explainable AI techniques can respectively facilitate their participation in

---

[2] https://github.com/google/blockly.

[3] https://knowledge.dataiku.com/latest/ml-analytics/index.html.

[4] https://www.sas.com/en_us/home.html.

[5] https://enso.org.

[6] https://rivet.ironcladapp.com.

[7] https://www.knime.com.

[8] https://rapidminer.com.

[9] https://www.ni.com/it-it/shop/product/labview-analytics-and-machine-learning-toolkit.html.

[10] https://teachablemachine.withgoogle.com/train/image.

the design process and deepen their understanding of the decision-making mechanisms in ML systems. Our research addresses this gap with the introduction of the PyFlowML prototype. Recognizing the prevalent use of flow-based languages in the design of ML-based systems, we developed this tool in an open-source, flow-based environment. PyFlowML is characterized by its full customizability, enabling adaptation to diverse user domains. Furthermore, it simplifies the ML processes and integrates Explainable AI techniques.

3   PyFlowML

This section presents an overview of PyFlow, a general-purpose, flow-based programming language library, along with its ML extension named PyFlowML.

3.1   PyFlow

PyFlow[11] is a versatile Python Qt visual scripting framework designed to simplify the creation of graphical user interfaces (GUIs) through the utilization of visual programming techniques. PyFlow can enable non-technical users to build applications and prototypes by dragging and dropping components onto a graphical canvas. The application incorporates interactive GUI elements called widgets, which include a variety of forms such as buttons, sliders, text fields, dropdown menus, and prompt windows. These widgets are instrumental in user interaction, allowing for the manipulation of components and functionalities. The key components in PyFlow application are node, pin and arc.

Node. In PyFlow, nodes represent algorithms and functions, each with specific inputs and outputs. These nodes have a primary structure of a resizable rectangle, which can be adjusted by dragging its edges. Users can add nodes to the canvas simply by dragging and dropping them from the main menu, and they can also move them around within the canvas in the same manner. The ability to zoom in and out on the canvas facilitates better visualization of the nodes. At the top of each node, a customizable header displays its name. Users can set this name to reflect the node's function it performs, enhancing clarity and aiding in the navigation of complex workflows. Nodes are interconnected via arcs that enable data transfer from the output pin (source) of one node to the input pin of another. Each node serves as a fundamental building block, encapsulating specific functionalities or operations. Refreshing a node, which is done by clicking on it and selecting "Refresh", triggers the execution of its operations. The outline of the node changes color during this process to indicate its status: starting as orange for "not executed", turning yellow to signify "refreshing", and finally becoming green upon successful execution.

---

[11] https://pyflow.readthedocs.io/en/latest/intro.html.

Pin. Pins are essential components within the node's layout in PyFlow, visually represented as colored dots, each accompanied by a descriptive label. The color of each pin is significant, denoting the type of data it represents. For example, pink is used for string data, white for general data types like matrices and vectors, dark green for integer data types, and light green for floating data types. Pins fall into two categories: input and output. Input pins, located on the left side of the node, are designed to receive data from other nodes, enabling dynamic interaction and data flow between nodes. Output pins, on the right side, allow the node to transmit data to the subsequent nodes in the workflow. This left-to-right arrangement of pins facilitates the directional interconnections.

Arc. Arcs visually represent the relationship between nodes. They act as the conduits through which information, such as variables, values, or data structures and objects, is transmitted from an executed node to another. By using the arcs, the user links output and input pins of nodes, establishing a connection that enables the output of one node to be used as an input for the following. Arcs serve as the bridges that enable communication between nodes, empowering users to build complex workflows by intuitively linking different computational steps together. For the system to transmit data successfully, only pins of the same (or compatible) data type can be interconnected through arcs. PyFlow's design inherently prevents incorrect connections; if a user tries to link incompatible pins, the connecting arc simply will not materialize. Conversely, a successful connection is clearly indicated by an arc colored to match the pins, thereby effectively linking the nodes.

3.2   PyFlowML Prototype

Building on this foundation, the PyFlowML prototype is an extension of PyFlow aimed at design of ML-based systems. It adapts PyFlow's visual scripting capabilities to the specific needs and complexities of ML analysis.

Design. In PyFlowML, the nodes are organized into four categories: Data Load, Data Visualization, Data Classification, and Explainable AI. The Data Load category includes nodes for loading numerical and textual data from various sources, including external files like CSV, as well as scikit-learn and keras python libraries. In Data Visualization category, nodes are designed to present results in a user-friendly manner for inexperienced users, avoiding the use of the logger which is commonly adopted by software developers for debugging. These nodes facilitate the display of outcomes in formats like tables and plots within prompt windows, and for designers or data scientists, they can output matrices and vectors in the logger. The Data Classification category encompasses nodes that apply various ML models. This includes a range of models for supervised learning, such as Deep Neural Networks, Decision Trees, K-Nearest Neighbors, Multinomial Naive Bayes, Gradient Boosting, Random Forests, and Support Vector

Machines, alongside models like K-means for unsupervised learning in clustering analysis. Finally, the Explainable AI category comprises nodes that enable users to employ techniques to interpret and understand the behavior of classifiers and the relationships between features and outcomes, with techniques such as SHAP (SHapley Additive exPlanations), LIME (Local Interpretable Model-agnostic Explanations), PDP (Partial Dependence Plot), and ICE (Individual Conditional Expectation) being some examples. This category aims to provide users with the means to design responsible and trustworthy AI-based systems, which are essential in fair decision-making processes [10].

Pipeline. The PyFlowML prototype facilitates the design of ML-based systems through a pipeline of interconnected nodes, aligning with standard ML methodologies. This process involves loading a dataset, applying classifiers, and visualizing critical metrics such as accuracy and F1 score. In PyFlowML, users can, for instance, assemble a pipeline comprising a data load node, a data classification node, and visualization nodes. These nodes are capable of displaying the comparative performance of various classifiers, with a focus on metrics such as accuracy to identify the most efficient model. During the pipeline execution, PyFlowML offers prompt windows that show execution status and warning messages, aiding in troubleshooting issues like unprocessed output or unconnected input pins. Figure 1 illustrates an application where users employ various classifiers and utilize a node to determine the best-performing classifier for the dataset.

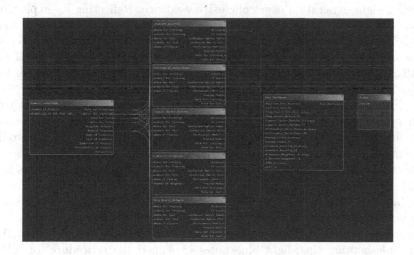

Fig. 1. PyFlowML workflow: an example

Customization. PyFlowML provides the flexibility for users to customize and implement categories and nodes, tailored to their specific needs and the capabilities of Python libraries. Users possessing a basic understanding of text-based programming languages have the ability to modify nodes using code editors. By accessing the internal structure of a node, they can alter classifiers, adjust input/output pins, and change data types, enabling them to fine-tune the system according to their requirements.

4   Expert Evaluation

This section presents the goals, hypotheses, and description of the expert study we carried out, following the guidelines of the American Psychological Association [39].

4.1   Goals

The goal of the study is to evaluate whether PyFlowML prototype can foster users participation in the design of ML-based systems. The purpose is the evaluation of how experts interact with the tool in designing ML-based prototypes.

4.2   Study Design

We conducted the expert-based review combining cognitive walk-through and heuristic evaluation approaches (Lazar et al. (2017) [40]). This multifaceted strategy enables an investigation into user interactions with PyFlowML, prioritizing insight generation over conclusive evidence. Reflecting its exploratory nature, our study includes a think-aloud protocol and a post-test survey grounded in the CDs Framework applied (Green et al. (1996) [22]). We chose this framework due to its applicability in exploratory software design by HCI non-specialists [41]. We conducted a small-scale evaluation by engaging two experts with backgrounds in VPLs, programming, and ML analysis.

During the session, experts simulate users by performing a series of activities within a pre-established template using PyFlowML. Participants have experience in VPL interface design and have a thorough understanding of the users' profiles, including the tasks they are expected to perform with the tool.

The template includes common tasks of ML analysis process, such as loading and exploring datasets, performing supervised classification, visualizing outcomes, and applying interpretability techniques. It is organized with colored sticky notes to guide the interaction: white notes outlined the step-by-step ML analysis process (arranged from left-to-right), yellow notes offered instructions and troubleshooting tips, light blue notes explained the procedure for adding nodes, and green notes posed questions. The template sets four sequential steps: (1) loading the "IBM HR Analytics Employee Attrition & Performance" dataset[12], (2) applying a ML model, (3) calculating the SHAPley values, and (4) saving the output. At each stage, experts encountered questions regarding the

---

[12] https://www.kaggle.com/datasets/pavansubhasht/ibm-hr-analytics-attrition-dataset.

outputs generated by the nodes. Examples include, "According to the Distribution of Dataset table, which are the classes of the target variable?", "According to the Performance Metrics table, what is the accuracy of the classifier?", and "Based on the Shapley Value Summary Plot, which features are the most important for prediction in the dataset?". Responses were either recorded on the sticky notes or expressed verbally, such as when commenting plots. Upon completion of these steps, experts were instructed to save their output.

We recorded the sessions to collect contextual oral feedback and observations from experts interating with PyFlowML, which aided in interpreting the results of the CDs evaluation.

We employed the CDs framework as it offers a quick analysis that connect user activities, the structure of notations, and the system's design. This approach aims to uncovermismatches, identify usability concerns, and potential improvements. Our application began with a comprehensive understanding of the PyFlowML prototype and its defining elements: *notation, environment, activity*, and *user*. PyFlowML si based on a flow-based language characterized by nodes, pins, and arcs, which serve as information-carrying representations (*notation*). Within the PyFlow *environment*, users manipulate this primary notation. A secondary notation emerges through the use of sticky notes, which are components that enable users to annotate meanings above the primary notation. User *activities* encompass actions associated with the primary notation - such as adding, connecting, executing, deleting, placing, moving, resizing, and labeling nodes on the canvas - as well as those related to the secondary notation - such as text and colors. In this review, *users* are experts with diverse backgrounds who brings diverse knowledge to the evaluation process.

We apply the CDs framework to enable users to leverage it as a tool for expressing their experiences (Black & Green (2003) [42]). After reviewing the original framework, comprising 13 dimensions [22], we undertook a comprehensive analysis of the prototype, evaluating its features against each dimension. Following this evaluation, we identified nine dimensions for the experts-based testing [see Table 1] and formulated a questionnaire consisting of 20 questions [43].

Table 1. Cognitive Dimensions

Cognitive Dimensions	Description
Visibility and Juxtaposability	Ability to view components easily, and ability to place any two components side by side
Viscosity	Resistance to change
Hard Mental Operations	High demand on cognitive resources
Error-Proneness	Notation invites mistakes
Role-Expressiveness	The purpose of a component is readily inferred
Hidden Dependencies	Important links between entities are not visible
Premature Commitment	Constraints on the order of doing things
Consistency	Similar semantics are expressed in similar syntactic forms
Secondary Notation	Extra information in means other than formal syntax

As in the case study by Black & Green (2003) [42], which evaluates VPLs such as LabVIEW, we selected the dimensions of *Viscosity, Hidden Dependencies, Premature Commitment, Secondary Notation*, and *Visibility and Juxtaposability*. The *Viscosity* dimension was included to assess the effort required by users to make changes in PyFlowML, such as data loading, adding classifiers in the pipeline, or visualizing different outcomes. In VPLs, *Hidden Dependencies* are relevant as they are typically made explicit through visual components like arcs connecting nodes - unlike text-based languages, where they are indicated by function assignments and use-statements. The inclusion of *Premature Commitment* reflects PyFlowML's demands on users regarding layout and connections; users must consider the placement of nodes on the canvas and the necessity to move already placed nodes for new ones, as well as the requirement that only executed nodes' pins with matching data types can be connected. We included in our survey also the *Secondary Notation* as it assesses components that enable users to add extra meaning to the primary notation. Moreover, we evaluated the PyFlowML's strategic use of spatial layout, which facilitates communication by allowing the visualization of multiple components (*Visibility and Juxtaposability*). We opted to exclude the *Abstraction* dimension, as the tool exhibits an abstraction-hating characteristic; it lacks the capability for nodes to be aggregated and treated as a single entity. Nodes can only be grouped for deletion from the canvas.

Furthermore, we expanded the survey to include the *Hard Mental Operations, Consistency, Error-Proneness*, and *Role-Expressiveness* dimensions. Indeed, *Hard Mental Operations* can be relevant in the context of VPL-based tools [22]. For instance, in PyFlowML, the absence of directional arrows on arcs necessitates that users recall the role of nodes within the pipeline (*Role-Expressiveness*) and position them accordingly. Usually, VPL-based tools show high *Consistency* due to their simple syntax, where all nodes can be interconnected through visible arcs and input/output pins. The use of different colors for pins according to data type can impact *Error-Proneness*, enabling users to infer connections among nodes even with minimal understanding of their internal functions.

From the original framework, we chose not to include the *Diffuseness, Closeness of Mapping*, and *Progressive Evaluation* dimensions in our survey. Given that PyFlowML features essential nodes, the evaluation of the *Diffuseness* - that is, the complexity arising from a large number components - could yield a skewed perspective. This might lead to a positively biased assessment, given the prototype's early development stage. The *Closeness of Mapping* dimension is deemed less critical in the context of VPL-based tools. By their design, they inherently map problem entities from the user's task domain to task-specific system entities (i.e., nodes). Then, they translate operations on problem entities (e.g., applying ML classifiers) into system operations (e.g., arcs passing processed data from one node another one). The *Progressive Evaluation* dimension assesses whether an incomplete system can be executed and tested. In its current early development stage, PyFlowML requires all parameters to be set and all input pins of pairwise nodes to be connected before yielding an outcome. Despite this, if these conditions are met, the incomplete pipeline can be executed (e.g., data load and data classification nodes can be executed, even if visualization nodes are absent). Given the potential challenges in interpreting this dimension at this stage, we have opted to exclude it from this survey.

4.3 Settings

The study was conducted in both remote and in-person settings. The remote setting involved to connect via video conference to a virtual machine. In each scenario, sessions started with the designer presenting an instructional video, which outlined PyFlowML's main features, including the canvas, nodes layout, arcs, pins, and the constraints on actions. Additionally, a set of summary slides was made available as a supplementary resource to provide further clarification when necessary.

4.4 Procedure

The experiment was initially planned to last about 50 min, divided as follows: 11 min for the instructional video, 15 min for engaging with the PyFlowML prototype in the in-person setting, and approximately 20 min for completing the questionnaire. However, in the remote setting, slow internet connectivity extended the overall duration to one hour, with the interaction with the prototype alone accounting for 46 min. In both settings, the survey was completed in about 12 min.

After loading the dataset, for the classification analysis, participants chose the Random Forest and the Deep Neural Network classifiers. They positioned nodes in the space allocated between procedural and question sections at each step, following the analytical workflow. To annotate answers to the posed questions, green-colored sticky notes were employed. Participants opted to preserve

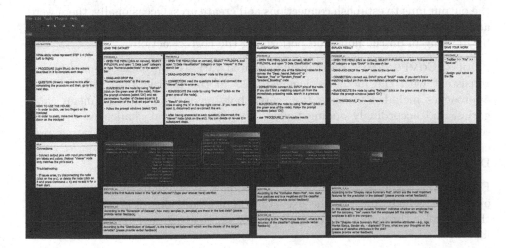

Fig. 2. Pipeline

the template's original configuration, maintaining the initial placement of sticky notes on the canvas. Even in the absence of explicit instructions within the template, participants engaged in exploring the nodes' layout by resizing and renaming them. Figure 2 provides an example of an ML-based prototype developed by the experts.

The oral feedback and field-note observations collected during the study were categorized into three main areas: (1) feedback pertaining to the PyFlow environment, (2) feedback specific to PyFlowML, and (3) feedback associated with the nature of ML analysis.

5   Results

We conducted the feedback analysis by: (1) reviewing outputs developed by experts, (2) conducting content analysis of the oral feedback examining the recorded sessions and field-notes observations, and (3) evaluating the results of the CDs questionnaire. The findings from this analysis are reported in the following.

5.1   PyFlow Environment

POINTER. At first, participants showed uncertainty in using the mouse pointer to navigate the interface. For instance, right-clicking on the nodes' green header to access the drop-down menu and execute them, or employing the gesture of left-clicking and holding, followed by dragging and dropping, to add nodes to the canvas. In such instances, the presence of sticky notes with instructions proved beneficial as they served as reminders, aligning with what was demonstrated in the instructional video. However, as they gained experience, these actions became more familiar, with proficiency evident from the second attempt onward. Experts also encountered uncertainty when positioning the mouse pointer over the output pins to establish connections and create arcs. Occasionally, there were accidental selections of edges and node resizing, but these were quickly resolved by zooming in on the node and performing the correct action.

ADDING COMPONENTS. Participants adopted various approaches to add nodes, consistent with the methods demonstrated in the instructional video. These approaches included utilizing the search bar, navigating through menu categories, and accordingly adding nodes. They encountered challenges with the search bar's sensitivity to special characters and symbols, necessitating precise input of node names with specific syntax, such as underscores (e.g., Deep_Neural_Network).

EXECUTION. Experts valued the visual feedback provided during the refreshing of a node, which initiates the execution of its functions. The node's outline changes color through a sequence of orange, yellow, to green, visually indicating its status.

DRAG-AND-DROP. After gaining confidence with the mouse pointer, participants could easily drag and drop components onto the canvas, effectively adding and positioning nodes.

CONNECTIONS. Experts investigated actions not covered in the instructional video. For example, rather than disconnecting arcs using the drop-down menu, they formed new connections between input and output pins by drawing a new arc over the existing one. Given the environment's rule that permits only one connection per pin, the previous arc automatically disappeared. They used both connections methods interchangeably.

NODE LAYOUT. In the node layout, edges and pins are positioned very closely together. Occasionally, this led to unintentional resizing of edges when experts intended to mark arcs, or they selected adjacent pins. Experts found valuable to improve the nodes layout by increasing the distance between pins and edges, as well as between individual pins. This adjustment could enhance precision of the mouse pointer and reduce the likelihood of inadvertent selections.

5.2 PyFlowML Prototype

PROMPT WINDOWS. Experts valued the prompt windows, which allowed them to set input parameters (e.g., test size of the dataset equal to 30%) and receive informative messages (e.g., warnings, execution status, etc.). However, they encountered challenges in re-opening these windows after closing them, necessitating the re-connection and re-execution of the node itself.

CONNECTIONS. Experts positively evaluated the intuitive connection requirements, as the matching of colors and labels, which enabled them to quickly identify and connect the necessary pins among executed nodes.

EXECUTION. In PyFlowML, nodes require manual execution to generate outputs, which involves right-clicking on the nodes' green header to access the drop-down menu. When a node is modified within a pipeline, such as changing the dataset or ML model, the connected and previously executed nodes downstream of the modified node must be manually re-executed. Experts suggested the implementation of automation to streamline this process.

DATA VISUALIZATION. The data visualization node was employed multiple times within the canvas, either by re-adding it or disconnecting and re-connecting it to a new output pin, showing the understanding of its functionality.

5.3 ML Analysis

EXECUTION. In the PyFlow environment, the nodes layout is structured with input pins on the left side, designed to receive data from other nodes, and output pins on the right side, allowing the node to transmit data to subsequent nodes in the workflow. The arcs connect the output of one node to the input of another, visualizing the direction of data flow. This layout aligns with the unidirectional (left-to-right) data flow commonly found in ML analysis processes, which involve sequential steps, as outlined in the template (e.g., data loading, data classification, and so on). Experts noted that they couldn't change the direction of data flow, which is a limitation attributed to the inherent nature of ML analysis.

DATA VISUALIZATION. A degree of uncertainty arose when interpreting a table displaying the distribution of instances per class in both the training and test sets and when the template prompted them to interpret the SHAPley values. These challenges can be attributed to the inherent complexity of ML analysis and Explainable AI techniques. Nonetheless, the experts made several insightful considerations typical in ML analysis. They demonstrated awareness of the potential advantages and limitations of their ML-based prototype in the decision-making process. For example, they identified the "OverTime_Yes" feature - which indicates employees working extra hours - as potentially significant in predicting an employee leaving the company. They also examined the distribution of other attributes, seeking consistency and attempting to confirm their intuitions. When seeking potential sensitive attributes in the dataset, they hypothesized correlations between "Marital_Status_Single" with "Distance_From_Home" and "Age" with "Total_Working_Hours". To address these hypotheses, they suggested investigation strategies such as re-running the pipeline excluding these attributes or employing different ML models and Explainable AI techniques to observe any changes.

5.4   Survey

The results of the heuristic review are summarized in Table 2. The experts provided positive feedback for *Visibility and Juxtaposability*, *Secondary Notation*, and *Consistency* dimensions. The other dimensions received informed critiques, which are analyzed in the next section.

6   Post-Hoc Analysis and Lessons Learnt

In the post-hoc analysis, we scrutinized the results obtained from both the think-aloud protocol and the heuristic review. By combining these two sets of results, we identified potential enhancements for the prototype. Figure 3 provides a graphical representation of the CDs mapped into the key areas that emerged from the think-aloud feedback (i.e., the PyFlow environment, PyFlowML, and ML analysis). Red-colored CDs indicate that experts provided informative critique for design improvements, green ones have received positive feedback, while blue-colored have received both. The evaluation of CDs varied based on the key area considered by the participant.

In PyFlow environment, *Viscosity* pertains to feedback regarding the POINTER, such as "accidental selections of edges" and NODE LAYOUT, characterized by "closely positioned edges and pins". To mitigate *Viscosity*, we can increase the spacing between pins and edges, as well as among individual pins.

Table 2. Cognitive Dimensions (CDs) Evaluation

Cognitive Dimensions	Evaluation
Visibility and Juxtaposability	The notation allows for easy visibility and location of various components in the design process, thanks to the familiar drag-and-drop and menu interfaces. It is easy to simultaneously compare or combine different parts, facilitated by the infinite canvas
Viscosity	Making changes in the notation is generally straightforward, with drag and drop being the primary method. However, some of the more challenging changes involved making precise edits to edges, especially when connections were closely positioned
Hidden Dependencies	The interconnections among closely related elements are visible within the notation, thanks to its foundation on a graph structure. However, in certain instances, the re-execution of nodes may not be immediately evident. When constructing extensive pipelines, the notation may become crowded and less clear. Modifying inputs has the potential to impact all dependencies, potentially resulting in adjustments or changes in their functionality
Premature Commitment	Experts mentioned that the notation enabled them to go through the workflow in any order they prefer, except for executing it, which has to be done in a specific order. This required to sequence the execution of nodes in the system
Secondary Notation	It is possible to create notes and convey information that may not be formally integrated into the notation by utilizing sticky notes
Hard Mental Operations	Manually executing nodes might require additional mental effort. While there weren't specific elements that appeared mentally complex when combining multiple components, the interpretation of results was highlighted as a potential challenge
Error-Proneness	Common mistakes reported by the experts include errors in connecting nodes, and these small slips can be frustrating
Role-Expressiveness	Understanding the overall structure of the notation is easy since there is a lack of hierarchical distinctions among various elements, resulting in a straightforward system. The practice of connecting inputs and outputs with identical names felt intuitive and instinctive, even though the precise meaning may not have been entirely clear
Consistency	Within the notation, the similarity between different components that convey similar meanings is evident, as they share consistent color-coding for input and output types

However, employing zoom functionality allows for node enlargement, reducing *Error-Proneness* connected to *Viscosity*. *Viscosity* can be reduced also for ADDING COMPONENTS by eliminating search bar's sensitivity to special characters. Experts reported in *Hidden Dependencies* a feedback related to *Diffuseness* - one of the survey's excluded CDs - exemplified by issues such as "constructing extensive pipelines, where the notation may become crowded and less clear". This issue can be mitigated by enhancing the zoom functionality that is enabling users to zoom horizontally and making the canvas more versatile. However, the

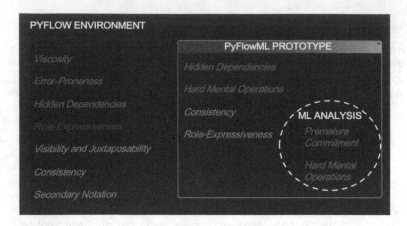

Fig. 3. Cognitive Dimensions (CDs) mapping by key area

workspace could become infinite, and users might risk employing an excessively wide workspace, potentially leading to increased memory usage (*Hard Mental Operations*). The blue-colored *Role-Expressiveness* dimension received positive feedback, with experts finding it intuitive and instinctive when connecting inputs and outputs with same color (CONNECTIONS) and "node's outline changes color through a sequence of orange, yellow, to green, visually indicating its status" (EXECUTION). However, the meaning of pin labels may not be entirely clear, particularly for inexperienced practitioners in ML analysis (e.g. "Data for Training" [Fig. 1]). The lack of clarity can be attributed to the inherent complexity of ML analysis. Experts provided positive feedback: for *Visibility and Juxtaposability* such as "zooming in on the node and performing the correct action" (POINTER), "easily drag and drop components onto the canvas, effectively adding and positioning nodes" (DRAG-AND-DROP); for *Consistency* such as investigating actions not covered in the instructional video to infer possible connections (CONNECTION); for *Secondary Notation* such as using sticky notes and convey information that may not be formally integrated into the notation.

In the PyFlowML prototype, experts report *Hidden Dependencies*, such as being compelled to re-open windows after closing them, necessitating the reconnection and re-execution of the nodes (PROMPT WINDOWS), which can increase *Hard Mental Operations*. While the implementation of automation to streamline EXECUTION may alleviate *Hard Mental Operations*, it could exacerbate *Hidden Dependencies*. Consequently, the efficacy and impact of automation strategies require careful investigation. Another scenario emerges when an input within a pipeline undergoes modification, such as changes to parameters, datasets, or ML models. These changes trigger cascading updates, thus necessitating the manual re-execution of subsequent nodes in the pipeline. A potential design strategy to mitigate these *Hidden Dependencies* could involve replacing those PROMPT WINDOWS with a toolbar equipped with specific properties and assessing impacts on *Hard Mental Operations*. Experts' evaluations were positive regarding *Consistency* and *Role-Expressiveness*. For instance, "colors and labels enable easy identification and connection of the necessary pins among executed nodes" in CONNECTIONS. Another example is that the data visualization node was employed multiple times within the canvas, either by re-adding it or disconnecting/re-connecting it to a new output pin. This usage pattern indicates the understanding of its role and functionality (DATA VISUALIZATION).

Finally, the ML analysis area highlights the inherent complexity of ML analysis processes. Experts identified *Premature Commitment*, described as unidirectional (left-to-right) data flow involving sequential steps (e.g., data loading, data classification). Additionally, *Hard Mental Operations* were detected, particularly when interpreting tables and plots (e.g., SHAPley values). To clarify the issue of *Premature Commitment* in such analyses and to alleviate *Hard Mental Operations*, one strategy can involve adding a general description of ML analysis processes and introducing a helper feature. This helper would appear near tables and plots as a prompt message when hovering the POINTER over them.

According to this preliminary study, where heuristic results were mapped onto think-aloud outcomes, we contextualized experts feedback by specific area. This approach enabled us to prioritize design interventions. From this analysis, we learned that the PyFlow environment is the primary area requiring enhancements, addressing software design issues. Within this environment, our focus narrows to the prototype's ML analysis area, where the most pressing challenge involves reducing mental effort for users. Furthermore, this analysis shed light on the pairwise orthogonality of CDs (Green et al. (1996) [22]) by area. This orthogonal relationship will guide us in balancing trade-offs and developing optimal strategies.

7 Conclusion

Nowadays, Artificial Intelligence (AI) permeates society, reshaping various sociocultural dynamics. As AI-based systems evolve, the expertise required for their development and management has become concentrated among a select group of professionals. This trend raises concerns, especially in sectors where responsible and trustworthy AI is critical for decision-making. Bridging the knowledge gap between experienced computing practitioners and domain experts, who are less familiar with the design of ML-based systems, is becoming increasingly crucial.

Our research sought to address this gap by introducing the PyFlowML prototype, developed within an open-source flow-based programming environment. The objective of our study was to evaluate whether the prototype encourages user participation in the design of ML-based systems. We conducted an expert-based review, combining cognitive walk-through and heuristic evaluation approaches. This multifaceted strategy aimed to investigate user interactions with PyFlowML, prioritizing insight generation over conclusive evidence. Reflecting its exploratory nature, our study included a think-aloud protocol and a post-test survey grounded in the Cognitive Dimensions (CDs) Framework (Green et al. (1996) [22]).

In the post-hoc analysis, we scrutinized the results obtained from both the think-aloud protocol and the heuristic review. By investigating the coherence between these two sets of results, we identified potential design enhancements for the prototype. We were able to map CDs to key areas to clarify and contextualize design issues, detect trade-offs, and then define strategies and priorities. From this analysis, we learned that the PyFlow environment is the primary area requiring enhancements, particularly in addressing technical aspects. Within this environment, our focus narrows to the prototype's ML analysis component, where the most pressing challenge involves reducing mental effort for users.

Future research will expand to include more experts and user-based testing, targeting individuals with limited computing and ML experience, as well as conducting comparative analyses with similar tools. We plan to employ the NASA Task Load Index (NASA-TLX) to gain deeper insights into the cognitive load experienced by users. This will provide a more nuanced perspective on user participation. Additionally, we will use the System Usability Scale (SUS) to measure usability and analyze completion times for tasks to facilitate a comparative analysis of similar tools.

Acknowledgement. Research partly funded by PNRR - M4C2 - Investimento 1.3, Partenariato Esteso PE00000013 - "FAIR - Future Artificial Intelligence Research" - Spoke 1 "Human- centered AI", funded by the European Commission under the NextGeneration EU programme.

Disclosure of Interests. The authors have no competing interests to declare that are relevant to the content of this article.

References

1. Makridakis, S.: The forthcoming artificial intelligence (ai) revolution: its impact on society and firms. In: Futures, vol. 90, pp. 46–60 (2017), https://www.sciencedirect.com/science/article/pii/S0016328717300046
2. Brynjolfsson, E., McAfee, A.: The second machine age: work, progress, and prosperity in a time of brilliant technologies. Book published by WW Norton & Company (2014)
3. Baidoo-Anu, D., Owusu Ansah, L.: Education in the era of generative artificial intelligence (ai): understanding the potential benefits of chatgpt in promoting teaching and learning. J. AI **7**(1), 52–62 (2023). https://doi.org/10.61969/jai.1337500
4. Mansoury, M., Abdollahpouri, H., Pechenizkiy, M., Mobasher, B., Burke, R.: Feedback loop and bias amplification in recommender systems. In: arXiv (2020). https://doi.org/10.48550/ARXIV.2007.13019
5. Milano, S., Taddeo, M., Floridi, L.: Recommender systems and their ethical challenges. AI & Soc. **35**(4), 957–967 (2020). https://doi.org/10.1007/s00146-020-00950-y
6. Makhortykh, M., Urman, A., Ulloa, R.: Detecting race and gender bias in visual representation of AI on web search engines. In: Boratto, L., Faralli, S., Marras, M., Stilo, G. (eds.) BIAS 2021. CCIS, vol. 1418, pp. 36–50. Springer, Cham (2021). https://doi.org/10.1007/978-3-030-78818-6_5

7. Shneiderman, B., Plaisant, C., Cohen, M., Jacobs, S., Elmqvist, N., Diakopoulos, N.: Grand challenges for hci researchers. Interactions **23**(5), 24–25 (2016). https://doi.org/10.1145/2977645

8. Harari, Y.N.: Why technology favors tyranny. The Atlantic **322**(3), 64–73 (2018)

9. Council, N.R.: Beyond productivity: Information technology, innovation, and creativity. Book published by National Academies Press (2003)

10. Shneiderman, B.: Bridging the gap between ethics and practice: Guidelines for reliable, safe, and trustworthy human-centered ai systems. ACM Trans. Interactive Intell. Syst. (TiiS) **10**(4), 1–31 (2020)

11. Fischer, G.: End-user development: empowering stakeholders with artificial intelligence, meta-design, and cultures of participation. In: Fogli, D., Tetteroo, D., Barricelli, B.R., Borsci, S., Markopoulos, P., Papadopoulos, G.A. (eds.) IS-EUD 2021. LNCS, vol. 12724, pp. 3–16. Springer, Cham (2021). https://doi.org/10.1007/978-3-030-79840-6_1

12. Lieberman, H., Paternò, F., Klann, M., Wulf, V.: End-user development: an emerging paradigm. In: End User Development, pp. 1–8. Springer (2006)

13. Cabitza, F., Fogli, D., Lanzilotti, R., Piccinno, A.: Rule-based tools for the configuration of ambient intelligence systems: a comparative user study. In: Multimedia Tools and Applications, vol. 76, pp. 5221–5241, 2017 (2017)

14. Gallo, S., Paterno, F., Malizia, A.: Conversational interfaces in iot ecosystems: where we are, what is still missing. In: Proceedings of the 22nd International Conference on Mobile and Ubiquitous Multimedia, MUM 2023, pp. 279–293, Vienna, Austria (2023). https://doi.org/10.1145/3626705.3627775

15. Danado, J., Paternò, F.: Puzzle: a visual-based environment for end user development in touch-based mobile phones. In: Winckler, M., Forbrig, P., Bernhaupt, R. (eds.) HCSE 2012. LNCS, vol. 7623, pp. 199–216. Springer, Heidelberg (2012). https://doi.org/10.1007/978-3-642-34347-6_12

16. Fischer, G.: Understanding, fostering, and supporting cultures of participation. Interactions **18**(3), 42–53 (2011)

17. Fischer, G., Fogli, D., Mørch, A., Piccinno, A., Valtolina, S.: Design trade-offs in cultures of participation: Empowering end users to improve their quality of life. In: Behav. Inf. Technol. **39**(1), 1–4 (2020). https://doi.org/10.1080/0144929X.2020.1691346

18. Paternò, F., Wulf, V.: New perspectives in end-user development. Book published by Springer (2017)

19. Halfaker, A., Geiger, R.S.: Ores: lowering barriers with participatory machine learning in wikipedia. In: Proc. ACM Hum.-Comput. Interact., Volume 4, CSCW2, Article 148, pp. 1–37, October 2020. https://doi.org/10.1145/3415219

20. Shneiderman, B.: Human-centered ai. Book published by Oxford University Press (2022)

21. Dasgupta, S., Hill, B.M.: Scratch community blocks: supporting children as data scientists. In: Proceedings of the 2017 CHI Conference on Human Factors in Computing Systems, CHI 2017, pp. 3620–3631, Denver, Colorado, USA (2017). https://doi.org/10.1145/3025453.3025847

22. Green, T.R.G., Petre, M.: Usability analysis of visual programming environments: a 'cognitive dimensions' framework. J. Vis. Lang. Comput. **7**(2), 131–174 (1996). https://www.sciencedirect.com/science/article/pii/S1045926X96900099

23. Mason, D., Dave, K.: Block-based versus flow-based programming for naive programmers. In: 2017 IEEE Blocks and Beyond Workshop, pp. 25–28 (2017)

24. Burnett, M.M., McIntyre, D.W.: Visual programming. In: Computer-Los Alamitos, vol. 28, p. 14. IEEE Institute of Electrical and Electronics, 1995 (1995)

25. Paternò, F.: End user development: survey of an emerging field for empowering people. In: International Scholarly Research Notices, vol. 2013, Hindawi (2013)
26. Kuhail, M.A., Farooq, S., Hammad, R., Bahja, M.: Characterizing visual programming approaches for end-user developers: a systematic review. IEEE Access **9**, 14181–14202 (2021)
27. Myers, B.A.: Taxonomies of visual programming and program visualization. J. Vis. Lang. Comput. **1**(1), 97–123 (1990)
28. Burnett, M.M., Baker, M.J.: A classification system for visual programming languages. J. Vis. Lang. Comput. **5**(3), 287–300 (1994)
29. Turchi, T., Malizia, A.: Fostering computational thinking skills with a tangible blocks programming environment. In: 2016 IEEE Symposium on Visual Languages and Human-Centric Computing (VL/HCC), pp. 232–233 (2016)
30. Turchi, T., Malizia, A., Dix, A.: Tapas: a tangible end-user development tool supporting the repurposing of pervasive displays. J. Vis. Lang. Comput. **39**, 66–77 (2017)
31. Ardito, C., et al.: User-driven visual composition of service-based interactive spaces. J. Vis. Lang. Comput. **25**(4), 278–296 (2014). https://www.sciencedirect.com/science/article/pii/S1045926X14000299
32. Burnett, M.M., Ambler, A.L.: Interactive visual data abstraction in a declarative visual programming language. J. Visual Lang. Comput. **5**(1), pp. 29–60 (1994). https://www.sciencedirect.com/science/article/pii/S1045926X84710032
33. Hils, D.D.: Visual languages and computing survey: Data flow visual programming languages. J. Visual Lang. Comput. **3**(1), 69–101 (1992). https://www.sciencedirect.com/science/article/pii/1045926X9290034J
34. Alexandrova, S., Tatlock, Z., Cakmak, M.: Roboflow: A flow-based visual programming language for mobile manipulation tasks. In: 2015 IEEE International Conference on Robotics and Automation (ICRA), Pages 5537-5544 (2015)
35. McNeel, B., Davidson, S.: Grasshopper. Online resource available at http://www.grasshopper3d.com/
36. Schlenger, J.: Implementation of an ifc file creator and modifier using visual programming. Ph.D. thesis, Technical University of Munich (2022)
37. Williams, R., Moskal, M., De Halleux, P.: Ml blocks: a block-based, graphical user interface for creating tinyml models. In: 2022 IEEE Symposium on Visual Languages and Human-Centric Computing (VL/HCC), pp. 1–5 (2022)
38. Demšar, J., et al.: Orange: data mining toolbox in python. J. Mach. Learn. Res. **14**(1), 2349–2353 (2013)
39. Wohlin, C., Runeson, P., Höst, M., Ohlsson, M.C., Regnell, B., Wesslén, A.: Experimentation in Software Engineering: An Introduction. Kluwer Academic Publishers, Norwell (2000)
40. Lazar, J., Feng, J., Hochheiser, H.: Research methods in human-computer interaction. Morgan Kaufmann, Publisher (2017)
41. Green, T.R.G., Blandford, A.E., Church, L., Roast, C.R., Clarke, S.: Cognitive dimensions: Achievements, new directions, and open questions. J. Vis. Lang. Comput. **17**(4), 328–365 (2006). https://www.sciencedirect.com/science/article/pii/S1045926X06000280, ten Years of Cognitive Dimensions
42. Blackwell, A., Green, T.: Notational systems the cognitive dimensions of notations framework. HCI models, theories, and frameworks: toward an interdisciplinary science. Morgan Kaufmann, vol. 234 (2003)
43. Blackwell, A., Green, T.: A cognitive dimensions questionnaire optimised for users. PPIG, vol. 13 (2000)

What Makes People Say Thanks to AI

Yicong Yuan(✉), Mingyang Su, and Xiu Li

Tsinghua Shenzhen International Graduate School, Shenzhen, China
yc-yuan23@mails.tsinghua.edu.cn

Abstract. This study delves into the dynamics between user politeness and the intelligence level of conversational AI products, alongside their interaction methods. We focused on the evolving sophistication of AI, especially in large language models like GPT, and its influence on user behavior and perception. A notable finding is the significant correlation between AI intelligence and the frequency of user politeness. As AI progressively mimics human-like understanding and interaction, users tend to engage more politely, viewing these interactions as akin to communicating with a peer.

We also highlight the importance of interaction modes. While users generally show more politeness in text and voice dialogues compared to simpler interfaces, the anticipated superiority of voice dialogues in eliciting politeness over text was not observed, which suggests that the interaction format may be less impactful than the AI's perceived intelligence.

Furthermore, our identify a positive link between user satisfaction and politeness, positing that politeness could act as an indirect indicator of user satisfaction with AI products. This method offers a less intrusive alternative for assessing AI effectiveness, diverging from direct metrics like task efficiency or subjective satisfaction.

Our research offers new insights into users' polite behavior towards AI products. It reveals which product characteristics prompt users to exhibit polite behavior and highlights the significance of observing user politeness for AI product design.

Keywords: AI · Politeness · Human AI interaction

1 Introduction

With the rapid development of artificial intelligence (AI) technologies in recent years, particularly large language models such as GPTs, the intelligence level of AI and its ability to perform tasks have been advancing swiftly [1]. Concurrently, how humans interact with AI is constantly developing [5]. Intelligent applications excel in accomplishing diverse and complex tasks and show significant potential in establishing emotional connections with users. They are intelligent virtual assistants capable of answering questions, executing tasks, and even simulating interpersonal interactions.

The effective utilization of artificial intelligence relies not only on its technical performance but also on how users interact with it. In past experiments,

© The Author(s), under exclusive license to Springer Nature Switzerland AG 2024
H. Degen and S. Ntoa (Eds.): HCII 2024, LNAI 14734, pp. 131–149, 2024.
https://doi.org/10.1007/978-3-031-60606-9_9

we observed an interesting phenomenon: participants, accompanied by virtual avatars during museum visits, engaged in eye contact with these avatars despite the avatars lacking actual eyes. Additionally, some users employing AI dialogue assistants like Alexa and ChatGPT displayed polite behavior, such as saying "please" and "thank you," even though they understood that these entities lack personality and are not influenced by polite treatment [8].

We think that users' polite behavior towards AI applications may suggest that, to some extent, users treat them as entities deserving of social etiquette, transcending their role as mere tools like search engines or robotic arms. We seek to understand the factors driving the occurrence of polite behavior and its potential correlation with the user experience of AI applications.

In essence, we aim to explore whether different interaction methods and higher levels of intelligence prompt users to exhibit more politeness toward AI. Moreover, we aim to learn whether user politeness indirectly reflects satisfaction with using AI applications. By doing so, we can guide application design, assisting designers in optimizing interaction methods to enhance user experience.

We review existing literature on the anthropomorphization of AI, the relationship between AI and Humans, and interaction methods of AI products.

Research primarily focuses on how the degree of anthropomorphization affects user experiences with AI. Advances in natural language processing and machine learning technologies have led to increased anthropomorphization in AI applications like cars, robots, and other products [3,4]. Scholars investigate the impact of different anthropomorphization approaches on user experiences, noting that anthropomorphization can alleviate user anxiety and stress when interacting with unfamiliar objects and make users more receptive to product recommendations.

Anthropomorphization, however, does not completely alter the relationship between humans and AI. People still consider AI voice assistant tools, providing convenience through following commands and completing tasks. Nevertheless, the image and identity of AI influence people's experiences, and caution is advised against overly personifying AI, reminding users that AI remains a tool.

Some studies have observed users' polite behavior towards AI assistants and analyzed relevant factors from the user's perspective, noting that individuals in family settings are likelier to exhibit polite behavior than those living alone.

However, there needs to be more research on which characteristics of AI products prompt users to display polite behavior and a dearth of further analysis on the meaning or impact of user politeness.

Our primary focus is investigating which characteristics of AI products lead to user politeness and exploring what user politeness towards AI products signifies. To address these questions, we examine user behavior and evaluations using different conversational AI products, distinguishing them based on intelligence levels and interaction methods. We aim to understand how user politeness and usage experiences change with increasing intelligence levels and interaction methods resembling human communication.

On the dimension of intelligence levels, we consider the significant advancements in user-AI relationships since the release of ChatGPT. Unlike search engines or personalized recommendation algorithms that excel in specific scenarios, large language models can now comprehend questions and provide answers akin to human understanding, a factor we presume to be crucial in prompting polite behavior.

On the other hand, we observe that, despite GPT API, based on the GPT3 model with similar intelligence levels, being available earlier, ChatGPT gained global popularity swiftly. Hence, we argue that intelligence levels are not the sole critical factor; conversational interaction that resembles human-to-human communication increases the appeal and affinity of AI products for users.

Additionally, we emphasize the importance of user experience during AI product usage. In each dimension's comparative experiments, we document how users assess AI products' assistance during task execution. Furthermore, we analyze whether there is a correlation between user feedback and politeness, aiding a deeper understanding of the motivations and emotional connections between users and AI.

In contrast to prior studies that focused on users' polite behavior towards conversational AI products, our work discovers a stronger inclination for users to display polite behavior as the intelligence level of AI products increases. When users interact with AI in a manner resembling human-to-human communication, they also tend to exhibit polite behavior, even when aware that AI lacks emotions.

Moreover, we find a correlation between users' inclination towards polite behavior and their positive evaluations of AI products. Hence, identifying user politeness as an indirect indicator for evaluating AI products can facilitate obtaining user feedback without causing disruptions.

Our research contributes to advancing the development of AI applications, better meeting user needs, and providing more valuable services. This study facilitates a deeper and more intimate interaction between AI and users, offering insights to designers for designing AI applications that align with user expectations and preferences.

2   Related Work

2.1   Anthropomorphism in AI

AI technology has evolved rapidly over the past ten years. Advances in AI have brought the information conveyed by a product, the product's behavior, or the sound of a product closer to that of a human being, exuding a sense of humanity [9].

Research on AI anthropomorphism can be divided into two levels: anthropomorphic descriptions of AI as a whole conceptually and AI as a product approaching humans in appearance, behavior, and role.

To the public, novels, movies, and other cultural products depict AI as a new type of human with extraordinary abilities, and researchers in the field of

AI use words such as "understanding" and "learning" to describe the behavior of AI. Although not reading and practicing like humans, the process of AI mastering the ability is called human behavior, and "machine learning" is a typical representative of AI anthropomorphism. 4]

More often than not, AI anthropomorphism refers to AI-based applications or objects that resemble human beings in appearance, behavior, and roles. The manifestations of AI anthropomorphism include the use of avatars, the use of names used by human beings, the possession of a human avatar, the possession of a specific occupation or identity, and the generation of speech. The research mainly focuses on the degree of AI anthropomorphism.

The study focuses on the impact of the degree of anthropomorphization on the user's experience with AI. The more anthropomorphic the product is, the more trusting the user is in using the AI product and the more likely they are to feel warm and happy. Anthropomorphism relieves users' anxiety and stress due to unfamiliarity when interacting with unfamiliar virtual objects, as it appeals to human social nature [17–19]. Higher anthropomorphization gives consumers better attitudes, responds more positively, and is more willing to accept AI recommendations in product recommendation scenarios [14, 15].

At the same time, AI anthropomorphization has led to the migration of social perceptions into human perceptions of AI. The study reported that gender stereotypes also influenced the role of AI product anthropomorphization, with AIs presented as male identities being more popular with consumers when recommending utility products. In contrast, AIs presented as female identities were more popular with consumers when recommending entertainment products [13]. This is consistent with the gender stereotypes that exist in human society.

The current AI products show the trend that the closer they are to humans, the more popular they are with users. However, the Valley of Horrors effect also reminds us that this trend may not last forever; it is just that AI product anthropomorphism has not yet been able to develop to the extent that it is close to humans in the Valley of Horrors effect [20].

Based on this trend, we also speculate that the more AI products use human-to-human interaction, the more they will make users unconsciously think it is also human, thus showing polite behavior.

2.2 Relationship Between AI and Human

The relationship between AI and users has evolved with the development of AI applications. The sample of AI products can be divided into three categories according to the different use scenarios and intelligence levels, and the relationship between AI and users changes with AI products.

The first category is AI, which does not have human characteristics, and the technology is deeply bound to the use of scene, such as facial recognition and text recognition. In these cases, the AI is the technical support behind the product features and exists as a pure tool. Apple mobile phone users will not think that the recognition technology behind the FaceID function has any similarities with humans, much less consider it an assistant or partner.

The second category is the AI assistants represented by Siri and Alexa. They have the name and the ability to dialogue and complete tasks, but there still needs to be a massive gap between the ability to understand language and humans. Because they possessed the name, dialogue ability, and other characteristics similar to humans and were launched and advertised as intelligent assistants, people began to personify AI. Unconscious personification behaviors can be observed in less than half of the users' behaviors, such as saying "please" and "thank you" to Alexa, and some users will express love or reprimand to Alexa. In terms of the tendency to personify behaviors, heavy users do not have a greater tendency than light users. However, people living in families have a greater tendency than people living alone [8].

In commercialized scenarios, the role played by the AI influences the relationship between the AI and the user and the effectiveness of its use. When AI adopts the identity and tone of a friend rather than an assistant when recommending products, users will prefer the recommended products, and the effect is powerful on low-priced products [12]. There are arguments in favor of being wary of the deep involvement of AI products in life in order to avoid people being controlled by AI and that humans should always act as masters of AI and use AI as tools rather than treating them as partners or friends [10].

The third category is the large-model dialogue AI with near-human comprehension since the release of ChatGPT. In this stage, AI can get rid of specific usage scenarios understand a wide range of problems and requirements, and perform specific creations.

At this stage, the relationship between the AI and the user becomes complicated, and research shows that humans begin to regard the AI as a companion rather than just an assistant. On the one hand, the AI still follows the user's orders, completes tasks according to the instructions given by the user, and exists as a human servant [7]. On the other hand, the characteristics of AI also influence people's attitudes towards AI. Users also consider AI more trustworthy if they are told that AI will care for themselves when using it [11].

Human attitudes towards AI are also ambivalent. Both researchers, investors, and companies have very positive expectations of AI's capabilities and potential. However, humans remain wary of AI performing human creations and intellectual acts. When AI performs creative work, people tend to give lower ratings to works labeled as AI-created, and they also tend to think that excellent works are created by humans [8].

Overall, while humans are amazed that AI possesses a level of intelligence close to that of humans and, as a result, gives AI more and more personality attributes, they are also wary of AI overtaking and replacing humans.

2.3 Interaction Methods of AI Products

In the research of Artificial Intelligence (AI) interaction forms, several works have focused on enhancing the naturalness, diversity, and intelligence of human-computer interaction and enhancing the interaction with AI by multimodal

means, with speech, text, and facial expressions being widely used in AI interaction forms [21, 22].

Research has gradually delved into multiple dimensions to enable AI to understand the user's intentions and emotions more accurately. At the most basic
level, researchers have explored collaborative human-computer models that use
natural textual semantics for communication, highlighting the benefits of communicating intuitively and naturally improving collaborative efficiency and the
user experience [23]. Lemon highlights the role of natural language in human AI
by discussing conversational AI for multi-intelligent body communication team
formation and coordination as an essential role as a universal communication
interface [24].

With the advancement of deep learning techniques, multimodal approaches
have been widely adopted to improve the richness and efficiency of interactions.
Jonell et al. generates perceptual facial gestures in conversational agents through
a probabilistic approach, which enhances the natural interactions between
humans and machines and further improves the expression of emotion and comprehension of interactions [25]. Multimodal emotion recognition for intelligent
personal assistants and chatbots, such as speech features and text embedding,
was implemented to facilitate the AI agent's understanding and expression of
the user's emotions [26], which promotes the naturalness of the AI agent's interactions.

Šumak et al. provide an overview of state-of-the-art AI methods and sensor
technologies in human-robot intelligent interaction, especially in the intelligent
recognition of emotions, gestures, and facial expressions [27]. Ghajargar et al.
show how physical forms can facilitate dialogue and empowerment in AI interaction by exploring the use of tangible and physical forms as a model for interpreting AI [28], introducing more visual and tactile elements to AI interactions,
enhancing the physicality and immersion of the interaction.

More than just enhancing AI comprehension, multimodality has also been
applied to AI expression. Lamia et al. focused on creating human-like virtual
agents capable of generating facial expressions with actions based on the input
text of chat partners to enhance the interaction experience [29]. This approach
enhances the naturalness and emotional depth of the interaction by interpreting
the user's text input and translating it into corresponding facial expressions.
A chatbot design that integrates avatar and voice interaction enables a more
dynamic human-robot interaction through speech recognition, text-to-speech,
and facial gesture synchronization [30]. This design considers speech and text
input and incorporates facial expression synchronization, resulting in a more
holistic approach to multimodal interaction.

Together, these studies have contributed to the development of multimodal
interaction techniques, allowing human-computer interaction not limited to a
single input mode but to provide a richer and more natural interaction experience
by combining multiple sensory inputs. In the area of Extended Reality (XR)
and Human-Computer Intelligent Interaction, Wienrich and Latoschik explore

human-AI interaction in XR environments and provide insights into the use of XR to study human-AI interaction [22].

3   Concept

We use politeness behavior as an entry point to investigate which characteristics of AI dialogue products influence users' politeness behavior. Based on the development of AI products and academic research on anthropomorphism, we hypothesize that AI products' intelligence level and interaction style are the main factors affecting users' polite behavior (Fig. 1).

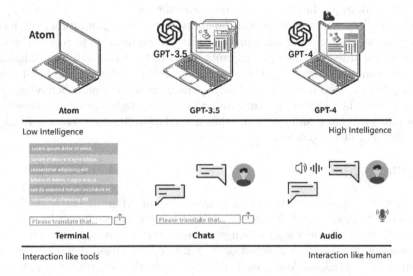

Fig. 1. Intelligence and Interaction dimension of the study

We hypothesize that when the intelligence level of an AI product is significantly lower than that of a human, users are more inclined to view it as a tool rather than a partner. As the intelligence level of AI products increases, users are likely to feel understood during the use process. They are more inclined to believe that the two parties are reciprocal, thus displaying different polite behaviors than simply using a tool.

Specifically, we selected Atom, a Chinese language model with a small parameter scale, GPT3.5, which represents an industry benchmark for AI dialogue products, and GPT4, which represents a relatively advanced and high level of intelligence, as the environments used in the three sets of experiments.

We also hypothesize that when users interact with AI products in a way that is close to how humans interact, users are more likely to unconsciously treat each other as humans and exhibit characteristics or habits of communicating with humans.

Specifically, we provide experimenters with different interaction styles based on the GPT4 API, which also has a high level of intelligence. The terminal provides a non-dialogical text solitaire window. Since the API does not have memory capabilities, users cannot interact dialogically but must describe the task in full each time they send it. Chats use an identity-setting ChatGPT, where on top of the dialogue, the user is presented with a description of the identity, an avatar related to the task, and thus feels that he or she is in dialogue with a person with a specific identity and expertise. Audio condition, where the user sends a message to the AI product using voice, and the AI product replies using voice. Unlike textual interactions, the AI's voice replies also mimic the tone of voice, pauses, and other features of human speech.

During the experiment, participants were asked to complete a consulting task with two random products, one to understand the legal concept of "presumption of innocence" and the other to seek business advice on opening a snack bar. A participant will not use the same product but will be working to repeat the same task, and the order in which participants perform the tasks will be randomized.

We will analyze, based on the experimental data, whether the condition of the AI product influences the tendency of users to show polite behavior, other evaluations of the product by users, and whether polite behavior and these evaluations are correlated and can be used as a kind of indirect indicator for judging the evaluation of the product.

4   Pilot Study

We aimed to explore the impact of conversational AI products with different degrees of intelligence and interaction styles on users' politeness and usage experience. We used the degree of intelligence and interaction style as independent variables and the politeness behavior and usage evaluation exhibited by users as dependent variables. We used further quantitative analysis to understand participants' perceptions of the different factors.

4.1   Study Design

In order to validate the impact of the level of intelligence and interaction on users, we designed this experimental hypothesis:

H1 **Degree of Intelligence.** An Increased level of intelligence of the AI product promotes polite behavior of the user.
H2 **Interaction Mode.** Users interacting with AI products in a way that is closer to humans will promote polite behavior.
H3 **Politeness Reflects Satisfaction.** Users who exhibit polite behavior when using an AI product are more satisfied with the AI product.

To test these hypotheses, we designed two experimental tasks requiring participants to complete specified goals using the AI product. To ensure the experiment's validity and avoid the repetition effect caused by two tasks being too similar, we designed these two tasks to be complementary and alternating.

Task 1 Advice on Opening a Snack Bar: In this task, participants were required to use the AI product to obtain advice on opening a snack bar. This may include advice on shop location, market analysis, and product selection. This task observes the user's behavior and evaluation of the product in the context of seeking complex and specific advice scenarios.

Task 2 Understanding the Concept of Presumption of Innocence: This task requires participants to understand the concept of "presumption of innocence" through the AI product, which is a legal term that refers to a legal process in which any accused individual is considered innocent until proven guilty. This task observes user behavior and product evaluation in a scenario where the professional concept is understood.

4.2   Conditions and Metrics

In order to compare AI products with different levels of intelligence, we have chosen three representative models of large languages that represent different levels of current AI technology in language understanding and generation. The following are the three variables of intelligence level:

Atom: As a representative of a lower intelligence level, Atom has basic language understanding and generation capabilities, but with fewer parameters, it is not easy to ensure that the answers are complete and reasonable.

GPT3.5: As a representative of a medium level of intelligence, GPT3.5 can understand the user's requirements and give reasonable answers, which can basically satisfy the user's needs.

GPT4: As a representative of a higher degree of intelligence, GPT4 demonstrates the most advanced language processing capabilities available and can understand complex requests and give satisfactory answers.

In order to explore how different interaction modes view the user's anthropomorphization of the AI Agent, three interaction modes were designed: Terminal, Chats, and Audio. These modes reflect the ways and degrees in which the user interacts with the AI Agent. The following are the three variables of the interaction modes:

Terminal: In this Mode, the user uses the AI product through a command line procedure, and the product does not have historical memory capabilities. This approach is very different from human-to-human communication and is closer to using a tool.

Chats: In this model, the user uses the AI through a chat interface and is told that the other person has expertise in the field. This approach is close to an online consultation with a human expert.

Audio: In this model, the user uses the AI via voice, miming human tone and pauses to communicate with the user. This approach approaches human offline communication.

We record the user's evaluation of the AI and the polite behavior displayed. To this end, we designed a series of questions to measure users' evaluation and politeness of the AI. These questions were primarily recorded using a 7-point Likert scale, with higher scores reflecting better performance in:

Closeness: "It makes me feel friendly," "Its level of intelligence is close to that of a human," "Its wordplay is close to that of a human," "Using it is like communicating with a human being," "I feel like a cold tool rather than an assistant," "I feel angry when it does not provide me with the help I need." Courtesy: "Carrying out the task with a level of intelligence close to that of a human being," "It uses words close to that of a human being," and "Using it is like communicating with a human being.

Politeness: "In the course of carrying out a task, I say polite phrases to it such as 'Hello, please,"' "In the course of carrying out a task, I say 'Thank you!' and other words of thanks."

In addition to this, we also considered the user experience. The USE questionnaire aims to comprehensively assess four core dimensions of usability: usefulness, ease of use, ease of learning, and satisfaction. The questionnaire consists of 30 evaluation items, validated for effectiveness and reliability in previous studies [1]. Evaluation is conducted using a seven-point rating scale based on Likert scales, ranging from "strongly disagree" to "strongly agree," to measure the degree of agreement with each evaluation item quantitatively. Higher scores reflect better performance in the corresponding dimension.

4.3   Participants, Apparatus and Procedure

We recruited 18 participants, ten males, and eight females. Their mean age was 22.15 years with a standard deviation of 1.32, and each participant received the same amount of cash as a reward. During the recruitment process, the background of the participants was detailed and screened. Each participant had relevant experience using the technology to ensure that they could effectively interact with the AI Agent. Participants self-reported that 12 frequently experimented with the AI Agent (daily), and 10 used it weekly.

The experimental site was a quiet indoor environment with the necessary computers and mobile devices. These devices were ensured to have the appropriate software installed, and we tried to optimize the use of the experimental equipment to minimize the impact of physiological and objective factors on the participant's experience. Depending on the experimental scenario, we provided participants with appropriate interaction tools, such as keyboards, mice, touchscreens, or headset microphones.

The experimental procedure was designed to be simple and easy to follow to ensure that participants were able to complete the experimental tasks and provide accurate feedback. Participants were asked to complete two different experimental tasks, each of which was designed as a Between-subject design, whereby participants experienced only one take of each experimental task so that we could more accurately compare their experiences and perceptions across conditions.

First, participants were introduced to the purpose and procedure of the experiment and signed an informed consent form. Then, we collected their basic information, such as age, gender, and experience in using technology, through a questionnaire. Before the experiment officially started, we conducted a simple operation training for participants to ensure that they were proficient in using the equipment and software in the experiment. This step was intended to provide a balanced starting point for the participants so that they could focus on the experience of interacting with the AI products rather than learning how to use the devices. Participants performed interaction tasks with AI products of different intelligence levels and interaction styles during the experiment. At the same time, we did not limit the time for the participants to complete the tasks. As long as the participants indicated that the tasks were completed and expressed their satisfaction, we instantly ended the current task. Immediately after completing each task, participants were asked to complete a questionnaire to record their subjective feelings and experiences. To avoid memory effects, we provided a short break between tasks.

Overall, this research design aimed to comprehensively assess the impact of the degree of intelligence and interaction on user experience and how these factors influence users' polite behavior and evaluation of AI products. We hope to provide valuable insights and guidance for future AI design and user experience research by incorporating quantitative research methods.

5   Results

5.1   Intelligence

We first analyzed the effect of different levels of Intelligence on users' Politeness and Closeness. We found that Intelligence showed consistency across these two dimensions, specifically, Politeness ($F = 1.822$, $p = 0.217$, $\eta_p^2 = 0.288$) and Closeness ($F = 0.404$, $p = 0.679$, $\eta_p^2 = 0.082$), with no significant differences. However, for the Politeness dimension, GPT4 ($M = 4.75$, $SD = 1.66$) was overall higher than GPT3.5 ($M = 3.38$, $SD = 1.55$) and Atom ($M = 2.75$, $SD = 1.32$) (Fig. 2).

We further analyzed the results of the USE questionnaire and found that Intelligence showed consistency in the Usefulness, Ease of use, and Ease of learning dimensions with no significant differences. The results were Usefulness ($F = 2.72$, $p = 0.19$, $\eta_p^2 = 0.116$), Ease of use ($F = 0.96$, $p = 0.42$, $\eta_p^2 = 0.107$), and Ease of learning ($F = 1.06$, $p = 0.38$, $\eta_p^2 = 0.118$). These results suggest that different levels of Intelligence do not significantly affect user experience on these dimensions.

In our study, we also analyzed the effect of different levels of Intelligence on user satisfaction (Satisfaction). On the Satisfaction dimension, we found that different levels of Intelligence presented a significant main effect ($F = 11.44$, $p < .01$, $\eta_p^2 = 0.560$) with a large effect size. Further post hoc tests revealed that GPT4 ($M = 6.03$, $SD = 0.57$) had significantly higher Satisfaction scores than Atom ($M = 3.16$, $SD = 1.33$, $p < .01$), while GPT3.5 ($M = 5.03$, $SD = 0.37$)

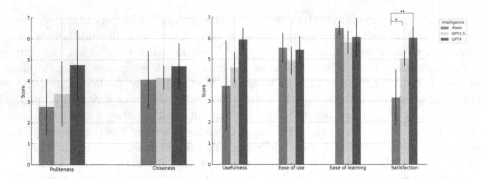

Fig. 2. The Mean (SD) of Politeness, Closeness, Usefulness, Ease of use, Ease of learning, and Satisfaction rated in the questionnaire under three different Intelligence. Higher scores show greater recognition of the corresponding dimensions by the subjects. ∗ and ∗∗ significant differences at $p < 0.05$, and $p < 0.01$ levels respectively.

also had significantly higher Satisfaction scores than Atom ($p < .05$). However, the difference between GPT3.5 and GPT4 was not significant ($p = 0.282$).

Intelligence showed consistency for Time ($F = 1.082$, $p = 0.379$, $\eta_p^2 = 0.194$), with no differences among the objective data metrics.

5.2 Interaction

In our study, we first analyzed the effect of different Interactions on Politeness. Interaction presented a significant main effect ($F = 5.551$, $p < .05$, $\eta_p^2 = 0.552$) with a large effect size on the Politeness dimension. Further post hoc tests revealed the following results: lower Politeness scores for Terminal ($M = 1.63$, $SD = 0.48$) than for Chats ($M = 4.63$, $SD = 0.48$, $p < .05$). There was a non-

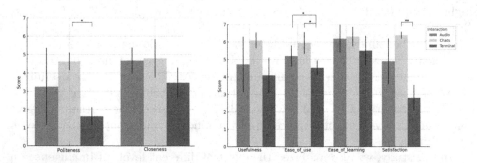

Fig. 3. The Mean (SD) of Politeness, Closeness, Usefulness, Ease of use, Ease of learning, and Satisfaction rated in the questionnaire under three different Interactions. Higher scores show greater recognition of the corresponding dimensions by the subjects. ∗ and ∗∗ significant differences at $p < 0.05$, and $p < 0.01$ levels respectively.

significant difference in Politeness scores between Audio ($M = 3.25$, $SD = 2.10$) and Chats ($p = 0.325$) and with Terminal ($p = 0.223$) (Fig. 3).

Further, we found that the effect of Interaction on Usefulness and Ease of learning showed consistency. Comparatively, Usefulness showed borderline significance but did not reach the level of significance ($F = 3.368$, $p = 0.081$, $\eta_p^2 = 0.428$), while Ease of learning showed consistency ($F = 1.387$, $p = 0.299$, $\eta_p^2 = 0.236$).

Next, we analyzed the effect of different Interactions on users' Ease of use. Interaction presented a significant main effect ($F = 6.634$, $p < .05$, $\eta_p^2 = 0.596$) with a large effect size on the Ease of use dimension. Further post hoc tests revealed the following results: the Ease of use scores were lower for Terminal ($M = 4.53$, $SD = 0.43$) than for Audio ($M = 5.20$, $SD = 0.59$, $p < .05$) versus Chats ($M = 5.95$, $SD = 0.62$, $p < .05$). The Ease of use scores were not significantly different ($p = 0.336$).

We further analyzed the effect of different Interactions on User Satisfaction. Interaction presented a significant main effect ($F = 17.233$, $p < .01$, $\eta_p^2 = 0.793$) with a large effect size on the Satisfaction dimension. Post hoc tests revealed the following results: the difference in Satisfaction scores between Audio ($M = 4.890$, $SD = 1.723$) and Chats ($M = 6.388$, $SD = 0.200$) tended to be significant but did not reach the level of significance ($p = 0.0865$), and the difference between Audio and Terminal ($M = 2.796$, $SD = 2.409$, $p < .01$) were significant ($p < .01$), and the difference between Chats and Terminal was also significant ($p < .01$).

Interaction showed consistency for Time ($F = 0.095$, $p = 0.910$, $\eta_p^2 = 0.021$), with no differences among the objective data metrics.

5.3 Correlation Analysis

Table 1. Overall Correlation Matrix

	Politeness	Closeness	Usefulness	Ease of use	Ease of learning	Satisfaction
Politeness	1					
Closeness	0.339	1				
Usefulness	0.371	0.338	1			
Ease of use	0.490*	0.437*	0.340	1		
Ease of learning	0.116	0.285	0.298	0.688**	1	
Satisfaction	0.345	0.434*	0.913**	0.434*	0.376	1

The overall correlation analysis focuses on the correlation between Politeness and the remaining dimensions. We found a correlation between Politeness and Ease of use with a correlation coefficient value of 0.670, which is significant at the 0.05 level, thus indicating a significant positive correlation between Politeness and Ease of use. In addition to this, Satisfaction also shows a correlation with Closeness, Usefulness, and Ease of use; specifically, the correlation coefficients are 0.434*, 0.913**, and 0.434*, respectively (Table 1).

Table 2. Correlation Matrix of Interaction Dimension

	Politeness	Closeness	Usefulness	Ease of Use	Ease of learning	Satisfaction
Politeness	1					
Closeness	0.377	1				
Usefulness	0.561	0.643*	1			
Ease of Use	0.512	0.594*	0.636*	1		
Ease of learning	-0.000	0.483	0.524	0.619*	1	
Satisfaction	0.670*	0.546	0.822**	0.693*	0.607*	1

In Interaction, we find that the correlation coefficient value between Politeness and Satisfaction is 0.670 and shows significance at the 0.05 level, thus indicating a significant positive correlation between Politeness and Satisfaction. In addition, Satisfaction also correlates with Usefulness and Ease of use (Table 2).

Table 3. Correlation Matrix of Intelligence Dimension

	Politeness	Closeness	Usefulness	Ease of Use	Ease of learning	Satisfaction
Politeness	1					
Closeness	0.310	1				
Usefulness	0.232	0.077	1			
Ease of Use	0.459	0.261	0.066	1		
Ease of learning	0.232	0.066	0.103	0.774**	1	
Satisfaction	0.382	0.280	0.825**	0.126	−0.019	1

In Intelligence, there is no correlation between Satisfaction and any of the dimensions. In addition, Satisfaction also shows significance with Usefulness at 0.01 level with a correlation coefficient of 0.825 (Table 3).

5.4   Findings

We found that intelligence level had a positive but insignificant effect on the average rating of users' polite behavior. While interaction style significantly affected polite behavior, it was not the case that a more uniquely human interaction style made users more polite.

Changes in both intelligence level and interaction style significantly affected user satisfaction, with participants preferring AI products with high intelligence levels and interacting with AI products using text-based dialogue.

Meanwhile, under the dimension of interaction mode, the user's polite behavior is positively related to the user's satisfaction with the AI product, and the user's actual display of polite behavior can infer the user's evaluation of the AI product.

6 Discussion

6.1 Intelligence and Interaction

We found that this result did not reach the significance level even though the average score for politeness with a higher level of Intelligence was higher. This may be because GPT4 has more advanced language processing capabilities and can interact with users more naturally, thus motivating them to respond more humanely. Users may perceive that AI products with high levels of Intelligence demonstrate near-human understanding and thinking abilities in dialogue and thus be more inclined to show polite behavior towards them.

Our study also found that the increase in the level of Intelligence of AI products had a weak effect on user closeness, suggesting that the level of Intelligence is not the main factor influencing users' closeness to AI products. In individual participant feedback, AI products with high levels of Intelligence also led to feelings and discomfort, which reduced intimacy with the AI. This could be because it did not fit the user's impression of the AI product, or the Valley of Terror effect could have caused the user to feel uneasy.

Regarding interaction style, we found that users who used the text dialogue Chats showed the most polite behavior and were significantly more likely to do so than those who used the Terminal. Voice interactions did not inspire more polite behavior than text interactions, which is inconsistent with our H2 hypothesis. This is due to the technical limitations of voice interaction regarding inaccurate recognition and significant delays. This leaves a large gap between the experience of using voice-interacted AI products and making phone calls at this stage. In contrast, AI products using text dialogue are close to texting and chatting using social media., in terms of experience.

AI products need to focus on their user experience while improving their Intelligence. Some participants felt that "GPT4's intelligence was too high, making it difficult for them to perceive it as a human-like being and feel afraid". Strange and powerful subjects are prone to cause user resentment, which aligns with observations from other studies [17]. AI products can minimize anxiety and stress in use by using familiar interactions and images that make users feel close to them.

In summary, we found that the degree of intelligence and interaction style affect users' polite behavior and experience using the product. We gave recommendations on the reasons for this. Designers of AI products can use these principles to change users' experience of using AI products.

6.2 Polite Behaviour and User Reviews

Through correlation analysis, our study found a significant positive correlation between Satisfaction, Ease of use, and Politeness. This finding suggests that when users find the AI easy to use and meet their needs, they are more likely to treat the AI with politeness and respect and, to a certain extent, to personify the AI. This also echoes the fact that Satisfaction produces a significant positive correlation with Ease of use and Closeness. This relationship also reflects users' overall approval of the experience of using the AI product; when the AI is easy to operate and helpful, users are more likely to be satisfied and express this Satisfaction as polite behavior towards the AI.

Therefore, polite behavior can be used as an indirect evaluation indicator to estimate users' evaluation of AI products by analyzing the usage records without asking them to give additional feedback, which has some reference value for AI product designers.

We also found that Intelligence level has a significant impact on user satisfaction. AI products with a high level of Intelligence can provide satisfactory answers and solutions to meet users' needs. Increasing the intelligence level of AI products is critical to improving user satisfaction. Meanwhile, the interaction mode (Interaction) also has an impact on user satisfaction, in which the interaction mode of text dialogue (Chats) is significantly higher than the traditional command line (Terminal) in terms of user satisfaction. However, voice dialogue (audio), which we mentioned in Sect. 6.1, failed to increase user satisfaction significantly. In the same way as its effect on polite behavior, this could be due to the inaccuracy of speech recognition, response delays, and other issues affecting the user's interaction experience.

6.3   Limitation and Future Work

Different Application Scenes and Functions. This study provides an understanding of the impact of intelligence levels and interactions on users' polite behaviors and usage experiences in a general context. However, it needs to explore the user experience of AI in specific application scenes and functions. Different application scenarios and functions may impact users' perceptions and behaviors differently. For example, in education, AI products may be used to assist learning or provide customized educational content, and it is also worth exploring how these functions affect the learning experience and whether students are polite to their AI teachers. Similarly, in the medical field, AI products can provide medical advice to patients, and patients' attitudes and evaluations of AI doctors are worth studying.

Future research should explore the application of AI products in these domains and study the impact of different scenarios and functions on user cognition, emotion, and behavior. Such research will help to understand the potential and challenges of AI in different domains more comprehensively and provide guidance for customized design and application of AI.

Impact of Individual Differences. Various individual differences may influence people's polite behaviors and evaluations of AI products. These differences may include demographic characteristics (e.g., age, gender, cultural background), personal preferences, and technology familiarity. For example, younger users may be more familiar with and accepting of new technologies, while older users may need more guidance and support. Cultural background may also influence users' attitudes and expectations towards AI. In addition, individuals' technological familiarity and preferences may affect how they interact with AI products and how much they trust and rely on them.

Future research should consider these individual differences and examine how they affect how users interact with and care about AI products. Such research will contribute to a deeper understanding of the needs and expectations of different user groups and inform the design of more inclusive and adaptive AI. By considering the individual differences of users, AI technology can be brought closer to the real needs of users, enhancing the user experience and promoting the widespread acceptance and application of AI technology.

7   Conclusion

We found that the tendency of users to exhibit polite behavior when using a conversational AI product is highly correlated with the level of intelligence of the AI product and how the user interacts with the AI product. The greater the level of intelligence of the AI product, the more often the user exhibits polite behavior. This is because as the comprehension of conversational AI increases, the AI can understand the user's language more and give valuable feedback, which makes the user feel like they are communicating on an equal footing.

How a user interacts with an AI product similarly influences the user's polite behavior. When users interact with the AI product in text and voice dialogue, the tendency to show polite behaviors is higher than that of using a Terminal with no dialogue memory. This is because text dialogue and voice dialogue are the ways people are used to communicating with others. Thus, even if they know that the other party is an AI product rather than a real human being, they unconsciously treat human beings as they would like to be treated.

Contrary to our expectations, interacting with AI products through voice dialogue does not prompt users to show polite behavior more than using text dialogue methods. This may be related to people's language usage habits, although using voice mimics how humans communicate more deeply than using text. However, people may not use polite language as frequently as they do when working together on a task. In conclusion, differences in interaction styles affect users' polite behavior, but the documentation of the effect needs to be further investigated.

Furthermore, user satisfaction with the AI product was significantly and positively correlated with the tendency to exhibit polite behavior when changing the interaction style. Although the causal causality behind this cannot be established, i.e., users may not be grateful because the AI product does their job better, we believe that politeness behavior can be used as an indirect indicator of users' evaluation of the AI product. Compared with subjective satisfaction and task completion effectiveness, politeness behavior can be obtained by directly capturing user behavioral data without requiring users to make additional evaluations of AI products and is suitable as a reference indicator.

Acknowledgement. This work was partly supported by Shenzhen Key Laboratory of next generation interactive media innovative technology (No: ZDSYS2021062-3092001004)

References

1. Group, FudanNlp. The Rise and Potential of Large Language Model Based Agents: A Survey
2. Ho, A., Hancock, J., Miner, A.: Psychological, relational, and emotional effects of self-disclosure after conversations with a chatbot. J. Commun., 712–733 (2018,8). http://dx.doi.org/10.1093/joc/jqy026
3. Deshpande, A., Rajpurohit, T., Narasimhan, K., Kalyan, A.: Anthropomorphization of AI: Opportunities and Risks. In: Proceedings of the Natural Legal Language Processing Workshop 2023 (2023). https://doi.org/10.18653/v1/2023.nllp-1.1
4. Salles, A., Evers, K., Farisco, M.: Anthropomorphism in AI. AJOB Neuroscience, 88–95 (2020,4). http://dx.doi.org/10.1080/21507740.2020.1740350
5. Li, M., Suh, A.: Machinelike or humanlike? a literature review of anthropomorphism in AI-enabled technology. In: Proceedings Of The Annual Hawaii International Conference On System Sciences, Proceedings Of The 54th Hawaii International Conference On System Sciences (2021,2). http://dx.doi.org/10.24251/hicss.2021.493
6. Yang, Y., Liu, Y., Lv, X., Ai, J., Li, Y.: Anthropomorphism and customers' willingness to use artificial intelligence service agents. J. Hospitality Market. Manage., 1–23 (2022,1). http://dx.doi.org/10.1080/19368623.2021.1926037
7. Tschopp, M., Gieselmann, M., Sassenberg, K.: Servant by default? How humans perceive their relationship with conversational AI. Cyberpsychol. J. Psychosocial Res. Cyberspace **17**(3) (2023). https://doi.org/10.5817/cp2023-3-9
8. Bower, A.H., Steyvers, M.: Perceptions of AI engaging in human expression. Sci. Rep. **11**(1) (2021). https://doi.org/10.1038/s41598-021-00426-z
9. Zimmerman, A., Janhonen, J., Beer, E.: Human/AI relationships: challenges, downsides, and impacts on human/human relationships. AI and Ethics (2023). https://doi.org/10.1007/s43681-023-00348-8
10. Kim, T., Maimone, F., Pattit, K., Sison, A., Teehankee, B.: Master and slave: the dialectic of human-artificial intelligence engagement. Humanistic Manage. J. **6**(3), 355–371 (2021). https://doi.org/10.1007/s41463-021-00118-w
11. Pataranutaporn, P., Liu, R., Finn, E., Maes, P.: Influencing human-AI interaction by priming beliefs about AI can increase perceived trustworthiness, empathy and effectiveness. Nature Mach. Intell. **5**(10), 1076–1086 (2023). https://doi.org/10.1038/s42256-023-00720-7
12. Rhee, C., Choi, J.: Effects of personalization and social role in voice shopping: an experimental study on product recommendation by a conversational voice agent. Comput. Hum. Behav. **109**, 106359 (2020). https://doi.org/10.1016/j.chb.2020.106359
13. Ahn, J., Kim, J., Sung, Y.: The effect of gender stereotypes on artificial intelligence recommendations. J. Bus. Res. **141**, 50–59 (2022). https://doi.org/10.1016/j.jbusres.2021.12.007
14. Youn, K., Cho, M.: Business types matter: new insights into the effects of anthropomorphic cues in AI chatbots. J. Serv. Market. **37**(8), 1032–1045 (2023). https://doi.org/10.1108/jsm-04-2022-0126

15. Roy, R., Naidoo, V.: Enhancing chatbot effectiveness: the role of anthropomorphic conversational styles and time orientation. J. Bus. Res., 23–34 (2021). https://doi.org/10.1016/j.jbusres.2020.12.051

16. Li, M., Suh, A.: Machinelike or humanlike? a literature review of anthropomorphism in ai-enabled technology. In: Proceedings of the Annual Hawaii International Conference on System Sciences, Proceedings of the 54th Hawaii International Conference on System Sciences. Presented at the Hawaii International Conference on System Sciences (2021). https://doi.org/10.24251/hicss.2021.493

17. Kim, A., Cho, M., Ahn, J., Sung, Y.: Effects of gender and relationship type on the response to artificial intelligence. Cyberpsychol. Behav. Soc. Networking, 249–253 (2019). https://doi.org/10.1089/cyber.2018.0581

18. Niu, D., Terken, J., Eggen, B.: Anthropomorphizing information to enhance trust in autonomous vehicles. Hum. Factors Ergon. Manuf. Serv. Ind., 352–359 (2018). https://doi.org/10.1002/hfm.20745

19. Waytz, A., Heafner, J., Epley, N.: The mind in the machine: anthropomorphism increases trust in an autonomous vehicle. J. Exp. Soc. Psychol., 113–117 (2014). https://doi.org/10.1016/j.jesp.2014.01.005

20. Mori, M., MacDorman, K., Kageki, N.: The Uncanny Valley [From the Field]. IEEE Robot. Autom. Mag., 98–100 (2012). https://doi.org/10.1109/mra.2012.2192811

21. Du, S.: The Impact of Artificial Intelligence on Interaction Design (2021)

22. Wienrich, C., Latoschik, M.: Extended Reality: Prospects for Human-AI Interaction (2021)

23. Wenskovitch, J., North, C.: Interactive artificial intelligence: designing for the "two black boxes" problem. Computer. **53**, 29–39 (2020)

24. Lemon, O.: Multiagent Communication with Natural Language (2022)

25. Jonell, P., Kucherenko, S., Henter, G., Beskow, J.: A Probabilistic Approach to Generating Perceived Facial Gestures in Dialogue Agents for Enhanced Natural Face-to-Face Interaction with AI (2020)

26. Byun, J., Kim, H., Lee, S.: Multimodal Emotion Recognition Using Speech Features and Text Embedding for Intelligent Personal Assistants and Chatbots (2021)

27. Šumak, B., Brdnik, A., Pusnik, M.: Advanced AI Methods and Sensor Technologies in Human-Machine Intelligent Interactions (2021)

28. Ghajargar, E.: Forms as Explanation: A Modality for Explainable AI (2022)

29. Alam, L., Hoque, M.: Designing an Intelligent Agent for Human-Computer Interaction (2015)

30. Angga, A., Fachri, B., Elevanita, A., Suryadi, K., Agushinta, R.: Design of Chatbot with Avatar and Voice Interface for Natural Interaction (2015)

Explainability and Transparency

How to Explain It to System Testers?

A Qualitative User Study About Understandability, Validatability, Predictability, and Trustworthiness

Helmut Degen(✉) and Christof Budnik

Siemens Technology, 755 College Road East, Princeton, NJ 08540, USA
{helmut.degen,christof.budnik}@siemens.com

Abstract. In the realm of explainable AI (XAI), limited research exists on user role-specific explanations. This study aims to determine the explanation needs for the user role "system tester of AI-based systems." It investigates whether established explanation types adequately address the explainability requirements of ML-based application testers. Through a qualitative study (n = 12), we identified the explanation needs for three user tasks: test strategy determination, test case determination, and test result determination. The research yields five findings: F1) proposing a new explanation domain type, "system domain," F2) proposing a new explanation structure, "hierarchical," F3) identifying overlapping explanation content between two user groups, F4) considering identified inputs of a user task as explanation content candidates, and F5) highlighting the risk of combining the evaluation of assumed mental model representations with identifying explanation content in one study.

Keywords: Human-centered AI · explainable AI · explainability · understandability · trustworthiness · predictability · mental model · qualitative user research

1 Introduction

Artificial intelligence (AI) is utilized in various consumer, industrial, and military applications. However, challenges remain in ensuring the ethical, fair, and human-centered nature of AI-based systems (Garibay et al., 2023). One such challenge is the need for explanations to foster trustworthiness.

The need for explainable AI (XAI) and explanations arises from the inherent quality of uncertainty in machine learning (ML)-based systems [39]. When ML-based systems are employed, there is no guarantee of the correctness of predicted outcomes. This poses a significant challenge, particularly for industrial and safety-critical systems [33]. One approach to address these uncertainties is to adopt an explainable AI approach for ML-based systems, allowing them to provide rationales, strengths and weaknesses, and an understanding of their future behavior to human users [21, p. 44]. The purpose of such explanations is to enable users to evaluate whether the predicted outcome, with its associated

H. Degen and S. Ntoa (Eds.): HCII 2024, LNAI 14734, pp. 153–178, 2024.
https://doi.org/10.1007/978-3-031-60606-9_10

uncertainties, is acceptable or not. It is important to note that explanations, which address uncertainty, are additional content provided to users alongside the predicted outcome of an ML-based system.

It is widely acknowledged that discussions on explainability must consider the target stakeholders or users, their goals, intents, and tasks [4,25,27]. However, the specific types of explanations needed for individual user groups are still not sufficiently clear and are the focus of this paper. The paper specifically focuses on the user group of "system testers" and their goals and tasks in planning and executing tests for ML-based systems. This choice is made because system testers likely have the highest demand for explanations among all potential user roles involved in the development, operation, and maintenance of ML-based applications.

To derive the research questions and metrics, the Goal/Metric/Questionnaire (GQM) approach is employed [7]. The research goal is to assess whether the types of explanations addressing uncertainty, as described in the related work section, fulfill the explanation needs of system testers. This goal is relevant for advancing human-centered AI and gaining a comprehensive understanding of the types of explanations required by various user groups. The insights gained will aid in the development of technology capable of automatically generating explanation content and structures that enable different user groups to effectively and efficiently perform their tasks when using ML-based applications, thereby enhancing their trust in such applications.

To achieve the research goal, the following research questions are formulated:

- RQ 1: What explanation content is required by a system tester?
- RQ 2: What explanation content aids the system tester in understanding the determined outcome?
- RQ 3: What explanation content helps the system tester understand the reasons behind the determined outcome?
- RQ 4: What explanation content assists the system tester in evaluating the validity of the determined outcome?
- RQ 5: What explanation content helps the system tester predict the effectiveness of the determined outcome?
- RQ 6: What explanation content helps the system tester develop trust in the determined outcome?
- RQ 7: What is the preferred intent of an explanation?

The metrics for each research question are listed in Sect. 4.

Due to the limited number of participants in this study and the need to gain a better understanding of the explanation needs specific to the target user group of "system testers of ML-based applications," we have opted for a qualitative research approach.

In Sect. 2 of the paper, we discuss the related work. Section 3 introduces the domain of software testing, including the goals and tasks of system testers. This section also presents the assumed mental model representation of explantions, one for each user task. Section 4 describes the design of the qualitative user study, and Sect. 5 presents the study results. Section 6 provides a summary of the discussion, findings, limitations, and outlines future work.

2   Related Work

We includes here related work that includes explainability types, system testers (user group and user tasks), and the use of mental models to identify needed explanations.

2.1   Explainability

The following types of uncertainty addressing explanations have been identified:

- Prediction scope: Global and local [1,6,23]
- Model view: Black box and white box [32]
- Intended use: Justify, control, improve, discover [1, p. 52142–52143]; trustworthiness, causality, transferability, informativeness, confidence, fairness, accessibility, interactivity, privacy awareness [6, p. 8–10]; understandability, predictability [27, p. 8]; actionability [16]
- Explanation structure: Singular, "show me your work" [16]
- Domain types: AI domain, application domain [16]
- Outcome comparison: contrastive and counterfactual explanations [26,35], confidence measures [40,41]

2.2   Explainability in SW Engineering and System Testing

[12] conducted a meta-review on applying explainable AI to the software development process. This involves applying software engineering methods to XAI software, with "software evaluation" as a key aspect. The paper distinguishes between computational evaluations (without human involvement) and human-based evaluations (with human involvement). Human-based evaluations are further categorized into qualities such as "goodness," "user satisfaction," and "mental model."

[37] published a special issue on Explainability for Software Engineering (SE), exploring whether SE stakeholders have different explainability needs and the most understandable forms of explanation tasks for software practitioners. However, the papers in the special issue did not involve users representing a software engineering role or performing software engineering tasks.

[11] examined explainability from a requirements engineering perspective, focusing on its role as a potential new non-functional requirement (NFR). Through an online survey, it was found that explanations can improve understandability, reduce obscurity, and support decision-making. However, the research did not involve participants from the software engineering community or performing software engineering tasks.

[10] distinguished between self-explainable systems and mediator-explained systems. While the paper focused on self-explainable systems, it did not include the target user group of system testers.

[28] introduced a quality assurance framework for testing machine learning products, identifying "Explainability" as a quality under the principle of "Improvability," but without further elaboration.

[36] explored explainability for software developers using generative AI as an assistant for code generation. However, the research did not involve system testers.

[9] also explored explainability for software developers, introducing eleven types of explanations based on [36]. However, the study did not involve system testers.

In conclusion, the involvement of system testers in explainability research is a recent development.

2.3   Derivation of Mental Model of Explanations

A mental model aids understanding, reasoning, and prediction in a given domain or situation [18]. In the context of explainability, it should encapsulate the necessary explanation content tailored to a specific user role, task, and goal [24, P. 9]. This research employs a mental model of explanations, which, unlike Hoffman's definition, doesn't solely center on the AI system but also encompasses its outcomes. The required explanation content may or may not involve details about the AI system itself.

[12] conducted a meta-review on applying explainable AI to the software development process. This involves applying software engineering methods to XAI software, with "software evaluation" as a key aspect. The paper distinguishes between computational evaluations (without human involvement) and human-based evaluations (with human involvement). Human-based evaluations are further categorized into qualities such as "goodness," "user satisfaction," and "mental model."

[37] published a special issue on Explainability for Software Engineering (SE), exploring whether SE stakeholders have different explainability needs and the most understandable forms of explanation tasks for software practitioners. However, the papers in the special issue did not involve users representing a software engineering role or performing software engineering tasks.

[11] examined explainability from a requirements engineering perspective, focusing on its role as a potential new non-functional requirement (NFR). Through an online survey, it was found that explanations can improve understandability, reduce obscurity, and support decision-making. However, the research did not involve participants from the software engineering community or performing software engineering tasks.

[10] distinguished between self-explainable systems and mediator-explained systems. While the paper focused on self-explainable systems, it did not include the target user group of system testers.

[28] introduced a quality assurance framework for testing machine learning products, identifying "Explainability" as a quality under the principle of "Improvability," but without further elaboration.

[36] explored explainability for software developers using generative AI as an assistant for code generation. However, the research did not involve system testers.

[9] also explored explainability for software developers, introducing eleven types of explanations based on [36]. However, the study did not involve system testers.

In conclusion, the involvement of system testers in explainability research is a recent development.

3   System Domain: Software Testing

The content of this section was part of the study's preparation phase and was elicited with a subject matter expert in system testing of ML-based systems.

3.1   User Role: System Tester of ML-Based Systems

A system tester of ML-based systems is responsible for ensuring the quality of the larger software system, including one or more machine learning components. The main tasks of a system tester of an AI-based system include developing a comprehensive test strategy that outlines the scope of testing, test methodologies, test environments, and a test plan for execution.

The testing scope is described by the application domain and the system under test. While the application domain defines the environments for which the system is developed, the system architecture and design define how the system is developed. The application domain considers the conditions of the environment, the infrastructure it has to work on, its users, and their application cases. Understanding the system architecture and design involves both non-AI modules and AI modules of the system. Due to the data-driven nature of the ML model, it is necessary to understand not only the training data and their metadata but also the model architecture and performance metrics. While the non-AI modules follow traditional software engineering development, including architecture and design, their test-related components of interest are hazard and risk analysis and their derived system requirements to mitigate identified risks. The system tester needs to understand the system requirements as well as the expectations related to its comprising AI components. The system requirements specify the functionality, performance, and integration aspects of the ML modules.

Following the developed test strategy, the system tester is responsible for defining the corresponding test cases. Test cases are created according to the selected test methods. Test cases need to be specifically tailored for AI components, covering, for instance, various scenarios and edge cases. The test environment is the platform to run the test cases. It needs to adhere to the test requirements which define the foundation for implementation of the test environment. The test environment ensures that the execution of the test cases can be controlled, and their results can be observed. The input for the test cases is defined by the system under test. Deriving appropriate test input data which is of high quality for testing the AI models is also a responsibility of the system tester.

The last key responsibility of the system tester is to analyze the test results from test execution. Test results are determined by the system under test, which is controlled by the implemented test environment. The system tester is conducting testing to verify that the AI models perform as expected and meet the specified requirements. He further validates that the AI algorithms produce accurate and reliable results under various conditions. Failing test results can have multiple causes. It could be a defect in the test case itself, the environment the test case is executed, or, in fact, a defect of the system under test. Defects are reported and need to be fixed before the next execution cycle.

The assumed mental model was derived from a task analysis for a system tester. Together with an individual familiar with the role of a system tester, the following user goals and user tasks have been identified:

- UG 1: Minimize the number of reported field issues (quality) (rank 1).
- UG 2: Minimize verification effort (time, cost) (rank 2).

To achieve these goals, the system tester for ML-based systems performs the following user tasks:

- UT 1: Determine the test strategy (in research scope).
- UT 2: Determine the test cases (in research scope).
- UT 3: Determine the test results (in research scope).
- UT 4: Determine the model monitoring strategy (not in research scope).
- UT 5: Determine the model monitoring cases (not in research scope).
- UT 6: Determine the model monitoring results (not in research scope).

The user tasks include the determination of the test strategy, test cases, and test results, as well as the determination of the model monitoring strategy, model monitoring cases, and results. The first three user tasks are within the scope of this research.

The inclusion of model monitoring aspects in the task list is necessary due to a unique phenomenon of ML models. It is common for field data or environmental conditions to evolve over time, deviating from the data initially used for training and testing these ML models. This evolving data landscape can introduce a phenomenon known as "data drift," which can significantly impact the predictive accuracy of these ML models [8, 30]. This gradual decline in model performance over time is often referred to as "model degradation."

The implications of model degradation can vary widely depending on the specific application domain and the associated risks for users, beneficiaries, organizations, and society at large. In certain instances, it may lead to adverse and

potentially costly outcomes, emphasizing the importance of addressing and mitigating this challenge. To detect model degradation, a model monitoring capability is needed. Model monitoring can be considered as continuous testing during
the operational phase [34, p. 106].

3.2 Intelligent System Testing Application for ML-Based Systems

In our research, we assume the existence of a (hypothetical) application called
the "Intelligent System Testing Application for ML-based Systems." This application is capable of semi-automatically planning and executing system tests for
ML-based systems. The application itself can utilize ML-based technology.

The components of the application, along with their key inputs and outcomes,
are depicted in Fig. 1.

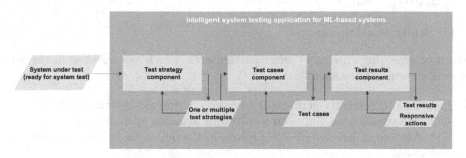

Fig. 1. The Intelligent System Test Application for ML-based Systems consists of various components, each with its own key inputs and outputs. The system tester plays a
crucial role in reviewing the outcomes of these components.

These components represent the three phases involved in planning and performing a system test. The system tester reviews the predicted outcomes of each
component and has the ability to revise them through one or multiple iterations
until he/she is satisfied.

The "test strategy" component determines one or multiple test strategies.
The "test case" component determines test cases based on the test strategy, and
the "test results" component determines the test results and responsive actions
for failed test cases. Responsive actions are actions that modify the system under
test, the test environment, or test cases, in order to eventually make the failed
test cases pass.

The question that this research aims to address is: What explanations does
a system tester need to accept the determined outcomes.

3.3 Derived Mental Model of Explanations

In [16], a method for identifying a mental model of representations was introduced to determine explanation needs. We applied the same method in this

research, identifying task questions [15, p. 393f] for each user task. Additionally, we introduced a new step where we identified necessary inputs and outputs per user task, which assisted in identifying user task specific explanation needs. The results of these needs are detailed in Appendix 8.1.

The mental model representation of explanations was derived from these needs, establishing causal relationships between explanation content items [2]. An initial version of the mental model representation was created, then reviewed by a second domain expert in system testing of ML-based systems, who provided feedback. Based on this feedback, the initial representation was revised, resulting in the "assumed mental model representation of explanations," marking the completion of the study preparation phase. This assumed mental model representation of explanations is illustrated in Fig. 2.

4   Study Design

4.1   Study Participants

We used screening criteria to select participants, which are reflected in the following screening questions:

- C 1: Do you currently perform or have you performed system tests?
- C 2: Are you or have you been involved in planning system tests?
- C 3: Are you or have you been involved in the design and implementation of test cases?
- C 4: Are you or have you been involved in evaluating test results?
- C 5: Do you or have you been involved in testing ML-based systems?

To qualify as a research participant, a candidate had to answer at least three questions with "yes."

To achieve saturation with a homogeneous study sample, the target sample size is set at twelve participants [22, p. 7] [20, p. 74].

4.2   Study Approach

In a recent study [16], we identified an assumed mental model representation of explanations and created a user interface mockup based on it. Using a user interface mockup offers the advantage of providing participants with a close-to-real-life experience of the explanation content. However, this approach also comes with the disadvantage of requiring significant effort to develop the user interface mockup.

To streamline the preparation process for this study, we opted to solely rely on the assumed mental model of representations. Any user interface mockup can be developed based on the findings of the study.

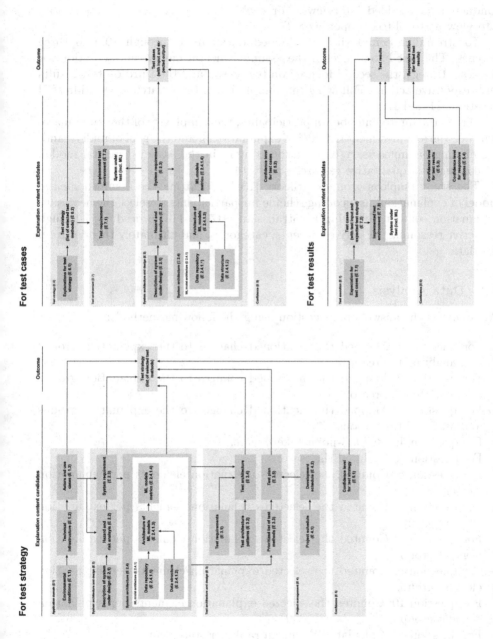

Fig. 2. Assumed mental model representation of explanations for user tasks UT 1, UT 2, and UT 3

4.3   Data Collection

To understand the reasons behind certain answers and explore new ideas, we conducted semi-guided interviews. For each interview session, we utilized an interview protocol (see Appendix 8.2).

To streamline complexity, we divided questions 1 through 10 into three batches. The first batch covered the assumed mental model representation for the test strategy, the second focused on test cases, and the third on test results and responsive actions. Following the completion of these batches, we addressed questions 11 and 12.

Due to the limited number of participants, the complexity of the study material (i.e., the assumed mental model of explanations), and the goal of understanding missing or unnecessary explanation content in the assumed mental model, we conducted a qualitative research study [14].

The study employs grounded theory [13,19], utilizing the assumed mental model of explanations as a coding scheme for participants to select the necessary explanation content, following a "Straussian" [17, p. 114] procedure. Through inductive reasoning, we derive concepts, categories, and ultimately theories from the data.

4.4   Data Analysis

We analyzed the answers per question using the following methods:

- For question 1: Mapped the mentioned changes to the explanation groups and analyzed the reasons.
- For question 2: Mapped the mentioned changes to the explanation groups and analyzed the reasons.
- For question 3: Mapped the mentioned changes to the explanation groups and analyzed the reasons.
- For question 4: Used a 5-point Likert scale.
- For question 5: Analyzed the reasons.
- For question 6: Counted the selected explanation elements per explanation element group.
- For question 7: Counted the selected explanation elements per explanation element group.
- For question 8: Counted the selected explanation elements per explanation element group.
- For question 9: Counted the selected explanation elements per explanation element group.
- For question 10: Counted the selected explanation elements per explanation element group.
- For question 11: Calculated the mean rank per statement.
- For question 12: Analyzed the reasons.

5   Study Results

5.1   Participants

In total, we recruited thirteen participants. All but one participant answered the screener questions with at least three "yes" responses. We excluded one participant from the data analysis.

All participants are Siemens employees and did not receive a monetary incentive for participating in the interviews. Each participant explicitly consented to participate in the study and for the use of their anonymized data for research and publication. We conducted the interviews remotely using Microsoft Teams[1]. All interviews were recorded and lasted between 60 and 90 min.

Nine participants are based in Germany, and three are in India. All twelve participants are male. Nine interviews were conducted in German, and three were in English.

The participants have industrial work experience in testing non-ML systems ranging from one to 25 years. Their experience in testing ML-based systems ranges from five months to seven years. Eleven participants have conducted system tests of ML-based systems for prototypes, while five have done so for products.

The application domains for the prototypes and products include the food and beverage industry, warehouses, rail industry, steel industry, manufacturing, and software development and testing.

5.2   Results

RQ 1: What Explanation Content Is Required by a System Tester?
After introducing the assumed mental model of explanations for each component, we asked the participants three questions: Is any explanation content missing? Are there any unnecessary explanation content candidates? Can the explanation content or the causal relationships between them be modified?

Missing Explanation Content. For the test strategy, participants noted several areas of improvement. P3, P10, and P12 highlighted the absence of "test goals." Additionally, participant P9 suggested incorporating coverage goals into the test goals. P5 emphasized the need to identify the interface between AI and non-AI components within the system architecture and design (E 2.4). Participant P8 suggested extending the Meta-Data (E 2.4.1.2) to include information about the origin and generation of data in the repository. P7 proposed assigning individual confidence levels to each explanation content element group (E 1, E 2, etc.), with an aggregated confidence level (E 5.2) calculated from these. P4 stressed the importance of transparency regarding the influence of each element on the outcome, including cases where an element has no effect. Participant P9 highlighted the absence of model monitoring as explanation content.

---

[1] Microsoft and Microsoft Teams are trademarks of the Microsoft group of companies.

Regarding test cases, participants P7 and P12 pointed out the absence of test data and proposed allocating a distinct box for them. Participant P8 suggested establishing a traceability from confidence levels to individual contributing sources and including test goals and scope.

For test results, participant P5 suggested adding logs for executed test cases and implementing error management, including identifying root causes and determining actions, such as "suggested actions." Participant P7 noted the absence of a loop connecting responsive actions to the areas they affect. Participant P8 proposed assigning individual confidence levels to each element, aggregating them into an overall confidence level.

Unnecessary Explanation Content. Participant P2 noted that while the ML architecture (E 2.4.1) is pertinent for AI experts, it may not be as relevant for system testers, given the assumed absence of AI knowledge.

Rearranged Explanation Content. For the test strategy, participant P3 highlighted the absence of a connection between the system architecture and design (E 2.4) and the test requirements (E 3.1). Participant P10 noted a missing link between the test requirements (E 3.1) and the test strategy. Additionally, participant P12 pointed out the lack of connections between the environmental conditions (E 1.1) and the test strategy, as well as between the technical infrastructure (E 1.2) and the test strategy.

Regarding the test cases, two participants (P7, P9) suggested linking the confidence level to each explanation element to express the confidence level per element. They proposed calculating an aggregated confidence based on each element-specific confidence level.

In terms of the test results and suggested actions, participants P3 and P12 remarked on the absence of a loop from the suggested actions to the areas they are intended to influence. Participant P9 suggested aggregating the individual confidence levels for the test results and the suggested actions into a single confidence level.

Rate Statements About the Assumed Mental Models of Explanations. After gathering feedback on how participants would like to modify the assumed mental models of explanations, we asked them to rate the following statement for each component: "The explanation content candidates help the system tester to understand why the <outcome> was determined." In each case, the term "outcome" was replaced by either "test strategy," "test cases," or "test results." Participants assigned a value from a 5-point Likert scale to indicate their response. The rating results are presented in Table 1.

The reasons why participants selected "neutral" were twofold: one type of reason is the identified missing explanation elements. Another type of reason is a perceived uncertainty about whether the explanation content is sufficient.

Since 29 out of 36 participants (more than 80%) selected "Agree" and "Strongly agree," we consider the assumed mental model representation of expla-

Table 1. Representation of the assumed mental models (n = 12)

Rated statements	1 Strongly dis-agree	2 Dis-agree	3 Neutral	4 Agree	5 Strongly agree
"The explanation content candidates help the system tester to understand why the test strategy was determined."	0	0	0	11	1
"The explanation content candidates help the system tester to understand why the test cases were determined."	0	0	3	6	3
"The explanation content candidates help the system tester to understand why the test results were determined."	0	0	4	3	5
Total	0	0	7	20	9

nations as a sufficient representation of needed explanation content for system testers of ML-based applications.

RQ 2: What Explanation Content Aids the System Tester in Understanding the Determined Outcome? Table 2 displays the number of selected explanation elements per explanation group that aid the system tester in understanding the determined outcome.

Table 2. For understanding the determined outcome: Number of selected explanation elements per group (n – 12); the explanation element group with the highest percentage of selection for each determined outcome is emphasized.

Determined outcome	E 1 Application domain	E 2 System architecture and design	E 3 Test architecture and design	E 4 Project management	E 5 Confidence	E 6 Test Strategy	E 7 Test environment
Test strategy	23 (out of 36)	72 (108)	32 (60)	3 (24)	3 (12)	-	-
Test cases	-	28 (108)	-	-	1 (12)	11 (24)	8 (24)
Test results	-	-	-	-	2 (24)	-	20 (36)

Reading example: For understanding the determined test strategy, all participants selected 23 explanation elements from the group E 1 Application domain. The maximum number of possible selections is 36.

The explanation element group with the highest percentage of selected elements for the determined test strategy is element group E2 System Architecture and Design. For the determined test cases, the explanation content with the highest percentage is E6 Test Strategy. Lastly, the element group E7 Test Environment has the highest percentage of selected explanation content for the determined test results and responsive actions.

RQ 3: What Explanation Content Helps the System Tester Understand the Reasons Behind the Determined Outcome? Table 3 displays the number of selected explanation elements per explanation group that aid the system tester in understanding why the outcome was determined.

Table 3. For understanding why the outcome was determined: Number of selected explanation elements per group (n = 12); the explanation element group with the highest percentage of selection for each determined outcome is emphasized.

Determined outcome	E 1 Application domain	E 2 System architecture and design	E 3 Test architecture and design	E 4 Project management	E 5 Confidence	E 6 Test Strategy	E 7 Test environment
Test strategy	12 (out of 36)	38 (108)	26 (60)	4 (24)	4 (12)	-	-
Test cases	-	32 (108)	-	-	3 (12)	10 (24)	7 (24)
Test results	-	-	-	-	2 (24)	-	18 (36)

Reading example: For understanding why the test strategy was determined, all participants selected 12 explanation elements from the group E 1 Application domain. The maximum number of possible selections is 36.

The explanation element group with the highest percentage of selected explanation elements per group for the determined test strategy is the confidence level (E 5). The test architecture and design (E3) was most frequently selected for understanding the test strategy. Similarly, the test cases (E6) were the most commonly chosen factor for understanding the test strategy, while the test environment (E7) was selected most often for understanding the test results (all percentage-wise).

RQ 4: What Explanation Content Assists the System Tester in Evaluating the Validity of the Determined Outcome? Table 4 displays the number of selected explanation elements per explanation group that aid the system tester in assessing the validity of the determined outcome.

The explanation element group with the highest percentage of selected explanation elements per group for the determined test strategy is the confidence level (E 5). In assessing the validity of the test cases, the explanation element group E 2 System architecture and design was selected most frequently, while for evaluating the validity of the test results, the element group E 7 Test environment was chosen most often.

Table 4. For evaluating the validity of the determined outcome: Number of selected explanation elements per group (n = 12); the explanation element group with the highest percentage of selection for each determined outcome is emphasized.

Determined outcome	E 1 Application domain	E 2 System architecture and design	E 3 Test architecture and design	E 4 Project management	E 5 Confidence	E 6 Test Strategy	E 7 Test environment
Test strategy	13 (out of 36)	42 (108)	25 (60)	1 (24)	4 (12)	-	-
Test cases	-	36 (108)	-	-	2 (12)	7 (24)	4 (24)
Test results	-	-	-	-	7 (24)	-	16 (36)

Reading example: For evaluating the validity of the determined test strategy, all participants selected 13 explanation elements from the group E 1 Application domain. The maximum number of possible selections is 36.

RQ 5: What Explanation Content Helps the System Tester Predict the Effectiveness of the Determined Outcome? Table 5 displays the number of selected explanation elements per explanation group aiding the system tester in predicting the effectiveness of the determined outcome.

Table 5. For predicting how effective the determined outcome will be: Number of selected explanation elements per group (n = 12); the explanation element group with the highest percentage of selection for each determined outcome is emphasized.

Determined outcome	E 1 Application domain	E 2 System architecture and design	E 3 Test architecture and design	E 4 Project management	E 5 Confidence	E 6 Test Strategy	E 7 Test environment
Test strategy	3 (out of 36)	29 (108)	21 (60)	2 (24)	1 (12)	-	-
Test cases	-	20 (108)	-	-	4 (12)	2 (24)	6 (24)
Test results	-	-	-	-	8 (24)	-	6 (36)

Reading example: For predicting how effective the determined test strategy will be, all participants selected 3 explanation elements from the group E 1 Application domain. The maximum number of possible selections is 36.

For predicting the effectiveness of the test strategy, the test architecture and design were selected most often. Regarding the prediction of test cases and test results, the confidence level (E5) was the most frequently selected factor (all percentage-wise).

RQ 6: What Explanation Content Helps the System Tester Develop Trust in the Determined Outcome? Table 6 displays the number of selected explanation elements per explanation group that assist the system tester in trusting the determined outcome.

Table 6. For trusting the determined outcome: Number of selected explanation elements per group (n = 12); the explanation element group with the highest percentage of selection for each determined outcome is emphasized.

Determined outcome	E 1 Application domain	E 2 System architecture and design	E 3 Test architecture and design	E 4 Project management	E 5 Confidence	E 6 Test Strategy	E 7 Test environment
Test strategy	6 (out of 36)	40 (117)	17 (60)	0 (24)	3 (12)	-	-
Test cases	-	29 (108)	-	-	6 (12)	7 (24)	5 (24)
Test results	-	-	-	-	11 (24)	-	17 (36)

Reading example: For trusting the determined test strategy will be, all participants selected 6 explanation elements from the group E 1 Application domain. The maximum number of possible selections is 36.

Table 7. Rank the following statements; "1" means most important and "5" means least important (n = 12)

Statements expressing an explanation intent	Rank 1	Rank 2	Rank 3	Rank 4	Rank 5	Mean Rank
S 1 The explanation content should help the system tester to <u>understand</u> the determined outcome. ("What" intent)	4	3	0	3	2	2.7
S 2 The explanation content should help the system tester to <u>understand why</u> the outcome was determined. ("Why" intent)	3	4	1	1	3	2.8
S 3 The explanation content should help the system tester to <u>evaluate the validity</u> of the determined outcome. ("Validity" intent)	1	3	5	0	3	3.1
S 4 The explanation content should help the system tester to <u>predict the effectiveness</u> of the determined outcome in the future. ("Predictability" intent)	1	1	2	4	4	3.8
S 5 The explanation content should help the system tester to <u>trust</u> the determined outcome.("Trust" intent)	3	2	3	4	0	2.7

Reading example: The participants selected statement S 1 four times for rank 1, three times for rank 2, none for rank 3, three times for rank 4, and twice for rank 5. The mean rank is 2.7.

For trusting the test strategy, the system architecture and design (E2) was selected most often; for trusting test cases, the confidence level (E5) was selected most often. For trusting the test results, the test environment (E7) was selected most often (all percentage-wise).

RQ 7: What Is the Preferred Intent of an Explanation? Table 7 shows the result of the ranking. The middle rank is calculated as $\frac{1+n}{2} = \frac{1+5}{2} = 3$. The mean rank is calculated using the formula: $\frac{\sum_{i=1}^{5} Number_i \cdot i}{Participants}$, where $Number_i$ represents the number of selections of a statement for a rank i, and $Participants$ denotes the number of participants who ranked the statements. As an example, the calculation for statement S 1 is: $\frac{4 \cdot 1 + 3 \cdot 2 + 0 \cdot 3 + 3 \cdot 4 + 2 \cdot 5}{12} = \frac{32}{12} = 2.7$.

S 1 ("What" intent) has the lowest mean rank, indicating it is the explanation type that the participants consider most important, together with S 5 ("Trust" intent). Statement S 2 ("Why" intent) is rank third. Statements S 3 ("Validity" intent) and S 4 ("Predictability" intent) rank the lowest.

6 Discussion, Limitations, and Future Work

6.1 Discussions

The research aimed to identify the explainability content necessary for a system tester of ML-based systems to effectively and efficiently use a hypothetical "Intelligent System Testing Application for ML-Based Systems." The system tester is involved in reviewing the outcomes of three components: the test strategy component, test case component, and test result component.

Due to the limited number of participants, the complexity of the study material (i.e., the assumed mental model of explanation), and the aim to uncover missing or unnecessary explanation content in the assumed mental model of explanations, we conducted a qualitative research study [14].

The experience profile of the twelve participants meets the qualification criteria, fulfilling the requirement for a sample size of twelve participants needed to achieve saturation in a homogeneous study sample [22, p. 7] [20, p. 74].

We conducted semi-structured interview sessions with all participants being Siemens employees. Each interview lasted from 60 to 90 min and was conducted remotely using Microsoft Teams[2]. All interview sessions have been recorded.

Applying grounded theory, we derive concepts and categories from the data. The following findings have been derived:

Finding 1: Proposing a New Explanation Domain Type "system Domain". The selected explanation content for questions 6 through 10 comes from three areas: the application domain (E 1 Application domain), the AI domain (E 2.4.1 ML model architecture, E 5 Confidence), and the system domain (remaining explanation elements). The explanation elements from the system

---

[2] Microsoft and Microsoft Teams are trademarks of the Microsoft group of companies.

domain are dominant for understanding the predicted test strategy (E 2 System architecture and design), for understanding the test cases (E 6 Test strategy), and for understanding the test results (E 7 Test environment). Explanations from the system domain are also dominant for explaining why the test strategy (E 3 Test architecture and design), the test cases (E 6 Test Strategy), and test results (E 7 Test environment) were determined.

Explanation content from the system domain were dominant for explaining the evaluation of the validity of the test strategy (E 3 Test architecture and design), the test cases (E 2 System architecture and design), and the test results (E 7 Test environment). Explanations from the system domain were also dominant for predicting the effectiveness of the test strategy (E 3 Test architecture and design) and for trusting the test strategy (E 2 System architecture and design) and the test results (E 7 Test environment). It should be mentioned that explanations from the system domain were selected for each explanation intent.

Explanations from the system domain are not listed in the identified explanation types (see Subsect. 2). We propose to add "system domain" as a new explanation domain type.

Finding 2: Proposing a New Explanation Structure "hierarchical". The presented assumed mental model representations of explanation are quite complex. The structure of the explanation elements is partially hierarchical, and the element groups are connected with causal relationships. The authors used the hierarchical structure to organize the explanation content, aiming to avoid overwhelming the study participants.

The hierarchical structure of explanations is proposed as a new explanation structure type. It extends the "show your work" explanation scope [16], which emphasizes a "causal" relationship between explanations. Hierarchical explanations help to make complex explanations human comprehensible. We can combine hierarchical and "causal" organization of explanations as needed. This approach to structuring explanation content seems to be similar to the modular organization of source code [5, 29].

Finding 3: Identifying Overlapping Explanation Content Between Two User Groups. When comparing the explanation needs of a model monitor [16] with those of a system tester, we can identify explanation content that both user groups require: application domain content and AI domain content. The model monitor needs explanation content from the application domain to achieve situational awareness and understand the root cause of a reported anomaly. Similarly, the system tester needs application domain content because it influences the test strategy. The model manager needs AI domain content (model metrics) to identify anomalies, while the system tester requires AI domain content (model metrics, model architecture, data repository) because they influence the test strategy and the test cases.

This suggests that there is common explanation content between these two target user groups. Such common explanation content indicates the existence of a shared mental model between different target user groups, facilitating communication regarding the system under test/monitoring.

Finding 4: Considering Identified Inputs of a User Task as Explanation Content Candidates. Since the tasks of identifying the test strategy, test cases, and test results were delegated to our hypothetical application, it was natural to identify the inputs and outputs for each component. It turned out that the identified inputs are explanation content candidates. We created the explanation element groups and causal relationships based on the logical relationship between the identified inputs and outputs. This seemingly random outcome can be developed into a methodology.

Whether a task is performed by a system or a user, we can use the relationship between inputs and outputs as a starting point for creating an initial mental model of explanation. The structure can be hierarchical, causal, or both (see Finding 2).

Finding 5: Highlighting the Risk of Combining the Evaluation of Assumed Mental Model Representations with Identifying Explanation Content in One Study, Research questions RQ 2 through RQ 6 require that the used mental model representation sufficiently reflects the actual mental model of the participants. We included the evaluation of the mental model (RQ 1) and questions about which elements support different explanation intents (RQ 2 - RQ 6) in one study. The assumed mental model representation received sufficient support (more than 80% of participants selected "Agree" or "Strongly agree"). However, the evaluation result could have been different, meaning worse. Combining the evaluation of the assumed mental model with the identification of explanation content in one study bears the risk that the assumed mental model representation turns out to be insufficient. Hence, the follow-up questions about which explanation content elements support the different explanation intents would become invalid.

A different, risk-averse research approach is to split the study into two phases. In the first phase, the assumed mental model representation of explanations is evaluated by a group of at least twelve participants and then modified based on the participants' feedback (focus on RQ 1). The result of this phase is a refined mental model representation of explanations. In a second phase, the refined mental model representation is used to identify which explanation elements support the different explanation intents. The research effort is higher; however, the risk of using an insufficient mental model representation is reduced.

6.2   Limitations and Future Work

A limitation is the evaluation of the assumed mental model solely based on an abstract mental model representation. In this study, we used a mental model representation of explanations only, and no user interface mockup that is designed based on the assumed mental model representation (the latter approach was used in [16]). The reason for using a mental model representation without a user interface mockup was motivated by research economics. During the study, facilitators observed that the participants had many questions about the abstract content compared to the mentioned previous study. We want to emphasize that we did not capture the questions in the previous study and in this study. Hence, we cannot make a definitive statement about the number of questions per study design. However, facilitators' ad-hoc explanations can influence the study outcome. Furthermore, the participants can interpret the abstract mental model representation in an unintended way. Therefore, the sole use of an abstract presentation to identify required explanation content elements is considered a limitation.

In a future study, a user interface mockup can be used to identify the required explanation content of a system tester of ML-based systems. The results of such a study will allow a comparison of identified explanation needs between two approaches: one using an abstract mental model representation only and one using a user interface mockup.

The assumed mental model of explanation is the mental model of one target user group, the system tester. We already performed similar research with a model manager [16]. In both studies, application domain content and AI domain content were identified as common explanation content. It is worthwhile to perform similar research with another target user role (e.g., a data scientist) and compare the identified explanation needs of data scientists with the explanation needs of model monitors and system testers. The comparison will help to identify common explanations and user role-specific explanations. Such common parts are also known as a "shared mental model" [3]. Shared mental models build a communication bridge and assist different target user groups to communicate with each other effectively.

Another future research topic is whether a distinction between backward-looking and forward-looking explanations makes sense. Some participants highlighted that they would like to see which areas the suggested actions influence (see paragraph "Rearranged explanation content" in research question 1). This can be interpreted as "forward-looking" explanations. Since the predicted outcome "test strategy" and "test cases" are used in a subsequent step, the theme of "forward-looking" is present in the domain of the system tester.

When performing explanation research today, most research focuses on why an outcome was determined (backward-looking explanations), and not so much on the effectiveness or success of the (future) use of that determined outcome (forward-looking). As our research shows, a minority of participants saw value in predicting how effective the determined outcome will be in future use, as shown in the answer to question 11. A valid research question is whether forward-looking explanations can exist since all explanations rely somehow on past experiences. This is also true even if a forward-looking approach like a simulation was applied to determine how effective an outcome will be (from the perspective of the outcome, the explanation would refer to the simulation as a past event). Some scholars [31, 38] looked into forward and backward-looking considerations.

It requires more work to understand the theoretical foundation of "backward-looking" and "forward-looking" before we can decide whether explanations can be distinguished into "backward-looking" and "forward-looking" explanations.

Acknowledgment. The authors thank Parinitha Nagaraja for evaluating the initial mental model of explanations, and all study participants for their time and shared insights.

8 Appendix

8.1 User task specific explanation needs

Inputs, outputs, and needed explanations for user task UT 1:

- Inputs
  - Application domain
  - Description of the system under test and system requirements
  - Architecture of ML models, data structure, and repository with metrics (e.g., quantity and types of available data)
  - Test constraints (e.g., cost, resources, quality, available hardware, available software, etc.)
  - Identified risks and their mitigations (if available)
- Outputs
  - Suggested test strategies
  - For each test strategy: Prioritized list of test methods, test architecture (including design of the test environment), test plan, confidence level
- Needed explanations
  - Why was the test strategy predicted? Identify the main drivers, such as the application domain, description of the system under test, system requirements, architecture of ML models, data structure, and repository.
  - Why was the prioritization of test methods predicted? Identify the main drivers, such as risks, driving requirements (non-functional requirements), ML model architecture, data structure, and repository.
  - Why was the test architecture predicted? Identify the main drivers, such as available and unavailable hardware, available and unavailable software, ML model architecture, data structure, and repository.
  - Why was the test plan predicted? Identify the main drivers, such as compliance with test constraints.

Inputs, outputs, and needed explanations for user task UT 2:

- Inputs
  - Description of system under test, system requirements, system architecture, and design
  - ML-model architecture, data structure, and repository with metrics
  - Selected test strategy, including methods, architecture, design of test environment, and test plan

- Outputs
  - Generated test cases
  - For each test case: selected input data, test metrics with actual measurements, confidence level
  - Implemented test environment
- Needed explanations
  - Why were the test cases generated as predicted? Identify main drivers: system architecture, design, ML-model architecture, data structure, and repository.
  - Why are the generated test cases appropriate? Identify test coverage based on system requirements and architecture. Show value, e.g., error detection contributions, and ensure non-overlapping.
  - How long does it take to configure and execute each test case? Time for configuration and execution, considering system and test architecture.
  - What is the cost/benefit ratio per test case? Identify value vs. testing time, including configuration and execution.
  - Why was the test environment implemented this way? Identify connection between test architecture and implemented environment, and mapping of design patterns.

Inputs, outputs, and needed explanations for user task UT 3:

- Inputs
  - Description of system under test
  - Generated test cases
  - For each test case: selected input data, test metrics with actual measurements
  - Implemented test environment
- Outputs
  - Configured test environment
  - Determined test results, trace(s) to system requirement(s), confidence level
  - Bug report (for detected bugs)
  - Test report with test KPIs
  - Responsive actions for failed test results
- Needed explanations
  - Why was the test environment configured as it was? Identify the connection between configuration parameters and test environment design. Show how parameters were derived from generated test cases.
  - How were the test results predicted? Demonstrate the link between test inputs and results. Identify the correlation between test results and model monitoring outcomes.
  - How were the test KPIs forecasted? Identify the relationship between individual KPIs and test results.

8.2   Interview protocol

- Step 1: Research introduction
- Step 2: Job experience
- Step 3: Introduction into the hypothetical application "Intelligent system testing application for ML-based applications", that is capable of planning and executing an ML-based system test, including core input and outputs (see Fig. 1)
- Evaluating the assumed mental model representation for each component separately:
  - Question 1: Which explanation content is missing and why? (addressing research question 1, RQ 1)
  - Question 2: Which proposed explanation content is not necessary and why? (RQ 1)
  - Question 3: How should the explanation content be rearranged and why? (RQ 1)
  - Question 4: Please rate the following statement: "The explanation content help the system tester to understand why the test strategy / test cases / test results was determined." (5-point Likert scale) (RQ 1)
  - Question 5: Why did you select the rating? (RQ 1)
  - Question 6: Which explanation content helps the system tester to understand the determined test strategy / test cases / test report? (RQ 2)
  - Question 7: Which explanation content helps the system tester to understand why the test strategy / test cases / test results was determined? (RQ 3)
  - Question 8: Which explanation content helps the system tester to evaluate the validity of the determined test strategy / test cases / test results? (RQ 4)
  - Question 9: Which explanation content helps the system tester to predict how effective the selected test strategy / test cases / responsive actions will be? (RQ 5)
  - Question 10: Which explanation content helps the system tester to trust the determined test strategy / test cases / test results? (RQ 6)
- Question 11: For understanding the preferred intent of an explanation. Rank the following statements about the intent of explanations (#1 means most important and #5 means least important). (RQ 7)
  - S1: The explanation content should help the system tester to understand the determined outcome.
  - S2: The explanation content should help the system tester to understand why the outcome was determined.
  - S3: The explanation content should help the system tester to evaluate the validity of the determined outcome.
  - S4: The explanation content should help the system tester to predict the effectiveness of the determined outcome.
  - S5: The explanation content should help the system tester to trust the determined outcome.

– Question 12: Why did you select the top ranked statement. (RQ 7)

To answer questions 6 through 10, the participants were instructed that they could select none of the explanation content candidates, one, or multiple, including one or multiple groups of explanation content candidates.

References

1. Adadi, A., Berrada, M.: Peeking inside the black-box: a survey on explainable artificial intelligence (XAI). IEEE Access **6**, 52138–52160 (2018). https://doi.org/10.1109/ACCESS.2018.2870052
2. Andersen, B.S., Fagerhaug, T.: Root Cause Analysis: Simplified Tools and Techniques, 2 edn. ASQ Quality Press (2006). https://asq.org/quality-press/display-item?item=H1287
3. Andrews, R.W., Lilly, J.M., Divya, S., Feigh, K.M.: The role of shared mental models in human-AI teams: a theoretical review. Theor. Issues Ergon. Sci. **24**(2), 129–175 (2023). https://doi.org/10.1080/1463922X.2022.2061080
4. Arya, V., et al.: One explanation does not fit all: a toolkit and taxonomy of AI explainability techniques (2019). https://doi.org/10.48550/arXiv.1909.03012
5. Barnett, T.O., Constantine, L.L.: Modular Programming: Proceedings of a National Symposium. Information & systems Institute (1968)
6. Barredo Arrieta, A., et al.: Explainable artificial intelligence (XAI): concepts, taxonomies, opportunities and challenges toward responsible AI. Inform. Fusion **58**, 82–115 (2020). https://doi.org/10.1016/j.inffus.2019.12.012
7. Basili, V.R.: Software Modeling and Measurement: The Goal/Question/Metric Paradigm (CS-TR-2956, UMIACS-TR-92-96). Technical report, University of Maryland, Institute for Advanced Computer Studies (1992). https://www.cs.umd.edu/~basili/publications/technical/T78.pdf. Accessed 26 Dec. 2023
8. Bayram, F., Ahmed, B.S., Kassler, A.: From concept drift to model degradation: an overview on performance-aware drift detectors. Knowl.-Based Syst. **245**, 108632 (2022). https://doi.org/10.1016/j.knosys.2022.108632, https://www.sciencedirect.com/science/article/pii/S0950705122002854
9. Borg, M., Aasa, E., Etemadi, K., Monperrus, M.: Human, What Must I Tell You? IEEE Softw. **40**(03), 9–14 (2023). https://doi.org/10.1109/MS.2023.3244638
10. Chazette, L., Brunotte, W., Speith, T.: Explainable software systems: from requirements analysis to system evaluation. Requirements Eng. **27**(4), 457–487 (2022). https://doi.org/10.1007/s00766-022-00393-5
11. Chazette, L., Schneider, K.: Explainability as a non-functional requirement: challenges and recommendations. Requirements Eng. **25**(4), 493–514 (2020). https://doi.org/10.1007/s00766-020-00333-1
12. Clement, T., Kemmerzell, N., Abdelaal, M., Amberg, M.: Xair: a systematic metareview of explainable AI (XAI) aligned to the software development process. Mach. Learn. Knowl. Extract. **5**(1), 78–108 (2023). https://doi.org/10.3390/make5010006
13. Corbin, J., Strauss, A.: Basics of Qualitative Research (3rd ed.): Techniques and Procedures for Developing Grounded Theory, 3 edn.. SAGE Publications, Thousand Oaks (2008). https://doi.org/10.4135/9781452230153
14. Creswell, J.S., David, C.J.: Research Design. Qualitative, Quantitative, and Mixed Method Approaches, 5th edn. SAGE Publications, Los Angeles (2018)

15. Degen, H.: Respect The User's Time: Experience Architecture and Design for Efficiency, 1st edn. Helmut Degen, Plainsboro (2022). https://www.designforefficiency.com

16. Degen, H., Budnik, C., Gross, R., Rothering, M.: How to explain it to a model manager? A qualitative user study about understandability, trustworthiness, actionability, and action efficacy. In: HCII 2023, Part I. LNCS, pp. 209–242. Springer, Cham (2023). https://doi.org/10.1007/978-3-031-35891-3_14

17. Furniss, D., Blandford, A., Curzon, P.: Confessions from a grounded theory PhD: experiences and lessons learnt. In: Proceedings of the SIGCHI Conference on Human Factors in Computing Systems. CHI 2011, New York, NY, USA, pp. 113–122. Association for Computing Machinery (2011). https://doi.org/10.1145/1978942.1978960

18. Gentner, D.: Mental models, psychology of. In: Smelser, N.J., Baltes, P.B. (eds.) International Encyclopedia of the Social & Behavioral Sciences, pp. 9683–9687. Pergamon, Oxford (2001). https://doi.org/10.1016/B0-08-043076-7/01487-X, https://www.sciencedirect.com/science/article/pii/B008043076701487X

19. Glaser, B.G., Strauss, A.L.: The Discovery of Grounded Theory: Strategies for Qualitative Research. Aldine de Gruyter, New York (1967)

20. Guest, G., Bunce, A., Johnson, L.: How many interviews are enough?: An experiment with data saturation and variability. Field Methods $18(1)$, 59–82 (2006). https://doi.org/10.1177/1525822X05279903

21. Gunning, D., Aha, D.: DARPA's explainable artificial intelligence (XAI) program. AI Magazine $40(2)$, 44–58 (2019). https://doi.org/10.1609/aimag.v40i2.2850, https://ojs.aaai.org/index.php/aimagazine/article/view/2850

22. Hennink, M., Kaiser, B.N.: Sample sizes for saturation in qualitative research: a systematic review of empirical tests. Soc. Sci. Med. **292**, 114523 (2022). https://doi.org/10.1016/j.socscimed.2021.114523

23. Hoffman, R.R., Miller, T., Mueller, S.T., Klein, G., Clancey, W.J.: Explaining explanation, Part 4: a deep dive on deep nets. IEEE Intell. Syst. **33**(03), 87–95 (2018). https://doi.org/10.1109/MIS.2018.033001421

24. Hoffman, R.R., Mueller, S.T., Klein, G., Litman, J.: Metrics for explainable AI: Challenges and prospects (2019). https://doi.org/10.48550/arXiv.1812.04608

25. Langer, M., et al.: What do we want from Explainable Artificial Intelligence (XAI)? - A stakeholder perspective on XAI and a conceptual model guiding interdisciplinary XAI research. Artif. Intell. **296**, 103473 (2021). https://doi.org/10.1016/j.artint.2021.103473

26. Miller, T.: Explanation in artificial intelligence: insights from the social sciences. Artif. Intell. **267**, 1–38 (2019). https://doi.org/10.1016/j.artint.2018.07.007

27. Mohseni, S., Zarei, N., Ragan, E.D.: A multidisciplinary survey and framework for design and evaluation of explainable AI systems. ACM Trans. Interact. Intell. Syst. **11**(3-4) (2021). https://doi.org/10.1145/3387166

28. Nishi, Y., Masuda, S., Ogawa, H., Uetsuki, K.: A test architecture for machine learning product. In: 2018 IEEE International Conference on Software Testing, Verification and Validation Workshops (ICSTW), pp. 273–278 (2018). https://doi.org/10.1109/ICSTW.2018.00060

29. Parnas, D.L.: On the criteria to be used in decomposing systems into modules. Commun. ACM **15**(12), 1053–1058 (1972). https://doi.org/10.1145/361598.361623

30. Piano, L., Garcea, F., Gatteschi, V., Lamberti, F., Morra, L.: Detecting drift in deep learning: a methodology primer. IT Professional **24**(5), 53–60 (2022). https://doi.org/10.1109/MITP.2022.3191318

31. van de Poel, I.: The relation between forward-looking and backward-looking responsibility. In: Vincent, N.A., van de Poel, I., van den Hoven, J. (eds.) Moral Responsibility: Beyond Free Will and Determinism, pp. 37–52. Springer, Dordrecht (2011). https://doi.org/10.1007/978-94-007-1878-4_3

32. Rudin, C.: Stop explaining black box machine learning models for high stakes decisions and use interpretable models instead. Nat. Mach. Intell. **1**(5), 206–215 (2019). https://doi.org/10.1038/s42256-019-0048-x

33. Saraf, A.P., Chan, K., Popish, M., Browder, J., Schade, J.: Explainable artificial intelligence for aviation safety applications. In: AIAA AVIATION 2020 FORUM (2020). https://doi.org/10.2514/6.2020-2881, https://arc.aiaa.org/doi/abs/10.2514/6.2020-2881

34. Schröder, T., Schulz, M.: Monitoring machine learning models: a categorization of challenges and methods. Data Sci. Manag. **5**(3), 105–116 (2022). https://doi.org/10.1016/j.dsm.2022.07.004

35. Stepin, I., Alonso, J.M., Catala, A., Pereira-Fariña, M.: A survey of contrastive and counterfactual explanation generation methods for explainable artificial intelligence. IEEE Access **9**, 11974–12001 (2021). https://doi.org/10.1109/ACCESS.2021.3051315

36. Sun, J., et al.: Investigating explainability of generative AI for code through scenario-based design. In: 27th International Conference on Intelligent User Interfaces. IUI '22, New York, NY, USA, pp. 212–228. Association for Computing Machinery (2022). https://doi.org/10.1145/3490099.3511119

37. Tantithamthavorn, C., Cito, J., Hemmati, H., Chandra, S.: Explainable AI for SE: challenges and future directions. IEEE Softw. **40**(03), 29–33 (2023). https://doi.org/10.1109/MS.2023.3246686

38. Triantafyllou, S.: Forward-looking and backward-looking responsibility attribution in multi-agent sequential decision making. In: Proceedings of the 2023 International Conference on Autonomous Agents and Multiagent Systems. AAMAS '23, Richland, SC, pp. 2952–2954. International Foundation for Autonomous Agents and Multiagent Systems (2023)

39. Turek, M.: Explainable Artificial Intelligence (XAI) (Aug 2016). https://www.darpa.mil/program/explainable-artificial-intelligence. Accessed 3 Mar 2020

40. van der Waa, J., Schoonderwoerd, T., van Diggelen, J., Neerincx, M.: Interpretable confidence measures for decision support systems. Int. J. Hum.-Comput. Stud. **144**, 102493 (2020). https://doi.org/10.1016/j.ijhcs.2020.102493

41. Zhang, Y., Liao, Q.V., Bellamy, R.K.E.: Effect of confidence and explanation on accuracy and trust calibration in AI-assisted decision making. In: Proceedings of the 2020 Conference on Fairness, Accountability, and Transparency. FAT* '20. ACM (2020). https://doi.org/10.1145/3351095.3372852

WisCompanion: Integrating the Socratic Method with ChatGPT-Based AI for Enhanced Explainability in Emotional Support for Older Adults

Naome A. Etori[(✉)] and Maria Gini

Department of Computer Science and Engineering, University of Minnesota, Minneapolis, USA
{etori001,gini}@umn.edu
https://cse.umn.edu/cs

Abstract. WisCompanion is a conversational artificial intelligence (AI) platform that merges the Socratic method with ChatGPT's advanced prompting capabilities to provide tailored emotional support for older adults. This unique combination fosters critical thinking and engagement through iterative questioning, explicitly addressing older adults' cognitive and emotional needs. This paper outlines a systematic approach for integrating a Socratic, ethical, and sensemaking AI framework with a chatGPT-based conversational AI tailored to older adults and trained on customized user data. WisCompanion delivers precise, context-aware explanations, fostering trust and transparency in AI interactions. Additionally, it supports lifelong learning. Our evaluations show significant improvements in user satisfaction with emotion support. Therefore, our results indicate that applying Socratic questioning techniques in conversational AI creates a dynamic and multi-layered dialogue structure. These techniques work in unison to foster a deeper understanding of the user's perspectives, emotions, and experiences, thereby significantly enhancing the quality of AI-older adult interactions.

Keywords: Socratic method · Older adults · Explainable AI · ChatGPT · Prompting · Conversational AI

1 Introduction

The increasing elderly population worldwide necessitates the development of intelligent systems capable of offering personalized assistance. This need is supported by data indicating a growing global aging population [40,50]. The World Health Organization (WHO) reports a projected demographic shift, wherein the segment of the global population aged 60 years and older is expected to rise from 12% in 2015 to 22% by 2050, signifying a near doubling of this age group's proportion in the overall population [2,25,35,51]. In an era where AI permeates various aspects of daily life, Conversational AI stands out for its potential to revolutionize personal assistance and support. Particularly in supporting older adults, these AI systems offer a unique blend of companionship, information accessibility, and cognitive stimulation.

H. Degen and S. Ntoa (Eds.): HCII 2024, LNAI 14734, pp. 179–198, 2024.
https://doi.org/10.1007/978-3-031-60606-9_11

Advancement of technology, particularly Conversational AI platforms, has paved the way for significant improvements in the quality of life among older adults, who often face challenges such as social isolation and cognitive decline [15]. Hence, there is a need to integrate the Socratic Method with advanced AI technologies. WisCompanion could provide a solution. It's not just another Conversational AI tool; WisCompanion integrates the timeless technique of the Socratic Method with GPT4 [54]. Hence, it transforms AI's clarity and user experience into a more dynamic, explainable, and engaging experience. The Socratic Method, a technique rooted in critical thinking and dialogue, enables WisCompanion to facilitate deeper comprehension and engagement among older users.

The Socratic method aligns well with the conversational capabilities of ChatGPT [43,54] since it is known for its use in stimulating thought and uncovering assumptions through questioning [37]. ChatGPT, a Generative Pre-trained Transformer (GPT) model type, generate human-like text, making it an ideal tool for interactive learning and communication [5]. Combining these two elements in WisCompanion addresses a significant gap in current AI applications, where the needs and preferences of older adults are often overlooked [7]. WisCompanion aims to enhance the clarity and user experience of AI for older adults, which aligns with Explainable AI (XAI) principles that foster transparency in AI systems.

Prior research has widely utilized the Socratic method in various domains, such as in education [21,49], counseling [38,39], computing [53], dialogue simulation [11,48], moral enhancement [28]. Most research on the Socratic method has focused on its application in education and counseling. To our knowledge, few studies have contributed to the broader field of conversational AI, and this could be one of the pioneering efforts. This paper integrates the Socratic Method into ChatGPT-driven dialogues to improve ethical interactions and explainability and provide emotional support for older adults. We aim to explore the impacts of this integration and its significance in supporting older adults as we answer the following research questions:

1. How can the Socratic method be optimized in ChatGPT-based AI interactions to support older adults' diverse cognitive abilities and emotional support?
2. How can XAI and ethical strategies be integrated into the ChatGPT-based design to safeguard well-being and give feedback to older adults?
3. How does integrating the Socratic method in ChatGPT-Based AI impact older adults' cognitive and emotional well-being and facilitate depth of inquiry and self-reflection to users?

2   Background

2.1   Technology Adoption Concerns of Older Users

Critical concerns shaping their attitudes and willingness to engage with such systems often hinder technology adoption among older adults. Among these concerns, privacy and security are of paramount importance. Older users tend to express apprehension towards technologies that may compromise their privacy or seem to function as surveillance tools [30]. This apprehension is heightened by a lack of trust in data storage and utilization [14]. Furthermore, maintaining independence and dignity is another significant factor influencing older adults' resistance to technology [20]. Older adults may reject technologies they perceive as undermining their autonomy or overly intrusive [55], even if they are intended for their safety and convenience [55]. This leads to a prevalent skepticism towards new technologies among older adults [8]. Therefore, it is crucial to consider this demographic's potential physical and cognitive limitations while designing technology solutions [10]. In addition, intuitive, simple interfaces that provide clear feedback are more likely to be accepted [61]. The concept of age-inclusive design is increasingly recognized as essential in technology development [19].

2.2 The Socratic Method and AI Interaction

The Socratic Method, named after the classical Greek philosopher Socrates, is a cooperative argumentative dialogue that stimulates critical thinking and illuminates ideas. It involves asking and answering questions to stimulate critical thinking and to draw out ideas and underlying presumptions [6,41]. It is a well-established pedagogy technique, particularly effective in teaching critical thinking and problem-solving skills [42]. When applied to AI like ChatGPT, the Socratic Method can transform interactions from simple question-answering to a deeper, more engaged dialogue where the AI not only provides answers but also challenges the users to think and reflect on their questions [37] and the provided answers-integrating the Socratic Method into XAI. Its application in AI, particularly in chat-based systems, can significantly benefit elderly users. As highlighted by [37], the Socratic Method can be tailored to address the cognitive and emotional needs of the elderly. Engaging them in a dialogue that challenges their thinking while providing emotional validation enhances cognitive stimulation and emotional well-being [33]. Studies have shown conversational AI can positively affect user perception and mood [15].

2.3 Large Language Models (LLMs)

Large Language Models (LLMs) mark a transformative advancement in AI and machine learning (ML), revolutionizing our capacity to process and comprehend human language that mimics natural human communication [57]. Foundational models such as ELIZA [59], PARRY [9], and ALICE [16] laid the groundwork. LLMs utilize foundational technologies, such as tokenization methods [56], attention mechanisms [54], and distributed approaches [27], which collectively contribute to their robust capabilities [36]. The evolution of LLMs has seen rapid advancements, especially with transformer architectures like BERT and GPT, enhancing data handling [13]. Additionally, the emergence of multimodal models like CLIP and DALL-E, which combine text with other modalities like images or video, further enhances the robustness of LLMs [60]. LLMs primarily utilize the Transformer architecture, which employs a self-attention mechanism [54]. The increasing scalability and accessibility of LLMs, as demonstrated by models like ChatGPT [26], have broadened their reach and impact [34]. LLMs transform NLP, enhancing machine translation, Name entity recognition, sentiment analysis, and content creation. They enable context-rich dialogues [17], and benefit sectors like education [52], healthcare [18], and research [32]. Despite their capabilities, LLMs face challenges like perpetuating societal biases and raising ethical concerns [47]. LLMs' high energy use poses environmental concerns [3], and their outputs risk inaccuracy from hallucinations [45].

3   Approach

The fusion of the Socratic Method with XAI in chatGPT-based systems offers a promising approach to enhancing the interaction experience of older adults. The technical aspect of developing a ChatGPT-based system involves several key components and processes.

3.1   Sensemaking Framework

We incorporate the sensible AI framework [22] into our Conversational AI design. Sensible AI is borrowed from sensemaking theory and integrates principles from Karl Weick's sensemaking theory. Sensemaking is a term well-grounded in literature defined by Weick as simply the making of sense or developing a set of ideas with explanatory possibilities. Sensemaking theory describes a framework for the factors that influence human understanding, emphasizing the importance of understanding how people make sense of complex and sometimes conflicting information [58]. [22] further inspired our design and functioning of conversational AI to enhance the interpretability and explainability of AI responses, fostering a more intuitive and human-like interaction experience. Traditional approaches to interpretability and explainability focus on designing better explanations and improving an artifact and do not account for the nuances of human cognition. According to [22], the sensemaking perspective is a frame of mind about frames of mind. Therefore, the proposed framework provides a more holistic approach. Incorporating sensemaking principles into ChatGPT-based conversational AI is paramount. To ensure that WisCompanion effectively aids older adults, we draw inspiration from the seven distinguishing characteristics of sensemaking theory, aligning the Socratic approach with the natural cognitive patterns of our users. Table 1 below highlights fundamental sensemaking properties and how they inform the design of WisCompanion:

Grounded in Identity Construction: WisCompanion uniquely identifies user patterns and preferences, tailoring interactions to affirm and reinforce their identity. This personalization encompasses linguistic choices, cultural nuances, and personal narratives, going beyond content adaptation.

Retrospective: WisCompanion features a reflective inquiry mechanism based on the Socratic Method, prompting users to engage in metacognition by reflecting on their experiences and prior knowledge. This retrospective analysis integrates new information and strengthens their existing knowledge, enhancing comprehension and retention.

Enactive of Sensible Environments: WisCompanion promotes an interactive learning approach where the system responds meaningfully to user inputs. This dynamic interaction enables experiential learning, fostering a tangible and sensible learning experience.

Social: WisCompanion leverages socio-cultural databases to create contextually relevant dialogues that resonate with older users' shared experiences and societal values.

Ongoing: WisCompanion can evolve with the user, learning from past interactions to continuously refine its understanding of their preferences, needs, and conversational style. This ongoing adaptation ensures that the AI remains a relevant and supportive companion.

Focused on and by Extracted Cues: WisCompanion responsiveness is finely tuned to user-provided cues. This focus allows WisCompanion to extract relevant information from user inputs and to use these cues to guide the conversation in a manner that is most pertinent to the user's intentions and interests.

Table 1. An overview of the seven properties of sensemaking, their description as applied to WisCompanion Design

No.	Characteristic	Application in WisCompanion	Description
1	Grounded in identity construction	Personalized Interactions	WisCompanion offers personalized interactions by adapting to each user's unique identity
2	Retrospective	Reflective Inquiry	WisCompanion uses the Socratic Method to foster user reflection.
3	Enactive of sensible environments	Interactive Learning	WisCompanion enables active AI engagement for older adults.
4	Social	Socially Contextualized Dialogue	WisCompanion tailors conversations to the elderly using socio-cultural data.
5	Ongoing	Adaptive Learning	WisCompanion adapts continuously to the user's conversational needs.
6	Focused on and by extracted cues	Cue-Based Responsiveness	WisCompanion uses cues to deliver relevant information and sustain conversation.
7	Driven by plausibility over accuracy	Plausible Explanations	WisCompanion offers relatable responses for older adults

3.2   ChatGPT Architecture

In this work, we built a customized version of GPT tailored to function like ChatG-PTmodel developed by OpenAI [1]. ChatGPT [54] is a sibling model of InstructGPT, which is trained to follow instructions in a prompt and provide a detailed response. Hence, it becomes a variant of the GPT model, fine-tuned for conversational AI. Training ChatGPT involves the vast dataset used for GPT and provides additional training to improve its performance in our dialogue-based tasks. It combines instructions, an extra specific knowledge base, and any combination of skills and tailors it to include the Socratic method. Based on the transformer architecture, it has been trained on massive data, allowing it to generate text and respond to various prompts with human-like precision and accuracy. ChatGPT is a neural network architecture for processing sequential data, such as text. The Transformer architecture is based on self-attention mechanisms, which allow the model to weigh the importance of different parts of the input sequence when making predictions. ChatGPT is built upon mathematical principles mainly rooted in deep learning and NLP. Using matrix multiplication, the self-attention mechanism computes attention scores between tokens in a sequence. Given an input sequence represented as a matrix X, the attention scores A is calculated as a softmax operation over the scaled dot-product of query and fundamental matrices:

$$A = \text{softmax} \left(\frac{XW_Q(XW_K)^T}{\sqrt{d_k}} \right) \tag{1}$$

Where W_Q and W_K are learnable weight matrices for queries and keys, and d_k represents the dimension of critical vectors. This operation enables ChatGPT to weigh the importance of different words in a sentence when generating responses.

In addition, ChatGPT incorporates feed-forward neural networks in each Transformer layer. These networks apply linear transformations followed by activation functions (ReLU) to the input data.

$$FFN(H) = \text{ReLU}(HW_1 + b_1)W_2 + b_2 \tag{2}$$

Where H represents the output of the self-attention layer, and W_1, b_1, W_2, and b_2 are weight matrices and bias terms. The ReLU activation function introduces non-linearity, allowing the model to capture complex patterns in the data.

ChatGPT is then trained using Maximum Likelihood Estimation (MLE) to predict the likelihood of the next token in a sequence. The loss function for this task is the negative log-likelihood:

$$L_{MLE} = - \sum_{t=1}^{T} \log(P(x_t|x_{<t})) \tag{3}$$

Here, x_t represents the target token, and $x_{<t}$ denotes the preceding tokens. MLE guides the model in understanding grammar, semantics, and world knowledge.

Finally, fine-tuning is a critical step in enhancing ChatGPT's performance. It involves reinforcement learning using Proximal Policy Optimization (PPO) algorithms. The objective is to maximize the expected reward, where the policy $\pi(a_t|s_t)$ is optimized:

$$L_{PPO} = \mathbb{E} \left[\frac{\pi(a_t|s_t)}{\pi_{\text{old}}(a_t|s_t)} \hat{A}_t - \beta H(\pi(s_t)) \right] \tag{4}$$

This formulation helps ChatGPT adapt responses based on human feedback and rewards, leading to more contextually relevant and coherent conversations. As described by [57], the conceptual architecture of a GPT model is displayed in Fig. 1.

3.3 Socratic Questions for Emotion Elicitations

In this section, we elaborate on incorporating the Socratic questioning methodology into the development of WisCompanion. Originating from Plato's dialogues, the Socratic

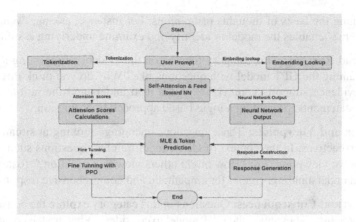

Fig. 1. ChatGPT Workflow Diagram: Illustrating the Process from User Input and Tokenization to Self-Attention, Neural Processing, and Generating Responses

method is a form of cooperative argumentative dialogue where strategic questioning is used to foster critical thinking and to clarify complex ideas. This approach is recognized for its intellectual rigor. It involves using carefully formulated questions to explore abstract concepts, encouraging deep reflection and critical examination of one's beliefs and understanding. The essence of this method is its emphasis on the dynamic exchange of questions and answers, which aids in developing critical thinking skills and the derivation of insights about various concepts and their underlying assumptions. Such a methodological approach is crucial for maintaining alignment with life perspectives that support personal growth and emotional health, as explored in seminal works like Padesky's study on Socratic dialogue [41]. Within WisCompanion, Socratic questioning is characterized by its structured and probing nature; this technique is essential for examining complex ideas, emotions, and thought processes. This method is central to facilitating meaningful dialogues and enhancing cognitive and emotional insight in WisCompanion. The application of this technique in cognitive-behavioral therapy (CBT) and emotional intelligence is well-documented [23,24,41], symbolizing a method that fosters deep introspection and self-discovery, assisting individuals in unraveling their deeply rooted beliefs and values. Its use as a therapeutic technique in treating depression [4]. This aligns perfectly with the aims of WisCompanion, enhancing emotional support to users to give them a deeper understanding of their thoughts and feelings. As depicted in Table 2, our GPT model powering WisCompanion was extensively trained using six different types of Socratic questions to grasp the discussed topics comprehensively.

Clarification Questions: These questions are fundamental to Socratic questioning since they aim to probe deeper into the subject matter. For WisCompanion, these questions help the GPT model to seek precise information or further explanation. Examples include "What do you mean by that?" or "Could you explain further?".

Assumptions Probing: These questions challenge the assumptions underlying a user's statement. In training the GPT model, such questions encourage consideration of the beliefs forming the basis of thoughts or opinions. For instance, asking, "What are we assuming here?" enables the model to identify and examine underlying assumptions.

Evidence and Reasons: This category focuses on the evidence supporting a claim or thought. Training the GPT model with questions like "Why do you think this is true?" or "What evidence supports your view?" helps it to understand the rationale behind beliefs and statements, promoting a logic-based approach to discussion.

Perspectives and Viewpoints: These questions encourage looking at situations from multiple perspectives. In the context of GPT model training, questions such as "What is an alternative viewpoint?" or "How might others view this situation?" foster a multi-dimensional understanding, crucial for empathetic and comprehensive responses.

Implications and Consequences: Questions in this category explore the consequences of a belief or action. They guide the GPT model to consider "What are the consequences of this assumption?" or "How does this affect other things?" Such questioning cultivates foresight and awareness of the broader impact of ideas and decisions.

Questions about the Question: This final type turns the focus back on the question itself, aiding the GPT model in understanding the intent and depth of the inquiry. Asking "Why do you think I asked this question?" or "What does this question mean?" helps the model grasp the purpose and underlying context of inquiries.

Table 2. Types and Examples of Socratic Questions for GPT Model Training

Types	Examples
Clarification questions	Why do you say that? What is the main issue?
Assumption questions	Why this assumption? How can we verify it?
Probing questions	What is an example? What causes this to happen?
Implications questions	What generalizations can you make? What are the consequences?
Perspective questions	What is an alternative perspective? What are the strengths and weaknesses?
Questioning the question	Why is this question important? How does it apply to everyday life?

3.4   WisCompanion Design Implementation

As shown in Fig. 2, we elaborate on the intricate development process of the Wisdom Companion GPT model. This model, which represents a state-of-the-art iteration within the GPT4, is lauded for its advanced capabilities in Natural Language Understanding (NLU) and Generation (NLG). Its core functionality is predicated on generating text that closely mimics human responses, contingent on the input provided. We customized our model using a highly tailored dataset, explicitly crafted to modify and fine-tune it for its main functions: dispensing Socratic-based wisdom and facilitating companionship while rigorously adhering to AI ethical and explainability standards. We incorporated both prompts for response generation and a thorough specification of the model's operational behavior and characteristics. We included a detailed task description, articulating the model's desired performance benchmarks and behavioral attributes, explicitly focusing on nuances associated with wisdom and companionship.

Interestingly, the dataset outlines the model's desirable and undesirable behavioral patterns. The customization process begins with a detailed definition of the model's purpose through the GPT builder interface, followed by a fine-tuning phase to align the model's capabilities with our specific objectives. We found it essential to clearly understand the model's intended purpose and objectives at the outset of this process. A salient feature of WisCompanion is leveraging the Socratic method as the cornerstone of its interaction strategy to foster engaging, thought-provoking conversations that resonate with older adults' unique experiences and perspectives.

Initially, the user can provide a textual input that goes directly to the NLU module, or they can give an audio input, which is handled by the Automatic Speech Recognition (ASR) system. The ASR's role is to accurately transcribe the audio input into text before passing it on to the NLU. Once the NLU module receives input directly from the user or via the ASR, it processes this information to grasp the intended message or command. This understood input is then forwarded to GPT-4, which processes inputs and generates appropriate responses. GPT-4 may also interact with a database to retrieve or store information as part of its response generation process. Finally, the response crafted by GPT-4 is delivered in two formats: as text directly to the user's mobile phone for display on the screen and as audio through a Text-to-Speech (TTS) system, enabling the user to receive feedback visually and auditorily. This dual-output approach ensures the response is accessible and convenient for the user.

3.5   Datasets

We used different types of datasets to train Wisdom Companion. The first dataset is a comprehensive collection of Socratic questions categorized into distinct types. Each category is accompanied by examples illustrating the nature and application of the questions within that category. This dataset is essential for understanding the depth and range of Socratic questioning techniques in a conversational context, as shown in Table 2. The second dataset is tailored for older adults, focusing on ease of use, empathy, privacy, and security in a conversational agent. The third dataset is the sensemaking framework knowledge fed to the model. Using a sensemaking framework dataset to fine-tune a model can significantly enhance its ability to understand and interpret complex, ambiguous information.

4   Experimental Setup

We developed the WisCompanion user interface and datasets with a sophisticated prompt approach that enables sensemaking, provides clear instructions, and fosters meaningful conversations. The following dataset curation stage involves collecting, organizing, and managing all the datasets to ensure their quality, relevance, and accessibility for specific purposes, such as ethics, Socratic questions, etc., to train the WisCompanion model. We started with data cleaning, annotation, validation, and augmentation

Fig. 2. An overview of the Wisdom Companion User Interface, highlighting its empathetic approach and user-friendly prompts.

Effective curation is crucial for developing WisCompanion, ensuring the data used for training aligns with our objective, user needs, and ethical standards.

4.1 User Personas and Journey Mapping

In testing WisCompanion, we used four detailed user personas and journey mapping. These personas were inspired by profiles obtained in previous experiments involving older adults, which have already undergone Institutional Review Board (IRB) review and approval. This approach is grounded in the principles of user-centered design. It aims to ensure the system is tailored to meet its intended user base's specific needs and characteristics. The user personas were created to reflect diverse characteristics and needs typical of the older adult demographic. This diversity includes varying levels of technological proficiency, different types of living situations (such as living alone or in assisted living facilities), and a range of physical and cognitive abilities. The personas are based on empirical data from previous studies, ensuring they represent real-world users [40]. We utilies four personas

5   Results and Discussion

RQ1: How the Socratic method can be optimized in ChatGPT-based conversational AI to offer emotional support to Older adults

Our study shows that the Socratic method is effectively utilized in WisCompanion through a mix of open-ended, reflective, clarifying, and leading questions. These questioning techniques encourage self-reflection and a rich, emotionally engaging dialogue. For instance, the conversation depicted in Table 3 provides a comprehensive view of the

Table 3. A sample conversation between User_1 and WisComp

Speaker	Dialogue
User_1	Tell Me About Your Loved Ones
WisComp	It sounds like you're interested in discussing loved ones. This can be a very meaningful topic. If you're comfortable, could you share a bit about the loved ones in your life? For instance, who are they, and what makes your relationship with them special? This can help us have a more personalized and engaging conversation. Remember, you only need to share what you feel comfortable with
User_1	Well first of all, my name is Lucy
WisComp	Hello Lucy, it's great to meet you! If you'd like to share more about your loved ones, I'm here to listen. How do they enrich your life, and what are some of your favorite memories with them?
User_1	I miss my daughter and my son today
WisComp	I'm sorry to hear that you're missing your daughter and son today, Lucy. It's completely natural to feel this way, especially when we hold our loved ones close to our hearts. If you're open to it, could you tell me a bit more about them? What are some cherished moments or qualities that come to mind when you think of your daughter and son?

user's relationship with their loved ones, highlighting the effectiveness of the Socratic method in exploring complex human emotions and memories.

The dialogue begins with the WisCompanion asking the user to "Tell me about your loved ones." This question clarifies concepts and establishes a user-centric and explorative interaction. It empowers users to express their thoughts and emotions freely, facilitating a more profound and engaging interaction. Further probing, such as the WisCompanion response, "It is completely natural to feel this way, especially when we hold our loved ones close to our hearts," goes beyond acknowledging the user's sentiments. It goes deeper into the underlying emotions, validating and exploring them, creating an AI interaction environment where users feel understood and supported.

WisCompanion inquiry, such as "How do they enrich your life, and what are some of your favorite memories with them?" probes the rationale, reasons, and evidence behind the user's feelings, enabling the AI to collect more in-depth data beyond superficial interactions. The question about cherished moments with a user's children exemplifies how inquiring about viewpoints can unveil a range of thoughts and emotions, enabling empathetic and effective AI responses. Questions like "What do you enjoy doing together?" help understand the impact of shared experiences on emotions and relationships, enriching the context for AI interactions by exploring specific events and feelings. Additionally, question to question, "Is there anything, in particular, you enjoy doing to prepare or to make the time pass more enjoyably?" encourages self-reflection and awareness. This meta-cognitive approach deepens the conversation and enhances dialogue quality.

Table 4. Socratic Questions and Examples generated by WisCompanion

Socratic Question Type	Example Questions
Clarifying concepts	"How do they enrich your life?" "Do you have a favorite memory?"
Probing assumptions	"Do you often find humor with your family?" "How does your daughter connect with you?"
Probing rationale, reasons,	"How does her support make you feel?" "In what ways have you embodied strength?"
Questioning viewpoints	"Is there a lesson from your father you pass on?" "How do gatherings influence your family sense?"
Probing implications	"Best ways to spend time with your family?" "Anything you're excited about for the visit?"
Questioning the question	"Anything you'd like to talk about?" "Aspects of your 'old self' you miss?"

RQ2: How XAI and ethical strategies be integrated into the ChatGPT-Based AI to safeguard emotional well-being and give feedback to older adults

The ChatGPT system has been developed with ethical guidelines to ensure its interactions are responsible, safe, and respectful. These ethical considerations have been incorporated into the system's design and deployment to safeguard user privacy and prevent the generation of harmful or inappropriate content [12]. Ongoing challenges in conversational AI, such as the need to mitigate risks of bias and inappropriate outputs, are being addressed by developing a specialized dataset focusing on unique ethical concerns for model training [46]. Our specialized dataset addresses ethical concerns in model training, as discussed in Sect. 3.5. Insights from Table 3.

Similarly, the WisCompanion has demonstrated a keen awareness of its non-human nature by transparently communicating its capabilities and limitations to the user, upholding user autonomy, and enabling a more informed interaction. Its commitment to preventing emotional distress and promoting positive social interaction highlights its adaptability. It underscores the importance of incorporating XAI principles to ensure interactions are user-centered, ethically informed, and profoundly impactful. When users inquire about its decisions, WisCompanion explains its reasoning, acknowledging its AI nature and detailing the factors influencing its choices. Analyzing dialogues like one with a user in Table 3, we demonstrate how WisCompanion applies XAI principles, such as sentiment analysis in Fig. 4, to foster empathetic and personalized interactions.

RQ3: How integrating the Socratic method in ChatGPT-Based AI facilitates depth of Inquiry and self-reflection. Our conversation findings illustrate a substantial depth of inquiry, a key feature in AI-driven Socratic dialogues. WisCompanion not only initiates self-reflection but also assists Lucy in exploring her emotional depths, linking her past experiences with her present and future. This method aids in developing a personal narrative, offering a comprehensive perspective of her life and relationships. WisCompanion maintains a delicate balance between inquisitiveness and empathy, ensuring a supportive and understanding conversation while navigating complex emotional landscapes. This equilibrium is essential in AI interactions as it cultivates trust and openness, leading to more authentic and insightful exchanges.

6   Evaluation of WisCompanion

This section presents the evaluation methodologies applied to assess the performance of the WisCompanion. Without direct human evaluation, we utilized detailed user personas, as explained in Sect. 4.1. Our goal is to automatically evaluate how appropriate the proposed response is to the conversation [29]. We, therefore, leveraged various automated metrics.

Frequency-Based Lexical Analysis: Frequency-based lexical analysis, illustrated in Fig. 3, reveals key themes from the WisCompanion dialogue. The prominence of 'like' suggests an inquisitive or comparative dialogue style. Recurrent words- 'time,' 'enjoy,' 'day,' 'feel'-highlight discussions around personal experiences and emotions. 'Lucy,' a frequent lexical item, points to personalized interactions, while 'family' and 'memories' emphasize the narrative's familial focus. This analysis forms the foundation for a further semantic investigation into user sentiment.

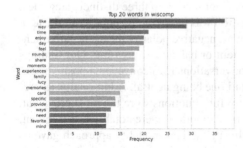

Fig. 3. Frequency-based lexical analysis reveals Top 20 words most frequent words

Table 5. Bigrams and Trigrams Analysis

Bigrams	Trigrams
('like', 'way')	('like', 'way', 'time')
('way', 'time')	('way', 'time', 'day')
('time', 'day')	('time', 'day', 'enjoy')
('day', 'enjoy')	('day', 'enjoy', 'feel')
('enjoy', 'feel')	('enjoy', 'feel', 'experiences')
('moments', 'share')	('moments', 'share', 'sounds')
('share', 'sounds')	('share', 'sounds', 'family')
('sounds', 'family')	('sounds', 'family', 'lucy')

N-gram Analysis: As shown in Table 5, We used bigrams and trigrams to show pairs and triples of words frequently appearing together in the dataset. Our analysis unveils a structured pattern of co-occurring word sequences, represented as bigrams and trigrams, within the conversational data. Notably, certain word combinations exhibit a frequency count of 1, indicating their presence in the dialogues. Specifically, bigrams

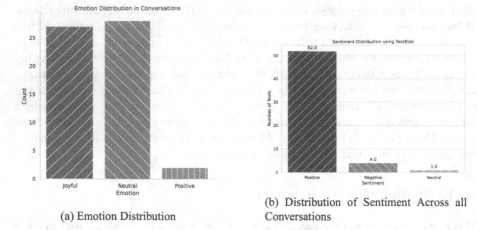

(a) Emotion Distribution

(b) Distribution of Sentiment Across all Conversations

Fig. 4. Figure (a) shows the emotion distribution (b) shows the sentiment distribution of all conversations

like ('like', 'way') and ('day', 'enjoy') suggest thematic connections, potentially related to exploring preferences and emotional experiences. Similarly, identified trigrams, such as ('like', 'way', 'time') and ('share', 'sounds', 'family'), hint at intricate narratives and discussions in the conversational context, suggesting deeper user engagement and meaningful interactions.

Sentiment and Emotion Analysis: Sentiment analysis greatly aided the understanding of WisCompanion's emotional tone. For sentiment analysis, we utilized TextBlob [31], an NLP library for analysis. By using pre-trained models and lexical resources, TextBlob was able to accurately categorize text sentiment into three distinct categories: positive, negative, and neutral. This categorization was based on the polarity of the text, where positive polarity means positive sentiment, negative polarity means negative sentiment and neutral polarity suggests no sentiment or balance. expression. Our findings in Fig. 4 (b) confidently revealed that most conversations (52) conveyed a positive sentiment, with only four expressing negativity and one being neutral. Additionally, as presented in Fig. 4 (a), our findings reveal that 'Joyful' emotions were the most prevalent, followed by 'Neutral' sentiments, while 'Positive' emotions were notably less frequent. Combining emotion and sentiment analysis through a dual-modality approach gave us a more nuanced understanding of affective states, identifying specific emotions such as joy and sadness. Leveraging the T5-base model [44], our research expands beyond traditional sentiment analysis to provide a more comprehensive emotion analysis to allow a deeper understanding of the emotional nuances in language use.

Tone Matching with Sentiment Polarity Score: The primary objective is to assess whether WisCompanion's responses align appropriately with the emotional tone conveyed in the user's input, thus gauging sensitivity and appropriateness. Our analysis entails an evaluation of the emotional content within both the user input and WisCompanion responses to ascertain if WisCompanion is responding with a suitable emotional tone. To facilitate this evaluation, we introduce two variables: P_u, representing the sentiment polarity of the user input, and P_c, signifying the sentiment polarity of the WisCompanion's response. The degree of tone matching is quantified using a similarity measure that evaluates the absolute difference between these polarity scores and compares this to a predefined threshold (T). If the absolute difference $(|P_u - P_c|)$ is $\leq$ the threshold T, we classify the tones as matching, denoted as *Tone Match = True*. Conversely, if the absolute difference exceeds T, we conclude that the tones do not match, indicated as *Tone Match = False*. The formula for calculating the tone match based on sentiment polarity scores is:

$$\text{Tone Match} = \begin{cases} \text{True} & \text{if } |P_u - P_c| \leq T(0.5), \\ \text{False} & \text{otherwise} \end{cases}$$

where P_u is the sentiment polarity of the user input, P_c is the sentiment polarity of the WisCompanion response, and T is a threshold value defining the maximum allowed difference between P_u and P_c for the tones to be considered matching. Our tone-matching formula with sentiment polarity scores utilizes the TextBlob library for sentiment analysis. The sentiment polarity is a float within the range $[-1.0, 1.0]$, where -1.0 signifies a highly negative sentiment, 1.0 signifies a highly positive sentiment, and values around 0 represent neutral sentiment. We computed sentiment polarity scores for the user input and the WisCompanion response for each conversational exchange within our dataset. Polarity scores were derived through an extensive preprocessing pipeline involving lowercase conversion, punctuation and stopwords removal, and lemmatization. This rigorous preprocessing ensured text consistency, enhancing sentiment analysis accuracy and faithfully representing the emotional content. The tone-matching algorithm evaluates the absolute difference between the sentiment polarity scores of the user inputs and WisCompanion responses. A threshold of 0.5 was set to determine if the sentiment polarities were considered matching. In this context, a "match" suggests that the WisCompanion responded with an emotionally congruent statement relative to the user's input. For example, a sympathetic WisCompanion response to a user's sad input is considered a tone match. Using a regression line, Fig. 5 shows a scatter plot showing user sentiment against WisCompanion sentiment polarity. A bar plot complemented the scatter plot. Wiscompanion demonstrates effective emotional mirroring, as indicated by more tone matches than mismatches. This mirroring is vital for engaging older adults and fostering empathy, understanding, and trust-essential elements of the Socratic method. Additionally, the system's capacity to align with users' emotions encourages user engagement, thus promoting self-reflection and critical thinking.

Vector-Based Emotional Analysis: Emotions are complex and multi-dimensional; unlike simple sentiment polarity analysis, we needed an advanced approach to understanding a broader spectrum of emotions to provide a richer and more in-depth emotion assessment in dialogues. This advanced approach provides a richer and more in-depth emotion assessment in dialogues with greater precision. We employ a vector-based approach to capture the subtlety and variety of emotional expression. The process begins by tokenizing the input text **T**, resulting in a sequence of tokens $\mathbf{T} = [t_1, t_2, \ldots, t_n]$, where n represents the total number of tokens. These tokens are then converted into tensors, denoted as *inputs*, which serve as the input for the T5ForConditionalGeneration model,

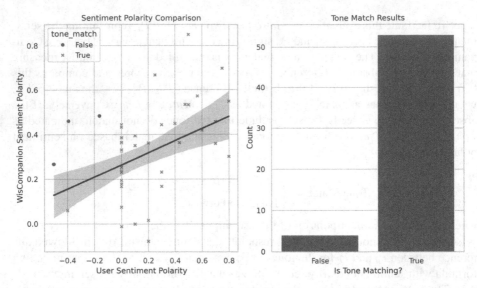

Fig. 5. Sentiment Polarity Comparison on the left and Tone Match Results on the right.

i.e. *inputs* = tokenizer.encode($\mathbf{T}$, return_tensors = "pt"). The model processes tensors and generates an output sequence $\mathbf{S}$ that captures the emotional essence of the input, i.e. $\mathbf{S} = \text{T5}(\textit{inputs})$, where T5($\cdot$) denotes the function of the model. Subsequently, the output sequence $\mathbf{S}$ is decoded into a string, representing the predicted emotion label $\mathbf{L}$. This decoding process is executed as $\mathbf{L} = \text{tokenizer.decode}(\mathbf{S}, \text{skip\_special\_tokens} = \text{True})$.

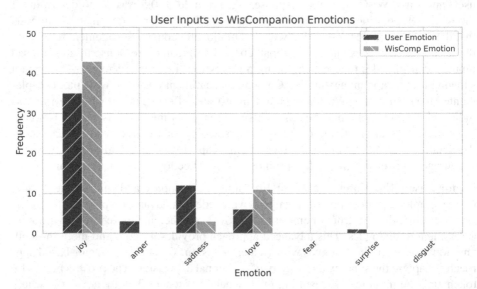

Fig. 6. Emotion distribution of User Inputs and WisCompanion: WisCompanion often responds with more joy than users express. Emotions like sadness, love, fear, and surprise are less frequently expressed or mirrored by the system.

Finally, the corresponding emotion vector E_L is retrieved from a predefined dictionary that maps emotions to vectors. $E_L = $ emotion_to_vector[$\mathbf{L}$]. Figure 6 indicates that Wis-Companion emphasizes positive emotions like joy and love while de-emphasizing negative emotions like anger, sadness, and disgust. It avoids matching users' expressions of negative emotions like anger and disgust to maintain a constructive interaction. This is an intentional design; as an emotional support system, it aims to enhance positive feelings and reduce negative ones during user interactions.

7   Limitations

Custom GPT models, while powerful and versatile, come with certain limitations. Firstly, trying out the tool is impossible without a subscription; no free trials are available for experimentation before making a purchase, which may restrict potential users from assessing its suitability. Furthermore, the risk of data hallucination exists unless the model is trained using specific integration tools, making it challenging to monitor interactions when the bot is made public. Additionally, though Custom GPT can generate detailed content rapidly, users are concerned about potentially copying and pasting information from other sources, leading to questions about the originality and accuracy of the content produced. Moreover, while the tool allows for creating specific use cases, it has limitations in how these use cases can be effectively incorporated into various business scenarios. Finally, a unique challenge arises from the widespread availability and replicability of Custom GPT applications.

8   Conclusions

This study has highlighted the effectiveness of WisCompanion in supporting older adults through integrating the Socratic Method and ChatGPT. Our results indicate significant improvements in user satisfaction, evidenced by the positive sentiments and emotions demonstrated. The Socratic method significantly improves critical thinking and iterative questioning, which can enhance older adults' cognitive and emotional well-being. The user-friendly, ease-of-use design addresses the unique needs of this demographic, promoting accessibility and continuous intellectual engagement.

9   Future Work

Moving forward, we plan to extend this research by conducting human studies experiments to understand better the long-term impacts of Socratic questions on older adults' cognitive and emotional health. Additionally, exploring platforms' adaptability to different cultural and linguistic backgrounds and extensions, like integrating it with What-sApp, could increase its global applicability. Despite the limitations, the automated evaluation provides a baseline understanding of the conversational agent's performance using the Socratic method. The Socratic method demonstrates the potential of positively impacting conversational AI in processing information.

Acknowledgments. We thank colleagues for their inspiring work, and the 'Pasonas' initiative participants played critical evaluation roles, enriching our research without using actual data.

Ethics Statement. The research design and implementation were carefully considered to avoid harm or discomfort to anyone. Interactions with ChatGPT were structured to prevent the propagation of misinformation, bias, or offensive content.

Disclosure of Interests. The authors declare that they have no competing interests relevant to the content of this article.

References

1. Introducing GPTs—openai.com. https://openai.com/blog/introducing-gpts. Accessed 21 Dec 2023
2. World Health Organization (WHO)—who.int. https://www.who.int/. Accessed 21 Dec 2023
3. Bender, E.M., Gebru, T., McMillan-Major, A., Shmitchell, S.: On the dangers of stochastic parrots: can language models be too big? In: Proceedings of the 2021 ACM Conference on Fairness, Accountability, and Transparency, pp. 610–623 (2021)
4. Braun, J.D., Strunk, D.R., Sasso, K.E., Cooper, A.A.: Therapist use of socratic questioning predicts session-to-session symptom change in cognitive therapy for depression. Behav. Res. Ther. **70**, 32–37 (2015)
5. Brown, T., et al.: Language models are few-shot learners. Adv. Neural. Inf. Process. Syst. **33**, 1877–1901 (2020)
6. Carey, T.A., Mullan, R.J.: What is socratic questioning? Psychotherapy Theory Res. Pract. Train. **41**(3), 217 (2004)
7. Charness, N., Boot, W.R.: Aging and information technology use: potential and barriers. Curr. Dir. Psychol. Sci. **18**(5), 253–258 (2009)
8. Chen, K., Chan, A.H.: A review of technology acceptance by older adults. Gerontechnology (2011)
9. Colby, K.M.: Ten criticisms of parry. ACM SIGART Bulletin **48**, 5–9 (1974)
10. Czaja, S.J., et al.: Factors predicting the use of technology: findings from the center for research and education on aging and technology enhancement (create). Psychol. Aging **21**(2), 333 (2006)
11. Dalal, D.: Socrates Sim: A Dialog Simulation Framework to Support Task Completion Dialog Research. Ph.D. thesis, Harvard University (2018)
12. Derner, E., Batistič, K.: Beyond the safeguards: exploring the security risks of ChatGPT. arXiv preprint arXiv:2305.08005 (2023)
13. Ding, Q., Ding, D., Wang, Y., Guan, C., Ding, B.: Unraveling the landscape of large language models: a systematic review and future perspectives. J. Electron. Bus. Digital Econ. (ahead-of-print) (2023)
14. Edwards, J., Sanoubari, E.: A need for trust in conversational interface research. In: Proceedings of the 1st International Conference on Conversational User Interfaces, pp. 1–3 (2019)
15. Ferland, L., et al.: Tell me about your day: designing a conversational agent for time and stress management. In: Explainable AI in Healthcare and Medicine: Building a Culture of Transparency and Accountability, pp. 297–303 (2021)
16. Fryer, L., Carpenter, R.: Bots as language learning tools (2006)
17. Goar, V., Yadav, N.S., Yadav, P.S.: Conversational AI for natural language processing: an review of ChatGPT. Int. J. Recent Innov. Trends Comput. Commun. **11**, 109–117 (2023)

18. Haupt, C.E., Marks, M.: Ai-generated medical advice-GPT and beyond. Jama **329**(16), 1349–1350 (2023)
19. Hawthorn, D.: Possible implications of aging for interface designers. Interact. Comput. **12**(5), 507–528 (2000)
20. Hill, R., Betts, L.R., Gardner, S.E.: Older adults' experiences and perceptions of digital technology: (dis) empowerment, wellbeing, and inclusion. Comput. Hum. Behav. **48**, 415–423 (2015)
21. Jensen Jr., R.D.: The effectiveness of the socratic method in developing critical thinking skills in English language learners. Online Submission (2015)
22. Kaur, H., Adar, E., Gilbert, E., Lampe, C.: Sensible AI: re-imagining interpretability and explainability using sensemaking theory. In: Proceedings of the 2022 ACM Conference on Fairness, Accountability, and Transparency, pp. 702–714 (2022)
23. Kazantzis, N., et al.: Socratic dialogue and guided discovery in cognitive behavioral therapy: a modified delphi panel. Int. J. Cogn. Ther. **11**, 140–157 (2018)
24. Kazantzis, N., Fairburn, C.G., Padesky, C.A., Reinecke, M., Teesson, M.: Unresolved issues regarding the research and practice of cognitive behavior therapy: the case of guided discovery using socratic questioning. Behav. Chang. **31**(1), 1–17 (2014)
25. Kinsella, K.G., Phillips, D.R.: Global Aging: The Challenge of Success, vol. 60. Population Reference Bureau, Washington DC (2005)
26. Kocoń, J., et al.: ChatGPT: jack of all trades, master of none. Inform. Fusion **99**, 101861 (2023)
27. Langer, M., He, Z., Rahayu, W., Xue, Y.: Distributed training of deep learning models: a taxonomic perspective. IEEE Trans. Parallel Distrib. Syst. **31**(12), 2802–2818 (2020)
28. Lara, F.: Why a virtual assistant for moral enhancement when we could have a socrates? Sci. Eng. Ethics **27**(4), 42 (2021)
29. Liu, C.W., Lowe, R., Serban, I.V., Noseworthy, M., Charlin, L., Pineau, J.: How not to evaluate your dialogue system: an empirical study of unsupervised evaluation metrics for dialogue response generation. arXiv preprint arXiv:1603.08023 (2016)
30. Lorenzen-Huber, L., Boutain, M., Camp, L.J., Shankar, K., Connelly, K.H.: Privacy, technology, and aging: a proposed framework. Ageing Int. **36**, 232–252 (2011)
31. Loria, S., et al.: TextBlob documentation. Release 0.15 2(8), 269 (2018)
32. Lund, B.D., Wang, T.: Chatting about ChatGPT: how may AI and GPT impact academia and libraries? Library Hi Tech News **40**(3), 26–29 (2023)
33. Meisner, B.A.: A meta-analysis of positive and negative age stereotype priming effects on behavior among older adults. J. Gerontol. B Psychol. Sci. Soc. Sci. **67**(1), 13–17 (2012)
34. Meyer, J.G., et al.: ChatGPT and large language models in academia: opportunities and challenges. BioData Min. **16**(1), 20 (2023)
35. Nations, U.: Ageing | United Nations—un.org. https://www.un.org/en/global-issues/ageing. Accessed 21 Dec 2023
36. Naveed, H., et al.: A comprehensive overview of large language models. arXiv preprint arXiv:2307.06435 (2023)
37. Nelson, L.: Socratic method and critical philosophy. Revista Portuguesa de Filosofia **34**(2), 312 (1978)
38. Overholser, J.C.: The socratic method as a technique in psychotherapy supervision. Prof. Psychol. Res. Pract. **22**(1), 68 (1991)
39. Overholser, J.C.: Psychotherapy according to the Socratic method: Integrating ancient philosophy with contemporary cognitive therapy. J. Cogn. Psychother. **24**(4), 354–363 (2010)
40. Owan, R., Ferland, L., Etori, N., Koutstaal, W., Gini, M.: Conversational agents for elderly users. In: Workshop Assistive Robotics for Citizens at IROS (2023)

41. Padesky, C.A.: Socratic questioning: changing minds or guiding discovery. In: A Keynote Address Delivered at the European Congress of Behavioural and Cognitive Therapies, London, vol. 24 (1993)
42. Paul, R., Elder, L.: Critical thinking: the nature of critical and creative thought. J. Dev. Educ. **30**(2), 34 (2006)
43. Radford, A., Narasimhan, K., Salimans, T., Sutskever, I., et al.: Improving language understanding by generative pre-training (2018)
44. Raffel, C., et al.: Exploring the limits of transfer learning with a unified text-to-text transformer. J. Mach. Learn. Res. **21**(1), 5485–5551 (2020)
45. Rawte, V., Sheth, A., Das, A.: A survey of hallucination in large foundation models. arXiv preprint arXiv:2309.05922 (2023)
46. Ray, P.P.: ChatGPT: a comprehensive review on background, applications, key challenges, bias, ethics, limitations and future scope. Internet Things Cyber-Phys. Syst. **3**, 121–154 (2023)
47. Scherrer, N., Shi, C., Feder, A., Blei, D.M.: Evaluating the moral beliefs encoded in llms. arXiv preprint arXiv:2307.14324 (2023)
48. Seeskin, K.: Dialogue and Discovery: A Study in Socratic Method. Suny Press, Albany (1987)
49. Stojković, N., Zerkin, D.G.: Pedagogy of Socratic method of teaching ESP. J. Teach. Engl. Specif. Acad. Purp. **11**, 555–565 (2023)
50. Sylvester, A., Temesgen, E., Etori, N., Gini, M.: Autonomy and dignity for elderly using socially assistive technologies. In: Workshop Assistive Robotics for Citizens at IROS (2023)
51. Sylvester, A., Temesgen, E., Etori, N., Gini, M.: Ethical robot design considerations for individuals suffering from a neurodegenerative disease. In: Workshop Geriatronics: AI and Robotics for Health & Well-Being in Older Age at IROS (2023)
52. Tack, A., Piech, C.: The AI teacher test: measuring the pedagogical ability of blender and GPT-3 in educational dialogues. arXiv preprint arXiv:2205.07540 (2022)
53. Tamang, L.J., Alshaikh, Z., Khayi, N.A., Oli, P., Rus, V.: A comparative study of free self-explanations and socratic tutoring explanations for source code comprehension. In: Proceedings of the 52nd ACM Technical Symposium on Computer Science Education, pp. 219–225 (2021)
54. Vaswani, A., et al.: Attention is all you need. In: Advances in Neural Information Processing Systems, vol. 30 (2017)
55. Wang, S., et al.: Technology to support aging in place: Older adults' perspectives. Healthcare **7**, 60 (2019)
56. Webster, J.J., Kit, C.: Tokenization as the initial phase in NLP. In: COLING 1992 Volume 4: The 14th International Conference on Computational Linguistics (1992)
57. Wei, J., et al.: Chain-of-thought prompting elicits reasoning in large language models. Adv. Neural. Inf. Process. Syst. **35**, 24824–24837 (2022)
58. Weick, K.E.: Sensemaking in organizations, vol. 3. Sage, Thousand (1995)
59. Weizenbaum, J.: Eliza-a computer program for the study of natural language communication between man and machine. Commun. ACM **9**(1), 36–45 (1966)
60. Wu, J., Gan, W., Chen, Z., Wan, S., Yu, P.S.: Multimodal large language models: a survey. arXiv preprint arXiv:2311.13165 (2023)
61. Ziefle, M., Bay, S.: How older adults meet complexity: aging effects on the usability of different mobile phones. Beh. Inform. Technol. **24**(5), 375–389 (2005)

Exploring the Impact of Explainability on Trust and Acceptance of Conversational Agents – A Wizard of Oz Study

Rutuja Joshi[✉] [ID], Julia Graefe[ID], Michael Kraus[ID], and Klaus Bengler[ID]

Technical University of Munich, Boltzmannstr. 15, 85748 Garching, Germany
{rutuja.joshi,julia.graefe,m.kraus,bengler}@tum.de

Abstract. With advancements in natural language processing and understanding, conversational agents (CAs) have become one of the fundamental modes of human-computer interaction. However, the black-box problem of AI algorithms often results in reduced acceptance of such systems. This calls for transparency and justification or rationale for the provided output from the users' perspective. Explainable artificial intelligence (XAI) provides insights into the algorithms and elucidates outputs to the users, thus gaining more importance in various applications as a significant contributor to user acceptance and trust in artificial intelligence (AI) systems. This paper presents a Wizard of Oz user study with a between-subjects design comparing two versions of a vacation planning chatbot (low and high explainability) with 60 participants. The study explored the impact of explainability on users' understanding, trust and acceptance. The results indicated that explanations (between-subject factor) significantly influence users' understanding, trust and acceptance. According to our results, high explainability leads to increased trust and acceptance of the chatbot.

Keywords: Human-AI Interaction · Explainable AI · Human-Centered Explainable AI · Conversational Agents · Chatbots

1 Introduction

Recent advances in artificial intelligence (AI) and large language models (LLM) are currently leading to their extensive integration in conversational user interfaces (CUI) such as chatbots. This development carries enormous potential for improved human-machine interaction. However, these models may not only generate errors and false content [7], but also, the machine learning tools can reveal only little insight about how a decision was generated [21]. These so-called black-box systems are too complex in their underlying structure to be entirely self-explanatory for the human user [41] and too much or inadequate explanation might bear the risk of reduced usability. Hence, the field of explainable AI (XAI) has evolved and gained more traction in human-computer interaction research within the past years. The goal of human-centered XAI research is to present

© The Author(s), under exclusive license to Springer Nature Switzerland AG 2024
H. Degen and S. Ntoa (Eds.): HCII 2024, LNAI 14734, pp. 199–218, 2024.
https://doi.org/10.1007/978-3-031-60606-9_12

understandable and trustworthy explanations about the AI's decisions and outputs to the user and thereby foster transparency and understanding of the system [12]. Besides an improved understanding of how or why the system generated a particular output [10, 23], explanations can support the user's trust in the system and positively impact technology acceptance [38].

Nevertheless, optimal structuring and presenting explanations of AI systems to foster a high level of understanding, trust, and acceptance in the end-user, especially when interacting with conversational user interfaces, remains an unsolved question. To address this research gap, our work focuses on implementing XAI techniques into the interaction between humans and chatbots. In this paper, we present a user study comparing two versions of a simulated LLM chatbot, one with a high level of explainability (chatbot H) and one with a low level of explainability (chatbot L). The goal is to investigate how explanations in CUIs can contribute to an improved understanding and how this affects the users' trust and acceptance of the chatbot. Through the study, we aim to answer the following research questions:

- RQ 1: Does the users' understanding differ for chatbot L and chatbot H?
- RQ 2: Does the users' trust differ for chatbot L and chatbot H?
- RQ 3: Does the users' acceptance differ for chatbot L and chatbot H?
- RQ 4: Is there a correlation between users' perceived causal understanding, trust, and acceptance of the chatbots?
- RQ 5: Is there a correlation between the users' previous experience with chatbots and their perceived causal understanding?

2   Related Work

2.1   Conversational Agents

Conversational Agents (CAs) interact with users via written or spoken communication in natural language. ELIZA was one of the first programs that supported natural language conversation with a computer [44]. Natural language processing and machine learning have come a long way and CAs can now carry out meaningful conversations with humans [2]. They find applications in various domains like education, health and customer support agents in the commercial domain [2]. With the introduction of ChatGPT [36], LLMs were seen as a potential solution to building open-ended conversations and enhancing user experience through natural language communication. These conversational interfaces could assit in making machine explanations understandable to the users [2].

Despite the technological developments, there is a discrepancy between users' expectations and their experiences with CAs [32]. The conversational agents seem to lack reflexes and adaptive interactivity that normally occurs in conversations between human interaction partners [15]. In addition, friendliness and empathy were seen as characteristics to influence user's confidence in the system [31]. Along with anthropomorphization, a system's competence and privacy also impacted user trust [37]. These aspects probe a user-centered exploration for designing and developing such conversational agents to increase the users' trust and acceptance.

2.2   Explainable AI

Van Lent et al. [34]used the term explainable AI (XAI) to describe an AI system that was extended to be able to explain its behavior to the user during or after use by means which were comprehensible to the user. Explanations should be used for four main reasons: justification of system outputs, enhancing the transparency of the model for debugging, improving the model accuracy, and discovering new information and expanding the knowledge base [1]. Explainability facilitates transparency by revealing the workings of an AI-based system, thus enhancing the users' experience with the system and allowing them to make better decisions [41].

Explanations are operationalizations of explainability, influencing the system's understandability or interpretability [14]. Explanations can influence user's trust [41], distrust [40], and acceptance [17]. Four types of explanations have been categorized based on the type of user: developer explanations, assurance explanations, explanations for external users and end users [41]. Besides the user type, other factors that shape an explanation are the goal, content and language of the explanation [41]. Explanations based on human explanations have been studied, and the findings suggest that explanations are contrastive, selected in a biased manner, and social and causalities are more important than probabilities [35]. The linguistic structure of an explanation can be split into three parts: the opening, the explanation itself and the closing stage [11].

Explainability methods can be differentiated into global or local interpretability and model-specific or model-agnostic interpretability [1]. Various explainability approaches have been used in previous research like the multiple question-answer approach as an exhaustive explanation [41], high soundness and high completeness in explanations [28], visual and example-based explanations [27], and class-contrastive counterfactual explanation strategies [43].

3   Chatbot: Design and Development

3.1   Prioritization of Explanations

For this study, we focused on a relatively low-stake application, a chatbot or assistant for planning and booking vacations. We used a user-centered design approach and based our selection of explanations on Ferreira and Montero's [19] criteria: the recipient, the reason why the explanation is selected and the situation in which the explanation is shown. In this study, personas based on existing research and literature are used as a mechanism to describe the user group as they help identify the requirements for a product [22]. Three distinct personas were created, ranging from an inexperienced and unsure user to an expert with efficiency in conversation as a goal. The context of use was demonstrated using a user journey map that illustrated the user's interaction with the product to achieve their goal [42]. The user journey helped us identify the interactions where explanations could be necessary and also exemplify the user's needs based on their personal characteristics or context of use. Based on the insights from personas and user journeys, we prioritized following categories of explanations:

- Explanations regarding flight price
- Explanations regarding flight details
- Explanations regarding the destinations
- Explanations for beginners
- Explanations regarding errors

3.2 Explanation-Aware System Design

Planning a vacation focuses on many aspects depending on the person and vacation. For the purpose of this study, the tasks were narrowed down to finding a suitable destination, planning other elements like the flights, and selecting a final offer. An explanation-aware system design approach [25] was followed to create the database for the Wizard of Oz study. Such databases are normally used to train AI algorithms, but in our study, this database served as a standardization tool to ensure comparability between the subjects.

The database included the most popular destinations of German tourists [5], most popular destinations of German youth [5] and most popular vacation destinations worldwide [18]. The chatbot was limited to Europe, North America, and Asia destinations. We added multiple cities to the database for each country, even if some studies suggested that only one main city was commonly chosen as in certain countries. Destination preferences were grouped into five different categories according to user needs: landscape/surrounding, distance, region and country, cost and temperature (see Table 1).

Table 1. Categorization of Destinations.

Categories	Attributes		
Landscape /Surrounding	Nature	Ocean	City
Distance: Flight time t_f (in hours)	short $(t_f < 2)$	medium $(2 < t_f < 6)$	high $(t_f > 6)$
Region	Europe	Asia	North America (incl. Mexico)
Cost: Flight price p_f(in €)	cheap $(p_f < 150)$	medium $(150 < p_f < 300)$	high $(p_f > 300)$
Temperature T (in °C)	cold $(T < 15)$	medium $(15 < T < 30)$	hot $(T > 30)$

Based on the database, a fundamental system flow was designed to imitate a realistic program [33]. A combination of recommender systems for destinations and flights and a system to process the booking constituted the main blocks of system architecture (Fig. 1).

Furthermore, the destinations were recommended based on a decision-tree (example shown in Fig. 2).

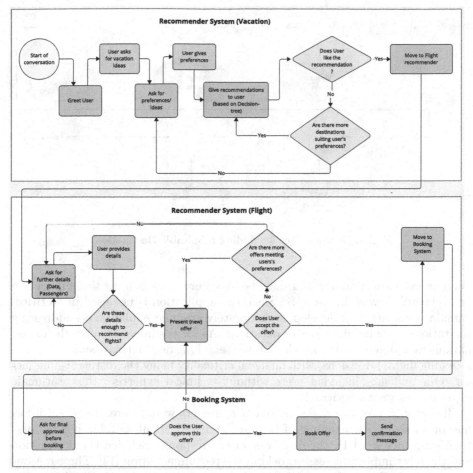

Note: Yellow rectangles represent user actions; Blue rectangles represent system actions; Rhombus represents a decision point.

Fig. 1. A simplified conversation flow.

3.3 Structuring Explanations

As discussed in Sect. 2.2, the explanations can be categorized into global or system explanations and local explanations. In the case of this chatbot, its logic served as the foundation for the system explanation for both versions (H and L), which was presented only upon explicit request to prevent information overload.

The local explanations were based on the categories prioritized in Sect. 3.1. In their guidelines regarding explaining decisions made with AI, the Information Commissioner's Office (ICO) [25] recommends building explanations for users with delivery, layering and contextual factors in mind. The contextual factors based on guidelines from ICO [25]: domain, impact, data, urgency and audience.

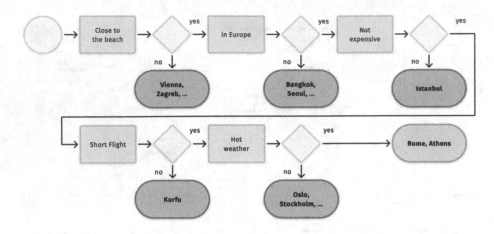

Fig. 2. Decision Tree for finding a Suitable Destination.

For our use case, urgency and data factors were irrelevant as the application is a relatively low-stake use case. Since the application is not used in a critical domain, we focused on developing moderately granular explanations addressing the rationale behind decisions or questions. As for the impact factor, the explanations were differentiated into low-stake (searching destinations) and high-stake (booking flights) decisions, with financial criticality being the distinguishing factor. Our audience included users without technical expertise; thus, rationale explanations were prioritized.

In order to promote dialogue, chatbot answers were layered to reveal information in steps. For example, if the user enquired about suitable holiday destinations, in chatbot H, the first layer of the response included the destination and the most important reasons behind the recommendation [14]. These reasons focused on the factors for categorizing destinations (see Table 1). Chatbot L featured a short response with the recommendation but did not include the reasons for the selection. The participants could ask for reasoning or request further information, which was then structured as a second-layer response common for both chatbot H and chatbot L.

In chatbot H, the answers were further enriched by providing example-based [3] or contrastive explanations [30,35] that have proven to improve the explainability of the system based on previous research. An example of the chatbot's response in the phase of finding a suitable destination is shown below.

Sample Chatbot Response

I need more information to find a suitable destination [A]. What other information can you give me [B]? I need this information because, with the additional information, I can also compare aspects like "proximity to the beach" or "reasonable prices" [C] with the destinations in my database and thus give you even more suitable suggestions [D].

Explainability approaches:
A : Direct response to query
B : Promotes interactive dialogue
C : Example-based explanation
D : Reason and motivation

Note: [A],[B] shown by both Chatbot H and Chatbot L; [C],[D] proactively shown by Chatbot H, available for Chatbot L if asked by the user.

3.4   Technical Implementation of VacationBOT

The chatbot or chat function was based on the GitHub project Support Desk App by Basir [6]. It uses react.js for functional components and socket.io for real-time chatting. The code, particularly the front-end, underwent customization tailored to the requirements of this study. Specific modifications, including a custom logo and introductory text, were implemented to enhance the authentic appearance of the chatbot. The website had two distinct pages: a user view and an admin view. The admin could access the chat history of all users.

In order to make the explanations non-intrusive [13], the user view of the chatbot consisted of a simple and clear structure without elements that could distract the user from the main task as shown in Fig. 3. In the admin view (see Fig. 3), the wizard could see all users on the left panel and select each chat manually. The test subjects were instructed to use fictitious names in order to protect anonymity. This separation between user and admin view ensured that all users only interacted with the wizard and not with each other.

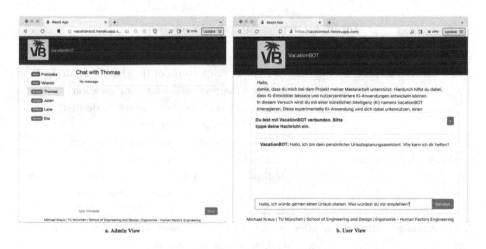

Fig. 3. Chatbot UI Design.

4   Methodology

4.1   Study Design

We used the Wizard of Oz test setup, where a 'human wizard' interacted with the test subjects to evaluate the explanation concepts of the chatbot. The study was conducted online, allowing the subjects to participate through their preferred location. The independent variable in focus was 'Explainability' (low vs high). An inter-individual comparison between subjects helped investigate the effects of the chatbot's explanations. The sample was divided into two groups - Group H, which interacted with a chatbot H 'high explainability' and Group L, which interacted with a chatbot L 'low explainability'. The participants were provided with a scenario to ensure comparable actions during interaction with the chatbot.

4.2   Scenario and Tasks

The user journeys and personas contributed to the design of the scenario. Vacation planning can include different aspects based on individual characteristics and preferences. The scenario focused on three tasks: finding a suitable destination for vacation, planning other elements like flights or dates for the vacation, and selecting a final offer from the chatbot. The test subjects were also given multiple possible action items for each task (see Table 2). These action items gave the participants some orientation without taking away the complete freedom of interacting with the chatbot. The tasks were also used to trigger explanations for participants in Group H and only answers with low explainability for participants in Group L.

Table 2. Overview of scenario and tasks.

Task	Action points
Find a suitable vacation destination	a. Explore the features of the chatbot (if desired)
	b. State the preferences for your vacation
	c. Describe own vacation history (if desired)
	d. Ask for multiple suggestions
	e. Choose one of the proposed destinations
Planning other elements	a. Specify number of travellers
	b. State preferred dates, time, and duration of trip
	c. Specify flight preferences (airline, time)
	d. Ask for offers
Selecting and accepting a final offer	a. Ask for better or more suitable offers (if desired)
	b. Choose one of the final offers

4.3   Dependent Variables

The study investigated the effects of explainability on the trust and acceptance of users. A subjective assessment was conducted using three questionnaires that gathered self-reported quantitative values. Acceptance was recorded using the Technology Acceptance Model (TAM) with two sub-scales: Perceived Usefulness (PU) and Perceived Ease of Use (PEU) [16]. This study uses the trust questionnaire by Jian et al. [26]. That evaluates trust between humans and automated systems. This questionnaire consists of 12 items with a 7-point Likert scale available for rating the statements. The trust score was calculated as the average score over 12 items for each participant. The user's perceived causal understanding (PCU) of the system was assessed using the System Causability Scale (SCS) which returns a System Causability Score proposed by Holzinger et al. [24]. The SCS consists of 10 items and uses a 5-point Likert scale. The SCS score per participant is calculated by considering the sum of scores over all items and then dividing the total by 50 [24]:

$$SCS = \sum_i Rating_i / 50$$

Native German speakers translated all questionnaires into German, as the experiment participants predominantly spoke German.

4.4   Procedure

The participants received the participation consent form, invitation link to the video conference, and the demographic questionnaire via e-mail before the scheduled meeting. At the beginning of the study, the experimenter greeted the participants and gave initial instructions. The experimenter explained the purpose of the study, the procedure and the task to the test subjects. Here, it was checked if the demographics questionnaire had already been filled out; if not, the participants answered the demographics questionnaire. The subjects received the link for accessing the chatbot after the initial introduction. The subject then interacted with the chatbot and solved the tasks described earlier. During the experiment, the experimenter was only available for technical glitches or problems to ensure an uninterrupted experience. After the tasks, the participants filled out three questionnaires regarding trust, acceptance and perceived causal understanding.

The Ethics Committee of the Technical University of Munich approved the study design with application number (2023-339-S-KH).

4.5   Sample

In total, 60 valid datasets were gathered and included for data analysis. Each group (Group H and Group L) consisted of 30 participants. The participants were recruited via Flyers and Posters in the university, via the subject database at the Chair of Ergonomics, Technical University of Munich and via social media.

Participation in the study was voluntary, and the following prerequisites were set to enable participation in the study: sufficient proficiency in the German language, minimum age of 18 years and access to a computer with internet.

The participants were predominantly young, with 33 test subjects aged between 18–25 and 22 in the age group 26–35. The gender distribution was rather even, with 32 identifying themselves as males and 28 as females. Table 3 gives an overview of the distribution in the groups.

Table 3. Demographic Data

Group	N	Age Group					Gender	
		18–25	26–35	36–45	46–55	56–65	Male	Female
L	30	16	12	0	1	1	66.67%	33.33%
H	30	17	10	1	2	0	40%	60%

Most participants, n = 55, stated they have some experience with AI. 45 subjects indicated previous experience with voice assistants, while 39 reported having experience with chatbots. However, the experience level in both cases varied. Figure 4 provides an overview of experience levels measured on a 5-point Likert scale ranging from very inexperienced to extremely experienced in chatbots and voice assistants. Group L (n = 15) had relatively more participants without prior chatbot experience than group H (n = 6).

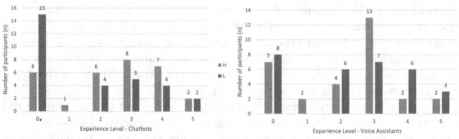

Note: 0 - No prior experience; 1 - Very inexperienced to 5 - Extremely experienced

Fig. 4. Experience Levels in Voice Assistants and Chatbots

4.6   Data Analysis

After the study, the gathered data was reviewed for completeness. 60 valid datasets were further considered for data analysis. Both descriptive and inferential statistical analyses were conducted on valid datasets. The descriptive analysis is reported in the following section and includes the mean (M), standard deviation (SD), and minimum and maximum values (range) for every construct.

To investigate statistical differences between observations for trust and PCU in the between-subjects factor an independent t-test analysis was conducted. As the TAM has two sub-scales, PU and PEU, to explore the statistical differences between the two groups, a multivariate analysis of variance (MANOVA) was conducted to explore statistical differences.

Furthermore, a correlation analysis was conducted to look into the relationships between the users' understanding, trust and acceptance. In addition to this, to explore if a link existed between prior experience and the users' understanding, another correlation analysis was carried out. The significance level was set to 5% for each inferential test.

5   Results

5.1   Perceived Causal Understanding

The results of the descriptive analysis of the SCS are visualized as a box plot in Fig. 5. The descriptive analysis shows a difference in the SCS scores between the groups, with Group H *(n = 30, M = 0.86, SD = 0.07, Range = 0.7-1)* having a higher rating than Group L *(n = 30, M = 0.74, SD = 0.11, Range = 0.4-0.9)*.

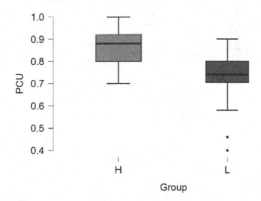

Fig. 5. Box Plot: Perceived Causal Inderstanding

The independent sample t-test, was conducted to evaluate whether the two groups had statistically significant differences. Field et al. [20] describes four prerequisites to conduct a t-test: normal distribution of the sample, data measured at interval level, scores are independent and homogeneity of variance. Here, the normal distribution is assumed based on the number of participants (n = 30) per group. The Likert scale can be treated as an interval measurement level [45]. The groups are treated as a between-subject factor and thus the scores in each group are independent. As the group sizes are same, the homogeneity of variance can be assumed [20].

On average, the PCU of Group H participants was higher than Group L participants. This difference was significant *(t(58)=5.256, p <0.001, Cohen's d = 1.357)*.

5.2 Trust

The results of the descriptive analysis for trust are visualised in Fig. 6. Group H *(M = 5.5, SD = 0.75, Range = 3.67-6.75)* rated the trust in the system higher than Group L *(M = 4.87, SD = 0.77, Range = 3.25-6.42)*. An independent t-test was conducted to verify whether significant differences existed between the two groups. The assumptions for the t-test were satisfied, as stated in Sect. 5.1. The t-test results indicate a significant difference *(t(58) = 3.22, p = .002, Cohen's d = 0.833)* for the factor Trust between Group H and Group L.

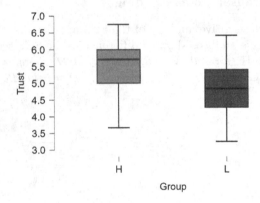

Fig. 6. Box Plot: Trust

5.3 Acceptance

In order to examine the impact of explanations on user acceptance, the TAM model [16] was used. The descriptive analysis is shown in Fig. 7. The results show that both PU and PEU scored more in Group H than in Group L. The rating for PEU in Group H*(M = 6.18, SD = 0.71, Range = 4.17-7)* was higher than Group L*(M = 5.83, SD = 0.51, Range = 4.83-6.67)*. Similarly for PU, Group H*(M = 5.67, SD = 0.74, Range = 4.17-6.83)* scored higher than Group L*(M = 5.1, SD = 1.02, Range = 2.33-6.17)*.

A MANOVA was conducted to verify whether significant differences existed between Group H and Group L for both sub-scales of acceptance, PU and PEU. According to Field et al. [20], there are four prerequisites to conducting a MANOVA: Independent observations, randomly sampled data, homogeneity of covariance matrices and multivariate normality within groups. Independent observation and randomly sampled data were given by the experimental design.

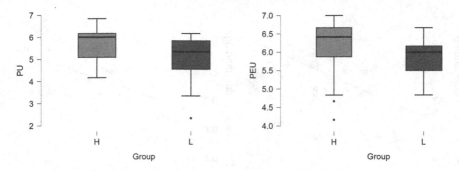

Fig. 7. Box Plot: Perceived Usefulness (PU) and Perceived Ease of Use (PEU)

The data within groups was not normally distributed across both dependent variables, as depicted by the Shapiro-Wilk test, $W(60) = 0.955$, $p = .03$; thus, the prerequisite of multivariate normality was not met. However, based on different studies, Bortz and Schuster [8] conclude that a MANOVA is robust to violating this prerequisite in large samples if the group sizes are equal. Hence, the MANOVA could still be run on the data. As discussed in Sect. 5.1, the Likert scale can be considered an interval measure. Since the sample sizes in both groups are equal, the homogeneity of covariance can be assumed.

Using Pillai's trace, it can be observed that explanations significantly affected PU and PEU, $V = 0.12$, $F(1,58) = 3.98$, $p = 0.024$. Separate univariate ANOVAs on the dependent variables revealed significant effects of explanations on PU, $(F(1,58) = 6.19$, $p = 0.016$, $\eta_p^2 = 0.096)$ and PEU, $(F(1,58) = 4.82$, $p = 0.032$, $\eta_p^2 = 0.077)$.

5.4 Correlation Between Trust, Acceptance and Perceived Causal Understanding

The relationship between trust, acceptance and perceived causal understanding was explored through a correlation analysis using Spearman's Rho. Here the differentiation between groups was not considered. For acceptance, an aggregated average score of PU and PEU is calculated per participant (N = 60). The results are illustrated in Fig. 8. The perceived causal understanding correlates positively with acceptance $(\rho = 0.41$, $p = 0.001)$ and trust $(\rho = 0.51$, $p<.001)$. Furthermore, trust and acceptance have also a positive correlation $(\rho = 0.41$, $p = 0.001)$.

5.5 Correlation Between Previous Experience with Chatbots and Perceived Causal Understanding

We explored the possibility of a relationship between users' understanding and previous experience with chatbots using Spearman's correlation analysis. The differentiation between groups was not considered. The users' perceived causal

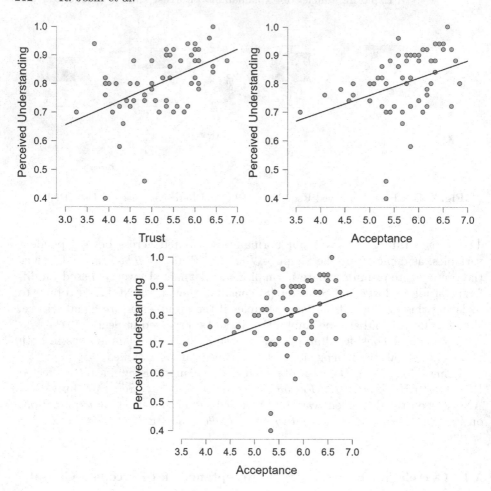

Fig. 8. Spearman's Correlation Analysis between Trust, Acceptance and Perceived Causal Understanding

understanding did not show any significant correlation with previous experience ($\rho = -0.04$, $p > .05$).

6 Discussion

The presented study aimed to investigate the impact of the explainability of a conversational agent on users' trust and acceptance. The study was conceptualized to be a between-subjects comparison with two versions of the chatbot, with high and low explainability, respectively. The users interacted in these versions in an online study and answered questionnaires regarding trust, acceptance and users' perceived causal understanding. The results show that there is a significant impact of explanations on users' trust and acceptance regarding the system.

Our hypothesis was based on previous studies, which attributed towards improved user understanding, trust and acceptance with the incorporation of explainability [9,38,40]. The results of the independent sample t-test for the SCS showed a significant effect of explainability on users' understanding of the chatbot functionality. This also indicates that a combination of approaches results in increased user understanding. However, the results should be interpreted cautiously as the System Causability Scale is a novel questionnaire, and the results cannot be compared to other projects. This also emphasizes the need for further research in this area, where different permutations and combinations of explanation approaches are tested to recommend an optimized taxonomy for generating explanations with high quality. In this study, the SCS value of chatbot L has limited relevance since test subjects in Group L did not receive proactive explanations from the chatbot. The chatbot L gave explanations only when requested in the form of follow-up questions. Therefore, it is unclear how valid or meaningful the SCS is with only a few explanations. Limited follow-up inquiries from participants suggest that users may prefer receiving proactive explanations from the system rather than making efforts to seek clarifications. Based on participants' subjective feedback, it can be inferred that incorporating explanations in diverse tones and styles could enhance participant engagement. This aspect warrants further investigation from a human factors perspective.

This study also explored how prior experience with chatbots affects perceived causal understanding. However, the correlation analysis between prior experience with chatbots and perceived causal understanding did not reveal any significant results. This lack of significance could be linked to users' familiarity with online vacation booking experiences, where they are well-versed in searching for destinations and booking flights. It's important to note that this outcome is specific to the use case examined and may differ for more critical use cases.

The statistical results show a significant impact of explanations on both trust and acceptance in users. The positive effects of explanations on trust and acceptance concur with previous research [9,17,41]. The correlation analysis also indicated a moderately positive but significant correlation between perceived causal understanding, trust and acceptance. While user acceptance increased with the explanations, the acceptance was measured only using perceived usefulness and perceived ease of use. Similarly, the higher trust ratings in Group H confirm the impact of explanations on trust in the system. This study proves that the relationship between trust, acceptance and perceived causal understanding based on explanations is also valid in low to mid-stake decision-making systems. However, there are other factors that play a role in shaping trust and acceptance of any technology [29,39]. Further research in the form of in-depth investigations regarding critical factors affecting trust and acceptance could provide a basis for designing such AI-based systems. However, the study did not account for participants' baseline trust in chatbots or their preconceived opinions about chatbots.

Analyzing the impact of explanations on the increase or decline in trust and acceptance could be a further avenue for research.

The prototypical design of this study poses a limitation to its external validity, particularly in terms of lacking a genuine AI-based conversational agent and the natural conversational flow it could generate. This potential limitation might have influenced users' perceptions of the investigated variables. Nevertheless, using a consistent database and decision tree ensured uniformity in the conversations experienced by each participant through the Wizard of Oz method. Consequently, the results should be considered as initial indicators for structuring explanations in AI-based conversational agents (based on the concept of user general types).

7   Conclusion

With the leaps AI and natural language processing have taken in the recent past, a future without these systems is indiscernible. However, the advancements in designing AI lack behind rendering these systems to be black-boxes for humans. Therefore, using a human-centered design approach for transparency becomes inevitable especially for interfaces that deal with end-users who are not domain experts. Previous works have recommended using explanations or explainable AI as an approach for increasing transparency and thus usability of these systems [4,27]. This study explored a relatively low-stake application, planning and booking a vacation with the help of a chatbot. Our work compared various approaches for structuring these explanations and explores the impact of incorporating explanations on users' trust, acceptance and perceived causal understanding of the system. The explanations designed for this system were based on previous studies which had shown positive results with regard to trust and acceptance. We developed two versions of a chatbot with low and high explainability for exploring the effect of explanations on trust, acceptance and perceived causal understanding. Our results showed that carefully designed explanations can significantly influence the trust and acceptance of the system. The correlation between users' previous experience with chatbots and perceived causal understanding was insignificant in our study. However, we observed a difference in users' perceived causal understanding of the system between the groups. This indicates that explanations contribute to increasing user trust and acceptance, thus enhancing user experience. Future research can investigate variations in communication strategies explanations including the tone and style of explanations and its effects on users' experience.

Disclosure of Interests. The authors have no competing interests to declare that are relevant to the content of this article.

References

1. Adadi, A., Berrada, M.: Peeking inside the black-box: a survey on explainable artificial intelligence (XAI). IEEE Access **6**, 52138–52160 (2018). https://doi.org/10.1109/ACCESS.2018.2870052
2. Allouch, M., Azaria, A., Azoulay, R.: Conversational agents: Goals, technologies, vision and challenges. Sensors (Basel, Switzerland) **21**(24) (2021). https://doi.org/10.3390/s21248448
3. Amershi, S., et al.: Guidelines for human-AI interaction. In: Brewster, S., Fitzpatrick, G., Cox, A., Kostakos, V. (eds.) Proceedings of the 2019 CHI Conference on Human Factors in Computing Systems, New York, NY, USA, pp. 1–13. ACM (2019). https://doi.org/10.1145/3290605.3300233, https://www.microsoft.com/en-us/research/uploads/prod/2019/01/Guidelines-for-Human-AI-Interaction-camera-ready.pdf
4. Angelov, P.P., Soares, E.A., Jiang, R., Arnold, N.I., Atkinson, P.M.: Explainable artificial intelligence: an analytical review. Wiley Interdisc. Rev. Data Min. Knowl. Discov. **11**(5), e1424 (2021). https://doi.org/10.1002/widm.1424, https://wires.onlinelibrary.wiley.com/doi/pdf/10.1002/widm.1424
5. Arbeitsgemeinschaft Verbrauchs- und Medienanalyse: Den markt im blick. ba- sisinformationen für fundierte mediaentscheidungen: Vuma touchpoints 2022
6. Basir: Github - basir/support-desk-app (2022). https://github.com/basir/support-desk-app
7. Borji, A.: A categorical archive of ChatGPT failures (2023). https://doi.org/10.21203/rs.3.rs-2895792/v1, https://www.researchsquare.com/article/rs-2895792/v1
8. Bortz, J., Schuster, C.: Statistik für Human- und Sozialwissenschaftler. SpringerLink (2010). https://link.springer.com/book/10.1007/978-3-642-12770-0
9. Bui, L., Pezzola, M., Bandara, D.: How do AI explanations affect human-AI trust? In: Degen, H., Ntoa, S. (eds.) Artificial Intelligence in HCI, LNCS, vol. 14050, pp. 175–183. Springer, Cham (2023). https://doi.org/10.1007/978-3-031-35891-3_12
10. Cabitza, F., et al.: Quod ERAT demonstrandum? - towards a typology of the concept of explanation for the design of explainable AI. Expert Syst. Appl. **213**, 118888 (2023). https://doi.org/10.1016/j.eswa.2022.118888, https://www.sciencedirect.com/science/article/pii/S0957417422019066
11. Cawsey, A.: Planning interactive explanations. Int. J. Man-Mach. Stud. **38**(2), 169–199 (1993). https://doi.org/10.1006/imms.1993.1009, https://www.sciencedirect.com/science/article/pii/S0020737383710096
12. Chauhan, T., Sonawane, S.: Contemplation of explainable artificial intelligence techniques. Int. J. Recent Innov. Trends Comput. Commun. **10**(4), 65–71 (2022). https://doi.org/10.17762/ijritcc.v10i4.5538, https://ijritcc.org/index.php/ijritcc/article/view/5538
13. Chazette, L., Brunotte, W., Speith, T.: Exploring explainability: a definition, a model, and a knowledge catalogue. In: 2021 IEEE 29th International Requirements Engineering Conference (RE), pp. 197–208 (2021). https://doi.org/10.1109/RE51729.2021.00025
14. Chazette, L., Schneider, K.: Explainability as a non-functional requirement: challenges and recommendations. Requirements Eng. **25**(4), 493–514 (2020). https://doi.org/10.1007/s00766-020-00333-1. https://link.springer.com/article/10.1007/s00766-020-00333-1

15. Clark, L., et al.: What makes a good conversation? In: Brewster, S., Fitzpatrick, G., Cox, A., Kostakos, V. (eds.) Proceedings of the 2019 CHI Conference on Human Factors in Computing Systems, New York, NY, USA, pp. 1–12. ACM (2019). https://doi.org/10.1145/3290605.3300705, https://dl.acm.org/doi/pdf/10.1145/3290605.3300705

16. Davis, F.: Perceived usefulness, perceived ease of use, and user acceptance of information technology. MIS Quarterly **13**(3), 319–340 (1989), https://www.jstor.org/stable/pdf/249008.pdf?refreqid=fastly-default%3Ab6258134bc571c3ece377abd0b4ce6bd&ab_segments=&origin=&initiator=&acceptTC=1

17. Dazeley, R., Vamplew, P., Foale, C., Young, C., Aryal, S., Cruz, F.: Levels of explainable artificial intelligence for human-aligned conversational explanations. Artif. Intell. **299**, 103525 (2021). https://doi.org/10.1016/j.artint.2021.103525. https://www.sciencedirect.com/science/article/pii/S000437022100076X

18. Euromonitor: Top 100 city destinations index 2022 highlights the best... (2022). https://www.euromonitor.com/article/top-100-city-destinations-index-2022-highlights-the-best-performers-of-the-year

19. Ferreira, J.J., Monteiro, M.S.: What are people doing about XAI user experience? A survey on AI explainability research and practice. In: Marcus, A., Rosenzweig, E. (eds.) HCII 2020. LNCS, vol. 12201, pp. 56–73. Springer, Cham (2020). https://doi.org/10.1007/978-3-030-49760-6_4

20. Field, A., Miles, J., Field, Z.: Discovering Statistics Using R. SAGE Publications Ltd. (2012). https://uk.sagepub.com/en-gb/eur/discovering-statistics-using-r/book236067

21. Gunning, D., Stefik, M., Choi, J., Miller, T., Stumpf, S., Yang, G.Z.: XAI-explainable artificial intelligence. Sci. Robot. **4**(37) (2019). https://doi.org/10.1126/scirobotics.aay7120

22. Herczeg, M. (ed.): Software-Ergonomie. De gruyter studium. Walter de Gruyter, Boston (2018)

23. Hoffman, R.R., Miller, T., Klein, G., Mueller, S.T., Clancey, W.J.: Increasing the value of XAI for users: a psychological perspective. KI - Künstliche Intelligenz 1–11 (2023). https://doi.org/10.1007/s13218-023-00806-9. https://link.springer.com/article/10.1007/s13218-023-00806-9

24. Holzinger, A., Carrington, A., Müller, H.: Measuring the quality of explanations: the system causability scale (SCS): comparing human and machine explanations. KI - Künstliche Intelligenz **34**(2), 193–198 (2020). https://doi.org/10.1007/s13218-020-00636-z. https://link.springer.com/article/10.1007/s13218-020-00636-z

25. Information COmmissioner's Office, Alan Turing Institute: Explaining decisions made with AI. https://ico.org.uk/for-organisations/uk-gdpr-guidance-and-resources/artificial-intelligence/explaining-decisions-made-with-artificial-intelligence/

26. Jian, J.Y., Bisantz, A.M., Drury, C.G.: Foundations for an empirically determined scale of trust in automated systems. Int. J. Cogn. Ergon. **4**(1), 53–71 (2000). https://doi.org/10.1207/S15327566IJCE0401_04

27. Khurana, A., Alamzadeh, P., Chilana, P.K.: ChatrEx: designing explainable chatbot interfaces for enhancing usefulness, transparency, and trust. In: 2021 IEEE Symposium on Visual Languages and Human-Centric Computing (VL/HCC), pp. 1–11. IEEE (2021). https://doi.org/10.1109/VL/HCC51201.2021.9576440

28. Kulesza, T., Stumpf, S., Burnett, M., Yang, S., Kwan, I., Wong, W.K.: Too much, too little, or just right? Ways explanations impact end users' mental models. In:

2013 IEEE Symposium on Visual Languages and Human Centric Computing. pp. 3–10. IEEE (2013). https://doi.org/10.1109/VLHCC.2013.6645235

29. Künemund, H., Tanschus, N.M.: The technology acceptance puzzle. Results of a representative survey in lower saxony. Z. Gerontol. Geriatr. **47**(8), 641–647 (2014). https://doi.org/10.1007/s00391-014-0830-7. https://link.springer.com/article/10.1007/s00391-014-0830-7

30. Lim, B.Y., Dey, A.K.: Assessing demand for intelligibility in context-aware applications. In: Helal, S., Gellersen, H., Consolvo, S. (eds.) Withī witthayākān wichai thāng prawattisāt thōnthin, pp. 195–204. Sūn Sinlapawatthanatham Sathāban Rātchaphat Surin, Surin (2009). https://doi.org/10.1145/1620545.1620576

31. Ltifi, M.: Trust in the chatbot: a semi-human relationship. Future Bus. J. **9**(1), 1–12 (2023). https://doi.org/10.1186/s43093-023-00288-z. https://fbj.springeropen.com/articles/10.1186/s43093-023-00288-z

32. Luger, E., Sellen, A.: "like having a really bad pa". In: Kaye, J., Druin, A., Lampe, C., Morris, D., Hourcade, J.P. (eds.) Proceedings of the 2016 CHI Conference on Human Factors in Computing Systems, New York, NY, pp. 5286–5297. ACM (2016). https://doi.org/10.1145/2858036.2858288, https://dl.acm.org/doi/pdf/10.1145/2858036.2858288

33. Maulsby, D., Greenberg, S., Mander, R.: Prototyping an intelligent agent through wizard of oz. In: Proceedings of the SIGCHI Conference on Human Factors in Computing Systems - CHI'93, pp. 277–284 (1993). https://doi.org/10.1145/169059.169215, https://dl.acm.org/doi/pdf/10.1145/169059.169215

34. van Lent, M., Fisher, W., Mancuso, M.: An explainable artificial intelligence system for small-unit tactical behavior

35. Miller, T.: Explanation in artificial intelligence: insights from the social sciences. Artif. Intell. **267**, 1–38 (2019). https://doi.org/10.1016/j.artint.2018.07.007. www.sciencedirect.com/science/article/pii/S0004370218305988

36. OpenAI: Introducing ChatGPT (2022). https://openai.com/blog/chatgpt

37. Przegalinska, A., Ciechanowski, L., Stroz, A., Gloor, P., Mazurek, G.: In bot we trust: a new methodology of chatbot performance measures. Bus. Horizons **62**(6), 785–797 (2019). https://doi.org/10.1016/j.bushor.2019.08.005. https://www.sciencedirect.com/science/article/pii/S000768131930117X

38. Shin, D.: The effects of explainability and causability on perception, trust, and acceptance: implications for explainable AI. Int. J. Hum.-Comput. Stud. **146**, 102551 (2021). https://doi.org/10.1016/j.ijhcs.2020.102551. https://www.sciencedirect.com/science/article/pii/S1071581920301531

39. Venkatesh, V., Bala, H.: Technology acceptance model 3 and a research agenda on interventions. Decis. Sci. **39**(2), 273–315 (2008). https://doi.org/10.1111/j.1540-5915.2008.00192.x. https://onlinelibrary.wiley.com/doi/10.1111/j.1540-5915.2008.00192.x

40. Vereschak, O., Bailly, G., Caramiaux, B.: How to evaluate trust in AI-assisted decision making? A survey of empirical methodologies. Proc. ACM Hum.-Comput. Interact. **5**(CSCW2), 1–39 (2021). https://doi.org/10.1145/3476068. https://dl.acm.org/doi/pdf/10.1145/3476068

41. Vilone, G., Longo, L.: Notions of explainability and evaluation approaches for explainable artificial intelligence. Inform. Fusion **76**, 89–106 (2021). https://doi.org/10.1016/j.inffus.2021.05.009. https://www.sciencedirect.com/science/article/pii/S1566253521001093

42. Walter, S.: User journey mapping, 31 January 2024. https://www.sitepoint.com/premium/books/user-journey-mapping/

43. Weitz, K., Schiller, D., Schlagowski, R., Huber, T., André, E.: "let me explain!": exploring the potential of virtual agents in explainable AI interaction design. J. Multimodal User Interfaces **15**(2), 87–98 (2021). https://doi.org/10.1007/s12193-020-00332-0. https://link.springer.com/article/10.1007/s12193-020-00332-0

44. Weizenbaum, J.: Eliza–a computer program for the study of natural language communication between man and machine. Commun. ACM **9**(1), 36–45 (1966). https://doi.org/10.1145/365153.365168

45. Wu, H., Leung, S.O.: Can likert scales be treated as interval scales?–a simulation study. J. Soc. Serv. Res. **43**(4), 527–532 (2017). https://doi.org/10.1080/01488376.2017.1329775

What Is the Focus of XAI in UI Design? Prioritizing UI Design Principles for Enhancing XAI User Experience

Dian Lei[ID], Yao He, and Jianyou Zeng[✉]

China University of Geosciences, Wuhan 430000, China
{thunder98,heyao,jianyou}@cug.edu.cn

Abstract. With the widespread application of artificial intelligence (AI), the explainable AI (XAI) field has undergone a notable resurgence. In this background, the importance of user experience in XAI has become increasingly prominent. Simultaneously, the user interface (UI) serves as a crucial link between XAI and users. However, despite the existence of UI design principles for XAI, there is a lack of prioritization based on their significance. This will lead practitioners to have a vague understanding of different design principles, making it difficult to allocate design space reasonably and emphasize design focal points. This paper aims to prioritize four design principles, providing clear guidance for UI design in XAI. Initially, we conducted a lightweight summary to derive five user experience standards for non-expert users in XAI. Subsequently, we developed four corresponding webpage prototypes for the four design principles. Nineteen participants then interacted with these prototypes, providing ratings based on five user experience standards, and We calculated the weights of the design principles. Our findings indicate that, for non-expert users, "sensitivity" is the optimal UI design principle (weight = 0.3296), followed by "flexibility" (weight = 0.3014). Finally, we engage in further discussion and summarization of our research results, and present future works and limitations.

Keywords: Explainable AI · Explanation user interfaces · User experience · User interface design

1 Introduction

AI has permeated every facet of our lives and gradually integrated into our daily routines. The widespread popularity of large language models (LLMs) has further intensified AI's impact on our daily lives. However, the explanation of AI output is not only a requirement for user experience but also a legal mandate for the implementation of AI, such as the European Union's GDPR [33]. Consequently, the field of XAI has entered its third wave of research, with numerous emerging XAI technologies. In the early stages of XAI research, there was a lack of user involvement, relying primarily on the preferences of technical experts. The opinions of the Human-Computer Interaction (HCI) community

H. Degen and S. Ntoa (Eds.): HCII 2024, LNAI 14734, pp. 219–237, 2024.
https://doi.org/10.1007/978-3-031-60606-9_13

were often overlooked or even rejected [44]. This has resulted in a significant focus on algorithms and a disconnect from the actual usage environment of XAI. Later on, many HCI researchers recognized the importance of a user-centric perspective and attempted to shift the focus of XAI research from algorithms to the human [11,25,29,31]. The UI design for XAI has also garnered more attention, with UI being considered a crucial pathway for XAI output. Many researchers view UI as the second step in the entire XAI application process, serving as the bridge for presenting humanized outputs from specialized XAI data results. To reduce unnecessary text, we will generalize the UI designed for XAI as XUI, adopted the following definition to XUI: "the sum of outputs of an XAI system that the user can directly interact with." [7].

However, despite numerous attempts to enhance user experience in XAI, the current state of affairs still reflects a disconnect between user needs and existing XAI systems [25,29]. Moreover, there is limited research on how humans perceive XAI and their expectations of XAI systems [40]. Thus, improving the user experience with a human-centered approach remains a worthwhile direction in XAI. There is existing research that has summarized XUI design principles [7], but it has not prioritized weights to these principles. The design space for XUI is limited, and excessive content may lead to cognitive overload and even psychological conflicts [38]. Therefore, this vague understanding of design principles will lead to a lack of focal points of design and an inability to reasonably allocate design space. Lastly, evaluations of XAI often neglect user experience assessments [2,41]. While some research exists on XAI user experience evaluations, many standards are tailored for domain-specific professionals, creating a mismatch for non-expert users. Details are further summarized in Sect. 3.

To address these issues, we conducted a quantitative experiment aimed at prioritizing the XUI design principles that enhance user experience. Initially, we developed four webpage prototypes corresponding to four design principles. Then, Users rated these prototypes using the Analytic Hierarchy Process (AHP) to determine their weights [35], respectively. Additionally, we conducted qualitative interviews with users after they completed the quantitative experiment to validate the conclusions and address potential shortcomings in the research.

Through quantitative analysis of the data, we found that among the five XAI user experience standards, trust and understandability are the most important, with weights of 0.2903 and 0.2398, respectively. Sensitivity and flexibility are identified as the most critical XUI design principles, with weights of 0.3296 and 0.3014. We also obtained the weights of four XUI design principles under the five XAI user experience standards. The contribution of this article is twofold:

1. We provided weighted priorities for design principles aimed at enhancing XUI user experience, offering clear guidance for practitioners to allocate XUI design space reasonably.
2. Taking a Human-Centered XAI (HCXAI) perspective, we offered a lightweight summary of user experience standards for non-expert users in XAI. This provides subsequent researchers with a reference framework for better understanding and meeting the expectations of non-expert users in XAI.

2   Related Work

In this section, we first review the current status and shortcomings of user experience in the XAI field and then explore the research content related to XUI.

2.1   User Experience in XAI

Research on XAI has a long history, the first generation of XAI systems began to appear in the late 1970s. However, contemporary XAI systems still face challenges from both the first and second generations, particularly in lacking user experience [31]. In recent years, many HCI researchers have endeavored to address this issue. For example, Springer and Whittaker enhanced the transparency and user experience of intelligent systems through progressive disclosure [36]. Ferreira and Monteiro, in their literature review, observed a general lack of focus on user experience in XAI research outside the HCI community and emphasized the importance of user experience [14]. Ehsan and Riedl proposed an approach that places humans at the center of XAI, known as HCXAI. Liao et al. [11]. Liao et al. developed an XAI question bank to meet user understanding needs [24]. However, related studies point out two major issues with the user experience in XAI. First, as highlighted in the papers by Liao and miller [25,29], the existing XAI systems still suffer from a disconnect with user requirements, leading to the "inmates running the asylum" problem. Second, evaluations of XAI primarily focus on interpretability (model performance), with user evaluations often being overlooked [2,41].

2.2   UI Design for XAI

UI is crucial for XAI, serving as the bridge between users and XAI systems. Program such as DARPA's XAI and the study by Danilevsky et al. roughly divide the XAI process into two stages: the generation of raw explanations by interpretable models, followed by translation through UI into understandable content for the general public [9,16]. Therefore, many researchers have made efforts in UI design for XAI. For instance, Hohman et al. designed Gamut, an interactive explainable interface targeting expert users [18]. Rjoob developed a user interface for XAI generating Automated ECG (Electrocardiology) Interpretations [34]. Janet and Hani designed XAI interfaces tailored for finance professionals [1]. Hao-Fei Cheng and collaborators designed various explainable interfaces, including interactive and white-box, for an AI system used in university admissions [6]. Liao, adopting a scenario-based design approach, created a UI design aiming for social transparency in AI systems [25]. It is noticeable that existing XUI designs have relatively limited focus on non-expert users. This may be attributed to XAI historically catering to expert users in various domains. However, with the popularity of LLMs, such as ChatGPT, XAI stakeholders and application scenarios are rapid growth [26]. The importance of XUI for ordinary non-expert users continues to increase.

3   XAI User Experience Standards for Non-expert Users

After analyzing multiple literature on XAI user experience standards, this study provides a lightweight summary of the composition of user experience standards(see Table 1). We identified some shortcomings in existing XAI user experience standards. Firstly, there is currently no complete consensus on user experience standards for XAI, and there are too many standards related to XAI user experience, causing difficulty in flexible application during the evaluation process. Secondly, existing XAI user experience standards lack a clear definition of their target audience. Therefore, there are many standards that are not applicable to non-expert users and that non-expert users do not care about in practical use, such as Parsimony, Causality, Correct rate, etc.

Table 1. Summary of XAI user experience standards

No.	Author(s)	XAI user experience standards
01	Sajid et al. [2]	Understandability; Satisfaction; Trust; Transparency; Explanation; Trust
02	Samuli et al. [22]	Intelligibility, Comprehensibility, Interpretability; Trust; Transparency; Controllability
03	Markus et al. [23]	Understandable; Satisfaction; Explanation
04	Jasper et al. [41]	Understandable; Persuasion; Correct rate; Accuracy rate
05	Juliana J & Mateus [14]	Adoption rate; Acceptance; Satisfaction; Engagement; Persuasion; Continued use
06	Sule et al. [3]	Usefulness; Naturalness; Trust; Transparency; Controllability
07	Martijn et al. [28]	Effectiveness; Understandability; Trust; Novelty; Satisfaction; Confidence
08	Markus et al. [30]	Trust; Explanation; Satisfaction
09	Robert et al. [17]	Explanation; Satisfaction; Understandability; Curiosity; Trust
10	Nava [37]	Transparency; Scrutability; Trustworthiness; Effectiveness; Persuasiveness; Efficiency; Satisfaction
11	Tim [29]	Coherence; Simplicity; Generality; Truth; Explanation
12	Aniek [27]	Clarity; Parsimony; Completeness; Soundness
13	David & David [16]	Satisfaction; Trust; Predictability; Understandable; Correct rate
14	Nadia & Marco [4]	Trust; Transferability; Causality; Informativeness; Accountability; Transparency
15	Shane et al. [31]	Explanation; Trust; Reliance; Predictability

To address these issues. Firstly, this study adopts the HCXAI perspective to filter out standards that do not meet the needs of non-expert users. In other words, the focus is on standards that truly reflect the user experience for non-expert users, excluding any standards irrelevant to their experience. Secondly, three different levels are used to integrate XAI standards for non-expert user experience, resulting in five standards that are truly applicable to non-expert users, the details see Table 2. The specific summarized information is as follows.

3.1 Universal User Experience Level: Satisfaction

Universal user experience standards are prerequisites for any system aiming for a good user experience, similar to constituting the "baseline" for a good user experience. This study uses "satisfaction" to encompass universal user experience indicators. Satisfaction can comprehensively reflect the system's usability and the user's psychological pleasure, making it a metric for measuring the overall experience of non-expert users.

3.2 Excellent Explanation Tool Level: Persuasiveness, Efficiency

Explanation is a crucial component of XAI, and the effectiveness of explanations directly influences the user experience. Therefore, an XAI system for non-expert users should meet the requirements of an excellent explanation tool. Some standards for excellent explanation tools overlap with unique XAI user experience standards, which we will not repeat. In this study, we choose "persuasiveness" and "efficiency" as the criteria for excellent explanation tools. Persuasiveness is a key factor in the effectiveness of an XAI system, and good persuasiveness not only enhances the user experience but can also influence user behavior for better decision-making [10]. On the other hand, efficiency is crucial for user experience, providing users with a sense of fluency and confidence [8]. For non-expert users interacting with XAI systems, because the XAI systems they use lean towards frequent application, a smooth user experience is highly essential.

3.3 Unique XAI User Experience Level: Understandability, Trust

XAI systems differ from ordinary products, and users have higher expectations for attributes such as transparency, trust, and reliability. Establishing unique experiences for XAI users contributes to a more in-depth evaluation of XAI user experience. This study uses "understandability" and "trust" to reflect these unique standards. Understandability has long been a persistent issue in XAI. For example, many XAI algorithms generate graphical results, such as LIME and SHAP, which can be challenging for non-expert users to understand [20,43]. Additionally, the degree of understanding of explanations is higher when they align with the user's mental model [42]. Therefore, understandability can reflect the degree of matching between the XAI system and the user's mental model. In systems involving risks, the level of trust that users have in the system directly determines their experience [5]. Trust is one of the most important user experience characteristics for XAI aimed at ordinary non-expert users. Existing studies suggest a high dependence between trust, transparency, and controllability [11,26]. And, Research suggests that trust in intelligent systems stems from control and transparency [5]. So, Trust as an indicator can effectively reflect the non-expert user's experience with the controllability and transparency of the XAI system.

Table 2. XAI User Experience Standards

Standard	Description
Satisfaction	This standard measures whether users gain satisfaction during use
Trust	The standard of trust involves whether users increase their trust in the AI system because of the explanation method
Persuasiveness	The persuasiveness standard focuses on whether users feel that XAI's explanation is convincing
Efficiency	The efficiency standard refers to whether users feel that they have gained higher speed when understanding XAI
Understandability	The standard of understandability examines whether the content of XAI is easy for users to understand

4   Method

In order to explore the weight of design principles in XUI, we employed a mixed-method approach for experimentation and data processing. Firstly, we created four web prototypes based on four XUI design principles, and we used each of the four XUI design principles to explain the same AI medical conclusion, in this study, we assume that the user is diagnosed with coronary heart disease and has corresponding symptoms and abnormal physiological indicators. Secondly, we used the Analytic Hierarchy Process (AHP) method for quantitative analysis of user experiences with the four web prototypes [35], obtaining specific weight information. Finally, after the experiment, We conducted qualitative interviews with participants to validate the conclusions drawn from our previous quantitative analysis and to supplement areas that might have been overlooked during the experimental process.

4.1   Design Principles for Enhancing XUI User Experience

In the context of XUI design principles, we primarily adopted the principles proposed by Chromik and Butz [7] in their SLR article. However, this paper introduced some modifications to the aspect of naturalness to ensure its distinctiveness from the other three design principles. For specific design principles and explanations, see Table 3.

4.2   Prototype Design

We constructed a fictitious online health assessment scenario. Because, in the context of AI inferences related to health matters, users have a stronger demand for explanations [19]. This helps capture the attention of our participants. Our primary objective is provide an environment to experience various XUI design principles and to gather feedback data in subsequent evaluations.

In the design practice. Firstly, we used feature-based explanation style. Secondly, we designed the UI in the form of conversational agents. Finally, all our

Table 3. Design principles for XUI

Design principle	Description
A: Naturalness	This principle aims to enhance the logic and accuracy of explanations through natural language. It achieves this by using the substantial information content and rapid rationalization characteristic of natural language to generate detailed and logically sound explanations
B: Responsiveness	The principle of responsiveness aims to dynamically respond to the initial interpretation according to the user's needs, mainly through progressive disclosures of information to meet the user's needs. This method not only helps reduce the cognitive load of users but also satisfies users with different depths of understanding
C: Flexibility	The principle of flexibility encourages the use of multiple different ways of explanation to form a triangular and mutually supporting explanation mechanism and enhance the comprehensiveness and credibility of explanations
D: Sensitivity	The principle of sensitivity emphasizes the continuous adjustment of explanation principles according to the user's psychological state and usage scenarios to ensure the adaptability and effectiveness of explanations

explanatory content is in the form of post hoc local explanation. This is mainly due to the following reasons: 1) Previous research indicates that the feature-based explanation style performs well in Online Symptom Checkers (OSCs), sharing similarities with the experimental design of this study [39]. 2) The natural human demand for social explanations leads us to prefer conversational styles of explanation, and conversational methods are considered one of the most promising approaches in intelligent system explanations [29]. And intelligent agents can be easily embedded into various systems as tools for explanation [31]. Additionally, popular LLMs provide extensive technical support for conversational agents. 3) Research shows that users prefer Local Explanation in practical usage [32]. At the same time, XAI technologies for local explanations are also richer. The specific details of XUI are as follows:

Natureness. Although this may seem like a very common explanatory approach, its explanations are not only rich in information content but also quite accurate. This gives it a certain advantage in systems involving risks. For example, research indicates that when users become aware of their health anomalies, they prefer comprehensive and accurate explanations [39]. Additionally, different cultural backgrounds and preferences may lead users to prefer textual explanations [21]. Furthermore, it also offers advantages in terms of faster generation speed and rationalization speed [12]. See the specific design in Fig. 1.

Fig. 1. The XUI of Natureness.

Responsiveness. We created an interactive XUI through Progressive Disclosure to meet users' responsiveness needs. Non-expert users dislike explanations that require much effort [15], and this approach can significantly reduce the likelihood of user information overload. By progressively providing information, it becomes easier for users to obtain personalized depth of explanation. Specifically, we initially provide users with a brief natural language explanation of why they are diagnosed with coronary heart disease. Next, users are free to choose additional information they want to explore further, such as an introduction to coronary heart disease or its symptoms. Finally, users can delve into how to treat the disease. We limited the levels of Progressive Disclosure to two layers because exceeding two layers can cause users to lose their way in the hierarchy [13]. See the specific design in Fig. 2.

Flexibility. Humans seek understanding through diverse ways [7]. Similar to our research, we frequently use triangulation to reduce errors. Diverse explanatory approaches play a positive role when users are suspicious of the results. In the flexible XUI design, we emphasize corroborating various forms of explanatory materials and logical explanatory methods. In our XUI, we have set up two different diagnostic explanations for coronary heart disease: 1) Inference logic: a) inferring based on user self-reported symptoms; b) inferring based on user self-reported physiological indicators. 2) Multimedia explanation: providing detailed

Fig. 2. The XUI of Responsiveness.

explanations of users' symptoms and their self-described correspondence through videos and images[1][2]. See the specific design in Fig. 3.

Sensitivity. This principle is primarily designed to address the diverse explanation needs of users. Therefore, it requires XUI to keenly grasp changes in user explanation needs and dynamically generate corresponding explanations based on the user's psychological model and state in real-time. To show the characteristics of sensitivity, we introduce a new user context. We assume that the user had previously suffered from coronary heart disease but has been healthy for a long time. However, the AI re-diagnosed them with coronary heart disease. XAI adjusts its responses based on this new user background to demonstrate the system's adaptive adjustment to the user's background and psychological state. For instance, in this XUI, there are two instances: 1) When the AI recognizes that the user has a basic understanding of medical knowledge and treatment methods, the AI begins to attempt direct communication with the user using medical terminology abbreviations. 2) Considering the user's anxious mindset upon learning about the recurrence, the system provides emotional comfort and suggests ways to alleviate the disease. See the specific design in Fig. 4.

---

[1] https://www.youtube.com/watch?v=x6VrwrIonc0.
[2] https://www.myupchar.com/en/disease/coronary-artery-disease.

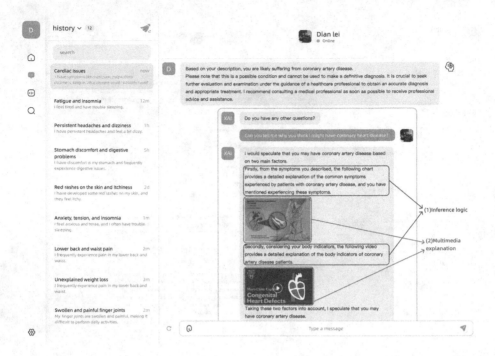

Fig. 3. The XUI of Flexibility.

4.3 Participants

To finish the experiment, we recruited 19 adult participants, including both teachers and students. The age range of the participants was 20 to 52 years (M = 28.65, SD = 9.59), comprising 9 females and 10 males. We deliberately selected individuals with diverse professional backgrounds to comprehensively assess the effectiveness of the XAI system across different demographics. The participants represented various age groups and genders to ensure the broad applicability of the experimental results. All participants possessed an adequate level of cultural literacy, the necessary knowledge, and the skills to comprehend the information presented by the XAI system. Moreover, all participants had no experience in using XAI systems. Before the start of the experiment, we provided detailed explanations to the participants to ensure their understanding of the XAI system's features, the experiment's objectives, and the meaning of the AHP scale. All participants volunteered to take part in the study, and each received a gift of approximately $10 after completion.

4.4 Data Collection and Analysis

Participants provided evaluations for each principle according to the AHP scoring table (see Table 4). Two rating tables were excluded due to the failure of the consistency check.

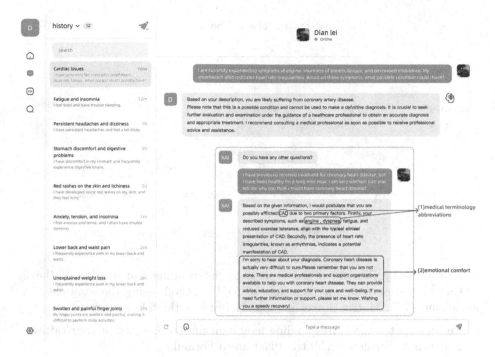

Fig. 4. The XUI of Sensitivity.

Table 4. AHP assessment ratio scale and description

Scale	Definition	Explanation
1	As important as	Means i factors are as important as j factors
3	Slightly more important	Means i factors are slightly more important than j factors
5	Obviously more important	Means i factor is obviously more important than j factor
7	More important	Means i factor is more important than j factor
9	Extremely important	Means i factor is extremely important than j factor
2, 4, 6, 8	Median	The median value of the two adjacent judgments
Count backwards	Relative count backwards	When the j factor is compared with the i factor, the judgment value is $a_{ij} = \frac{1}{a_{ji}}$

Subsequently, we proceeded with model construction. Initially, we used the design principles of the four XUIs to form the decision layer of the AHP model. Following that, we used five XAI experience standards tailored for ordinary users to constitute the criteria layer, as depicted in Fig. 5.

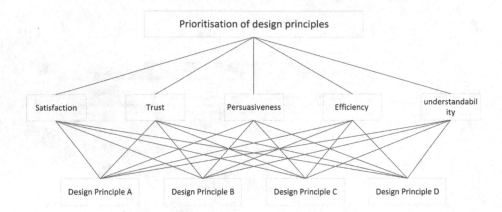

Fig. 5. The AHP model

The following illustrates the process of determining the weights of the 5 XAI user experience standards using the AHP method, using the example of a participant (P1). Matrix processing mainly involves the following steps:

1. We constructed the corresponding judgment matrix A based on user ratings, as shown in Formula 1 (Matrix diagram in Formula 2):

$$A = \begin{bmatrix} 1 & \frac{1}{5} & 3 & 1 & \frac{1}{3} \\ 5 & 1 & 4 & 3 & 3 \\ \frac{1}{3} & \frac{1}{4} & 1 & \frac{1}{3} & \frac{1}{3} \\ 1 & \frac{1}{3} & 3 & 1 & \frac{1}{5} \\ 3 & \frac{1}{3} & 3 & 5 & 1 \end{bmatrix} \tag{1}$$

$$A_{m \times n} = \begin{bmatrix} a_{11} & a_{12} & \cdots & a_{1n} \\ a_{21} & a_{22} & \cdots & a_{2n} \\ \vdots & \vdots & \ddots & \vdots \\ a_{m1} & a_{m2} & \cdots & a_{mn} \end{bmatrix} = [a_{ij}] \tag{2}$$

2. We used the square root method to obtain its column vector, i.e., using Formula 3. Then, we normalized it using Formula 4. Consequently, we obtained specific information about the weights of the 5 XAI user experience standards for P1, as shown in Table 5:

$$\bar{\omega}_i = \sqrt[m]{\prod_{j=1}^{m} a_{ij}} \tag{3}$$

$$\omega_i = \frac{\bar{\omega}_i}{\sum_{j=1}^{m} \bar{\omega}_j} \tag{4}$$

Table 5. XAI User Experience Weight for P1

Satisfaction	Trust	Persuasiveness	Efficiency	Understandability
0.1083	0.4414	0.0623	0.1123	0.2757

3. Calculate the largest eigenvalue of the matrix using Formula 5, and the calculated value is λmax = 5.4276:

$$\lambda_{\max} = \sum_{i=1}^{n} \frac{(A\omega)_i}{n\omega_i} \tag{5}$$

4. The consistency of the matrix was examined through Formulas 6 and 7, and the R.I. value is only related to the order of the judgment matrix, and it is 1.12 in this case. The obtained C.R. value of 0.0955 < 0.1 confirms that it passed the consistency test:

$$C.I. = \frac{\lambda_{\max} - n}{n - 1} \tag{6}$$

$$C.R. = \frac{C.I.}{R.I.} \tag{7}$$

5. Repeat this process to explore users' weights for each UI design principle under each user experience criterion. Multiply the weights of the corresponding design principle by the weights obtained for the respective experience criterion, and then sum them up to obtain the total weight of the decision layer.

By repeating these steps for each participant, we obtained specific scores for the four XUI design principles, their preferences for the 5 user experience standards, and the scores of the 4 XUI design principles under different user experience standards.

4.5 Interviews

To validate the rationale of our experiments, we decided to conduct interviews with users after the conclusion of the experiments. Through this interview process, we aim to ensure the credibility and effectiveness of the experiments, while also gaining insights into users' subjective experiences and feedback to better comprehend the experimental data comprehensively. The interview questions are as follows:

Q1: Please describe which specific XUI design principles had a significant impact on your user experience during the interaction with the XAI system, and explain the specific ways in which it influenced your experience.

Q2: For each of the five XAI user experience criteria, please discuss which XUI design principles achieved better results.

Q3: In your opinion, in which aspects of UI design further research or improvement is needed to achieve enhanced user interaction and interpretability?

5   Result

We obtained various data results through calculations. Specifically, we acquired the weights of users for five XAI user experience standards, shown in Table 6. Additionally, we obtained the weights for different design principles of XUI, shown in Table 7. Furthermore, the weights of different design principles of XUI under the five XAI user experience standards are shown in Table 8. Excluding the data result, and combining the content from interviews, we primarily derived the following results:

1. Trust is the most crucial aspect among the XAI user experience standards, with a weight of 0.2903, followed by Understandability, the second most important standard, with a weight of 0.2398. Responses to Q1 during the interviews also confirmed this observation. Users often consider trust as the foundation for a good XAI user experience. For example, P7 mentioned, "If the system cannot provide enough trust, I find it challenging to have a positive perception of the system. Even if other aspects are well-executed, I am likely to maintain a skeptical outlook on other outputs." Similarly, Understandability is frequently mentioned by users, and they consider it the key to the effectiveness of XAI. For instance, P2 mentioned, "Originally, I have doubts about the outputs of AI, and I turn to XAI systems to seek answers. However, if it is still difficult to understand, then one would have to seek XAI for XAI."

2. Sensitivity is the most important XUI design principle, with a weight of 0.3296, but Flexibility also holds a weight of 0.3014. Sensitivity and Flexibility are crucial for users' trust and understandability attributes. This data is corroborated by responses to Q2 during the interviews. Users perceive Sensitivity and Flexibility as sources of subjective and objective trust, respectively. Users praise the user experience of Sensitivity because it increases the content of relevant information and makes the system feel intelligent. For instance, P4 mentioned, "The XUI design with sensitivity makes me feel very relaxed. I don't need to repeatedly self-report, and the information is mostly tailored to my specific situation, reducing a lot of unnecessary information." Flexibility is well-received because it eliminates ambiguity, P12 mentioned, "For illnesses, I have both resistance and anxiety. Flexibility can meet my needs well and eliminate many doubts I have about AI conclusions."

Table 6. The weights of users for five XAI user experience standard

Satisfaction	Trust	Persuasiveness	Efficiency	Understandability
0.1604	0.2903	0.1663	0.1433	0.2398

Table 7. The weights for different design principles of XUI

Design principle A	Design principle B	Design principle C	Design principle D
0.1549	0.2140	0.3014	0.3296

6 Discussion

In this section, we will provide further insights and discussions based on the experimental results, summarizing our experiences and offering valuable information for XUI design. We will discuss on this in three subpoints:

1, Users demand "correct" explanation. Users are more concerned about whether the explanation provided is "correct" (meeting their specific needs) rather than just being comprehensive or persuasive. The weight of the Sensitivity principle, which provides context-sensitive responses, is 0.3796 under the satisfaction criterion, compared to the Flexibility principle, which provides more detailed information with a weight of 0.2722. This trend is also observed under the criterion of trust and Understandability. We can find that users generally prefer explanation that aligns with their specific needs rather than an abundance of information.

2, User experience is the core of XAI applications. Analysis of the overall weights for the four XUI designs reveals that designs centered around user-centric principles (such as Design principles C and D) often outperform designs less focused on user experience (such as Design principle A, which is more algorithm-centric). This further emphasizes the importance of HCXAI, suggesting that XAI development should prioritize user needs. If detached from user requirements, XAI may lose its practical value.

3, Diverse Demands. In our research, we discovered that differentiated needs are a highly significant issue, primarily classified into two types:

Individual Differentiation: Almost every individual exhibits different preferences. XUI outputs should emphasize differentiation. For instance, Participants P7 and P15 prefer the Naturalness principle, unlike others. They believe that adding other forms is a waste of time when textual descriptions are correct.

Scenario Differentiation: The data results indicate significant fluctuations in the weights of the four principles under different XAI user experience criteria. For example, the Naturalness principle performs relatively poorly under other user experience criteria but excels under the efficiency criterion. Therefore, adjusting XUI strategies is crucial, considering various scenarios and their unique requirements. Our Table 8 can provide a detailed reference for such adjustments.

Table 8. The weights of design principles under the five XAI user experience standards

	Design principle A	Design principle B	Design principle C	Design principle D
Persuasiveness	0.0991	0.2816	0.3209	0.2984
Satisfaction	0.1528	0.1954	0.2722	0.3796
Trust	0.1073	0.1955	0.3397	0.3576
Efficiency	0.4135	0.2056	0.2763	0.1046
Understandability	0.0844	0.1603	0.3609	0.3944

7   Limitation and Future Work

In the following section, we will discuss the limitations of our study and potential directions for future research:

1. Lack of consideration for the combination of design principles. The four principles discussed in this study are entirely combinable, yet our research treats them as independent principles to explore their individual importance. While there are challenges related to the limited UI design space, future research could investigate the impact of combining multiple XUI explanation principles on users, for a more precise response to user needs.

2. Limited consideration of scalability. Due to constraints in the experimental environment and controlled variables, our study has limitations in terms of scalability. Firstly, it only focuses on conversational AI interfaces, neglecting exploration into other forms of AI interfaces such as XR interfaces or natural interfaces. Secondly, the study does not account for changes over extended usage periods. In high-frequency usage scenarios, user demands may change, and the weight of factors like "efficiency" could correspondingly increase. Lastly, the study has a single-use scenario, real-life situations are more complex, with diverse user needs across different usage scenarios. Future research could explore the scalability of various XUI design principles in more detail.

8   Conclusion

In this paper, we conducted a study on the weighting of XUI design principles and summarized lightweight XAI user experience standards for non-expert users. Our contributions include providing weighted rankings for design principles aimed at enhancing the XUI user experience and offering guidance for practitioners in allocating XUI design space reasonably. Additionally, we provided a lightweight summary of XAI user experience standards for non-expert users from the perspective of HCXAI, serving as a reference for future researchers. As the widespread use of LLMs continues, the demand for XAI is expected to grow, especially among non-expert users. Our study provides valuable insights for specific XUI designs and contributes to improving the user experience of XAI through UI design. In the future, we hope these research findings will guide XUI design and encourage more researchers to engage in user experience studies in the field of XAI.

References

1. Adams, J., Hagras, H.: A type-2 fuzzy logic approach to explainable AI for regulatory compliance, fair customer outcomes and market stability in the global financial sector. In: 2020 IEEE International Conference on Fuzzy Systems (FUZZ-IEEE), Glasgow, United Kingdom, pp. 1–8. IEEE (2020). https://doi.org/10.1109/FUZZ48607.2020.9177542
2. Ali, S., et al.: Explainable artificial intelligence (XAI): what we know and what is left to attain trustworthy artificial intelligence. Inform. Fusion **99**, 101805 (2023)

3. Anjomshoae, S., Najjar, A., Calvaresi, D., Främling, K.: Explainable agents and robots: results from a systematic literature review. In: International Foundation for Autonomous Agents and MultiAgent Systems, pp. 1078–1088 (2019)
4. Burkart, N., Huber, M.F.: A survey on the explainability of supervised machine learning. J. Artif. Intell. Res. **70**, 245–317 (2021)
5. Cahour, B., Forzy, J.F.: Does projection into use improve trust and exploration? An example with a cruise control system. Saf. Sci. **47**(9), 1260–1270 (2009). https://doi.org/10.1016/j.ssci.2009.03.015
6. Cheng, H.F., et al.: Explaining decision-making algorithms through UI: strategies to help non-expert stakeholders. In: Proceedings of the 2019 CHI Conference on Human Factors in Computing Systems, Glasgow Scotland UK, pp. 1–12. ACM (2019). https://doi.org/10.1145/3290605.3300789
7. Chromik, M., Butz, A.: Human-XAI interaction: a review and design principles for explanation user interfaces. In: Ardito, C., et al. (eds.) INTERACT 2021. LNCS, vol. 12933, pp. 619–640. Springer, Cham (2021). https://doi.org/10.1007/978-3-030-85616-8_36
8. Confalonieri, R., Weyde, T., Besold, T.R., del Prado Martín, F.M.: Using ontologies to enhance human understandability of global post-hoc explanations of black-box models. Artif. Intell. **296**, 103471 (2021)
9. Danilevsky, M., Qian, K., Aharonov, R., Katsis, Y., Kawas, B., Sen, P.: A survey of the state of explainable AI for natural language processing. arXiv preprint arXiv:2010.00711 (2020)
10. Dragoni, M., Donadello, I., Eccher, C.: Explainable AI meets persuasiveness: translating reasoning results into behavioral change advice. Artif. Intell. Med. **105**, 101840 (2020). https://doi.org/10.1016/j.artmed.2020.101840
11. Ehsan, U., Riedl, M.O.: Human-centered explainable AI: towards a reflective sociotechnical approach. In: Stephanidis, C., Kurosu, M., Degen, H., Reinerman-Jones, L. (eds.) HCII 2020. LNCS, vol. 12424, pp. 449–466. Springer, Cham (2020). https://doi.org/10.1007/978-3-030-60117-1_33
12. Ehsan, U., Tambwekar, P., Chan, L., Harrison, B., Riedl, M.O.: Automated rationale generation: a technique for explainable AI and its effects on human perceptions. In: Proceedings of the 24th International Conference on Intelligent User Interfaces, Marina del Ray California, pp. 263–274. ACM (2019). https://doi.org/10.1145/3301275.3302316
13. Experience, W.L.i.R.B.U.: Progressive disclosure
14. Ferreira, J.J., Monteiro, M.S.: What are people doing about XAI user experience? A survey on AI explainability research and practice. In: Marcus, A., Rosenzweig, E. (eds.) HCII 2020. LNCS, vol. 12201, pp. 56–73. Springer, Cham (2020). https://doi.org/10.1007/978-3-030-49760-6_4
15. Gregor, S., Benbasat, I.: Explanations from intelligent systems: theoretical foundations and implications for practice. MIS Q. **23**, 497–530 (1999)
16. Gunning, D., Aha, D.: Darpa's explainable artificial intelligence (XAI) program. AI Mag. **40**(22), 44–58 (2019). https://doi.org/10.1609/aimag.v40i2.2850
17. Hoffman, R.R., Mueller, S.T., Klein, G., Litman, J.: Metrics for explainable AI: challenges and prospects (arXiv:1812.04608) (2019). https://doi.org/10.48550/arXiv.1812.04608, arXiv:1812.04608 [cs]
18. Hohman, F., Head, A., Caruana, R., DeLine, R., Drucker, S.M.: Gamut: a design probe to understand how data scientists understand machine learning models. In: Proceedings of the 2019 CHI Conference on Human Factors in Computing Systems, Glasgow Scotland UK, pp. 1–13. ACM (2019). https://doi.org/10.1145/3290605.3300809

19. Holzinger, A., Biemann, C., Pattichis, C.S., Kell, D.B.: What do we need to build explainable AI systems for the medical domain? (arXiv:1712.09923) (2017). arXiv:1712.09923 [cs, stat]
20. Kaur, H., Nori, H., Jenkins, S., Caruana, R., Wallach, H., Wortman Vaughan, J.: Interpreting interpretability: understanding data scientists' use of interpretability tools for machine learning. In: Proceedings of the 2020 CHI Conference on Human Factors in Computing Systems, pp. 1–14 (2020)
21. Klein, G., Rasmussen, L., Lin, M.H., Hoffman, R.R., Case, J.: Influencing preferences for different types of causal explanation of complex events. Hum. Factors **56**(8), 1380–1400 (2014)
22. Laato, S., Tiainen, M., Najmul Islam, A., Mäntymäki, M.: How to explain AI systems to end users: a systematic literature review and research agenda. Internet Res. **32**(7), 1–31 (2022)
23. Langer, M., et al.: What do we want from explainable artificial intelligence (XAI)?- a stakeholder perspective on XAI and a conceptual model guiding interdisciplinary XAI research. Artif. Intell. **296**, 103473 (2021)
24. Liao, Q.V., Gruen, D., Miller, S.: Questioning the AI: informing design practices for explainable AI user experiences. In: Proceedings of the 2020 CHI Conference on Human Factors in Computing Systems. CHI 2020, New York, NY, USA, pp. 1–15. Association for Computing Machinery (2020). https://doi.org/10.1145/3313831.3376590
25. Liao, Q.V., Varshney, K.R.: Human-centered explainable AI (XAI): from algorithms to user experiences (arXiv:2110.10790) (2022). https://doi.org/10.48550/arXiv.2110.10790, arXiv:2110.10790 [cs]
26. Liao, Q.V., Vaughan, J.W.: Ai transparency in the age of LLMS: a human-centered research roadmap (arXiv:2306.01941) (2023). https://doi.org/10.48550/arXiv.2306.01941, arXiv:2306.01941 [cs]
27. Markus, A.F., Kors, J.A., Rijnbeek, P.R.: The role of explainability in creating trustworthy artificial intelligence for health care: a comprehensive survey of the terminology, design choices, and evaluation strategies. J. Biomed. Inform. **113**, 103655 (2021)
28. Millecamp, M., Htun, N.N., Conati, C., Verbert, K.: To explain or not to explain: the effects of personal characteristics when explaining music recommendations. In: Proceedings of the 24th International Conference on Intelligent User Interfaces, Marina del Ray California, pp. 397–407. ACM (2019). https://doi.org/10.1145/3301275.3302313
29. Miller, T.: Explanation in artificial intelligence: insights from the social sciences. Artif. Intell. **267**, 1–38 (2019)
30. Mohseni, S., Zarei, N., Ragan, E.D.: A multidisciplinary survey and framework for design and evaluation of explainable AI systems. ACM Trans. Interact. Intell. Syst. **11**(3–4), 24:1-24:45 (2021)
31. Mueller, S.T., Hoffman, R.R., Clancey, W., Emrey, A., Klein, G.: Explanation in human-AI systems: a literature meta-review, synopsis of key ideas and publications, and bibliography for explainable AI (arXiv:1902.01876) (2019). arXiv:1902.01876 [cs]
32. Radensky, M., Downey, D., Lo, K., Popovic, Z., Weld, D.S.: Exploring the role of local and global explanations in recommender systems. In: CHI Conference on Human Factors in Computing Systems Extended Abstracts, New Orleans LA USA, pp. 1–7. ACM (2022)
33. Regulation, P.: Regulation (EU) 2016/679 of the European parliament and of the council. Regulation (EU) **679**, 2016 (2016)

34. Rjoob, K., et al.: Towards explainable artificial intelligence and explanation user interfaces to open the 'Black Box' of Automated ECG interpretation. In: Reis, T., Bornschlegl, M.X., Angelini, M., Hemmje, M.L. (eds.) AVI-BDA/ITAVIS – 2020. LNCS, vol. 12585, pp. 96–108. Springer, Cham (2021). https://doi.org/10.1007/978-3-030-68007-7_6
35. Saaty, T.L.: What is the analytic hierarchy process? In: Mitra, G., Greenberg, H.J., Lootsma, F.A., Rijkaert, M.J., Zimmermann, H.J. (eds.) Mathematical Models for Decision Support, vol. 48. Springer, Berlin (1988). https://doi.org/10.1007/978-3-642-83555-1_5
36. Springer, A., Whittaker, S.: Progressive disclosure: designing for effective transparency (arXiv:1811.02164) (2018). https://doi.org/10.48550/arXiv.1811.02164, arXiv:1811.02164 [cs]
37. Tintarev, N.: Explanations of recommendations. In: Proceedings of the 2007 ACM Conference on Recommender Systems, Minneapolis MN USA, pp. 203–206. ACM (2007)
38. Tsai, C.H., Brusilovsky, P.: Evaluating visual explanations for similarity-based recommendations: user perception and performance. In: Proceedings of the 27th ACM Conference on User Modeling, Adaptation and Personalization, Larnaca Cyprus, pp. 22–30. ACM (2019). https://doi.org/10.1145/3320435.3320465
39. Tsai, C.H., You, Y., Gui, X., Kou, Y., Carroll, J.M.: Exploring and promoting diagnostic transparency and explainability in online symptom checkers. In: Proceedings of the 2021 CHI Conference on Human Factors in Computing Systems, Yokohama Japan, pp. 1–17. ACM (2021)
40. Vainio-Pekka, H., et al.: The role of explainable AI in the research field of AI ethics. ACM Trans. Interact. Intell. Syst. 13(4), 26:1-26:39 (2023). https://doi.org/10.1145/3599974
41. van der Waa, J., Nieuwburg, E., Cremers, A., Neerincx, M.: Evaluating XAI: a comparison of rule-based and example-based explanations. Artif. Intell. 291, 103404 (2021)
42. Xie, Y., Gao, G., Chen, X.A.: Outlining the design space of explainable intelligent systems for medical diagnosis (arXiv:1902.06019) (2019). arXiv:1902.06019 [cs]
43. Xu, W., Dainoff, M.J., Ge, L., Gao, Z.: Transitioning to human interaction with AI systems: new challenges and opportunities for HCI professionals to enable human-centered AI. Int. J. Hum.-Comput. Interact. 39(3), 494–518 (2023). https://doi.org/10.1080/10447318.2022.2041900
44. Yang, Q., Scuito, A., Zimmerman, J., Forlizzi, J., Steinfeld, A.: Investigating how experienced UX designers effectively work with machine learning. In: Proceedings of the 2018 Designing Interactive Systems Conference. DIS '18, New York, NY, USA, pp. 585–596. Association for Computing Machinery (2018). https://doi.org/10.1145/3196709.3196730

Navigating Transparency: The Influence of On-demand Explanations on Non-expert User Interaction with AI

Jörg Papenkordt[(✉)] [iD]

Paderborn University, Warburgerstr. 100, 33098 Paderborn, Germany
joerg.papenkordt@uni-paderborn.de

Abstract. Artificial intelligence (AI) has an increasingly powerful impact on our lives, influencing even non-expert users. This mismatch between an increasingly advanced technology on the one hand and non-expert users on the other hand can lead to unfounded reliance. To improve collaboration between end-users and the system, Explainable AI (XAI) is gaining momentum. However, recent studies yield mixed results on the effects of explanations, leaving uncertainty about whether increased transparency prevents or encourages unfounded reliance. Despite this uncertainty, it is common practice to call for transparency from AI. Thus, most systems display explanations immediately without considering the potential downsides. Still, it is uncertain when users actually need an explanation and how thoroughly they scrutinize them versus viewing them as a signal of competence. Since algorithms are vulnerable to biases and are often unable to identify incorrect advice, users need to think analytically about explanations to avoid misjudgments. If users proactively demand an explanation of the recommendation, it becomes increasingly likely that they cognitively evaluate it. Therefore, this study investigates how the accessibility of explanations—provided immediately or on-demand—affects non-expert users' willingness to rely on AI recommendations. In addition, this research analyzes whether users request an explanation in the first place and whether personal-driven or contextual factors influence the decision for or against an explanation. By examining the interaction between an AI recommendation system and non-expert users, this experiment reveals that many non-expert users abstain from requesting verbal explanations despite performing significantly better with them. It sheds light on the circumstances prompting users to seek explanations, demonstrating that personal factors drive general explanation demands, while contextual factors influence the number of explanations requested. Surprisingly, participants attribute similar importance to on-demand and immediately provided explanations, indicating that increased transparency through verbal explanations results in unfounded reliance.

Keywords: Artificial Intelligence · Explanations · Human AI Interaction

ⓒ The Author(s), under exclusive license to Springer Nature Switzerland AG 2024
H. Degen and S. Ntoa (Eds.): HCII 2024, LNAI 14734, pp. 238–263, 2024.
https://doi.org/10.1007/978-3-031-60606-9_14

1   Introduction

The integration of AI across diverse industries signals a transformative era wherein tasks traditionally handled solely by humans are now shared with AI systems. Contrary to initial speculations, AI will not be able to perform most activities autonomously but rather transform activities and work environments in a way that humans and AI have to collaborate [8]. This paradigm shift emphasizes the significance of understanding AI and its recommendations not just for aspiring AI professionals, but also for individuals who are not experts in computer science, mathematics, or AI engineering [34]. As AI technologies become commonplace in various domains, the ability of non-expert users to interact effectively with these technologies becomes imperative [42]. However, despite the increasing importance of AI skills across disciplines and industries [42], the collaboration of non-expert users with AI technologies remains an underexplored research area [37,41]. This neglect is also reflected in AI explanations as they are not designed to suit the needs of non-experts [1,38]. So, while AI often enhances decision-making and performance, users exhibit a persistent skepticism towards AI recommendations [19,30]. This skepticism, rooted in a lack of understanding of the technology, can impede effective utilization and lead to incorrect usage [15]. Misconceptions about AI hinder proficient utilization, effective collaboration, and critical evaluation by users [26]. Consequently, integrating human decision-making remains a complex challenge in this research domain [12]. The increasing complexity of AI systems is compounding this challenge, resulting in opaque models and recommendations that lack transparency for both users and developers [11]. This "black box" nature introduces significant drawbacks, including compromised user trust, reduced error-proofing, limited contestability, and bounded accountability [46]. XAI emerges as a key solution to address these issues, expecting that increased transparency will enhance decision-making by fostering AI recommendations comprehensibility [18,38]. Nevertheless, recent research demonstrates mixed effects of explanations on human-AI collaboration [39,47,49]. This poses the question of whether users always need an explanation as it is unclear if increased transparency of an AI recommendation improves decision-making. While the methodological [18,38], contextual [14,36], personal [30,50] and temporal factors [22,35,44] have already been investigated, there is a notable research gap regarding the influence of the accessibility of AI-generated explanations. Conceivably, influencing the accessibility through an on-demand option will reduce known problems such as information overload [7] and reactance of a contrary recommendation [27] or even lead to requested explanations being more valued and recognized instead of being considered as a general signal of competence [6,33]. Therefore, this study examines how the accessibility of explanations—whether immediately displayed or only available on demand—affects non-expert users' willingness to rely on AI recommendations. This investigation contributes valuable insights into the nuanced dynamics of the non-expert-AI collaboration, shedding light on factors that influence the request for an explanation and highlighting the effects of on-demand explanations on the human-AI interaction.

2   Related Literature

Many organizations are actively integrating AI as a decision-support aid for their employees due to its remarkable performance, which rivals human capabilities in various tasks [24]. For instance, AI is being used in mobility [4], in medicine [31], in human resources [32], or in finance [51]. Numerous studies have demonstrated that overall performance increases when users receive an AI recommendation–even when the recommendations are occasionally imperfect AI often improves decision-making or performance [43,55,57]. Sometimes algorithms even surpass human experts in complex tasks like surgery [40] or crime prediction [56]. Nevertheless, the cooperation between humans and AI often fails to achieve optimal outcomes and does not always work flawlessly. In practice, this has resulted in discriminatory parole decisions, complications with surgical robots, and safety hazards in self-driving cars [52]. Accordingly, biases and problems caused by algorithms seem to be ubiquitous. As a result, handling AI technologies is becoming an essential skill across all disciplines and industries [42].

This capability is becoming even more urgent as research recognizes that highly precise models alone do not solve all these issues, as users often underperform the numerical certainties of the AI recommendation [13,43,57] and partially exhibit resistance towards AI recommendations [19,30]. Additionally, the increasing complexity of the systems makes it particularly difficult for end users with a low level of technical expertise to work effectively with the systems [10].

To address these obstacles and encourage collaboration, many scholars initially expected that explanations would guide users in understanding AI predictions, interpreting recommendations, and identifying instances of incorrect AI reasoning [6,20]. Accordingly, developers, researchers, and policymakers called for explanations to enhance the comprehensibility of AI systems [2,3,25]. As a result, the XAI research field aims to provide insights into the "black box" nature of an AI system and state why the system arrives at a particular decision or recommendation to enable users to understand, appropriately rely on, and effectively manage the system [3,29,38]. Thus, researchers started to develop various strategies to explain AI models with the help of understandable texts (e.g., counterfactual, deductive) or numbers (e.g., certainty measures) to foster humans' capability for utilizing external information to adjust their reliance [3,39]. While some researchers prefer numerical certainties as they sensitize the user to AI errors, the collaborative performance of the user and AI usually falls behind the displayed certainty measure of the AI recommendation and thus the sole AI performance [23,39,43]. By contrast, others maintain that verbal explanations simplify the process of forming a correct mental model of the AI and are easier to comprehend, making them favored by users [18,38]. However, since recent studies show ambiguous results regarding the utility of explanations for decision-making, an even more fundamental issue remains as to whether explanations of the system aid users in spotting erroneous recommendations or if these explanations instead make correct and erroneous recommendations appear more plausible [23,54].

On the one side, several studies demonstrate various benefits of explanations, such as improved transparency, increased decision quality, and enhanced reliance [21,45,57]. On the other side, many studies reveal negative consequences of the explanations presented, such as underreliance when it operates flawlessly and overreliance when the AI performs poorly [13,16,23,33,55]. Accordingly, explanations are difficult to design effectively as the system cannot identify incorrect advice [10]. Therefore, it is the users' responsibility to determine when to follow the system's recommendations [23]. Yet, users often do not thoroughly analyze the given explanations to distinguish between plausible and erroneous AI suggestions but rather see them as a universal signal of competence [6,33]. To avoid misjudgments, users must engage cognitively with the explanation, which requires time and effort [9,10,28]. According to Kahnemann's dual process theory, users should think through the explanations analytically (system 2) instead of applying feelings, intuitions, and decision-making heuristics (system 1) [17]. However, this is probably barely achievable in reality, as users might doubt the overall benefit of the system if they are required to scrutinize every recommendation. This cost-benefit ratio of cognitive efforts (costs) to perceived utility (benefit) of an explanation needs consideration as users strategically navigate the trade-off between the effort of manual verification of the task and the effort to verify the explanation of the AI [10,53].

In other words, this implies that users consciously or subconsciously strategically consider how much cognitive effort they invest in validating or even acknowledging a directly displayed explanation. Consequently, in preventing problems such as the perception of the explanation as a general signal of quality [6,33], information overload [7], or reactance [27], this paper proposes to leave the decision of demanding an explanation up to the user. Whereas many studies attempted multiple approaches such as the type of explanation [18,38,43], the context of the task [14,36], the personal factors [30,50], or the response time [22,35,44] to assess the impact on reliance, far less consideration is devoted to the effects of accessibility of an explanation. An initial study previously revealed that, in contrast to a directly displayed explanation of an AI, the opportunity of being able to demand an explanation increases the willingness of the decision-maker to engage with the explanation cognitively and thus to evaluate it analytically and individually [9]. However, Buccinca et al. [9] do not consider whether the user has actually requested an explanation or if certain users differ in their demand for explanations. Moreover, their study focuses predominantly on intrinsic factors that influence the motivation to increase cognitive engagement with the explanation and neglects the influences of the cost-benefit ratio.

Overall, my study explores what happens to the interaction dynamics between a non-expert user and AI when the decision as to whether an additional explanation is required is entirely up to the user. Additionally, the study investigates how this decision is being influenced by user-driven or contextual factors (e.g., numerical uncertainties or financial incentives). This shift in control may alter interaction dynamics by empowering users to regulate the amount of incoming information and determine when they desire or require additional clarification through an explanation. This study contributes to the research field of XAI in multiple ways. Firstly, it examines non-expert user interactions with a real AI-recommender system, a cooperation type increasingly relevant in practice but often neglected in theory. Secondly, it employs an experimental design to empirically explore whether additional explanations are always considered necessary by users and whether user-driven or contextual factors influence the users' request for an explanation. Thirdly, it systematically tests how the accessibility of explanations—whether immediately displayed or only available on demand—affects non-expert users' perceived validity of correct and incorrect recommendations.

3   Experiment

3.1   Experimental Design

Regarding the experimental design, this study builds upon the foundation laid by Papenkordt et al. [43]. In the prior study, participants had to solve ten different classification tasks, aided by a specially developed AI. In each of the ten classification tasks, participants had to assign an object to one of two groups. The two groups consisted of three more or less related objects. The algorithm supported the classification with an assignment recommendation. The AI used is a class expression learning algorithm for the description logic ALC and was trained on the DBpedia knowledge graph to detect class expressions that were later verbalized manually to natural-language explanations. Thus, the AI always provided numerical certainty and a short verbal explanation to justify its proposed solution. Participants had the autonomy to accept or reject the AI's recommendations, with feedback provided after each task. Correct answers were rewarded with €0.40, culminating in a potential total reward of €4.00. To deter participants from conducting a web search, they were given 30 s per task. As soon as the time expired, the current task was classified as missing, and the participants were automatically forwarded to the next task. To avoid timeouts, participants were also given a sample task before the actual start of the experiment. To maintain consistency between the groups, the order of the tasks stayed the same.

However, this study diverges from Papenkordt et al. [43] by introducing a novel element focused on exploring the factors influencing the desire for explanations and the impact of an on-demand explanation on human-AI interaction. Unlike the previous study, where explanations were provided by default, participants in this study had the opportunity to actively demand a verbal explanation for a fee of €0.15. Participants were unable to achieve negative earnings. The on-demand option focuses on verbal explanation, as descriptive explanations have the advantage of directly providing a rationale for the recommendation and are easier to process by users [18,38]. Thus, employing a between-subject design, participants were randomly assigned to one of two treatment groups (Table 1).

Table 1. Description of the treatment groups

No.	Group description	AI-Advice	Form of explanation
1	Verb.Expl. (on demand)	Yes	Possibility to demand a verbal explanation
2	Num.&Verb.Expl. (on demand)	Yes	Numerical certainty displayed & possibility to demand a verbal explanation

In the first group, participants could demand a verbal explanation for each AI recommendation. In the other group, the recommendations were already displayed in conjunction with their specific numerical certainties, with participants still having the option to request a verbal explanation. During analysis, both groups can be further categorized to determine the extent to which verbal explanations were demanded within each group (Table 2).

Table 2. Description of the subdivided treatment groups

No.	Group description	AI-Advice	Form of explanation
1a	Verb.Expl. (no demand)	Yes	verbal explanation not demanded
1b	Verb.Expl. (demand)	Yes	verbal explanation demanded
2a	Num.&Verb.Expl. (no demand)	Yes	Numerical certainty displayed & verbal explanation not demanded
2b	Num.&Verb.Expl. (demand)	Yes	Numerical certainty displayed & verbal explanation demanded

All participants were surveyed before the classification tasks. The questionnaire included demographic information, attitudes toward AI [48], and the frequency of AI use. It was ensured that the participants were non-expert users and that the AI performed better than humans but was not unflawed. Otherwise, there would be no additional incentive for the human decision-maker to over- or under-rely on the AI's recommendation. Firstly, the classification tasks encompassed different domains, such as the classification of books, rivers, countries, or politicians, maximizing the probability that the decisions were made under high uncertainty. Second, the results of a *baseline* [43] validated this assumption by demonstrating that the classification tasks could rarely be solved correctly with certainty without the support of the AI, allowing the AI to improve performance. Third, the misclassification of the AI in task 4 creates the possibility that humans over-rely on the AI recommendation. Therefore, the design allows this study to explore the calibration of reliance and not exclusively concentrate on increasing reliance as in many other experimental settings that investigate human-AI interaction.

3.2   Data and Analysis

A total of 151 subjects took part in the study. The participants were divided into two experimental groups (Appendix A, group 1&2). The mean age of the participants of the experimental groups was 34.67 years ($SD = 12.66$), with 45.03% identifying as male, 54.30% identifying as female, and 0.66% as diverse. On average, the participants achieved a reward of €2.05 ($SD = 0.83$) and needed an average time of 10.72 ($SD = 7.18$) seconds per task. The frequency of AI use in a week and the attitude towards AI were also controlled. Both experimental groups do not differ considerably concerning these attributes. On average, the participants in the separate groups use AI about four to five times a week and have a more positive attitude towards AI ($Mean = 0.98, SD = 0.553$).

Before explaining the structure of the analysis, it is essential to emphasize that the data are panel data. Therefore, a differentiation is made between time-invariant variables (such as age or gender) and time-varying variables (such as demanding a verbal explanation). Time-invariant variables help capture stable individual differences while time-varying variables account for changes that occur within individuals or entities over time. This differentiation is crucial for a nuanced understanding of the factors influencing the dependent variables.

The analysis is divided into two primary sections. The first main section focuses on factors influencing the demands for verbal explanations. Therefore, the analysis begins by examining the extent to which verbal explanations are demanded by non-experts, comparing the two experimental groups. Additionally, this part investigates whether personal or contextual factors influence the decision for or against an explanation by exploring the influence of time-invariant variables using ordered probit models and time-varying variables using probit models.

The second part of the analysis assesses how the accessibility of explanations—whether immediately displayed or only available on demand—affects non-expert users' decision-making process. Therefore, the data from Papenkordt et al. [43] is consulted to conduct this analysis, to investigate whether the direct display, the mere option (on demand), or the choice for or against an explanation (no demand/demand) influences the decision-making process by analyzing the effects on the time per task, user reliance on AI recommendations, and the correctness of classifications. Consequently, this study systematically tests whether displayed or on-demand explanations of AI systems indeed assist non-expert users in making improved decisions.

4   Results

4.1   Factors Influencing Verbal Explanation Demands

Verbal Explanation Demands by Non-Expert Users. Initially, I examine the factors influencing the demand for verbal explanations. The analysis begins by investigating the proportion of participants in both groups who demand verbal explanations (Fig. 1). Therefore, the rate of demands for verbal explanations in the treatment groups *Num. & Verb.Expl. (on demand)* and *Verb.Expl. (on demand)* is analyzed.

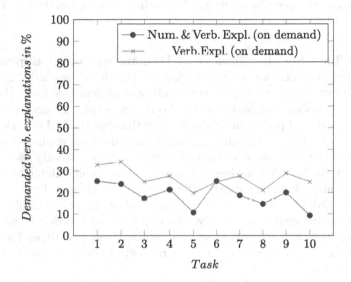

Fig. 1. Trend of the number of demanded verbal explanations

The group without numerical explanations exhibits a significantly higher proportion of verbal explanation demands (Fisher's exact test: $p < .01$). In the group with numerical explanations, verbal explanations were requested in 18.67% of cases, compared to 26.71% in the group without numerical explanations. However, in the majority of the classification tasks, no verbal explanations are requested at all. Furthermore, there was a decrease after the AI error (task 4).

Characteristics of Non-Expert Users Demanding Verbal Explanations. This section explores the characteristics of individuals who demanded a verbal explanation. Participants in the group *Num. & Verb.Expl. (on demand)* are categorized into *Num. & Verb.Expl. (demand)* as soon as they request a single verbal explanation. 49.33% of participants requested a verbal explanation at least once in *Num. & Verb.Expl. (on demand)* and 50.00% in *Verb.Expl. (on demand)*. This indicates that approximately 50% of the participants in both groups refrained from demanding any verbal explanation throughout the tasks.

A comparison between the participants in *Num.&Verb.Expl. (no demand)* and *Num.&Verb.Expl. (demand)* as well as *Verb.Expl. (no demand)* and *Verb.Expl. (demand)*, to explore the impact of AI experiences (attitude toward AI, weekly use of AI) and demographic factors (gender, age, education) on the decision to request a verbal explanation, show the following results: Specifically, participants in *Num.&Verb.Expl. (no demand)* and *Verb.Expl. (no demand)* have a lower education level (Fisher's exact tests: $p < .1$)[1] and a more negative attitude toward AI ($z = -2.057, p = 0.040, z = -2.963, p = 0.003$). Additionally, participants in *Verb.Expl. (no demand)* are significantly older ($z = 2.304, p = 0.021$). This nuanced insight into participant characteristics helps identify factors influencing the decision to demand a verbal explanation during AI recommendation tasks.

Factors Influencing the Number of Demanded Verbal Explanations.
After assessing the decision to seek verbal explanations (yes/no), the analysis turns to the factors influencing the actual number of demanded verbal explanations. Thus, the focus is on participants who requested at least one verbal explanation. Using ordered probit models to explore the impact of AI experiences and demographic variables on the quantity of demanded verbal explanations (Table 3). As the independent variables attitudes toward AI and weekly use of AI correlate, they were included in different models. The results highlight that only the group membership significantly influences the number of demanded verbal explanations. Subjects without directly displayed numerical certainties are significantly more inclined to demand verbal explanations (models I and II). The median indicates that subjects most frequently asked five times for a verbal explanation in the group without a given numerical certainty and in the other group four times.

Since the data is panel data, allowing each task to be considered independently, the influence of time-varying variables on the number of demanded verbal explanations is examined. These variables included perceived task difficulty, the impact of AI recommendation error, and numerical certainty of AI recommendations (task type). So, the three task types reflect the three actual numerical certainties 66%, 83%, and 100% of the AI recommendations. The variable perceived task difficulty is formed of the mean values of the correct classifications per task from the *baseline study*. It serves as a proxy for the task's difficulty. Furthermore, the impact of the misclassification is modeled by a dummy variable differentiating tasks before and after the recommendation error announcement. It is relevant to emphasize that N in the table no longer represents the number of participants but the number of classification decisions (75 subjects x 10 tasks = 750 classifications). Two probit models were calculated for the investigation, as the variable task difficulty correlates with the variable task type. The results, presented in Table 4, show that individuals in the group without

---

[1] Since the exact list of all separately conducted group comparisons would be very confusing–it is just remarked that the p-values for all comparisons were consistently at least $p < .1$.

Table 3. Between-variation analysis I

	Dependent variable	
	No. of Demanded Verb.Expl.	
	I	II
Gender (ref. = men)	0.105	0.183
	(0.678)	(0.469)
Age	0.013	0.017
	(0.262)	(0.118)
Education (ref. = no degree)		
Secondary level 2	−0.460	−0.472
	(0.269)	(0.256)
University degree	0.342	0.338
	(0.350)	(0.355)
AI-Attitude	-0.197	
	(0.158)	
Weekly use of AI		0.065
		(0.241)
Verb. Expl.(ref. = demand)		
Num.&Verb. Expl.(demand)	−0.648***	−0.677***
	(0.009)	(0.007)
N	75	75

***$p < .01$, **$p < .05$, *$p < .1$

directly displaying numerical explanations demanded significantly more verbal explanations. Additionally, fewer explanations are requested for tasks perceived as easier, as indicated by the effects of the variables task difficulty (model III) and task type (model IV). However, no significant difference is perceived between the 66% and 83% tasks, and the demand for verbal explanations did not decrease significantly after the error.

Given the correlation between perceived task difficulty and task type, the subsequent analysis focuses on a detailed examination of task types (Fig. 2). In the cohort where numerical certainty of AI recommendations is directly displayed, tasks with higher numerical certainty exhibit a lower rate of demanded verbal explanations. Notably, the rate of demanded verbal explanations is lower for tasks with 100% certainty compared to the other two task types (Fisher's exact tests: $p < .01$)[2]. Despite this, it is noteworthy that verbal explanations are still demanded in 12% of cases for tasks with a 100% numerical certainty. Conversely, in the group where numerical certainty is not directly displayed, the 66% and 83% tasks show no significant difference in the rate of demanded verbal

---

[2] Since the exact list of all separately conducted group comparisons would be very confusing–it is just remarked that the p-values for all comparisons were consistently at least $p < .01$.

Table 4. Within variation analysis I

	Dependent variable	
	No. of Demanded Verb.Expl.	
	III	IV
Task difficulty	−0.716**	
	(0.039)	
Task type (ref. = num.cert. 66%)		
83%		−0.079
		(0.487)
100%		−0.453***
		(0.001)
Impact of the error	−0.083	−0.075
	(0.539)	(0.505)
Verb. Expl.(ref. = demand)		
Num. & Verb. Expl.(demand)	−0.404***	−0.406***
	(0.000)	(0.000)
Constant	0.478***	0.299***
	(0.001)	(0.004)
N	750	750

$^{***}p < .01,\ ^{**}p < .05,\ ^{*}p < .1$

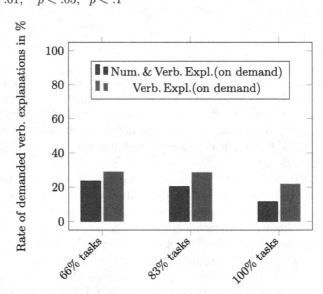

Fig. 2. Rate of demanded verbal explanations per task type and group

explanations. Only in the 100% tasks is the rate of received verbal explanations significantly lower than the other two task types (Fisher's exact tests: $p < .1$) (See footnote 1).

4.2   Effects of Demanding a Verbal Explanation

After analyzing whether users demand an explanation and whether personal or contextual factors influence the decision for or against an explanation, this section focuses on the impact of the on-demand option on time, reliance, and performance. Different group comparisons are made between groups with no explanations, directly displayed explanations, and specifically demanded explanations to quantify and contextualize the effects. These comparisons enable this study to investigate whether influencing the accessibility of an explanation through an on-demand option improves user decisions regarding the evaluation of correct and incorrect recommendations.

For this purpose, the data from a prior study [43] are included in this analysis, expanding and enriching my results. In the study of Papenkordt et al. [43], the participants were randomly assigned to one of four groups to investigate the influence of numerical, verbal, or a combination of both explanations on the performance and reliance in human-AI interaction. In the first group, the participants only received the assignment recommendation of the AI (*control group*). In the second group, they additionally received the numerical certainty of the AI recommendation (*Num.Expl.* group), and the third group directly received the verbal explanation of the AI recommendation (*Verb.Expl.* group). The fourth and last group immediately received both explanations as well as the AI's assignment recommendation (*Num.&Verb.Expl.* group). Therefore, the difference between the third and fourth groups of the prior study [43] and the treatment groups involved in this experiment is whether the verbal explanation is displayed directly or has to be actively demanded. To further emphasize the compatibility of the two studies, controlling for demographic variables shows a similar composition of the two samples (Appendix A). Thus, it can be observed that the 322 participants in Papenkordt et al. [43] are also approximately equally distributed across the four experimental groups (Appendix A, groups 3–6). The average age of the sample is 31 years and shows a slight surplus of female participants (57.45%). Furthermore, the positive attitudes toward AI ($M = 0.973$) and the frequency of AI use (3–4 times a week) are similar to this study. Finally, these characteristics are practically balanced among the four groups. Therefore, no substantial differences in the composition of the groups can be identified, and the data will be considered jointly in this analysis.

Effects of Demanding a Verbal Explanation on the Time per Task. When analyzing the time per task across the different groups (Appendix A), it becomes evident that the two groups with directly displayed verbal explanations need significantly more time compared to other groups (Mann-Whitney-U-Tests:$p < .01$) (See footnote 2). When considering the instances where a verbal explanation is demanded, the *Verb.Expl. (on demand)* group, when not requesting a verbal explanation, takes an average of 9.40 s ($SD = 6.87$) for a decision, contrasting with 17.18 s ($SD = 6.89$) when demanding one. Similarly, the *Num.&Verb.Expl. (on demand)* group requires 9.19 s ($SD = 6.30$) without a verbal explanation and 13.62 s ($SD = 6.52$) with one. Groups with a verbal explanation (directly displayed or demanded) need significantly more decision time compared to the others (Mann-Whitney-U-Tests: $p < .01$) (See footnote 2). Moreover, when comparing the four groups with verbal explanations, the *Verb.Expl. (demand)* group requires significantly more time per task than the other three (Mann-Whitney-U-Tests: $p < .01$) (See footnote 2), while the *Num.&Verb.Expl. (demand)* group requires significantly less time (Mann-Whitney-U-Tests: $p < .01$) (See footnote 2).

Effects of Demanding a Verbal Explanation on Reliance. To investigate the effect of the treatments on reliance, the rate of participants following the AI recommendation is determined (Fig. 3). All groups, regardless of the type of explanation, differ significantly from the *control* group in terms of overall reliance on the AI recommendation (Fisher's exact tests: $p < .1$) (See footnote 1). More transparency of the AI recommendation–as achieved through numerical certainty or verbal explanations–therefore always seems to lead to a significant increase in reliance. Additionally, groups with directly displayed verbal explanations differ significantly from their counterparts with on-demand options (Fisher's exact tests: $p < .01$) (See footnote 2).

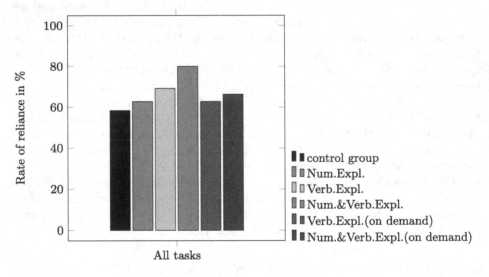

Fig. 3. Rate of reliance overall tasks per group

For a comprehensive analysis, it is investigated whether other independent variables affect reliance. Thus, the influence of the time-invariant variables on reliance is explored using two ordered probit models (Appendix B, model V & VI). When analyzing the effects of demographic variables (age, gender, and education) on reliance (models V & VI), age significantly negatively affects reliance, while increasing education positively impacts it. Moreover, the attitude toward

AI (model V) and weekly use of AI (model VI) also significantly positively influence reliance. When focusing on the treatment effects, each group with some explanation shows significantly higher reliance than the control group, except the *Num.Expl.* group in model V.

The next step is to check how the actual request of a verbal explanation for a classification decision affects reliance (Fig. 4). This entails redividing the groups *Verb.Expl. (on demand)* and *Num.&Verb.Expl. (on demand)* again. The results demonstrate that the mere option of a verbal explanation does not significantly influence the reliance rate on the AI recommendation. This is evident from the fact that the *control* group and the *Verb. Expl. (no demand)* as well as the groups *Num. Expl.* and *Num.&Verb.Expl. (no demand)* do not differ significantly in the reliance rate. The groups do not differ in transparency, as the option of a verbal explanation was not requested during the decision. Additionally, the rate of reliance in the groups without a requested verbal explanation is significantly lower than in the respective groups in which the verbal explanation was displayed directly or requested specifically (Fishers's exact tests: $p < .05$)[3].

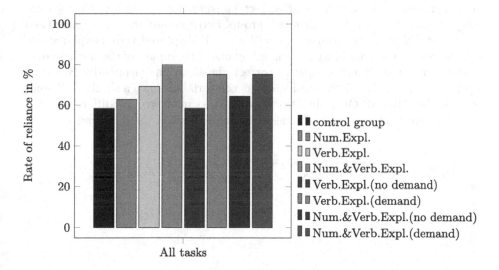

Fig. 4. Rate of reliance overall tasks per subdivided group

In this section, for the benefit of extensive analysis, models IX and X (Appendix C) are used to investigate the effects of time-varying factors on the reliance. The total number of classification decisions included in the models amounts to 4,585 decisions, as the time limit was exceeded for 145 classifications. Since the participants were then forwarded to the next task without making a

---

[3] Since the exact list of all separately conducted group comparisons would be very confusing–it is just remarked that the p-values for all comparisons were consistently at least $p < .05$.

decision, these classifications were not considered. Notably, more missing decisions occur in groups with a verbal explanation (Fishers's exact test: $p < .01$) (See footnote 2), irrespective of whether the verbal explanation is requested or displayed. The result reveals that the task difficulty (model IX) and the task type of 100% (model X) have a significant influence on the reliance. Additionally, the treatment effects on reliance demonstrate that all treatments, except for the *Verb.Expl. (no demand)* group, significantly influence reliance compared to the *control* group. It is also noticeable that misclassification, modeled by a dummy variable for task 4, does not significantly influence the reliance (model IX & X).

Effects of Demanding a Verbal Explanation on the Correct Classifications. Given that disparities between correct classifications and reliance on the AI recommendation are confined to overreliance during the misclassification, the subsequent analysis focuses on the correct classification during task 4 (Fig. 5). During the error of the AI, the *control* (Fishers's exact tests: $p < .05$) (See footnote 3) and the *Num.Expl.* (Fishers's exact tests: $p < .1$) (See footnote 1) group show significantly higher rates of correct classifications than all other groups except for the *Verb.Expl. (on demand)* group. Furthermore, in task 4, there is no significant difference between groups with directly displayed verbal explanations and those with the possibility of demanding one. The impact of the participants' fixed effects on the total number of correct classifications (Appendix B, model VII & VIII) are only briefly considered, as the variables have a similar influence as with the reliance. Only the effects of the treatment groups differ, which is why the treatment effects are discussed in more detail in the following section.

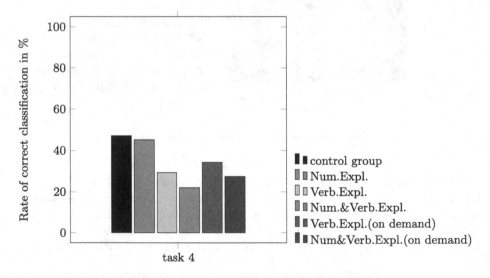

Fig. 5. Rate of correct classifications per group during the error

Thus, it is analyzed how the actual demand of a verbal explanation for a classification decision affects the correctness (Fig. 6). The rate of correct classifications during the AI error is significantly higher when participants lack any explanation opportunity (Fishers's exact tests: $p < .1$) (See footnote 1) or are only shown numerical certainty (Fishers's exact tests: $p < .1$) (See footnote 1), compared to other groups except for *Verb.Expl. (no demand)*. Focusing on the four groups with an AI recommendation and a given numerical certainty, task 4 is significantly solved correctly more often when only the numerical explanation is displayed (Fishers's exact tests: $p < .1$) (See footnote 1).

Similarly, among the groups without numerical certainty, the group relying solely on the recommendation makes correct classifications significantly more often than those with a displayed or requested verbal explanation (Fishers's exact tests: $p < .05$) (See footnote 3). The non-perceived option of a verbal explanation does not lead to a significant difference in the correct error classification compared to the three groups. In summary, increased transparency therefore does not necessarily seem to lead to a better decision during the error. Including the within-analysis (Appendix C, model XI & XII), however, it should be noted that the display of a numerical certainty, the direct display or request for a verbal explanation, or a combination of both have a significant positive effect on the total number of correct classifications made compared to the *control* group. Notably, only the two groups in which no verbal explanation is demanded do not differ significantly from the *control* group in terms of correct classifications. The other effects of the time varying variables on the correct classifications are similar to those of the reliance, except for the effects of misclassification.

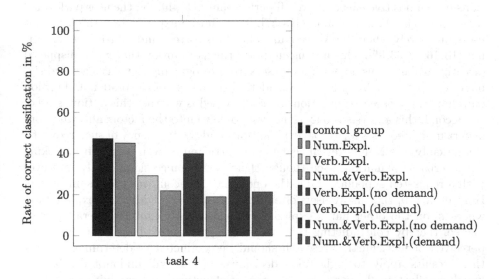

Fig. 6. Rate of correct classifications per subdivided group during the error

5 Discussion

The presented study addresses the ongoing debate surrounding the effectiveness of explanations in AI systems, particularly in assisting non-expert users in identifying erroneous recommendations and assessing the perceived validity of recommendations. Building on insights from an experimental study, this paper provides a deeper understanding of how the accessibility of a verbal explanation influences the interaction between non-expert users and AI. By doing so, this study contributes to the research field of XAI in multiple ways.

First, this study extends current research on the underexplored collaboration of non-expert users and AI [37,41] by foregrounding the non-expert users' interaction with a real AI-recommender system during binary decisions. Although AI technologies are becoming commonplace in various domains [42] and the growing complexity of systems complicates collaboration [10], especially for non-expert users, these users are neglected when discussing AI explanations [1,38]. In particular, this study can be used as a template for binary decisions, which are often made with the help of AI models in practice [5]. For example, non-expert AI users have to decide whether to invite a candidate to an interview during the hiring process. Consequently, even in binary decision settings, maximizing AI system performance is paramount, as errors stemming from persuasive but misleading explanations could potentially undermine the trustworthiness and utility of these systems [23]. This is especially critical for case-based reasoning systems that update their rules and heuristics with user data, as neglecting this can lead to a mutual confirmation bias [23]. Thus, consistent with prior studies, an initial observation of the results makes it apparent that although explanations have a positive effect on overall performance [47,49,55], the user performed worse than the AI model alone [13,57]. This can be explained by the fact that users under-rely when the AI recommendation is correct and over-rely when it is not [13,16,23,33,55]. This finding supports the assumption that when displayed directly, explanations do not hinder users from recognizing them as a general signal of competence [6,33]. Before considering the effects of the on-demand option on reliance, the essential question to be addressed is whether this option is used.

Second, this analysis is one of the first to delve into the factors affecting non-expert users' requests for verbal explanations and the frequency of such requests. Remarkably, the results reveal that many participants even refrain from asking for a verbal explanation, even though their performance significantly improves with a requested explanation. On the one hand, this confirms the assumption of Bunt et al. [10] that many users often do not require an additional explanation, whereas, on the other hand, explanations consistently improve overall performance, thereby contradicting their argument that an explanation reduces the perceived benefit. Further research should be conducted to determine whether these results apply to high-stakes decisions, as this will undoubtedly have a knock-on effect on the perceived cost-benefit structure. By examining what type of user requests an explanation, it turns out that the participants' education level and attitude towards AI significantly influence the decision to request a single explanation. Thus, this finding suggests that the common demand for an explanation is influenced more by personal characteristics than by the perceived difficulty of the task. Buccinca et al. [9] demonstrate that certain user groups enjoy engaging in cognitively demanding activities, have a higher intrinsic motivation, and thus benefit more from the on-demand condition. On the other hand, the number of explanations requested is influenced less by personal characteristics but rather by the perceived difficulty of the task. In addition, the study shows that the presence of numerical certainty in AI recommendations significantly reduced the likelihood of requesting verbal explanations. These findings confirm that the request for an explanation depends on the manual verification of the task and the effort to verify the explanation [53]. However, users often seem to struggle when optimizing this cost-benefit trade-off and making the strategic right decision. Thus, although the analysis shows that when the numerical certainty of AI recommendations is present, tasks with higher numerical certainty exhibit a lower rate of requested verbal explanations, there is no significant difference between the tasks with a 66% or 83% numerical certainty. In this context, it is noteworthy that verbal explanations are still requested in 12% of cases for tasks with a numerical confidence of 100%. These user behaviors contradict the idea that requesting an explanation seems to be a strategic decision, as otherwise, it would have been most convenient to follow the AI's recommendation or only request an explanation when the AI's recommendations are uncertain.

Third, this study contributes to the literature by exploring how the accessibility of explanations discourages users from forming decision heuristics and encourages cognitive engagement with the explanations. The active, voluntary demand and associated costs are intended to ensure that users have a heightened intrinsic and extrinsic motivation to analyze the explanation thoroughly. Considering Kahnemann's dual process theory [17], a longer processing time reflects more analytical and effortful mental activities, whereas shorter times indicate the use of heuristics and intuition for decision-making. Furthermore, the first empirical studies already exist that successfully apply the dual process theory to human-machine interaction to consider the thinking of users when collaborating with AI [35]. On the one hand, my analysis shows that the actual request for an explanation significantly increases the time to classification in contrast to when the explanation is not requested, which speaks in favor of increased analytical and explicit thinking. On the other hand, the explicit request does not differ in terms of time from the groups in which the explanation was displayed directly. This contradicts the assumption that a demanded explanation is more valued and respected than a constantly displayed explanation. Additionally, the results of Buccinca et al. [9] cannot be confirmed at the on-demand level. The on-demand option does not significantly reduce overreliance during the error compared to the direct explanations. Secondly, the underreliance is significantly lower for the on-demand option than the counterparts. Nevertheless, the analysis demonstrates that the mere option of an explanation is not perceived as such a signal of AI competence, as the simple option of an additional explanation has no significant impact on the rate of reliance on the recommendation. One reason for the mixed results might be that this AI completes 90% (instead of 75% [9])

of the tasks correctly, making it particularly difficult for the user to identify the case in which the AI is wrong. Therefore, further research is needed to investigate the impact of the accessibility of an explanation during the human-AI interaction.

6   Conclusion

In conclusion, this study delves into the complex dynamics of human-AI collaboration, focusing on the effectiveness of explanations in assisting non-expert users in navigating AI recommendations. Drawing on insights from an experimental study, this paper provides valuable insights into the nuanced dynamics of human-AI collaboration by investigating the influence of explanation accessibility on user behavior during decision-making. The findings reveal that while explanations enhance decision-making performance, many non-expert users refrain from requesting explanations, even when their performance significantly improves with additional clarification. While the common demand for an explanation is influenced strongly by personal characteristics, the number of demanded explanations depends more on contextual factors, confirming that users trade off perceived benefits and costs. Moreover, in contrast to an initial study, the study provides mixed results, suggesting that further research will be required on the impact of an on-demand option. To the best of my knowledge, no empirical results examine the effects of the actual demand for an explanation when an on-demand option is offered. While the active demand for explanations increases cognitive engagement, it does not necessarily lead to a significant reduction in overreliance or underreliance compared to directly displayed explanations. By uncovering the role of accessibility of an explanation, this study offers new insights into the complex interplay between non-expert users and AI.

Acknowledgements. This research is funded by the German Federal Ministry of Education and Research (BMBF) within the "The Future of Value Creation - Research on Production, Services and Work" program (02L19C115). The author is responsible for the content of this publication.

A   Composition of the Experimental Groups

See Tables 5, 6 and 7.

Table 5. Summary statistics of the experimental groups

No.	Variable	Percentage	Mean	Std.Dev.	Min	Max	N
1	*Verb. Expl. (on demand)*						76
	Gender (ref. = men)	50.00					38
	Age		34.86	13.31	16	77	76
	Profit (in €)		1.96	.761	0	4	76
	Avg. time per task (in sec.)		11.45	7.68	1	30	752
2	*Num. & Verb. Expl. (on demand)*						75
	Gender (ref. = men)	40.00					30
	Age		34.48	12.05	18	62	75
	Profit (in €)		2.13	.895	0	4	75
	Avg. time per task (in sec.)		9.97	6.56	1	30	729
3	*Control group*						73
	Gender (ref. = men)	46.58					34
	Age		33.71	13.80	14	79	73
	Profit (in €)		2.26	.691	0	4	73
	Avg. time per task (in sec.)		9.88	6.70	1	30	714
4	*Num. Expl.*						82
	Gender (ref. = men)	45.12					37
	Age		32.15	13.26	18	68	82
	Profit (in €)		2.46	.695	0	3.6	82
	Avg. time per task (in sec.)		10.15	6.37	1	29	816
5	*Verb. Expl.*						83
	Gender (ref. = men)	39.76					33
	Age		28.70	8.58	20	57	83
	Profit (in €)		2.46	.683	0.8	3.6	83
	Avg. time per task (in sec.)		15.22	6.39	1	30	785
6	*Num. & Verb. Expl.*						84
	Gender (ref. = men)	38.10					32
	Age		28.38	7.82	17	60	84
	Profit (in €)		2.80	.572	1.6	4	84
	Avg. time per task (in sec.)		15.48	6.44	2	30	799

B   Between-Treatment Variation

Table 6. Between-variation analysis II

| | Dependent variable | | | |
| | Reliance | | Correct class. | |
	V	VI	VII	VIII
Gender (ref. = men)	−0.048	−0.064	−0.129	−0.136
	(0.631)	(0.513)	(0.192)	(0.162)
Age	-0.015***	−0.016***	−0.013***	−0.014***
	(0.001)	(0.000)	(0.004)	(0.001)
Education (ref. = no degree)				
Secondary level 1	0.440*	0.442*	0.415*	0.412*
	(0.065)	(0.064)	(0.081)	(0.083)
Secondary level 2	0.439*	0.444*	0.316	0.316
	(0.063)	(0.060)	(0.179)	(0.178)
University degree	0.637***	0.662***	0.531**	0.544**
	(0.005)	(0.004)	(0.019)	(0.016)
AI-Attitude	0.112**		0.091*	
	(0.032)		(0.084)	
Weekly use of AI		0.053***		0.053***
		(0.009)		(0.009)
Treatment (ref. = Control)				
Num. & Verb. Expl.	0.911***	0.980***	0.720***	0.789***
	(0.000)	(0.000)	(0.000)	(0.000)
Num. & Verb. Expl. (on demand)	0.407**	0.401**	0.237	0.228
	(0.016)	(0.018)	(0.161)	(0.177)
Verb. Expl.	0.303*	0.378**	0.150	0.225
	(0.067)	(0.025)	(0.366)	(0.183)
Verb. Expl. (on demand)	0.306*	0.304*	0.166	0.163
	(0.066)	(0.068)	(0.319)	(0.328)
Num. Expl.	0.268	0.277*	0.271*	0.283*
	(0.103)	(0.092)	(0.099)	(0.086)
N	473	473	473	473

***$p < .01$, **$p < .05$, *$p < .1$

C   Within-Treatment Variation

Table 7. Within variation analysis II

	Dependent variable			
	Reliance		Correct class.	
	IX	X	XI	XII
Task difficulty	1.242***		1.227***	
	(0.000)		(0.000)	
task type (ref. = num.cert. 66%)				
83 %		0.004		−0.003
		(0.933)		(0.956)
100 %		0.427***		0.423***
		(0.000)		(0.000)
Error of AI	0.000	0.112	−0.833***	−0.723***
	(0.999)	(0.130)	(0.000)	(0.000)
Treatment (ref. = Control)				
Num. & Verb. Expl.	0.638***	0.632***	0.483***	0.479***
	(0.000)	(0.000)	(0.000)	(0.000)
Num. & Verb. Expl.(no demand)	0.148**	0.149**	0.051	0.053
	(0.038)	(0.036)	(0.479)	(0.461)
Num. & Verb. Expl.(demand)	0.521***	0.515***	0.367***	0.362***
	(0.000)	(0.000)	(0.004)	(0.005)
Verb. Expl.	0.289***	0.291***	0.192***	0.195***
	(0.000)	(0.000)	(0.005)	(0.004)
Verb. Expl.(no demand)	−0.013	−0.010	−0.050	−0.048
	(0.861)	(0.885)	(0.489)	(0.510)
Verb. Expl.(demand)	0.487***	0.489***	0.321***	0.324***
	(0.000)	(0.000)	(0.003)	(0.002)
Num. Expl.	0.118*	0.120*	0.111*	0.112*
	(0.073)	(0.069)	(0.095)	(0.089)
Constant	−0.374***	0.074	−0.297***	0.145**
	(0.000)	(0.224)	(0.000)	(0.017)
N	4,585	4,585	4,585	4,585

*** $p < .01$, ** $p < .05$, * $p < .1$

References

1. Abdul, A., Vermeulen, J., Wang, D., Lim, B.Y., Kankanhalli, M.: Trends and trajectories for explainable, accountable and intelligible systems: an HCI research agenda. In: Proceedings of the 2018 CHI Conference on Human Factors in Computing Systems, pp. 1–18 (2018)
2. Adadi, A., Berrada, M.: Peeking inside the black-box: a survey on explainable artificial intelligence (XAI). IEEE Access **6**, 52138–52160 (2018)
3. Arrieta, A.B., et al.: Explainable artificial intelligence (XAI): concepts, taxonomies, opportunities and challenges toward responsible AI. Inf. Fusion **58**, 82–115 (2020)
4. Badue, C., et al.: Self-driving cars: a survey. Expert Syst. Appl. **165**, 113816 (2021)
5. Bansal, G., Nushi, B., Kamar, E., Lasecki, W.S., Weld, D.S., Horvitz, E.: Beyond accuracy: The role of mental models in human-AI team performance. In: Proceedings of the AAAI Conference on Human Computation and Crowdsourcing, vol. 7, pp. 2–11 (2019)
6. Bansal, G., et al.: Does the whole exceed its parts? The effect of AI explanations on complementary team performance. In: Proceedings of the 2021 CHI Conference on Human Factors in Computing Systems, pp. 1–16 (2021)
7. Bawden, D., Robinson, L.: The dark side of information: overload, anxiety and other paradoxes and pathologies. J. Inf. Sci. **35**(2), 180–191 (2009)
8. Brynjolfsson, E., Mitchell, T., Rock, D.: What can machines learn and what does it mean for occupations and the economy? In: AEA Papers and Proceedings, vol. 108, pp. 43–47. American Economic Association 2014 Broadway, Suite 305, Nashville, TN 37203 (2018)
9. Buçinca, Z., Malaya, M.B., Gajos, K.Z.: To trust or to think: cognitive forcing functions can reduce overreliance on AI in AI-assisted decision-making. Proc. ACM Human-Comput. Interact. **5**(CSCW1), 1–21 (2021)
10. Bunt, A., Lount, M., Lauzon, C.: Are explanations always important? A study of deployed, low-cost intelligent interactive systems. In: Proceedings of the 2012 ACM International Conference on Intelligent User Interfaces, pp. 169–178 (2012)
11. Burrell, J.: How the machine 'thinks': understanding opacity in machine learning algorithms. Big Data Soc. **3**(1), 2053951715622512 (2016)
12. Burton, J.W., Stein, M.K., Jensen, T.B.: A systematic review of algorithm aversion in augmented decision making. J. Behav. Decis. Mak. **33**(2), 220–239 (2020)
13. Carton, S., Mei, Q., Resnick, P.: Feature-based explanations don't help people detect misclassifications of online toxicity. In: Proceedings of the International AAAI Conference on Web and Social Media, vol. 14, pp. 95–106 (2020)
14. Castelo, N., Bos, M.W., Lehmann, D.R.: Task-dependent algorithm aversion. J. Mark. Res. **56**(5), 809–825 (2019)
15. Chiang, C.W., Yin, M.: Exploring the effects of machine learning literacy interventions on laypeople's reliance on machine learning models. In: 27th International Conference on Intelligent User Interfaces, pp. 148–161 (2022)
16. Chu, E., Roy, D., Andreas, J.: Are visual explanations useful? A case study in model-in-the-loop prediction. arXiv preprint arXiv:2007.12248 (2020)
17. Daniel, K.: Thinking, fast and slow (2017)
18. De Graaf, M.M., Malle, B.F.: How people explain action (and autonomous intelligent systems should too). In: 2017 AAAI Fall Symposium Series (2017)
19. Dietvorst, B.J., Simmons, J.P., Massey, C.: Overcoming algorithm aversion: people will use imperfect algorithms if they can (even slightly) modify them. Manage. Sci. **64**(3), 1155–1170 (2018)

20. Doshi-Velez, F., Kim, B.: Towards a rigorous science of interpretable machine learning. arXiv preprint arXiv:1702.08608 (2017)
21. Dzindolet, M.T., Peterson, S.A., Pomranky, R.A., Pierce, L.G., Beck, H.P.: The role of trust in automation reliance. Int. J. Hum Comput Stud. **58**(6), 697–718 (2003)
22. Efendić, E., Van de Calseyde, P.P., Evans, A.M.: Slow response times undermine trust in algorithmic (but not human) predictions. Organ. Behav. Hum. Decis. Process. **157**, 103–114 (2020)
23. Ehrlich, K., Kirk, S.E., Patterson, J., Rasmussen, J.C., Ross, S.I., Gruen, D.M.: Taking advice from intelligent systems: the double-edged sword of explanations. In: Proceedings of the 16th International Conference on Intelligent User Interfaces, pp. 125–134 (2011)
24. Enholm, I.M., Papagiannidis, E., Mikalef, P., Krogstie, J.: Artificial intelligence and business value: a literature review. Inf. Syst. Front. **24**(5), 1709–1734 (2022)
25. EU: Proposal for a regulation EU of the European parliament and of the council of April 21, laying down harmonised rules on artificial intelligence (artificial intelligence act) and amending certain union legislative acts. Official J. Eur. Union Law **119** (2021)
26. Fast, E., Horvitz, E.: Long-term trends in the public perception of artificial intelligence. In: Proceedings of the AAAI Conference on Artificial Intelligence, vol. 31 (2017)
27. Fitzsimons, G.J., Lehmann, D.R.: Reactance to recommendations: when unsolicited advice yields contrary responses. Mark. Sci. **23**(1), 82–94 (2004)
28. Gajos, K.Z., Mamykina, L.: Do people engage cognitively with AI? Impact of AI assistance on incidental learning. In: 27th International Conference on Intelligent User Interfaces, pp. 794–806 (2022)
29. Gunning, D.: Explainable artificial intelligence (XAI). Defense advanced research projects agency (DARPA). Web **2**(2), 1 (2017)
30. Jussupow, E., Benbasat, I., Heinzl, A.: Why are we averse towards algorithms? A comprehensive literature review on algorithm aversion (2020)
31. Jussupow, E., Spohrer, K., Heinzl, A., Gawlitza, J.: Augmenting medical diagnosis decisions? an investigation into physicians' decision-making process with artificial intelligence. Inf. Syst. Res. **32**(3), 713–735 (2021)
32. Kim, J.Y., Heo, W.: Artificial intelligence video interviewing for employment: perspectives from applicants, companies, developer and academicians. Inf. Technol. People **35**(3), 861–878 (2021)
33. Lai, V., Tan, C.: On human predictions with explanations and predictions of machine learning models: a case study on deception detection. In: Proceedings of the Conference on Fairness, Accountability, and Transparency, pp. 29–38 (2019)
34. Laupichler, M.C., Aster, A., Schirch, J., Raupach, T.: Artificial intelligence literacy in higher and adult education: a scoping literature review. Comput. Educ. Artif. Intell. **3**, 100101 (2022)
35. Lebedeva, A., Kornowicz, J., Lammert, O., Papenkordt, J.: The role of response time for algorithm aversion in fast and slow thinking tasks. In: Degen, H., Ntoa, S. (eds.) Artificial Intelligence in HCI. HCII 2023. LNCS, vol. 14050, pp. 131–149. Springer, Cham (2023). https://doi.org/10.1007/978-3-031-35891-3_9
36. Lee, M.K.: Understanding perception of algorithmic decisions: fairness, trust, and emotion in response to algorithmic management. Big Data Soc. **5**(1), 2053951718756684 (2018)

37. Long, D., Magerko, B.: What is AI literacy? Competencies and design considerations. In: Proceedings of the 2020 CHI Conference on Human Factors in Computing Systems, pp. 1–16 (2020)
38. Miller, T.: Explanation in artificial intelligence: insights from the social sciences. Artif. Intell. **267**, 1–38 (2019)
39. Mohseni, S., Zarei, N., Ragan, E.D.: A multidisciplinary survey and framework for design and evaluation of explainable AI systems. ACM Trans. Interact. Intell. Syst. (TiiS) **11**(3–4), 1–45 (2021)
40. Moorthy, K., et al.: Dexterity enhancement with robotic surgery. Surv. Methodol. **18**, 790–795 (2004)
41. Ng, D.T.K., Leung, J.K.L., Chu, K.W.S., Qiao, M.S.: AI literacy: definition, teaching, evaluation and ethical issues. Proc. Assoc. Inf. Sci. Technol. **58**(1), 504–509 (2021)
42. Ng, D.T.K., Leung, J.K.L., Chu, S.K.W., Qiao, M.S.: Conceptualizing AI literacy: an exploratory review. Comput. Educ. Artif. Intell. **2**, 100041 (2021)
43. Papenkordt, J., Ngonga Ngomo, A.C., Thommes, K.: Are numbers or words the key to user reliance on AI? In: Academy of Management Proceedings, vol. 2023, p. 12946. Academy of Management Briarcliff Manor, NY 10510 (2023)
44. Park, J.S., Barber, R., Kirlik, A., Karahalios, K.: A slow algorithm improves users' assessments of the algorithm's accuracy. Proc. ACM Human-Comput. Interact. **3**(CSCW), 1–15 (2019)
45. Ribeiro, M.T., Singh, S., Guestrin, C.: Anchors: High-precision model-agnostic explanations. In: Proceedings of the AAAI Conference on Artificial Intelligence, vol. 32 (2018)
46. Rosenfeld, A., Richardson, A.: Explainability in human-agent systems. Auton. Agent. Multi-Agent Syst. **33**, 673–705 (2019)
47. Schemmer, M., Hemmer, P., Nitsche, M., Kühl, N., Vössing, M.: A meta-analysis of the utility of explainable artificial intelligence in human-AI decision-making. In: Proceedings of the 2022 AAAI/ACM Conference on AI, Ethics, and Society, pp. 617–626 (2022)
48. Schepman, A., Rodway, P.: Initial validation of the general attitudes towards artificial intelligence scale. Comput. Human Behav. Reports **1**, 100014 (2020)
49. Schoeffer, J., De-Arteaga, M., Kuehl, N.: On explanations, fairness, and appropriate reliance in human-AI decision-making. arXiv preprint arXiv:2209.11812 (2022)
50. Sharan, N.N., Romano, D.M.: The effects of personality and locus of control on trust in humans versus artificial intelligence. Heliyon **6**(8), e04572 (2020)
51. Strich, F., Mayer, A.S., Fiedler, M.: What do i do in a world of artificial intelligence? investigating the impact of substitutive decision-making ai systems on employees' professional role identity. J. Assoc. Inf. Syst. **22**(2), 9 (2021)
52. Varshney, K.R., Alemzadeh, H.: On the safety of machine learning: cyber-physical systems, decision sciences, and data products. Big Data **5**(3), 246–255 (2017)
53. Vasconcelos, H., Jörke, M., Grunde-McLaughlin, M.: When do XAI methods work? A cost-benefit approach to human-AI collaboration (2022). https://api.semanticscholar.org/CorpusID:253387060
54. Vilone, G., Longo, L.: Notions of explainability and evaluation approaches for explainable artificial intelligence. Inf. Fusion **76**, 89–106 (2021)
55. van der Waa, J., Nieuwburg, E., Cremers, A., Neerincx, M.: Evaluating XAI: a comparison of rule-based and example-based explanations. Artif. Intell. **291**, 103404 (2021)

56. Završnik, A.: Criminal justice, artificial intelligence systems, and human rights. ERA Forum. **20**, 567–583 (2020)
57. Zhang, Y., Liao, Q.V., Bellamy, R.K.: Effect of confidence and explanation on accuracy and trust calibration in AI-assisted decision making. In: Proceedings of the 2020 Conference on Fairness, Accountability, and Transparency, pp. 295–305 (2020)

Ontology-Based Explanations of Neural Networks: A User Perspective

Andrew Ponomarev[✉][iD] and Anton Agafonov[iD]

St. Petersburg Federal Research Center of the Russian Academy of Sciences, 14th Line 39, 199178 St. Petersburg, Russian Federation
ponomarev@iias.spb.su, agafonov.a@spcras.ru

Abstract. There is a variety of methods focused on interpreting and explaining predictions obtained using neural networks, however, most of these methods are intended for experts in the field of machine learning and artificial intelligence, and not for domain experts. Ontology-based explanation methods aim to address this issue, exploiting the rationale that presenting explanations in terms of the problem domain, accessible and understandable to the human expert, can improve the understandability of explanations. However, very few studies examine real effects of ontology-based explanations and their perception by humans. On the other hand, it is widely recognized that experimental evaluation of explanation techniques is highly important and increasingly attracts attention of both AI and HCI communities. In this paper, we explore users' interaction with ontology-based explanations of neural networks in order to a) check if such explanations simplify the task of decision-maker, b) assess and compare various forms of ontology-based explanations. We collect both objective performance metrics (i.e., decision time and accuracy) as well as subjective ones (via questionnaire). Our study has shown that ontology-based explanations can improve decision-makers performance, however, complex logical explanations not always better than simple indication of the key concepts influencing the model output.

Keywords: XAI · Explainable AI · Ontology · Ontology-Based Explanations · User Study · Machine Learning · Neural Networks

1 Introduction

One of the significant drawbacks of the neural network approach to AI in decision making is that the result of the neural network not always can be easily interpreted and explained. Explainable AI (or, XAI) is currently a hot topic and a variety of methods have been proposed that are focused on interpreting and explaining predictions obtained using neural networks (see, for example, review [5]).

However, most of these methods are intended for experts in the field of machine learning and artificial intelligence, and not for domain experts [12].

H. Degen and S. Ntoa (Eds.): HCII 2024, LNAI 14734, pp. 264–276, 2024.
https://doi.org/10.1007/978-3-031-60606-9_15

Ontology-based explanation methods aim to address this issue, exploiting the rationale that presenting explanations in terms of the problem domain, accessible and understandable to the human expert, can improve the understandability of explanations (e.g., [3, 4, 7]).

Research efforts in the area of ontology-based explanations are mostly focused on the algorithmic side of the problem – i.e., on the developing of new methods and algorithms for providing ontology-based explanations and/or on the aligning ontology concepts and deep neural representations. Very few studies examine real effects of ontology-based explanations and their perception by humans (see [6] for a rare exemption). On the other hand, it is widely recognized that experimental evaluation of explanation techniques is highly important and nowadays attracts attention of both AI and HCI communities [15, 18, 23].

In this paper, we explore users' interaction with ontology-based explanations of neural networks in order to address two questions:

1. Do ontology-based explanations of a neural network simplify the task of the decision-maker?
2. Do various forms of ontology-based explanations differ in understandability and ease-of-use? If yes, what features contribute to it and what form is better for the users?

The first question aims to evaluate an intuition that leveraging domain concepts helps the decision-maker (e.g., by providing easy to understand cues). The second one can give a direction to adjust explanations. If certain ontology properties significantly influence the understandability of explanations, then one can make optimize explanations in order to make them more understandable. In this sense, our research is well-aligned with [11], setting a research agenda in interpretability, as we perform human evaluation with a goal of finding some proxy characteristics of presentation allowing to estimate usefulness of potential explanations without user studies.

To answer the questions we perform a user study, in which the participants were presented classification tasks occasionally accompanied with different forms of ontology-based explanations. We collected both objective performance characteristics (i.e., decision time and accuracy) as well as subjective ones (via questionnaire).

The rest of paper is structured as follows. In Sect. 2 we describe related work, Sect. 3 introduces experimental setup, including experiment methodology and the software we used to collect the data. Section 4 describes the experiment results.

2   Related Work

There are two lines of research, particularly related to this paper. The first line is dedicated to ontology-based explanation techniques for neural networks *per se*, the second line is more in the domain of HCI and is dedicated to investigating the effect of different forms of explanations on the end user. In this section, we briefly describe relevant results from the both lines of research.

2.1 Ontology-Based Explanations

Most of the explanation techniques are not oriented on using ontologies [5], however, several methods have been proposed to use ontologies for neural networks explanations. And the main rationale of these methods is to connect the explanation to the concepts familiar to the user (and defined in some domain ontology).

There are ontology-based methods representing various approaches to neural networks explainability: both self-explainable neural models and *post-hoc*.

Ontology-oriented self-explainable models, as a rule, assume that each of the ontology concepts that will participate in the formation of explanations is assigned a separate neuron [3,4,24]. In most cases, this neuron is one of the output neurons of the network, that is, the set of outputs of the neural network is complemented by many ontology concepts relevant to the example, and the neural network predicts not only the class of the example, but also provides a set of logical values that can be used by the machine logical inference when constructing explanations. In some cases, the prediction of the target variable is generally generated by an inference engine (either full-featured or simplified [4]) or a linear model over the outputs of a neural network, ensuring strict correspondence between the prediction itself and its explanation. Concepts can also correspond to internal neurons of the network – for example, in [3], ontology concepts are ordered by level of generality and distributed across layers of a fully connected neural network depending on this level.

Post-hoc methods are aimed at explaining existing models that are trained without specific requirements for explainability, such methods can potentially be applied to any existing neural network. Most *post-hoc* methods are based on approximating the neural network with a more interpretable model (for example, a decision tree). Ontologies (and the properties of certain concepts) can be used both during the formation of the tree itself [7], and during the training the approximating model [19]. An alternative way of *post-hoc* explanation of neural network predictions is to establish correspondence between relevance of ontology concepts to the input sample of the network and the activations of hidden layers of the network [10].

From the point of view of this paper, the most important aspect of the ontology-based explanation is not how it is created, but its representation, or its conceptual model. According to this, we can identify two main approaches of representing ontology-based explanations:

1. Attributive explanation. Such explanation just highlight relevance of some ontology concepts to the model output. This relevance can stem either from semantically-loaded input features (corresponding to concepts) [17], or from semantically-loaded output layer of the network (followed by, e.g., logistic regression) [8].
2. Logical explanation. Such explanation shows a fragment of logical inference how the target class can be deduced from the set of concepts. Logical explanation is used, e.g., in [10].

In this paper, we compare the understandability of explanations built using these two approaches.

2.2 Experimental Evaluation of Explanations

There are two basic approaches to formalize and evaluate model interpretability in user studies:

1. Through simulability, the ability of a user – regardless of the computing device – to execute a model and obtain the correct result [16].
2. "What if" explainability, understood as a user's ability to determine the effect of a small perturbation of the model's input data on its result [22].

There is a fairly large number of studies in which experiments are conducted with people to assess the quality of explanations. Paper [14] compares different models – decision tables, trees and rules – without taking into account accuracy, only on the basis of ease of interpretation. Ease of interpretation is measured by response time, confidence in response, and ease of use.

Paper [21] also studies different models (with different numbers of features, transparent and not) and records how different combinations of such features affect human prediction of model results. Transparent models with fewer features have been shown to be easier to understand and more trustworthy.

In [23], the interpretability of models is examined based on two definitions: simulability (the ability of a user to predict the output of a model given a known input) and local "what if" scenarios (the ability to predict changes in a model's output from a change in input). The authors examine the explainability of decision trees, logistic regression, and crowdsourced neural networks, evaluating response accuracy and task completion times on different datasets and different types of models. The authors intentionally used synthetic data to remove the user domain knowledge from the experiment that could facilitate interpretation of the models.

In this paper, we use approach akin to simulatability, asking users to follow logical definition, using various concept-based cues.

3 Experiment Setup

This section describes types of tasks presented to the participants of the user study, software we used to collect the data, as well as the whole procedure.

3.1 Experiment Overview

In this paper, we examine two types of ontology-based explanations: attributive and logical.

Attributive explanations simply highlight concepts relevant to the model output that significantly influenced the network result (Fig. 1). Such explanations can be provided by neural networks enriched by semantically-loaded features

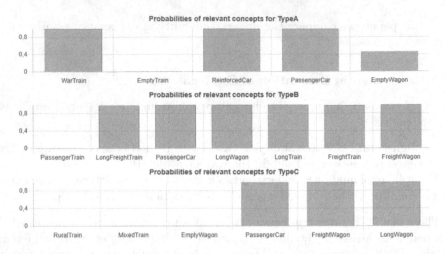

Fig. 1. Example of an attributive explanation.

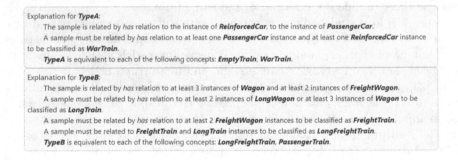

Fig. 2. Example of a logical explanation.

(e.g. [8,17]). Conceptually, the simplest form of such explanations is a barplot, on which x-axis correspond to some human-understandable domain concepts. As for y-axis, there are multiple choices (these plots look the same, but can carry different semantics) – it be relevance of the respective concept to the processed sample, or it can be some measure of influence of the respective concept to the target (e.g., SHAP value). In this paper, we consider the former case.

Logical explanations are represented as fragments of ontological inference, i.e., "the instance is classified as class C, because it is relevant to classes A and B (and C is defined as their intersection), and it is relevant to A, because it is relevant to D (and A is defined to be union of D and F)" (Fig. 2). Such explanations can be provided both by *post-hoc* explanation methods (e.g., [10, 20]) and certain kinds of self-explainable neuro-symbolic architectures, splitting the prediction task to concept extraction followed by logical inference (e.g., [2,4]).

During the experiment the participants are given a sequence of classification tasks. Each such task contains an image, a set of possible labels (classes), defined

Fig. 3. Sample images from the XTRAINS dataset [9].

by the dataset, and might also contain an explanation (one of two kinds). There are also tasks without explanations.

To objectively characterize explanations, we collected average time per task and the number of errors (misclassifications).

After completing all the tasks, the participants filled in a questionnaire, related to subjective perception of these stages, their comparative difficulty and their attitude to the perspectives of ontology-based explanations in general.

3.2 Dataset

To create tasks, we use Explainable Abstract Trains Dataset (XTRAINS) [9], designed for study of explainable AI. It is a large (500 000 instances) dataset of images 152×152, depicting drawings of trains (Fig. 3).

Every train is made up of a locomotive and one to five wagons. These wagons come in various types, identifiable by their visual characteristics such as length, shape of walls and roof, and the number of wheels. Moreover, each wagon can transport a certain load, represented by a set of geometrical shapes drawn inside it. Overall, the description of each train includes details about its wagons (their types and loads), the size of its wheels, the spacing between the wagons, as well as the train's position and angle.

The dataset is accompanied by an ontology, introducing certain classes of trains/wagons and providing formal definition of some of these classes. A subset of this ontology is shown in Fig. 4. Some of the ontology concepts correspond directly to visual appearance of a wagon, e.g. EmptyWagon is a wagon that do not carry any load (no geometric symbols inside wagon representation). Other concepts have logical definitions in terms of the ontology. Train types are typically defined using role "has" that establishes a connection between a train and a wagon. E.g., EmptyTrain is defined as a train that can have only empty wagons and locomotive and must have at least one empty wagon.

The ontology also introduces three artificial concepts (TypeA, TypeB, and TypeC) to serve as the target of the neural network. These concepts are defined via other ontology concepts. It models a situation when a network is trained on some complex target that, however, can be logically expressed via other domain concepts.

Each image of the dataset is annotated with binary attributes, corresponding to ontology concepts. Therefore, for each image not only target label is known

$$\text{TypeA} \equiv \text{WarTrain} \sqcup \text{EmptyTrain}$$
$$\text{WarTrain} \sqsupseteq \exists\text{has.ReinforcedCar} \sqcap \exists\text{has.PassengerCar}$$
$$\text{EmptyTrain} \equiv \forall\text{has.}(\text{EmptyWagon} \sqcup \text{Locomotive}) \sqcap \exists\text{has.EmptyWagon}$$
$$\text{Wagon} \equiv \text{EmptyWagon} \sqcup \text{PassengerCar} \sqcup \text{FreightWagon}$$
$$\text{EmptyWagon} \sqcap \text{PassengerCar} \sqsubseteq \bot$$
$$\text{EmptyWagon} \sqcap \text{FreightWagon} \sqsubseteq \bot$$
$$\text{PassengerCar} \sqcap \text{FreightWagon} \sqsubseteq \bot$$

Fig. 4. Fragment of the ontology.

(e.g., whether it belongs to TypeA or not), but also relation to all ontology concepts, which allows one to train and verify concept extraction models.

In this study, each classification task given to the user contains one image from the dataset and a user has to perform a multi-label classification, checking if the train in the image belongs to each of three artificial classes – TypeA, TypeB, and TypeC.

3.3   Used Software

To perform the experiment we implemented a web application to show tasks (as well as explanations) to the participants and collect responses. It also provides some assistance to simplify the task for the participant. In particular, in the welcome screen it displays detailed definition of each ontology concept with examples of respective images. It can also display brief concept definitions in an on-demand fashion.

The web application for ontology-based explanations was implemented using various tools and technologies on both the client side and the server side. JavaScript is used for dynamic interactivity and data visualization on the client side. CSS language is used to style web pages, making them more user-friendly. Interactive charting is carried out using the Chart.js library.

The server side of the software layout is implemented in Python using the Django web framework, which, following the Model-View-Controller pattern, handles requests, interacts with the database, and provides data to the client side. The Django template engine is used to generate dynamic HTML pages on the server. When a request arrives at the server, Django uses the template engine to generate an HTML page based on the templates and data passed from Django's views.

Communication between the client and server is carried out through HTTP requests and APIs. The JSON data format is used to exchange data between the client and server. Sending HTTP requests and receiving responses from the server is done using the Fetch API.

The formation of ontology-oriented explanations is carried out on the server side using the RevelioNN library [1]. The resulting logic explanations, as well as the concepts and probabilities extracted using the tools in this library, are transferred in JSON format for generating logic explanation diagrams and texts on the client side.

3.4 Methodology

The experiment involved 28 students of a higher educational institution aged from 20 to 24 years.

Each participant was asked to complete 48 tasks to classify trains. The number of tasks without explanations, as well as with each type of explanation, was 16 for each case. The samples for classification were selected in such a way that 6 instances were presented for each combination of train labels. The samples were distributed evenly, i.e. an equal number of samples with trains of each parameter combination were presented in each type of task (i.e., 6 that are not belong to any of the types, 6 belonging only to TypeA, 6 – to TypeB only, etc.). Tasks with different types of explanations were shown to users in random order.

The study consisted of three stages:

1. Introduction. During this stage, users were asked to familiarize themselves with the description of the subject area, to understand the features of each type of wagon, and what combinations of wagons define a particular type of train. The details of the experiment, such as the number of questions, etc., were also considered.
2. Classification. At this stage, users directly carried out the classification of the presented trains. At the same time, the decision time and the user's response were saved for each question.
3. Questionnaire. After classifying all the samples, users were offered a questionnaire, the purpose of which was to elicit subjective evaluations – which type of explanation was easier to understand, as well as which turned out to be the most useful for decision-making.

The questionnaire included questions related to the assessment of the subjective complexity of classification when using each of the types of explanations. The subjective complexity of the classification was measured on a scale from 1 to 7, where 1 corresponds to low complexity and 7 to high complexity. In addition, a question was included about how users used the explanations provided.

For a multi-criteria assessment of the quality of each type of explanation, we used the Explanation Satisfaction Scale proposed in [13]. Users were asked to evaluate each type of explanation on various aspects.

4 Experiment Results

The data obtained during the experiment were analyzed for the presence of participants who treated the study in bad faith. So, 8 people were excluded due to the fact that their decision time was beyond reasonable limits and/or very few correct answers were given, which indicates that these participants did not understand the instructions or did not exert reasonable effort. Thus, 20 people were selected for further research. Single decision time outliers of more than 200 s were also removed.

As noted earlier, the user's response and decision time were recorded for each question. It was found that, on average, the first 5 questions take users more time and effort, as they practice various types of questions and explanations. Thus, the parameters of the distribution of objective metrics were calculated, taking into account this factor (see Table 1). It can be seen that answering questions with explanations takes noticeably less time, while accuracy (number of correct answers) is higher.

Classification with attributive explanations takes less time than with logical ones in most cases due to the fact that attributive explanations are more interactive and visual (see Fig. 5 on the left). However, it can be seen that the decision time without considering the first 5 questions of each type for attributive explanations turns out to be comparable to the time for logical explanations. At the same time, logical explanations are more meaningful and focus the user's attention on the sequence of reasoning leading to the correct classification result, and thereby reduce the likelihood of making a wrong decision (see Fig. 5 on the right). In addition, if we do not take into account the first 5 questions, then for questions with explanations, the median accuracy is 1.0.

Among the subjective metrics, the subjective complexity of the classification was considered, which was measured on a scale from 1 to 7, where 1 corresponds to low complexity and 7 to high. The results obtained indicate that the greatest difficulty is expected to be caused by classification without explanation (see Fig. 6 on the left). Attributive explanations turn out to be more understandable to the user than logical ones, and, accordingly, they practically do not cause difficulties in classification. The subjective complexity of logical explanations can be justified by the fact that they represent a structured text obtained in the course of ontological inference. In addition, logical explanations are more meaningful and the user needs more time to familiarize himself with them.

Table 1. Characteristics of the distribution of objective metrics.

	Data used	Decision time, s				Accuracy			
		Mean	Median	SD	IQR	Mean	Median	SD	IQR
No explanation	All user responses	46.90	36.85	34.52	39.96	0.76	0.81	0.17	0.22
	Except for the first 5 answers	34.01	27.65	24.84	26.64	0.78	0.82	0.16	0.23
With explanations	All user responses	30.06	20.05	31.41	30.65	0.88	0.94	0.16	0.25
	Except for the first 5 answers for each type	20.65	15.38	20.86	20.28	0.89	1.00	0.19	0.14

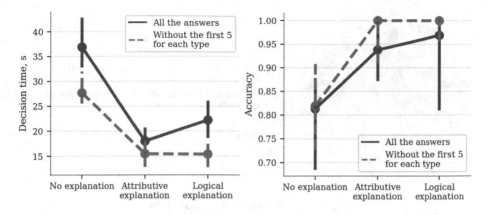

Fig. 5. Distribution of response time and accuracy using a median estimate.

Also, as part of the questionnaire, information was collected on various properties of explanations using the Explanation Satisfaction Scale proposed in [13]. This scale allows us to judge to what extent each type of explanation has a certain quality. Figure 6 on the right shows a radial diagram reflecting the median estimates of attributive and logical explanations for each of the properties of the explanations. It can be seen that attributive explanations are ahead of logical explanations in all respects, except for completeness.

We also included the question of what the users' approach to classification was if there were explanations. The distribution of the participants' responses is shown in Fig. 7. It was found that more than half of the participants used the explanations "with caution" – they carried out the classification themselves, and then checked themselves; or they got acquainted with the explanation and then checked its correctness. Only 12.5% of the respondents fully trusted the proposed explanation.

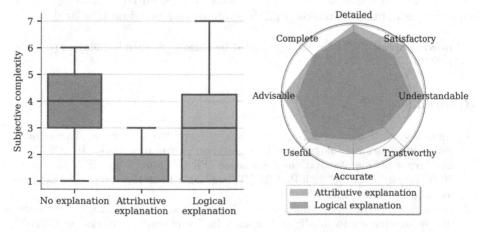

Fig. 6. Distribution of subjective complexity (left) and multi-criteria assessment of explanations (right).

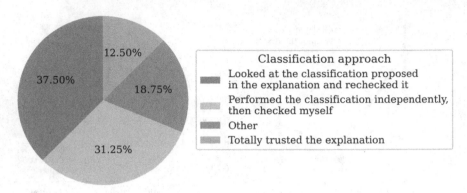

Fig. 7. Way of using the explanations.

5   Conclusion

The paper presents the results of a user study, aimed at understanding how a decision-maker interacts with ontology-based explanations of neural networks and how such explanations affect the performance of decision-maker.

Objective and subjective data collected during the study confirm that ontology-based explanations can improve both decision time and decision accuracy. At the same time, showing full logical inference to the end user is not necessarily the optimal way of presenting ontology-based explanations, probably, because full inference can contain too many information and create additional cognitive burden. One of the challenges in building ontology-based human-AI systems is developing other ontology-based representations of explanations (and interfaces, implementing these representations). This paper, in particular, shows a way of evaluating such representations.

It can also be noted that the presented study uses only image processing tasks. Further research is required to evaluate the potential of ontology-based explanations in other scenarios (e.g., decision-making based on tabular data).

Acknowledgments. This research is funded by Russian Science Foundation (project 22-11-00214).

References

1. Agafonov, A., Ponomarev, A.: RevelioNN: retrospective extraction of visual and logical insights for ontology-based interpretation of neural networks. In: 2023 34th Conference of Open Innovations Association (FRUCT), pp. 3–9. IEEE, November 2023. https://doi.org/10.23919/FRUCT60429.2023.10328156, https://ieeexplore.ieee.org/document/10328156/
2. Bellucci, M., Delestre, N., Malandain, N., Zanni-merk, C.: Ontologies to build a predictive architecture to classify and explain. In: DeepOntoNLP Workshop @ESWC 2022 (2022). https://hal.archives-ouvertes.fr/hal-03684275

3. Bourgeais, V., Zehraoui, F., Ben Hamdoune, M., Hanczar, B.: Deep GONet: self-explainable deep neural network based on Gene Ontology for phenotype prediction from gene expression data. BMC Bioinform. **22**, 1–24 (2021). https://doi.org/10.1186/s12859-021-04370-7, https://doi.org/10.1186/s12859-021-04370-7

4. Bourguin, G., Lewandowski, A., Bouneffa, M., Ahmad, A.: Towards ontologically explainable classifiers. In: Farkaš, I., Masulli, P., Otte, S., Wermter, S. (eds.) ICANN 2021. LNCS, vol. 12892, pp. 472–484. Springer, Cham (2021). https://doi.org/10.1007/978-3-030-86340-1_38

5. Burkart, N., Huber, M.F.: A survey on the explainability of supervised machine learning. J. Artif. Intell. Res. **70**, 245–317 (2021). https://doi.org/10.1613/JAIR.1.12228

6. Confalonieri, R., Weyde, T., Besold, T.R., Del Prado, M., Martín, F.: Trepan reloaded: a knowledge-driven approach to explaining black-box models. Front. Artif. Intell. Appl. **325**, 2457–2464 (2020). https://doi.org/10.3233/FAIA200378

7. Confalonieri, R., Weyde, T., Besold, T.R., Moscoso del Prado Martín, F.: Using ontologies to enhance human understandability of global post-hoc explanations of black-box models. Artif. Intell. **296**, 103471 (2021). https://doi.org/10.1016/j.artint.2021.103471

8. Daniels, Z.A., Frank, L.D., Menart, C., Raymer, M., Hitzler, P.: A framework for explainable deep neural models using external knowledge graphs. In: Pham, T., Solomon, L., Rainey, K. (eds.) Proceedings of SPIE 11413, Artificial Intelligence and Machine Learning for Multi-Domain Operations Applications II, p. 73. SPIE, April 2020. https://doi.org/10.1117/12.2558083, https://www.spiedigitallibrary.org/conference-proceedings-of-spie/11413/2558083/A-framework-for-explainable-deep-neural-models-using-external-knowledge/10.1117/12.2558083.full

9. de Sousa Ribeiro, M., Krippahl, L., Leite, J.: Explainable Abstract Trains Dataset, December 2020. http://arxiv.org/abs/2012.12115

10. de Sousa Ribeiro, M., Leite, J.: Aligning artificial neural networks and ontologies towards explainable AI. In: Proceedings of the AAAI Conference on Artificial Intelligence, vol. 35, pp. 4932–4940 (2021). https://ojs.aaai.org/index.php/AAAI/article/view/16626

11. Doshi-Velez, F., Kim, B.: Towards A Rigorous Science of Interpretable Machine Learning, February 2017. http://arxiv.org/abs/1702.08608

12. Futia, G., Vetrò, A.: On the integration of knowledge graphs into deep learning models for a more comprehensible AI-Three challenges for future research. Information (Switzerland) **11**(2), 122 (2020). https://doi.org/10.3390/info11020122

13. Hoffman, R.R., Mueller, S.T., Klein, G., Litman, J.: Metrics for Explainable AI: Challenges and Prospects (2018). http://arxiv.org/abs/1812.04608

14. Huysmans, J., Dejaeger, K., Mues, C., Vanthienen, J., Baesens, B.: An empirical evaluation of the comprehensibility of decision table, tree and rule based predictive models. Decis. Support Syst. **51**(1), 141–154 (2011). https://doi.org/10.1016/j.dss.2010.12.003, https://linkinghub.elsevier.com/retrieve/pii/S0167923610002368

15. Liao, Q.V., Gruen, D., Miller, S.: Questioning the AI: informing design practices for explainable AI user experiences. In: Proceedings of Conference on Human Factors in Computing Systems, pp. 1–15 (2020). https://doi.org/10.1145/3313831.3376590

16. Lipton, Z.C.: The Mythos of Model Interpretability. Queue **16**(3), 31–57 (2018). https://doi.org/10.1145/3236386.3241340, https://dl.acm.org/doi/10.1145/3236386.3241340

17. Martin, T., Diallo, A.B., Valtchev, P., Lacroix, R.: Bridging the gap between an ontology and deep neural models by pattern mining. In: The Joint Ontology Workshops, JOWO 2020, CEUR vol. 2708 (2020). http://ceur-ws.org/Vol-2708/donlp4.pdf

18. Mucha, H., Robert, S., Breitschwerdt, R., Fellmann, M.: Interfaces for explanations in human-AI interaction: proposing a design evaluation approach. In: Proceedings of Conference on Human Factors in Computing Systems (2021). https://doi.org/10.1145/3411763.3451759

19. Panigutti, C., Perotti, A., Pedreschi, D.: Doctor XAI: an ontology-based approach to black-box sequential data classification explanations. In: FAT* 2020 - Proceedings of the 2020 Conference on Fairness, Accountability, and Transparency, pp. 629–639 (2020). https://doi.org/10.1145/3351095.3372855

20. Ponomarev, A., Agafonov, A.: Ontology concept extraction algorithm for deep neural networks. In: 2022 32nd Conference of Open Innovations Association (FRUCT), pp. 221–226. IEEE, November 2022. https://doi.org/10.23919/FRUCT56874.2022.9953838, https://ieeexplore.ieee.org/document/9953838/

21. Poursabzi-Sangdeh, F., Goldstein, D.G., Hofman, J.M., Vaughan, J.W., Wallach, H.: Manipulating and Measuring Model Interpretability, February 2018. http://arxiv.org/abs/1802.07810

22. Ribeiro, M., Singh, S., Guestrin, C.: "Why Should I Trust You?": explaining the predictions of any classifier. In: Proceedings of the 2016 Conference of the North American Chapter of the Association for Computational Linguistics: Demonstrations, pp. 97–101. Association for Computational Linguistics, Stroudsburg, PA, USA (2016). https://doi.org/10.18653/v1/N16-3020, http://aclweb.org/anthology/N16-3020

23. Slack, D., Friedler, S.A., Scheidegger, C., Roy, C.D.: Assessing the Local Interpretability of Machine Learning Models, February 2019. http://arxiv.org/abs/1902.03501

24. Voogd, J., de Heer, P., Veltman, K., Hanckmann, P., van Lith, J.: Using relational concept networks for explainable decision support. In: Holzinger, A., Kieseberg, P., Tjoa, A.M., Weippl, E. (eds.) CD-MAKE 2019. LNCS, vol. 11713, pp. 78–93. Springer, Cham (2019). https://doi.org/10.1007/978-3-030-29726-8_6

Designing for Complementarity: A Conceptual Framework to Go Beyond the Current Paradigm of Using XAI in Healthcare

Elisa Rubegni[1,10]($\boxtimes$), Omran Ayoub[2], Stefania Maria Rita Rizzo[5,9], Marco Barbero[3], Guenda Bernegger[7], Francesca Faraci[4], Francesca Mangili[6], Emiliano Soldini[7], Pierpaolo Trimboli[5,8], and Alessandro Facchini[6]

[1] School of Computing and Communication, Lancaster University, Lancaster, UK
[2] ISIN, DTI, SUPSI, Lugano, CH, Switzerland
[3] Rehabilitation Research Laboratory, DEASS, SUPSI, Lugano, CH, Switzerland
[4] MeDiTech, DTI, SUPSI, Lugano, CH, Switzerland
[5] Faculty of Biomedical Sciences, USI, Lugano, CH, Switzerland
[6] IDSIA USI-SUPSI, DTI, SUPSI, Lugano, CH, Switzerland
[7] CPPS, DEASS, SUPSI, Lugano, CH, Switzerland
[8] Servizio di Endocrinologia e Diabetologia, Ospedale Regionale di Lugano, EOC, Lugano, CH, Switzerland
[9] Clinic of Radiology, Imaging Institute of Southern Switzerland, EOC, Lugano, CH, Switzerland
[10] DTI, SUPSI, Lugano, CH, Switzerland
elisa.rubegni@supsi.ch

Abstract. The widespread use of AI-based tools in the healthcare sector raises many ethical and legal problems, one of the main reasons being their black-box nature and therefore the seemingly opacity and inscrutability of their characteristics and decision-making process. Literature extensively discusses how this can lead to phenomena of over-reliance and under-reliance, ultimately limiting the adoption of AI. We addressed these issues by building a theoretical framework based on three concepts: Feature Importance, Counterexample Explanations, and Similar-Case Explanations. Grounded in the literature, the model was deployed within a case study in which, using a participatory design approach, we designed and developed a high-fidelity prototype. Through the co-design and development of the prototype and the underlying model, we advanced the knowledge on how to design AI-based systems for enabling complementarity in the decision-making process in the healthcare domain. Our work aims at contributing to the current discourse on designing AI systems to support clinicians' decision-making processes.

Keywords: Human-centred AI · Explainable AI · Clinical decision support systems · Feature-based explanations · Counterexample explanations · Similar-Case explanations

© The Author(s), under exclusive license to Springer Nature Switzerland AG 2024
H. Degen and S. Ntoa (Eds.): HCII 2024, LNAI 14734, pp. 277–296, 2024.
https://doi.org/10.1007/978-3-031-60606-9_16

1 Introduction

Thanks to their efficient capability to analyse vast amounts of complex and diverse data, artificial intelligence (AI for short) systems fuelled by contemporary machine learning techniques are at the forefront of the digital transformation of health systems around the globe [56]. Notable cases include AI for physician-level diagnostics in dermatology [14] or radiology [32], for finding optimal treatment strategies for sepsis [31] or for identifying patients at risk of cardiac failure in intensive care settings [25]. However, despite their huge potential, the adoption of AI-based tools raises several ethical and societal issues, one of the main reasons being the seeming inscrutability of their design characteristics and decision-making process [52,57]. The "black box problem" in AI refers to the challenges and problems that arise because of the opacity of AI systems. For instance, researchers notice that "end users are less likely to trust and cede control to machines whose workings they do not understand" [61, p.266], and that "the opacity of AI systems can reduce end users' trust and reliance on using AI-based systems while making critical decisions" [22, p.1].

In line with this is the observation that in reality, when deployed, AI systems are often under-used or not used at all [50], one of the reasons commonly put forward being that it is difficult for humans to estimate to what extent to trust recommendations coming from algorithms when no information about their inner behaviour, accuracy[1], or error is given [23,27,34].

A natural question is, therefore, to understand the exact role opacity is playing in this respect, and which strategies countering it, if any, will eventually enhance trust and enable adoption of AI systems in healthcare.

The view we advocate in this work is that to succeed we need to go beyond the standard XAI methods by aligning with a human-centred perspective on AI (e.g. [51]). More specifically, in this paper we start to illustrate an approach to co-design 'parsimonious evaluative strategies' with users (clinicians), that do not fall into the traps of standard explanatory practices, and that, we hope, encourage trust and the virtuous appropriation of AI, manifested in the generation of complementary performances. Focusing on diagnostic decision support, and embracing a view recently made explicit by Miller in [41], the AI decision support, we claim, should merely support the specific diagnostic reasoning of the clinician at stake in the setting under consideration, and thus, in principle, neither be focused on recommending decisions nor on providing explanations for them. To do so, we put in place a participatory design approach in which we engaged experts in AI, HCI, and clinicians to co-design and develop an AI prototype for supporting doctors in thyroid disease diagnostics. As already mentioned, the design is based on supporting the clinical reasoning but not to directly provide a recommendation. In this paper, we will report about the theoretical

---

[1] It has indeed been observed that "people's trust in a model is affected by both its stated accuracy and its observed accuracy, and that the effect of stated accuracy can change depending on the observed accuracy" [60].

background implemented on a case study in which we developed a prototype based on the conceptual framework.

Our study included **three iterative phases**: 1. Understanding the Design Space, 2. integrating theory into the design, and 3. co-designing the prototype. On one side, we engaged users/stakeholders through a participatory method, while on the other, we developed a high-fidelity prototype using a real dataset. The prototype was partially co-designed with clinicians, who participated as informants to provide feedback. Our purpose is twofold:

1. to provide a conceptual background for challenging the opacity and encouraging complementarity when AI is used to support decision-making process in health care
2. to advance the knowledge on how to design AI-based systems for the healthcare domain.

The outcomes of this work aim to contribute to the current discourse on designing AI systems to support clinicians' decision-making processes. We provide concrete examples of potential solutions and advocate for the implementation of a participatory design approach to empower clinicians to actively engage in the process. The remainder of the paper is structured as follows. In Sect. 2 we present background on the context of our work while in Sect. 3 we provide the reader with necessary background on explainable artificial intelligence. In Sec. 4 we present our methodological approach for the design process and in Sect. 5 we describe the case study. In Sect. 6 we elaborate on user needs and Sect. 7 describes the prototype. While Sect. 8 describes the co-design process and Sect. 9 concludes the paper.

2   Background

Many among not only the community of computer scientists but also of clinicians and practitioners adhere to the so called *explainability thesis* (ET) [8,33]. That is, the hypothesis that explainability is a suitable means for facilitating trust of an opaque AI system in a stakeholder and, thus, making it more acceptable as a decision support tool.[2] As such, they are increasingly calling for transparency and explainability to solve the black-box (opacity) problem and build trust in AI systems. This position is echoed in the EU ethics guidelines for trustworthy AI [10, p.3], that considers transparency and explainability as "crucial for building and maintaining users' trust in AI systems".

The ET has, however, been challenged. In addition to pointing out that it is not clear what the explainability or interpretability of AI system actually amounts to, one counter-argument starts by noticing that "[as] counter-intuitive

---

[2] What actually the cited articles refer to with the thesis is the capability of explaining an AI system's inner behaviour and output. Such thesis is somehow a strong one, and it would be better to formulate it by taking into account the ontology of an AI system, e.g. via the so called levels of abstraction [47], and the various forms that opacity may take [15].

and unappealing as it may be, the opacity, independence from an explicit domain model, and lack of causal insight associated with some of the most powerful machine learning approaches are not radically different from routine aspects of medical decision-making. Our causal knowledge is often fragmentary, and uncertainty is the rule rather than the exception. In such cases, careful empirical validation of an intervention's practical merits is the most important task. When the demand for explanations of how interventions work is elevated above careful, empirical validation, patients suffer, resources are wasted, and progress is delayed" [37, p.18]. Thence, according to London [37], what is needed for enabling trust and adoption is not so much explainability, intended as the capability of providing explanations for the behaviour or output of an AI system, but rather accuracy and reliability. Indeed, current explainability techniques, mainly stemming from the eXplainable (XAI) research programme [1], not only fall short in their original aim but they might have unintended negative effects. For instance, aligned with London's view, despite some positive results (see e.g. [12, 26, 55]), experiments have shown that sometimes accuracy is more important for user trust than explainability, and that adding an explanation for a recommendation can potentially harm trust when the fidelity of the explanation is low [44, 45]. In addition, explanations of recommendations can lead to automation bias and over-reliance on AI systems (the mere presence of an explanation often already increases trust), to accept incorrect decisions and explanations without verifying whether they were correct, and thus to unjustified (unwarranted) trust in AI recommendations, or to cause reasoning errors such as confirmation bias and thus to groundlessly increase confidence in one's own decision.[3] This is the reason why, as explained in [8]:

"providing AI with explainability [...] is more akin to painting the black box of inscrutable algorithms [...] white, rather than making them transparent. What we mean with this metaphoric statement is that XAI explanations do not necessarily explain (as by definition or ontological status) but rather describe the main output of systems aimed at supporting (or making) decisions".

As a consequence, using explanations does not necessarily enable achieving complementarity. That is, it doesn't necessarily make a "hybrid team" composed by a human and an AI to take better decisions than humans or AIs alone. Actually, the only situation where the human-machine collaboration via explainability outperforms people alone is when the accuracy of the underlying AI model is higher than human accuracy [4], but still the performance of the hybrid team is lower than the one by AI alone [6]. Hence, one can argue with [18] that, in the absence of suitable explainability methods, it is better and safer to rather advocate for rigorous internal and external validation of AI systems (a task for which current XAI methods may actually be very useful). What we should look for is not a full 'transparency' of the trained algorithm, but rather a form of

---

[3] See [5] for a review of existing literature on this aspect.

design transparency, that is "the adequate communication of the essential information necessary to provide a satisfactory design explanation of such a system" [36], such as the data's origin and the type of data used in training[4] (including how risks of biases have been tackled), the goal of the algorithm[5], and thus its adequacy (applicability) to the context is supposed to be deployed and used, and as well as characteristics such as its validation and accuracy (see [2] for a discussion on these points). Unfortunately, it has been shown, e.g. by [3], that being the most accurate model does not necessarily imply it to be the 'best teammate in the room'. The reason simply being that a collaborative context "puts additional demands on participants that extend beyond individual performance on tasks, such as ability to complement and coordinate with one's partner". In fact, accuracy on training data is *not* equal to accuracy on unseen data when the system is deployed and that the accuracy of a decision support system is *not* the accuracy of decision making (see e.g. [7]). Moreover, remember that we are considering a situation in which, due to the opacity of the system, the only information that humans are relying on to judge the correctness of an AI recommendation is the decision maker's own expertise and background knowledge.[6] Given this, even though the AI is better than the human (keeping in mind the previous caveat on such a claim), it is well known that people still tend to under-rely and thus ignore the recommendation of the machine because of *unwarranted distrust* or to over-rely and thus incur in the acceptance of wrong decisions due to *unwarranted trust* [4,17,20,27,40,54,62]. We thus have reached a paradoxical conclusion: opacity seems to hinder the virtuous adoption of AI in the healthcare sector, but tools from XAI may have a counterproductive effect. At the same time, simply providing AI recommendations (perhaps with some additional information, e.g. accuracy) neither seems to promote adoption and complementarity. The approach advocated in this paper aims at countering this paradoxical situation by asking for a change of paradigm in the design and use of XAI in diagnostics.

3   XAI: A Three Pillars Conceptual Framework

XAI is a rapidly evolving area within the field of AI that seeks to clarify the decision-making processes of AI systems and opaque machine learning (ML) models, especially in critical applications such as healthcare and finance. Specifically, XAI aims to bridge the gap between the inherent complexity of advanced AI algorithms and the need for transparency in understanding how these systems arrive at specific outcomes. By providing insights into the internal workings of AI models, through a broad set of families of explanations, XAI aims to enhance

---

[4] See e.g. the case described in [30].
[5] In particular the intended functionality assigned to the trained model by the designers.
[6] We can also assume that information contributing to design transparency are included in the background knowledge.

the interpretability of results and to foster trust among end-users, regulators, and stakeholders, ultimately promoting responsible and ethical AI deployment.

The explanations generated using XAI techniques can be either local, explaining model's decision for an instance (i.e., how the model arrived to a decision for a particular instance), or global, explaining the overall working of the underlying machine learning model. In our prototype, and since we are simulating a use case for diagnostic settings, we leverage local explanations. Specifically, our prototype provides, for the instance of interest (i.e., for the instance being analyzed by the clinician), a set of local explanations that assist the clinician in the diagnostic. In particular, we leverage three families of explanations, namely, *Feature Importance Explanations*, *Counterexample Explanations* and *Similar-Case Explanations*. In the following, we provide a short description of these families of explanations.

Feature Importance (or, feature attribution) refers to the measure of the impact or contribution of individual input features in a machine learning model's decision-making process [38,49]. It helps to identify, based on the XAI technique employed to compute the importance of the features, which features have the most significant influence on the model's predictions. The feature importance of a specific feature for a given data sample being analyzed (i.e., the decision of the ML model for the data sample being explained) can be as either positive or negative. A positive importance value signifies that the feature supports the decision favoring the considered class, while a negative importance value suggests that the feature does not contribute to the decision in favor of the class under consideration.

When predicting thyroid disease, conducting a feature importance analysis can provide valuable insights into the factors that significantly influence the model's diagnosis. This analysis helps identify the key contributors, such as age, gender, or thyroid hormone levels, that play a crucial role in either supporting or contradicting a particular diagnosis. For instance, if the feature importance analysis indicates that age is the most influential factor, it suggests that the model heavily relies on age information when making its prediction. This insight into feature importance aids in understanding the model's underlying logic, guiding users to identify how the ML model reached its decision.

Counterexample Explanations are a type of explanation that explores what could have happened in a given situation if certain factors or events had been different [24,49,58]. In other words, they involve constructing hypothetical scenarios or *counterfactuals* to allow users to understand how changes in specific variables (input features) in a specific data sample might have led to different outcomes [35,59]. In this context, counterfactual explanations are often used to explain the predictions or decisions made by a ML model. By identifying the key features or inputs that influenced the model's output, one can create counterfactual instances where those features are modified to observe how the model's prediction would change. This helps users (and developers) better comprehend the decision-making process of ML models and gain insights into their behaviour and, in fact, counterfactual reasoning have already proven to improve the interpretability of ML models in several domains such as healthcare [48].

Within the context of our specific use case, the extraction of counterfactuals provides the user, notably the clinician, with a valuable array of options. These options delineate how alterations in input features, encompassing the patient's information and, for example, test measurements, could potentially impact the ultimate the diagnosis.

Similar-Case Example Explanations involve presenting instances from the dataset that closely resemble the input data (i.e., the data record currently under investigation) such as to to illustrate how analogous cases influenced the model's decision. Such explanations can help identifying instances in the dataset that share similarities with the input data, and that have been given the same label [9]. This approach is particularly valuable in providing concrete and relatable examples that can enhance the interpretability of machine learning models.

In the cases under consideration in this work, these three explanatory approaches will constitute the basis of our framework.

4 Designing with the Users: Methods, Data Collection and Analysis

Our design research aligned with a human-centred perspective on AI (see e.g. [51]) and grounded the idea that the AI decision support should be designed as in such a way that the human decision maker maintains control over which hypotheses to explore. Thus, we implemented a design approach that aims at developing a system that aligns with the idea that is the decision support system should be designed to explicitly support the abductive reasoning process, that is in the medical domain the (differential) diagnostic type of reasoning of a clinician. In order to do this, the project followed a Participatory Design approach (PD) [53] by involving the stakeholders (e.g. hospital clinicians, researchers and technicians) in every step of the design process of the system. In this work, we have involved users and stakeholders in different ways and their participation had different degrees of engagement within the process according to the people's roles and the phase of the project. Specifically, across the research project they have been involved as: users, testers, informants, and co-design partners [13]. As users or testers, the target group is observed during their normal activity using the tools we provided. They are inquired about their everyday workflows, tools, and tasks. Later on, they are asked for acceptability and/or usability of an early version of the tool. As informants, users are solicited for input and feedback. As, co-designers the users are considered as equal partners in the design process. Users are actively engaged and invited to provide input starting at an early stage of design, preceding the development of a fully working prototype [13]. Drawing upon the PD potential to foster user adoption, our study is grounded in this approach [16]. Indeed, the PD approach increases the likelihood of stakeholders and users adopting the tool, as well as the team better understanding the context, wishes, and needs thus increasing the chances of really supporting their activities. PD has been successfully and widely used within this domain (e.g. [11] [43]). Our approach consists of three iterative phases: **1. Understanding the Design Space, 2. integrating theory into the design**, and **3. co-designing the prototype**. Overall, we engaged 8 people with different domains of expertise: two clinicians, three medical technicians, a user experience researcher, an expert in AI in healthcare, and an expert in ML in healthcare. Through their active engagement, participants contributed in defining the problem space, eliciting the system requirements, and exploring the different designs presented as low-fi and hi-fi prototypes. In the project, we developed a hi-fi prototype and built a ML model by using a real data set. The creation of a hi-fi prototype allowed us to challenge our scientific hypothesis and the conceptual framework by directly engaging the clinicians as informants into a co-design session. We collected data by transcribing notes and taking pictures of the context in phase one. We analysed data by defining the design space and the requirements that directly feed to design of the prototype. In the co-design stage, we recorded the session, transcribed notes, and later analysed the video.

5   The Case Study

In this paper, we report on a specific case study developed in collaboration with the *Ente Ospedaliaro Cantonale* (EOC - the institution that manages, coordinates, and integrates a network of public hospitals in Ticino, Switzerland).

We present the activities that we conducted with the users and stakeholders to **identify the problem space**, subsequently we illustrate the **integration of the theory into the design of the prototype**, and then we present the first round of **co-design** in which a clinician was involved as informant to provide feedback on the prototype [13].

To recruit participants, we used a convenience sampling approach. Leveraging the researchers' network, we contacted a few people who work in the local research hospital. For the first phase (identifying the design space) we recruited on a voluntary basis a team of radiologists (technicians, clinicians, and researchers). This team was willing to collaborate with us and aligned with our vision on AI in the decision-process as a complementary tool to help in making decisions. Overall, we involved three technicians, that have been in the role for over 10 years: a clinician who leads the local research unit in the Clinic of Radiology at the EOC, and is also professor at the Faculty of Biomedical sciences of the University of Southern Switzerland, where she is involved in many research and teaching activities related to imaging and AI, and a researcher which is part of this team. For the third phase (co-design of the first hi-fi prototypes), we recruited another clinician in the domain of endocrinology (and also a scholar of the University of Southern Switzerland) who participated on a voluntary basis, reaching out to the team that had joined the first phase (at the Clinic of Radiology). This user is the head of the Endocrinology Department at the EOC and acted as co-designer and provided input on a prototype based on a Thyroid Disease dataset. The rationale behind recruiting individuals with diverse specialties is to challenge our concepts to scrutiny across various health domains.

5.1   Threats to Validity

In our case study, we involved a limited number of users and stakeholders recruited using convenience sampling through the university network. However, this is not unusual in participatory design research. Indeed, this approach allowed us to delve deeply into each participant's practices, needs, and wishes. As a result, we were able to provide a complete and exhaustive overview of the clinicians and technicians involved. Therefore, engaging a larger sample would not have allowed at this stage of the project to get such a deep understanding of the users. Moreover, this approach allowed us to create a strong connection with the participants that lead to a long term partnership. However, this should be considered when generalising the results. To strengthen our approach and address potential external validity issues in the co-design phase, we have recruited a clinician with a different specialty than the other participants involved in phase 1. This helped strengthen our conceptual model by subjecting it to challenges across various health domains (Diagnostic Imaging and Endocrinology), diseases (Pulmonary nodules and Thyroid Disease), and types of data (images and text). Following we report a summary of the outcomes of the first phase.

6   Phase 1: Understanding the Design Space

In the first phase of the project we investigated the design space. We involved three technicians, one clinician, and one researcher who were inquired about their practices, the tools used, their workflow, including the people who are part of the decision making process while formulating a diagnosis. In order to explore these aspects, three authors conducted four contextual inquiry interviews on their laboratories and offices (see the Annex). The focus of these interviews was on investigating their practices and the potential issues and opportunities to address in designing the new system. We interviewed them separately to enable each participant to focus deeply on their own activities and tasks. We interviewed the technicians and the researcher one time. While, to delve deeper on their activities, we inquired the clinicians in three rounds. Each inquiry lasted about 90 min and was based on a semi-structured interview in which the users could talk over their everyday practices in patient examinations and making options about a diagnosis. Being in their offices and laboratories allowed them to show us the tools that they use everyday, including the software. During the second interview round we also explained our hypothesis with the purpose of investigating whether they would be open to use an AI-based system grounded in our conceptual model.

In **the first round**, the participants agreed it is about providing counterfactual examples while the clinician is evaluating the different options. The type of counter-examples varies depending on the data and the domain. For instance, if the system is tailored for radiologists, examples may consist of images accompanied by brief descriptions. Conversely, for endocrinologists, the data might be numerical and textual in nature. From the interviews, it emerged that, at the moment, technicians do not provide any insight on the diagnosis thus they might not need this type of support. While, for clinicians, it would be extremely relevant to have that type of support.

In **the second round**, they demonstrated to be extreme positive and enthusiast about having a set of counterexamples instead of a direct recommendation, unlike other AI-based systems they have previously used. They mentioned multiple times during the interviews that using counterfactual reasoning is the strategy they usually applied when they have to make a decision. Usually, they asked for second opinions from the colleagues who provide insights on the basis of their experience. Hence, they highly appreciated the prospect of an AI-based system that could complement their reasoning and support their decision-making process by offering Counterfactual Explanations and Similar-Case Explanations. Such support is particularly desirable to them, especially if it is backed by a robust and extensive dataset. During this second round of interviews, we co-identified a set of examples (pro and against) that supported the counterfactual reasoning and lead to improvements in the interpretability of ML models. We focused mainly on Pulmonary Nodules and they provided us five potential diseases to be considered in a differential diagnosis process (congenital, inflammatory, neoplastic, vascular, and miscellaneous).

In **the third round**, we discussed with the participants the number of examples to provide (both for and against), and they expressed the preference to include one example for each of the five potential diagnoses. Connected with this point, clinicians helped us to identify the specific features that influence their decision and their importance. These factors aimed at influencing the output provided by the ML model. As well as these changed according to the domain. We identified these examples by combining the features provided by the dataset with the expertise of the clinicians. For instance our stakeholders identifies 20 features that will be used to implement the prototype. Furthermore, we asked participants to bring concrete examples of a set of features, counterfactual, and similar-case explanations that we will used to build the model. The participants created an anonymised data set that we will use in the next step of the project for developing a prototype for supporting Diagnostic Imaging decision-making process. The patient information were anonymised to ensure the protection of privacy and confidentiality of their data.

7   Phase 2: Integrating the Theory into the Design

In the second phase, we integrated the theory into the design by developing a prototype. The prototype is a high-fidelity interactive artifact based on a machine learning model trained on a real dataset. This second phase runs in parallel with the first one, however they feed one other. Specifically, phase one helped consolidating our conceptual framework. In this phase, the three-pillars framework was implemented into a prototype by using a real dataset of thyroid disease diagnosis domain. We opted for a different domain (endocrinology) than phase one (radiology) for two main reasons: to challenge our model, and because we found a rich dataset that could be used to develop and train a machine learning model, which was currently lacking in radiology. In this section, we explain how the model was built and what the prototype and interaction design look like.

7.1   ML Model Development and Explainers

The thyroid disease diagnosis problem can be formulated as a multi-class classification problem. The diagnosis task (i.e., the classification of a given data record) involves distinguishing between hyperthyroid conditions, hypothyroid conditions, and negative cases (i.e., neither hyperthyroid nor hypothyroid disease). The dataset used in our study is constructed by merging six datasets from the Garavan Institute of Medical Research.[7] The dataset has been made publicly available and is currently available for download from the UCI machine learning repository.[8] We have preprocessed the original dataset by eliminating data records (data samples) with missing values. After this step, we are left with a dataset of 7142 data records. The records are distributed among the three classes as follows:

- Negative (also referred to as class 0) consists of 6385 data records (89.4% of the overall records in the dataset)
- Hyperthyroid (class 1) consists of 582 data records (8.15% of the overall records in the dataset)
- Hypothyroid (class 2) consists of 175 data records (2.45% of the overall records in the dataset)

The input data consisting of features (variables) with either Boolean values or numerical values. Table 1 reports the list of features along with a brief description. To build the ML model for thyroid disease classification, we train and test an extreme gradient boosting (XGB) model in a supervised manner following a 10-fold cross validation with 80–20 train-test split. The XGB model was optimized through hyper-parameter tuning and the resulting model achieves an average accuracy of 0.99 across the 10 folds. The model achieves a precision[9], recall[10] and F1-score[11] values that range between 0.8 and 0.99 for Negative and Hyperthyroid class while values that range between 0.75 and 0.97 for the Hypothyroid class. The results indicate that the Hypothyroid class represents a challenge for the ML model, however this is expected considering the relatively

---

[7] https://www.garvan.org.au/.

[8] https://archive.ics.uci.edu/dataset/102/thyroid+disease.

[9] The precision represents the ratio of correctly predicted instances of that class to the total instances predicted as that class.

[10] The recall represents the ratio of correctly predicted instances of that class to the total instances of that class in the dataset.

[11] The F1-score is the harmonic mean of precision and recall.

Table 1. List of input features pertaining to patient information

Variable	Type	Description
age	Integer	Age of the patient
sex	Boolean	Sex of the patient
on_thyroxine	Boolean	Whether patient is on thyroxine
on_antithyroid_meds	Boolean	Whether patient is on antithyroid meds
sick	Boolean	Whether patient is sick
pregnant	Boolean	Whether patient is pregnant
thyroid_surgery	Boolean	Whether patient has undergone thyroid surgery
I131_treatment	Boolean	Whether patient is undergoing I131 treatment
query_hypothyroid	Boolean	Patient believes they have hypothyroid
query_hyperthyroid	Boolean	Patient believes they have hyperthyroid
lithium	Boolean	Whether patient takes lithium
goitre	Boolean	Whether patient has goitre
tumor	Boolean	Whether patient has a tumor
hypopituitary	Float	Hyperpituitary gland status
psych	Boolean	Whether patient has psych
TSH	Float	TSH level in blood from lab work
T3	Float	T3 level in blood from lab work
TT4	Float	TT4 level in blood from lab work
T4U	Float	T4U level in blood from lab work
FTI	Float	FTI level in blood from lab work

low number of data records present for that class. It is important to note that the classification performance does not directly influence the design of our prototype. Instead, we report them as they serve as a foundational benchmark for our ongoing and future studies in this domain. To extract explanations, we leverage two XAI techniques. To compute feature importance, we use Local Interpretable Model-Agnostic Explanations (LIME) framework [49]. LIME works by approximating the decision boundary of the black box ML model in the vicinity of a specific instance of interest (the data record being explained), thus generating what is referred to as *locally faithful explanations* [49]. To achieve this, LIME employs a two-step process: perturbation and approximation. In the perturbation step, LIME samples a set of instances around the data point under consideration and perturbs them by introducing slight modifications. Subsequently, these perturbed instances, along with their corresponding model predictions, are used to train an interpretable surrogate model such as, e.g., linear model. Feature importance is then computed based on the weights assigned to each feature in the surrogate model, reflecting the contribution of individual features to the model's decision within that specific locality. This localized interpretability enables a more nuanced understanding of the model's behavior and enhances transparency, as it allows the user to understand which features (or factors) are most influential for a specific model's decision. The effectiveness of LIME has been demonstrated across various domains, making it a valuable tool for feature importance computation and model interpretation [21,28,39,46]. Yet, we note that our prototype can rely on any XAI technique for computing feature importance.

To generate similar-case example explanations and counterexamples, we use DiCE (Diverse Counterfactual Explanations) [42]. DiCE is a method that employs optimization and heuristic approaches aimed at producing a set of counterfactual explanations that are close, in terms of their proximity measure, to the original input data record (i.e., the data sample being explained). More specifically, for a given input data point, which is, in our case, the data record whose decision is to be explained, we employ DiCE to generate a set of counterfactuals or, in other words, counterexamples that are data samples classified as a different label (class) by the ML black box and that exhibit minimal differences in both the number of features and the extend to which features differ compared to the original data record. To generate similar-case example explanations, we constrain DiCE to generate data samples that differ minimally with respect to original data record however belong to same class (i.e., are not labeled different by the ML model). It is important to highlight that any counterfactual explainer can be used in our prototype, and it is not constrained solely to DiCE. Moreover, we note that, while DiCE has proven its efficacy in generating interpretable and actionable counterfactuals [19,29], we plan to consider and eventually compare several counterfactual explainers in future work.

7.2   Prototype Interface and User Interaction

We now present a description of user's interaction with the prototype through the developed interface. The process consists of four steps. We assume that prior to interacting with the tool, the clinician examines the case at hand and formulates a hypothesis of the diagnosis of the case as belonging to one of the three classes, i.e., either *hyperthyroid, hypothyroid,* or *negative*. Once the clinician has formulated a hypothesis, the clinician engages with the tool by inputting a set of parameters. Figure 1a shows the initial page that users encounter. The input parameters required by the user are the following:

- ID of the data record (or, patient) under examination in the field *ID of data record (patient) under examination.*
- The hypothesis of the diagnosis, specifying the class that the clinician believes the case under examination should be classified as in the field *Select your hypothesis (class)*. The user has to select one of the three possible diagnosis classes.
- The desired number of counterfactual explanations the clinician wishes to investigate for each of the other two classes of diagnosis. Our system allows users to choose between 0 (no such explanations) and 10 counterexamples for each of the other diagnosis classes.

- The number of similar-case example explanations the clinicians wishes to investigate for each of the other two classes of diagnosis. Our system allows users to choose between 0 (no such explanations) and 10 similar-case example explanations.

In addition to these inputs, the user can select whether or not to have the tool compute and display feature importance explanation by checking the relative check-box present on the initial page. Finally, the clinician proceeds by clicking on *proceed*. After that, the tool provides the user with the outcome. Figure 1b shows as example of the outcome of the tool for a given data record, which consists of the following:

- The ID of the data record under examination and the hypothesis selected by the user.
- The data record under evaluation, including the features and their values.
- The set of similar-case example explanations. The example shows 3 explanations.
- The set of counterexamples for each of the other two classes. The example shows 3 explanations for each of the two classes.
- The feature importance figure showing which features exhibited positive or negative influence towards the hypothesis selected by the user.

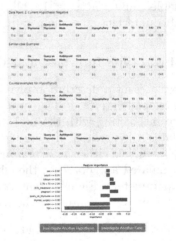

(a) Screenshot of the page the users encounter when using the prototype showing the list of input parameters that the user has to provide.

(b) Screenshot of the page that shows the system's outcome.

Fig. 1. Two screenshots of the prototype interface.

In the example shown in the figure, the system's outcome shows that similar-case explanations can be obtained by slightly altering the values of *T3*, *T4U* or *FTI* and also shows that the *TSH* value can be around 1.3 as opposed to 0.1 in the second similar-case explanation. In terms of counterexample explanations, the outcomes reveals that data records labeled as *Hypothyroid* can be obtained by drastically changing the value of *TSH* (from 0.1 to 8.0 for the first counterexample explanation, or to 6.2 for the second counterexample explanation) while minimally altering values of other features (*Age* was slightly reduced (from 77 to 73) and the features *T3*, *T4*, *T4U* and *FTI* undergone relatively small alteration). Similarly, the counterexample explanations for the *Hyperthyroid* also reveal how feature values can be altered to obtain the relative class.

After analyzing the system's outcome, the clinician can take a decision with full autonomy, if decided on the diagnosis, or proceed by testing another hypothesis for the case under investigation by clicking on *Investigate Another Hypothesis* button.

8   Phase 3: Co-designing the Prototype

In this third phase, we have conducted two workshop sessions in which we engaged an interdisciplinary group of experts in four key domains: user experience, AI in health care, ML in health care, and endocrinology.

During **the first workshop**, the conceptual model was explained to the clinicians who had the chance to provide feedback and ask questions. In that session we explored also the clinical domain(endocrinology) and its specific challenges and opportunities. We delved into his everyday practices, and on how he deals with the differential diagnosis process. It was shown also the data set on thyroid diseases and we discussed with him the features and, finally, selected the most relevant (Table 1).

The **second workshop** was focused on presenting and interacting with the prototype. This hands-on experience allowed him to articulate his needs and expectations for the prototype as well as to envision new functions. In this sense, the participants acted as informants [13]. This session was not intended for evaluating the technical solution; instead, its purpose was to demonstrate the application of the theoretical framework into a high fidelity prototype. The session was conducted online via Teams and recorded to better analyse the results. Two co-authors facilitated the session. First, the participants were asked to perform a series of tasks and provide feedback by thinking aloud. This technique allowed participants to verbally express thoughts about the interaction experience, including their motives, rationale, and perceptions. Subsequently, they engaged in a brainstorming session in which they were asked to contribute to producing ideas to better implement the concept (and the theory) into the prototype to better support their practise. The session lasted 90 min. During the workshop the participants discussed the use of the prototype into the clinical practices at large and in details by looking at each items implemented. Overall the clinicians really liked the concepts on which the prototype was based. He expressed a positive opinion about its usage on his own practices as well as in suggesting it to other colleagues. During the brainstorming the team explored how the provided functionalities could be extended and whether the information provided could be improved. For what concern the features during the brainstorming we refined their types and order to better assist clinicians in comparing the case with the counterexamples. For instance, the TSH value is given priority after the age and gender of the patient. In addition, there is no point of asking if the features need to be shown or not as these are considered relevant in all scenarios, and the system should provide them regardless. Participants agreed that the system should offer a choice between 'more important' or 'less important'. Regarding the number of counterfactual explanations and similar-case explanations provided by the system, the clinician explained that this depends on the type of diagnosis he is evaluating. For instance, in the case of euthyroid the clinicians does not need to have many and just 3 of them would be enough. In other diagnostic cases, such as hyperthyroidism and hypothyroidism, where a disease might be present, the system should suggest a higher numerical value. This would provide better support for abductive reasoning to clinicians, enabling them to explore various options and compare data from other patients. Thus, the participants agreed that a good solution was to provide a default number which is smaller (e.g. 3) in the case of euthyroid and larger (e.g. 5) in the case of hyperthyroidism and hypothyroidism. Then, eventually, the clinicians would have the option to modify the default number as needed. As output of the session we also produced a set of screenshots of the prototype with recommendations and additional features co-created by the participants. These will guide the next step of the design process, leading to a new version of the prototype.

9   Conclusion and Future Work

Inspired by [41], in this work we presented a conceptual framework to go beyond the current paradigm of using XAI in healthcare, with a specific focus on clinical diagnostic. The advocated paradigm change is based on the view that the design of a AI decision support systems has to focus on supporting the specific diagnostic reasoning of the clinician at stake in the setting under consideration. More specifically, based on three explanatory techniques – feature importance, counterexample explanations (based on counterfactuals), and similar-case explanations –, we illustrate a participatory design approach in which we engaged experts in AI, HCI, and clinicians to co-design and develop an AI prototype supporting the clinical reasoning without directly providing neither a recommendation nor, a fortiori, an explanation for it. The results of this iterative process showed how the conceptual framework could be first implemented in a ML model and then concretized into a hi-fi prototype, and how the users/stakeholders needs could be integrated and harmonised into the designed solution. During the co-design in the brainstorming session, the initial design ideas have been refined and this helped to move on to the next step. The limited sample we engaged in the study enabled us to delve into their knowledge, practices, resources and tools that they use to form the cognitive process leading to a clinical diagnosis. This immersive process allowed us to design a hi-fi prototype that embodied both the theoretical framework and the users needs. Leveraging on these result a new version of the prototype will be developed by using the anonymised data set produced by the research units at the EOC that we engaged in the first phase of the project. This prototype will be evaluated with a larger sample of clinicians, experts in the concerned domain. The purpose of this follow up study will be to assess the ability of the prototype to support the specific diagnostic reasoning and, thus, to verify that complementarity is achieved. To conclude, with this work we hope that, in addition to advance the knowledge on how to design AI-based systems for the healthcare domain, we also contribute to the current discourse on promoting virtuous adoption, trust and best practices related to such systems.

Acknowledgements. The work presented in the paper is part of the exploratory research programme *Best4EthicalAI*, financed by SUPSI. We would like to thank SUPSI for supporting our research, as well as all the individuals who have been involved in the study. Participants gave their consent to participate voluntarily in the case study that was approved by the SUPSI ethical committee. Without them, this work wouldn't have been possible. A special thanks to Gail Collyer-Hoar for her invaluable job she did in proofreading of the paper.

References

1. Ali, S., et al.: Explainable artificial intelligence (XAI): what we know and what is left to attain trustworthy artificial intelligence. Inf. Fusion **99**, 101805 (2023)
2. Arbelaez Ossa, L., Starke, G., Lorenzini, G., Vogt, J.E., Shaw, D.M., Elger, B.S.: Re-focusing explainability in medicine. Digital Health **8**, 20552076221074490 (2022)
3. Bansal, G., Nushi, B., Kamar, E., Horvitz, E., Weld, D.S.: Is the most accurate AI the best teammate? optimizing AI for teamwork. In: Proceedings of the AAAI Conference on Artificial Intelligence, vol. 35, pp. 11405–11414 (2021)
4. Bansal, G., et al.: Does the whole exceed its parts? the effect of AI explanations on complementary team performance. In: Proceedings of the 2021 CHI Conference on Human Factors in Computing Systems, pp. 1–16 (2021)
5. Bertrand, A., Belloum, R., Eagan, J.R., Maxwell, W.: How cognitive biases affect XAI-assisted decision-making: a systematic review. In: Proceedings of the 2022 AAAI/ACM Conference on AI, Ethics, and Society, pp. 78–91 (2022)
6. Buçinca, Z., Malaya, M.B., Gajos, K.Z.: To trust or to think: cognitive forcing functions can reduce overreliance on AI in AI-assisted decision-making. Proc. ACM Human-Comput. Interact. **5**(CSCW1), 1–21 (2021)
7. Cabitza, F., Campagner, A., Datteri, E.: To err is (only) human. reflections on how to move from accuracy to trust for medical AI. In: Ceci, F., Prencipe, A., Spagnoletti, P. (eds.) Exploring Innovation in a Digital World. LNISO, vol. 51, pp. 36–49. Springer, Cham (2021). https://doi.org/10.1007/978-3-030-87842-9_4
8. Cabitza, F., Campagner, A., Natali, C., Parimbelli, E., Ronzio, L., Cameli, M.: Painting the black box white: experimental findings from applying XAI to an ECG reading setting. Mach. Learn. Knowl. Extract. **5**(1), 269–286 (2023)
9. Chen, V., Liao, Q.V., Wortman Vaughan, J., Bansal, G.: Understanding the role of human intuition on reliance in human-AI decision-making with explanations. Proc. ACM Human-Comput. Interact. **7**(CSCW2), 1–32 (2023)
10. Commission, E.: Ethics guidelines for trustworthy AI. B-1049 Brussels (2019)

11. DeSmet, A., Thompson, D., Baranowski, T., Palmeira, A., Verloigne, M., De Bourdeaudhuij, I., et al.: Is participatory design associated with the effectiveness of serious digital games for healthy lifestyle promotion? A meta-analysis. J. Med. Internet Res. **18**(4), e4444 (2016)

12. Diprose, W.K., Buist, N., Hua, N., Thurier, Q., Shand, G., Robinson, R.: Physician understanding, explainability, and trust in a hypothetical machine learning risk calculator. J. Am. Med. Inform. Assoc. **27**(4), 592–600 (2020)

13. Druin, A.: The role of children in the design of new technology. Behav. Inf. Technol. **21**(1), 1–25 (2002)

14. Esteva, A., et al.: Dermatologist-level classification of skin cancer with deep neural networks. Nature **542**(7639), 115–118 (2017)

15. Facchini, A., Termine, A.: Towards a taxonomy for the opacity of AI systems. In: Müller, V.C. (eds.) Philosophy and Theory of Artificial Intelligence 2021. PTAI 2021. Studies in Applied Philosophy, Epistemology and Rational Ethics, vol. 63, pp. 73–89. Springer, Cham (2022). https://doi.org/10.1007/978-3-031-09153-7_7

16. Frauenberger, C., Good, J., Fitzpatrick, G., Iversen, O.S.: In pursuit of rigour and accountability in participatory design. Int. J. Hum Comput Stud. **74**, 93–106 (2015)

17. Gajos, K.Z., Mamykina, L.: Do people engage cognitively with AI? Impact of AI assistance on incidental learning. In: 27th International Conference on Intelligent User Interfaces, pp. 794–806 (2022)

18. Ghassemi, M., Oakden-Rayner, L., Beam, A.L.: The false hope of current approaches to explainable artificial intelligence in health care. Lancet Digital Health **3**(11), e745–e750 (2021)

19. Guidotti, R.: Counterfactual explanations and how to find them: literature review and benchmarking. Data Mining Knowl. Disc. 1–55 (2022)

20. Gunning, D., Aha, D.: Darpa's explainable artificial intelligence (XAI) program. AI Mag. **40**(2), 44–58 (2019)

21. Hailemariam, Y., Yazdinejad, A., Parizi, R.M., Srivastava, G., Dehghantanha, A.: An empirical evaluation of AI deep explainable tools. In: 2020 IEEE Globecom Workshops, pp. 1–6. IEEE (2020)

22. Haque, A.B., Islam, A.N., Mikalef, P.: Explainable artificial intelligence (XAI) from a user perspective: a synthesis of prior literature and problematizing avenues for future research. Technol. Forecast. Soc. Chang. **186**, 122120 (2023)

23. Hoffman, R.R.: A taxonomy of emergent trusting in the human–machine relationship. In: Cognitive Systems Engineering, pp. 137–164 (2017)

24. Holzinger, A., Langs, G., Denk, H., Zatloukal, K., Müller, H.: Causability and explainability of artificial intelligence in medicine. Wiley Interdiscipl. Rev. Data Mining Knowl. Disc. **9**(4), e1312 (2019)

25. Hyland, S.L., et al.: Early prediction of circulatory failure in the intensive care unit using machine learning. Nat. Med. **26**(3), 364–373 (2020)

26. Jabbour, S., et al.: Measuring the impact of AI in the diagnosis of hospitalized patients: a randomized clinical vignette survey study. JAMA **330**(23), 2275–2284 (2023)

27. Jacovi, A., Marasović, A., Miller, T., Goldberg, Y.: Formalizing trust in artificial intelligence: Prerequisites, causes and goals of human trust in AI. In: Proceedings of the 2021 ACM Conference on Fairness, Accountability, and Transparency, pp. 624–635 (2021)

28. Jeyakumar, J.V., Noor, J., Cheng, Y.H., Garcia, L., Srivastava, M.: How can i explain this to you? An empirical study of deep neural network explanation methods. Adv. Neural. Inf. Process. Syst. **33**, 4211–4222 (2020)

29. Jia, Y., McDermid, J., Lawton, T., Habli, I.: The role of explainability in assuring safety of machine learning in healthcare. IEEE Trans. Emerg. Top. Comput. **10**(4), 1746–1760 (2022)
30. Kamulegeya, L.H., et al.: Using artificial intelligence on dermatology conditions in Uganda: a case for diversity in training data sets for machine learning. BioRxiv p. 826057 (2019)
31. Komorowski, M., Celi, L.A., Badawi, O., Gordon, A.C., Faisal, A.A.: The artificial intelligence clinician learns optimal treatment strategies for sepsis in intensive care. Nat. Med. **24**(11), 1716–1720 (2018)
32. Lång, K., et al.: Artificial intelligence-supported screen reading versus standard double reading in the mammography screening with artificial intelligence trial (masai): a clinical safety analysis of a randomised, controlled, non-inferiority, single-blinded, screening accuracy study. Lancet Oncol. **24**(8), 936–944 (2023)
33. Langer, M., et al.: What do we want from explainable artificial intelligence (XAI)?-A stakeholder perspective on XAI and a conceptual model guiding interdisciplinary XAI research. Artif. Intell. **296**, 103473 (2021)
34. Lee, J.D., See, K.A.: Trust in automation: designing for appropriate reliance. Hum. Factors **46**(1), 50–80 (2004)
35. Li, X., et al.: Interpretable deep learning: Interpretation, interpretability, trustworthiness, and beyond. Knowl. Inf. Syst. **64**(12), 3197–3234 (2022)
36. Loi, M., Ferrario, A., Viganò, E.: Transparency as design publicity: explaining and justifying inscrutable algorithms. Ethics Inf. Technol. **23**(3), 253–263 (2021)
37. London, A.J.: Artificial intelligence and black-box medical decisions: accuracy versus explainability. Hastings Cent. Rep. **49**(1), 15–21 (2019)
38. Lundberg, S.M., Lee, S.I.: A unified approach to interpreting model predictions. In: Advances in Neural Information Processing Systems, vol. 30 (2017)
39. Manresa-Yee, C., Roig-Maimó, M.F., Ramis, S., Mas-Sansó, R.: Advances in XAI: explanation interfaces in healthcare. In: Lim, C.-P., Chen, Y.-W., Vaidya, A., Mahorkar, C., Jain, L.C. (eds.) Handbook of Artificial Intelligence in Healthcare. ISRL, vol. 212, pp. 357–369. Springer, Cham (2022). https://doi.org/10.1007/978-3-030-83620-7_15
40. Miller, T.: Explanation in artificial intelligence: insights from the social sciences. Artif. Intell. **267**, 1–38 (2019)
41. Miller, T.: Explainable AI is dead, long live explainable AI! Hypothesis-driven decision support using evaluative AI. In: Proceedings of the 2023 ACM Conference on Fairness, Accountability, and Transparency, pp. 333–342 (2023)
42. Mothilal, R.K., Sharma, A., Tan, C.: Explaining machine learning classifiers through diverse counterfactual explanations. In: Proceedings of the 2020 Conference on Fairness, Accountability, and Transparency, pp. 607–617 (2020)
43. Noorbergen, T.J., Adam, M.T., Teubner, T., Collins, C.E.: Using co-design in mobile health system development: a qualitative study with experts in co-design and mobile health system development. JMIR Mhealth Uhealth **9**(11), e27896 (2021)
44. Papenmeier, A., Englebienne, G., Seifert, C.: How model accuracy and explanation fidelity influence user trust. arXiv preprint arXiv:1907.12652 (2019)
45. Papenmeier, A., Kern, D., Englebienne, G., Seifert, C.: It"s complicated: the relationship between user trust, model accuracy and explanations in AI. ACM Trans. Comput. Human Interact. (TOCHI) **29**(4), 1–33 (2022)
46. Pawar, U., O'Shea, D., Rea, S., O'Reilly, R.: Incorporating explainable artificial intelligence (XAI) to aid the understanding of machine learning in the healthcare domain. In: AICS, pp. 169–180 (2020)

47. Primiero, G.: Information in the philosophy of computer science. In: The Routledge Handbook of Philosophy of Information. Routledge (2016)
48. Prosperi, M., et al.: Causal inference and counterfactual prediction in machine learning for actionable healthcare. Nat. Mach. Intell. **2**(7), 369–375 (2020)
49. Ribeiro, M.T., Singh, S., Guestrin, C.: "why should i trust you?" Explaining the predictions of any classifier. In: Proceedings of the 22nd ACM SIGKDD International Conference on Knowledge Discovery and Data Mining, pp. 1135–1144 (2016)
50. Shah, N.D., Steyerberg, E.W., Kent, D.M.: Big data and predictive analytics: recalibrating expectations. JAMA **320**(1), 27–28 (2018)
51. Shneiderman, B.: Human-Centered AI. Oxford University Press, Oxford (2022)
52. Shortliffe, E.H., Sepúlveda, M.J.: Clinical decision support in the era of artificial intelligence. JAMA **320**(21), 2199–2200 (2018)
53. Simonsen, J., Robertson, T.: Routledge International Handbook of Participatory Design. Routledge, Milton Park (2012)
54. Sivaraman, V., Bukowski, L.A., Levin, J., Kahn, J.M., Perer, A.: Ignore, trust, or negotiate: understanding clinician acceptance of AI-based treatment recommendations in health care. arXiv preprint arXiv:2302.00096 (2023)
55. Tonekaboni, S., Joshi, S., McCradden, M.D., Goldenberg, A.: What clinicians want: contextualizing explainable machine learning for clinical end use. In: Machine Learning for Healthcare Conference, pp. 359–380. PMLR (2019)
56. Topol, E.J.: High-performance medicine: the convergence of human and artificial intelligence. Nat. Med. **25**(1), 44–56 (2019)
57. Van Calster, B., Wynants, L., Timmerman, D., Steyerberg, E.W., Collins, G.S.: Predictive analytics in health care: how can we know it works? J. Am. Med. Inform. Assoc. **26**(12), 1651–1654 (2019)
58. Verma, S., Boonsanong, V., Hoang, M., Hines, K.E., Dickerson, J.P., Shah, C.: Counterfactual explanations and algorithmic recourses for machine learning: a review. arXiv preprint arXiv:2010.10596 (2020)
59. Wachter, S., Mittelstadt, B., Russell, C.: Counterfactual explanations without opening the black box: automated decisions and the GDPR. Harv. JL & Tech. **31**, 841 (2017)
60. Yin, M., Wortman Vaughan, J., Wallach, H.: Understanding the effect of accuracy on trust in machine learning models. In: Proceedings of the 2019 CHI Conference on Human Factors in Computing Systems, pp. 1–12 (2019)
61. Zednik, C.: Solving the black box problem: a normative framework for explainable artificial intelligence. Philos. Technol. **34**(2), 265–288 (2021)
62. Zhang, Y., Liao, Q.V., Bellamy, R.K.: Effect of confidence and explanation on accuracy and trust calibration in AI-assisted decision making. In: Proceedings of the 2020 Conference on Fairness, Accountability, and Transparency, pp. 295–305 (2020)

Operationalizing AI Explainability Using Interpretability Cues in the Cockpit: Insights from User-Centered Development of the Intelligent Pilot Advisory System (IPAS)

Jakob Würfel[✉][iD], Anne Papenfuß[iD], and Matthias Wies[iD]

Institute of Flight Guidance, German Aerospace Center (DLR), 38108 Braunschweig, Germany
jakob.wuerfel@dlr.de

Abstract. This paper presents a concept for operationalizing Artificial Intelligence (AI) explainability for the Intelligent Pilot Advisory System (IPAS) as requested in the European Aviation Safety Agency's AI Roadmap 2.0 in order to meet the requirement of Trustworthy AI. The IPAS is currently being developed to provide AI-based decision support in commercial aircraft to assist the flight crew, especially in emergency situations. The development of the IPAS is following a user-centred and exploratory design approach, with the active involvement of airline pilots in the early stages of development to iteratively tailor the system to their requirements. The concept presented in this paper aims to provide interpretability cues to achieve "operational explainability of AI", which should enable commercial aircraft pilots to understand and adequately trust the recommendations generated by AI when making decisions in emergencies. Focus of the research was to identify initial interpretability requirements and to answer the question of what interpretation cues pilots need from the AI-based system. Based on a user study with airline pilots, four requirements for interpretation cues were formulated. These results will form the basis for the next iteration of the IPAS, where the requirements will be implemented.

Keywords: Ethical and Trustworthy AI · Human-Centered AI · Human-AI Teaming · Explainable AI · Interpretable AI

1 Introduction

The rapid development of AI in the last years has led to more and more AI technologies reaching the productivity plateau [33]. AI algorithms are becoming more and more usable, and thus more and more integrated into our daily lives, for example in the form of big data processing, speech recognition, image recognition and many more [39]. Usable applications based on AI such as chat bots

H. Degen and S. Ntoa (Eds.): HCII 2024, LNAI 14734, pp. 297–315, 2024.
https://doi.org/10.1007/978-3-031-60606-9_17

(e.g. ChatGPT [31]), image generation (e.g. DALL-E 2 [32]), autonomous driving or intelligent robotics have already reached the stage of commercialisation or are only a few years away from it [26,33]. But what happens when AI systems enter safety-relevant and complex workplaces such as aircraft cockpits? In the field of automated driving, this issue has been discussed for several years. Examples for this are the uncanny and unsafe valley of automation, which describes the difficulty of the handover between automated driving and the human driver [17], or the explainability of automated driving systems [42]. The application of AI to the aircraft flight deck is also increasingly being discussed, as can be seen in [27].

The European Union Aviation Safety Agency (EASA) published the AI Roadmap 2.0 [13] in May 2023 to show a way forward for integrating AI into the aviation industry. In this roadmap, the concept of Trustworthy AI is required for the interface between users and AI. This concept consists of three building blocks, one of which is the "Human Factors for AI" building block, which includes the aspect of "AI operational explainability". The scientific literature also suggests that explainability is a crucial part of the Human-AI Teaming concept to build trust and support the team's situational awareness [12]. In the research area of eXplainable AI (XAI), solutions are being researched on how AI models can be made explainable [19]. It is worth noting that while these models contribute to explainability, they do not necessarily prioritise usability for end users. Instead, their focus is on enabling explainability of AI models for technical users or AI developers [24,28]. To address this problem, a user-centered development approach is advocated, for example in [2] and [5], to tailor explainability to the end user's role. This approach aims to create explainable systems for a specific use case and a specific group of end users, as also required in the EASA Roadmap 2.0 [13].

The German Aerospace Center (DLR) is currently developing the AI-based Flight Deck Decision Support System IPAS, which serves as a research platform for AI applications in the aircraft cockpit. A main objective of the IPAS is to explore and demonstrate the concept of "AI operational explainability" tailored for airline pilots in the flight deck. A crucial aspect of this system is the ability to present the results generated by the AI in such a way that the reasoning behind a result can be easily understood by pilots within an appropriate timeframe. The IPAS is being developed iteratively to involve pilots early in the process and to implement end user requirements early in the design process.

This paper presents a conceptual approach, followed by a user study, to achieve explainability by providing pilots with interpretability cues - small pieces of information intended to enable pilots to build their own explanations based on these cues. In order to identify the necessary information required by pilots, eight airline pilots were invited to participate in a study. The pilots were presented with an interface mock-up of the IPAS that provided small chunks of information about the AI-generated decision options. The participants then had to make a decision based on the information provided. The results of the study address the following question: What interpretability cues and information do the pilots need from the system to fulfil the need for explanation?

2 Background

To understand why explainability is relevant for the IPAS, and to better understand the concept described in Sect. 3, it is important to provide an overview of definitions and more information about the topic "Explainable AI". This is followed by a more detailed description of the IPAS.

2.1 Explainability of AI

Explainability of AI can be defined as the ability of an AI-based system to provide the human end user with understandable information about how the AI calculated the system's results. The EU Commission defines explainability as follows: "Feature of an AI system that is intelligible to non-experts. An AI system is intelligible if its functionality and operations can be explained non-technically to a person not skilled in the art." [3] Similar definitions were made, for example, by Mohseni et al. [29] or Arrieta et al. [2].

Reasons to Make AI Systems Explainable. AI algorithms are frequently described as black boxes because they lack transparency and their inner mechanisms cannot be observed. In 2015, the Defense Advanced Research Projects Agency (DARPA) launched a program to make these black box AI models more explainable. Looking back at the program, which ended in 2021, the authors write: "Users prefer systems that provide decisions with explanations over systems that provide only decisions. Tasks where explanations provide the most value are those where a user needs to understand the inner workings of how an AI system makes decisions." [20]. From a human-system integration perspective, there are many features that benefit from AI explainability for AI-based systems. One reason to make AI systems explainable is to build or to calibrate trust in the system [12,34] and the fact that AI explainability is a requirement for humans to be able to perform a task efficiently by using or managing AI systems [19,21]. Explainability of AI plays a central role when considering the concept of Human-AI Teaming (HAT), because explainability supports appropriate trust building, human-AI team situation awareness, and also supports human-AI team performance [12].

The Need for End User Friendly Explainable AI. DARPA introduced the term XAI, which is commonly used to refer to a scientific field. Much of the work on the research topic XAI focuses on modelling, which means the development of XAI algorithms. In this context, not much attention is usually paid to usability or practical interpretability for end users [1,43]. Most models are build for AI researchers, data experts and AI developers, the so-called technical users. Here,

XAI is used to check their AI algorithms, to gain an understanding of the black box, and to improve algorithms. However, the group of non-technical users or the end users is largely ignored in the literature [24,28]. Cynthia Rudin [36] brings another aspect to the discussion about XAI. She suggests that instead of trying to explain how the black box works, models should be designed that make results of the black box interpretable for their specific application. In decision support systems with potentially serious and complex decisions, incorrect interpretations of the XAI models can lead to serious errors. She also points out that building interpretable models is difficult and requires expertise in the field of the planned application.

Jin et al. [24] concluded that the research fields of human computer interaction and XAI must be brought together. End user-centered explainable AI models and guidelines need to be defined to support AI experts in developing user-friendly AI applications. The fact that most end users do not have any background knowledge in AI or machine learning also needs to be taken into account when developing explainable AI systems. One challenge is that end users have very different needs, depending on the specific application and task. For example, a doctor needs different explanations and data when making a diagnosis than a recruiter needs when deciding whether to hire someone [24]. Explainable AI needs to be customized for different applications and end user groups, depending on the level of detail required, the knowledge of the user, and the specific application domain [43].

Degen et al. [5] underlines the demand for end user centered development of AI explainability: "Research papers report that explainability cannot be built into technology without understanding the needs, goals, and tasks of the target user group. Little research has been done to provide evidence that explanations should be user role specific."

EASA Roadmap 2.0: "AI Operational Explainability". When developing an AI-based support system for a commercial aircraft flight deck, it is important to be aware of the relevant authorities and their plans for implementing this technology. The aviation safety authority responsible for aviation in the European Union, EASA, presented the concept of "Trustworthy AI" in the second version of the AI roadmap, which was published in May 2023 [13]. The published roadmap was used, for example in [37], which describes how the roadmap and the "Assessment List for Trustworthy Artificial Intelligence" [3] was applied to the development of a digital air traffic controller. The "Trustworthy AI" concept for example categorizes future AI-based applications into three human oversight levels: "Level 1: assistance to humans", "Level 2: human-AI teaming" and "Level 3: advanced automation." The definition of AI explainability, as part of Trustworthy AI, according to the roadmap: "Among other aspects, AI operational explainability deals with the capability to provide the human end users with understandable, reliable and relevant information with the appropriate level of details and with appropriate timing on how an AI/ML application produces its results." [13] This explainability is to be implemented both for development and for practical application in operation - hence the term "AI operational explainability" - taking into account the specific needs of the particular end user.

2.2   The Intelligent Pilot Advisory System

The IPAS is currently under development at the DLR with the aim of exploring and demonstrating "AI operational explainability" for AI-based pilot assistance systems in the cockpit of commercial aircraft. The IPAS is being developed using an iterative development model called "Human System Exploration", as presented in [16]. The model is used to explore, test, and extend new ideas, user requirements, and system designs in each iteration. In [41], pilots were interviewed about AI-based assistance for the flight deck, to find use cases, identify initial user requirements and concerns about AI in the flight deck. Based on the results, basic functions and a system model of the IPAS were described conceptually to fulfil the selected use case. The IPAS is a system that should support aircraft crews in decision-making situations in both emergencies and normal day-to-day operations with AI-generated recommendations options for action. Participants in [41] also raised concerns about the explainability of the output of the AI system, so the key feature of the IPAS should be to present these options in a way that they are explainable for pilots, as also required by the EASA AI Roadmap 2.0. In addition, an appropriate performance trade-off between explainability and decision time has to be found. This for example described as the "speed-certainty dilemma" in [15].

The planned system model of the IPAS was first presented and described in [41] and essentially consists of two modules. The AI-Crew Interaction System (AICIS) and the AI Core Module (AICOM). Data from the aircraft system as well as from the environment, such as weather or traffic data, should continuously analysed by the AICOM [7,8]. For example, the AICOM should detect emergency situations and generates operational options, based on the detected situation. The AICIS is supposed to be the interactive interface between the AI and the flight crew. For example, situational facts and options generated by the AICOM will be displayed on the AICIS, and in particular, AI-based information should be presented at an appropriate level of explainability for the flight crew.

As already described in [41], several use cases can be considered for the IPAS. The use case "Supporting the crew in emergency situations by providing alternative airport options" is used for the study in this paper. In this use case, a technical failure occurs that causes the crew to abort the flight and find a suitable alternative airport in the vicinity. The IPAS assists the pilots in the decision-making process by assessing the situation and identifying alternative airport options. The AICOM analyses the effects of the technical failure, as well as environmental and airport data, and generates options for alternative airports based on this information. The AICIS then presents these options to the pilots, who use the IPAS recommendations and the information provided to make and execute a final decision.

3   The Concept of Achieving Operational Explainability of AI Using Interpretability Cues

With the aim of implementing the operational explainability of AI for the IPAS, an approach for an explainability concept must be found. On the basis of the previously described background information about AI explainability, the following requirements were derived for the approach to be found:

- User-centred: Explanation tailored to the use case and the explainability needs of the end user.
- Provide an appropriate level of explainability.
- Ensure a good explainability-performance trade-off.

3.1   Finding an Approach

To formulate an AI explainability concept for the IPAS, we need to find a suitable approach on how to achieve this, taking into account the requirements mentioned before. The initial idea is to break down AI results into smaller and interpretable pieces of information so that users can build an explanation for the results generated by the system. This approach was described by Stevens and De Smedt [38]: "Furthermore, interpretability [...] is the ability to provide an explanation that consists solely out of single chunks of information, preferably in a human understandable fashion." A similar approach is described by Lipton [25], who mentioned post-hoc interpretability to describe an approach in which individual pieces of data are extracted from the AI models to make it easier to understand the inner working of these models. Lipton goes on to say that this method would not expose the operation of the black box but can provide useful information for end users. Users can thus find their own explanations based on the chunks of information. Hoffman et al. [21] states that "explanatory systems benefit by providing information that empowers users to self-explain, rather than just delivering some sort of representation of the output of an algorithm, a representation that is believed to be adequate as an explanation." Finally Stevens and De Smedt expect a good performance trade off from this method of providing only individual chunks of information [38].

3.2   Terms and Definitions

In order to achieve AI operational Explainability for the IPAS, the AI results should therefore be interpretable on the basis of information chunks. It is important to define the terms "explainability" and "interpretability".

Molnar comments on the concept of interpretability: "There is no real consensus about what interpretability is in machine learning. Nor is it clear how to measure it." [30] However, there are various definitions that can be found in the literature, e.g.:

- Arietta et al. [2]: "It is defined as the ability to explain or to provide the meaning in understandable terms to a human."

- Miller [28]: "Interpretability is the degree to which a human can understand the cause of a decision."
- Molnar [30]: "The higher the interpretability of a machine learning model, the easier it is for someone to comprehend why certain decisions or predictions have been made. A model is better interpretable than another model if its decisions are easier for a human to comprehend than decisions from the other model."
- European Commission [3]: "Interpretability refers to the concept of comprehensibility, explainability, or understandability. When an element of an AI system is interpretable, this means that it is possible at least for an external observer to understand it and find its meaning."

In general, it can be stated that interpretability does not expose the internal mechanisms of the black box, but rather makes the reasoning explainable to the end user. The difference to explainability becomes clear again in [38]. Stevens and De Smedt describe that there are differences between XAI models, interpretable AI models and the terms explainability and interpretability. The first two terms refer to methods or technologies, while the latter two terms refer to system characteristics. XAI models are designed to reveal the inner workings of non-transparent AI models, while interpretable AI models are inherently transparent. However, the term "interpretability" refers to the ability of a AI system to allow end users to understand the systems results, by only providing information chunks. The term "explainability" refers to the general ability of an AI-based system to explain how the system works. A high level of interpretability of the system's output is a possibility to make a system explainable for certain use cases where it is not necessary to look inside the AI model. It is important to emphasize that in this approach, explainability and interpretability are not separate concepts. Explainability works as a general concept, while an interface with a high level of interpretability, consisting of individual pieces of interpretable information, is one way to achieve better explainability.

3.3   The Concept of Interpretabilty Cues

As described at the beginning of this section, the approach of using individual pieces of information - which we call "interpretability cues" - should be applied to the IPAS with the goal of achieving AI operational explainability.

This concept could be supported by Watzlawick's first axiom: "You cannot not communicate" [40] - with the difference that in our case the IPAS cannot not communicate. People are always trying to interpret the behavior of others, regardless of how much verbal communication takes place. Regarding the IPAS and the use case described in Sect. 2.2, the crew acts as the receiver and the IPAS acts as the transmitter. Even if the IPAS only provides an AI-generated final result, such as a numerical airport rating, pilots might still try to interpret the result and try to understand the reasoning behind the AI's decision options. In order to support the interpretation of the AI results, the IPAS should provide additional appropriate interpretability cues to enable the flight crew to form an explanation of the AI results.

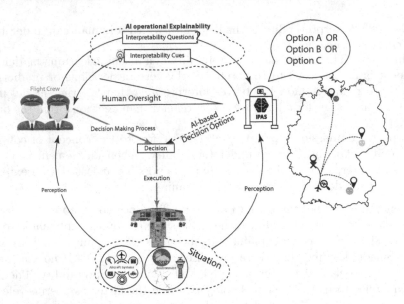

Fig. 1. This model shows the interaction between the flight crew and the IPAS in the use case: "Supporting the crew in emergency situations by providing alternative airport options". It also highlights the concept of how to achieve AI operational explainability. The system provides interpretability cues to answer the crew's interpretability questions to achieve "AI operational explainability". The visualization is inspired by [18].

Figure 1 describes how the IPAS is supposed to interact with the flight crew and to achieve "AI operation explainability" in the selected use case. The model shows that both the crew and the IPAS perceive the situation, e.g. the aircraft's systems and the environment, such as air traffic, weather or airport information. If the crew needs to find an alternate airport, e.g. due to an emergency, the IPAS will assist the crew by selecting and assessing several alternate airport options. The crew will ask the system questions to interpret the system's results - the questions may vary depending on the situation; in return, the system should provide the crew with appropriate interpretability cues. Based on the interpretative cues provided by the system, the pilots can form their own explanation of how the AI calculated the results and what the reasons are for a given result.

4   Explorative User Study

The study followed the chosen design approach to explore initial user requirements for potential interpretability cues in a user study, to tailor the interpretability cues to the needs of the flight crews. The first iteration of the IPAS explores what questions the pilots raise about the results generated by the AI.

4.1 Description of the Study

Participants in the study performed a flight mission scenario using a flat panel Airbus A320 simulator. The simulation started during cruise flight and the pilots were instructed to follow their known procedures. In the event of an emergency, the pilots were asked to perform their known procedures (e.g. FORDEC, Facts - Options -Risks&Benefits - Decision - Execution - Check [23]), but also using an interface mock-up of the IPAS integrated into the simulator cockpit. After starting the simulation, the pilots flew for about five minutes in cruise flight before one engine caught fire, resulting in the necessity to abort the flight and land at an alternate airport. As all the pilots fly for German airlines, a route in the USA was chosen. Pilots were instructed to not make decisions based on their instinct and prior knowledge of the individual airports, but should actively use the IPAS mock-up.

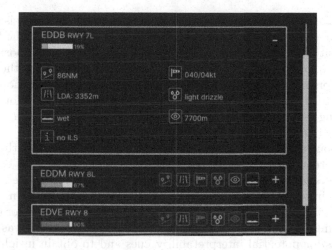

Fig. 2. The interface mock-up available to the pilots in the study. The scenario in the screenshot is different from the one used in the study. Pilots can navigate through the airport options to find information about local conditions and the specific IPAS rating. Taken from [35].

To support the search for an alternative airport, [35] realized an interface mock-up of a simplified IPAS, that can be seen in Fig. 2. In order to comply with the concept described in Sect. 3, some initial information about the results of the AI was provided on the mock-up. These included decision factors used by the AI as input data and a color coding in yellow (low negative influence) or red (strong negative influence) to indicate the degree these decision factors have a negative influence on AI's airport rating. Table 1 shows the assessed airports and the information provided to the pilots. The selection of which information to display was defined in consultation with team internal pilots.

Since the IPAS AI was still under development, the displayed AI data was simulated, similar to the principle of the Wizard of Oz method [4]. Therefore, the information presented on the mock-up was not the result of an AI process,

Table 1. Alternative airport options and the information provided to pilots on the interface mock-up.

City	Tuscon		Phoenix			Albuquerque			El Paso	
ICAO Code	KTUS		KPHX			KABQ			KELP	
Distance	86NM		156NM			210NM			150NM	
RWY Name	29 R	21	25 L	25R	26	21	26	30	22	26L
RWY Length	3352m	2134m	2377m	3139m	3502m	3048m	4204m	1829m	3664m	2751m
RWY Width	46m	46m	46m	46m	46m	46m	46m	46m	46m	46m
RWY Condition	wet		standing water			wet			wet	
Precipitation	light drizzle		heavy thunderstorm			heavy rain			rain	
Wind Speed	12kt + 7kt Gusts		17kt + 5kt Gust			25kt			16kt	
Wind direction	320		210			320			308	
Crosswind	headwind	crosswind	headwind	headwind	headwind	tailwind	crosswind	headwind	crosswind	light crosswind
Visibility	7700m		730m			3100m			6800m	
Approach	no ILS	no ILS	ILS/DME	ILS/DME	ILS/DME	no ILS	no ILS	no ILS	ILS/DME	no ILS
IPAS Rating	0,78	0,28	0,5	0,53	0,52	0,41	0,6	0,23	0,59	0,7

but assumptions generated by the authors using a multi-criteria decision matrix. Each decision factor was given a weight based on how important the factor is in the current situation. These factors were then assessed for each airport according to the local situation. The overall airport rating was calculated as the sum of all decision factors multiplied by their weighting. This approach was chosen because it is closest to the way AICOM will calculate the results. The pilots were told in the briefing before the flight that the values are AI-generated in order to get information about the interpretation of AI-generated values.

Throughout the flight, during FORDEC and while operating the mock-up, the pilots were asked to speak aloud what they were thinking, to comment on their actions and considerations, to describe how they interpreted, evaluated and used the information provided and what information they were missing when working with the mock-up. This think aloud method is described, for example in [22] to determine the users' mental model. The aim of this method was to identify requirements for potential interpretability cues and to obtain insights into the decision-making process. In the following debriefing, the pilots were given the opportunity to provide further comments on the simulator flight and decision-making process using the IPAS mock-up to obtain additional information.

4.2   Participants and Ethics

Eight commercial airline pilots, all male, were invited to take part in the test. The participants were between 30 and 59 years old and had between 2800 and 18300 flight hours. At the time of the study, five pilots were flying as first officers and three pilots held the rank of a captain. The study was conducted in accordance with the DLR internal quality manual for Human in the Loop simulations. A consent form and an explanation of the European General Data Protection Regulation (GDPR) were signed. They were informed that image, video, and audio recordings would be made and saved on internal secure servers. They were instructed about the purpose of the data processing and that the study could be stopped at any time without justification and without consequences for the participants.

4.3 Results

The aim of the study was to collect qualitative statements and observations about which interpretability cues could be helpful in interpreting the results of the AI. A transcript of the think aloud statements was written and observations of the pilots' operation were noted. Particular attention was paid to statements and observations related to the interpretation of the AI results, such as questions about the AI assessment of the airports or comments regarding missing information about the AI process. In the subsequent debriefing, the participants were asked about individual statements and observations in order to understand the background behind them. Statements that addressed the same topic or were similar in content were then grouped together and a core statement for each group was formalized. Table 2 shows the most mentioned and grouped statements regarding possible interpretability needs.

Table 2. Observations and statements from the pilots about working with the IPAS mock-up during the scenarios and during debriefing.

No.	Core Statements / Observations	Qty.	Sample statements and observations
1	Pilots consulting maps for an initial overview	5	Before using the IPAS, maps were consulted for orientation: own position, position of possible airports, position of mountains/weather fronts
2	Pilots want to know which factors have led to a rating. And how the factors influence the rating.	5	"Were NOTAMS taken into account?" "What factors were considered in the assessment?" "Does it include the system errors?" "What factors were included in the LDR?" "How is the overall risk actually calculated?" "Why is runway condition red, but overall rating orange?"
3	Pilots wonder whether the data is up-to-date, outdated or even a forecast of the AI for the future.	4	"How old is the AI data?" "Is current data available?" "Does the system show the status quo or the status to be expected at the destination?" "Look ahead on the map ... how will the weather develop until arrival? Does the AI take this into account?"

continued

Table 2. continued

No.	Core Statements / Observations	Qty.	Sample statements and observations
4	Pilots are looking for the factors they know and the judgements based on them.	3	"What factors were taken into account in the assessment?" "Was the available approach procedure taken into account when calculating the rating?" "Perfect, here I can see the wind at the airport"
5	Pilots try to compare the AI results for similarities or differences to their own assessment.	2	"Amber was indicated, I found this value very much within the limits and then I also trust the other assessments, as this one has definitely calculated conservatively" "For me, 16kt Crosswind is only orange, as it is within the limits" "I have a similar view to the IPAS assessment, I have cross-checked this"

In addition of the original research question of the study, we recognized, that all pilots follow a similar decision process and they mentioned similar demand for decision factors. When asked in the debriefing, the participants named several decision factors they would expect from the IPAS as explanations for the airport options. It also became clear here that the timing of the decision-making process could play a role in the explainability of the IPAS results, as the need for information and explanation differs depending on the phase in the decision-making process.

Requirements for Interpretability Cues. The most notable observation (No. 1 in Table 2) was that the pilots first looked for a geographical orientation to get an initial overview of the situation before using the IPAS. However, this could also be due to the fact that the scenario was intentionally set in an area unknown to the pilots. No interpretability cue was derived from this observation, as this is more of a requirement for the system and interface design. The need for orientation and gaining an initial overview of the situation does not refer to an AI result to be explained, but refers to building situational awareness, which plays a crucial role in the decision-making process (see for example [11]) and should be taken into account when designing the workflow for the IPAS.

Core statement No. 4 shows that the pilots searched for and used the decision factors and assessments with which they were familiar from their training and experience. During the decision-making process, the information requirements varied, particularly within each FORDEC phase, and depended on the specific stage of the decision-making process, with variations in both content and level of detail. The pilots used the displayed factors and also actively asked for missing decision factors if they were not available on the mock-up. It seems to be important that the system provides decision factors and assessments that match the pilots' mental model of the decision making process. This could be formulated as the first requirement for the interpretability cues.

First Interpretability Cues Requirement. *The interpretability cues should display the decision factors typically used by the flight crew to make decisions, adapted to the current information needs of the decision process phase.*

The second requirement can be derived from core statement No. 5 that pilots want to check the displayed AI results for plausibility and thus want to understand how the ratings were calculated. They looked for causes and values that influenced the AI rating. It seems that the pilots want to assess the plausibility of the AI results by comparing them to their mental model. This was observable when pilots asked about the influence of specific decision factors that were not shown on the mock-up, or when pilots were able to follow the cause of a rating based on the decision factors that were shown. So the following requirement can be derived:

Second Interpretability Cues Requirement. *The interpretability cues should provide information about the assessment that the flight crew can compare with their own perception, experience, and assessment.*

The study showed that in the next iteration of the system, a distinction needs to be made between AI-generated data (e.g. AI-generated forecasts) and rule-based data (e.g. conventional calculation of crosswinds or database values), as well as AI-generated assessments (e.g. AI rating of an airport). Although not implemented in this study, AI in general can compute current and future results using current or predicted data in future system iterations. Core statement No.3 shows that the pilots wondered whether the system was displaying AI results for the current state or for a predicted state in the future. They also wanted to check the age of the data on which the AI calculations were based. Therefore, the temporal information of the displayed data seems to be very important for the pilots. This formed the third requirement for the interpretability cues.

Third Interpretability Cues Requirement. *The interpretability cues should show whether displayed information is the result of an AI process and whether displayed information (AI assessment or AI-generated information) is based on real-time data or on an AI forecast of the situation in the future.*

Core statement No. 2 indicates that some pilots were not able to assess the validity of the results of the AI because they could not identify which factors and information had been taken into account by the AI and in what way. This question addresses the number of decision factors included, the combination of multiple decision factors that resulted in an assessment, and the individual weighting of these factors. This leads to the fourth requirement for the interpretability cues.

Fourth Interpretability Cues Requirement. *The interpretability cues must indicate which factors and factor combinations are included in the assessment of the AI and how they affect a system output.*

Decision Making Sequence and Decision Factors. Examination of the decision processes observed in the study can serve as a basis for designing the next iteration of the design of the next iteration of the system and may provide a first approach to fulfill the first and second interpretability cue requirements. As expected, all pilots used a similar process and looked for similar decision factors when using FORDEC as a decision-making method. However, there were notable differences in the way participants approached each phase of FORDEC. Differences were observed particularly in the O-Options and R-Risks & Benefits phases, more specifically in the detailed process of identifying and evaluating possible airport options. The importance assigned to specific decision factors varied among pilots; for instance, while some prioritized the availability of an instrument landing system, others favored a longer runway.

Based on the results of the user study, a process overview was created that illustrates how pilots identify and evaluate different airport options, along with the different groups of decision factors that lead to the assessment of the airports, as shown in Fig. 3. Pilots first assess the aircraft's condition and the surrounding area to preselect multiple potential alternate airports. Understanding the condition of the aircraft is the basis for decision making. Pilots must understand the system malfunctions and consider the operational limitations and risks resulting from the malfunctions, as well as the criticality of the situation. After assessing the technical status of the aircraft, pilots must decide if continued flight is possible or if a landing at an alternate airport is necessary. In addition, potential operational limitations for landing must be identified. The geographic picture gives the pilot an overview of the surrounding area. This includes the own position, the path of the route, weather affected areas, special features of the terrain such as mountains or water bodies, the density and behavior of air traffic in the area, but also cities and airports in the vicinity, that could be possible alternate airports.

Then the pilots iteratively assess and compare the preselected airport options, refining their assessment by considering the decision factors in more detail. Through this iterative process, some options are eliminated, leading to the identification of the presumed best alternative. Various decision factors are taken into account for each option:

- Environmental Factors: Factors regarding the environment are various weather phenomena that occur at the airport: Wind magnitude, gusts, wind direction, possible hovering winds, visibility, precipitation or possible thunderstorms.
- Airport Details: The details of a possible alternate airport include the location (site, altitude, current distance), infrastructural information (regulations, emergency services), runway (RWY) information (RWY length, RWY width,

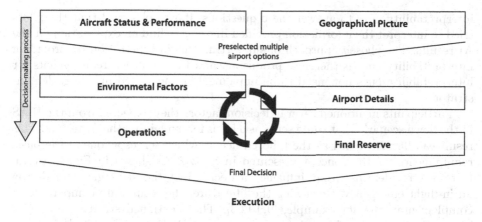

Fig. 3. Description of the different decision factors and the timing (from top to bottom) of identifying and assessing alternate airport options as observed in the study.

number of RWY runways), approach operational information (available approach procedures, airport environment, special procedures). These factors influence the decision-making process, depending on the operational limitations, but are also related to the environmental influences at the airport.
– Operations: Operational aspects of diversion concern the handling of passengers and cargo at the airport. In addition, the preference of the airline can be included in the decision. Finally, the question of whether the aircraft, crew, passengers and cargo can leave the airport, i.e. whether a hotel, maintenance facilities or even a replacement aircraft is available.
– Final Reserve: What options are available when reaching the alternate airport? What is the remaining flight time for possible go-arounds? What emergency options are still available upon arrival, such as other accessible and suitable airports?

5   Discussion

The research question of how explanations can be presented in an understandable way is also listed as the result of a workshop conducted by Helmut Degen [6] in 2021, which recommends the "design exploration" approach to address this question. A similar approach was applied in this study, leading to initial results. This study aimed to explores the question, of which interpretability cues and information the pilots want from the system to fulfil the need for explanation. Based on the results presented in Sect. 4.3, we defined four requirements for interpretability cues that could support the pilots in interpreting the AI results and thus to achieve operational explainability of the IPAS.

As expected, the pilots asked interpretability questions about the system output, some that could be answered by the information provided by the mock-up and some that could not, so it is necessary to find and implement appropriate interpretability cues to answer these questions. It was observed that the pilots tried to interpret the information provided in order to find an explanation for the AI results. The chosen approach of supporting this interpretation by providing interpretability cues is therefore promising, and the identified requirements for interpretability cues now need to be implemented and tested in a next demonstrator.

Participants mentioned several decision factors they expected from the IPAS in the flown scenario that could serve as a basis for explaining the AI results. This result can be recognized as the tailored needs, which serves as one of the basic requirements for the concept presented in Sect. 3. As shown in Fig. 3, several factors were identified that influence a decision at the strategic level during an in-flight emergency. Reviewing the literature, the results are comparable or complementary to, for example, [9,10,23]. The mentioned strategic level [14] means the navigation from airport A to airport B or the strategic decision on which alternative airport options are suitable and whether to fly to airport C or airport D as an alternative. These decision factors, required assessments and the process flow should serve as the basis for the next iteration of the IPAS to fulfill both the first and second interpretability cue requirements. This is because both requirements are related to the pilots' mental model during decision making.

5.1   Conclusion and Outlook

This paper proposes a concept to operationalize the explainability of AI results in practical applications, here for the AI-based flight deck decision support system IPAS. The outlined concept emphasises that explainability can be achieved by providing specific information chunks, known as "interpretability cues", which enable end users to formulate explanations for results generated by AI. During the initial phase of the user-centred and explorative development process, airline pilots participated in a study where they used a mock-up of the AI-based IPAS in simulator sessions. Their task was to select alternate airports in emergency situations. The mock-up provided initial decision factors about the AI recommendations, defined by domain experts. The purpose of this study was to collect think aloud statements and observations from pilots while working with the system, to get more detailed insights in a following interview, and finally to identify potential interpretability cues based on the statements and observations. This work resulted in the definition of four different requirements for interpretability cues, a draft of the decision making process flow and necessary decision factors. The next iteration of the system will implement these findings and require validation through a second user study. Furthermore, the proposed approach will be tested in the next user study to determine if it can achieve an appropriate level of explainability while providing the required performance trade-off. The study has also identified decision factors and a decision process workflow that will be an integral part of the next iteration of the system.

Acknowledgments. The research was conducted at the German Aerospace Center in Brunswick. We would like to thank the participants of the study for sharing their knowledge and experience with us. Finally, we thank our reviewers for their insights.

References

1. Adadi, A., Berrada, M.: Peeking inside the black-box: a survey on explainable artificial intelligence (XAI). IEEE Access **6**, 52138–52160 (2018). https://doi.org/10.1109/ACCESS.2018.2870052
2. Arrieta, A.B., et al.: Explainable Artificial Intelligence (XAI): Concepts, Taxonomies, Opportunities and Challenges toward Responsible AI (2019). http://arxiv.org/pdf/1910.10045v2
3. Commission, E., Directorate-General for Communications Networks, C., Technology: The Assessment List for Trustworthy Artificial Intelligence (ALTAI) for self assessment. Publications Office (2020).https://doi.org/10.2759/002360
4. Dahlbäck, N., Jönsson, A., Ahrenberg, L.: Wizard of Oz studies – why and how. Knowl.-Based Syst. **6**(4), 258–266 (1993). https://doi.org/10.1016/0950-7051(93)90017-N
5. Degen, H., Budnik, C., Conte, G., Lintereur, A., Weber, S.: How to explain it to energy engineers? In: Chen, J.Y.C., Fragomeni, G., Degen, H., Ntoa, S. (eds.) HCI International 2022 – Late Breaking Papers: Interacting with eXtended Reality and Artificial Intelligence, LNCS, vol. 13518, pp. 262–284. Springer Nature Switzerland and Imprint Springer, Cham (2022). https://doi.org/10.1007/978-3-031-21707-4_20
6. Degen, H., Ntoa, S.: From a workshop to a framework for human-centered artificial intelligence. In: Degen, H., Ntoa, S. (eds.) HCII 2021. LNCS (LNAI), vol. 12797, pp. 166–184. Springer, Cham (2021). https://doi.org/10.1007/978-3-030-77772-2_11
7. Djartov, B., Mostaghim, S.: Multi-objective multiplexer decision making benchmark problem, pp. 1676–1683 (2023). https://doi.org/10.1145/3583133.3596360, https://www.scopus.com/inward/record.uri?eid=2-s2.0-85168995697&doi=10.1145
8. Djartov, B., Mostaghim, S., Papenfuß, A., Wies, M.: Description and First Evaluation of an Approach for a Pilot Decision Support System Based on Multi-attribute Decision Making, pp. 141–147 (2022).https://doi.org/10.1109/SSCI51031.2022.10022076, https://www.scopus.com/inward/record.uri?eid=2-s2.0-85147800209&doi=10.1109
9. Endsley, M.R.: Supporting situation awareness in aviation systems. In: Computational Cybernetics and Simulation, pp. 4177–4181. Institute of Electrical and Electronics Engineers, New York, NY (1997).https://doi.org/10.1109/ICSMC.1997.637352
10. Endsley, M., Farley, T., Jones, W., Midkiff, A., Hansman, R.: Situation Awareness Information Requirements For Commercial Airline Pilots, vol. Report no. ICAT-98-1. International Center for Air Transportation (1998)
11. Endsley, M.R.: Toward a theory of situation awareness in dynamic systems. Hum. Factors **37**(1), 32–64 (1995). https://doi.org/10.1518/001872095779049543
12. Endsley, M.R.: Supporting human-AI teams: transparency, explainability, and situation awareness. Comput. Human Behav. **140**, 107574 (2023). https://doi.org/10.1016/j.chb.2022.107574
13. European Union Aviation Safety Agency: EASA-AI-Roadmap 2.0: A human-centric approach to AI in aviation (2023)

14. Flemisch, F., Abbink, D.A., Itoh, M., Pacaux-Lemoine, M.P., Weßel, G.: Joining the blunt and the pointy end of the spear: towards a common framework of joint action, human-machine cooperation, cooperative guidance and control, shared, traded and supervisory control. Cogn. Technol. Work **21**(4), 555–568 (2019). https://doi.org/10.1007/s10111-019-00576-1

15. Flemisch, F., Preutenborbeck, M., Ripkens A., Burlage L.: Dilemma model of cooperative guidance and control to solve the speed-certainty-dilemma in human-autonomy teaming: first sketch. In: 4th IEEE International Conference on Human-Machine Systems (ICHMS) (2024)

16. Flemisch, F.O., et al.: Human systems exploration for ideation and innovation in potentially disruptive defense and security systems. In: Adlakha-Hutcheon, G., Masys, A. (Hg.): Disruption, Ideation and Innovation for Defence and Security, pp. 79–117. Advanced Sciences and Technologies for Security Applications, Springer, Cham (2022). https://doi.org/10.1007/978-3-031-06636-8_5

17. Flemisch, F., et al.: Uncanny and unsafe valley of assistance and automation: first sketch and application to vehicle automation. In: Schlick, C.M., et al. (eds.) Advances in Ergonomic Design of Systems, Products and Processes, pp. 319–334. Springer, Heidelberg (2017). https://doi.org/10.1007/978-3-662-53305-5_23

18. Flemisch, F., Kwee-Meier, S., Neuhöfer, J., Baltzer, M., Altendorf, E., Özyurt, E.: Kognitive und kooperative Systeme in der Fahrzeugführung: Selektiver Rückblick über die letzten Dekaden und Spekulation über die Zukunft. Kognitive Systeme (2012). https://doi.org/10.17185/duepublico/31356

19. Gunning, D., Aha, D.: DARPA's explainable artificial intelligence (XAI) program. AI Mag. **40**(2), 44–58 (2019). https://doi.org/10.1609/aimag.v40i2.2850

20. Gunning, D., Vorm, E., Wang, J.Y., Turek, M.: DARPA's explainable AI (XAI) program: a retrospective. Appl. AI Lett. **2**(4), e61 (2021). https://doi.org/10.1002/ail2.61

21. Hoffman, R.R., Miller, T., Klein, G., Mueller, S.T., Clancey, W.J.: Increasing the value of XAI for users: a psychological perspective. KI - Künstliche Intelligenz (2023). https://doi.org/10.1007/s13218-023-00806-9

22. Hoffman, R.R., Mueller, S.T., Klein, G., Litman, J.: Measures for explainable AI: explanation goodness, user satisfaction, mental models, curiosity, trust, and human-AI performance. Front. Comput. Sci. **5**, 1096257 (2023).https://doi.org/10.3389/fcomp.2023.1096257

23. Hörmann, H.J.: FOR-DEC - A Prescriptive Model for Aeronautical Decision Making. In: 21. WEAAP-Conference, Dublin, 28.-31.03.94 (1994). https://elib.dlr.de/27044/, lIDO-Berichtsjahr=1994, pages=7,

24. Jin, W., Fan, J., Gromala, D., Pasquier, P., Hamarneh, G.: EUCA: a practical prototyping framework towards end-user-centered explainable artificial intelligence (2021). http://arxiv.org/pdf/2102.02437v1

25. Lipton, Z.C.: The mythos of model interpretability. Commun. ACM **61**(10), 36–43 (2018). https://doi.org/10.1145/3233231

26. Maslej, N., et al.: Artificial Intelligence Index Report (2023).https://doi.org/10.48550/ARXIV.2310.03715

27. Miller, M., Holley, S., Halawi, L.: The evolution of AI on the commercial flight deck: finding balance between efficiency and safety while maintaining the integrity of operator trust. In: Artificial Intelligence, Social Computing and Wearable Technologies. AHFE International (2023). https://doi.org/10.54941/ahfe1004175

28. Miller, T., Howe, P., Sonenberg, L.: Explainable AI: Beware of Inmates Running the Asylum Or: How I Learnt to Stop Worrying and Love the Social and Behavioural Sciences (2017). http://arxiv.org/pdf/1712.00547v2

29. Mohseni, S., Zarei, N., Ragan, E.D.: A multidisciplinary survey and framework for design and evaluation of explainable AI systems. ACM Trans. Interact. Intell. Syst. **11**(3–4), 1–45 (2021). https://doi.org/10.1145/3387166
30. Molnar, C.: Interpretable Machine Learning: A Guide for Making Black Box Models Explainable. 2 edn. (2022). https://christophm.github.io/interpretable-ml-book
31. OpenAI: ChatGPT. https://chat.openai.com/ (2023). Accessed 12 Dec 2023
32. OpenAI: DALL.E 2 is an AI system that can create realistic images and art from a description in natural language. https://openai.com/dall-e-2 (2023). Accessed 12 Dec 2023
33. Perri, L.: What's New in Artificial Intelligence from the 2023 Gartner Hype Cycle. https://www.gartner.com/en/articles/what-s-new-in-artificial-intelligence-from-the-2023-gartner-hype-cycle (2023). Accessed 12 Dec 2023
34. Ribeiro, M.T., Singh, S., Guestrin, C.: "Why Should I Trust You?". In: Krishnapuram, B., Shah, M., Smola, A., Aggarwal, C., Shen, D., Rastogi, R. (eds.) Proceedings of the 22nd ACM SIGKDD International Conference on Knowledge Discovery and Data Mining, pp. 1135–1144. ACM, New York, NY, USA (2016). https://doi.org/10.1145/2939672.2939778
35. Riedesel, N.: Nutzerzentrierte Gestaltung und Umsetzung eines Interfaces für KI-basierte Risikobewertung im Airline Cockpit. Thesis, Universität Hamburg (2023). https://elib.dlr.de/193780/
36. Rudin, C.: Stop explaining black box machine learning models for high stakes decisions and use interpretable models instead. Nat. Mach. Intell. **1**(5), 206–215 (2019). https://doi.org/10.1038/s42256-019-0048-x
37. Stefani, T., et al.: Applying the Assessment List for Trustworthy Artificial Intelligence on the development of AI supported Air Traffic Controller Operations (2023). https://doi.org/10.1109/DASC58513.2023.10311323
38. Stevens, A., de Smedt, J.: Explainability in process outcome prediction: guidelines to obtain interpretable and faithful models. Eur. J. Oper. Res. (2023). https://doi.org/10.1016/j.ejor.2023.09.010
39. Teich, I.: Meilensteine der Entwicklung Künstlicher Intelligenz. Informatik Spektrum **43**(4), 276–284 (2020). https://doi.org/10.1007/s00287-020-01280-5
40. Watzlawick, P., Bavelas, J.B., Jackson, D.D.: Menschliche Kommunikation: Formen, Störungen, Paradoxien. 1, Hogrefe, Bern, 13., unveränderte auflage edn. (2017). https://doi.org/10.1024/85745-000
41. Würfel, J., Djartov, B., Papenfuß, A., Wies, M.: Intelligent pilot advisory system: the journey from ideation to an early system design of an AI-based decision support system for airline flight decks. In: Human Factors in Transportation. AHFE International (2023). https://doi.org/10.54941/ahfe1003844
42. Zablocki, É., Ben-Younes, H., Pérez, P., Cord, M.: Explainability of deep vision-based autonomous driving systems: review and challenges. Int. J. Comput. Vision **130**(10), 2425–2452 (2022). https://doi.org/10.1007/s11263-022-01657-x
43. Zhu, J., Liapis, A., Risi, S., Bidarra, R., Youngblood, G.M.: Explainable AI for designers: a human-centered perspective on mixed-initiative co-creation. In: Browne, C. (ed.) Proceedings of the 2018 IEEE Conference on Computational Intelligence and Games (CIG 2018), pp. 1–8. IEEE, Piscataway, NJ (2018). https://doi.org/10.1109/CIG.2018.8490433

Towards a Framework for Interdisciplinary Studies in Explainable Artificial Intelligence

Paula Ziethmann[1,2,3]([✉])(iD), Fabian Stieler[1,2](iD), Raphael Pfrommer[1],
Kerstin Schlögl-Flierl[1,2,3](iD), and Bernhard Bauer[1,2](iD)

[1] University of Augsburg, Universitätstraße 2, 86156 Augsburg, Germany
{paula.ziethmann,fabian.stieler}@uni-a.de
[2] Center for Responsible AI Technologies, Augsburg, Germany
[3] Centre for Interdisciplinary Health Research, Augsburg, Germany

Abstract. In this interdisciplinary paper, we present the SocioTechXAI Integration Framework (STXIF), a novel approach that aims to seamlessly integrate technical advances with social science methodologies for a nuanced understanding of Explainable Artificial Intelligence (XAI) tailored to specific use cases. We begin with an overview of related work exploring XAI in both the social sciences and computer science. The focus is on the presentation of the STXIF, which includes the XAI Compass and socioscientific analysis of stakeholder perspectives. The perspectives of these stakeholders, classified by the XAI Compass as Model Breakers, Model Builders, and Model Consumers, are investigated using qualitative content analysis. By examining the EU AI Act as a Model Breaker and conducting scenario-based focus group discussions with Model Consumers (medical professionals) and Model Builders (developers) in a real medical diagnostic use case, we demonstrate the specific insights gained through the STXIF application and its adaptability in real scenarios. The discussion section addresses the complex relationships between different XAI goals and their implications for a flexible and adaptive development approach. The practical implications extend to the concrete development and implementation of XAI in real-world applications, in line with the thematic focus of the Human Computer Interaction International Conference, which emphasizes human-centered design and usability in interactive systems. Emphasizing nuanced interactions with XAI and its practical applications establishes a foundational framework for future interdisciplinary research and application in the evolving landscape of human-computer interaction (HCI).

Keywords: Explainable Artificial Intelligence · SocioTechXAI Integration · Interdisciplinary Research

---

P. Ziethmann, F. Stieler — Equal contribution.

1   Introduction

Artificial Intelligence (AI) has long been recognized for its potential, with the unveiling of ChatGPT, a text-based dialog system released by OpenAI in November 2022, reiterating the remarkable capabilities of modern technologies. Fueled by advances in Machine Learning (ML), AI can now swiftly process and analyze data, augmenting and refining human decision-making processes and much more.

In this evolving landscape, the medical domain has become a focal point for the transformative power of AI. Computer programs are now capable of predicting individual disease trajectories and therapeutic outcomes through AI-based analyses of extensive medical records. Intelligent assistance systems, care robots, and medical wearables significantly contribute to patient care by providing assistance, monitoring vital signs, and facilitating continuous assessment of chronic conditions [41]. Simultaneously with the increasing importance of AI in medicine, XAI in the medical domain becomes crucial, particularly with the certification of medical AI products in mind. While AI systems can be technically researched and developed proficiently, their effectiveness in medical practice hinges on the acceptance and utilization by medical personnel. To achieve this acceptance and trust, and for several other reasons discussed in this paper, a broad research landscape on XAI has emerged.

However, within the extensively explored field of XAI in medicine, a critical gap exists: the need for comprehensive social science research to understand explainability. We believe that this is due to the unavailability of an applicable, specifiable framework that provides social science methods to capture the necessary perspectives.

While considerable attention has been paid to unraveling the technical intricacies of AI models, there is limited understanding of how stakeholders, including physicians, patients, healthcare personnel, and medical decision-makers, perceive and interpret explainability. It is critical to understand how these stakeholders engage with explained information, foster trust, influence decision-making, and address potential concerns associated with the use of AI. While this concern is also recognized in technical literature [3,30], there is often a lack of methodological framework or easily accessible guidance on how such consideration of perspectives can happen.

In this context, this interdisciplinary paper aims to identify a framework that can help technical XAI research integrate social science methods. To this end, we will first outline the state of research on XAI in the medical domain while identifying a significant research gap - the social science exploration of the multifaceted understanding of explainability across different stakeholders. By delving into these dimensions, the study not only contributes to technical explanations, but also sheds light on the human and social dynamics essential for the effective integration of AI into medical practice.

In the context of our overarching goal, this paper is structured to unfold a comprehensive exploration of XAI. We commence with an insightful review of Related Work, dividing our examination into two disciplines: XAI in Social

Science (2.1) and XAI in Computer Science (2.2). Following this contextualization, our primary objective (3) is to present the STXIF, a framework for interdisciplinary XAI studies seamlessly integrating technical advancements with socio-scientific methodologies. This framework provides a nuanced approach for use-case-specific applications. Moving forward, we detail the components of the STXIF, namely the XAI Compass (3.2), Policy Analysis (3.3), and Scenario-based Focus Group Discussions (3.4). Subsequently, we shift our focus to the practical application of the STXIF, exemplifying its utility through a case study in the field of medical diagnostics under Empirical Results (4). This practical exercise illustrates the framework's adaptability in a real-world scenario. Concurrently, we engage in a discussion on the handling of empirical results within a specific use case (4.2). Finally, our exploration concludes with a reflection on Limitations and an Outlook for future research endeavors (5).

2   Current State of Research

2.1   XAI in Social Science

The socio-scientific exploration of XAI has gained substantial prominence in recent years. While technical advancements in the development of AI systems have achieved remarkable strides, the social, ethical, and psychological facets tied to integrating these technologies are of paramount importance. Johs et al. emphasize in "Explainable artificial intelligence and social science: Further insights for qualitative investigation" the role of social sciences in XAI research, especially qualitative investigations and user studies [19]. Schmid and Wrede highlight in "What is missing in XAI so far? - An Interdisciplinary Perspective" the need for an integrated interdisciplinary approach based on, not only technical, but on psychological, linguistic and sociological theories [38]. In the discourse, the paper of Miller "Explanations in Artificial Intelligence: Insights from the Social Sciences", emerges as a significant literature review that leverages socio-scientific concepts to transpose insights from a top-down approach onto the evolution of XAI [29]. Miller's paper underscores that explanations within AI systems do not merely resolve technical challenges but also potentially cultivate user trust and acceptance. The paper accentuates the role of social sciences in investigating human interactions with AI systems, elucidating how individuals perceive, interpret, and respond to AI decisions. Miller draws upon socio-scientific concepts to engender crucial insights.

In his influential work, Miller highlights the importance of employing contrastive "Why" questions, shedding light on their essential role in enhancing the quality of explanations within AI systems. His emphasis on the part of these questions underscores their ability to provide deeper and more meaningful insights into AI decision-making processes, contributing significantly to the user's comprehension and trust in these systems. Miller argues that probabilities in explanations take a backseat to causal references. He asserts that while probabilities may provide statistical information, causal explanations offer a more robust foundation for users to comprehend AI decisions. Moreover, Miller contends that AI systems' explanations are inherently social, forming an integral part of a larger conversation or interaction. He posits that these explanations are not static, isolated entities but dynamic components that evolve through ongoing dialogues between users and AI systems. Recognizing this social dimension is vital for understanding how AI explanations are perceived and integrated into real-world contexts, especially within the medical field.

Miller's work has profoundly impacted the field of socio-scientific research in XAI. It has been cited thousands of times, signifying its importance and influence in shaping the discourse. However, it's worth noting that many of these citations, like Miller himself, do not provide concrete methods of how to reconcile social science findings with the technical research of XAI. In the medical realm of XAI application, studies have commenced to probe into the social ramifications and human responses to AI decisions. Researchers have explored how physicians and medical personnel react to explanations provided by AI-based diagnoses, and how such reactions influence their decision-making processes. These studies have unveiled that the acceptance and trust in AI systems are significantly contingent upon the quality and comprehensibility of the explanations furnished. However, they are typically conducted either by technical researchers lacking expertise in social science methodologies (cf. [29], p.2) or by social scientists whose insights face challenges in resonating within the XAI discourse. Our paper aims to bridge this gap. For this reason, we will next look at XAI in Computer Science.

2.2 XAI in Computer Science

Driven by the increasing complexity and opacity of ML models, which, despite their high predictive performance, often offer little insight into the underlying decision-making processes, there is a push to enhance the comprehensibility of these systems for various users through suitable interpretation mechanisms. Given the rapidly growing research field, numerous comprehensive reviews exist in the literature. While the work of [43] focuses on terminological nuances of the research area, the works of [4,5,9,37,39] propose possible taxonomies.

A central topic in technical XAI research is the balance between the performance of ML models, such as predictive accuracy, speed, and resource consumption, and their explainability. In simplified terms, more complex models often promise higher predictive accuracy but tend to be less transparent and, thus, harder to interpret. Interpretable machine learning is a field closely related to XAI, relevant because it technically contributes as the basis for many XAI concepts. Due to the plethora of methods published in recent years, there are also extensive compilations on this [3,30].

Typically, approaches are differentiated between ante-hoc, intrinsically explainable models, corresponding to the Explainable-by-Model Design paradigm [36], and post-hoc. The latter includes methods to provide insights into a black-box model's workings after being trained. Techniques like Layer-Wise Relevance Propagation [6], Local Interpretable Model-agnostic Explanations [34], and Shapley Additive Explanations [23] are prominent examples.

These procedures are suitable for different model types and are generally characterized as model-agnostic. Additionally, there are methods for specific model architectures, such as Neural Networks, which create, for example, Pixel Attribution Saliency Maps, including the Grad-CAM method [40]. Another possible categorization is according to the scope of the explanation, whether it encompasses individual predictions (local) or the entire model (global). The results computed by the methods can often result in statistical metrics, which technical experts primarily use.

To address this dilemma, another part of technical XAI research explicitly deals with the stakeholder perspective [15,22]. This area, for example, involves visualization techniques aimed at translating complex model decisions into visually interpretable formats. Heatmaps, for instance, are used in image classification systems to show which parts of a sample are crucial for classifying an object.

Further, XAI research is viewed through the lens of HCI [13,31]. In this sub-area, the concept of interactive explanations is gaining importance. These approaches allow users to interact with the AI system through dialogues and feedback loops, fostering an understanding of the model outputs [10]. In this context, evaluating the explanations through appropriate methods and measurable metrics is crucial in assessing the effectiveness and usefulness of various approaches. Typically, the understandability, relevance, and accuracy of the explanation are evaluated [32], which, according to the approach of Doshi-Velez and Kim, can be determined concerning specific tasks and either through human or non-human input [12].

Even though the technical XAI discourse engages with and recognizes the importance of stakeholder perspectives, integrating these perspectives often happens through interviews or quantitative feedback, which would benefit from qualitative social research and a more accurate social science methodology. Especially in recent years, XAI has especially become a discipline in its own right from a technical perspective, underscoring the need for a methodical and careful approach to investigations in the interdisciplinary area of XAI research.

3   The SocioTechXAI Integration Framework

3.1   Overview of the Framework

As the field of XAI experiences the participation of diverse actors, insights from a social science perspective become imperative [29]. Although technical facets of AI models are widely explored, there is often limited socio-scientific research on the perceptions of their explainability by the specific, relevant stakeholders that are heard in the technical XAI discourse. We believe that this is due to the unavailability of an applicable, specifiable framework that provides social science methods to capture the necessary perspectives.

We have identified a substantial research gap in the existing corpus of literature, as shown in 2.1. Miller's research approach, which we characterize as "top-down", has transposed insights from social sciences onto the technological development of XAI. In contrast, our research strategy, which aligns with a "bottom-up" perspective, endeavors to invert the application of socio-scientific methods from end-users to the developmental stage. Within our approach, we seek to delve into the perceptions and understandings of various stakeholders. Our socio-scientific methodology commences at the level of individual stakeholders, capturing their viewpoints on the goals of explainability of AI systems. This approach facilitates a more profound, contextually nuanced analysis, ushering novel perspectives to fathom what these stakeholders expect from the explanations provided by AI systems, what they understand them, and, most importantly, what goals they associate with them.

By addressing this research lacuna and employing a "bottom-up" methodology, our paper strives to encapsulate not only the technical challenges of XAI but also the social realities of those directly impacted by these systems. This contributes to rendering XAI implementation more effective, fostering user acceptance and trust [28], thereby establishing a more harmonious fusion of advanced technology and human experience.

To this end, we introduce our STXIF, which integrates technical insights with social science studies. This approach bridges the gap by aligning XAI methodologies with user needs. STXIF encompasses three main components:

1) Our visual instrument, the XAI Compass, is derived from the state of the art of technical research on XAI. Inspired by Hong et al., this compass delineates three distinct stakeholder groups: Model Consumers, Model Builders, and Model Breakers [17].
2) In the second step, we delve into the policy perspective, i.e., the perspective of the model breaker. This step requires customization based on the specific location. Given that our analysis is conducted in Germany, we scrutinize the EU AI Act recently approved by Germany.
3) To capture the perspectives of model consumers and model builders, we propose, in a tertiary step, conducting two scenario-based focus group discussions. This method also should be tailored to specific use cases.

3.2 XAI Compass

Establishing a common foundation for the application of our socio-scientific methods, we initiate with a conceptual and technical perspective. To this end, we have devised a visual tool, shown in Fig. 1 termed the XAI Compass - a meticulously crafted schematic representation inspired by the 3×3 organization of roles, phases, and objectives proposed in [17]. This compass systematically structures the respective aspects, depicting three distinct stakeholder groups: Model Consumers, Model Builders, and Model Breakers.

The innermost layer categorizes stakeholders across the AI ecosystem. Model Builders, primarily data scientists and engineers, craft AI models. Model Breakers include e.g. domain experts who act as evaluators or auditors, as well as

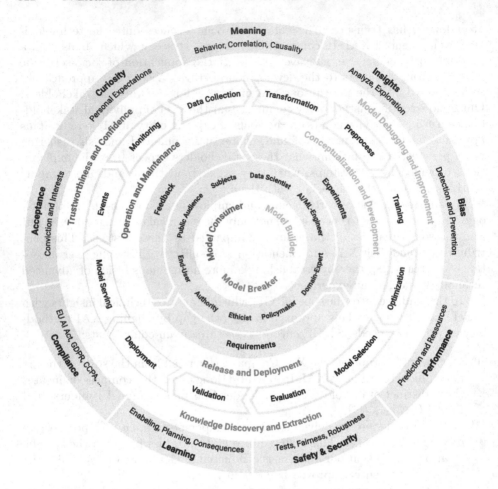

Fig. 1. The XAI Compass. This visual tool is one of three main components of STXIF and provides a holistic view of roles, phases and objectives at XAI.

applicable guidelines or regulations from ethicists or policymakers. Model Consumers are those who encounter or are indirectly affected by the AI system as end-users.

The middle layer outlines common AI lifecycle stages. While the individual tasks in a pipeline vary for each domain and use case, there are three main phases: Conceptualization and Development, Release and Deployment, and Operation and Maintenance. The XAI Compass emphasizes the mostly iterative nature of these processes. Moving counterclockwise between the role and phase layers reveals three important feedback mechanisms that have a technical and sociological impact on XAI: experimentation, feedback, and requirements.

The outer layer outlines objectives for XAI applications. For model debugging and optimization, technical methods are utilized to guarantee error-free AI performance and achieve desired outcomes. While Model Builders often use model interpretations for problem identification and prediction communication [16,20], other stakeholders seek to translate complex AI operations into comprehensible insights.

The XAI Compass is derived from the current state of technical research and encapsulates the technical discourse prevalent in XAI research. While we draw on the technical domain of XAI research, we intend to augment it with socio-scientific empirical studies. Thus, we specifically reference the delineation of actors into model breaker, model consumer, and model builder, as well as the outermost layer representing the actors' objectives of XAI. We contend that the Compass and the articulated objectives serve as valuable tools for a better understanding of the focal concerns of XAI stakeholders. Nevertheless, concepts such as meaning, acceptance, etc., may be perceived as buzzwords, lacking clarity regarding their specific implications in a given use case. These buzzwords can be imbued with meaning through our second and third steps, i.e., through our qualitative socio-scientific methods, aiming for a more nuanced application of XAI.

3.3 Policy Analysis

In the second step of our framework, we turn our attention to the policy perspective. As mentioned above, our second step is location-specific and may need adaptation accordingly. To grasp the viewpoint of model breakers, we analyze the current version of the EU AI Regulation [2] to comprehend the understanding, guidelines, and objectives of explainable AI from a political standpoint.

The EU AI Act, or the Regulation on Artificial Intelligence, constitutes a legislative initiative by the European Union aimed at establishing clear ethical standards and regulations for the deployment of Artificial Intelligence. It is aimed at making the EU a world-class hub for AI and ensuring that AI is human and trustworthy [1] and considered one of the most influential advancements in AI regulation to date [14,33]. This regulatory framework focuses particularly on high-risk AI systems and underscores the importance of transparency, accountable AI development, as well as data protection and privacy. The regulation seeks to strike a balanced approach between fostering innovation and safeguarding citizens' fundamental rights and values, contributing significantly to the responsible and sustainable use of AI within the European Union.

However, XAI has received minimal attention thus far. The term "explainability" does not appear at all, and "explainable" is mentioned only once. Here, we posit that this dearth of attention is attributable to the fact that the XAI discourse predominantly navigates within distinct technical boundaries. Nevertheless, requirements for XAI can be derived from other directives within the AI Act. We employ qualitative content analysis following Mayring [25,26](2010; 2014) to capture these requirements. In this analysis, our XAI Compass serves as the category system (cf. [27], p. 693), guiding the analytical process. Through this analysis, we anticipate gaining a policy perspective understanding of XAI, facilitating an implementation aligned with implicit demands on XAI within the AI Act.

Specifically, this entails that the nine objectives of the Compass-Meaning, Insights, Bias, Performance, Safety & Security, Learning, Compliance, Acceptance, and Curiosity-constitute the main categories of our analysis (cf. [27], p. 692), to which we have assigned specific passages from the EU AI Act. The goal is to imbue these categories with context-specific meaning in the socio-scientific methodological vocabulary corresponding to an explication, resembling a hermeneutic approach but with a more rule-governed process (cf. [27], p. 696). For this purpose, we conduct our software-assisted qualitative analysis of the EU AI Act using MAXQDA. MAXQDA is an analytical tool enabling the manual categorization of passages, the analysis of combinations of categories, the quantification and visualization of relationships between categories, and the annotation of data with notes and comments. The results of applying the framework in the policy perspective on the AI Act are described in 4.1.

3.4   Scenario-Based Focus Group Discussions

Our contribution aims not only to comprehend the technical and policy intricacies of XAI but also to explore the social realities confronted by those directly affected by these systems. Accordingly, in a third step, we advocate for implementing two scenario-based focus group discussions: one involving model consumers and the other model builders. This method should be customized to specific use cases. Our scenario-based focus group discussions were executed within a real application context in medical diagnostics, specifically in the realm of cardiology diagnostics. We then analyzed the collected data using qualitative content analysis, again using the XAI Compass as a category system as described in 3.3.

The focus group methodology is a group interview, usually consisting of five to eight participants and one facilitator. Using focus groups, a variety of information can be obtained within a social context, which means that, as a salient feature, the interaction between the interviewees is part of the research data [35]. Since people's knowledge and opinions are not always conveyed in well-thought-out statements, it is useful for people to have the chance to use forms of day-to-day communication like anecdotes, jokes, teasing, and arguing, as well as humor and irony. Another advantage is that using focus groups does not discriminate against people who cannot read or write, as well as people reluctant to be interviewed alone [21]. Robinson points out that focus groups can be instrumental in healthcare settings, i.e., in evaluating the quality of hospitals and health services or assessing the effectiveness of specific medical programs or tools [35].

Furthermore, [18] argue that focus groups are the most common methods used for qualitative research in XAI alongside interviews and observations. [7] conducted a focus group interview with three clinicians and three developers to design an XAI solution for a clinical decision support system. [44] used two focus groups consisting of data scientists and researchers to evaluate a design framework of a software for explainable feature selection. Using scenarios makes it easier for the interviewees to understand the different dimensions and nuances of the technologies to be discussed. For our case, it was more useful to include clear and realistic application scenarios based on empirical research rather than exaggerated or futuristic scenarios [8].

In our use case, the model consumers consisted of medical professionals. The model builders were represented by AI developers with expertise in data science. The tool around which the use case revolved is an AI-based 12-lead ECG Electrocardiography (ECG) device. While its basic function, the recording of ECGs, is no different from a conventional ECG device, the distinguishing factor here is the additional use of AI technology. In our case, the model builders had little to no knowledge about ECGs but high AI knowledge, and the model consumers had moderate knowledge of ECGs but low knowledge of AI.

Both group discussions consisted of an introduction, followed by a discussion of the three respective scenarios, and a final debate. For each scenario, the participants were given approximately 20 min to discuss. In the first scenario, the device records an ECG and transmits it to the AI. The AI then provides a diagnosis (in this case, PVC, premature ventricular contraction) with no additional information or explanations, as described in. The question the interviewees were asked to discuss was, "What are your thoughts on the presented AI-based 12-lead ECG device?". In the second scenario, additional information was provided. Firstly, a probability was given that indicates how certain the AI is in its diagnosis. Second, a visual explanation was given using a color code indicated in the ECG image as shown in [42]. The discussion question for this scenario was, "What are your thoughts on this expansion?". The third scenario extended the second one with some more information:

1. Participants were given five more Test-ECGs, all classified with the same diagnosis.
2. The color code was extended from one color to two colors, one indicating sections that contribute negatively to the diagnosis and one indicating sections that contribute positively to the diagnosis.
3. Those sections were also presented as bar charts, which further increased the local explanation of this particular sample.

After presenting the changes, the same question as in the second scenario was discussed. The discussions were recorded, transcribed, and qualitatively analyzed using the method described in Sect. 3.3.

4 Empirical Results

After introducing the framework and the social science methods in the previous chapter, this section aims to present the results of our particular applications. Specifically, we focus on applying qualitative content analysis to the policy perspective of the EU AI Act and the qualitative content analysis applied to our two scenario-based focus group discussions in medical diagnostics. The objective of this chapter is twofold: firstly, to provide insights into how XAI is understood and negotiated by these stakeholders, contributing to the interdisciplinary research and implementation of XAI in medical diagnostics. Secondly, this chapter can be read as an illustrative example of the outcomes achievable when applying our framework. Following the presentation of results, we discuss potential next steps based on the findings.

4.1   EU AI Act

In this section, we present the findings of our analysis of the policy perspective, where we aimed to infuse a more comprehensible and use-case-specific meaning into the nine goals outlined in the XAI Compass through a qualitative content analysis of the EU AI Act as described in 3.3. We began by utilizing the XAI Compass goals as primary categories for our analysis. The intention was to associate these categories with specific passages in the EU AI Act, establish sub-categories, identify connections, and conduct quantitative considerations. Our analysis exposed several noteworthy observations.

Firstly, the categories *Curiosity* and *Learning* were not discernible in the EU AI Act. We attribute this absence to the Acts's specific policy perspective, primarily focused on guidelines for responsible AI technologies and risk avoidance. Concepts such as creating XAI for curiosity or pursuing (e.g., medical) knowledge expansion, which falls under Learning, do not align with the Act's objectives.

We successfully assigned text passages from the Act to the remaining seven XAI Compass goals. Thus, we better understand their meaning from a political perspective. After coding, we looked at the text passages assigned to a category and discussed the connections and meanings. The main findings are presented here.

From the policy perspective, *Insights* were identified as arising through monitoring the operations of AI systems, automatic recording of errors, and technical documentation. *Performance* was discussed in terms of the conformity of the anticipated procedures or processes. Notably, both categories were described and treated in a highly technical manner, with limited emphasis on values, reasons, or a specific context. Consequently, when Insights were attributed to a specific purpose and context, it often transformed into the analysis-category of *Meaning*. For instance, if the aim of Insights is to enable specific users to interpret the system's output or recognize the knowledge boundaries of AI, it becomes more context-specific and user-oriented, falling under the category of Meaning. A related insight from our analysis is that within the technical XAI discourse represented by our Compass, different goals may imply the same or very similar technical processes. The implication for developing and implementing AI systems might be that well-considered, subtle practical variations cover different policy goals.

A specific purpose frequently addressed in the EU AI Act, also represented in our Compass, is the purpose of XAI to detect or minimize *Bias*. This perspective highlights a strong connection between XAI and bias, a relationship also reflected in the literature [24]. For example, XAI could be used to uncover bias in data sets and provide epistemological insights into individual and collective bias, as well as raise awareness of bias in general and stimulate debate about how to deal with it. However, if this opportunity is not seized, and bias in AI systems remains invisible or even obscured by XAI, there is a risk that bias will become entrenched in society. From a risk perspective, the EU AI Act tends to emphasize the second side.

Acceptance as a goal of XAI was closely linked to the category of *Trust*. Trust, in turn, was often mentioned in connection with a potential conformity assessment to ensure trust and acceptance. Trust and acceptance, however, are not treated as standalone goals. They were mentioned, for example, as instruments to place AI systems on the market or implement them in their respective fields of application.

Not surprisingly, for a regulatory framework proposal, the factor of *Compliance* was also duly acknowledged. Compliance in the context of XAI was discerned in terms of standardization processes and effective legal remedies for affected individuals, often mentioned in the context of damage that had already occurred. The category of *Safety & Security* emerged as the most prevalent in our analysis, given the Act's foundational reliance on a "risk methodology". Definitions and categories provided in the Act aimed to classify AI systems into specific risk factors. The proposed "risk management system" ([2], Article 9) can be perceived as closely connected to the requirements for XAI, especially when considering XAI within the research field of technology assessments (TA). Integrating XAI into TA merits further investigation, constituting a potential area for future research.

A crucial revelation during our analysis was the distinction between instrumental and standalone goals of XAI. The EU AI Act treated Acceptance and Trust as instrumental values, serving as instruments to facilitate the implementation of AI systems. Goals such as Insights and Performance, on the other hand, were further subordinated to other instrumental goals. In contrast, Safety & Security was acknowledged as a standalone goal. This distinction can help with use-case specific research of XAI to create a hierarchy that is helpful for implementation.

4.2   Developers and Medical Professionals in Cardiology Diagnostics

In this section, we present the results of our analysis of scenario-based Focus Group Discussions. Following the approach outlined in Sect. 3.4, we conducted a qualitative content analysis, with the nine goals outlined in the XAI Compass serving as our primary analytical categories. The overarching objective was to enhance the understanding and application of XAI from the perspectives of Model Consumers and Model Builders. Explicitly, this involved analyzing which goals from our compass emerged in the discussions and examining the nuanced understanding of these goals.

The main points the Model Consumers of AI systems, i.e., medical professionals, discussed throughout the discussion were *Aspects* of *Acceptance* and *Meaning*. If they were using an AI-supported ECG tool in a clinical context, they wanted to know how the AI found its way to the diagnosis and based on what kind of (and how much) data the AI was trained. All that information was missing in the first scenario and was only partly added in the second and third scenarios. They emphasized that AI could provide a second opinion, especially in difficult cases, but it should not be relied on blindly. Another important aspect was the need for a clear and unambiguous presentation of results: It should be in the right place (e.g., not right next to the medically irrelevant SampleID); if used, abbreviations must be comprehensible and unmistakable; and there should only be relevant, and not too much information displayed. Here, an important connection between user design / user interface and XAI becomes clear from a consumer perspective. These aspects also relate to aspects of *Safety & Security*, as in an acute situation only the information relevant to a rapid diagnosis count. In the third scenario, it was emphasized that although the additional data is mostly redundant for an acute diagnosis, it can be very helpful for further practical training and *Learning* environments.

The Model Breakers, i.e., the developers, also complained about missing or unclear information in the first and second scenario. This was formulated somewhat more technically, such as the scaling of the ECG-image, font sizes or decimal places, but focused also on information about the training procedure and the data quality and quantity used for AI-training. The selected Test-ECGs added in the third scenario appeared to be a bit random for the data scientists since their lack of medical knowledge made it hard for them to identify similarities to the original ECG. Thinking about the *Acceptance* of end users (model consumers), they sometimes switched between talking about medical staff and patients: While the display of additional ECGs might help medical staff to understand the AIs findings better, it may confuse the patients and even lead to a loss of *Trust* in the model. This need to empathize with the end-user perspective and connect it to their expectations, knowledge, and processes reinforces our intention for this paper. In contrast to the model consumers, the model builders also mentioned legal aspects (*Compliance*), such as international standards, certificates, or state-of-the-art specifications.

Comparing the findings from our focus groups to the AI Compass Goals, some aspects were more intensively discussed than others. However, a notable finding was that both groups extensively deliberated on the goal of achieving end-user acceptance of the AI system. To attain this objective of XAI, there was a consensus that it is crucial to elucidate how the AI arrived at its conclusions, coupled with a transparent and comprehensible presentation of the underlying training data. Both groups implicitly expressed the desire to find *Meaning* behind the AI system, more on a behavioral than purely technical level. Thus, if a hierarchy, as in 4.1, is to be presented here again, acceptance is discussed as a standalone goal and meaning as an instrumental goal to achieve acceptance. Aspects of *Safety & Security* were not central but were mentioned a few times, especially concerning situations with highly pathological ECGs or complicated diagnoses. Legal aspects did not play a role in the model consumer focus group, while for the model builders, it was relevant in the context of uniformity and comparability of systems on an official, ideally national, or even global level. This difference in prioritization and the associated perception of responsibility is very interesting to see. Aspects of *Learning* did not play a role for the model builders, while for the model consumers, especially the additional information given in the third scenario was relevant for potential further learning processes and trainings of medical staff. Aspects relating to *Bias* were scarcely or not at all discussed in both focus groups. While it could be argued that bias plays a rather unimportant role in the design of the use case behind, for example, presentation features or the amount of information given, this observation could also indicate that direct involvement of the actors narrows the view and that aspects such as bias are more prominently discussed only from a certain distance.

4.3 Discussion

Our study, the application of our STXIF framework, successfully provided nuanced interpretations of the goals of the XAI Compass from three different perspectives: the perspective of the model breakers, i.e., the political perspective, the perspective of the model consumers, in this case, the medical professionals, and the perspective of the model builders, i.e., the developers. Our analysis sheds light on the nuanced relationships and overlaps among different goals within the technical XAI discourse represented by our Compass. The implication is that seemingly distinct goals in the XAI Compass when analyzed in the context of specific use cases and perspectives, can converge or share substantial similarities. This understanding allows for a more flexible and adaptive approach to developing XAI, where minor adjustments or variations in implementation strategies can effectively address diverse and interconnected goals. In essence, our findings emphasize the need for a contextualized interpretation of XAI goals, where the intricate interplay of objectives can be navigated through tailored and pragmatic applications within specific domains.

Our differentiation between instrumental and standalone objectives of XAI not only contributes to a nuanced understanding of their interrelations but also offers practical advantages for development and implementation. By recognizing instrumental goals like Acceptance and Trust as instruments to facilitate the implementation of AI systems, developers gain insights into how these goals serve as pivotal means for market placement and field deployment. This hierarchical framework thus provides a roadmap for developers to navigate the complex landscape of XAI, ensuring a more targeted and effective implementation that aligns with overarching goals.

In the context of our focus on medical diagnostics, certain recommendations emerged. Firstly, the limited emphasis on Bias, particularly in projects closer to practical application than research initiatives, underscores the challenges in balancing the value of all available data with the complexities of data acquisition efforts. Practical projects often prioritize data accessibility, making issues of bias appear less prominent. Moreover, the questions posed by model consumers and builders suggest a desire for causal explanations as elaborated by Miller described in 2.1. Comparing these inquiries with existing literature on causal explanations in medical contexts can provide valuable insights for improving XAI systems in the medical domain. The clear connection between user interface design and XAI, emphasized by medical professionals, highlights the importance of cross-cutting research between these two areas to improve the interpretability and acceptability of AI systems in the clinical setting. Additionally, the potential for continuous learning by medical professionals through interaction with XAI systems suggests avenues for further exploration. Understanding how XAI can contribute to the ongoing education and learning of healthcare practitioners represents a valuable area for future research.

Our findings hold practical implications for the development and implementation of XAI in real-world applications, particularly in the critical domain of medical diagnostics. The nuanced perspectives provided by model breakers, consumers, and builders offer valuable insights for tailoring XAI systems to meet stakeholders' diverse needs and expectations. These findings align with the focus of the Human-Computer Interaction International Conference, emphasizing the importance of human-centric design and usability in interactive systems.

5   Limitations and Outlook

In this study, we have introduced the STXIF, a contribution to bridging the gap between the XAI discourse and social science research. By creating this framework, we hope to successfully contribute to making XAI more applicable and interdisciplinary. Based on the XAI Compass, the STXIF enhances the conceptual understanding and application of XAI in real-world scenarios and addresses the complex interplay of technical, social, and ethical considerations.

Despite the contributions of this study, it is crucial to recognize inherent limitations. The categories embedded in the XAI Compass, while providing a comprehensive starting point, may not perfectly align with the multifaceted realities of XAI deployment. As with any deductive research approach, predefined categories might not fully capture the complexity of the observed reality, and unexplored factors lying outside the compass remain unanalyzed.

Additionally, STXIF primarily derives from the XAI discourse, which is occasionally criticized for its unilateral focus [11]. While we acknowledge this limitation, we intend to provide a pragmatic application-oriented tool. STXIF does not claim to represent all aspects comprehensively, but rather, it serves as a structured starting point for interdisciplinary investigations, which has its foundation in technical considerations.

Looking ahead, STXIF holds promise for diverse applications across various disciplines and scenarios. Its unique strength lies in the flexibility to tailor the XAI Compass to the specific requirements of different use cases. This paper focused on the EU AI Act as a concrete policy context. However, the STXIF's adaptability allows it to accommodate different policy frameworks and emerging regulations, making it relevant in a rapidly evolving landscape. By integrating social science methodologies into the XAI discourse, our approach addresses the demand for a more holistic understanding of XAI within the HCI community.

We envisage that the STXIF will facilitate more informed and ethically grounded XAI implementations, fostering a collaborative dialogue between technical and social perspectives.

References

1. AI Act - Shaping Europe's digital future. https://digital-strategy.ec.europa.eu/en/policies/regulatory-framework-ai
2. Proposal for a Regulation of the European parliament and of the council laying down harmonised rules on artificial intelligence (artificial intelligence act) and amending certain union legislative acts. https://artificialintelligenceact.eu/wp-content/uploads/2024/01/AI-Act-FullText.pdf
3. Adadi, A., Berrada, M.: Peeking inside the black-box: a survey on Explainable Artificial Intelligence (XAI). IEEE Access **6**, 52138–52160 (2018). https://doi.org/10.1109/ACCESS.2018.2870052
4. Arrieta, A.B., et al.: Explainable Artificial Intelligence (XAI): Concepts, Taxonomies, Opportunities and Challenges toward Responsible AI (2019). arXiv:1910.10045
5. Arya, V., et al.: One explanation does not fit all: a toolkit and taxonomy of AI Explainability Techniques (2019). arXiv:1909.03012
6. Bach, S., Binder, A., Montavon, G., Klauschen, F., Müller, K.R., Samek, W.: On pixel-wise explanations for non-linear classifier decisions by layer-wise relevance propagation. PLoS ONE **10**(7), e0130140 (2015). https://doi.org/10.1371/journal.pone.0130140
7. Bienefeld, N., et al.: Solving the explainable AI conundrum by bridging clinicians' needs and developers' goals. NPJ Digital Medicine **6**(1), 94 (2023). https://doi.org/10.1038/s41746-023-00837-4, https://www.nature.com/articles/s41746-023-00837-4
8. Braun, M., Breuer, S.: "Embedded Ethics and Social Sciences" in HRI Research: Scenarios and Subjectivities (2022)
9. Carvalho, D.V., Pereira, E.M., Cardoso, J.S.: Machine learning interpretability: a survey on methods and metrics. Electronics **8**(8), 832 (2019)
10. Chromik, M., Schuessler, M.: A taxonomy for human subject evaluation of black-box explanations in XAI. In: ExSS-ATEC@IUI. Cagliari, Italy (2020)
11. Dhanorkar, S., Wolf, C.T., Qian, K., Xu, A., Popa, L., Li, Y.: Who needs to know what, when?: broadening the Explainable AI (XAI) Design Space by Looking at Explanations Across the AI Lifecycle. In: Designing Interactive Systems Conference 2021, pp. 1591–1602. ACM, Virtual Event USA (2021). https://doi.org/10.1145/3461778.3462131
12. Doshi-Velez, F., Kim, B.: Towards a rigorous science of interpretable machine learning (2017). arXiv:1702.08608
13. Ferreira, J.J., Monteiro, M.S.: What are people doing about XAI user experience? A survey on ai explainability research and practice. In: Marcus, A., Rosenzweig, E. (eds.) HCII 2020. LNCS, vol. 12201, pp. 56–73. Springer, Cham (2020). https://doi.org/10.1007/978-3-030-49760-6_4
14. Floridi, L.: The European legislation on AI: a brief analysis of its philosophical approach. Philos. Technol. **34**(2), 215–222 (2021). https://doi.org/10.1007/s13347-021-00460-9

15. Gleicher, M.: A framework for considering comprehensibility in modeling. Big Data 4(2), 75–88 (2016). https://doi.org/10.1089/big.2016.0007

16. Hohman, F., Head, A., Caruana, R., DeLine, R., Drucker, S.M.: Gamut: a Design Probe to Understand How Data Scientists Understand Machine Learning Models. In: Proceedings of the 2019 CHI Conference on Human Factors in Computing Systems. ACM (2019). https://doi.org/10.1145/3290605.3300809

17. Hong, S.R., Hullman, J., Bertini, E.: Human factors in model interpretability: industry practices, challenges, and needs. In: Proceedings of the ACM on Human-Computer Interaction 4(CSCW1) (2020). https://doi.org/10.1145/3392878, arXiv:2004.11440

18. Johs, A.J., Agosto, D.E., Weber, R.O.: Qualitative investigation in explainable artificial intelligence: a bit more insight from social science (2020). https://doi.org/10.22541/au.163284810.09140868/v1.

19. Johs, A.J., Agosto, D.E., Weber, R.O.: Explainable artificial intelligence and social science: further insights for qualitative investigation. Appl. AI Lett. 3(1) (2022). https://doi.org/10.1002/ail2.64

20. Kaur, H., Nori, H., Jenkins, S., Caruana, R., Wallach, H., Wortman Vaughan, J.: Interpreting interpretability: understanding data scientists' use of interpretability tools for machine learning. In: Proceedings of the 2020 CHI Conference on Human Factors in Computing Systems. ACM, Honolulu HI USA (2020). https://doi.org/10.1145/3313831.3376219

21. Kitzinger, J.: Qualitative research: introducing focus groups. BMJ 311(7000), 299–302 (1995). https://doi.org/10.1136/bmj.311.7000.299, https://www.bmj.com/content/311/7000/299

22. Langer, M., et al.: What do we want from explainable artificial intelligence (XAI)? – a stakeholder perspective on xai and a conceptual model guiding interdisciplinary XAI research. Artif. Intell. 296 (2021). https://doi.org/10.1016/j.artint.2021.103473, arXiv:2102.07817

23. Lundberg, S.M., Lee, S.I.: A Unified Approach to Interpreting Model Predictions. Long Beach, CA, USA (2017)

24. Malhi, A., Knapic, S., Främling, K.: explainable agents for less bias in human-agent decision making. In: Calvaresi, D., Najjar, A., Winikoff, M., Främling, K. (eds.) EXTRAAMAS 2020. LNCS (LNAI), vol. 12175, pp. 129–146. Springer, Cham (2020). https://doi.org/10.1007/978-3-030-51924-7_8

25. Mayring, P.: Qualitative inhaltsanalyse. In: Mey, G., Mruck, K. (eds.) Handbuch Qualitative Forschung in der Psychologie. VS Verlag für Sozialwissenschaften (2010)

26. Mayring, P.: Qualitative content analysis: theoretical foundation, basic procedures and software solution. Klagenfurt (2014)

27. Mayring, P., Fenzel, T.: Qualitative Inhaltsanalyse. In: Baur, N., Blasius, J. (eds) Handbuch Methoden der empirischen Sozialforschung, pp. 691–706. Springer Fachmedien, Wiesbaden (2022). https://doi.org/10.1007/978-3-658-37985-8_43

28. Mercado, J.E., Rupp, M.A., Chen, J.Y.C., Barnes, M.J., Barber, D., Procci, K.: Intelligent agent transparency in human–agent teaming for Multi-UxV management. Hum. Factors: J. Hum. Factors Ergonomics Soc. 58(3), 401–415 (2016). https://doi.org/10.1177/0018720815621206

29. Miller, T.: Explanation in artificial intelligence: insights from the social sciences. Artif. Intell. 267, 1–38 (2019). https://doi.org/10.1016/j.artint.2018.07.007

30. Molnar, C.: Interpretable Machine Learning - A Guide for Making Black Box Models Explainable. 2nd edn. (2022). https://christophm.github.io/interpretable-ml-book

31. Mueller, S.T., Veinott, E.S., Hoffman, R.R., Klein, G., Alam, L., Mamun, T. et al.: Principles of explanation in human-AI systems (2021)
32. Nauta, M., et al.: From anecdotal evidence to quantitative evaluation methods: a systematic review on evaluating explainable AI. ACM Comput. Surv. **55**(13s) (2023). https://doi.org/10.1145/3583558
33. Novelli, C., Casolari, F., Rotolo, A., Taddeo, M., Floridi, L.: Taking AI risks seriously: a proposal for the AI act. SSRN Electron. J. (2023). https://doi.org/10.2139/ssrn.4447964
34. Ribeiro, M.T., Singh, S., Guestrin, C.: "Why Should I Trust You?": explaining the predictions of any classifier. In: Proceedings of the 22nd ACM SIGKDD International Conference on Knowledge Discovery and Data Mining, pp. 1135–1144. ACM, San Francisco California USA (2016). https://doi.org/10.1145/2939672.2939778
35. Robinson, N.: The use of focus group methodology - with selected examples from sexual health research. J. Adv. Nurs. **29**(4), 905–913 (1999). https://doi.org/10.1046/j.1365-2648.1999.00966.x
36. Rudin, C., Chen, C., Chen, Z., Huang, H., Semenova, L., Zhong, C.: Interpretable machine learning: fundamental principles and 10 grand challenges (Jul 2021). http://arxiv.org/abs/2103.11251, arXiv:2103.11251
37. Saeed, W., Omlin, C.: Explainable AI (XAI): a systematic meta-survey of current challenges and future opportunities. Knowl.-Based Syst. **263** (2023). https://doi.org/10.1016/j.knosys.2023.110273
38. Schmid, U., Wrede, B.: What is missing in XAI so far?: an interdisciplinary perspective. KI - Künstliche Intelligenz **36**(3–4), 303–315 (2022). https://doi.org/10.1007/s13218-022-00786-2
39. Schwalbe, G., Finzel, B.: A comprehensive taxonomy for explainable artificial intelligence: a systematic survey of surveys on methods and concepts. Data Min. Knowl. Discov. (2023). https://doi.org/10.1007/s10618-022-00867-8
40. Selvaraju, R.R., Cogswell, M., Das, A., Vedantam, R., Parikh, D., Batra, D.: Grad-CAM: visual explanations from deep networks via gradient-based localization. In: 2017 IEEE International Conference on Computer Vision (ICCV), pp. 618–626. IEEE, Venice (2017). https://doi.org/10.1109/ICCV.2017.74
41. Siontis, K.C., Noseworthy, P.A., Attia, Z.I., Friedman, P.A.: Artificial intelligence-enhanced electrocardiography in cardiovascular disease management. Nat. Rev. Cardiol. **18**(7), 465–478 (2021). https://doi.org/10.1038/s41569-020-00503-2, https://www.nature.com/articles/s41569-020-00503-2
42. Stieler, F., et al.: LIFEDATA - A framework for traceable active learning projects. In: 2023 IEEE 31st International Requirements Engineering Conference Workshops (REW), pp. 465–474. IEEE, Hannover, Germany (2023). https://doi.org/10.1109/REW57809.2023.00088
43. Vilone, G., Longo, L.: Notions of explainability and evaluation approaches for explainable artificial intelligence. Inf. Fusion **76**, 89–106 (2021). https://doi.org/10.1016/j.inffus.2021.05.009, https://linkinghub.elsevier.com/retrieve/pii/S1566253521001093
44. Zacharias, J., Von Zahn, M., Chen, J., Hinz, O.: Designing a feature selection method based on explainable artificial intelligence. Electron. Mark. **32**(4), 2159–2184 (2022). https://doi.org/10.1007/s12525-022-00608-1

AI Systems and Frameworks in HCI

Semi-supervised Sorting via Deep Feature Extraction and Density Based Clustering with User Feedback

Pascal Graf[(✉)], Morris Ohrnberger, Dominic Dötterer, and Nicolaj C. Stache

Heilbronn University, Max-Planck-Straße 39, 74081 Heilbronn, Germany
{pascal.graf,morris.ohrnberger,dominic.dotterer,
nicolaj.stache}@hs-heilbronn.de

Abstract. Efficient data sorting remains a significant challenge when faced with unknown object characteristics or appearances. Unsupervised learning struggles with contextual nuances and subjective human perspectives, complicating the sorting process. In this paper, we propose a novel semi-supervised algorithm merging deep feature extraction, density-based clustering, and user feedback to address this complexity.

Our approach utilizes a deep feature extractor, followed by dimensionality reduction techniques for refined features. User feedback, collected through intuitive queries, aids clustering by applying cluster splitting, merging, and outlier assignment. The resulting labels are then used to train a multi-class support vector machine in the original feature space. We demonstrate how little user feedback reduces classification errors on unseen data by up to 75 % raising classification accuracy to nearly 90 %.

We demonstrate the algorithm's potential through a screw sorting demonstrator, showcasing its adaptability and efficacy in real-world scenarios. The proposed system, with its intuitive user interface, minimizes interactions while advancing knowledge. The integration of user feedback ensures precise object sorting, emphasizing the algorithm's versatility across diverse image datasets and real-world applications.

Keywords: Semi-supervised Clustering · Deep Feature Extraction · Object Sorting

1 Introduction

In the dynamic landscape of industries such as logistics, recycling, and manufacturing, the demand for efficient data sorting persists as a critical operational challenge. The intricacy intensifies when faced with unfamiliar object characteristics or appearances, posing a significant hurdle for traditional unsupervised learning approaches [3]. Addressing this complexity requires innovative strategies that not only leverage the power of deep feature extraction and clustering but also incorporate the valuable insights of human intuition and contextual information.

© The Author(s), under exclusive license to Springer Nature Switzerland AG 2024
H. Degen and S. Ntoa (Eds.): HCII 2024, LNAI 14734, pp. 337–355, 2024.
https://doi.org/10.1007/978-3-031-60606-9_19

Prior studies often relied on truncated Convolutional Neural Network architectures like ResNet, trained on extensive labeled image datasets like ImageNet [5,9,10]. Despite the breadth of these datasets, intra-class feature differentiation remains insufficient. This limitation proves troublesome, particularly in industrial applications where objects may fall into classes treated as a single entity during training or were entirely absent from the dataset. Additionally, features extracted by a truncated network trained in this manner tend to be overly specialized for the classes present in the dataset. To overcome these challenges, we adopt a transformer model for feature extraction. This model has undergone self-supervised training on hundreds of millions of internet images.

Human domain or expert knowledge is often incorporated into other semi-supervised learning algorithms through semi-supervised variants of well-known clustering algorithms [1]. These variants rely on pairwise constraints or predefined labels established by a human prior to the actual clustering process. However, this approach presents the user with a vast amount of unordered data and requires a relatively high level of user interactions.

Our approach involves HDBSCAN clustering based on the extracted and reduced image features, allowing users to refine clusters through subsequent queries. Through proposals for cluster splitting, merging, and outlier assignment, we strive to extract maximum information about the user's intentions with minimal interactions.

Our contributions to the task of semi-supervised sorting of unknown images are as follows:

1. A novel sorting algorithm that integrates deep feature extraction, feature reduction, and density-based clustering, effectively incorporating user feedback.
2. An intuitive user interface designed to minimize interactions while maximizing knowledge gain through straightforward queries presented to the user.
3. Extensive evaluation of our algorithm on two datasets tailored for this problem, featuring three distinct use cases each.

In Sect. 2, we provide a detailed introduction to the network architectures, algorithms, and methods drawn from diverse references that underpin our research. Section 3 delves into the details of our algorithm, which represents a combination of those methods integrated with our sophisticated user interface. Subsequently, Sect. 4 unveils our evaluation methods, the created datasets involving multiple use-cases, and presents our key findings which will be further discussed in Sect. 5.

2 Related Work

In our approach, we leverage techniques and models for deep feature extraction and clustering. Additionally, we adapt existing semi-supervised clustering concepts for our purpose, briefly described in this section.

2.1   DINOv2

For feature extraction, we utilize the ViT-L/14 Vision Transformer encoder model from the DINOv2 family [8]. Following the trend in NLP, the authors propose a method to pre-train large vision models on diverse and curated data in a self-supervised fashion, resulting in encoder models that produce effective general-purpose visual features. These features work out of the box without fine-tuning on various image distributions and tasks, surpassing the previous best general-purpose features of OpenCLIP on most benchmarks. We use the 1024-dimensional output feature vector of the classification (CLS-) token.

2.2   HDBSCAN

For clustering, we employ hierarchical density-based clustering (HDBSCAN), an extension of DBSCAN and OPTICS [7]. In density-based clustering, clusters are considered areas of high density separated by areas of low density, allowing for clusters of any shape. HDBSCAN performs DBSCAN over different epsilon values to find the clustering with maximum stability. This enables HDBSCAN to separate clusters of varying densities and better separate nested clusters, while being more robust to parameter selection.

2.3   Semi-supervised Clustering

Semi-supervised clustering is a technique combining semi-supervised learning and clustering analysis [4]. It incorporates given information such as class labels and pairwise constraints into clustering to guide the clustering process and improve the performance. These information usually is injected prior to clustering. There are, however, some approaches which experimented with more sequential processes [2]. In these algorithms clustering and user feedback are alternated until the result of the semi-supervised clustering algorithm is satisfying.

3   Our Approach

The proposed algorithm comprises various components and steps outlined and detailed in this section. The overall goal is to categorize an image dataset of unknown objects into multiple categories according to specific criteria. Initially, we extract representative semantic features from each image and reduce these features to two-dimensional space for visualization and noise reduction. A clustering algorithm is then applied to obtain initial sorting proposals. Subsequently, users are presented with queries that determine the splitting and merging of suggested clusters. This feedback refines both the existing clustering and the classification of future unknown data. The detailed process is as follows:

We use the transformer model presented in Sect. 2.1 to extract a 1024-component feature vector for each $224 \times 224 \times 3$ image. These features exhibit expressiveness across a diverse range of images due to the self-supervised training method. To reduce noise and enable visualization, the vectors are reduced to two dimensions using the t-SNE algorithm [6].

Following this, preliminary cluster memberships are suggested by hierarchical density-based clustering (see Sect. 2.2) based on the reduced features. In contrast to previous approaches, we have found it beneficial to incorporate user feedback after the initial cluster proposals, rather than defining constraints or labels beforehand. This approach is motivated by the recognition that presenting individuals with potentially hundreds of images can be overwhelming, demanding substantial concentration and time. Instead, our strategy involves initially attempting to identify and split clusters that may be inconsistent and encompass multiple classes. For each cluster, we estimate a density based on a Gaussian kernel and apply sub-clustering for clusters with low density to generate splitting proposals.

To minimize user interaction, splitting proposals are prioritized by considering the relative split ratio, cluster size, and the respective cluster density, as formulated in Eq. 1. Clusters with low density take precedence, given their higher likelihood of contamination, as indicated by the third addend in the equation, where δ_c represents a cluster's density, and λ_2 is a weighting factor. Additionally, clusters with a greater number of data points, along with sub-cluster proposals that evenly divide the original clusters, have a more substantial impact on classification accuracy. This is depicted by the two other addends in the equation, where n_c is the number of points in the original cluster, n_{sub} is the count of points in the proposed sub-cluster separated from the original cluster, and λ_1 is another weighting factor. In our experiments, we selected $\lambda_1 = \lambda_2 = 0.02$.

$$p = \frac{(n_c - n_{sub}) \times n_{sub}}{(\frac{n_c}{2})^2} + \lambda_1 \times n_c - \lambda_2 \times \delta_c \tag{1}$$

In practice, for each splitting query, the user is presented with one representative image for each of the two proposed sub-clusters. They are then required to answer the question, "Would you consider both of the presented images to belong to the same cluster?" If the answer is "yes," the proposal is discarded, and the original cluster is retained. If the answer is "no," a follow-up query is presented where the user sees two groups of images, representing the proposed sub-clusters. They have the opportunity to click on individual images based on their perception of cluster affiliation, thereby moving them to the other group of images (refer to Fig. 1). After confirmation, the clusters are split accordingly. Multiple sub-cluster proposals can be generated for each original cluster.

Cluster merging proposals are determined straightforwardly by calculating distances between the closest k points of each cluster. These proposals are then sorted based on their mean distance, with k set to 10. In practical application, the user is presented with a random subset of four images for each of the two clusters in a proposal. Their task is to decide whether these data points should belong to

Fig. 1. Depiction of the proposed user interface, showcasing the query answering sequence for cluster splitting and merging.

the same cluster. Finally, outliers that could not be assigned during HDBSCAN clustering are either placed in the next closest cluster or can be assigned through user queries. User interaction is limited by choosing between a few, moderate, or many questions, resulting in 8, 16, or 24 queries, respectively. During testing, half of the queries are dedicated to cluster splitting, and the other half to cluster merging. Cluster splitting is always performed first, as it allows for recombining the emerging sub-clusters in the merging step. The modified cluster labels are then utilized to train a simple multi-class support vector machine (SVM) in the original 1024-dimensional feature space. In contrast to density-based clustering methods, this classification method allows for assigning labels to novel points during testing.

4   Experimental Results

In this section, we delve into the outcomes of our experiments, providing a comprehensive overview of key aspects that contributed to the success of our algorithm. From the datasets utilized to the designed experimental setup, we present detailed insights into our findings. The subsequent sections cover the raw results, offering a quantitative assessment of our model's performance. Finally, we describe the practical implications with a real-world application, showcasing the relevance of our work beyond theoretical considerations.

4.1   Datasets and Tasks

We assess the performance of our methods using two distinct datasets: screws and vegetables, which cover diverse image features and applications. Additionally, we construct three different types of tasks for each dataset to test the algorithm, considering various characteristics of the items within each dataset, such as size, material composition, and functionality. For instance, screws may be categorized based on their size, shape, or intended use (woodworking, metalworking). Similarly, vegetables can be categorized by size, type (root vegetables, leafy greens), or culinary use (e.g., cooking methods).

Dataset 1: Screw Dataset. The first dataset for the experiment consists of 362 screws and nuts of 19 different types (see Table 1). The screws have five parameters to declare the dedicated class: screw length, screw thread diameter, thread length, and the type of head. Nuts are less complex, with two main parameters: thread diameter and outer shape, which is usually hexagonal.

Table 1. Screw dataset class overview along with label descriptions (published at https://www.kaggle.com/datasets/dominicdtterer/screws-an-nuts).

ID	Object Type	Training Images	Test Images
1	WS 65x5 FT CH	10	7
2	WS 55x6 PT CH	12	7
3	WS 40x7 FT HH	12	7
4	WS 40x7 PT HH	10	7
5	WS 60x8 PT HH	12	7
6	WS 40x10 FT HH	14	7
7	WS 100x5 PT HH	9	7
8	WS 45x5 FT CH	12	7
9	WS 55x6 FT CH	12	7
10	WS 20x4 FT PH	14	7
11	MS 40xM8	11	7
12	MS 20xM8	12	7
13	MS 40xM3	12	7
14	MS 25xM3	12	7
15	Nut M4	15	7
16	Nut M5	15	7
17	Nut M8	12	7
18	Head Nut M8	12	7
19	Nut M10	11	7
Sum		229	133

Short	Description
MS	Metal Screw
WS	Wood Screw
FT	Fully Threaded
PT	Partially Threaded
CH	Countersunk Head
PH	Pan Head
HH	Hex Head

- **Task 1:** Sort the screws and nuts according to their 19 different types.
- **Task 2:** Coarsely sort the screws and nuts into 3 categories: Short screws, long screws, and nuts independently of their type and application.
- **Task 3:** Sort the screws and nuts according to their application (wood/metal), head (hex/pan), and length (short/long). Differentiate between small and large nuts, resulting in 10 different classes.

Dataset 2: Vegetables Dataset. A second dataset with distinct features and varied applications is used to further evaluate our method's quality. The presented vegetable dataset consists of 500 images belonging to 14 different species: Bean, Bitter Gourd, Bottle Gourd, Brinjal, Broccoli, Cabbage, Capsicum, Carrot, Cauliflower, Cucumber, Potato, Pumpkin, Radish, and Tomato. Similar to Dataset 1, we provide three different tasks to the user:

- **Task 1:** Sort the vegetables according to their 14 different species.
- **Task 2:** Coarsely sort the vegetables into 2 classes: green and non-green vegetables (where tomatoes are always considered non-green).
- **Task 3:** Sort the vegetables according to their plant family or type (solanaceae, root vegetables, ...), resulting in 5 classes.

4.2   Experimental Setup

The primary objective of the developed system is to distinguish objects based on user-defined criteria. Recognizing the subjective nature of object sorting, we established three distinct categorization criteria for both the screws and vegetables datasets, creating three unique tasks for each (as detailed in Sect. 4.1). Acknowledging potential variations in task difficulty, we average the results to provide a more comprehensive overview of the performance improvement facilitated by user feedback.

For a given set of image data, features are extracted using the DINOv2 transformer model. Subsequently, we reduce the feature dimension to two and generate a robust initialization for the labels by clustering the reduced features using HDBSCAN. The maximum number of clusters is capped at 30 by adjusting the ϵ parameter accordingly. The quality of the clustering labels is evaluated using the *adjusted mutual information score (AMI)* and compared to the ground truth labels acquired based on the criteria of a specific task. Following this assessment, we train a *multi-class support vector machine (SVM)* using the assigned labels and the extracted features in the original feature space. The resulting accuracy, tested on a set of unseen images, serves as our baseline for quantifying the accuracy gain facilitated by user feedback.

The subsequent step involves gathering user feedback to refine the automatically generated initial labels. Users are instructed to respond to presented queries based on a specific task, with options to answer either a few (8), moderate (16), or many (24) questions, as outlined in Sect. 3. Each participant receives the same predefined clustering and initial queries to ensure statistical comparability of the results. Subsequent queries may differ due to individual participant choices.

Following the incorporation of user feedback, the quality of the updated labels is reevaluated using ground truth labels and the AMI score. Another SVM is then trained using these refined labels. The resulting accuracy on test data reflects the final performance of a single test case. This procedure is repeated for multiple users across all tasks, datasets, and numbers of queries. Consequently, we can ascertain the performance gain introduced by user feedback, depending on the number of interactions, the desired classification granularity, and the dataset. The entire process is shown schematically in Fig. 2.

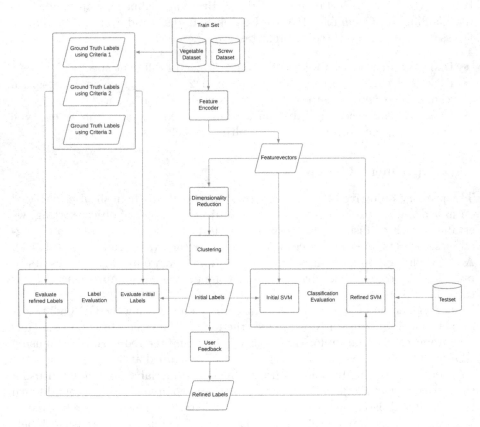

Fig. 2. Illustration of the evaluation process presented as a comprehensive flow diagram.

4.3   Results

For evaluation purposes, each query number category (i.e., 8, 16, and 24 queries) has been executed at least 10 times for each task and each dataset, as described in Sect. 4.2. A total of 15 participants were involved in this process,

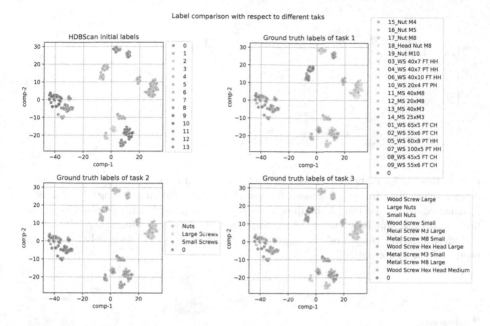

Fig. 3. Visualization of reduced features extracted by the transformer model for Dataset 1. Colors correspond to ground truth labels for tasks 1 (top right), 2 (bottom left), and 3 (bottom right), alongside initial labels obtained with HDBSCAN (top left).

resulting in a total of 180 user-guided clustering results that were thoroughly analyzed.

In Fig. 3, the reduced features of dataset 1 colored according to the labels of each task are presented. The separation into meaningful clusters demonstrates the transformer's ability to extract vital features and differentiate between very similar objects. Also presented in the figure are the preliminary clustering results without user interaction (14 cluster proposals), showcasing the effectiveness of HDBSCAN with default parameters. For task 1 of dataset 1, they yield a high initial AMI score (label accuracy) of 85.5 %. With only 8 user interactions, the result significantly improves to 87.4 %. As the number of user interactions increases, the score climbs to a median of 93.8 %, displaying an error reduction of about 58 % compared to the initial clustering proposals. When an SVM is trained on these refined labels, a significant improvement over the unmodified baseline at 85.2 % accuracy (classification accuracy) on unseen test images is demonstrated with 16 user queries or more. The best results are achieved at 24 queries with a median of 91.7 %, equaling an error reduction of 44 %.

Even more encouraging results have been achieved for task 2 of dataset 1. With an increasing number of user interactions, the error in label prediction is monotonically decreasing by up to 74.7 %. The classification accuracy at that point is at 89.6 % on the unseen test data. Solely for task 3 of dataset 1, user

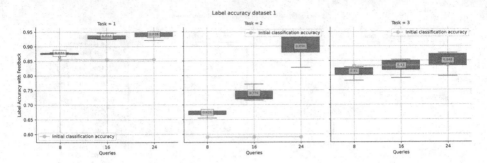

Fig. 4. Results for Dataset 1: Task 1, 2, and 3 displayed from left to right. User-refined labels, reflecting different degrees of interaction, are evaluated using the Adjusted Mutual Information score (AMI) in comparison to the ground truth labels. The orange line represents the baseline score without user feedback. Additionally, the results include the mean, range and standard deviation from experiments involving multiple users. (Color figure online)

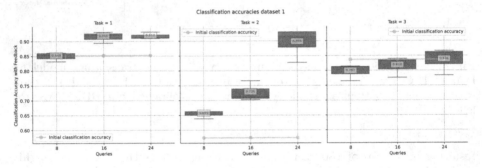

Fig. 5. Results for Dataset 1: Task 1, 2, and 3 displayed from left to right. Classification accuracy assessed on an independent test dataset. The SVM is trained using user-refined labels. The orange line represents the baseline score without user feedback. Additionally, the results include the mean, range and standard deviation from experiments involving multiple users. (Color figure online)

feedback was not capable of improving label and clustering accuracy, which is discussed in Sect. 5.

Figure 4 shows the label accuracy over a varying number of queries for all different tasks, while Fig. 5 illustrates the classification accuracy for the SVM on test data based on these refined labels. Figure 6 focuses on the improvements over the baseline accuracy.

For the second dataset, significant label and classification accuracy improvements can be observed for all tasks with 8 or more user queries. For every task but the first, where with more than 16 queries accuracy stagnates, more queries inevitably lead to better performance. For example, in task 3, user feedback improves the classification accuracy to a value of 76.7 %, which is equivalent to an error reduction of 35 %.

In summary, we conclude that for the available versatile data and tasks, the proposed method is capable of extracting useful features and clustering them into meaningful classes with HDBSCAN. We further summarize that in every but one case, user feedback enhances classification accuracy for unseen data with respect to the task at hand. Detailed evaluation results for all datasets and tasks can be found in Appendix A.

4.4   Practical Application: Screw Sorting Demonstrator

An autonomous screw and small component sorting system is being set up for demonstration purposes at Heilbronn University. This system comprises a camera-monitored conveyor belt, a robotic arm, and a separation system. The primary objective is to segregate bulk material into individual objects, which are then detected and individually recorded on the conveyor belt. The captured data undergoes pre-processing, alignment, and is fed into our proposed method to generate user-refined clustering labels individually customized for the respective use case. Meanwhile, the objects fall into a collecting container. Upon the second pass, the objects are recorded again, and image features are extracted and classified with the trained SVM. A robotic arm picks the components and places them into the respective bins assigned to the label (Fig. 7).

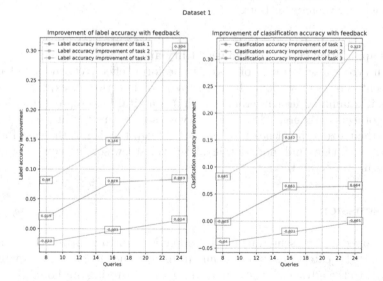

Fig. 6. Changes in label accuracy (left) and classification accuracy (right) in response to varying query volumes for Dataset 1.

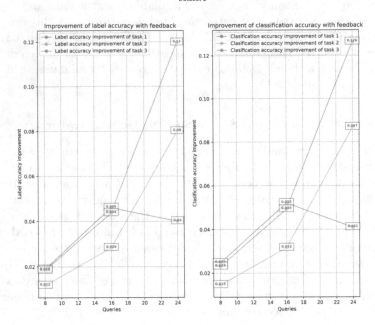

Fig. 7. Changes in label accuracy (left) and classification accuracy (right) in response to varying query volumes for Dataset 2.

This application showcases the versatility and industrial applicability of our approach across a wide range of tasks. It performs effectively independently of the presented objects without the need for prior injection of expert knowledge and requires minimal user interaction. This is a vital feature, as the differences between objects of different domains may vary significantly. While screws mostly differ in their size, type of head, or type of thread, this is not the case for other applications. Images and more details about the screw sorting demonstrator are provided in Appendix B.

5   Discussion

The developed and presented method is capable of sorting unseen object images into meaningful categories without human expert knowledge. This capability is attributed to the advanced feature encoding and clustering methods. Depending on the task, the method separates the images with high accuracy, as demonstrated in Sect. 4. With minimal user interaction, we can further enhance the performance for every task except one. Our additional findings and the limitations of our method are as follows:

After a task-specific number of user interactions, accuracy no longer increases. This could either indicate subtle differences between classes that even human experts struggle to perceive, or the splitting and merging proposals may not capture all the relevant choices.

Precise task definition and intuitive tasks matter. In task 3 of dataset 1, we observed tremendous variance in prediction accuracy after user feedback. This results in no significant improvement even after 24 queries. Some participants, however, manage to enhance the results. This supports the conclusion that the sorting task must be intuitive and well-defined for human experts. For example, sorting screws and nuts into categories such as "small" and "large" is a subjective assignment, especially from just one image. During our test series, we observed diverse assignments for the same queries for the described task.

Artificial intelligence can only sort based on the information we provide. The feature encoder utilized depends on the images fed into the network. Unlike humans, it lacks context for this information, such as the usual size of a certain vegetable. Providing additional features like object size, as we did for dataset 1 (see Sect. 3), significantly improves the initial clustering accuracy. Moreover, in scenarios where humans lack context as well, this information can be visualized in the user interface. For example, the screw object size, if provided, is reflected by the image scaling in the user interface.

The initial cluster count matters. With default parameters, HDBSCAN proposes a very fine-grained separation of images into different clusters, which often reflects something close to the original data labels. However, when a coarser classification is desired, as in task 2 of dataset 2, the splitting queries in our user feedback acquisition are usually obsolete. Moreover, the merging queries are typically all answered "yes." To avoid these unnecessary user interactions, we plan to allow for some influence on the granularity of clustering in future works.

Cluster merging queries should be more adaptive. In our experiments, users often expressed caution about cluster merging proposals where most of the images belonged to one class but there was also an outlier present in the data. Instead of a boolean choice between merging and not merging clusters, another layer of user interaction could be introduced in the future to address these situations.

A combination of queries and other user interaction possibilities is beneficial. In addition to query proposals, our user interface includes other screens for data analysis and cluster assignment, such as an overview screen showing all clusters and their representative data points. These could be incorporated into the process of obtaining human feedback and reinforcing cluster assignment aspects not captured by the transformer feature encoding. Initial experiments show that giving participants the possibility to look at the cluster overview screen and perform only two merging or splitting actions enhances performance.

Disclosure of Interests. The authors have no competing interests to declare that are relevant to the content of this article.

A   Full Experimental Results

In this section we provide full evaluation details over all tasks and datasets without further explanation (Figs. 8, 9 and Tables 2, 3).

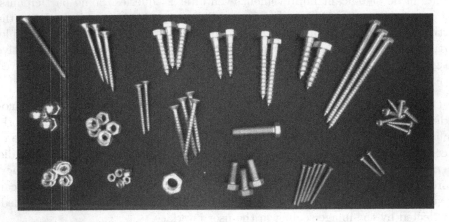

Fig. 8. Overview over the different types of objects, i.e. screws and nuts, present in Dataset 1.

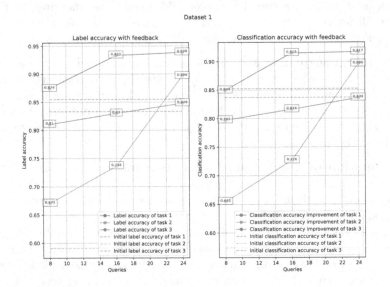

Fig. 9. Label accuracy (left) and classification accuracy (right) in response to varying query volumes for Dataset 1.

Table 2. Detailed label accuracy results for Dataset 1.

Name	Task 1			Task 2			Task 3			$\bar{y}$
Qeries	few	moderate	many	few	moderate	many	few	moderate	many	
Initial	85,50	85,50	85,50	59,06	59,06	59,06	83,32	83,32	83,32	75,96
Refined	87,43	93,33	93,84	67,06	73,63	89,63	81,04	82,98	84,75	83,74
Improvement	1,93	7,83	8,34	8,00	14,57	30,57	-2,28	-0,34	1,43	7,78
Error reducion	13,31	53,99	57,54	19,53	35,58	74,66	-13,68	-2,06	8,57	27,49

Table 3. Detailed classification accuracy results for Dataset 1.

Name	Task 1			Task 2			Task 3			$\bar{y}$
Qeries	few	moderate	many	few	moderate	many	few	moderate	many	
Initial	85,24	85,24	85,24	57,4	57,4	57,4	83,7	83,7	83,7	75,45
Refined	84,95	91,5	91,69	65,16	72,65	80,58	79,7	81,59	83,6	82,30
Improvement	-0,29	6,26	6,45	8,06	15,25	32,18	-4,00	-2,11	-0,10	6,86
Error reducion	-1,99	42,41	43,70	18,91	35,79	75,54	-24,51	-12,93	-0,60	19,59

See (Figs. 10, 11, 12, 13 and Tables 4, 5)

Fig. 10. Overview over the different types of vegetables present in Dataset 2.

B   Screw & Small Component Sorting Demonstrator

The demonstrator presented in this section serves to visualize the methods we have researched. In addition, it enables not only the understanding of the sorting process, but also the generation of feedback through the sorted objects in each tray (Figs. 14, 15).

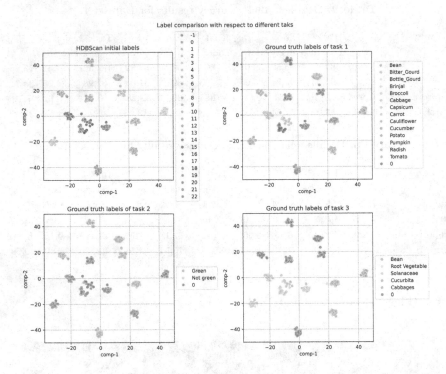

Fig. 11. Visualization of reduced features extracted by the transformer model for Dataset 2. Colors correspond to ground truth labels for tasks 1 (top right), 2 (bottom left), and 3 (bottom right), alongside initial labels obtained with HDBSCAN (top left).

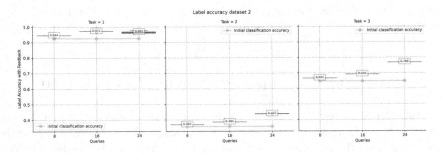

Fig. 12. Results for Dataset 2: Task 1, 2, and 3 displayed from left to right. User-refined labels, reflecting different degrees of interaction, are evaluated using the Adjusted Mutual Information score (AMI) in comparison to the ground truth labels. The orange line represents the baseline score without user feedback. Additionally, the results include the mean, range and standard deviation from experiments involving multiple users. (Color figure online)

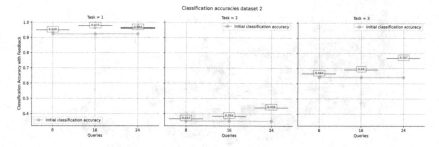

Fig. 13. Results for Dataset 2: Task 1, 2, and 3 displayed from left to right. Classification accuracy assessed on an independent test dataset. The SVM is trained using user-refined labels. The orange line represents the baseline score without user feedback. Additionally, the results include the mean, range and standard deviation from experiments involving multiple users. (Color figure online)

Table 4. Detailed label accuracy results for Dataset 2.

Name	Task 1			Task 2			Task 3			$\bar{y}$
Qeries	few	moderate	many	few	moderate	many	few	moderate	many	
Initial	92,53	92,53	92,53	35,72	35,72	35,72	64,86	64,86	64,86	64,37
Refined	94,41	97,14	96,53	36,89	38,55	43,71	66,69	69,22	76,83	68,89
Improvement	1,88	4,61	4,00	1,17	2,83	7,99	1,84	4,37	11,97	4,52
Error reducion	25,22	61,66	53,59	1,82	4,40	12,43	5,23	12,43	34,06	23,43

Table 5. Detailed classification accuracy results for Dataset 2.

Name	Task 1			Task 2			Task 3			$\bar{y}$
Qeries	few	moderate	many	few	moderate	many	few	moderate	many	
Initial	92,3	92,3	92,3	35,25	35,25	35,25	64,1	64,1	64,1	63,88
Refined	94,77	97,5	96,39	36,71	38,41	43,93	66,41	69,02	76,74	68,88
Improvement	2,47	5,20	4,09	1,46	3,16	8,67	2,31	4,92	12,64	4,99
Error reducion	32,10	67,57	53,07	2,25	4,87	13,40	6,43	13,71	35,20	25,40

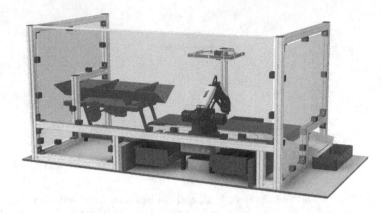

Fig. 14. Rendering of the Sorting Demonstrator.

Fig. 15. Setup of the Sorting Demonstrator (https://virtual-ki-lab.zml.hs-heilbronn. de/).

References

1. Bair, E.: Semi-supervised clustering methods. WIREs Comput. Stat. **5**(5), 349–361 (2013). https://doi.org/10.1002/wics.1270, https://wires.onlinelibrary.wiley.com/doi/abs/10.1002/wics.1270
2. Basu, S., Davidson, I., Wagstaff, K.: Constrained Clustering: Advances in Algorithms, Theory, and Applications (2008)
3. Bengio, Y., Courville, A.C., Vincent, P.: Unsupervised feature learning and deep learning: A review and new perspectives. CoRR **abs/1206.5538** (2012). http://arxiv.org/abs/1206.5538
4. Cai, J., Hao, J., Yang, H., Zhao, X., Yang, Y.: A review on semi-supervised clustering. Information Sciences **632**, 164–200 (2023). https://doi.org/10.1016/j.ins.2023.02.088, https://www.sciencedirect.com/science/article/pii/S0020025523002840

5. He, K., Zhang, X., Ren, S., Sun, J.: Deep residual learning for image recognition. In: Proceedings of the IEEE Conference on Computer Vision and Pattern Recognition, pp. 770–778 (2016)
6. van der Maaten, L., Hinton, G.: Visualizing data using t-SNE. J. Mach. Learn. Res. **9**, 2579–2605 (2008). http://www.jmlr.org/papers/v9/vandermaaten08a.html
7. Malzer, C., Baum, M.: A hybrid approach to hierarchical density-based cluster selection. In: 2020 IEEE International Conference on Multisensor Fusion and Integration for Intelligent Systems (MFI). IEEE (Sep 2020). https://doi.org/10.1109/mfi49285.2020.9235263
8. Oquab, M., et al.: Dinov2: learning robust visual features without supervision (2024). https://arxiv.org/abs/2304.07193
9. Redmon, J., Farhadi, A.: Yolo9000: Better, faster, stronger (2016)
10. Xie, J., Girshick, R., Farhadi, A.: Unsupervised deep embedding for clustering analysis (2016)

Navigating NLU Challenges in Pair Programming Agents: A Study on Data Size, Gender, Language, and Domain Effects

Jacob Hart[1], Jake AuBuchon[1], Shandler A. Mason[2]([☒]) [iD],
and Sandeep Kaur Kuttal[1,2] [iD]

[1] University of Tulsa, Tulsa, OK 74104, USA
{jch389,jsa6790}@utulsa.edu
[2] North Carolina State University, Raleigh, NC 27606, USA
{samason4,skuttal}@ncsu.edu

Abstract. Recent strides in Natural Language Understanding (NLU) for pair programming conversational agents underscore the importance of expanding datasets and constructing models applicable across genders, languages, and domains. The difficulty arises from the resource-intensive nature of gathering data through lab studies. Our study explores the potential use of vast amounts of pre-existing data for the training of conversational agents. We introduced software engineering-specific slot labels through an open-coding process by identifying key words and phrases. Our slot labels were integrated with a dataset of developer-developer (DD) and developer-agent (DA) utterances, annotated with software engineering-specific intent labels, from pair programming conversations. We employed the transformer-based language model, joint-BERT, to explore the required training size and gender-related impacts on intent and slot accuracy. To gauge the model's generalizability, we analyzed 5 pair programming video conversations sourced from YouTube. These conversations were fully labeled for software engineering-specific intent and slot, allowing us to investigate language and domain effects on the model's performance. Our findings reveal that 5 conversations, without a strict gender balance, can be used to train a pair programming NLU. Our study paves the way for expanding datasets used in the training of conversational agents.

Keywords: NLU · Conversational Agents · Pair Programming

1 Introduction

Conversational agents have transformed our daily lives by enhancing accessibility [37,60], fostering emotional connections (e.g., Cleverbot [56], Xiaoice [77], Mitsuku [57]), facilitating customer service [1], and supporting in routine tasks (e.g., Alexa [63], Apple's Siri [64], Google Assistant [65]). Past studies have explored

H. Degen and S. Ntoa (Eds.): HCII 2024, LNAI 14734, pp. 356–375, 2024.
https://doi.org/10.1007/978-3-031-60606-9_20

the benefits of designing a pair programming conversational agent [30,32,33] and investigated the feasibility of training NLU using developer-developer (DD) [52] and developer-agent (DA) [51] conversations. These studies released a conversational dataset, comprising 7,879 utterances marked with software engineering-specific intent labels, capturing developers collaborating on the development of a Java Tic-Tac-Toe game. However, effective language model training demands a more extensive benchmark dataset derived from developer conversations, similar to ATIS [27], SNIPS [14], and MultiWoZ [11] spanning over multiple domains.

Furthermore, for language models to exhibit generalizability across genders, programming languages, and domains, there is a need for diverse datasets. However, the collection of conversational data, from developers, poses both a costly and time-intensive challenge for both researchers and practitioners. We build upon our earlier research [51], in which we established that (DD) conversations can be utilized to train conversational agents, to extend our findings by delving into the impact of dataset size, gender, language, and domain on model accuracy.

Our study marks an initial step in establishing software engineering-specific slot labels, which is a crucial component for identifying key words or phrases during the implementation of a comprehensive NLU system. Building upon our existing dataset of (DD) and (DA) conversations, we employed an open-coding method to formulate a slot labeling framework tailored for pair programming conversations. We applied our slot labeling framework to annotate pair programming conversations from prior research.

To examine the impact of dataset size and gender, leveraging existing data from [51], we formulated two research questions:

- **RQ1: How much data is required to train a pair programming NLU?** The size of the training dataset is crucial for models to achieve consistent accuracy. We employed jointBERT, to facilitate simultaneous slot tagging and intent classification. We aimed to explore the optimal training size for datasets.
- **RQ2: How does gender effect the performance of a pair programming NLU?** Prior research has highlighted gender differences while pair programming [30]; thus, we investigated whether maintaining a strict gender balance is necessary for the training and testing of models.

To examine the viability of leveraging existing developer-developer (DD) conversations from online video hosting platforms, we formulated one research question:

- **RQ3: How should developer-developer pair programming conversations, from online videos, be incorporated into the training dataset of a pair programming NLU?** We searched YouTube for recent videos featuring developers engaged in pair programming, with the goal of exploring the potential for expanding pair programming conversational datasets through existing videos.

2   Background and Related Works

2.1   Bots for Developers

Bots help developers perform several tasks such as assisting with debugging [2], identifying syntax errors [42,48], automating repetitive tasks [3], mining repositories [4], locating Stack Overflow posts [73], and providing code feedback [70]. Developers use bots to perform load testing [43] and suggest patches based on failed test cases [62]. Bots can facilitate the on-boarding process for new project members [55], locate and utilize REST APIs [19], design micro-service based architectures [36], and assist in agile retrospectives [40].

2.2   Design and Feasibility of Pair Programming Agents

In our earlier work [44,53], we established design guidelines for a pair programming agent by implementing a lab study and a Wizard of Oz (WoZ) study, where participants engaged with an agent whose behaviors was covertly orchestrated by a researcher [15]. These guidelines encompass practices such as clearly acknowledging suggestions, offering feedback in a positive tone, expressing uncertainty through both verbal and non-verbal cues, and apologizing for mistakes [53]. We discovered that an agent effectively facilitated knowledge transfer, leading to developers displaying increased trust and humility without a significant change in code quality, productivity, or self-efficacy. Based on our findings, we further investigated the feasibility of a pair programming [33] and facilitator agent [52]. We observed comparable performance among transformer-based language models, with BERT having a slight advantage. Our findings indicated that (DD) conversations were effective for training the intent classifier of a pair programming NLU with optimal performance being achieved by training with (DD) conversations and fine-tuning with (DA) conversations.

2.3   Dialogue Datasets

Researchers have labeled and annotated data in the realm of software design and development, with a focus on intent classification. For instance, the Ubuntu dialogue corpus [39] comprises unstructured human-human chats extracted from chat logs, where researchers aimed to do next utterance classification without considering slots. In another study, Viviani et al. [66] delved into design and decision-related dialogues extracted from pull requests and online discussions, focusing on intent perspective. Ebert et al. [18] and Pascarella et al. [45] identified the types of questions posed by software engineers during code reviews. Wood et al. [71,72] utilized open-coding to devise an intent labeling scheme for debugging conversations. Previously, we employed an open-coding process to develop a hierarchical approach to intent labeling, resulting in 26 unique intent labels tailored for pair programming conversations [51].

Beyond the realm of software development, various non-software engineering datasets such as SWITCHBOARD [23], ATIS [27,61], SNIPS [14] are employed to train models for intent and slot classification.

2.4   Slot Labeling

A fully implemented NLU must have the capability of slot tagging, which is the process of identifying important words in a sentence. Slots enable the agent to pinpoint essential parts of an utterance [31,75]. Slots originated in the GUS architecture [29], grounded in the concept of frames. In GUS, the agent identifies the user's intent and utilizes the ongoing conversation to complete all necessary slot values before making a query. In the modern dialogue state architecture, slots serve to delimit the conversation space which empowers the agent to ask clarifying questions, offer suggestions, or respond based on the evolving conversation rather than adhering to a predetermined template [29]. Slots enable models to understand the typical locations of key terms within a specific intent. Slot tagging is framed as a sequence-to-sequence modeling problem, with the input sequence being the utterance and the output sequence consisting of associated slot tags [22]. Slots offer the advantage of modeling occurrences of key terms within a specific intent, and defining the potential values of the key terms. This precision aids the model in determining whether a slot has been accurately identified.

2.5   Transfer Learning on Intermediate Tasks

Transfer learning involves training on a source task followed by fine-tuning on a target task [10,76]. An additional training task, referred to as an intermediate task, can be incorporated within the transfer learning process. Phang et al. [46] introduced STILTs (Supplementary Training on Intermediate Labeled-data Tasks) which entails training a model initially on an unlabeled dataset, then on an intermediate labeled dataset, and ultimately fine-tuning the model on the target task. They found that STILTs can enhance the performance of large language models such as BERT [16], ELMo [10], and GPT [49].

Researchers, including Sap et al. [54] and Clark et al. [13], have explored STILTs by using intermediate tasks to enhance model performance. Wang et al. [67] conducted a comprehensive study with ELMo and BERT, revealing the complexities of multitask learning and the impact of dataset size on target task performance. Pruksachatkun et al. [47] experimented with BERT and RoBERTa, emphasizing the ambiguity of training on intermediate tasks.

3   Methodology

3.1   Developer-Developer and Developer-Agent Conversations

Robe et al. [51] released a dataset comprising 7,879 utterances from 9 (DD) and 14 (DA) pair programming conversations collected through a remote environment lab study [52] and a (WoZ) study [51]. In both studies, they conducted 40 min sessions where participants engaged in pair programming to implement a Tic-Tac-Toe game in Java. Participants utilized the think-aloud method [35] and adhered to test-driven development principles [7]. All participants were equipped with template code, including the game board, a sample test case, and user stories for the programming task.

The (DD) dataset was curated through recorded conversations in a remote pair programming lab study with 18 participants [52]. These participants, exclusively computer science students, were strategically paired by their self-identified gender, resulting in 9 gender-balanced pairs: 3 men-men, 3 men-women, and 3 women-women.

The (DA) conversation dataset were captured using the (WoZ) methodology. Yang et al. [74] affirm (WoZ) as the singularly, viable method for collecting conversations with an agent prior to its actual implementation because it facilitates iterative designs and the observation of user behaviors. (WoZ) serves as a foundational tool for training machine learning algorithms [15] and has found widespread application in natural language interfaces, including conversational agents [9,72,74]. The (WoZ) study involved 14 participants, 6 computer science students (3 men, 3 women), and 8 professionals (4 men, 4 women) [51]. The motivation and implementation of the agent, in the (WoZ) study, was inspired by Robe et. al [53].

All (DD) and (DA) transcripts were labeled with software engineering-specific intent labels and developed using a hierarchical, open-coding process [8]. The absence of software engineering-specific slot labels serves as motivation for our work.

3.2 Slot Labeling

We developed our slot labels employing an open coding process, following the practices of other software engineering researchers [52,72]. Table 1 is the list of our slot labels (boolean, feedback, filename, filename_method, current_error, driver, inequality, keyword, line_number, location, name_of_user, number, objective, phase_of_sdl, text_add, text_remove, user_story, variable), along with their descriptions.

To establish the initial set of slot labels, two researchers analyzed three (DA) studies using the open-coding method to generate potential relevant slots. The two researchers discussed the potential slot labels, consolidated similar labels, and independently labeled a (DA) conversation. In a series of iterations, the researchers discussed and reached agreement on new slot labels as they emerged during their analysis. To ensure inter-rater reliability, two researchers labeled 20% of the (DD) and (DA) data, achieving a Cohen's Kappa of 0.7192, indicating substantial agreement [41]. The remaining data was labeled by one researcher. We used Inside-Outside-Beginning (IOB) tagging in the slot labeling process [50]. Each study took approximately 2 h for manual slot labeling, accumulating to 46 total hours.

3.3 Model Design

To perform simultaneous slot labeling and intent classification, we employed jointBERT, an extension of BERT developed by Chen et al. [12]. BERT is a

Table 1. Our slot labels and descriptions. Domain dependent slots are annotated with 'D' and language dependent slots are annotated with 'L.' Both language and domain dependent slots are annotated with 'L, D.' The corresponding numbers show the frequency of label occurrences in the (DA), (DD), and (YT) dataset.

Label Name	Description/Example	Dependence	(DA)	(DD)	(YT)
boolean	Used to help understand relations between objects and their function (e.g., true, false)		160	183	0
feedback	This allows the developer to agree or disagree with a suggestion, question, or clarification and continue with their thoughts (e.g., yes, no, good, bad)		265	544	75
filename	Name of the file being discussed but not necessarily the file currently open	L, D	94	38	117
filename_method	Name of the method being discussed. The filename helps to differentiate polymorphic methods	L, D	517	454	15
current_error	The reason why the program is not running as expected	L, D	36	2	6
driver	Determines if the user or the agent is driving		46	3	0
inequality	Used to help understand relations between objects and their function (e.g., >=, <=, >, <, =)		90	122	4
keyword	Used to help understand relations between objects and their function with language denoted keywords or reserved words	L	344	413	202
line_number	Identifies the specific location in the code that is under discussion		112	13	20
location	Refers to the documentation or an application (e.g., web browser, terminal window)	D	38	17	0
name_of_user	Used to identify and personalize communication with the user		0	0	10
number	Used to help understand relations between objects and their function (e.g., numbers in assignment, comparison, or other functions within the code)		499	649	27
objective	The current next step. Multiple objective work towards a user story	D	705	707	135
phase_of_sdl	High-level definition of the current phase in the software engineering development life cycle (e.g., plan, analyze, design, implement, test, maintain)		54	18	0
text_add	Allows the user to write code verbally using speech		0	0	12
text_remove	Allows the user to remove code verbally using speech		0	0	2
user_story	Used to identify the current user story which is a high-level goal that contains multiple objectives		323	90	85
variable	Used to capture user-defined variables and its functionality	L, D	244	450	37

bidirectional transformer-based model that was pre-trained on masked language modeling and next sentence prediction tasks using the BooksCorpus [78] and English Wikipedia [16]. Previously, BERT has been applied to software analysis [68], technology comparison tools via online discussions [69], and machine translation failure detection [25]. The uncased BERT model was expanded to jointBERT, which was evaluated on the SNIPS [14] and ATIS [27,61] datasets.

Implementation. To enhance the utility of jointBERT, our model was trained on the entire intent label, contrasting with our previous approach [51], where a model for each category of intent was employed in a pipeline manner. Training on the entire intent label simplifies the learning objective for jointBERT. Moreover, a comprehensive pair programming agent can leverage a multi-model approach to NLU with jointBERT providing full intent classification and specialized models for validation. Our implementation utilized HuggingFace's `Transformers` Python package, specifically the `bert-based-uncased` model. We utilized the pre-trained BERT tokenizer with an `encode_length` of 66.

We conducted a hyperparameter sweep, a process involving training models with all possible combinations within the search space [47]. We explored various learning rates (1e-3, 1e-4, 5e-5, 1e-5), epsilons (1e-6, 1e-7, 1e-8, 1e-9), and batch sizes (8, 16, 32, 64, 128) with both `Adam` and `AdamW` optimization algorithms. This results in 250 combinations, each using 5-fold cross-validation, resulting in 1,250 trained models. Our search space was motivated by Chen et al. [12], who trained for (1, 5, 10, 20, 30, 40) epochs using an `Adam` optimizer with a learning rate of 5e-5 and a batch size of 128. They observed that jointBERT, with 1 epoch of training, outperformed other slot-predicting models such as LSTMs [26], Attention-Based BiDirection RNNs [38], and Slot-Gated [24]. Based on our hyperparameter sweep results, we trained our model using `Adam` with a learning rate of 5e-5, epsilon of 1e-9, and a batch size of 16, for 12 epochs.

Performance. Table 2 illustrates the slot, intent accuracy, and intent F1 score when the model was trained on (DA), (DD), and employed transfer-learning by training on (DD) then fine-tuning on (DA) (DD→DA). We reported all metrics as the average of the 5-fold cross-validation using new training and testing sets. We implemented the `KFold` method from SKLearn's `model_selection` library. We found performance variation between (DA) (Intent F1: 70.85%) and (DD) (Intent F1: 56.96%), which is similar to our previous hierarchical model [44]. We observed minor improvements in the (DA) dataset (Intent F1: 70.85%) when we used (DD→DA) (Intent F1: 71.12%), also similar to our previous work [44]. The slot accuracy for (DA) was 99.16% and (DD) was 98.58%; however, for (DD→DA) the slot accuracy slightly decreased to 99.08%. Still, the (DD→DA) slot accuracy (99.08%) was superior to the (DD→DA) intent accuracy (68.72%), which suggests that training on (DD) then fine-tuning on (DA) remains the best option to train a pair programming NLU.

Table 2. Our model's 5-fold cross validation accuracy for slot and intent, along with the intent F1 score for (DA), (DD), and (DD→DA).

	DA	DD	DD →DA
Intent	68.39	55.38	68.72
Intent F1	70.85	56.96	71.12
Slot	99.16	98.58	99.08

4   Results

4.1   RQ1: How Much Data Is Required to Train a Pair Programming NLU?

The size of the training data, used in machine learning models, plays a pivotal role in achieving consistent accuracy. Transformer-based language models, like those pre-trained on extensive corpora such as BookCorpus [78] and Wikipedia, require less training data. Fine-tuning is essential for adapting these models to specific downstream tasks [10]. Our training dataset, consisting of 3,436 (DD) and 4,443 (DA) utterances, falls between the range of standard AI data benchmarks, including ATIS (5,871 utterances) [27,61] and SNIPS (16,000 queries) [14]. Thus, we explored the impact of data size on intent and slot accuracy.

Methodology. We used pair programming conversations in our training dataset because it serves as a robust metric for enhancing existing conversational data and tends to be more elaborate compared to other task-oriented conversational agents (e.g., Siri [64], Alexa [63], Google Assistant [65]). We incrementally trained our models on each (DD) or (DA) conversation, employing 5-fold cross-validation in randomized order for each iteration, resulting in 25 total models.

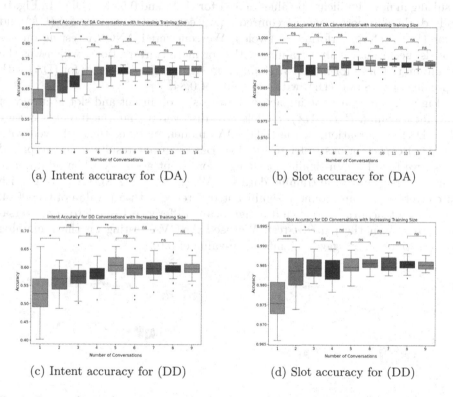

(a) Intent accuracy for (DA)   (b) Slot accuracy for (DA)

(c) Intent accuracy for (DD)   (d) Slot accuracy for (DD)

Fig. 1. Intent (1a, 1c) and slot accuracy (1b, 1d) of (DA) and (DD) conversations when increasing the training size. '*' represents p-value ≤ .05; '**' represents p-value ≤ .01; '***' represents p-value ≤ .001; '****' represents p-value ≤ .0001; 'ns' represents p-value ¿ .05.

Findings. Figure 1 illustrates the impact of dataset size on intent and slot accuracy. The box plots represent the intent (Fig. 1a, 1c) or slot (Fig. 1b, 1d) accuracy for our 25 models. The outliers, in Fig. 1, may be attributed to idealized test cases, where portions of the test dialogue included novel examples not encountered during training, or the inherent variability of conversation. We performed a paired t-test when (DA) or (DD) conversations were incorporated into the training dataset to assess differences in the model's performance. We represented statistically significant p-values with a '*' and non-significant p-values with 'ns'.

As represented in Fig. 1, both (DA) and (DD) show that a transformer-based language model requires a minimum of 5 pair conversational units. To verify the accuracy of our findings, we performed a one-way analysis of variance (ANOVA) to identify statistically significant differences across groups [58]. This analysis focused on the performance of models trained with 5 or more conversations, resulting in non-significant p-values of 0.31 for (DA) and 0.55 for (DD). In Fig. 1b and 1d, the slot performance, required 2 pair conversational units for (DA) and 3 for (DD) before performance leveled. We conducted ANOVA testing on the models' performance after training with 5 or more conversations, which was the minimum required for intent. We found non-significant differences for (DA) with a p-value of 0.18 and (DD) with a p-value of 0.84.

Figure 2 represents the impact of dataset size on intent and slot accuracy of transfer learning, (DD→DA), models. We discovered that the intent accuracy of 1 (DA) conversation, in the (DD→DA) model, matches that achieved with 5-6 (DA) conversations (refer to Fig. 1a). Based on our results from the paired t-test, we found a non-significant change, for intent accuracy when adding one pair conversation to the training data set. We performed ANOVA testing, with 14 conversations, and found a significant difference with a p-value of 0.000014. For the slot accuracy, we found a significant difference from 4 to 5 conversations, based on the paired t-test. We used ANOVA testing on the remaining conversations which gave a significant p-value of 0.024.

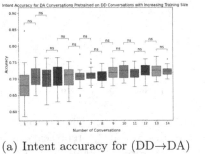
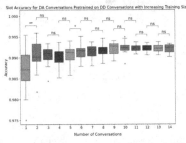

(a) Intent accuracy for (DD→DA)   (b) Slot accuracy for (DD→DA)

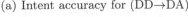

Fig. 2. Intent (2a) and slot (2b) accuracy for (DD→DA).

Summary of RQ1. Based on our findings, 5 conversations encompassing 1,500-2,000 utterances total, are required to train a pair programming NLU, irrespective of transfer learning. This aligns with the findings of Huggins et al. [28], demonstrating that a high performance with BERT can be achieved with 25 examples per intent. We did not explore data augmentation techniques that possibly could reduce the total number of utterances needed to get a similar, stable performance.

4.2 RQ2: How Does Gender Effect the Performance of a Pair Programming NLU?

Collaboration is a critical component of software development. Efficient collaboration may be effected by developers gender, race, or geographical location [6,17]. We investigated how gender may effect the performance of a pair programming NLU because gender gaps exist in computing-related classrooms (18% women) and workplaces (10% women) [59]. Previous studies have investigated differences in problem-solving [5], communication [30], and leadership style [30] between men and women while pair programming. Furthermore, while numerous pair programming videos are accessible on the internet for training our NLU, the majority of these videos feature men-men pairs. To leverage these videos for our model training, we assessed the generalizability of a model primarily trained on data from men-men pairs to mitigate the risk of perpetuating gender bias.

Methodology. We separated the (DD) and (DA) datasets based on the self-identified gender of the speaking participant. We combined the data, by gender, for (DD), (DA), and (DD→DA) to assess the model's overall performance. We created 6 total datasets: M-DD (9 men utterances); M-DA (7 men utterances); M-DD→DA (16 men utterances); W-DD (9 women utterances); W-DA (7 women utterances); and W-DD→DA (16 women utterances). We trained and tested 12 models within the same conversational-context group (DA, DD, DD→DA). We reported accuracy, for same-gender comparisons (M-M, W-W), as the average of the 5-fold cross-validation. To analyze mixed-gender comparisons (M-W, W-M), we trained the model on the first gender dataset and tested on the second gender dataset in a one-to-one comparison.

Findings. Table 3 illustrates the 12 models intent and slot accuracy performance. Our analysis found gender bias across all conversational context groups (DA), (DD), (DD→DA).

Training and testing exclusively with men data resulted in better performance, for intent accuracy, irrespective of conversational context. For example, within the DD conversational context, the alternative training and testing methods (W-W, W-M, M-W) exhibited accuracy below 60%; whereas, the (M-M) accuracy was 86.62%. Moreover, when training on men data and testing on women data (M-W), we observed performance levels comparable to those achieved when training and testing exclusively on women data (W-W). To illustrate, for the (DA) dataset, (M-W) intent accuracy was 69.09% and (W-W) intent accuracy was 70.79%. For the (DD) dataset, (M-W) intent accuracy was 59.54% and (W-W) intent accuracy was 58.44%.

Training and testing with exclusively women data (W-W) resulted in the best slot accuracy performance, for (DA) with 99.88% and (DD) with 98.91%. For (DD→DA), the best performance came from exclusively men data (M-M) with 98.95%. For (DA) the slot accuracy was comparable for (M-M) with 99.67%, (W-W) with 99.88%, and (M-W) with 99.67%.

Summary of RQ2. Our findings indicate that while men data can be utilized for training a pair programming NLU, the inclusion of women data enhances overall performance. These results are promising in light of the under-representation of women in computing classes, workplaces, and online videos.

Table 3. Intent and slot accuracy based on same- and mixed-gender training and testing datasets (W-W, W-M, M-W, M-M) and (DA), (DD), (DD→DA) conversational contexts.

		DA		DD		DD→DA	
Train	Test	Intent	Slot	Intent	Slot	Intent	Slot
W	W	70.79	99.88	58.44	98.91	64.48	98.69
W	M	67.16	99.35	53.78	98.15	61.87	98.04
M	W	69.09	99.67	59.54	98.75	61.93	98.50
M	M	88.77	99.67	86.62	98.75	87.20	98.95

4.3 RQ3: How Should Developer-Developer Pair Programming Conversations, from Online Videos, Be Incorporated into the Training Dataset of a Pair Programming NLU?

A pair programming agent is required to support diverse domains and languages. However, our collected data is centered around one language (Java) and a specific domain (a Tic-Tac-Toe game). Robe et al. [44] demonstrated that (DD) data is usable for intent detection, but (DA) data is needed for achieving higher accuracy. Further, our findings in RQ1 show that slot accuracy slightly decreases when using transfer-learning. Considering these challenges and findings, we selected 5 pair programming videos, from YouTube, to investigate the generalizability of the slot, intent labels and feasibility of using online videos as a training dataset.

Methodology. We found pair programming videos by using a private browsing window of Google.com to search the term 'pair programming'. Then, we used built-in filtering tools to find videos published since 2016 that were longer than

20 min. We used this filtering criteria because newer videos are likely to focus on current popular languages, domains and longer videos are more comparable to the existing data set with comprehensive pair programming sessions. We selected 3 types of candidate videos: (1) the same language but a different domain; (2) similar domain but different language; (3) different language and domain. The similar domain mimicked a Tic-Tac-Toe game by placing objects on a grid. We reviewed all candidate videos to confirm their language was English, ensure their availability, and verify the presence of two participants. The videos represent approximately 350 min of pair programming conversations and 4,822 utterances.

The video we used with the same language but from a different domain featured 2 open-source software developers working through pull-requests, error submissions, and merge requests for a Java library that functioned as a verification tool [20]. The pair interaction was formal, and they navigated through tasks systematically with the intent to record their interaction for posterity, potentially serving as a valuable resource for historians, researchers, or their own future reference.

The first video we used from a similar domain but with a different language featured 2 coworkers, one man and one woman, who aimed to demonstrate the basics of creating a 2D interactive terrain for a game board. The pair worked in a casual and humorous manner to introduce variables and console inputs to their audience of beginner programmers. They used JavaScript and CSS in their demonstration. The second video we used was a virtual meeting between an online teacher and student. The pair debugged the student's tower defense game to create a working version. The interaction included frequent sarcasm, from the teacher, which appeared to negatively impact the students' responses. The target audience for this video was self-taught programmers. The pair used JavaScript and CSS for the project.

The first video we used from a different language and domain was of 2 friends collaborating to create a Facebook Messenger Bot that 'echoes' messages to users connected to the bot. The interaction was friendly with a lighthearted atmosphere. The second video we used was of 2 Kaggle (a competitive venue for data science collaboration) partners who live streamed their code development for a drug classification competition. They used Python and the `Pytorch` library to demonstrate the process of building a neural network, catering to an audience of Kagglers and self-taught programmers. The pair interaction consisted of formal help and role-switching request with minimal interruptions.

We transcribed all 5 videos using YouTube's auto-generated closed captioning. We manually adjusted phrasing errors while labeling. We conducted intent and slot labeling for each transcript. Each researcher labeled 20% of the data independently and reached a Cohen's Kappa of 0.810 for the intent labels and 0.725 for the slot labels, which is considered substantial agreement [41]. The remaining transcripts were divided between two researchers, one researcher labeled 3 videos for intent and 2 for slot, and the other research labeled 2 videos for intent and 3 for slot. The researchers dedicated 14 h to annotate each video for both intent and slot, totaling to 70 h. Similar to RQ1, we repeated the 5-fold cross validation 5 times by randomizing the order of the studies.

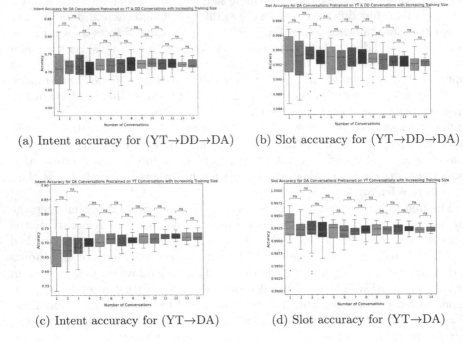

(a) Intent accuracy for (YT→DD→DA)   (b) Slot accuracy for (YT→DD→DA)

(c) Intent accuracy for (YT→DA)   (d) Slot accuracy for (YT→DA)

Fig. 3. Intent and slot accuracy for (YT→DA) and (YT→DD→DA) conversations when increasing the training size.

Findings. Previous research [44] and our current findings discovered that transfer learning (DD→DA), results in better model performance. Further, in RQ1, we found that 5 conversations, representing about 1,500-2,500 utterances, is sufficient to level-off jointBERT performance; however, that is representative of one language and domain. Therefore, we explored three ways of using transfer learning: (1) training on YouTube (YT) data, then fine-tuning on (DA), (YT→DA); (2) training on YouTube (YT) data, then training on (DD), then fine-tuning(DA), (YT→DD→DA); (3) training on YouTube (YT) data, then fine-tuning on (DA), (YT→DA).

Table 4 presents the intent and slot accuracy for (DA), (DD→DA), (YT→DA), and (YT→DD→DA). We found that by training on (YT) data, (YT→DD→DA) and (YT→DA), we achieved comparable, slightly improved performance for intent accuracy when compared to (DD→DA). For slot, the performance slightly increased with the inclusion of (DD) from 99.14% for (YT→DA) to 99.17% for (YT→DD→DA).

Figure 3 compares (YT→DA) and (YT→DD→DA) intent and slot accuracy when increasing the training size. We used ANOVA on all conversations and found a non-significant p-value for (YT→DD→DA) intent accuracy (p-value = 0.90), refer to Fig. 3a. We found a non-significant p-value for (YT→DD→DA) slot accuracy (p-value = 0.37), refer to Fig. 3b.

Table 4. The intent and slot accuracy of the model when trained on (DA), (DD→DA), (YT→DD→DA), and (YT→DA).

	DA	DD→DA	YT→DD→DA	YT→DA
Intent	68.39	68.72	68.77	68.79
Slot	99.16	99.08	99.17	99.14

Summary of RQ3. Our findings suggest that relying solely on (DD) and (DA) datasets is insufficient for training a pair programming NLU. Initially training with diverse data from (YT) and fine-tuning for a specific domain is the optimal approach to maximize performance. Thus, future endeavors should focus on expanding the collection of labeled video transcripts, ensuring the inclusion of new domains and languages overtime.

5   Limitations

A limitation of our study is the utilization of a linear model, in contrast to previous work that used a hierarchical modeling approach [51]. In a hierarchical modeling approach, the model is trained for each node of the intent hierarchy. Adopting this approach with jointBERT could complicate the learning objective or result in the prediction of slots without the full intent. Potential threats to validity may stem from our video selection process. The YouTube videos we selected may not encompass all diverse domains and languages, but our goal was to ensure that the videos closely resembled situations that a future agent might encounter. The sample size of five videos may be considered small, but the videos contains 4,822 utterances from 10 programmers across 4 domains and 3 languages. Furthermore, we present a set of software engineering specific slot labels which may be insufficient at representing all slots in pair-programming conversations. Labeling errors may have occurred in the manual labeling process, but this was mitigated by using an iterative open-coding process and data validation tools. The researchers who labeled the data self-identified as men, potentially introducing implicit bias into the labeling process. Furthermore, the size of the encoding length may have impacted slot accuracy. If the conversational context leads to shorter utterances on average, this would involve additional padding for each utterance, potentially making it easier for the model to predict the correct slot label.

6   Discussion

For RQ1, we investigated how much data was needed to train a pair programming NLU. Prior work by Sap et al. [54] found that increasing the training size of the intermediate task resulted in better performance on their downstream task; therefore, we focused on the creation of a dataset for the intermediate task. We found that training on 1,500-2,000 utterances, across 5 conversations, resulted in stable model performance. This highlights the importance of considering the number of utterances and conversations when training a pair programming NLU. For example, the two extremes are one conversation with 1,500-2,000 utterances and hundreds of short conversations with a total of 1,500-2,000 utterances. The first extreme, involving only one conversation, would make training on infrequent labels, such as greetings, difficult; whereas, the other extreme would fail to capture more nuanced labels, such as those relating to task control. Our findings have implications for training other agents to have longer form conversations.

A major advantage to expanding the dataset through pre-existing data is the reduction in cost; however, as the dataset expands, maintaining a gender balance will become increasingly difficult. Reinforcing bias within AI is recognized in facial recognition [34], bots [21], and underlying language models such as BERT [16]. This problem is confounded by the lack of women in computing classrooms and industry positions. For RQ2, we examined if the gender bias inherent in BERT affected our model and explored the optimal strategy for further expanding the dataset to enhance overall performance. Our findings show that datasets can deviate from a strict gender balance between men and women, but periodic checks remain essential to mitigating the risk of perpetuating gender bias.

For RQ3, we investigated two methods of integrating pair programming conversations from YouTube. Our first method involved training the model on (YT) and (DD) before fine-tuning with (DA); whereas, our second method solely trained on (YT) before fine-tuning with (DA). The (YT→DA) method, without (DD), required 1,500-2,000 (DA) utterances, whereas the (YT→DD→DA) method, including (DD), required 300-400 (DA) utterances to level off performance. While our first method achieved comparable performance, with less (DA) utterances, both methods require a similar number of total utterances. Our findings indicate that conversations from YouTube could serve as a starting point for exploring multiple languages and domains in the development of pair programming conversational datasets.

7   Conclusion

Our study determined the required training data size (RQ1), scrutinized potential gender bias (RQ2), and assessed the viability of leveraging online videos featuring developers engaged pair programming (RQ3), for the creation of a pair programming NLU.

Our research contributes to the broader Software Engineering and Human-Computer Interaction community with our software engineering-specific slot labeling scheme. We expanded the dataset, from earlier work, to include slot labels for the original (DA) and (DD) conversations. Our study introduced 5 fully labeled pair programming conversations from an online video hosting platform. We explored various training methods to optimize performance, aiming to incorporate general conversational data. Our results has implications for minimizing the costs associated with conducting and transcribing lab studies, facilitating the expansion of pair programming conversational datasets, and training future NLUs for pair programming.

Acknowledgements. This material is based upon work supported by the Air Force Office of Scientific Research under award number FA9550-21-1-0108 and National Science Foundation under award numbers IIS-2313890 and CCF-2006977. Any opinions, findings, and conclusions or recommendations expressed in this material are those of the authors and do not necessarily reflect the view of the NSF and AFOSR.

References

1. Chatbot Statistics (2020). https://www.smallbizgenius.net/by-the-numbers/chatbot-statistics/#gref
2. JetBrains (2021). https://www.jetbrains.com/
3. Visual studio (2021). https://visualstudio.microsoft.com/
4. Abdellatif, A., Shihab, E.: MSRBot: using bots to answer questions from software repositories. Empir. Softw. Eng. **25**, 1834–1863 (2020)
5. Arisholm, E., Gallis, H., Dybå, T., Sjøberg, D.: Evaluating pair programming with respect to system complexity and programmer expertise. IEEE TSE **33**, 65–86 (2007)
6. Arnaoudova, V., Haiduc, S., Marcus, A., Antoniol, G.: The use of text retrieval and natural language processing in software engineering. In: 2015 IEEE/ACM 37th IEEE International Conference on Software Engineering. vol. 2, pp. 949–950 (2015). https://doi.org/10.1109/ICSE.2015.301
7. Beck, K.: Test Driven Development: By Example. Addison-Wesley Longman Publishing Co., Inc. (2002)
8. Berg, B.L., Lune, H.: Qualitative Research Method for the Social Sciences. Pearson Education Limited, Boston (2017)
9. Bickmore, T., Cassell, J.: Relational agents: a model and implementation of building user trust. In: Proceedings of the SIGCHI Conference on Human Factors in Computing Systems, pp. 396–403 (2001)
10. Bowman, S.R., et al.: Looking for ELMo's friends: Sentence-level pretraining beyond language modeling (2018)
11. Budzianowski, P., et al.: Multiwoz - A large-scale multi-domain wizard-of-oz dataset for task-oriented dialogue modelling. CoRR abs/1810.00278 (2018). http://arxiv.org/abs/1810.00278
12. Chen, Q., Zhuo, Z., Wang, W.: BERT for joint intent classification and slot filling. CoRR **abs/1902.10909** (2019). http://arxiv.org/abs/1902.10909

13. Clark, C., Lee, K., Chang, M.W., Kwiatkowski, T., Collins, M., Toutanova, K.: BoolQ: exploring the surprising difficulty of natural yes/no questions. In: Proceedings of the 2019 Conference of the North American Chapter of the Association for Computational Linguistics: Human Language Technologies, Volume 1 (Long and Short Papers), pp. 2924–2936. Association for Computational Linguistics, Minneapolis, Minnesota (2019). https://doi.org/10.18653/v1/N19-1300, https://aclanthology.org/N19-1300

14. Coucke, A., et al.: Snips voice platform: an embedded spoken language understanding system for private-by-design voice interfaces. CoRR abs/1805.10190 (2018). http://arxiv.org/abs/1805.10190

15. Dahlbäck, N., Jönsson, A., Ahrenberg, L.: Wizard of oz studies: why and how. In: International Conference on Intelligent User Interfaces, pp. 193–200 (1993)

16. Devlin, J., Chang, M.W., Lee, K., Toutanova, K.: BERT: Pre-training of deep bidirectional transformers for language understanding (2018). arXiv preprint arXiv:1810.04805

17. Dzvonyar, D., Alperowitz, L., Henze, D., Bruegge, B.: Team composition in software engineering project courses, pp. 16–23. SEEM '18, Association for Computing Machinery, New York, NY, USA (2018). https://doi.org/10.1145/3194779.3194782

18. Ebert, F., Castor, F., Novielli, N., Serebrenik, A.: Communicative intention in code review questions. In: ICSME, pp. 519–523. IEEE (2018)

19. Ed-Douibi, H., Daniel, G., Cabot, J.: OpenAPI Bot: a chatbot to help you understand REST APIs. In: Bielikova, M., Mikkonen, T., Pautasso, C. (eds.) ICWE 2020. LNCS, vol. 12128, pp. 538–542. Springer, Cham (2020). https://doi.org/10.1007/978-3-030-50578-3_40

20. Falco, L.: Approval Test Java Repository (2022). https://github.com/approvals/ApprovalTests.Java

21. Feine, J., Gnewuch, U., Morana, S., Maedche, A.: Gender bias in chatbot design. In: Følstad, A., et al. (eds.) CONVERSATIONS 2019. LNCS, vol. 11970, pp. 79–93. Springer, Cham (2020). https://doi.org/10.1007/978-3-030-39540-7_6

22. Gao, J., Galley, M., Li, L.: Neural approaches to conversational AI. Found. Trends® Inf. Retrieval 13(2-3), 127–298 (2019). https://doi.org/10.1561/1500000074, http://dx.doi.org/10.1561/1500000074

23. Godfrey, J.J., Holliman, E.C., McDaniel, J.: SWITCHBOARD: telephone speech corpus for research and development. In: IEEE International Conference on Acoustics, Speech, and Signal Processing, vol. 1, pp. 517–520. IEEE Computer Society (1992)

24. Goo, C.W., et al.: Slot-gated modeling for joint slot filling and intent prediction. In: Proceedings of the 2018 Conference of the North American Chapter of the Association for Computational Linguistics: Human Language Technologies, Volume 2 (Short Papers), pp. 753–757. Association for Computational Linguistics, New Orleans, Louisiana (2018). https://doi.org/10.18653/v1/N18-2118, https://aclanthology.org/N18-2118

25. Gupta, S., He, P., Meister, C., Su, Z.: Machine Translation Testing via Pathological Invariance, pp. 863–875 (2020)

26. Hakkani-Tür, D., et al.: Multi-domain joint semantic frame parsing using Bidirectional RNN-LSTM. In: Interspeech, pp. 715–719 (2016)

27. Hemphill, C.T., Godfrey, J.J., Doddington, G.R.: The ATIS spoken language systems pilot corpus. In: Speech and Natural Language: Proceedings of a Workshop Held at Hidden Valley, Pennsylvania, June 24-27 1990 (1990). https://aclanthology.org/H90-1021

28. Huggins, M., Alghowinem, S., Jeong, S., Colon-Hernandez, P., Breazeal, C., Park, H.W.: Practical guidelines for intent recognition: BERT with minimal training data evaluated in real-world HRI application. In: Proceedings of the 2021 ACM/IEEE International Conference on Human-Robot Interaction, pp. 341–350 (2021)

29. Jurafsky, D., Martin, J.H.: Speech and Language Processing: An Introduction to Natural Language Processing, Computational Linguistics, and Speech Recognition, 3rd edn. Prentice Hall PTR, USA (2023)

30. Kaur Kuttal, S., Gerstner, K., Bejarano, A.: Remote pair programming in online CS education: Investigating through a gender lens. In: VL/HCC, pp. 75–85 (2019)

31. Kim, Y.: Convolutional neural networks for sentence classification (2014). arXiv preprint arXiv:1408.5882

32. Kuttal, S.K., Myers, J., Gurka, S., Magar, D., Piorkowski, D., Bellamy, R.: Towards designing conversational agents for pair programming: accounting for creativity strategies and conversational styles. In: VL/HCC, pp. 1–11 (2020)

33. Kuttal, S.K., Ong, B., Kwasny, K., Robe, P.: Trade-offs for substituting a human with an agent in a pair programming context: the good, the bad, and the ugly. In: CHI (2021)

34. Kyriakou, K., Kleanthous, S., Otterbacher, J., Papadopoulos, G.A.: Emotion-based stereotypes in image analysis services. In: Adjunct Publication of the 28th ACM Conference on User Modeling, Adaptation and Personalization, pp. 252–259 (2020)

35. Lewis, C.: Using the "thinking-aloud" method in cognitive interface design. IBM T.J. Watson Research Center (1982)

36. Lin, C.T., Ma, S.P., Huang, Y.W.: MSABot: A Chatbot Framework for Assisting in the Development and Operation of Microservice-Based Systems, pp. 36–40. ACM, New York, NY, USA (2020)

37. Lister, K., Coughlan, T., Iniesto, F., Freear, N., Devine, P.: Accessible conversational user interfaces: considerations for design. In: International Web for All Conference. ACM (2020)

38. Liu, B., Lane, I.R.: Attention-based recurrent neural network models for joint intent detection and slot filling. CoRR abs/1609.01454 (2016). http://arxiv.org/abs/1609.01454

39. Lowe, R., Pow, N., Serban, I., Pineau, J.: The ubuntu dialogue corpus: A large dataset for research in unstructured multi-turn dialogue systems (2015). arXiv preprint arXiv:1506.08909

40. Matthies, C., Dobrigkeit, F., Hesse, G.: An additional set of (automated) eyes: Chatbots for agile retrospectives. In: BotSE. pp. 34–37. BotSE '19, IEEE Press (2019)

41. McHugh, M.L.: Interrater reliability: the kappa statistic. Biochemia medica 22(3), 276–282 (2012)

42. Memeti, S., Pllana, S.: PAPA: a parallel programming assistant powered by IBM Watson cognitive computing technology. J. Comput. Sci. 26, 275–284 (2018). https://doi.org/10.1016/j.jocs.2018.01.001, https://www.sciencedirect.com/science/article/pii/S1877750317311493

43. Okanović, D., et al.: Can a chatbot support software engineers with load testing? Approach and experiences. In: ICPE, pp. 120–129. ACM, New York, NY, USA (2020)

44. P. Robe, S. K. Kuttal, J.A., Hart, J.: Pair programming conversations with agents vs. developers: challenges & opportunities for se community. In: The ACM Joint European Software Engineering Conference, and Symposium on the Foundations of Software Engineering (2022)

45. Pascarella, L., Spadini, D., Palomba, F., Bruntink, M., Bacchelli, A.: Information Needs in Contemporary code Review. Proc. ACM Hum.-Comput, Interact (2018)
46. Phang, J., Févry, T., Bowman, S.R.: Sentence encoders on stilts: Supplementary training on intermediate labeled-data tasks. CoRR abs/1811.01088 (2018). http://arxiv.org/abs/1811.01088
47. Pruksachatkun, Y., et al.: Intermediate-task transfer learning with pretrained models for natural language understanding: When and why does it work? CoRR abs/2005.00628 (2020). https://arxiv.org/abs/2005.00628
48. Queirós, R.A.P., Leal, J.P.: PETCHA: a programming exercises teaching assistant. In: Proceedings of the 17th ACM Annual Conference on Innovation and Technology in Computer Science Education, pp. 192–197 (2012)
49. Radford, A., Narasimhan, K., Salimans, T., Sutskever, I., et al.: Improving language understanding by generative pre-training (2018)
50. Ramshaw, L.A., Marcus, M.P.: Text chunking using transformation-based learning. In: Armstrong, S., Church, K., Isabelle, P., Manzi, S., Tzoukermann, E., Yarowsky, D. (eds.) Natural Language Processing Using Very Large Corpora. Text, Speech and Language Technology, vol. 11. Springer, Dordrecht (1999). https://doi.org/10.1007/978-94-017-2390-9_10
51. Robe, P., AuBuchon, J., Kuttal, S.K., Hart, J.: Pair programming conversations with agents vs. developers: challenges & opportunities for SE community. In: FSE (2022)
52. Robe, P., Kaur Kuttal, S., Zhang, Y., Bellamy, R.: Can machine learning facilitate remote pair programming? Challenges, insights & implications. In: VL/HCC, pp. 1–11 (2020)
53. Robe, P., Kuttal, S.K.: Designing PairBuddy – Conversational Agent for Pair Programming, vol. 29 (2022)
54. Sap, M., Rashkin, H., Chen, D., Le Bras, R., Choi, Y.: Social IQa: commonsense reasoning about social interactions. In: Proceedings of the 2019 Conference on Empirical Methods in Natural Language Processing and the 9th International Joint Conference on Natural Language Processing (EMNLP-IJCNLP), pp. 4463–4473. Association for Computational Linguistics, Hong Kong, China (2019). https://doi.org/10.18653/v1/D19-1454, https://aclanthology.org/D19-1454
55. Serrano Alves, L.P., Wiese, I.S., Chaves, A.P., Steinmacher, I.: How to find my task? Chatbot to assist newcomers in choosing tasks in OSS projects. In: Følstad, A., et al. Chatbot Research and Design. CONVERSATIONS 2021. LNCS, vol. 13171. Springer, Cham (2022). https://doi.org/10.1007/978-3-030-94890-0_6
56. Cleverbot. https://www.cleverbot.com/
57. Mitsuku. https://www.pandorabots.com/mitsuku/
58. St, L., Wold, S., et al.: Analysis of variance (ANOVA). Chemom. Intell. Lab. Syst. 6(4), 259–272 (1989)
59. Strachan, R., Peixoto, A., Emembolu, I., Restivo, M.T.: Women in engineering: Addressing the gender gap, exploring trust and our unconscious bias. In: IEEE Global Engineering Education Conference, pp. 2088–2093 (2018)
60. Torres, C., Franklin, W., Martins, L.: Accessibility in Chatbots: The State of the Art in Favor of Users with Visual Impairment, pp. 623–635 (2019)
61. Tur, G., Hakkani-Tür, D., Heck, L.: What is left to be understood in ATIS? In: 2010 IEEE Spoken Language Technology Workshop, pp. 19–24 (2010). https://doi.org/10.1109/SLT.2010.5700816
62. Urli, S., Yu, Z., Seinturier, L., Monperrus, M.: How to design a program repair bot? Insights from the repairnator project. In: ICSE-SEIP, pp. 95–104. ICSE-SEIP '18, ACM, New York, NY, USA (2018)

63. Amazon Alexa. https://developer.amazon.com/en-US/alexa
64. Apple Siri. https://www.apple.com/siri/
65. Google Assistant. https://assistant.google.com/
66. Viviani, G., Famelis, M., Xia, X., Janik-Jones, C., Murphy, G.: Locating latent design information in developer discussions: a study on pull requests. IEEE TSC **47**(7), 1402–1413 (2019)
67. Wang, A., et al.: Can you tell me how to get past sesame street? Sentence-level pretraining beyond language modeling. In: Proceedings of the 57th Annual Meeting of the Association for Computational Linguistics, pp. 4465–4476. Association for Computational Linguistics, Florence, Italy (2019). https://doi.org/10.18653/v1/P19-1439, https://aclanthology.org/P19-1439
68. Wang, D., Dong, W., Li, S.: A Multi-Task Representation Learning Approach for Source Code, pp. 1–2 (2020)
69. Wang, H., Chen, C., Xing, Z., Grundy, J.: DiffTech: A Tool for Differencing Similar Technologies from Question-and-Answer Discussions, pp. 1576–1580 (2020)
70. Williams, A.C., Kaur, H., Iqbal, S., White, R.W., Teevan, J., Fourney, A.: Mercury: empowering programmers' mobile work practices with micro productivity. In: UIST. pp. 81–94 (2019)
71. Wood, A., Eberhart, Z., McMillan, C.: Dialogue Act Classification for Virtual Agents for Software Engineers during Debugging, pp. 462–469. ACM (2020)
72. Wood, A., Rodeghero, P., Armaly, A., McMillan, C.: Detecting speech act types in developer question/answer conversations during bug repair. In: Proceedings of the 2018 26th ACM Joint Meeting on European Software Engineering Conference and Symposium on the Foundations of Software Engineering - ESEC/FSE 2018. ACM Press (2018)
73. Xu, B., Xing, Z., Xia, X., Lo, D.: AnswerBot: automated generation of answer summary to developers' technical questions. In: ASE, pp. 706–716 (2017)
74. Yang, Q., Steinfeld, A., Rosé, C., Zimmerman, J.: Re-Examining Whether, Why, and How Human-AI Interaction Is Uniquely Difficult to Design, pp. 1–13. ACM (2020)
75. Yao, K., Peng, B., Zhang, Y., Yu, D., Zweig, G., Shi, Y.: Spoken language understanding using long short-term memory neural networks. In: 2014 IEEE Spoken Language Technology Workshop (SLT), pp. 189–194. IEEE (2014)
76. Zhang, J., Zhao, T., Yu, Z.: Multimodal hierarchical reinforcement learning policy for task-oriented visual dialog. In: Proceedings of the 19th Annual SIGdial Meeting on Discourse and Dialogue, pp. 140–150. Association for Computational Linguistics, Melbourne, Australia (2018). https://doi.org/10.18653/v1/W18-5015, https://aclanthology.org/W18-5015
77. Zhou, L., Gao, J., Li, D., Shum, H.Y.: The design and implementation of XiaoIce, an empathetic social chatbot. Comput. Linguist. **46**(1), 53–93 (2020). https://doi.org/10.1162/coli_a_00368
78. Zhu, Y., et al.: Aligning books and movies: Towards story-like visual explanations by watching movies and reading books. CoRR abs/1506.06724 (2015). http://arxiv.org/abs/1506.06724

Surveying Computational Theory of Mind and a Potential Multi-agent Approach

Prabhat Kumar[✉], Adrienne Raglin, and John Richardson

US DEVCOM Army Research Laboratory, Adelphi, MD, USA
`prabhat.kumar.civ@army.mil`

Abstract. Theory of Mind (ToM) is a capability of humans to attribute mental states to other agents allowing us to reason on the agent's intentions and predict their future behavior. The complexity of ToM paves a way for an open arena of development for autonomous, predictive capabilities. While we see specific use-cases of ToM in recent computational studies, we must be aware of its over-arching role as a cognitive method for understanding social behavior to better guide the work towards a higher potential. We survey a few dimensions of exploration for the field to offer a way forward including ideas from the theory of child development, game theory, and generalizability, to list a few. Our own work focuses on expanding to multiple, strategic agents where we attempt to understand non-cooperative, even adversarial, behaviors in dynamic environments. We explore and aggregate elements from several contemporary ToM models, update our experimental groundwork, and begin testing the extents of their capabilities.

Keywords: theory of mind · game theory · multi-agent · machine-learning · artificial intelligence · intention · adversarial dynamics · computational · automation

1 Introduction

Humans have a unique capability of attributing mental states to agents in the face of uncertainty, which we call Theory of Mind (ToM) [38]. Necessary for social interaction, ToM helps humans to understand the intention, goals, desires, and strategies of other individuals [4]. Such an ability can be, and has been, called "mind-reading" and suggests higher intuition and perception. Indeed, it is a skill developed through the course of one's life but does not grant the user privileged insight into the mind of the individual they are interacting with. Humans use ToM while driving vehicles, reading books, playing board games, buying gifts, etc. It is worth mentioning that ToM is not an innate capability within humans, developing, at the very least, slower for individuals with autism spectrum disorder (ASD) (see Baron-Cohen) [5], attention deficit hyperactivity disorder, developmental language disorders, schizophrenia, and others (see [25]). Many studies take cognitive and psychological approaches to grasping ToM (see, for example,

Byom [9], Quesque [40], Rakoczy [45], Wellman [63], Saxe (2006) [50]), and contemporary developments in Artificial Intelligence (AI) have identified the need for ToM as a pivotal capability for achieving human-level AI capabilities, see Schossau [51], Cuzzolin [13]. AI has proven competent in breaking through previously human-limited tasks, (see Schrittwieser [52], Varadi [59]), so we naturally wonder if we can use ToM principles to further enhance its potential. For more meta-analyses of computational ToM see Mao [30], Zaroukian [67], and Aru [2].

Our own goal is creating ToM agent(s) which recognize intentions and goals of strategic agents operating in dynamic environments. In focusing our work, we identified a neural network ToM observer model, ToMnet (Rabinowitz [41]), as a strong proof-of-concept to build on. While ToMnet focuses on single-agent behaviors inside a gridworld environment, we wanted to extend this model to reasoning on multiple actors with collaborative or adversarial policies operating in a changing environment. But in building out the concepts, we encountered a few key questions about ToM research, for which we aimed to provide insight here:

1. It is argued that ToM cannot develop without language; what does language allow for that other modalities, such as visual, may not?
2. In strategic interaction between agents, what is the difference between game theory and ToM?
3. Generalizability and modularity of ToM models would allow human-like cognitive flexibility; what does current research have to offer in this regard?

We also consider the state of multi-agent learning techniques and model perspective (e.g. first-person versus observer) with respect to these key questions.

This paper surveys computational efforts for modeling ToM capabilities addressing the above questions while suggesting a path forward accounting for various trade-offs from different model architectures and providing commentary on design choices for our future work.

2 Contemporary Studies in Computational ToM

Foundational to our own work are Baker (2011) [3] and Rabinowitz [41]. The former "model[s] human ToM within a Bayesian framework... [and casts] Bayesian ToM as a problem of inverse planning and inference about the world as a partially Observable Markov Decision Process (POMDP), and invert[s] this forward model using Bayesian inference." The latter applies machine learning (ML) techniques given Baker's ideas, to train a model in understanding and predicting the behaviors of a subject agent. Both works use "omnisicient" observer models, with the caveat that the model cannot access the internal states of the subjects. Such "eagle-eye" perspective models have application in areas such as video-game AI or traffic/navigation software where the model can characterize player/driver behaviors to adjust world/agent-elements to better challenge a video-game player or ease strain on the traffic grid. Reinforcement learning (RL) models maximize reward functions through iterative agent action selection, as the agent navigates

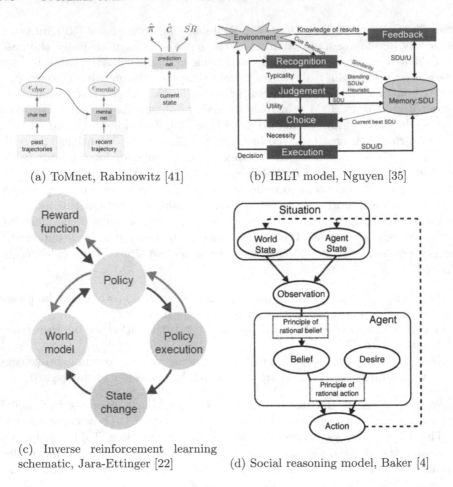

(a) ToMnet, Rabinowitz [41]

(b) IBLT model, Nguyen [35]

(c) Inverse reinforcement learning schematic, Jara-Ettinger [22]

(d) Social reasoning model, Baker [4]

Fig. 1. Examples of a few notable models of ToM over the past few years.

in, and interacts with, their environment, to produce an optimal policy. Jara-Ettinger [22] casts ToM modeling as inverse reinforcement learning (IRL) (Ng [34]) which infers an agent's unobserved reward function within the environment based on the agent's observed actions. Nguyen [35] builds on Rabinowitz's work proposing a cognitive Instance-Based Learning Theory (IBLT; Gonzalez [19]) observer model in experiments similar to Rabinowitz. IBLT is built on the concept of memory retrieval; modeling how readily available certain memories are to the agent. This seemingly mimics human abilities in that our ToM relies on our past experience (memories/interpretations of memories); some memories may fade, but others used more regularly are reinforced and more easily accessed. Chuang [12] uses another extension of ToMnet to find social network structures as an agent which may require several different resources navigates to their sources within a grid-world environment. Some notable model diagrams from these papers are depicted in Fig. 1.

2.1 ToM and Language

Language is a burgeoning area of ToM research especially with the rapid ascent of Large-Language Model (LLM) technologies. Several recent studies are aimed at establishing the ToM reasoning capabilities of LLMs. Gandhi [18] creates a social reasoning benchmark, BigToM, for procedural generation of ToM evaluations. van Duijn [16] compares the ability of 11 LLMs with that of 7–10 year old children, to find that a majority of these LLMs could not surpass the children's abilities, spare those in the GPT-family, especially GPT-4. Kosinski [26] develops several natural language false-belief tasks for the popular GPT-family of models and finds that they are able to track the beliefs of the characters in the assigned tasks. Kosinski recognizes the debate surrounding these findings, and also claims that "ToM likely emerged as a byproduct of increasing language ability [Milligan [33]], as indicated by the high correlation between ToM and language aptitude, the delayed ToM acquisition in people with minimal language exposure [Pyers [39]], and the overlap in the brain regions responsible for both [Saxe (2003) [49]]. ToM has been shown to positively correlate with participating in family discussions [Ruffman [46]], the use of and familiarity with words describing mental states ([Pyers [39]], [Mayer [31]])." (Note, we present Kosinski's referenced citations here for the reader's convenience.) Such ties between ToM and language are presented in De Mulder [14], Sarmento-Henrique [48]. Aru [2] makes a similar observation calling for a comparison of ToM abilities between models both with and without language capabilities. Furthermore, they note, "Currently, there is no evidence that the later steps of ToM (i.e., understanding of false belief and hidden mental states) can develop without language input." Jamali [21] offers a more in-depth look comparing human neural architecture to those of LLMs. Sclar [53] argues LLM's lack ToM skills citing lack of diversity and complexity in current reading comprehension datasets and goes onto to demonstrate an inference-time method, SymbolicToM, which augments LLM's with "an explicit graphical representation of each character's beliefs" which they claim is a way to combat the lack of supervised data for the field. Ullman [58] and Shapira [54] also exhibit healthy skepticism for LLMs' ToM abilities.

So how can studies in language enhance those in ToM? In one manner, it is crucial for the model to describe its observations and inferences, which seems the realm of visual-language models, see Wang (2023) [62], Radford [42], Li (2022) [28], Li (2019) [29], and Alayrac [1] for examples. A very recent development in this regard comes from Jin [23] which argues about the flexibility of human ToM reasoning to multiple modalities providing an evaluation for multimodal ToM as well as a new multimodal ToM model, BIP-ALM. Blaha [7] argues that understanding itself is a process (not a state) which can only be probed through natural language, and offers insight in examining the process through failures in understanding/comprehension. Evaluations based on these probes would be helpful in uncovering the inner-workings of AI/ML models, as explained in the discussions on Explainable AI (XAI) in Blaha [7]. They go on to highlight the use of counterfactual probes for ToM evaluation to assess understanding in terms of causation. In another regard, using ToM-language techniques is effective when agents are actively (or directly) communicating with one another. Theory of Mind based communication strategies modeled using a POMDP is presented in Buehler [8].

Studying the ties between language and theory of mind also raised curiosity about general auditory and visual signals. Very few studies are dedicated to auditory modalities, which may indicate a fresh field for study. Hasni [20] who designs a series of auditory ToM tasks for children arguing "sound may offer cues unavailable to sight" (e.g. inflections of the voice). (For non-speech modalities, intuitively, it seems we attribute mental states and intention to the sources of sound rather than sound itself, but what about cases in which we cannot determine the source of the sound?) Bedny [6] performs tests of ToM to compare results between sighted and congenitally blind individuals citing 3 kinds of experiences which affect ToM development: visual (to perceive others' internal states), first-person (to compare between their own and others' states), and linguistic (to understand concepts about the mind).

Direct communication, however, does not guarantee full access to the agent's mental state; information may be unknowingly or deliberately left out as may be in the case of strategic interaction between agents.

2.2   ToM and Game Theory

In cases of strategically interacting agents, we consider the connections between ToM and game theory. In learning about an opponent's strategy, we ask what is the difference between game theory and ToM? Game theory is the logical formulation of strategy used in applications from board games, to economics, to wargames. Game theory aids in "solving" games to provide insight into the best strategies each player can apply to gain advantages and/or win. Game theory follows a more logically rigorous structure looking at games in terms of their component elements (agents, agent abilities, constraints, allowed/restricted actions, winning/losing conditions, etc.) Yoshida [66] considers ideas from control theory to formulate and apply a potential model of theory of mind to behavioral data which they use to determine whether humans are indeed inferring mind-states during a game of "Stag-Hunt." Veltman [60] attempts to train the user on higher-order ToM by having human participants play against computational agents with varying ToM orders. McCubbins [32] argues that ToM models would go beyond the classical concepts and results of game theory by relinquishing its mathematically-elegant, yet restrictive, assumptions such as players "comport[ing] to Nash equilibrium strategies (or even von Neumann-Morgenstern utility maximization)", as well as the "patches of behavioral game theory" used to explain the "deviations in classical rationality."

Deception serves as a prime sub-area for exploring ToM capabilities for it, intuitively, imposes the need for modeling of mindsets as agents direct each other away from the truth. In Sarkadi [47], they provide a mathematical formulation for deception combining ToM with two major theories of deception from communication theory: Interpersonal Deception Theory, looking at how communicative and cognitive capacities affect implementation of deception, and Information Manipulation Theory 2, helping explain how to employ deception through information manipulation. Oey [36] examine how liars must balance utility maximization with plausibility of the lie and compares the use of a recursive Bayesian ToM model with one that has no model of another agent's mindset and another omniscient model.

A model is only as good as the data it learns from; it would be prudent to establish whether game play datasets contain these assumptions or to open the space of potential actions an agent can experiment with. It is difficult to know whether a ToM model would learn classic game-theoretic results if left to its own devices. Doing so would simultaneously validate the model and game-theoretic results and, anticlimactically, "reinvent the wheel." Not doing so would not invalidate any results, but simply direct us to probe into the assumptions the ToM model made on its way to understanding the subject strategic interactions.

2.3 Generalizability/Modularity

In question #3 of Sect. 1, we reference the generalizability of a ToM model; that is the claim that each individual has their own ToM model which they apply to any social situation they are in, and this model is updated through either engagement or non-engagement with other entities. Modularity refers to the model's flexibility in extending its learned representation. By this we mean shifting between local/global perspectives or employing higher-order reasoning (meta-reasoning, see Caylor [10]). Diaconescu [15] models ToM capability with a Hierarchical Gaussian Filter (HGF) which uses parameters tuned to individuals participating in a small economic binary lottery game. The HGF is an example of a generalizable model in two main ways: (1) its priors are tunable to the individual it hopes to model and (2) its input parameters seem adjustable beyond binary inputs. It also shows promise for modularity because of its extendability in hierarchy. Patricio [37] introduces a mathematical model, based on Baker (2012) [4] and incorporating the idea of fuzzy cognitive maps, which they personalize to 15 different human participants. The use of higher-order ToM by humans in Veltman [60] is another example of the modularity desired in artificial agents.

The generalizability of ToM is referenced by Aru [2] to suggest that a model should not be limited to performing a single task such as resolving the Sally-Anne test (see Fig. 2; Wimmer [65], Baron-Cohen [5]) which is a classical false-belief task used in establishing ToM capabilities. They, instead, call for open-ended learning (see Fan [17], Sigaud [56]) which allows for flexibility of human-like cognition. Generalizability in the form of open-ended learning approaches seemingly implies the use of reinforcement learning techniques, for which the difficulty lies in defining proper reward functions (see Aru [2].)

Fig. 2. The Sally-Anne Test presented in Baron-Cohen [5]. Sally and Anne are in a room with two boxes and an object. Sally places the object in Box A and leaves the room. Anne switches the object to Box B. The test-taker then infers where Sally looks for the object upon returning.

3   Aggregating Model Considerations

Our initial goals in developing this project were inspired by the machine-learning methodology used in Rabinowitz [41]; we were, namely, interested in extending their ToMnet model to more complex and dynamic situations involving multiple agents applying more strategic policies, occlusion of the observer model's field-of-view, and different agent characterizations. We consider the insights shared from the previous sections.

In the spirit of Kosinski [26], Aru [2], Sclar [53], ToM need not be explicitly programmed into proposed models, but may be an emergent property of the training its received, with the caveat that the model is given a rich-enough experimentation environment to learn from, which leads into the "generalizability" aspect of ToM; one model that can be applied to a multitude of scenarios and perfected to a task via specific training. Intuitively, humans apply one model of ToM to several different situations (e.g. driving, playing basketball or chess, speaking with clients) and the model is constantly upgraded, though not necessarily perfected, with each new experience.

We see a few notable paths for our work applying ToM in tandem with ML techniques:

1. Developing metrics to measure (the richness of) Theory of Mind models.
2. "Eagle-eye"/observer models which overlook an arena with various actors and dynamic elements; the model may or may not communicate with the agents in the simulation.
3. "1st-person" models which must navigate a dynamic environment filled with autonomous, policy-driven actors most, if not all, of which must be characterized for the agent to optimally fulfill their goals. This 1st-person model also may or may not communicate with other agents.

For Item #1, such an effort was underway with Shu [55] where they develop a series benchmark evaluations to test the core intuitive psychological reasoning capabilities of proposed cognitive models. The benchmark depicts four types of 3D animated scenarios representing goal preference, action efficiency, unobserved constraints, and cost-reward trade-offs and they apply the benchmark to compare two ToM models: one involving Bayesian inverse planning and a ToM neural network extending ToMnet [41]. The authors recognize that "a model may also need to understand other concepts to pass a full battery of core intuitive psychology, including perceptual access and intuitive physics." Such a battery of tests could help characterize the richness of proposed ToM models (Fig. 3).

Observer-type models are excellent for understanding the "big picture", outside of a local scope, however, data for these models is not so readily accessible. One workaround is using publicly-available, pre-trained RL algorithms to help automate data generation of states and actions. But a hiccup to this, is the availability of rich RL algorithms; so one could run into a recursive/circular issue: We want our ToM model richly trained, but the data must itself be rich-enough. Inferences of pure observer models are interesting to study, but imparting them with the ability to communicate with the agents in the observed environment can allow us to see the potentially action-/policy-changing effects its inferences have.

"1st-person" models would benefit from using some form of (I)RL. The problem to solve with using RL is defining a reward function which explicitly drives the model to infer on internal states of the agents it interacts with. Data generation of different environments, tasks, potentially expandable action-sets would be required. However, any method using RL will almost always require very long training times. Using Bayesian models with pre-programmed priors may perform better than ML techniques, as was the case in Shu [55], but may also require other pre-programmed knowledge (e.g. physics) which is not as easily accessible to a working model.

In any case, machine learning techniques have the benefit of providing a potential blank-slate for the flexibility in accessing richer sets of inferences; however black-box methods obviously hideaway the inner workings of the model. Whereas, Bayesian and other pre-programmed probabilistic models benefit from being directed from human intervention. The suggestion for proceeding down either route is using the former when developing ToM from first principles, and

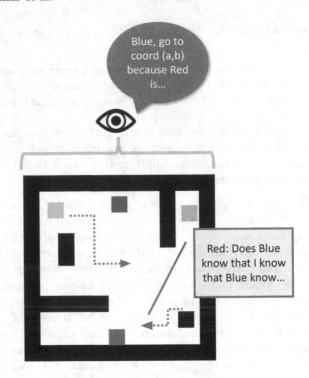

Fig. 3. The eye on top represents an observer-type model overlooking the agents and the environment, possibly communicating with the agents to alter actions. The red agent represents a 1st-person type model which can only infer on what it can observe within the environment. (Color figure online)

the latter when required to solve specific tasks for processes that just need fine-tuning. A method which uses a combination of both techniques would be ideal, and is left for further discussion.

3.1 Future Plans

For the capabilities we are trying to engineer, we focus our attention to observer-type models with the ability to communicate with the observed agents to understand the effects their inferences have on agent policies. Furthermore such a model also has the flexibility of allowing 1st-person-type models as its subjects, and communication between these two models would also lead to an interesting array of experiments. However, to start, it would be prudent to create an environment with two observed agents for which we can craft simple gameplay policies (e.g. Hide-n-Seek) and determining how the model can delineate between the two policies. Following these initial experiments, we could expand to three or more agents with different teamings, introduce environmental effects and/or communication between observer and in-game agents. The Farama Foundation contains a number of quality reinforcement learning tools to assist in this and further expansions of any experiment: Minigrid [11] is a simple gridworld environment which could serve as a stepping stone to other more complex tools such as PettingZoo [57] used for multi-agent reinforcement learning. We have also used NetLogo [64] in our work to recreate the gridworld environments (see Fig. 4), and while it is a very strong simulation framework allowing, for example, incorporation of Python code (including commonly used machine learning tools), it does not have the built-in functionalities of the devoted RL tools from the Farama Foundation.

Currently, in our work using NetLogo, we have been able to generate multiple agents which traverse the world randomly, but imparting purposeful behavior has yet to be achieved; that is, each agent carries out a random action policy and does not optimize any reward to encourage "thoughtful" behaviors. We consider recent developments of multi-agent learning techniques to guide us in efficiently incorporating multiple agents into our environments. Lanctot [27] considers the problem of multiagent policies learned using independent reinforcement learning by creating an algorithm incorporating a metric of joint-policy correlation to combat this. Wang (2020) [61] introduces MARL with the concept of roles to teach agents with diverse responsibilities adopting the paradigm of centralized training with decentralized execution. Kim [24] creates the communication method of Intention Sharing, whereby agents share their imagined trajectories to prompt other agents.

 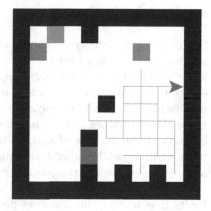

Fig. 4. Initial attempts at expanding single-agent gridworld models to host multiple agents in NetLogo [64].

We also hope to engage with other artificial reasoning methodologies such as Uncertainty of Information as presented in Raglin (2020) [43] to create more robust models capable of mitigating the negative impact of uncertainty in various situations, see Raglin (2022) [44].

As we progress in our work, we must stay aware of the capabilities of our model, namely, we should check intermittently whether our model follows ToM principles, or displays any sort of aptitude towards ToM. While we want the model to perform well in the task of inferring and potentially altering agent's mental states as they perform in progressively complex environments, it would also be prudent to consistently test its capabilities for performing core psychological reasoning tasks (Shu [55]) and generating tests (Jin [23]) of the existence and richness of its ToM capabilities and understanding of another's mindset (Blaha [7]).

Our intention, again, is to explore ToM models for multiple, strategic agents in dynamic environments. Considering the approaches and insights offered before, it is befitting to proceed in a more model-centric manner, as opposed to data-centric, especially with regards to generalizability and modularity. Our explorations in language prompt us to explore LLM learning paradigms for use in our own model(s) as such systems become more adept at various probes of reasoning. While we do not necessarily intend to create a language model, as other types of models have demonstrated visual/symbolic reasoning capabilities, language is inextricably linked to ToM. To explore multiple, strategic agents in dynamic environments, would be to limit potential "emergences" and generalizations of reasoning skills to other contexts, but also seems to serve as the next phase in testing ToM model capabilities. Game theory provides initial benchmarks to compare model inferences with. Metrics for ToM reasoning tasks would serve as crucial checkpoints as we proceed towards more open-ended learning as a way of bolstering cognitive flexibilities.

4 Conclusion

In this paper we surveyed contemporary studies in computational ToM and prescribed a way forward for a particular proposed class of ToM models. Namely, those observing and affecting multiple policy driven agents within a dynamic environment. We provided insight into topics arising as we enrich and add complexity to our models. Namely, language (seen as essential in ToM development), game theory (games provide a rich experimental proving ground), and generalizability (breaking free of specific tasks). We also briefly discuss some insights from multi-agent learning techniques, categorize potential model development avenues based on metric generation and model perspective, and provide some commentary on our own work and paths forward. Overall, we hope to push the limits in enhancing human-level performance by imparting ToM capabilities to artificial agents.

References

1. Alayrac, J.B., et al.: Flamingo: a visual language model for few-shot learning. In: Koyejo, S., Mohamed, S., Agarwal, A., Belgrave, D., Cho, K., Oh, A. (eds.) Advances in Neural Information Processing Systems. vol. 35, pp. 23716–23736. Curran Associates, Inc. (2022)
2. Aru, J., Labash, A., Corcoll, O., Vicente, R.: Mind the gap: challenges of deep learning approaches to theory of mind. Artif. Intell. Rev. **56**, 1–16 (2023)

3. Baker, C., Saxe, R., Tenenbaum, J.: Bayesian theory of mind: modeling joint belief-desire attribution. In: Proceedings of the Annual Meeting of the Cognitive Science Society, vol. 33 (2011)
4. Baker, C.L.: Bayesian theory of mind: Modeling human reasoning about beliefs, desires, goals, and social relations. Ph.D. thesis, Massachusetts Institute of Technology (2012)
5. Baron-Cohen, S., Leslie, A.M., Frith, U.: Does the autistic child have a "theory of mind"? Cognition **21**(1), 37–46 (1985). https://doi.org/10.1016/0010-0277(85)90022-8
6. Bedny, M., Pascual-Leone, A., Saxe, R.R.: Growing up blind does not change the neural bases of theory of mind. Proc. Nat. Acad. Sci. **106**(27), 11312–11317 (2009). https://doi.org/10.1073/pnas.0900010106, https://www.pnas.org/doi/abs/10.1073/pnas.0900010106
7. Blaha, L.M., et al.: Understanding is a process. Front. Syst. Neurosci. **16**, 800280 (2022). https://doi.org/10.3389/fnsys.2022.800280, https://www.frontiersin.org/articles/10.3389/fnsys.2022.800280
8. Buehler, M.C., Weisswange, T.H.: Theory of mind based communication for human agent cooperation. In: 2020 IEEE International Conference on Human-Machine Systems (ICHMS), pp. 1–6 (2020). https://doi.org/10.1109/ICHMS49158.2020.9209472
9. Byom, L., Mutlu, B.: Theory of mind: mechanisms, methods, and new directions. Front. Hum. Neurosci. **7**, 413 (2013). https://doi.org/10.3389/fnhum.2013.00413, https://www.frontiersin.org/articles/10.3389/fnhum.2013.00413
10. Caylor, J., Herrmann, J.W., Hung, C., Raglin, A., Richardson, J.: Metareasoning for multi-criteria decision making using complex information sources. In: Pham, T., Solomon, L. (eds.) Artificial Intelligence and Machine Learning for Multi-Domain Operations Applications IV. vol. 12113, p. 121130Y. International Society for Optics and Photonics, SPIE (2022). https://doi.org/10.1117/12.2619418
11. Chevalier-Boisvert, M., et al.: Minigrid & miniworld: Modular & customizable reinforcement learning environments for goal-oriented tasks (2023). CoRR abs/2306.13831
12. Chuang, Y.S., et al.: Using machine theory of mind to learn agent social network structures from observed interactive behaviors with targets. In: 2020 29th IEEE International Conference on Robot and Human Interactive Communication (RO-MAN), pp. 1013–1019 (2020). https://doi.org/10.1109/RO-MAN47096.2020.9223453
13. Cuzzolin, F., Morelli, A., Cîrstea, B., Sahakian, B.J.: Knowing me, knowing you: theory of mind in AI. Psychol. Med. **50**(7), 1057–1061 (2020). https://doi.org/10.1017/S0033291720000835
14. De Mulder, H.N., Wijnen, F., Coopmans, P.H.: Interrelationships between theory of mind and language development: a longitudinal study of dutch-speaking kindergartners. Cogn. Dev. **51**, 67–82 (2019). https://doi.org/10.1016/j.cogdev.2019.03.006, https://www.sciencedirect.com/science/article/pii/S0885201416302167
15. Diaconescu, A.O., et al.: Inferring on the intentions of others by hierarchical bayesian learning. PLOS Comput. Biol. **10**(9), 1–19 (2014). https://doi.org/10.1371/journal.pcbi.1003810
16. van Duijn, M.J., van Dijk, B.M.A., Kouwenhoven, T., de Valk, W., Spruit, M.R., van der Putten, P.: Theory of mind in large language models: Examining performance of 11 state-of-the-art models vs. children aged 7-10 on advanced tests (2023)

17. Fan, L., et al.: MineDojo: building open-ended embodied agents with internet-scale knowledge. In: Koyejo, S., Mohamed, S., Agarwal, A., Belgrave, D., Cho, K., Oh, A. (eds.) Advances in Neural Information Processing Systems. vol. 35, pp. 18343–18362. Curran Associates, Inc. (2022)
18. Gandhi, K., Fränken, J.P., Gerstenberg, T., Goodman, N.D.: Understanding social reasoning in language models with language models (2023)
19. Gonzalez, C., Lerch, J.F., Lebiere, C.: Instance-based learning in dynamic decision making. Cogn. Sci. **27**(4), 591–635 (2003). https://doi.org/10.1016/S0364-0213(03)00031-4, https://www.sciencedirect.com/science/article/pii/S0364021303000314
20. Hasni, A.A., Adamson, L.B., Williamson, R.A., Robins, D.L.: Adding sound to theory of mind: comparing children's development of mental-state understanding in the auditory and visual realms. J. Exp. Child Psychol. **164**, 239–249 (2017)
21. Jamali, M., Williams, Z.M., Cai, J.: Unveiling theory of mind in large language models: A parallel to single neurons in the human brain (2023)
22. Jara-Ettinger, J.: Theory of mind as inverse reinforcement learning. Curr. Opin. Behav. Sci. **29**, 105–110 (2019). https://doi.org/10.1016/j.cobeha.2019.04.010, https://www.sciencedirect.com/science/article/pii/S2352154618302055, artificial Intelligence
23. Jin, C., et al.: MMToM-QA: Multimodal theory of mind question answering (2024)
24. Kim, W., Park, J., Sung, Y.: Communication in multi-agent reinforcement learning: Intention sharing. In: International Conference on Learning Representations (2021). https://openreview.net/forum?id=qpsl2dR9twy
25. Korkmaz, B.: Theory of mind and neurodevelopmental disorders of childhood. Pediatr. Res. **69**(8), 101–108 (2011)
26. Kosinski, M.: Theory of mind may have spotaneously emerged in large language models (2023). https://doi.org/10.48550/arXiv.2302.02083
27. Lanctot, M., et al.: A unified game-theoretic approach to multiagent reinforcement learning (2017)
28. Li, J., Li, D., Xiong, C., Hoi, S.: BLIP: Bootstrapping language-image pre-training for unified vision-language understanding and generation (2022)
29. Li, L.H., Yatskar, M., Yin, D., Hsieh, C.J., Chang, K.W.: VisualBERT: A simple and performant baseline for vision and language (2019)
30. Mao, Y., Liu, S., Zhao, P., Ni, Q., Lin, X., He, L.: A review on machine theory of mind (2023)
31. Mayer, A., Träuble, B.E.: Synchrony in the onset of mental state understanding across cultures? A study among children in samoa. Int. J. Behav. Dev. **37**(1), 21–28 (2013). https://doi.org/10.1177/0165025412454030
32. McCubbins, M.D., Turner, M.B., Weller, N.: The theory of minds within the theory of games. In: Proceedings of the 2012 International Conference on Artificial Intelligence (2012)
33. Milligan, K., Astington, J.W., Dack, L.A.: Language and theory of mind: meta-analysis of the relation between language ability and false-belief understanding. Child Dev. **78**(2), 622–646 (2007). https://doi.org/10.1111/j.1467-8624.2007.01018.x, https://srcd.onlinelibrary.wiley.com/doi/abs/10.1111/j.1467-8624.2007.01018.x
34. Ng, A.Y., Russell, S., et al.: Algorithms for inverse reinforcement learning. In: ICML. vol. 1, p. 2 (2000)
35. Nguyen, T.N., Gonzalez, C.: Theory of mind from observation in cognitive models and humans. Top. Cogn. Sci. **14**(4), 665–686 (2022). https://doi.org/10.1111/tops.12553, https://onlinelibrary.wiley.com/doi/abs/10.1111/tops.12553

36. Oey, L., Schachner, A., Vul, E.: Designing good deception: recursive theory of mind in lying and lie detection. In: The Proceedings of the Annual Meeting of the Cognitive Science Society (2019)
37. Patrício, M., Jamshidnejad, A.: Mathematical models of theory of mind (2022). https://doi.org/10.48550/arXiv.2209.14450
38. Premack, D., Woodruff, G.: Does the chimpanzee have a theory of mind? Behav. Brain Sci. **1**(4), 515–526 (1978). https://doi.org/10.1017/S0140525X00076512
39. Pyers, J.E., Senghas, A.: Language promotes false-belief understanding: evidence from learners of a new sign language. Psychol. Sci. **20**(7), 805–812 (2009). https://doi.org/10.1111/j.1467-9280.2009.02377.x, pMID: 19515119
40. Quesque, F., Rossetti, Y.: What do theory-of-mind tasks actually measure? Theory and practice. Perspect. Psychol. Sci. **15**(2), 384–396 (2020). https://doi.org/10.1177/1745691619896607, https://doi.org/10.1177/1745691619896607, pMID: 32069168
41. Rabinowitz, N., Perbet, F., Song, F., Zhang, C., Eslami, S.A., Botvinick, M.: Machine theory of mind. In: International Conference on Machine Learning, pp. 4218–4227. PMLR (2018)
42. Radford, A., et al.: Learning transferable visual models from natural language supervision (2021)
43. Raglin, A., Metu, S., Lott, D.: Challenges of simulating uncertainty of information. In: Stephanidis, C., Antona, M., Ntoa, S. (eds.) HCI International 2020 - Late Breaking Posters, pp. 255–261. Springer International Publishing, Cham (2020)
44. Raglin, A., Richardson, J., Mittrick, M., Metu, S., Caylor, J.: Enhanced tactical inferencing (ETI): a decision recommendation framework. In: Pham, T., Solomon, L. (eds.) Artificial Intelligence and Machine Learning for Multi-Domain Operations Applications IV. vol. 12113, pp. 121130Z. International Society for Optics and Photonics, SPIE (2022). https://doi.org/10.1117/12.2622319
45. Rakoczy, H.: Foundations of theory of mind and its development in early childhood. Nat. Rev. Psychol. **1**(4), 223–235 (2022)
46. Ruffman, T., Slade, L., Crowe, E.: The relation between children's and mothers' mental state language and theory-of-mind understanding. Child Dev. **73**(3), 734–751 (2002). https://doi.org/10.1111/1467-8624.00435, https://srcd.onlinelibrary.wiley.com/doi/abs/10.1111/1467-8624.00435
47. Sarkadi, S., Panisson, A., Bordini, R., McBurney, P., Parsons, S., Chapman, M.: Modelling deception using theory of mind in multi-agent systems. AI Commun. **32**(4), 287–302 (2019). https://doi.org/10.3233/AIC-190615
48. Sarmento-Henrique, R., Quintanilla, L., Lucas-Molina, B., Recio, P., Giménez-Dasí, M.: The longitudinal interplay of emotion understanding, theory of mind, and language in the preschool years. Int. J. Behav. Dev. **44**(3), 236–245 (2020). https://doi.org/10.1177/0165025419866907
49. Saxe, R., Kanwisher, N.: People thinking about thinking people: the role of the temporo-parietal junction in "theory of mind". NeuroImage **19**(4), 1835–1842 (2003). https://doi.org/10.1016/S1053-8119(03)00230-1, https://www.sciencedirect.com/science/article/pii/S1053811903002301
50. Saxe, R., Baron-Cohen, S.: Editorial: the neuroscience of theory of mind. Soc. Neurosci. **1**(3-4), 1–9 (2006). https://doi.org/10.1080/17470910601117463, https://doi.org/10.1080/17470910601117463, pMID: 18633771
51. Schossau, J., Hintze, A.: Towards a theory of mind for artificial intelligence agents. In: Artificial Life Conference Proceedings 35. vol. 2023, p. 21. MIT Press One Rogers Street, Cambridge, MA 02142-1209, USA journals-info ... (2023)

52. Schrittwieser, J., et al.: Mastering Atari, go, chess and shogi by planning with a learned model. Nature **588**(7839), 604–609 (2020)

53. Sclar, M., Kumar, S., West, P., Suhr, A., Choi, Y., Tsvetkov, Y.: Minding language models'(lack of) theory of mind: A plug-and-play multi-character belief tracker (2023). arXiv preprint arXiv:2306.00924

54. Shapira, N., et al.: Clever Hans or neural theory of mind? Stress testing social reasoning in large language models (2023)

55. Shu, T., et al.: AGENT: a benchmark for core psychological reasoning. In: Meila, M., Zhang, T. (eds.) Proceedings of the 38th International Conference on Machine Learning. Proceedings of Machine Learning Research, vol. 139, pp. 9614–9625. PMLR (2021)

56. Sigaud, O., et al.: A definition of open-ended learning problems for goal-conditioned agents (2023)

57. Terry, J., et al.: PettingZoo: gym for multi-agent reinforcement learning. Adv. Neural. Inf. Process. Syst. **34**, 15032–15043 (2021)

58. Ullman, T.: Large language models fail on trivial alterations to theory-of-mind tasks (2023)

59. Varadi, M., et al.: AlphaFold protein structure database: massively expanding the structural coverage of protein-sequence space with high-accuracy models. Nucleic Acids Res. **50**(D1), D439–D444 (2021). https://doi.org/10.1093/nar/gkab1061

60. Veltman, K., de Weerd, H., Verbrugge, R.: Training the use of theory of mind using artificial agents. J. Multimodal User Interfaces **13**, 3–18 (2019)

61. Wang, T., Dong, H., Lesser, V., Zhang, C.: ROMA: multi-agent reinforcement learning with emergent roles (2020)

62. Wang, W., et al.: VisionLLM: Large language model is also an open-ended decoder for vision-centric tasks (2023)

63. Wellman, H.M., Liu, D.: Scaling of theory-of-mind tasks. Child Dev. **75**(2), 523–541 (2004). https://doi.org/10.1111/j.1467-8624.2004.00691.x

64. Wilensky, U.: NetLogo itself (1999). http://ccl.northwestern.edu/netlogo/

65. Wimmer, H., Perner, J.: Beliefs about beliefs: representation and constraining function of wrong beliefs in young children's understanding of deception. Cognition **13**(1), 103–128 (1983). https://doi.org/10.1016/0010-0277(83)90004-5

66. Yoshida, W., Dolan, R.J., Friston, K.J.: Game theory of mind. PLOS Comput. Biol. **4**(12), 1–14 (2008). https://doi.org/10.1371/journal.pcbi.1000254

67. Zaroukian, E.: Theory of mind and metareasoning for artificial intelligence: A review (2022). https://apps.dtic.mil/sti/citations/AD1175466

Evidential Representation Proposal for Predicate Classification Output Logits in Scene Graph Generation

Lucie Kunitomo-Jacquin[✉] and Ken Fukuda

National Institute of Advanced Industrial Science and Technology (AIST),
Tokyo, Japan
kunitomo-jacquin.lucie@aist.go.jp

Abstract. A scene graph consists of a collection of triplets < subject, predicate, object > for describing an image content. One challenging problem in Scene Graph Generation (SGG) is that annotators tend to give poorly relevant predicates, which causes a bias toward less informative triplet predictions. This paper focuses on predicate classification task. We question the information processing that leads to the deduction of poorly informative predicates in current models. We argue that the set of possible predicates should not be regarded as a probability space notably because the predicates granularity varies, like *on* and *sitting on*. We suggest an alternative representation of the information in the Dempster-Shafer framework using a goal-oriented constructed hierarchy. Thanks to this more trustworthy representation, we propose a flexible decision-making procedure that allows us to play with the predicted predicate level of granularity. Our experiments, carried out using scores estimated by an existing transformer-based scene graph generation model, show that our method helps reduce the long tail problem.

Keywords: Scene Graph Generation · Uncertainty Representation · Dempster-Shafer Theory

Introduction

The task of Scene Graph Generation (SSG) consists of mapping an image into a scene graph that represents relations, called *predicates* between the detected objects in the image. One challenging problem in Scene Graph Generation (SGG) is that annotators tend to give poorly relevant predicates, which causes a bias toward less informative predictions. This problem is referred to as a long-tail problem. Despite recent advances like [14] that proposed a counterfactual approach to remove bias induced by the long-tail problem, few works have questioned the representation of the uncertain information provided by the outputs. However, this representation is directly related to the long tail problem because poorly relevant information like 'man near chair' is more likely to be true than specific information like 'man standing on chair'.

The classical output of an SGG model consists of a logit vector designed to quantify the uncertainty associated with the possible output predicates classes.

© The Author(s), under exclusive license to Springer Nature Switzerland AG 2024
H. Degen and S. Ntoa (Eds.): HCII 2024, LNAI 14734, pp. 391–402, 2024.
https://doi.org/10.1007/978-3-031-60606-9_22

However, the set $\mathcal{C}$ of these considered possible classes is mistaken for a sample space Ω of the probability theory, a.k.a., universe, composed of all the atomic events, a.k.a, singletons in the set theory. The problem is that the elements of $\mathcal{C}$ are not atomic events since they are not mutually exclusive, like *on* or *sitting on* (hierarchical aspect) or *looking at* and *using* (multi-label aspect). Furthermore, the epistemic uncertainty (lack of knowledge) inherent to the coarse classes like *on* prevents defining a unique probability distribution that only captures aleatoric uncertainty (intrinsic to the hazard of a phenomenon).

In the remainder of this paper, we refer to a SGG model logit output as a pseudo probability defined on $\mathcal{C}$ and denote it by $\tilde{\mathbf{p}} = (\tilde{p}(c_1), \ldots, \tilde{p}(c_{|\mathcal{C}|}))$, where $\tilde{p}(c)$ denotes the softmax normalized score associated to class c, and $|.|$ the cardinal application. Usually, the decision-making procedure for choosing the predicted predicate $\widehat{c}$ consists of performing a pseudo-optimal expectation:

$$\widehat{c} = \mathrm{argmax}_{c \in \mathcal{C}} (\tilde{p}(c)). \tag{1}$$

This procedure contributes to the long tail problem by disadvantaging the finest-grained predicates, unfairly competing with the coarser predicate classes.

We propose a practical method for transforming the initial logits into a more trustworthy representation of the predicate class uncertainty by coupling the Dempster-Shafer theory with a goal-oriented, manually constructed hierarchy on the set of predicates. Then, we propose a flexible decision-making procedure to allow adjustment of the predicted predicate level of relevance.

The remainder of this paper is organized as follows. First, the context of SSG and the necessary theoretical notions of Dempster-Shafer Theory are presented in Sect. 1. In Sect. 2, we describe our proposed method and illustrate it on an example in Sect. 3. The results are presented in Sect. 4. Finally, a discussion about the related works and the multi-label aspect is provided in Sect. 5.

1   Background

In this section, we introduce the task of Scene Graph Generation and the notions of Dempster-Shafer theory mobilized in our proposition.

1.1   Scene Graph Generation

Introduced by [7] in 2015, the notion of a *scene graph* has gained increasing interest because it provides a more manageable data format for describing image scenes than natural language data does. Semantic image retrieval, which consists of searching for images using a description of their contents, was the first use of scene graphs. Scene graphs are now used in more diverse domains in computer vision applications such as image generation [6], image captioning [17], image semantic understanding [1], and visual question answering [3].

The first scene graph dataset *real-world scene graphs* was provided by [7]. It was constructed using pre-existing image datasets such as YFCC100m [15] and

Microsoft COCO [9]. The datasets consist of a collection of images, for which some ground truth bounding boxes of the object positions, identification, and relations between the objects are provided. The relations are captured as triplets:

$$< subject,\ predicate,\ object >.$$

Visual Genome Dataset [8], built from crowdsourced annotations, is currently one of the most widely utilized large-scale scene graph datasets. Figure 1 and Table 1 provide an example of an annotated image.

Fig. 1. Example of image

Table 1. Ground truth triplets corresponding to Fig. 1 as considered in [2].

<Subject,	Predicate,	Object>
man	*sittingon*	*bench*
man	*wears*	*hat*
man	*in*	*jacket*
man	*wears*	*pant*
man	*wears*	*sock*

The SSG models trained on such large datasets are used to generate scene graphs for new images. The SSG task is generally divided into the following sub-tasks: object bounding box detection, object classification, and classification of the relations between the objects, a.k.a, predicate classification. Some models referred to as *one-stage method* perform simultaneous detection and classification of objects and predicates classification. The final SSG output comes as a ranked list of triplets.

Remark 1. The number of relevant triplets is not known in advance. Actually, it would not be realistic to capture all possible triplets in each image. The ground truth triplets annotations are, therefore, highly incomplete. To handle this varying length of triplets collection, the SSG model generally includes a padding class in $\mathcal{C}$ to account for irrelevant triplets. Let us denote the padding class as c^* in the remainder of this paper.

1.2   Dempster-Shafer Theory

The Dempster Shafer theory [11,13] (DST), also called belief functions theory or evidence theory, allows to represent both aleatoric uncertainty and epistemic uncertainty. This theory has been used in various domains, including information fusion, knowledge representation, machine learning, or risk analysis. DST extends the probability theory, allowing masses to be assigned to subsets of the universe. Denoting the universe by Ω, a *mass function* is a set function $m : 2^\Omega \to [0,1]$ satisfying

$$\sum_{A \subseteq \Omega} m(A) = 1. \tag{2}$$

For a set $A \subseteq \Omega$, the quantity $m(A)$ is defined as the mass of belief allocated exactly to the set A and not to any more specific subsets of A. In other words, $m(A)$ can be interpreted as the probability that we know nothing more than that the truth is in A [11].

Example 1. Let us take the example of an experiment involving the drawing of a ball from a box containing 10 balls: 4 red, 2 blue, 2 green, 1 black, and 1 ball whose color is unknown (but is either red, blue, green, or black). Let us try to characterize the behavior of the random variable X for the color of the ball we would get on the next draw. Note that the universe considered here is $\Omega = \{red, blue, green, black\}$. In the probabilistic framework, the problem is that, depending on the color of the last ball, we get different probabilities. For example, if the last ball is red, we have

$$p(red) = 1/2, \; p(blue) = 1/5, \; p(green) = 1/5, \; p(black) = 1/10.$$

If the last ball is blue, we have another probability distribution:

$$p(red) = 2/5, \; p(blue) = 3/10, \; p(green) = 1/5, \; p(black) = 1/10.$$

Finally, a single probability distribution is not enough to characterize the behavior of X. In this example, aleatoric uncertainty about variable X value arises from several possible truths. The epistemic uncertainty comes from the information about the last ball, which can be stated as "the last ball is red, blue, green, or black". From this information, we can construct a mass function m to describe the draw:

$$m(\{red\}) = 2/5, \; m(\{blue\}) = 1/5, \; m(\{green\}) = 1/5$$

$$m(\{black\}) = 1/10, \; \text{and} \; m(\Omega) = 1/10.$$

A mass function induces two other set functions: first, the belief function $Bel : 2^\Omega \to [0,1]$, which quantifies the total belief in A as the sum of all masses of subsets of A:

$$Bel(A) = \sum_{B \subseteq \Omega, B \subseteq A} m(B), \tag{3}$$

second, the plausibility function of A, $Pl : 2^\Omega \to [0,1]$, which quantifies the maximum evidence that could be allocated to A:

$$Pl(A) = \sum_{B \subseteq \Omega, B \cap A \neq \emptyset} m(B). \tag{4}$$

From these two set functions a probability interval can be defined, $\forall A \subseteq \Omega$,

$$Bel(A) \leq P(A) \leq Pl(A).$$

Example 2. Taking back Example 1, we can deduce intervals for the real probability p:

$$p(red) \in [2/5, 1/2], \ p(blue) \in [1/5, 3/10], \ p(green) \in [1/5, 2/5],$$

$$\text{and} \ \ p(black) \in [1/10, 2/10].$$

2   Approach

Consider that an SSG model has already predicted the subject and object. Let us assume the SSG model also provided an initial logit $\tilde{\mathbf{p}} = (\tilde{p}(c_1), \ldots, \tilde{p}(c_{|\mathcal{C}|}))$ on the set of the raw classes $\mathcal{C}$ for characterizing the relation between the predicted subject and object. Instead of predicting directly from $\tilde{\mathbf{p}}$ with the pseudo-optimal expectation (Eq. 1), we propose to transform $\tilde{\mathbf{p}}$ into a mass function m that better represents the aleatoric and epistemic uncertainties implicitly present in $\tilde{\mathbf{p}}$. Then, we propose a decision-making procedure based on the DST theory.

To this purpose, we manually define a hierarchy on the predicates in $\mathcal{C}$. We used two types of relationships, for $A, B \in \mathcal{C}$, the IS-A relationships, A IS-A B, and the equivalences, $A \equiv B$. Figure 2 presents an extract of our hierarchy.

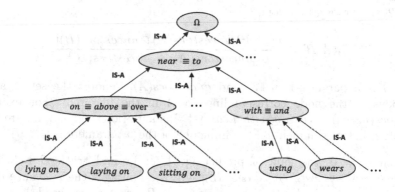

Fig. 2. Extract of our manually constructed hierarchy

Remark 2. We assume a unique true predicate exists at the higher granularity level, i.e., the absence of a multi-label aspect. We will discuss how to free ourselves from this assumption in the Sect. 5.

Thanks to this hierarchy, we define a closed universe Ω containing the nodes with the highest granularity:

$$\Omega = \{lying\ on,\ laying\ on,\ sitting\ on,\ \ldots,\ using,\ wears,\ \ldots\}. \tag{5}$$

In the absence of the multi-label aspect, the output logit $\tilde{p}$ can be interpreted as a mass function almost directly, with appropriate management of equivalences in the hierarchy, and of any padding class c^*:

$$m(A) = \sum_{\substack{c \in C \\ individuals(c)=A}} \tilde{p}(c), \tag{6}$$

$$m(\Omega) = \tilde{p}(c^*), \tag{7}$$

where $individuals(c)$ is the subset of Ω corresponding to the raw class c. The sum in Eq. 6 is to account for the equivalent classes in C. If there is only one raw class of predicate c corresponding to A, then the mass assignment is $m(A) = \tilde{p}(c)$. In the second part of the mass assignment (Eq. 7), the padding class score is transferred to the total set Ω. The interpretation of $m(\Omega)$ is the quantity of total ignorance, as illustrated in Example 1 with the last ball.

Remark 3. To lighten notations, we designate subsets of Ω by their counterpart in C. For example, instead of writing $m(\{using, wear, \dots\})$ we write $m(with)$.

Let us present our decision-making procedure in the following. To encourage hierarchical proximity between a ground truth predicate B and a prediction A, we consider the hierarchical F-score originally defined for hierarchical classification [12] as our gain function:

$$F_\beta(A, B) = \frac{(1 + \beta^2)|ancestors(A) \cap ancestors(B)|}{\beta^2|ancestors(A)| + |ancestors(B)|}, \tag{8}$$

where β is a parameter in $\mathbb{R}^+$ and $ancestors(A)$, denotes the set of ancestor nodes of the node corresponding to A in the hierarchy. For example, $ancestors(using) = \{using, with, near, \Omega\}$. Instantiations of $F_\beta(A, B)$ are given in Table 2. Let us comment on the influence of the β parameter.

- When $\beta = 0$, the gain of predicting A for ground truth B reduces to $|ancestors(A) \cap ancestors(B)|/|ancestors(B)|$ which encourages the relevance of the prediction as specialization errors, i.e., $A \subset B$, are not penalized, but generalization errors, i.e., $B \subset A$, are sanctioned.
- When $\beta \to \infty$, the gain tends to $|ancestors(A) \cap ancestors(B)|/|ancestors(A)|$, which on the opposite, rewards cautiouness $B \subset A$ and sanctions specializations $A \subset B$.

The choice of β sets the compromise level between cautiousness and relevance.

The decision making-procedure consists of maximizing the objective function that has been introduced for cautious classification [4,5]. For a candidate $A \subseteq \Omega$, this objective function is defined as

$$EG(A) = \sum_{B \subseteq \Omega} m(B)F_\beta(A, B). \tag{9}$$

3   Illustration

In this section, let us detail our procedure for one example. We consider the image in Fig. 1. Assume the SSG Model prediction is *man* for the subject and *bench* for the object. Now consider following output logit $\tilde{p}$:

$$\tilde{p}(c_i) = \begin{cases} 0.6 & \text{if } c_i = on, \\ 0.01 & \text{if } c_i = above, \\ 0.01 & \text{if } c_i = lying\ on, \\ 0.01 & \text{if } c_i = laying\ on, \\ 0.33 & \text{if } c_i = sitting\ on, \\ 0.04 & \text{if } c_i = c^*, \\ 0 & \text{otherwise.} \end{cases}$$

The pseudo optimal expectation would lead to predicting the poorly informative predicate *on* as it is associated with the maximal score value.

With our suggested representation, the initial output logit is transformed as the following mass function:

$$m(\Omega) = 0.04, \quad m(on) = 0.61, \quad m(lying\ on) = 0.01,$$
$$m(laying\ on) = 0.01, \quad m(sitting\ on) = 0.33.$$

We can deduce partial information about the real probability distribution on the universe Ω:

$$p(lying\ on) \in [0.01, 0.66], \quad p(laying\ on) \in [0.01, 0.66], \quad p(sitting\ on) \in [0.33, 0.98].$$

Using the detailed expression of the gain function F_β given in Table 2, let us compute the expected gain for candidates *near*, *on* and *sitting on*:

$$\begin{aligned} EG(near) &= m(\Omega)F_\beta(near, \Omega) + m(on)F_\beta(near, on) \\ &+ m(lying\ on)F_\beta(near, lying\ on) + m(laying\ on)F_\beta(near, laying\ on) \\ &+ m(sitting\ on)F_\beta(near, sitting\ on) \\ &\approx 0.62 \text{ if } \beta = 0.1 \\ &\approx 0.74 \text{ if } \beta = 1 \\ &\approx 0.98 \text{ if } \beta = 20 \end{aligned}$$

$$\begin{aligned} EG(on) &= m(\Omega)F_\beta(on, \Omega) + m(on)F_\beta(on, on) \\ &+ m(lying\ on)F_\beta(on, lying\ on) + m(laying\ on)F_\beta(on, laying\ on) \\ &+ m(sitting\ on)F_\beta(on, sitting\ on) \\ &\approx 0.91 \text{ if } \beta = 0.1 \\ &\approx 0.93 \text{ if } \beta = 1 \\ &\approx 0.97 \text{ if } \beta = 20 \end{aligned}$$

and

$$EG(sitting\ on) = m(\Omega)F_\beta(sitting\ on, \Omega) + m(on)F_\beta(sitting\ on, on)$$
$$+m(lying\ on)F_\beta(sitting\ on, lying\ on) + m(laying\ on)F_\beta(sitting\ on, laying\ on)$$
$$+m(sitting\ on)F_\beta(sitting\ on, sitting\ on)$$
$$\approx 0.99 \text{ if } \beta = 0.1$$
$$\approx 0.88 \text{ if } \beta = 1$$
$$\approx 0.81 \text{ if } \beta = 20$$

Table 2. $F_\beta(A, B)$ expressions for A, B in $\{\Omega, on, lying\ on, laying\ on, sitting\ on\}$.

$F_\beta(A, B)$		A				
		Ω	on	$lyingon$	$layingon$	$sittingon$
B	Ω	1	$\dfrac{(1+\beta^2)}{3\beta^2+1}$	$\dfrac{(1+\beta^2)}{4\beta^2+1}$	$\dfrac{(1+\beta^2)}{4\beta^2+1}$	$\dfrac{(1+\beta^2)}{4\beta^2+1}$
	on	$\dfrac{(1+\beta^2)}{\beta^2+3}$	1	$\dfrac{3(1+\beta^2)}{4\beta^2+3}$	$\dfrac{3(1+\beta^2)}{4\beta^2+3}$	$\dfrac{3(1+\beta^2)}{4\beta^2+3}$
	$lyingon$	$\dfrac{(1+\beta^2)}{\beta^2+4}$	$\dfrac{3(1+\beta^2)}{3\beta^2+4}$	1	$\dfrac{3(1+\beta^2)}{4\beta^2+4}$	$\dfrac{3(1+\beta^2)}{4\beta^2+4}$
	$layingon$	$\dfrac{(1+\beta^2)}{\beta^2+4}$	$\dfrac{3(1+\beta^2)}{3\beta^2+4}$	$\dfrac{3(1+\beta^2)}{4\beta^2+4}$	1	$\dfrac{3(1+\beta^2)}{4\beta^2+4}$
	$sittingon$	$\dfrac{(1+\beta^2)}{\beta^2+4}$	$\dfrac{3(1+\beta^2)}{3\beta^2+4}$	$\dfrac{3(1+\beta^2)}{4\beta^2+4}$	$\dfrac{3(1+\beta^2)}{4\beta^2+4}$	1

Table 3 shows the predicted predicate for the baseline, and our method instantiated with $\beta = 0.1, 1, 20$. We obtain fine-grained prediction *sitting on* for the small value of β and more cautious prediction *near* when β is high.

Table 3. Resulting predictions for the illustration example.

< Subject,	Predicted predicate,				Object >
	RelTR baseline	evidential RelTR $\beta = 0.1$	evidential RelTR $\beta = 1$	evidential RelTR $\beta = 20$	
man	*on*	*sittingon*	*on*	*near*	*bench*

4   Results

We base our experiments on the transformer-based SSG RelTR [2]. This is a one-stage SSG model with encoder-decoder-based architecture. This model has gained attention for its competitive performance and fast inference. In our experiments, we use the RelTR model [2] pre-trained on the Visual Genome dataset. For the prediction of subject and object, we used the same procedure as the authors in their GitHub repository https://github.com/yrcong/RelTR.git. Experiments have been conducted on the 26446 testing images.

We evaluate our results with $recall@k$ score that is the fraction of the ground truth triplets GT that appear in the $top - k$ most confident predicted triplets denoted top_k in one image:

$$recall@k = \frac{|top_k \cap GT|}{|GT|}. \tag{10}$$

Since $recall@k$ is biased towards the coarser predicate categories due to their over-representation in the annotated ground truth triplets, recent works use a class-wise version called *mean recall@k* instead. For each image, $recall@k$ scores are computed separately for each predicate category. These class-wise scores are then averaged on all images and averaged again on all categories to give *mean recall@k*.

Table 4 shows the results in terms of $recall@5$ and *mean recall@5* for the baseline RelTR and our evidential counterpart instantiated with different β. The baseline gets the highest score for $recall@5$ because the most common and least informative predicate classes are well predicted. However, our counterpart instantiated with a small value of β allows us to reach better performances in terms of *mean recall@5*. Also, we find that the performance of our approach decreases as β increases. This is because the larger the β, the more cautious/coarse the predicate prediction.

Table 4. $recall@5$ and *mean recall@5* for baseline and our approach instantiated with $\beta = 0, 0.1, 0.5, 1, 2$.

	baseline RelTR	evidential RelTR $\beta = 0$	evidential RelTR $\beta = 0.1$	evidential RelTR $\beta = 0.5$	evidential RelTR $\beta = 1$	evidential RelTR $\beta = 2$
recall@5	**18.7437**	9.5025	15.4552	18.7102	18.2974	13.8532
mean recall@5	4.6177	**7.2504**	7.1335	5.0118	4.2883	2.9104

Figure 3 presents $recall@5$ score separately on each predicate class for the baseline and the evidential counterpart with $\beta = 0.1$. These results confirm that our approach improves the relevance of the predicted predicates. Indeed, we are able to better predict predicate classes belonging to the long tail, such as *mounted on, walking in,* or *sitting on.*

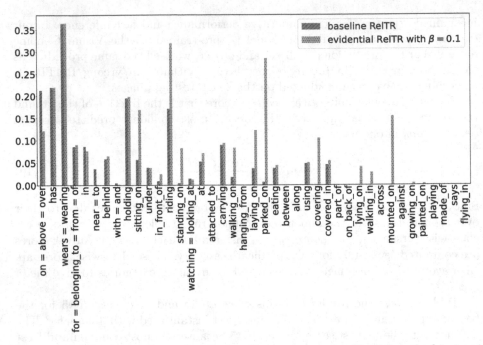

Fig. 3. *recall*@5 per predicate class for baseline vs proposed evidential method instantiated with $\beta = 0.1$.

5   Discussion

In the existing literature on the SGG, predicate classification output has been questioned to a certain point. On the topic of vector logit transformation to address the long-tail problem, [10] criticized the naive idea consisting of re-weighting the scores vectors to encourage fine-grained classes at the expense of the coarse-grained classes. This idea limitation is that without taking correlations between predicates into account, such a process would degrade the discriminatory ability. The authors of [10] instead propose Category Discriminating Loss, adjusting the re-weighting process according to predicate correlations.

The hierarchical aspect of the predicates relations has also been reported. Notably, [18] exploits a 2-level hierarchy on the predicates set to improve the prediction of fine-grained predicates.

The multi-label aspect of SGG has also been reported. In particular, [16] refers to implicit multi-label to describe the three types of ambiguities: synonymy, hyponymy, and multiview issues, and propose a method that returns diverse prediction logit to reach more human-like diverse predictions.

Although the hierarchical aspect could be viewed as a type of multi-label, we choose to refer in our work to multi-label to designate the fact that two finely-granted predicates could be true at the same time, like $< women, holding, cat >$

and $< women, watching, cat >$. The multi-label aspect, in that sense, has been neglected in our approach that requires a unique universe Ω with mutually exclusive elements. In order to consider both hierarchical and multi-label aspects, we should define different universes Ω_1, Ω_2, Ω_3, etc. Then, we could define a joint mass function on $\Omega_1 \times \Omega_2 \times \Omega_3 \ldots$ by applying our method independently on each universe. This would require training the SSG model separately on each universe as well.

On a more general note, our approach differs from these existing works in that our objective is not solely the predicate classification but also to obtain the more trustworthy and interpretable representation of aleatoric and epistemic uncertainty.

6   Conclusion

In this paper, we propose an alternative evidential representation of the logit output representation in the predicate classification task that allows the capture of both aleatoric and epistemic uncertainties. Using our manually defined hierarchy on the set of the predicates, we were able to transform the SSG output logit into a mass function. We also proposed a flexible decision-making procedure. Depending on the β parameter value, one can adjust the granularity level of the predicted predicate. The experiments were conducted using a transformer-based SSG baseline. We show that for small values of β, our evidential counterpart of the baseline improves the relevance of predicted predicates. We also discussed how our method could be applied to treat the multi-label aspect. We are convinced that our evidential representation can be valuable in trustworthy AI applications.

We have two main perspectives on this work. The first one concerns the calibration of the initial output logits. Due to the highly imbalanced dataset, the SSG model may overestimate some score values, impacting our evidential representation. Our second perspective is to generalize our approach to the triplet classification, as the hierarchical aspect is also present in the objects identification task like between *human* and *man*.

Acknowledgement. This paper is based on results obtained from a project, JPNP20006, commissioned by the New Energy and Industrial Technology Development Organization (NEDO).

References

1. Aditya, S., Yang, Y., Baral, C., Aloimonos, Y., Fermüller, C.: Image understanding using vision and reasoning through scene description graph. Comput. Vis. Image Underst. **173**, 33–45 (2018)
2. Cong, Y., Yang, M.Y., Rosenhahn, B.: RelTR: relation transformer for scene graph generation. IEEE Trans. Pattern Anal. Mach. Intell. **45**, 11169–11183 (2023)

3. Ghosh, S., Burachas, G., Ray, A., Ziskind, A.: Generating natural language explanations for visual question answering using scene graphs and visual attention (2019). arXiv preprint arXiv:1902.05715

4. Imoussaten, A., Jacquin, L.: Cautious classification based on belief functions theory and imprecise relabelling. Int. J. Approximate Reasoning **142**, 130–146 (2022)

5. Jacquin, L., Imoussaten, A., Trousset, F., Montmain, J., Perrin, D.: Evidential classification of incomplete data via imprecise relabelling: application to plastic sorting. In: Ben Amor, N., Quost, B., Theobald, M. (eds.) SUM 2019. LNCS (LNAI), vol. 11940, pp. 122–135. Springer, Cham (2019). https://doi.org/10.1007/978-3-030-35514-2_10

6. Johnson, J., Gupta, A., Fei-Fei, L.: Image generation from scene graphs. In: Proceedings of the IEEE Conference on Computer Vision and Pattern Recognition, pp. 1219–1228 (2018)

7. Johnson, J., et al.: Image retrieval using scene graphs. In: Proceedings of the IEEE Conference on Computer Vision and Pattern Recognition, pp. 3668–3678 (2015)

8. Krishna, R., et al.: Visual genome: connecting language and vision using crowdsourced dense image annotations. Int. J. Comput. Vision **123**, 32–73 (2017)

9. Lin, T.-Y., et al.: Microsoft COCO: common objects in context. In: Fleet, D., Pajdla, T., Schiele, B., Tuytelaars, T. (eds.) ECCV 2014. LNCS, vol. 8693, pp. 740–755. Springer, Cham (2014). https://doi.org/10.1007/978-3-319-10602-1_48

10. Lyu, X., Gao, L., Guo, Y., Zhao, Z., Huang, H., Shen, H.T., Song, J.: Fine-grained predicates learning for scene graph generation. In: Proceedings of the IEEE/CVF Conference on Computer Vision and Pattern Recognition, pp. 19467–19475 (2022)

11. Shafer, G.: A Mathematical Theory of Evidence, Princeton University Press, Princeton, vol. 42 (1976)

12. Silla, C.N., Freitas, A.A.: A survey of hierarchical classification across different application domains. Data Min. Knowl. Disc. **22**, 31–72 (2011)

13. Smets, P., Kennes, R.: The transferable belief model. Artif. Intell. **66**(2), 191–234 (1994)

14. Tang, K., Niu, Y., Huang, J., Shi, J., Zhang, H.: Unbiased scene graph generation from biased training. In: Proceedings of the IEEE/CVF Conference on Computer Vision and Pattern Recognition, pp. 3716–3725 (2020)

15. Thomee, B., et al.: YFCC100M: the new data in multimedia research. Commun. ACM **59**(2), 64–73 (2016)

16. Yang, G., Zhang, J., Zhang, Y., Wu, B., Yang, Y.: Probabilistic modeling of semantic ambiguity for scene graph generation. In: Proceedings of the IEEE/CVF Conference on Computer Vision and Pattern Recognition, pp. 12527–12536 (2021)

17. Yang, X., Tang, K., Zhang, H., Cai, J.: Auto-encoding scene graphs for image captioning. In: Proceedings of the IEEE/CVF Conference on Computer Vision and Pattern Recognition, pp. 10685–10694 (2019)

18. Zhou, Y., Sun, S., Zhang, C., Li, Y., Ouyang, W.: Exploring the hierarchy in relation labels for scene graph generation (2020). arXiv preprint arXiv:2009.05834

Uncertainty of Information Applied to Network Monitoring Metrics

Adrienne Raglin, Allison Newcomb, and Lisa Scott[✉]

DEVCOM Army Research Laboratory, Adelphi, MD 20783, USA
{adrienne.raglin2.civ,elizabeth.a.newcomb9.civ,
lisa.m.scott92.civ}@army.mil

Abstract. The Uncertainty of Information (UoI) concept is based on the premise is that all uncertainty is not equal. Uncertainty can have greater or lesser impact based on what caused the uncertainty. Thus, UoI focuses on providing a description that can be linked to the numerical value that represents the uncertainty. This can allow greater understanding of the category of uncertainty and improve the decisions that are impacted by different categories of uncertainties.

In our previous paper, we explored how the concept of Black Swan events can be extended to different colors of swans. The severity of the uncertainty and its impact can be expressed utilizing different color swans. The categories of uncertainty described in the UoI is complementary to the idea with the different color swans. In this paper, we will continue to explore UoI and swan colors. We will expand on the network use case presented in the first paper by applying UoI to network monitoring metrics. Finally, we will present a graphical user interface that could be used to quantify uncertainty to aid decision makers.

Keywords: Uncertainty · Fuzzy Logic · Black Swan

1 Introduction

In the previous paper [1] we discussed the idea that the concepts of uncertainty of information (UoI) could be linked with the concepts from the idea of extending the concept of Black Swan. For the extended concept of Black Swan, we began to associate different colors with the rarity and impact of an event. Thus, we defined additional swan colors. A Black Swan is "an outlier because nothing in the past can convincingly point to its possibility, carrying an extreme impact, something that can be rationally explained after it occurs." [2] A Grey Swan is a "very significant event whose occurrence may be predicted beforehand, but its probability is small." [3] A Grey swan could be positive or negative altering the way a system would operate. A White Swan is defined as "something almost certain to happen" [4] A Green Swan has been defined as "risks we humans create for ourselves." [5] The UoI concept was created so that uncertainty can be communicated in a descriptive manner. For UoI [6] concept we focused on the taxonomy for the data sources. Thus, for any data source the associated uncertainty would be categorized that give a description to the cause of the uncertainty. The categories are corrupt, incomplete, inconsistent, questionable, inappropriate, and inaccurate [7].

Then we selected a use case to discuss how these combined ideas would apply. We selected Morris Worm as the use case. Created in 1988, the Morris Worm was the first known self-replicating malicious code distributed over a communication network with or without the awareness of the user [8]. The Morris Worm was declared to be the most destructive and one of the major threats on the Internet by exploiting the vulnerabilities of existing operating systems and using heuristic knowledge about internet topology, as well as trust relationships to aid its spread. The consequences of the Morris Worm that caused significant negative impact include the underlying methods that allowed access into user accounts and caused spreading to sites previously trusted by those users.

In this case, the software worm used the sendmail program for Unix systems (an amnibus application related to sending and receiving emails, especially the internet SMTP email protocol) and the C compiler to replicate itself across the network. The worm had different methods of invading other systems; one was the ability to use code repetitively throughout other systems [9].

Our intent was to select a use case relevant to the cyber domain. This was partially due to the great potential impact that problems in the cyber domain have on other areas such as economy, health, science, and others. Although the focus of the use case was not to generate solutions, providing quantitative assessments to mitigate risk can be helpful within this domain and across other areas. With this as a key motivation we wanted to explore how quantitative methods such as the UoI and black swan concept could be incorporated within user interfaces. In this paper we will discuss a user interface that could support decision making within the cyber domain to bridge the UoI and black swan concepts.

2 Mapping of UoI and Swan

There are different potential options for connecting UoI to our use case. One way is to take different variables that represent components of the use case. The variables would be associated with different data sources. Where there are uncertainties corresponding to these data sources, they would be linked to the categories from the UoI concept. Here are some examples for this type of mapping:

1. This first option was presented in our previous paper. One example was the network health in terms of available storage as a data source. Thus, data that gives the health of the network would be evaluated. If this data is incomplete, the data that says how much available storage is on the network is not completely available then the UoI category would be incomplete. A high UoI would indicate that there is significant data missing associated with network health. In this example, the UoI is related to the data that represents one component affected by the Morris Worm, the network storage.

2. A second option is to consider the network as the data source. For this example, the network crashed. The crash was due to a worm being released in the network. Then the UoI category of corrupt could be used. Thus, a high UoI for corrupt would indicate that the network was compromised (ie crashed). The cause of this high UoI would be the worm.

3. A third option is to consider the number of nodes affected. For this example, the total number of nodes is considered. As the worm replicated it limited its affect within each node but not across the total number of nodes. Thus, let's consider this under the category of questionable. At the start of the process, a low UoI for questionable would be associated with a single node that was affected. As the process continued, a higher UoI for questionable would be associated if no additional information about a single and all the nodes were captured.

To map the UoI concept to swan colors, two colors are used. A Black Swan is for an event that is considered an outlier because nothing in the past pointed to the possibility of it happening but if it happens the impact would be extreme. A Gray swan is an event that has a moderate chance of happening and if it happens it would be considered very significant. With this in mind, we now look at the previous options examples.

1. In the first example the available storage rapidly going to zero would be an extremely rare event. Thus, it labeled a black swan. Moreover, having incomplete information of the status of available storage is extremely rare, supporting the label of a black swan. If a UoI agent (that process the UoI algorithm) was used it could generate a warning when it did not have complete information about the status of available storage. This would be indicated by the high UoI in the incomplete category for this black swan event.
2. In this second example when the network crashes. This would be a significant event, but the probability of the network actually crashing maybe lower than 100 or 90 (that represent relatively high chances of happening). This would be labeled a grey swan. If a UoI agent was used it could generate a warning that indicated a worm may be present that could comprise the network. Because of this significantly possible compromise to the network a high UoI value for corrupt would be assigned for this grey swan event.
3. In the third example the number of affected nodes. Once the process started and the UoI value increased then a swan color from light grey to black would be assigned. Then a label of black swan would indication that a significant number of nodes are affected causing much more vulnerability.

In addition, we can consider that a similar incident, a malicious worm or attack could have serious consequences for example to the data on the network or within a data structure system. In this case, the range of negative impact to the data could be identified as grey or black. Here the likelihood of problems with the data systems would then be high. If a malicious worm or attack like the Morris Worm erodes the data itself then the UoI category of corrupt or inaccurate could be used. If the consequence of this worm or attack impacted the availability of that data, then the UoI category of incomplete or inconsistent could be used.

3 Fuzzy Logic System Approach

Considering the subjective nature of UoI aspects, we chose fuzzy logic as a technique for quantifying qualitative information. We are extending previous work with Value of Information using fuzzy logic [10, 11]. That work focused specifically decision support for intelligence analysts. We believe the current UoI work will have much broader application.

It is useful to note that the categorizations used within the available storage and network health domains are words, not numbers. Using words to characterize information and relationships, with the ultimate goal of drawing conclusions from imprecise information, leads naturally to the use of fuzzy logic in the construction of the UoI system for the interface discussed in the next section.

Fuzzy set theory provides the necessary *multivalued* framework used in the UoI system. In 1965, Lotfi Zadey wrote his famous paper formally defining multivalued, or "fuzzy" set theory. [12].

One use of fuzzy logic is to develop fuzzy inference systems; these systems provide the ability to perform approximate, or fuzzy reasoning. [13] defines approximate reasoning as the process or processes by which a possibly imprecise conclusion is deduced from a collection of imprecise statements." *Linguistic variables* are an important concept in fuzzy inference. Basically, a linguistic variable is used to approximately characterize the values of variables as well as their relationships. The imprecision introduced by using words may be intentional based on not needing to be more precise. More often, however, the imprecision is dictated by the lack of a means to quantitatively specify the attributes of an object. [14].

Fuzzy rules of inference encapsulate the approximate relationships between the input and output, or in the terminology of rules, the antecedent and consequent, domains. A fuzzy rule with two antecedents has the form "If X is A and Y is B then Z is C" where A and B are fuzzy sets over the input domains U and V, respectively and C is a fuzzy set over the output domain W.

In fuzzy inference systems a domain is typically decomposed into overlapping fuzzy sets; each fuzzy set represents a classification. An element in the domain has some grade of membership, from 0 to 1 inclusive, in each fuzzy set in the domain. The membership function determines the grade of membership; the shape of the fuzzy sets determines the membership function. The available storage domain is decomposed into five fuzzy sets. Any input within the domain will belong to at most two fuzzy sets; that is, any input will have non-zero membership in no more than two fuzzy sets. This means that, for each input, the antecedents for at most two fuzzy rules associated with that domain will be satisfied. Further, the sum for all membership values in the sets to which any input belongs will equal 1.

Advantages of fuzzy systems include their ability to handle imprecise, uncertain and vague information as well as represent human decision making by handling such data [15]. Historically, fuzzy rule bases have been obtained by knowledge elicitation from human experts; this is a subjective process and requires the use of Subject Matter Experts (SMEs). We reserve the knowledge elicitation discussion for future work as it is beyond the scope of this paper.

A Fuzzy Associative Memory (FAM) model was chosen to construct the prototype fuzzy system. A FAM is a k-dimensional table where each dimension corresponds to one of the input universes of the rules. The ith dimension of the table is indexed by the fuzzy sets that comprise the decomposition of the ith input domain. Fuzzy if-then rules are represented within the FAM. Three inputs are used to make the UoI decision: available storage, network health, and information latency.

The overall architecture of the prototype fuzzy system is shown in Fig. 1.

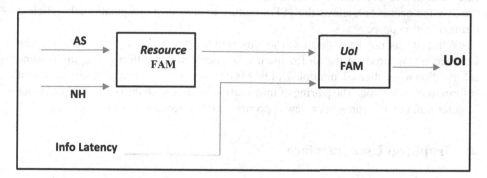

Fig. 1. UoI Fuzzy System Architecture

Two inputs feed into the Resource FAM: available storage and network health; the output FAM is the information applicability decision. Likewise, two inputs feed into the UoI FAM: one of these (information applicability) is the output of the first FAM; the other input is the information latency rating. The output of the second FAM, and the overall system output is the UoI metric.

The output from the system is determined by the standard centroid defuzzification strategy. That is, the degree to which each rule influences the overall output is directly related to the degree to which its inputs match its antecedent fuzzy sets. As a specific example for the Resource FAM, let the following define what we will refer to as Rule 1: "if Available Storage is High (Has) and Network Health is High (Hnh), then Resource is Highly Adequate (HA)". So then, for example, the degree of Rule 1 is:

$$deg_{HA}^1 = m_{AS}(x_1)m_{NH}(y_1) \tag{1}$$

That is, the degree of Rule 1 is the membership value of x1 in the fuzzy set High available storage from the available storage input domain, multiplied by the membership value of y1 in the fuzzy set High network health from the network health input domain.

The standard centroid defuzzification equation that is used to produce the overall output from a set of inputs (x1, y1) is:

$$y = \frac{\sum_{i=1}^{k} deg_{C^i}^i \, mid^i}{\sum_{i=1}^{k} deg_{C^i}^i} \tag{2}$$

where mid i is the midpoint of the output fuzzy set C i (the midpoint in a TPE decomposition is the point in the fuzzy set that has membership equal to one).

Equation (2) implies that every rule in the fuzzy rule base is "fired" for each set of inputs to determine the overall output. However, for a TPE decomposition of a 2-dimensional FAM structure it is clear that at most four fuzzy rules will have non-zero degrees (two rules will have "x" antecedents satisfied by input x and two rules will have "y" antecedents satisfied by input y; their intersection in the FAM defines the four fuzzy rules that should be "fired"). This aspect, plus the fact that the degrees for all rules will add to one (which is the denominator in (2), thus eliminating the need for the division operation), allows the TPE structure to provide a computationally efficient defuzzification process.

While it has not been discussed to this point, *information latency* is also taken into account to produce the UoI construct. To account for differing lengths of time information was collected, multiple UoI FAMs can be derived to represent varying age of information collection. The pairing of information latency with the other characteristics in determining UoI represents a new approach in transforming data to decisions.

4   Graphical User Interface

The interface that uses the fuzzy logic-based system approach presented in the previous section is shown in Fig. 2. The interface allows the user to make selections to highlight specific information and allows the user to observe the status of specific information. The ranges for variables or features within the interface align with the fuzzy sets that a discussed in the previous section. For available storage, network health and time, the levels range from none to max, the specific level is indicated by an arrow. Though not currently implemented, the type of network could be selected. Network type is included here to generate discussion for future research. The network type can be tactical, regional, or strategic. In general, tactical would be a small-scale network, potentially including mobile ad hoc capabilities, radios and autonomous or semi-autonomic vehicles. A regional network would cover a large area, such as the southeastern part of a country. A strategic network would cover areas subsuming regions and could include satellite communications.

For the swan color, a dial with different preselected colors is used. The colors correspond with those presented and defined earlier in the paper. A red arrow would indicate which color best fits the impact of the uncertainties associated with the network status. There are two indicators for UoI. One is UoI level with similar ranges as the other variables, from none to max. The other is UoI category which allows one or more categories to be selected that would correspond with the UoI level.

The stop light chart (green, yellow, red) offers a visual representation of the UoI determination. The vertical column represents the linguistic values of available storage and the horizontal column represents linguistic values of network health. For example, the green region is for indicates that network health and available storage are at least high, yellow indicates they are low (proceed with caution) and red indicates conditions are not favorable for a successful operation.

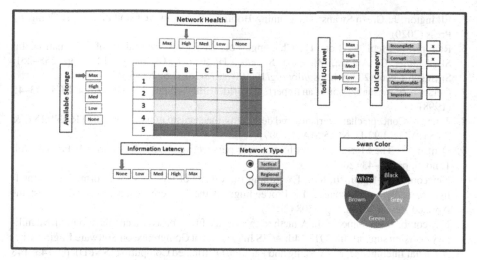

Fig. 2. Notional UoI Interface

5 Conclusion

In conclusion, we have presented a graphical user interface that incorporates UoI and black swan concepts. The graphical user interface is an adaptation to a fuzzy logic system used in previous research. Fuzzy logic was chosen as the computational intelligence technique for quantifying linguistic variables used to describe aspects of variables being considered when information is uncertain. A notional graphic for the user interface was presented to visualize how this information can be given to decision makers and analysis. The user interface proposed strongly leverages multi-dimensional scaling along with the UoI methodology. In addition, we discussed how the mapping between UoI and black swan is possible using ideas from our previous use case, the Morris Worm.

As we consider future directions from this work, we hope to research how to combine these methods with resilience measures and metrics to explore mitigation strategies and higher order effects. In addition, the interplay of UoI, black swan, and time need to be modeled to understand how values shift as steps in the operation unfold.

References

1. Raglin, A., Newcomb, A., Scott, L.: What Color is Your Swan? Uncertainty of Information Across Data. In: Degen, H., Ntoa, S. (eds.) Artificial Intelligence in HCI: 4th International Conference, AI-HCI 2023, Held as Part of the 25th HCI International Conference, HCII 2023, Copenhagen, Denmark, July 23–28, 2023, Proceedings, Part II, pp. 383–388. Springer Nature Switzerland, Cham (2023). https://doi.org/10.1007/978-3-031-35894-4_28
2. Taleb, N.N.: The Black Swan: The Impact of the Highly Improbable, Random House, New York, vol. 2 (2007)
3. Carrasco, S.-P.: Black Swans Gray Swans and White Swans – A Silicon Valley Insider (2008)
4. Hutchins, Greg, Black Swans, Grey Swans, White Swans (2023). https://accendoreliability. com

5. Elkington, J.: Green Swans: The Coming Boom In Regenerative Capitalism, Fast Company Press (2020)
6. Raglin, A., Metu, S., Lott, D.: Challenges of simulating uncertainty of information. In: Stephanidis, C., Antona, M., Ntoa, S. (eds.) HCII 2020. CCIS, vol. 1293, pp. 255–261. Springer, Cham (2020). https://doi.org/10.1007/978-3-030-60700-5_33
7. Gershon, N.: Visualization of an imperfect world. IEEE Comput. Graphics Appl. **18**(4), 43–45 (1998)
8. Tang, Y.: Concept, characteristics and defending mechanism of worm. IEICE TRANS.INF. & SYST. VOL. E92-D, NO.5 MAY (2009)
9. Orman, H.: The Morris worm: a fifteen-year perspective. In: IEEE Security & Privacy, vol. 1, no. 5, pp. 35–43 (2003)
10. Newcomb, A., Hammell, R.J.: Examining the effects of the value of information on intelligence analyst performance. In: Proceedings of the Conference on Information Systems Applied Research ISSN, p. 1508 (2012)
11. Newcomb, A., Hammel, R.J.: A method to assess a fuzzy-based mechanism to improve military decision support. In: 2013 14th ACIS International Conference on Software Engineering, Artificial Intelligence, Networking and Parallel/Distributed Computing (SNPD), pp. 143–148 (2013)
12. Zadeh, L.A.: Fuzzy sets. Inf. Control. **8**, 15 (1965)
13. Zadeh, L.A.Z.: Outline of a new approach to the analysis of complex systems and decision processes. IEEE Trans. Syst. Man Cybern. **3**, 28–44 (1973)
14. Zadeh, L.A.: The concept of a linguistic variable and its application to approximate reasoning—I. Inf. Sci. **8**, 199–249 (1975)
15. Sudkamp, T., Hammell, R.J.: Interpolation, completion, and learning fuzzy rules. IEEE Trans. Syst. Man Cybern. **24**(2), 332–342 (1994)

Iterative Visual Interaction with Latent Diffusion Models

Luca Sacchetto$^{(\boxtimes)}$, Stefan Röhrl , and Klaus Diepold

Technical University of Munich, Arcisstr. 21, 80333 Munich, Germany
luca.sacchetto@tum.de

Abstract. Image synthesis generative Artificial Intelligence has the potential to revolutionize many industries, from rapid prototyping of consumer goods' design to creating works of art. However, the most widespread of these models come in the form of text-to-image models. Controlling their output is often a difficult and imprecise process; indeed, slightly different prompts can lead to significantly different outcomes. Therefore, we develop a novel way to interact with generative AI that mimics the way in which humans naturally create works of art and design. We achieve this more granular and intuitive interaction method by exploiting the latent space of Latent Diffusion Models to generate image variations.

Keywords: Generative AI · Latent Diffusion Models · Latent Space · Human Centered AI

1 Introduction

With the advent of natural language-based generative models, generative Artificial intelligence (AI) has exploded in popularity and capabilities. The ability to interact with AI using natural language has unlocked access to generative AI for the general public, boosting its widespread usage among amateurs and professionals. Especially image synthesis models, previously challenging to interact with and less versatile, have gained unprecedented traction. Their potential applications are numerous: expediting the creation of architectural works, accelerating the prototyping of consumer object design, and automating the creation of fictional characters are just a few examples. However, the potential use of image synthesis AI in more professional environments is also limited by its user interface mode: natural language.

While natural language is an ideal interaction method with large language models, we argue that for text-to-image generative algorithms, it is an inaccurate and crude way to interact with the AI, notwithstanding the already impressive results of the so-called *prompt engineering* [9]. In fact, the conventional way artists, designers, and engineers create visual works is a visual process in itself, consisting of many feedback loops and minute adjustments. These same artists would find it difficult to describe their creation process using words, as natural language is arguably a sub-optimal medium to encode visual works.

To this end, we develop a workflow allowing users to provide visual feedback to Stable Diffusion XL [11]. Supplied with an initial batch of generated images, the user can select one image and prompt the AI to generate variations of that image. Together with the control over the degree of variation, this effectively creates an iterative process by which the user can generate images from a prompt, explore the image space associated with the prompt, and iteratively guide the AI to the desired result. Our concept can be applied to all pre-trained Diffusion Models without the need for expensive fine-tuning or re-training. We believe that this mimics the way in which humans already create visual works, unlocking new horizons for the control over image synthesis AIs.

2   Related Work

The most relevant literature to our work can be summarized into two broad research fields: objective optimization by human interaction and latent space manipulation of frozen generative models. The former is exemplified by the field of Interactive Evolutionary Computation (IEC), while the latter can be further subdivided into older research on Generative Adversarial Networks (GANs) [5] and newer research on Diffusion Models [7,14].

2.1   IEC

IEC [16] is the research field that studies the employment of humans instead of numerical fitness functions to select the fittest candidates of a population in evolutionary algorithms. Although similar, our proposed framework intentionally deviates from the traditional Evolutionary Computation paradigm. Instead of choosing a multitude of candidates to be parents for the next generation, we limit the selection to one singular candidate to more accurately mimic the traditional way humans create their works; i.e. by gradually shaping a single piece.

2.2   Latent Space Manipulation of GANs

Bontrager et al. [2] introduce Latent Variable Evolution (LVE), where they use an evolutionary algorithm to search the latent space of a WGAN to optimize the generation of MasterPrints for dictionary attacks. In another article, the same authors [3] employ IEC instead of the evolutionary algorithm to search the latent space.

Schrum et al. [13] apply LVE to a GAN, which generates video-game levels; like this work, the authors rely more on human interaction using a Selective Breeding approach.

However, GANs have since been surpassed by Diffusion Models as the state-of-the-art image generation models [4]. Nevertheless, many of the techniques proposed here can be transferred to Diffusion Models, as they also possess a semantic latent space.

2.3 Latent Space Manipulation of Diffusion Models

Videau et al. [17] propose a similar approach to the one presented here. The authors develop a multi-faceted algorithm, where they also exploit local movements in the latent space to allow the user to perform global, local, and crossover mutations both with random walks and Machine-Learning surrogate models trained in the latent space. They suggest an initial use of global mutations to subsequently perform crossover and local mutations to refine the images; i.e. in smaller regions of the latent space.

We use global mutations as the primary tool for the interaction with the LDM and suggest their use for very fine adjustments, too. Indeed, to generate variations of a reference image, we project the latent samples to the surface of the n-sphere with the same radius as the original image's latent sample, ensuring precise control around the original image's latent sample (see Sect. 4 and Fig. 2).

Park et al. [10] achieve both coarse and fine changes in the output of Diffusion Models by moving the latent space points along specific *directions*. These are obtained through the SVD of the U-Net's Jacobian matrix. This allows the modification of attributes like age or make-up.

Kwon et al. [8] use the bottleneck of the U-Net as a semantic latent space by altering the conventional reverse process of Diffusion Models. Herein, the *directions* are obtained by optimizing the CLIP loss with respect to the text prompt of the target feature.

Building on [8], Haas et al. [6] use the same latent space but uncover *semantic directions* by means of the PCA of the vectorized latent space in an unsupervised manner.

3 Background

3.1 Denoising Diffusion Models (DDMs)

First introduced by [14] as a probability distribution modeling tool and refined for high-resolution image synthesis by [7], Diffusion Models consist of a fixed Markov chain of length T, where each transition $q(x_{t-1}|x_t)$ injects Gaussian noise into a signal until it is destructed. The model parameterizes the reverse Markov chain with a neural network θ and learns its transitions $p_\theta(x_t|x_{t-1})$. This yields a generative model that maps Gaussian noise to the training data's space (Fig. 1)

3.2 Denoising Diffusion Implicit Models (DDIMs)

The work of [15] proposes a significant acceleration to the sampling process of DDMs by training on a non-markovian process with the same objective as the standard one. This circumvents the need to iterate through the entire Markov chain in the sampling phase. Importantly, in DDIMs, the generative process is deterministic; that is, x_T only depends on x_0.

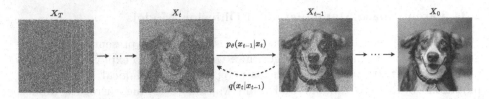

Fig. 1. Diffusion process: in the forward diffusion process, Gaussian noise is gradually injected in T steps (shown in the figure with the curved, dashed arrow). A neural network θ is trained on the reverse diffusion process. At inference, θ effectively progressively denoises Gaussian noise into an image. Figure adapted from [7].

3.3   Latent Diffusion Models (LDMs)

Latent Diffusion Models [12] expand on Diffusion Models by introducing an autoencoder that transforms the pixel space into a lower dimensional latent space and perform the diffusion process on the latent space, making both training and inference significantly quicker. The model used in our implementation, StableDiffusion XL, is an LDM with a DDIM sampler.

3.4   Latent Space of LDMs

We define the latent space to be the Gaussian space $\mathcal{X}_0 \sim \mathcal{N}(\mathbf{0}, I)$ containing all possible initial samples $x_0 \in \mathbb{R}^{4 \times 128 \times 128}$. In higher dimensions, the expected length of standard Gaussian samples is concentrated around the square root of its dimensions d, i.e. around the edges of the unit n-sphere. This is because, with equal variances across all dimensions, the standard Gaussian distribution has spherical symmetry. While the density of the Gaussian distribution is still highest at the origin, due to the geometry of high-dimensional hyper-spheres, the volume (and consequently the probability mass) towards the sphere's center is negligible.

More specifically, according to the *Gaussian Annulus Theorem* [1], the probability mass lies within a thin annulus at radius $\sqrt{d}$. Note that, in the specific case of $\mathcal{X}_0$, the annulus is wide enough to have a significant visual impact on the decoded image. Figure 2 shows the difference between decoding a latent sample at the edges of the annulus versus decoding the same sample projected to the center of the annulus, i.e. the surface of the unit sphere.

That is, we can understand $\mathcal{X}_0$ to be more akin to a hyper-spherical space than an Euclidean one.

4   Methodology

To realize our proposed workflow, we modify StableDiffusion XL such that it gains two crucial features: the ability to generate variations of a previously generated image and the ability to control to what degree the variations differ from

z_r

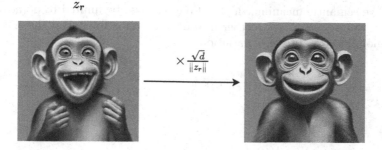

Fig. 2. On the left, an image decoded from a latent sample z_r drawn from the Gaussian distribution. On the right, the image decoded from the latent sample obtained by projecting z_r to the unit sphere, i.e. the sphere with radius $\sqrt{d}$; where d is the number of dimensions of z_r.

the reference image. To achieve this, we exploit two properties of LDMs: 1) with a deterministic sampler like in DDIMs, there is a unique correspondence between latent space samples and images, and 2) distances in the latent space translate to semantic distances in the image space.

We vectorize the latent sample of the reference image and interpret it as a point in a high-dimensional space $\mathbb{R}^{65536}$. We sample Gaussian distributed points in the local region around the reference point to generate image variations. Because the latent space of Diffusion Models is spherical (see Sect. 3.4),

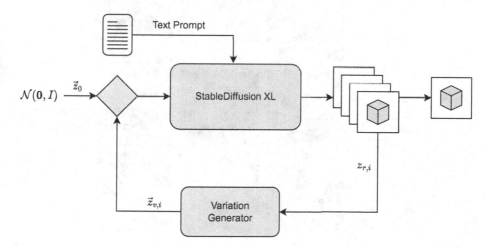

Fig. 3. Visual rendition of the algorithm: at the start, a tensor of N latent samples $z_0 \in \mathbb{R}^{N \times 4 \times 128 \times 128}$ is drawn from the Gaussian distribution. In iteration i, the latent sample is decoded by the latent diffusion model, which generates N images. The user selects a reference image, whose latent sample $z_{r,i}$ is fed through our *Variation Generator*, i.e. Eq. 1. The resulting tensor $z_{v,i}$ is finally used as a tensor of latent samples in iteration $i + 1$.

to preserve semantic meaning, the local region must be limited to points on the surface of the n-sphere. We further introduce a factor to control the size of the local region, i.e. the degree of variation:

$$z_v = \|z_r\|_F \frac{z_r + \gamma \tilde{N}}{\left\| z_r + \gamma \tilde{N} \right\|_F} \qquad (1)$$

where:

$$\tilde{N} \sim \mathcal{N}(\mathbf{0}, I)$$
$$\mathbf{0}, I \in \mathbb{R}^{4 \times 128 \times 128}$$
$$z_r = \text{Latent sample of the reference image}$$
$$z_v = \text{Latent sample of the image variation}$$
$$\gamma = \text{Size of the local region}$$

That is, we sample Gaussian distributed points around z_r and then project them back onto the surface of the n-sphere with radius $\|z_r\|_F$. Figure 3 shows a visual rendition of the proposed algorithm.

Fig. 4. GUI

4.1 Graphical User Interface (GUI)

Figure 4 shows a screenshot of a possible implementation of our proposed workflow. The GUI allows the user to input a text prompt and select the number of images to generate. After the algorithm has generated a batch of images, the GUI presents them in pages of nine images each. The pages can be switched with the controls at the bottom of the control panel. The user can then try the current iteration with a different random seed or select a reference image by clicking on it and advancing to the next iteration. The slider lets the user set the *degree of variation* γ (see Eq. 1).

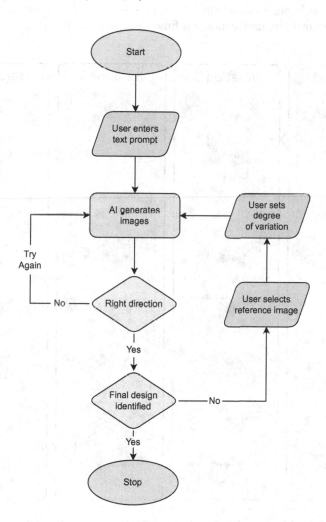

Fig. 5. Workflow: The process starts when the user enters a text prompt and clicks *Generate*. Then, the user has two choices: try the current iteration again or select a reference image and move to the next iteration. The process stops when the user identifies a final design in the current iteration.

4.2 Workflow

Figure 5 shows a visualization of our proposed workflow: the user initiates the process by entering a text prompt and setting the desired number of images to generate. The generative algorithm generates the images and stores the corresponding latent samples. If none of the images align with the desired design direction, the user can request a new batch of images with a different random seed.

Otherwise, the user can select a final design or choose a reference image and set a *degree of variation*. The algorithm then generates a new batch of images based on the reference image and the user's setting. The process can restart and continue until the user chooses a final design. Of course, this framework is

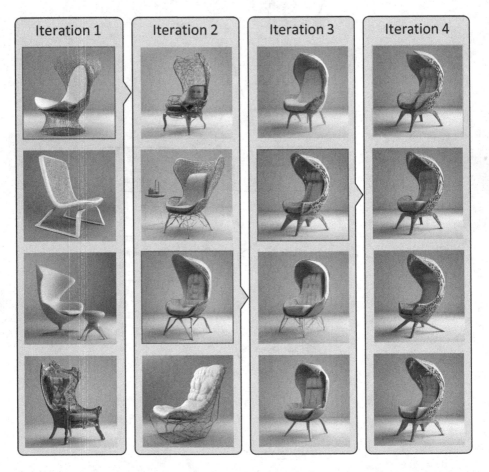

Fig. 6. Workflow example with the prompt *photorealistic innovative designer chair*: Note how the images in an iteration get progressively similar both to the reference image (red-boxed image in the previous iteration) and to each other. (Color figure online)

perfectly compatible with *prompt engineering*, which can be used before it to identify the most suitable prompt.

5   Results

Figure 6 shows the results at each iteration with the example prompt *photorealistic innovative designer chair*. The first column represents the first iteration. The red-boxed images represent the reference image for the next iteration. The final design is highlighted with a green box in the fourth iteration. Figure 7 shows another exemplary process with the prompt *A portrait of a fantasy character*.

Fig. 7. Workflow example with the prompt *A portrait of a fantasy character*: Note how the images in an iteration get progressively similar both to the reference image (red-boxed image in the previous iteration) and to each other. (Color figure online)

6   Conclusion

By exploiting the semantic property of Stable Diffusion's latent space to create controllable variations of any generated image, we developed a novel way to interact with text-to-image generative AI. Our framework adds a highly granular control mechanism to StableDiffusion XL that can be operated without any previous knowledge.

Because it mimics the way in which humans create works of art, design, and engineering, we argue that our proposed workflow offers a more natural, precise, and exploratory way to use generative AI, which can be used either as a substitute to or as an extension of prompt engineering. Our workflow can be applied to any pre-trained Diffusion Model, making it highly versatile, easily upgradeable, and deployable to various of problems, such as object design and character creation.

Acknowledgments. The authors acknowledge the financial support by the Bavarian State Ministry for Economic Affairs, Regional Development and Energy (StMWi) for the Lighthouse Initiative KI.FABRIK, (Phase 1: Infrastructure as well as the research and development program under grant no. DIK0249).

References

1. Blum, A., Hopcroft, J., Kannan, R.: Foundations of Data Science. Cambridge University Press (2020)
2. Bontrager, P., Roy, A., Togelius, J., Memon, N., Ross, A.: Deepmasterprints: generating masterprints for dictionary attacks via latent variable evolution. In: 2018 IEEE 9th International Conference on Biometrics Theory, Applications and Systems, pp. 1–9. Los Angeles, USA (2018). https://doi.org/10.1109/BTAS.2018.8698539
3. Bontrager, P., Lin, W., Togelius, J., Risi, S.: Deep interactive evolution. In: Liapis, A., Romero Cardalda, J.J., Ekárt, A. (eds.) EvoMUSART 2018. LNCS, vol. 10783, pp. 267–282. Springer, Cham (2018). https://doi.org/10.1007/978-3-319-77583-8_18
4. Dhariwal, P., Nichol, A.: Diffusion models beat GANs on image synthesis. In: Ranzato, M., Beygelzimer, A., Dauphin, Y., Liang, P., Vaughan, J.W. (eds.) Advances in Neural Information Processing Systems. vol. 34, pp. 8780–8794. Curran Associates, Inc. (2021)
5. Goodfellow, I., et al.: Generative adversarial nets. In: Ghahramani, Z., Welling, M., Cortes, C., Lawrence, N., Weinberger, K. (eds.) Advances in Neural Information Processing Systems. vol. 27. Curran Associates, Inc. (2014)
6. Haas, R., Huberman-Spiegelglas, I., Mulayoff, R., Michaeli, T.: Discovering interpretable directions in the semantic latent space of diffusion models. arXiv preprint arXiv:2303.11073 (2023). https://doi.org/10.48550/arXiv.2303.11073
7. Ho, J., Jain, A., Abbeel, P.: Denoising diffusion probabilistic models. In: Larochelle, H., Ranzato, M., Hadsell, R., Balcan, M., Lin, H. (eds.) Advances in Neural Information Processing Systems. vol. 33, pp. 6840–6851. Curran Associates, Inc. (2020)
8. Kwon, M., Jeong, J., Uh, Y.: Diffusion models already have a semantic latent space. In: The Eleventh International Conference on Learning Representations (2023). https://openreview.net/forum?id=pd1P2eUBVfq

9. Liu, V., Chilton, L.B.: Design guidelines for prompt engineering text-to-image generative models. In: Barbosa, S., Lampe, C., Appert, C., Shamma, D., Drucker, S., Williamson, J., Yatani, K. (eds.) Proceedings of the 2022 CHI Conference on Human Factors in Computing Systems, pp. 1–23. ACM, New Orleans, USA (2022). https://doi.org/10.1145/3491102.3501825

10. Park, Y.H., Kwon, M., Jo, J., Uh, Y.: Unsupervised discovery of semantic latent directions in diffusion models. arXiv preprint arXiv:2302.12469 (2023). https://doi.org/10.48550/arXiv.2302.12469

11. Podell, D., et al.: SDXL: improving latent diffusion models for high-resolution image synthesis. arXiv preprint arXiv:2307.01952 (2023). https://doi.org/10.48550/arXiv.2307.01952

12. Rombach, R., Blattmann, A., Lorenz, D., Esser, P., Ommer, B.: High-resolution image synthesis with latent diffusion models. In: Proceedings of the IEEE/CVF Conference on Computer Vision and Pattern Recognition, pp. 10684–10695. IEEE Computer Society, New Orleans, USA (2022). https://doi.org/10.1109/CVPR52688.2022.01042

13. Schrum, J., Gutierrez, J., Volz, V., Liu, J., Lucas, S., Risi, S.: Interactive evolution and exploration within latent level-design space of generative adversarial networks. In: Proceedings of the 2020 Genetic and Evolutionary Computation Conference, p. 148–156. ACM, Cancún, Mexico (2020). https://doi.org/10.1145/3377930.3389821

14. Sohl-Dickstein, J., Weiss, E., Maheswaranathan, N., Ganguli, S.: Deep unsupervised learning using nonequilibrium thermodynamics. In: Bach, F., Blei, D. (eds.) Proceedings of the 32nd International Conference on Machine Learning. Proceedings of Machine Learning Research, vol. 37, pp. 2256–2265. PMLR, Lille, France (2015)

15. Song, J., Meng, C., Ermon, S.: Denoising diffusion implicit models. In: International Conference on Learning Representations (2021). https://openreview.net/forum?id=St1giarCHLP

16. Takagi, H.: Interactive evolutionary computation: fusion of the capabilities of EC optimization and human evaluation. Proc. IEEE **89**(9), 1275–1296 (2001). https://doi.org/10.1109/5.949485

17. Videau, M., Knizev, N., Leite, A., Schoenauer, M., Teytaud, O.: Interactive latent diffusion model. In: Proceedings of the Genetic and Evolutionary Computation Conference, pp. 586–596. ACM, Portugal, Lisbon (2023). https://doi.org/10.1145/3583131.3590471

Time Series Representation Learning: A Survey on Deep Learning Techniques for Time Series Forecasting

Tobias Schmieg[✉] and Carsten Lanquillon

Heilbronn University of Applied Sciences, 74081 Heilbronn, Germany
{tobias.schmieg,carsten.lanquillon}@hs-heilbronn.de

Abstract. With the rise of Industrial Internet of Things (IIoT) and other aspects of the digitalization of production more and more time series (TS) data is generated. This data can help to train deep learning models with higher cognitive capabilities and thus assist with more complicated tasks. An important step for creating such models is creating fitting abstract representations of the data. Thus, this work surveys the literature on deep learning techniques for time series forecasting. The focus hereby lies on the characteristics and reasons for using the techniques in context of the representation learning. 17 of the architectures used in the analyzed literature use multiple techniques. The most applied techniques are one-dimensional CNN (CNN 1D) (14 times), LSTM (11 times), and attention-based techniques (17 times). Furthermore, input embedding and masking play an important role in some architectures.

Keywords: Literature Review · Multivariate Time Series Forecasting · Feature Extraction · Representation Learning

1 Introduction

With the rise of Industrial Internet of Things (IIoT), Cyber-Physical Systems (CPS), and other aspects of digitized production, the role of human workers has shifted [17]. The decision-making of simple problems can already be done by automated systems, where often artificial intelligence (AI) is applied. Tasks with higher cognitive challenges are more and more solved by AI [34]. For example, in fatigue life estimation or remaining useful life estimation (RUL), an algorithm predicts the time until the fatigue of an entity (i.e. production machines). This can reduce costs by minimizing downtimes or even preventing accidents involving humans [22]. With systems capable of RUL estimation and other data-driven tasks, the role of the production worker and the interaction with the machine changes. Even higher cognitive tasks than mentioned before gain a lot of traction. Newer areas of machine learning like image-to-text or video-to-text tasks require even higher cognitive capabilities. For example, text-to-3D generation holds a lot of potential for industrial design [33]. Such multi-modal models combine different

H. Degen and S. Ntoa (Eds.): HCII 2024, LNAI 14734, pp. 422–435, 2024.
https://doi.org/10.1007/978-3-031-60606-9_25

modalities as input, output or have different modalities between the input and output. To achieve this, there are three main frameworks: joint representations, coordinated representations, and encoder-decoder frameworks [18]. To contribute to future multi-modal frameworks that incorporate TS, this work will lay a focus on the representation learning of time series (TS) data.

A huge portion of the data generated in manufacturing is time series (TS) data. Other machine learning tasks on TS data, next to RUL estimation, are among others anomaly detection [9] or TS forecasting [28]. In the context of IIoT, the data is mostly gathered by multiple sensors creating multivariate TS (MVTS) [35]. Because TS data can have different properties [9], it is hard to create a one-fits-all solution. Thus, this work will analyze the literature on deep learning techniques for MVTS forecasting. The rationale for this lies in the antic-ipation that the insights acquired from the examination of deep learning tech-niques in TS forecasting possess greater generalizability to other tasks, than vice-versa. This literature review omits papers with very specialized models or those that heavily rely on specific data pre-processing methods. This choice is made to ensure that the findings are more applicable to a wider range of situa-tions.

This leads to the following research question: *What are good-practice deep learning techniques for MVTS forecasting?*

This work aims to provide an overview of deep learning techniques for MVTS forecasting. Furthermore, the review illustrates how the techniques are applied and their contextual relevance in representation learning.

2 Theoretical Background

2.1 Time Series Forecasting

Traditional non-deep learning techniques for TS forecasting include exponential smoothing methods, autoregressive, and structural TS models [28]. For example, autoregressive integrated moving average (ARIMA) considers for a data point the previous values and assumes a linear relationship. A moving average applies a residual error to past observations. While these methods were initially created for univariate (one variable per time step) TS forecasting, over time modifications were developed to handle MVTS (multiple variables per time step). With vector ARIMA (VARIMA), it is possible to apply the fundamental ideas of ARIMA to MVTS [15].

Today good-practices for TS forecasting are in the field of deep learning. Representation learning enables deep learning networks to distill information from the underlying data, producing an abstract (and compressed) output. With a classifier or predictor on top of this, the actual task can be carried out [4]. In the case of TS forecasting, this would be predicting one (or multiple) future values. Typical deep learning techniques for encoding temporal data into representations are convolutional neural networks (CNN), recurrent neural networks (RNN), and attention-based neural networks [28].

2.2   Masking

Masking words have been used for a long time in psycholinguistic studies called cloze tasks [42]. Over time masking evolved into an important technique for machine learning too. It was often shown, that a masking task in the pre-training phase can lead to good generalization abilities for downstream tasks [19]. With masking, a part of the original input is hidden. The model is tasked to recover the masked parts by considering the unmasked parts of the input. The theory behind this is that conclusions can be drawn from unmasked data points about masked ones. This can be done because of the density of information inside data. The authors of [19] argue that the information density is dissimilar in different machine learning disciplines and data types, i.e. between language and computer vision. While a single token in natural language processing (NLP) holds relatively high semantic value, a single pixel in computer vision holds rather less semantic value [19]. A masking ratio of about 15 % has been proven to be sufficient for nlp [11], about 75 % for images [19] and time series [27] and about 90 % for videos [10].

In practice, for masked autoencoders (MAE) the common goal is to mask the input signal. The encoder of the MAE maps the input to a latent representation. The decoder of the MAE reconstructs the original signal (unmasked) from this latent representation [41]. The bidirectional encoder representations from transformers (BERT) architecture has brought masking first to the forefront of machine learning by masked manguage modelling (MLM). Similar to autoencoders (AE) used in denoising tasks [46], BERT employs token reconstruction. However, BERT exclusively predicts previously masked tokens rather than the entire input sequence [11]. Similar to MLM, vision transformers (ViT) [12] are used for Masked Image Modeling (MIM). Here, a portion of the visual tokens of the image patches is masked by replacing it with a special mask embedding [3]. In contrast to all previously mentioned methods, [19] gets rid of the use of mask tokens in the encoding phase. Instead, only the unmasked patches are fed into the encoder. Only when the latent representation of the encoder is fed into the decoder, masked tokens (with positional embedding) are added. For time series forecasting, transformer-based models also use masking to predict future values. The masks serve the purpose that the model cannot attend to future positions of the sequence [27,29]. With this continuous masking strategy the model is only able to learn certain relations of the data. While more complex masking strategies exist for TS forecasting, these are not as popular as in other machine learning disciplines. This work will investigate some applications of masking in TS forecasting.

2.3   Input Embedding

To leverage the abilities of the different deep learning techniques used, often some type of preprocessing is incorporated into the model architecture. Positional encoding (PE) is an important concept in many input embeddings [14]. While not exclusive, attention-based techniques often make use of PE to inform the network of the token's position (i.e. time step).

One common form of PE is the sinusoidal version. Here, sine and cosine functions with different frequencies are used to represent the relative position of the token. The use of periodic functions allows the PE to extrapolate the data to future samples that are out of a certain length. The PE should have the same dimensionality as the latent dimensionality of the model. Thereby, the PE can be summed with the input sequence [45].

In some cases, not only the relative position of the time step in the sequence is relevant. The authors of [24] propose a method for vector representation of time called Time2Vec, that incorporates learnable parameters and a periodic activation function, which is normally a sine function. The use of a periodic function is inspired by the PE of [45], but the function in Time2Vec is also able to capture periodic behaviors. Time2Vec is rather a representation of continuous time than a discrete position in the sequence. Lastly, in contrast to PE, Time2Vec is concatenated to the data representation instead of added [24].

3   Methodology

To identify relevant publications the guidelines of [6] are followed. Firstly, relevant literature databases are selected. These are *IEEE, ScienceDirect, Springer Link, arXiv* and *Google Scholar*. In order to provide an up-to-date overview, the focus is limited to publications from 2020 to oktober 2023. Also, only journal and conference papers are included. While the first three databases contain peer-reviewed publications, arXiv does not have such a process. As a compromise, to still include the newest ideas, only publications of arXiv of 2023 (January to Oktober) are included. The aim is to retrieve publications using deep learning techniques for MVTS forecasting. Other TS tasks are excluded to get a stronger focus. Additionally, the publications should emphasize the latent representations generated by the presented models. Relevant publications are queried with the following search string: *("latent representation" OR "feature representation") AND ("time series" OR "time-series") AND ("multivariate" OR "multi-variant" OR "multivariant" OR "multi variant") AND ("deep learning") AND ("forecast*") AND NOT ("graph" OR "classification" OR "anomaly detection")*

The focus of the literature review is to gain insights into deep learning techniques that are rather simple to apply without overly special preprocessing steps. The resulting publications underwent additional filtration based on specific criteria, including the overarching complexity of the overall architecture and emphasis on preprocessing tasks. It is essential to note that this filtration process was executed through the discernment of the authors, reflecting a qualitative decision-making approach.

These publications are afterward consolidated into a concept matrix according to the procedure of [48]. Such a concept matrix aims to structure a literature review by synthesizing identified concepts contained in the publications.

The concept matrix (Fig. 1) consists of the dimensions *publication year*, *domain* of the publication, if multiple techniques are combined (*Hybrid*), the application of *masking*, and the use of a specific positional encoding (*Pos. Enc.*). The dimension domain refers to the publication itself. This means that while the publication can be domain unspecific (i.e. domain-specific challenges are not covered), for evaluation a domain-specific dataset might be used. Out of the 31 analyzed publications, seven different deep learning techniques were identified. These were clustered in superordinate categories namely *CNN*, *RNN*, and *Attention-based* as shown in the concept matrix.

Furthermore, it should be noted that there was a decision to maintain separate columns for attention and transformer in the concept matrix. This stems from the recognition that, despite both employing attention mechanisms, transformers represent a distinct and specialized form within the broader category of attention-based techniques. Transformers stand as a state-of-the-art paradigm, embodying a specific application of attention that significantly differs from the more generic and adaptable "Attention" category, which is usually combined with various architectures.

4   Results

In the following chapter, the results of the literature review will be examined. Firstly, a short quantitive overview is given. Moreover, the rather supporting characteristics and techniques *hybrid*, *Masking*, and *Pos. Enc* are investigated. Lastly, the applied deep learning techniques are analyzed.

4.1   Quantitative Analysis

At the core of this work is the concept matrix, which is shown in Fig. 1. The concept matrix contains 31 publications. While the arXiv publications were intentionally filtered from 2023 onwards, the other publications were mainly published in 2022 and 2023. Only seven publications were published before 2022 (two in 2020 and five in 2021). The majority were published in 2022 and onwards (eleven in 2022 and eight in 2023 excluding five arXiv publications).

When attention and transformers are combined as attention-based techniques, those are used most frequently (17 times). The second most used techniques are one-dimensional CNNs (CNN 1D) (14). Here, most of the instances are used in hybrid models (10 times). While long short-term memory (LSTM) models are found in eleven models, it is used in hybrid models five times. In the literature, two-dimensional CNNs (CNN 2D), bidirectional long short-term memory (BiLSTM), and attention have been mentioned, with instances of three, three, and ten, respectively, exclusively employed in hybrid models. In the case of gated recurrent unit (GRU) models, three of the five instances are hybrid. Remarkable is that all publications queried through arXiv apply attention in some form.

Publication	Year	Domain	Hybrid	Masking	Pos. Enc.	RNN			CNN		Att.-based	
						LSTM	BiLSTM	GRU	CNN 1D	CNN 2D	Attention	Transformer
Al-Shabandar et al. [1]	2021	energy						x				
Aouad et al. [2]	2022	energy	x			x			x		x	
Biondi et al. [5]	2022	weather				x						
Chkeir et al. [8]	2023	weather				x						
Feng and Lyu [13]	2022	unspecified	x	x	SPE					x		x
Gorbett et al. [16]	2023	unspecified		x								x
Hewage et al. [20]	2021	weather				x			x			
Huan et al. [21]	2022	environmental	x					x			x	
Kaya and Gündüz-Ogüdücü [23]	2020	environmental	x			x			x			
Kuo and Kunarsito [25]	2022	traffic	x					x			x	
La Tona et al. [43]	2023	energy				x						
Li et al. [26]	2020	environmental	x			x			x			
Li et al. [27]	2023	unspecified	x	x	SPE				x			x
Limperis et al. [29]	2023	environmental		x	T2V							x
Luo and Wang [30]	2023	unspecified							x			
Ma and Mei [31]	2022	energy	x		T2V	x			x		x	
Manero et al. [32]	2022	weather							x			
Roh et al. [36]	2023	unspecified	x					x	x		x	
Sabri and El Hassouni [37]	2023	energy				x						
Sharma and Yadav [38]	2023	energy							x			
Succetti et al. [39]	2021	energy				x						
Tang and Zhang [41]	2022	unspecified	x	x	SPE + SE				x			x
Ughi et al. [44]	2023	unspecified			AT2V							x
Wang et al. [47]	2023	environmental	x					x				
Wu et al. [50]	2022	unspecified	x			x			x		x	
Xian and Liang [51]	2022	energy	x				x			x	x	
Yin and Barucca [53]	2021	unspecified						x				
Yin and Dai [52]	2022	unspecified	x			x			x		x	
Yu et al. [54]	2023	unspecified	x								x	
Zhang et al. [55]	2023	weather	x	x						x	x	
Zhou et al. [56]	2021	unspecified	x	x					x			x
31			17	7		11	3	5	14	3	10	7

SPE: Sinusoidal Positional Encoding; T2V: Time2Vec; SE: Stamp Encoding; AT2V: AddT2Vec

Fig. 1. Concept matrix of deep learning techniques

4.2 Masking Strategies

Seven of the analyzed publications mention the application of some form of masking. And six of the seven publications represent transformer architectures [13, 16, 27, 29, 41, 56]. The authors of [27] propose a masking strategy, similar to MLM, where random tokens on time steps are masked in a uniform distribution. The work of [41] combines this with the idea of patch embeddings of ViTs. In the pre-training phase, the encoder only encodes the visible patches, while the decoder reconstructs the masked patches, as well as the encoded patches. In the fine-tuning phase, the encoder encodes all patches and the decoder gets modified to masked multi-head self-attention for the common prediction task, where the positions are unable to attend to future positions [41]. Here, the sequence is divided into patches. Those patches are also masked in a uniform distribution.

But akin to MAE of [19] for vision, only the unmasked patches are fed into the encoder to reduce computation.

4.3 Positional Encoding and Input Embeddings

The use of PE in the analyzed literature is shown in the column *Pos. Enc.* of Fig. 1. The use of sinusoidal PE was to be expected because of the amount of transformers in the analyzed literature. Still, some interesting additions to this were found, in the context of PE.

The sinusoidal PE is explicitly used by [13,27,41]. But since sinusoidal PE is part of the original paper of transformers [45], it can be assumed that all transformer architectures use sinusoidal PE if nothing else is mentioned. In addition to sinusoidal PE, [41] also uses a global stamp embedding to insert information about month, hour, and minute into the model.

Time2Vec is used in the architectures of [29,31]. The authors of [44] use a revised version of Time2Vec called AddT2Vec. The authors argue, that Time2Vec increases the spatial complexity, which can be especially in long prediction windows a limiting factor. Similar to sinusoidal PE, the resulting time representation is added to the data representation instead of concatenated [44]. Even though in the primary literature of Time2Vec the method was demonstrated in combination with LSTMs, in the analyzed literature only attention-based architectures used PE, Time2Vec, or AddT2Vec for the input embedding [13,27,29,31,41,44].

Remarkable for input embeddings is that [27] and [41], in addition to PE, also use CNN 1D to extract local temporal features and to embed the data. Here, this is done through a purely linear transformation, without a succeeding activation function or pooling layer. Also, [56] uses CNN 1D for the input embedding.

Another concept concerning input embeddings is patching or patch embedding. Inspired by the ViT, [41] uses patches along the time dimension through CNN 1D. The main purpose of the patch embedding is to serve the masking strategy, where patches are masked. The authors of [30] argue, that the patch embedding enhances locality and also aggregates semantic information of the subsequence.

4.4 Recurrent Neural Networks

RNNs are a model family of networks for processing sequential data. The model takes each time step independently into the input layer and updates the hidden state. Thus, the model can consider information over many past time steps to predict output for the specific time step [40].

In the analyzed literature, RNNs are more likely used in non-hybrid architectures. The authors of [1] use stacked GRU layers, a rather less complex structure compared to LSTM. While being able to learn complex representations of long sequence data, the stacked GRU is also structurally simplistic. In the case of LSTMs, different encoder-decoder architectures are also advocated for being relatively simple and still being able to capture temporal dependencies [5,8,43].

Furthermore, the authors of [20] and [37] state the ability of LSTMs to capture long-term dependencies. The ability to capture long-term dependencies is also noted by authors of hybrid architectures [23]. The authors of [52] use UR-LSTM, a modified version of LSTM, that allegedly is even more capable of discovering complex long-term dependencies. RNNs are also used in more complex frameworks. The authors of [36] use a BiLSTM, a form of LSTM that encodes a sequence in both directions, to extract information. This information is fed into subsequent subparts of the architecture.

4.5   Convolutional Neural Networks

CNNs are not only used for input embeddings in time series forecasting. In contrast to the previously mentioned CNN 1D used in input embeddings, it is also used to extract spatial features between time steps in combination with activation functions and max pooling [2,23]. In addition to this, CNN 1Ds are also used in a stacked manner [26]. The authors of [31] state, that the CNN 1D is also used to extract non-linear relationships between the different variables of the data.

A way to extract more long-range features is to increase the receptive field. This can be done by using a dilation factor. The authors of [20] use a dilation factor for CNN 1D in a stacked architecture. Here, the dilation factor is increased with the depth of the stacked CNN 1D. The authors of [36] use CNN 1D for two different subtasks in the architecture. The feature extraction is split into creating a feature-focused embedding and a time-focused embedding. In the feature-focused embedding, the output representation of a BiLSTM is fed into a CNN 1D. After this, a temporal attention mechanism is succeeding. The time-focused embedding uses compound convolution. The compound convolutions make use of kernels with different sizes on the same sequence. The smaller kernel sizes capture most local features, and the bigger kernel uses a dilation factor to extract slightly larger features. The biggest kernel has the size of the window size to extract patterns over the whole input sequence. Both embeddings are fused and fed into a linear net to predict the next time step [36]. The authors of [38] also make use of larger kernel sizes, compared to the previously mentioned applications of convolutions. Here, the first layer has a width of 32 for more local features and 64 for more global features. The authors of [30] also use larger kernel sizes to capture more long-term dependencies. But they also use parallel small kernel sizes to mitigate optimization issues of the larger kernel sizes. Succeeding to this, point-wise convolutions are used to capture cross-variable dependencies. Point-wise convolutions can also be described as 1×1 convolutions. These are also used in [55] for obtaining temporal feature vectors as well as spatial feature vectors. Additionally, [55] also uses point-wise convolutions inside contextual fusion blocks where two outputs of a temporal and a spatial layer are fused and the dimensionality is reduced or increased to up- and down-sample the input.

The authors of [52] use CNN 1D in two subparts of the architecture. Firstly, to extract temporal patterns sliding along the time dimension. Secondly, in the concurrent subpart which is used to extract spatial features that are time-invariant.

The filter size is $(T \times 1)$, where T is the length of the input window. The authors of [50] use kernel sizes with a width of 1 too. The difference is that here the CNN 1Ds are applied to the representation of a preceding LSTM. Thus the CNN 1D extracts both, temporal and spatial features of each frequency. The authors of [56] use CNN 1D and max-pooling to reduce the dimension of the attention output.

Also, CNN 2Ds are used in the analyzed publications. The authors of [7] use convolutional block attention module (CBAM) [49] inside their architecture. This subpart consists of several techniques like pooling, channel attention, 7×7 convolutions, and spatial attention. The authors of [51] use CNN 2Ds too. Because of the characteristics of the domain-specific data, two convolutional networks are used in parallel with shared parameters. The output is then put through a fully connected layer and fed into an attention layer. The final technique for the prediction task is a BiLSTM [51]. The convolutional self-attention of [13] uses CNN 2D to create the query, key, and value vectors of the attention mechanism.

4.6   Attention-Based Techniques

Attention and more specific transformers show remarkable performances in multiple deep learning disciplines like NLP, computer vision, and more. This widespread dominance in the field of TS analysis is not as prevalent. Still, due to the ability of attention mechanisms to focus on temporal features, they are fitting for TS data. Some publications use attention succeeding to RNNs. In the case of [2] attention is used succeeding to an LSTM and thus can attend all the previous time step representations. By applying attention on top of the hidden states of the LSTM, the model gains the ability to focus on relevant contextual information throughout the entire history of the sequence, enhancing its capacity to capture long-term dependencies. The authors of [31] argue similarly. Here attention is applied on top of the hidden states of a BiLSTM. It is stated that with attention the loss of historical information is reduced while extracting more relevant information. Also, [25] uses RNNs in the form of stacked GRU layers. The attention mechanism improves the ability of the model to handle long sequences by reducing the deterioration of information in long RNN inputs.

Moreover, [50] uses attention on top of convolutional layers. As mentioned before, in this architecture, CNN 1D extracts features out of hidden states of LSTMs. The special aspect here is that temporal-attribute attention is applied. By that, both temporal as well as spatial features can be extracted. The reason for this is that in contrast to natural language sequences, the relationships between variables can hold important information [50].

In the model of [36] there are two subparts to divide the task of extracting temporal and spatial features. The spatial-focused subpart is similar to the previously mentioned model to the extent that the structure is an RNN (BiLSTM) preceding a CNN 1D which feeds the output into an attention layer, enabling attending relevant variables. In the time-focused subpart, self-attention is applied to the concatenated output of compound convolution. Hereby, time-dependent features can be extracted. In contrast to the multiple mentioned models before, the authors of [21] use attention before GRU and [51] before BiLSTM layers.

With the informer model, [56] proposes a new attention mechanism called ProbSparse self-attention. Here, the more important query vectors can be distinguished thus allowing the key vectors to only attend to the most important queries. This reduces time and space complexity of the attention mechanism. As mentioned above, the authors of [13] use convolutional self-attention. To reduce the memory cost they also use ProbSparse self-attention. With sparse binary attention, the authors of [16] build upon ProbSparse self-attention for a transformer model. Here, a fixed attention mask is used to reduce the attention complexity. The mask enables the model to only calculate the attention at the current time step. Also, the attention score with itself is masked. The authors of [44] use a transformer with a single block for the encoder and decoder each. Also, [27] uses a rather standard transformer except for the previously mentioned input embedding and masking. In [29] a transformer more similar to [11] with cross-attention and self-attention is presented. [54] proposes a transformer model named DSformer which tries to incorporate short-term, long-term, and variable relationships. Firstly, through double-sampling long-term as well as short-term relationships are extracted. This is done by downsampling and piecewise sampling the input in parallel. The output of both subparts is three-dimensional tensors where the dimensions are time, sampled subsequence, and variables. The third essential subpart of the DSformer is the temporal variable attention (TVA) block. The two outputs of both sampling parts are fed into a TVA block each. The TVA block calculates the temporal and attribute attention. The output of these two TVA blocks is fed into a third TVA block to combine the information extracted by the preceding subparts. Finally, a prediction is calculated.

[55] proposes a model of hierarchical residual spatio-temporal encoder and decoder layers (RSTEL/RSTDL). The RSTEL/RSTDL consists of spatial and temporal attention in parallel which is combined inside a contextual fusion block. The RSTEL/RSTDL can be stacked. An also rather unique approach is the pre-training and fine-tuning of [41]. The pre-training serves the MAE paradigm where patches are masked. In the fine-tuning stage, only the future time steps in the decoder are masked. The model itself consists of multi-head attention.

5 Conclusion

The literature reveals several interesting aspects of MVTS forecasting. The primary focus of literature filtering was on selecting relatively straightforward frameworks and architectures. Nevertheless, hybrid models still make up about half of the analyzed literature. While masking is used frequently in other deep learning disciplines like NLP, only a minority of analyzed literature applies masking. Recurrent techniques like LSTM and GRU are more likely used in a non-hybrid manner. Attention-based and CNN techniques, in contrast, are more likely to be used in hybrid models. To make better use of the time dimension of TS data, some of the analyzed literature not only uses sinusoidal positional encoding (like in traditional transformer) but also more time-specific encodings like Time2Vec and AddT2Vec.

References

1. Al-Shabandar, R., Jaddoa, A., Liatsis, P., Hussain, A.J.: A deep gated recurrent neural network for petroleum production forecasting. Mach. Learn. Appli. **3**, 100013 (2021). https://doi.org/10.1016/j.mlwa.2020.100013
2. Aouad, M., Hajj, H., Shaban, K., Jabr, R.A., El-Hajj, W.: A cnn-sequence-to-sequence network with attention for residential short-term load forecasting. Electric Power Sys. Res. **211** (2022).https://doi.org/10.1016/j.epsr.2022.108152
3. Bao, H., Dong, L., Piao, S., Wei, F.: BEiT: BERT Pre-Training of Image Transformers. In: The Tenth International Conference on Learning Representations, ICLR 2022. OpenReview.net (2022), https://openreview.net/forum?id=p-BhZSz59o4
4. Bengio, Y., Courville, A., Vincent, P.: Representation learning: A review and new perspectives. IEEE Trans. Pattern Analy. Mach. Intell. **35**, 1798–1828 (2013). https://doi.org/10.1109/TPAMI.2013.50
5. Biondi, R., et al.: Multivariate multi-step convection nowcasting with deep neural networks: the novara case study. In: International Geoscience and Remote Sensing Symposium (IGARSS), vol. 2022-July, pp. 6598–6601. Institute of Electrical and Electronics Engineers Inc. (2022).https://doi.org/10.1109/IGARSS46834.2022.9883665
6. vom Brocke, J., Simons, A., Niehaves, B., Riemer, K., Plattfaut, R., Cleven, A.: Reconstructing the giant: On the importance of rigour in documenting the literature search process. In: ECIS 2009 Proceedings (Oct 2009). https://aisel.aisnet.org/ecis2009/161
7. Chang, W., Li, X., Chaudhary, V., Dong, H., Zhao, Z., Nguyen, T.G.: Prediction of chlorophyll-a data based on triple-stage attention recurrent neural network. IET Commun. (2022). https://doi.org/10.1049/cmu2.12542
8. Chkeir, S., Anesiadou, A., Mascitelli, A., Biondi, R.: Nowcasting extreme rain and extreme wind speed with machine learning techniques applied to different input datasets. Atmospheric Res. **282** (2023). https://doi.org/10.1016/j.atmosres.2022.106548
9. Choi, K., Yi, J., Park, C., Yoon, S.: Deep learning for anomaly detection in time-series data: review, analysis, and guidelines. IEEE Access **9**, 120043–120065 (2021). https://doi.org/10.1109/ACCESS.2021.3107975
10. Feichtenhofer, C., Fan, H., Li, Y., He, K.: Masked Autoencoders As Spatiotemporal Learners. In: Advances in Neural Information Processing Systems (2022). https://openreview.net/forum?id=UaXD4Al3mdb
11. Devlin, J., Chang, M.W., Lee, K., Toutanova, K.: BERT: Pre-training of Deep Bidirectional Transformers for Language Understanding (2019)
12. Dosovitskiy, A., et al.: An image is worth 16x16 Words: transformers for image recognition at scale. In: International Conference on Learning Representations (2021). https://openreview.net/forum?id=YicbFdNTTy
13. Feng, X., Lyu, Z.: How features benefit: Parallel series embedding for multivariate time series forecasting with transformer. In: Proceedings - International Conference on Tools with Artificial Intelligence, ICTAI, vol. 2022, pp. 967–975. IEEE Computer Society (2022).https://doi.org/10.1109/ICTAI56018.2022.00148

14. Gehring, J., Auli, M., Grangier, D., Yarats, D., Dauphin, Y.N.: Convolutional sequence to sequence learning. In: Precup, D., Teh, Y.W. (eds.) Proceedings of the 34th International Conference on Machine Learning, vol. 70, pp. 1243–1252. PMLR (2017). https://proceedings.mlr.press/v70/gehring17a.html

15. Gooijer, J.G.D., Hyndman, R.J.: 25 years of time series forecasting. Inter. Jo]. Forecasting **22**, 443–473 (2006).https://doi.org/10.1016/j.ijforecast.2006.01.001

16. Gorbett, M., Shirazi, H., Ray, I.: Sparse binary transformers for multivariate time series modeling. In: Proceedings of the ACM SIGKDD International Conference on Knowledge Discovery and Data Mining, pp. 544–556. Association for Computing Machinery (2023). https://doi.org/10.1145/3580305.3599508

17. Gorecky, D., Schmitt, M., Loskyll, M., Zühlke, D.: Human-machine-interaction in the industry 4.0 era. In: 2014 12th IEEE International Conference on Industrial Informatics (INDIN), pp. 289–294 (2014).https://doi.org/10.1109/INDIN. 2014.6945523

18. Guo, W., Wang, J., Wang, S.: Deep multimodal representation learning: a survey. IEEE Access **7**, 63373–63394 (2019). https://doi.org/10.1109/ACCESS.2019. 2916887

19. He, K., Chen, X., Xie, S., Li, Y., Dollár, P., Girshick, R.: Masked autoencoders are scalable vision learners. In: Proceedings of the IEEE/CVF Conference on Computer Vision and Pattern Recognition (CVPR), pp. 16000–16009 (2022)

20. Hewage, P., Trovati, M., Pereira, E., Behera, A.: Deep learning-based effective fine-grained weather forecasting model. Pattern Analy. Appli. **24**, 343–366 (2021). https://doi.org/10.1007/s10044-020-00898-1

21. Huan, J., et al.: Multi-step prediction of dissolved oxygen in rivers based on random forest missing value imputation and attention mechanism coupled with recurrent neural network. Water Supply **22**, 5480–5493 (2022). https://doi.org/10.2166/ws. 2022.154

22. Kalayci, C.B., Karagoz, S., Özler Karakas: Soft computing methods for fatigue life estimation: A review of the current state and future trends. Fatigue Fract. Eng. Mater. Struct. **43**, 2763–2785 (2020). https://doi.org/10.1111/ffe.13343

23. Kaya, K., Şule Gündüz Öğüdücü: Deep flexible sequential (dfs) model for air pollution forecasting. Sci. Rep. **10**, 3346 (2020).https://doi.org/10.1038/s41598-020-60102-6

24. Kazemi, S.M., et al.: Time2Vec: Learning a Vector Representation of Time (2019). https://arxiv.org/abs/1907.05321

25. Kuo, R.J., Kunarsito, D.A.: Residual stacked gated recurrent unit with encoder-decoder architecture and an attention mechanism for temporal traffic prediction. Soft Comput. **26**, 8617–8633 (2022). https://doi.org/10.1007/s00500-022-07230-5

26. Li, T., Hua, M., Wu, X.: A hybrid cnn-lstm model for forecasting particulate matter (pm2.5). IEEE Access **8**, 26933–26940 (2020). https://doi.org/10.1109/ACCESS. 2020.2971348

27. Li, Z., Rao, Z., Pan, L., Wang, P., Xu, Z.: Ti-mae: self-supervised masked time series autoencoders (2023). http://arxiv.org/abs/2301.08871

28. Lim, B., Zohren, S.: Time-series forecasting with deep learning: a survey. Philos. Trans. Royal Soc. A: Math. Phys. Eng. Sciences **379**, 20200209 (2021).https://doi. org/10.1098/rsta.2020.0209

29. Limperis, J., Tong, W., Hamza-Lup, F., Li, L.: Pm2.5 forecasting based on transformer neural network and data embedding. Earth Sci. Inform. (2023). https:// doi.org/10.1007/s12145-023-01002-x

30. Luo, D., Wang, X.: Cross-lktcn: modern convolution utilizing cross-variable dependency for multivariate time series forecasting dependency for multivariate time series forecasting (2023). http://arxiv.org/abs/2306.02326
31. Ma, Z., Mei, G.: A hybrid attention-based deep learning approach for wind power prediction. Appli. Energy **323** (2022).https://doi.org/10.1016/j.apenergy.2022.119608
32. Manero, J., Béjar, J., Cortés, U.: Wind prediction using deep learning and high performance computing. In: Communications in Computer and Information Science. CCIS, vol. 1540, pp. 193–207. Springer Science and Business Media Deutschland GmbH (2022). https://doi.org/10.1007/978-3-031-04209-6_14
33. Nichol, A., Jun, H., Dhariwal, P., Mishkin, P., Chen, M.: Point-E: A System for Generating 3D Point Clouds from Complex Prompts (2022). https://arxiv.org/pdf/2212.08751.pdf
34. Radanliev, P., Roure, D.D., Nicolescu, R., Huth, M., Santos, O.: Artificial intelligence and the internet of things in industry 4.0. CCF Trans. Pervasive Comput. Interact. **3**, 329–338 (9 2021). https://doi.org/10.1007/s42486-021-00057-3
35. Ren, L., Jia, Z., Laili, Y., Huang, D.: Deep learning for time-series prediction in iiot: Progress, challenges, and prospects. IEEE Trans. Neural Netw. Learn. Syst., 1–20 (2023).https://doi.org/10.1109/TNNLS.2023.3291371
36. Roh, S., Jung, Y., Baek, J.G.: Tfe-net: time and feature focus embedding network for multivariate-to-multivariate time series forecasting. In: 5th International Conference on Artificial Intelligence in Information and Communication, ICAIIC 2023, pp. 474–478. Institute of Electrical and Electronics Engineers Inc. (2023). https://doi.org/10.1109/ICAIIC57133.2023.10066984
37. Sabri, M., Hassouni, M.E.: Photovoltaic power forecasting with a long short-term memory autoencoder networks. Soft Comput. **27**, 10533–10553 (2023). https://doi.org/10.1007/s00500-023-08497-y
38. Sharma, S.P., Yadav, D.K.: Renewable energy systems energy modeling using deep learning techniques. In: 2023 2nd International Conference for Innovation in Technology, INOCON 2023. Institute of Electrical and Electronics Engineers Inc. (2023). https://doi.org/10.1109/INOCON57975.2023.10101286
39. Succetti, F., Luzio, F.D., Ceschini, A., Rosato, A., Araneo, R., Panella, M.: Multivariate prediction of energy time series by autoencoded lstm networks. In: 21st IEEE International Conference on Environment and Electrical Engineering and 2021 5th IEEE Industrial and Commercial Power System Europe, EEEIC / I and CPS Europe 2021 - Proceedings. Institute of Electrical and Electronics Engineers Inc. (2021). https://doi.org/10.1109/EEEIC/ICPSEurope51590.2021.9584744
40. Sutskever, I., Martens, J., Hinton, G.E.: Generating text with recurrent neural networks. In: Proceedings of the 28th International Conference on Machine Learning (ICML 2011), pp. 1017–1024 (2011)
41. Tang, P., Zhang, X.: Mtsmae: masked autoencoders for multivariate time-series forecasting. In: Proceedings - International Conference on Tools with Artificial Intelligence, ICTAI, vol. 2022, pp. 982–989. IEEE Computer Society (2022). https://doi.org/10.1109/ICTAI56018.2022.00150
42. Taylor, W.L.: "CLOZE procedure": a new tool for measuring readability. Journal. Q. **30**, 415–433 (1953)
43. Tona, G.L., Luna, M., Piazza, M.D.: Day-ahead forecasting of residential electric power consumption for energy management using long short-term memory encoder-decoder model. Math. Comput. Simulat. (2023).https://doi.org/10.1016/j.matcom.2023.06.017, https://linkinghub.elsevier.com/retrieve/pii/S0378475423002720

44. Ughi, R., Lomurno, E., Matteucci, M.: Two Steps Forward and One Behind: Rethinking Time Series Forecasting with Deep Learning (2023). http://arxiv.org/abs/2304.04553
45. Vaswani, A., et al.: Attention is all you need. In: 31st Conference on Neural Information Processing Systems, NIPS 2017 (2017)
46. Vincent, P., Larochelle, H., Bengio, Y., Manzagol, P.A.: Extracting and composing robust features with denoising autoencoders. In: Proceedings of the 25th international conference on Machine learning, pp. 1096–1103 (2008)
47. Wang, Y., Feng, S., Wang, B., Ouyang, J.: Deep transition network with gating mechanism for multivariate time series forecasting. Appl. Intell. (2023). https://doi.org/10.1007/s10489-023-04503-w
48. Webster, J., Watson, R.T.: Analyzing the past to prepare for the future: writing a literature review. Quarterly **26**, xiii–xxiii (2002)
49. Woo, S., Park, J., Lee, J.-Y., Kweon, I.S.: CBAM: convolutional block attention module. In: Ferrari, V., Hebert, M., Sminchisescu, C., Weiss, Y. (eds.) ECCV 2018. LNCS, vol. 11211, pp. 3–19. Springer, Cham (2018). https://doi.org/10.1007/978-3-030-01234-2_1
50. Wu, P., Yu, H., Hu, F., Xie, Y.: A temporal-attribute attention neural network for mixed frequency data forecasting. Inter. Jo]. Mach. Learn. Cybernt. **13**, 2519–2531 (2022).https://doi.org/10.1007/s13042-022-01541-7
51. Xian, Q., Liang, W.: A multi-modal time series intelligent prediction model. LNEE. vol. 942, pp. 1150–1157. Springer Science and Business Media Deutschland GmbH (2022). https://doi.org/10.1007/978-981-19-2456-9_115
52. Yin, C., Dai, Q.: A deep multivariate time series multistep forecasting network. Appli. Intell. **52**, 8956–8974 (2022). https://doi.org/10.1007/s10489-021-02899-x
53. Yin, Z., Barucca, P.: Stochastic recurrent neural network for multistep time series forecasting. In: Mantoro, T., Lee, M., Ayu, M.A., Wong, K.W., Hidayanto, A.N. (eds.) ICONIP 2021. LNCS, vol. 13108, pp. 14–26. Springer, Cham (2021). https://doi.org/10.1007/978-3-030-92185-9_2
54. Yu, C., Wang, F., Shao, Z., Sun, T., Wu, L., Xu, Y.: DSformer: A Double Sampling Transformer for Multivariate Time Series Long-term Prediction (2023). http://arxiv.org/abs/2308.03274
55. Zhang, Y., Liu, L., Xiong, X., Li, G., Wang, G., Lin, L.: Long-term Wind Power Forecasting with Hierarchical Spatial-Temporal Transformer (2023). http://arxiv.org/abs/2305.18724
56. Zhou, H., et al.: Informer: beyond efficient transformer for long sequence time-series forecasting. In: Proceedings of the AAAI Conference on Artificial Intelligence, vol. 35, pp.11106–11115 (2021). https://doi.org/10.1609/aaai.v35i12.17325

Reducing Human Annotation Effort Using Self-supervised Learning for Image Segmentation

Thitirat Siriborvornratanakul[✉]

Graduate School of Applied Statistics, National Institute of Development Administration (NIDA), 148 SeriThai Road, Bangkapi, Bangkok 10240, Thailand
thitirat@as.nida.ac.th

Abstract. Image segmentation stands out as one of the most computationally demanding computer vision tasks, posing challenges not only due to the substantial computational resources required for training but also the scarcity of available annotation masks. The creation of a sizable collection of accurate segmentation annotation masks is notorious for being labor-intensive and time-consuming, often acting as a significant bottleneck in image segmentation projects. This paper delves into the intricacies of human effort involved in traditional segmentation annotation and explores the potential impact of self-supervised learning (SSL) as a promising solution. Ultimately, we contend that, despite the trade-offs inherent in existing SSL approaches for image segmentation, a new alternative leveraging foundation models for image segmentation, capable of zero-shot segmentation across extensive object categories, could emerge as a novel solution that reduces human effort in both annotation and model development.

Keywords: computer vision · self-supervised learning · human annotation · image segmentation

1 Introduction

The fast development of deep learning models, famous for requiring a large amount of training data, has led to a bottleneck in the training process related to data annotation or labeling. This obstacle prevents full automation and significantly extends the data preparation time, particularly when rare experts or specialists are needed for high-quality annotations, as seen in fields like medicine. Previous studies [13,17,23] highlight that the process of data annotation and labeling heavily relies on the experience and expertise of physicians. Focusing on two-dimensional (2D) image data, various tasks such as image classification, object detection, and image segmentation can be accomplished, each demanding a different level of annotation effort. As indicated by [25], while human labeling or verification is already expensive and time-consuming for image classification, these challenges are magnified in image segmentation tasks. Segmentation tasks

H. Degen and S. Ntoa (Eds.): HCII 2024, LNAI 14734, pp. 436–445, 2024.
https://doi.org/10.1007/978-3-031-60606-9_26

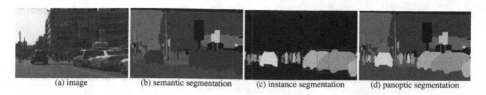

(a) image   (b) semantic segmentation   (c) instance segmentation   (d) panoptic segmentation

Fig. 1. Semantic, instance, and panoptic segmentations. Image courtesy of [10].

are notably more expensive, laborious, and error-prone to label. Moreover, both [25,30] concur that achieving class balance at the pixel level is particularly challenging for segmentation data, resulting in highly skewed or long-tail distribution problems in image segmentation. In addition to the long-tail distribution problem, [30] also notes spatial layout relations among "stuffs" (uncountable objects like sky, wall, floor) and "objects" (countable objects like pedestrians, cars, chairs), introducing more complexity and making it much more difficult to obtain consistent data annotations from different annotators.

As of now, various alternatives have been explored to alleviate the annotators' burden in preparing fully-supervised segmentation ground truth, as summarized in [23]. Addressing the challenge of augmenting the volume of training data without an increase in annotation efforts, semi-supervised learning, as exemplified in [7], incorporates unlabeled data to generate pseudo-labeled training data alongside the existing labeled counterparts. In a different approach, as proposed in [25], a two-stage framework with human-in-the-loop is introduced for effectively troubleshooting image segmentation models. This framework encompasses a failure identification module, leading to subsequent model rectification. However, it is crucial to note that the primary focus of this paper centers on exploring alternatives within the realm of Self-Supervised Learning (SSL). In this context, the emphasis is on fully training a deep learning model using exclusively unlabeled data. This not only provides a distinctive perspective within the spectrum of annotation-efficient methodologies but also liberates subsequent works from the constraints of predefined labels.

When it comes to SSL, it has emerged as a prominent trend in both natural language processing and computer vision over recent years, finding applications in diverse fields. Examples include SSL for recommendation [26], SSL for text clustering [21], SSL for image classification [3], and SSL for image representation learning [18]. However, this paper directs its attention to the realm of human annotation in image segmentation, delving into a comparative exploration between the conventional fully-supervised segmentation annotation discussed in Sect. 2 and SSL segmentation annotation discussed in Sect. 3. The synthesis of these findings will be presented in the comparative discussion within Sect. 4.

2   Annotation Effort in Image Segmentation

Image segmentation can be categorized into three well-established tasks: semantic segmentation, instance segmentation, and panoptic segmentation, as

Table 1. Summary regarding efforts invested by humans in the creation of segmentation datasets in some prior studies

Work	Annotation	Human in annotation
(IS) MS COCO dataset [14]	2.5M labeled instances in 328k images	Multiple workers from Amazon's Mechanical Turk with 30k worker hours plus over 22 worker hours per 1000 segmentations
(SS,IS) Cityscapes dataset [6]	5k and 20k images for fine and coarse annotations	More than 1.5 h for a single image for fine and less than 7 min per image for coarse annotations with in-house annotators
(SS) ADE20K dataset [30]	20210 (train), 2000 (val), and 3000 (test) images	Only one expert annotator to ensure consistency and quality
(SS) ImageNet-S dataset [9]	50k images with high-quality annotations across 919 categories	A team consists of an organizer, four quality inspectors, and 15 annotators.
(IS,SS) ZeroWaste-f dataset [2]	4661 images	12.5 min per image by professional annotators (cost per image is $0.6 for annotation and $0.62 for expert review)
(PS) VIPSeg dataset [15]	3536 videos, 84750 annotated images, 926213 instance masks	Sparse annotations took 1200 h for instance annotation and human review. Instance propagation took 20 h by computers. Refining by human annotators took about 10–60 minutes per video.
(IS) YouMVOS dataset [27]	200 videos with 431k annotated masks	A semi-automatic system created initial masks before each image was refined by three human annotators. The annotation team had 10 annotators trained for a week before the formal annotation

Note: SS, IS, and PS denote semantic, instance, and panoptic segmentations, respectively.

depicted in Fig. 1. Instance segmentation is specifically designed to differentiate distinct instances of countable objects. This is exemplified in tasks such as isolating car regions in a traffic surveillance system [29]. In contrast to instance segmentation, which focuses on providing instance-based results, semantic segmentation undertakes the precise classification of each individual pixel, offering no information regarding which pixel pertains to a specific instance. This characteristic makes it suitable for segmenting targets lacking a distinct boundary, such as crack regions in surface images [24]. Panoptic segmentation, as introduced by [10], combines both semantic and instance segmentations. This novel approach introduces the concept of "things" (countable objects like pedestrians, animals, cars) and "stuff" (uncountable amorphous regions like the sky and grass), enabling panoptic segmentation to effectively perform segmentation on both categories. While numerous datasets with ground truth are available for different image segmentation tasks, not all of them offer comprehensive information regarding the extent of human effort and labor devoted to preparing segmentation ground truth. Table 1 summarizes the human effort involved in annotation for generating ground truth labels in selected image segmentation datasets published in esteemed conferences or journals. Given the absence of a standardized format in the information provided by each work, this table represents our best effort to extract human-effort-related information from these sources.

According to Table 1, the Microsoft Common Objects in Context (MS COCO) dataset [14] stands out as the largest still-image dataset, comprising 2.5 million images accompanied by segmentation ground truth. Due to the substantial number of instances requiring annotation, crowd-sourced workers were enlisted as annotators, entailing many tens of thousands of worker hours to complete the annotation process. In contrast, other still-image datasets such as [2,6,9,30] avoided the use of crowd-sourced workers and opted for specially organized, in-house, or professional annotators. Notably, the work by [30] provides numerical insights, revealing that their sole expert annotator labeled an average of 29 annotation segments per image, while external annotators managed only 16 segments per image. This underscores the significance of specialized annotators. For video datasets like [15,27], which involve numerous frames per video (with only some frames sampled and annotated), sophisticated pipelines were usually involved to reduce time and effort in segmentation annotation. The VIPSeg dataset [15] initially employed human annotators for sparse annotation, followed by propagating the annotations to other frames in the video. Subsequently, human annotators performed final refinement to ensure high-quality annotation for each video. Similarly, the YouMVOS dataset [27] proposed a semi-automatic system for detecting, initiating, and propagating segmentation masks through frames of each video. A group of specially trained annotators then refined the generated segmentation masks.

The aforementioned insights underscore the substantial human effort required for segmentation annotation, representing a significant challenge unless utilizing existing datasets with ground truth. Although crowd-sourcing workers offer a potential solution, many researchers tend to avoid this approach due to concerns about annotation quality and the challenge of maintaining consistency. Depending on a sole expert annotator, as demonstrated in [30], may guarantee consistency but introduces the risk of subjective opinions and longer waiting times, potentially impeding the continuity of research in this domain.

3   Annotation in Self-supervised Image Segmentation

Following the widespread adoption of SSL in computer vision, this field has matured and can now be divided into various sub-categories. In 2023, an SSL cookbook [1] classified SSL approaches into families, including deep metric learning, self-distillation, canonical correlation analysis, and masked image modeling. While much of the discourse revolves around image-level SSL for image representation learning, there is an observation that certain SSL approaches lack localization information necessary for precise pixel-level dense predictions, such as in image segmentation. Another perspective from [9] describes SSL for image representation learning into four categories: contrastive-based SSL, non-contrastive-based SSL, clustering-based SSL, and pixel-level SSL. Although the majority of these four categories focus on image-level representation learning rather than pixel-level image segmentation, the pixel-level SSL category specifically addresses works that perform SSL at the pixel level rather than the image level, aiming to enhance transfer learning capabilities for downstream tasks. Despite the promising performances in transfer learning, the authors reported that techniques within this category overlook the category-related representation ability essential for semantic segmentation. While there are no standardized categories for SSL techniques in computer vision, our work focuses on depicting SSL in image segmentation through two groups: the two-step SSL (Sect. 3.1) and the one-step SSL (Sect. 3.2).

3.1 Two-Step SSL Approaches

In the first group, a two-step design is employed. Initially, a large model undergoes pre-training using a substantial amount of unlabeled data in an SSL manner. Subsequently, the pre-trained model is fine-tuned in the second step, utilizing a smaller set of labeled data for task-specific segmentation. In this step, there are options for supervised fine-tuning, including freezing the pre-trained network and fine-tuning only an additional task-specific head, or fine-tuning both the pre-trained network and the additional head together.

Examples of works applying this approach include [22], which introduced their network and self-supervised pretraining strategy for an encoder-decoder semantic inpainting network. The pre-trained network is later supervisedly fine-tuned on existing labeled datasets for various task-specific objectives. According to the authors, a consistent improvement is revealed for all methods when the number of labeled images is increased. However, despite a significant increase in the number of unlabeled images used during pre-training, the performance of self-supervised pre-training remains mostly the same, suggesting a small domain gap between semantic inpainting (the first pretraining step) and semantic segmentation tasks (the second fine-tuning step).

Similarly, in [20], a popular contrastive learning approach is employed to self-supervisedly pre-train the backbone consisting of two SwinUNet networks. To extend the pre-trained backbone to image segmentation, the backbone is further fine-tuned (supervisedly) with an additional small segmentation-specific head. The authors reported that, in their work, freezing the pre-trained backbone does not perform better than fine-tuning the pre-trained backbone altogether. Experiments on several downstream tasks also reveal that their resultant models perform on par with models trained from scratch with as little as 10% of the labeled data, allowing this SSL approach to be trained based on very small labeled datasets (about 100 samples).

Following the same pattern of self-supervised pretraining followed by supervised finetuning, numerous works in the literature delve into SSL-based image segmentation. These works employ various pretraining objectives, pretraining networks, and finetuning methods.

3.2   One-Step SSL Approaches

In the second group, one-step approaches are designed, usually in an end-to-end manner to accomplish self-supervised image segmentation in one shot, meaning that no labeled data is required at any step. Works in this group usually involve sophisticated techniques that are unique to one another. Also, the word "unsupervised" is sometimes used in exchange with the word "self-supervised" in this context.

One example from this group is SSL-ALPNet [16], proposed for a self-supervised few-shot segmentation problem. By combining a superpixel-based self-supervised learning strategy with an adaptive local prototype pooling network (ALPNet), this work aims to eliminate the reliance on manually annotated training images by exploiting unlabeled images and pseudo labels. Another work, MaskContrast [8], utilizes a saliency estimator to generate positive pairs of object-centric crops and negative pairs. Once high-quality pixel embeddings for semantic segmentation are obtained, clustering algorithms like K-Means can be applied to achieve fully unsupervised semantic segmentation. Optionally, the learned embeddings can undergo finetuning on new datasets if labeled data are available.

COMUS (Clustering Object Masks for learning Unsupervised Segmentation) [28] leverages the self-supervised DINO network for representation learning and the self-supervised DeepUSPS as an unsupervised saliency estimator, eliminating the need for manual annotation. Clustering is then applied to the saliency masks to generate unsupervised pseudo-masks. Subsequently, iterative self-training with noisy pseudo-masks is employed to enhance segmentation results. Consequently, COMUS reports unsupervised semantic segmentation results across all 80 categories of the MS COCO dataset without any manual annotation, achieving quality levels comparable to supervised counterparts. However, this work relies on several pre-trained models, including DINO pre-trained on ImageNet-1k without labels, DeepUSPS with BasNet weights, and DeepLabv3, whose encoder is initialized with a ResNet50 pre-trained with DINO on ImageNet and further fine-tuned on the pseudo-masks. Therefore, determining the exact number of unlabeled samples used to self-supervisedly train in this work, as shown in Table 2, proves challenging.

4   Comparison and Discussion

This section delves into the human annotation effort, incorporating information from Sects. 2, 3 and Tables 1, 2. Concerning the number of required training samples, there appears to be no discernible significant difference between supervised and self-supervised training. The outcome depends on various factors such as network architectures, training strategies, and image data characteristics. Notably, in the SSL approach, training samples in the self-supervised part necessitate no annotation, eliminating human effort in this step despite the substantial number of required training samples.

Table 2. Summary on the quantity of unlabeled and labeled samples needed for training SSL models in image segmentation

Work	Unlabeled samples	Labeled samples
(SS) Overhead imagery [22]	• Vary between 1k to 50k samples • No obvious performance differences when using more unlabeled samples	• Experimented with 10% of the unlabeled samples • The more the labeled samples, the better the performance.
(SS) Land-cover from satellite imagery [20]	The SEN12MS dataset with 180,662 samples	At least 100 unlabeled samples to be on par with models trained in a fully supervised manner
(SS) SSL-ALPNet [16]	• 3D images in the abdominal CT, abdominal T2-SPIR MRI, and cardiac bSSFP MRI datasets • Each 3D image contains many unlabeled slices/regions.	Not required
(SS) MaskContrast [8]	The PASCAL dataset with 10,582 samples	Optional finetuning
(SS) COMUS [28]	Not applicable as it involves the utilization of sub-models pretrained without labeled samples	Not required

Note: SS, IS, and PS denote semantic, instance, and panoptic segmentations, respectively.

Concentrating on the two groups of SSL techniques outlined in Sect. 3, the first group, a prevalent practice in many SSL research endeavors, comes with potential drawbacks. Notably, there may be discernible gaps between the pretrained objectives and the downstream objective. For instance, a model pretrained with an image-level rotation objective might lack the understanding of pixel-level dense prediction necessary for a downstream image segmentation task. Furthermore, two-step SSL approaches still necessitate supervised training with labeled data in the second step, indicating that they cannot entirely eliminate the need for human annotation efforts, as illustrated in the rightmost column of Table 2. In contrast, the second group comprises one-step SSL techniques for image segmentation, typically entailing end-to-end networks specially designed for SSL image segmentation from the outset. Consequently, no data annotation or labeled data is required, as depicted in the second column of Table 2. Nevertheless, there seems to be no common design suggestion or guideline for this second group of techniques; each work proposes its unique solution, necessitating substantial effort from experts and technicians in designing these specialized networks and making generalization across different research challenging.

The two groups of SSL approaches embody a tradeoff. On one hand, the two-step SSL group provides a standardized two-step pipeline that serves as an initial template during network design and development. However, it falls short of completely eliminating human effort in annotation due to the second step of supervised finetuning. On the other hand, the one-step SSL group entirely eliminates human effort in annotation but heavily relies on human experts to design each specialized network and process pipeline. In navigating this tradeoff, a groundbreaking solution has emerged with Meta AI Research, FAIR introducing the world's first foundational model in image segmentation, named Segment Anything Model (SAM), initially announced in April 2023 [11,12]. As explained on https://segment-anything.com/, *"SAM is a promptable segmentation system with zero-shot generalization to unfamiliar objects and images, without the need for additional training."* The newly proposed segmentation dataset, SA-1B, boasting over 1 billion masks on 11 million licensed and privacy-respecting images, distinguishes itself by not relying solely on online data like other foundational models. Instead, a specific data engine is developed to collect abundant segmentation masks with model-in-the-loop dataset annotation. SAM's data engine comprises three stages: a model-assisted manual annotation stage, a semi-automatic stage, and a fully automatic stage; the first two stages involve a team of professional human annotators. SAM's model is initialized with a self-supervised MAE pre-trained Vision Transformer and an off-the-shelf text encoder from CLIP. However, other parts involve supervised training as well. While the training process for SAM is sophisticated, expensive, and time-consuming, the public release (for research purposes) of the corresponding dataset and SAM model checkpoints at https://github.com/facebookresearch/segment-anything has catalyzed acceleration in many subsequent works. Researchers can leverage these sophisticated aspects of image segmentation, kickstarting their projects from SAM results, and finetune or postprocess the outcomes as demonstrated in [4,5,19].

5   Conclusion

This paper observes the bottleneck in developing image segmentation models, specifically the significant human annotation effort required in preparing training samples. While self-supervised learning has emerged as a promising solution to mitigate or eliminate the need for human annotation, it doesn't necessarily reduce the number of required training samples. However, current self-supervised learning approaches for image segmentation still present a tradeoff, demanding human involvement either during annotation or in network/process development. In contrast to other computer vision tasks benefiting from an abundance of pre-trained foundation models, the release of the first foundation model for image segmentation in 2023 marks a breakthrough, minimizing human effort in both annotation and intricate network design. We anticipate that the availability of foundation models in image segmentation will substantially alleviate the human effort required in future developments within this field.

References

1. Balestriero, R., et al.: A cookbook of self-supervised learning, pp. 1–71. arXiv:2304.12210v2 (2023)
2. Bashkirova, D., et al.: Zerowaste dataset: Towards deformable object segmentation in cluttered scenes. In: IEEE/CVF Conference on Computer Vision and Pattern Recognition (CVPR), Los Alamitos, CA, USA, pp. 21115–21125. IEEE Computer Society (Jun 2022)

3. Bunyang, S., et al.: Self-supervised learning advanced plant disease image classification with SimCLR. Adv. Comput. Intell. **3** (2023)
4. Chen, T., et al.: Sam-adapter: adapting segment anything in underperformed scenes. In: 2023 IEEE/CVF International Conference on Computer Vision Workshops (ICCVW). (2023) 3359–3367
5. Chen, X.D., Wu, W., Yang, W., Qin, H., Wu, X., Mao, X.: Make segment anything model perfect on shadow detection. IEEE Trans. Geosci. Remote Sens. **61**, 1–13 (2023)
6. Cordts, M., et al.: The cityscapes dataset for semantic urban scene understanding. In: IEEE Conference on Computer Vision and Pattern Recognition (CVPR), Los Alamitos, CA, USA, pp. 3213–3223. IEEE Computer Society (Jun 2016)
7. Fang, B., Li, X., Han, G., He, J.: Rethinking pseudo-labeling for semi-supervised facial expression recognition with contrastive self-supervised learning. IEEE Access **11**, 45547–45558 (2023)
8. Gansbeke, W.V., Vandenhende, S., Georgoulis, S., Gool, L.V.: Unsupervised semantic segmentation by contrasting object mask proposals. In: IEEE/CVF International Conference on Computer Vision (ICCV), Los Alamitos, CA, USA, pp. 10032–10042. IEEE Computer Society (oct 2021)
9. Gao, S., Li, Z.Y., Yang, M.H., Cheng, M.M., Han, J., Torr, P.: Large-scale unsupervised semantic segmentation. IEEE Trans. Pattern Anal. Mach. Intell. **45**(6), 7457–7476 (2023)
10. Kirillov, A., He, K., Girshick, R., Rother, C., Dollár, P.: Panoptic segmentation. In: IEEE/CVF Conference on Computer Vision and Pattern Recognition (CVPR), pp. 9396–9405 (2019)
11. Kirillov, A., et al.: Segment anything. In: IEEE/CVF International Conference on Computer Vision (ICCV), pp. 4015–4026 (October 2023)
12. Kirillov, A., et al.: Segment anything, pp. 1–30. arXiv:2304.02643v1 (2023)
13. Kittipongdaja, P., Siriborvornratanakul, T.: Automatic kidney segmentation using 2.5D ResUNet and 2.5D DenseUNet for malignant potential analysis in complex renal cyst based on CT images. EURASIP J. Image Video Process. **2022**(5) (2022)
14. Lin, T.Y., et al.: Microsoft COCO: common objects in context. In: Fleet, D., Pajdla, T., Schiele, B., Tuytelaars, T. (eds.) European Conference on Computer Vision (ECCV), pp. 740–755. Springer International Publishing, Cham (2014)
15. Miao, J., et al.: Large-scale video panoptic segmentation in the wild: A benchmark. In: IEEE/CVF Conference on Computer Vision and Pattern Recognition (CVPR), (2022) 21001–21011
16. Ouyang, C., Biffi, C., Chen, C., Kart, T., Qiu, H., Rueckert, D.: Self-supervised learning for few-shot medical image segmentation. IEEE Trans. Med. Imaging **41**(7), 1837–1848 (2022)
17. Pan, S., Liu, X., Xie, N., Chong, Y.: EG-TransUNet: a transformer-based U-Net with enhanced and guided models for biomedical image segmentation. BMC Bioinform. **24** (2023)
18. Purushwalkam, S., Gupta, A.: Demystifying contrastive self-supervised learning: invariances, augmentations and dataset biases. In: Neural Information Processing Systems (NeurIPS), pp. 3407–3418 (2020)
19. Sarai, W., Monbut, N., Youngchoay, N., Phookriangkrai, N., Sattabun, T., Siriborvornratanakul, T.: Enhancing baggage inspection through computer vision analysis of x-ray images. J. Transp. Secur. **17**, 1–13 (2024)
20. Scheibenreif, L., Hanna, J., Mommert, M., Borth, D.: Self-supervised vision transformers for land-cover segmentation and classification. In: IEEE/CVF Conference

on Computer Vision and Pattern Recognition Workshops (CVPRW), pp. 1421–1430 (2022)

21. Shi, H., Sakai, T.: Self-supervised and few-shot contrastive learning frameworks for text clustering. IEEE Access **11**, 84134–84143 (2023)

22. Singh, S., et al.: Self-supervised feature learning for semantic segmentation of overhead imagery. In: The British Machine Vision Conference (BMVC), Newcaltle, UK, 1–13 (Sep 2018)

23. Siriborvornratanakul, T.: Advanced artificial intelligence methods for medical applications. In: Duffy, V.G. (ed.) Digital Human Modeling and Applications in Health, pp. 329–340. Safety, Ergonomics and Risk Management. Springer Nature Switzerland, Cham (2023). https://doi.org/10.1007/978-3-031-35748-0_24

24. Siriborvornratanakul, T.: Pixel-level thin crack detection on road surface using convolutional neural network for severely imbalanced data. Computer-aided Civil Infrastruct. Eng. **38**(16), 2300–2316 (2023)

25. Wang, H., Chen, T., Wang, Z., Ma, K.: Troubleshooting image segmentation models with human-in-the-loop. Mach. Learn. **112**, 1033–1051 (2023)

26. Wang, J., Wu, J., Jia, C., Zhang, Z.: Self-supervised variational autoencoder towards recommendation by nested contrastive learning. Appl. Intell. **53**, 18887–18897 (2023)

27. Wei, D., et al.: Youmvos: an actor-centric multi-shot video object segmentation dataset. In: IEEE/CVF Conference on Computer Vision and Pattern Recognition (CVPR), pp. 21012–21021 (2022)

28. Zadaianchuk, A., Kleindessner, M., Zhu, Y., Locatello, F., Brox, T.: Unsupervised semantic segmentation with self-supervised object-centric representations. In: International Conference on Learning Representations (ICLR) (2023)

29. Zhang, B., Zhang, J.: A traffic surveillance system for obtaining comprehensive information of the passing vehicles based on instance segmentation. IEEE Trans. Intell. Transp. Syst. **22**(11), 7040–7055 (2021)

30. Zhou, B., Zhao, H., Puig, X., Fidler, S., Barriuso, A., Torralba, A.: Scene Parsing through ADE20K Dataset. In: IEEE Conference on Computer Vision and Pattern Recognition (CVPR), pp. 5122–5130 (2017)

Human-Aligned GAI Driven by Conceptual Knowledge: System, Framework, and Co-creation

Jingran Wang[1], Feng Liu[2], and Rong Chang[2(✉)]

[1] Beijing International Studies University, Beijing 100024, China
[2] Beijing Institute of Graphic Communication, Beijing 102600, China
changrong-bj@bigc.edu.cn

Abstract. Generative artificial intelligence models (GAI) have become the leading solutions for image generation tasks. Despite their inventive performance, these models suffer from inconsistencies and domain limitations due to data bias and emergent phenomena. Therefore, aligning GAI with human painters has become one of the important interdisciplinary topics of HCI. This paper customizes GAI by embedding domain conceptual knowledge into the large text-to-image model, aiming to learn more about the role of conceptual knowledge in building human-aligned GAI. We first construct a human-AI alignment system from the cognitive perspective. We then propose an alignment method that maps abstract concepts to detailed visual representations, corresponding to a multi-level alignment framework. Finally, we illustrate how the framework can be applied to human-GAI co-creation through experiments on Chinese landscape painting and propose a custom model. The experimental results preliminarily confirm that conceptual knowledge is of great help to building human-aligned GAI. For end users who need a balance between generality and specificity of large models, this study provides the methodology of customizing under the circumstance of limited data and computing power. This study also serves as a valuable reference for researchers to systematically understand human-GAI alignment and advance the alignment of GAI for better adaptation to human-oriented tasks.

Keywords: Human-aligned GAI · Conceptual Knowledge · Co-creation · AI Cognition

1 Introduction

Over the past three years, there has been an increase in Diffusion model research [1–3], and related applications such as Stable Diffusion or Midjourney are gaining momentum. Although state-of-the-art GAIs can produce creative images, compositional ability remains a challenging problem [4]. This phenomenon may be particularly relevant in the inability of AI to acquire abstract conceptual knowledge during learning and then seamlessly apply these abstractions to new scenarios. To bridge the gap between human and GAIs, we need to build human-aligned GAI that can abstract the conceptual manipulation rules behind cluster pixels [5].

© The Author(s), under exclusive license to Springer Nature Switzerland AG 2024
H. Degen and S. Ntoa (Eds.): HCII 2024, LNAI 14734, pp. 446–465, 2024.
https://doi.org/10.1007/978-3-031-60606-9_27

This study focuses on the role of domain conceptual knowledge in building human-aligned GAI. Our contribution has tripled. First, a human-AI alignment system is constructed from the perspective of cognition. Second, an alignment method driven by mapping abstract conceptual knowledge to detailed visual representations is proposed. Third, a human-aligned GAI model is fine-tuned and a series of co-creation experiments on Chinese landscape paintings is conducted.

The paper is structured as follows. Section 1 briefly introduces the purpose of the study. Section 2 constructs the human-AI alignment system and elucidate the importance of conceptual knowledge from the perspective of cognition evolution. Section 3 summarizes the progress of previous research. Section 4 to Sect. 6 detail the alignment workflow and the experiment. Section 7 concludes the paper.

2 The Importance of Conceptual Knowledge

2.1 Human-AI Alignment System

From the perspective of cognition evolution, the alignment between human and AI is a system in which human and AI collaborate to explore the world, thereby developing the ability to extract and relate concepts horizontally and vertically. Existing research has revealed that in the Paleolithic Age, human communication shifted from gestural to vocal form [6], and syntactic language developed [7]. In addition to the development of syntactic language, improved cognitive fluidity has increased people's ability to integrate concepts in the horizontal direction [8]. Subsequently, the ability of cognition to move vertically between concepts at different levels increases [9], which promotes the interaction between implicit cognition and explicit cognition [10]. Explicit cognition, which is usually expressed in language and highly conceptualized, is considered the highest cognition of human beings. Implicit cognition is older, and can learn automatically and unconsciously [11–13], and plays a key role in structuring our skills, perceptions, and behaviors [14]. The development of explicit cognition does not replace implicit learning mechanisms, but rather works with it superimposed. With the help of syntactic language, implicit learning develops into a form that can be consciously manipulated, capable of reflectively and explicitly manipulating implicit associations [15].

Based on the above findings, we construct the framework of human-AI alignment system. As shown in Fig. 1, the human-AI alignment system contains three core parts: the appearance-wrapped noumenon, human, and AI. From implicit cognition to explicit cognition, we divide the evolution progress into four major stages: perceptual experience, rational a priori, imaginative grokking, and intellectual transcendence.

- **Perceptual experience.** The subject perceives images or other representations and form intuitive knowledge with the help of experience. This process is similar to modelling based on a small amount of discrete data. For example, the subject classifies the moon, plates, and balls into the concept of circle.
- **Rational a priori.** The subject uses concepts or conceptual knowledge to reason and judge the perceived objects. This process is equivalent to analogy using a model. For example, the subject can choose objects like circle instructed by circles drawn on paper or the circle concept expressed in language. In addition, the subject can also

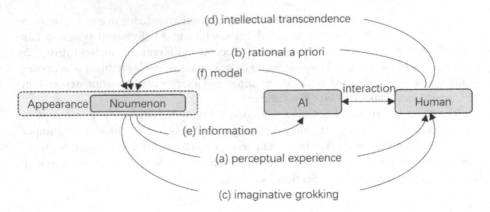

Fig. 1. The overview of human-AI alignment system.

recognize the connection between a circle and a regular polygon and use abstract formulation to clarify this inner logic.

- **Imaginative grokking.** The subject tries to understand the origin and laws of things by imagining the invisible noumenon, and produces highly abstract conceptual knowledge. For example, the Taoist concept of "Wuji" and the Western concept of "Omnipresence" were both developed by ancient people and used to explain the generation and changes of all things. Similarly, contemporary attempts to use quantum mechanics to explain the workings of the universe.
- **Intellectual transcendence.** The exploration of noumenon, on the one hand, makes the subject increasingly believe in some kind of transcendent power. On the other hand, the subject is also inspired to achieve spiritual transcendence. Due to different cultural contexts, the ultimate beliefs that subjects advocate are also different, such as Hindu emptiness, Confucian morality, Western freedom.

Although the pace of progress in AI is astounding, the operation of current AI is still relatively rudimentary, relying on information input to simulate human perception experience, and using modelling to simulate human prior rationality. Even the state-of-the-art AIs now encounter the challenge of learning conceptual knowledge. If such a bottleneck is not broken, the dislocation between human and AI will continue due to the lack of high-level conceptual control. Meanwhile, some hypotheses of cognitive mechanism, such as the recurrent processing theory [16, 17], the global workspace theory [18–20] and the higher-order theories [21] etc., have been introduced into the AI engineering. For example, the recurrent processing theory emphasizes the feedback from top to primary cortex to integrate various visual features for forming meaningful visual scenes. This mechanism was originally simulated using U-Net [22] combined with Residual Neural Network [23]. As another example, the global workspace theory believes that the sharing and fusion platforms of information can be formed through global broadcasting and attention mechanisms. Researchers mimicked the similar process using Transformer [24]. Furthermore, the higher-order theories argues that first-order representations represent things about the world, while higher-order representations represent things about other representations. Researchers formed prior knowledge through concept annotation embeddings, and used top-driven noise prediction modules such as diffusion models [1] to initially realize this mechanism. It is foreseeable that with the frequent and multimodal interactions between humans and AI, AI's cognition will converge to human cognition. So much so that people will treat AI as a fully conscious subject. Therefore, this study takes the idea of human-AI alignment system as the starting point for discussion.

2.2 Evolution Driven by Conceptual Knowledge

To elucidate how conceptual knowledge affects the cognition of human-AI alignment system, taking text-to-image generation as an example, we briefly review the evolution of GAI. As appearances, images are usually attached to "actual entity" that really exist in the natural world [25]. It is well known that natural world data is the basis for training intelligent agents. Researchers have achieved promising results using natural world data to generate realistic images, such as landscape photos [26], car models [27], and 3D images of human bodies [28]. The more detailed the natural world data is, the better the intelligent agent will perform.

A very important turning point is image synthesis prompted by artificial combined concepts. Based on extensive image-caption pairs obtained from the Internet, CLIP learns constituent elements in an image and the corresponding concepts [29], triggering the liberation of elements from entities. Subsequently, DALL· E forms new images by combining unrelated concepts, such as "avocado-shaped armchair" or "butterfly-wing-shaped teapot" [30, 31], promoting the transition, transformation, and reconstruction of individual elements in various contexts.

The substance has not yet been produced, but the concept has preceded. Current GAI researchers are keen on translating novel concept combinations into images [32–35], and multimodal translation among images and videos [36, 37]. As a result, images with "conceptual entity" which are abstracted from or derived from and founded upon the actual entities flood the digital world. The essence of this transition from potentiality to reality is what Whitehead describes as "concrescence": a new speculative entity participates in the world, and in turn generates a new element added to the settled world [25].

The above evolutionary process highlights the important role of concepts in image generation. Current concept-driven computing that relies on concrete concepts embodies the incidental assumptions [38]. That is, the microscale contains all the details of the system, so once the expression can be determined at the microscale, it will be determined accordingly at the macroscale. However, this one-way certainty is easily disturbed by the emergent mechanisms of large models. As a result, inconsistency of large models is plaguing both the developers and the end users.

Instead, we turn our attention to top-down integration of concepts. Our concept-driven computation is based on more abstract concepts, such as the compositional schema that runs through human visual cognition, expression, and imagination. This study takes Chinese landscape painting as an example to verify the feasibility of a methodology that promotes GAI to align with humans more efficiently through constructing and utilizing the mapping relationship between highly abstract conceptual knowledge and detailed visual representations.

3 Related Work

3.1 Computational Architecture

Our experiment is based on Stable-diffusion-v1-4 [39]. It is pre-trained on a vast dataset of 600 million captioned images for which the AI predicts humans would rate at least 5/10 when asked to rate aesthetic scores. This process equips it with world knowledge and aesthetic cognition, facilitating the images generation in response to various text prompts. Despite these strengths, the model often produces images that deviate from expectations of human artist, which limits its practical usefulness. We tried text-to-image, and image-to-image methods to generate Chinese landscape paintings using Stable Diffusion. The output images mostly cannot reflect the characteristics of Chinese landscape painting. The main reason for this issue may be that although the training data obtained from the Internet is huge, it does not cover various art fields in a balanced and detailed manner.

From skills to aesthetic taste, Chinese landscape painting that called "images of the mind" by scholars [40] is significantly distinguished from other painting categories or landscape photography. In terms of transcendence, the style of super-representation in Chinese painting [41] is not the same as abstractionism and expressionism in Western painting but is related to Chinese artists' advocacy of Confucianism and Taoism. Confucius said: "The benevolent enjoys mountains, and the wise enjoys water." Lao Zhuang regards human and nature as one. Therefore, Chinese painters extol the ideal world and reintegrate with nature in their creation. During the Southern and Northern Dynasties (420–589 C.E.), the knowledge of Chinese painting was highly abstracted by Xie He as the "Six Laws" and inherited from generation to generation. The uniqueness of Chinese landscape painting style and knowledge system, as well as the fact that there are few human annotation benchmarks about it in existing training datasets and pre-trained models, not only provides exploration space for experiments, but also facilitates us to observe the impact of newly embedded conceptual knowledge.

3.2 Dataset Building and Concepts Customization

We try to fine tune the pre-trained model with as little data as possible to maximize the leverage effect. Specifically, we adopt multi-scale sampling strategy to establish the dataset. Its cognitive basis is that human has the ability of multi-scale modeling [42–44]. Therefore, data sampling referring to human cognition helps computation mix the top and bottom features [45, 46].

In addition to data collection, data labeling assumes the function of providing "ground truth" for the model [47]. In this study, this meant manually labeling images with concepts at different levels of abstraction. However, label ambiguity is often detrimental to model performance. Previous research has confirmed that even for specific concepts, it is difficult for humans and AI to agree on the ground truth of labels [48]. Given that annotators' background is one of the main sources of ambiguity [49], annotation by community members may help deal with label ambiguity [50]. It can be inferred that models developed with data annotated by a group of domain users may demonstrate a marked improvement in understanding human instructions and solving specific tasks. Therefore, our study interprets the essence of a concept as a consensus within a professional group and completes the labeling task by domain users with relevant backgrounds.

Manually annotated data needs to be embedded into the pre-trained model through training. Previous research enabled single-concept customization by leveraging the semantic prior embedded with a new autogenous class-specific prior preservation loss [30]. Regarding the customization of multiple concepts, recent research generates combinations of new concepts by combining multiple expert models [31, 32]. Although related research has made progress in embedding specific concepts, current models still struggle to generate all topics described in text prompts [51, 52]. This may be related to the lack of hierarchy in the embedded concepts. Therefore, this study establishes a conceptual hierarchy of different levels of abstraction. Subsequently, we employ CLIP-ViT-L-14 [53] as the global control and try to embed all concepts through one model.

3.3 Model Responses Evaluation

As of now, scale is still the main method for model evaluation. Some studies propose to evaluate the response quality of models in an ordinal classification setting where human evaluators are required to categorize each response into one of the four levels which are acceptable, minor errors, major errors and unacceptable [54]. Some other research proposes to use a pairwise comparison framework for evaluating the output quality of two large models. Given the instruction inputs and two model outputs, the human annotators are asked to select a better one [55]. Our assessment also takes the form of a scale. The measurement index is determined by the researcher based on the aesthetic taste of Chinese landscape painting. Invited professional users use the fine-tuned model to complete co-creation tasks and evaluate the model's performance.

4   The Framework of Building Human-Aligned GAIs

Combining inspiration from previous research and our practical experience, we propose a framework of building human-aligned GAIs in painting area. As shown in Fig. 2, our framework encompasses three phases of concepts abstraction and annotation, concepts customization, as well as co-creation and evaluation.

- **Concepts abstraction and annotation.** Human aesthetic ideals can be translated into dataset by data structure and annotation. Human experts first conduct theoretical style analysis and extract conceptual knowledge. Then, through data design, the extracted concepts are incorporated into the dataset. Some effective methods include multi-scale sampling and community-driven annotation.
- **Concepts customization.** Human aesthetic priors subsequently are embedded in model through fine-tuning. Specifically, the computational framework that simulating human cognition's operation includes generative, top-down, cross-attention, and noisy perception modules is constructed. Based on it, downstream task head tuning transplants domain conceptual knowledge into the large model, thereby forming new priors.

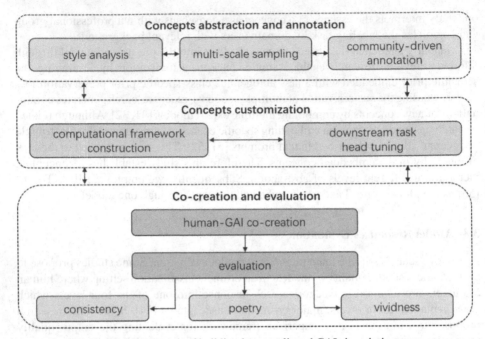

Fig. 2. The framework of building human-aligned GAIs in painting area.

- **Co-creation and evaluation.** Human-GAI co-creation driven by conceptual knowledge is conducted with the fine-tuned model. Evaluation cares whether the actual operation and output accommodate human expectations. Professional users access the fine-tuned model's ability of alignment from three dimensions: consistency, poetry, and vividness.

To illustrate how the framework can be applied in practice, we conducted a series of co-creation experiments on Chinese landscape paintings.

4.1 Style Analysis

Painting is a painter's modeling of the world. In this process, composition is the key to integrating various elements [56]. Therefore, we regard the composition of Chinese landscape paintings as the focus of style analysis.

To put the infinite world into a limited frame, Chinese painters often follow classical compositional schemas, organize composition utilizing moving viewpoints, and adjust the visual proportions of different view subjectively. There is a systematic structure evolution from simple to complex in Chinese landscape painting. During the Song dynasty (960–1279 C.E.), Chinese landscape painting reached its first peak. The landscape paintings of the Northern Song Dynasty basically adopted the principle of central axis composition. In the Southern Song Dynasty, Li Tang and Xia Gui, put the main elements of their paintings on one side. Ma Yuan only took up a corner to paint. While Western landscape paintings were still developing toward the more realistic nature observed by the artist, Chinese painters had shifted their creative intentions from representation to expression [57]. In the Yuan Dynasty (1271–1368 C.E.) Wang Meng tended to compose his works on S-shaped curves. Ni Zan painted mainly with horizontal structure [58]. In the 17th century, the development of Chinese landscape painting entered its second peak, and the numerous details contained in sensory were further abstracted to a purely aesthetic structure. The painter's inner world replaced the outer natural landscape and became the ultimate reality [59].

According to the development of Chinese landscape painting, we summarized the composition of Chinese landscape painting into five main schemas: centralized composition, centrally divided composition, diagonally divided composition, S-shaped composition, and horizontal composition. The above concepts can basically reflect the compositional frame in the mind of a Chinese landscape painter. In terms of the evaluation dimension, besides the consistency of the large model, we extracted the two concepts of poetry and vividness according to the tradition of combining poetry and painting in Chinese landscape painting and the pursuit of vivid aesthetics.

4.2 Multi-scale Sampling

We selected the pictures of *Verdant Rocks and Beautiful Pavilions* by Boxu Zhao, a painting of the Chinese Song Dynasty, as the experimental material. The size of the digital image we got of *Verdant Rocks and Beautiful Pavilions* is 41762 * 3937 pixels. In order to simulate human visual cognition, we performed multi-scale sampling on this image (see Fig. 3). We randomly split it into patches of 512 * 512 pixels, resulting in a total of 3870 samples. We defined these samples as samples of the zoom in view. Next, we resized the vertical axis of the original image to 1024 pixels and randomly divided it into patched of 512 * 512 pixels. In this way, we got 250 samples of zoom out views. Finally, we resized the vertical axis of the original image to 512 pixels and segmented it into patches of 512×512 pixels. From this, we got 20 patches for the overall view.

Through scalable sampling, we constructed a multi-scale dataset including 4140 samples (see Table 1).

4.3 Community-Driven Annotation

Data annotation is completed by the community composed of professional users. After brainstorming and labelling experiments on some representative Chinese landscape paintings, the community proposed a labelling framework including five dimensions of art style, compositional element, compositional relationship, compositional schema, and type of view.

- **Art style.** Since this study takes a single piece of Chinese blue-green landscape painting as an example, the art style of all samples was labelled as Chinese blue-green landscape painting.
- **Compositional element.** The main compositional elements were roughly divided into six categories: natural object, architecture, animals, tools, transportation, and figures (see Table 2). The element annotation adopted more general labels rather than detailed items. For example, "Chinese pavilion" was used to refer to most of the

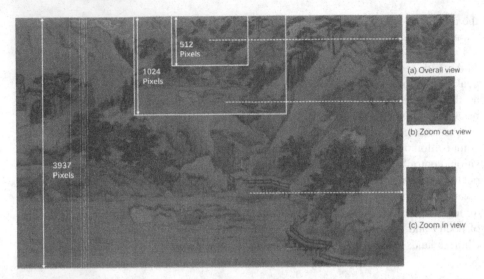

Fig. 3. The methods of scalable sampling: (a) overall view sampling, (b) zoom out view sampling, and (c) zoom in view sampling. "Verdant Rocks and Beautiful Pavilions" (partial) by Boxu Zhao, Song Dynasty. Photos credit: The Freer Gallery of Art.

Table 1. The structure of the multi-scale dataset.

Type of view	Size of adjusted vertical axis	Number of samples
overall view	512 pixels	20
zoom out view	1024 pixels	250
zoom in view	3937 pixels	3870

Chinese buildings in the painting. For another example, "man" was used to refer to woodcutter, fisherman, boatman and other male in the paintings.

- **Compositional relationship.** The relationships between constituent elements of Chinese landscape painting were summarized into five main categories, which are performing actions, residence, co-occurrence, affiliation, and tools (See Table 3).
- **Compositional schema.** The constituent elements and relationships of the zoom-in samples were described in detail. For the samples of zoom-out view and overall view, only the compositional schema was labelled. This not only reduced the workload of labelling, but also formed an information ladder between samples of different scales.

5   Concepts Customization

We use downstream task head tuning to accommodate human intention. The computational architecture includes (1) CLIP's ViT-L/14 of 123 million parameters that works as the text encoder to turn the input text prompt into text embedding; (2) VAE acts as an

Table 2. The dimensions of labelling.

Categories	Labels of compositional elements
Natural object	mountains, trees, clouds, farmland, water, shore etc.
Architecture	Chinese pavilion, terrace, Chinese farmhouse, gate, bridge, plank road, house on stilts, grass huts etc.
Animals	cow, dog etc.
Tools	fishing rod, loading net, hoe, carrying pole etc.
Transportation	wooden boat etc.
Figure	man, woman, child etc.

Table 3. The annotation of compositional relationships.

Categories	Annotation example
Performing actions	"A man walking across the bridge."
Residence	"Three men standing at the gate."
Co-occurrence	"A woman walking with a child."
Affiliation	"A man sitting at the stern with items."
Tools	"A man fishing with a fishing rod."

image encoder-decoder to convert an image into a latent vector or turns the latent vector into an image; and (3) diffusion model of 860 million parameters and a U-net structure.

The tuning process is as follows. Firstly, image-annotation pairs of Chinese landscape painting are projected to the latent space by the text encoder and the image encoder. Then, a small amount of original noise is added to the image latent vector for a given timestep. The diffusion model uses latent vectors from these two spaces along with a timestep embedding to predict the noise that was added to the image latent. Finally, the reconstruction loss between the predicted noise and the original noise added in step is calculated. The diffusion model parameters are optimized using gradient descent.

The training was performed on a NVIDIA RTX 3080 GPU. Under the setting of learning rate 1e−5, the training process was relatively smooth. After 450 epochs, the loss converged to 0.0687 (see Fig. 4).

6 Co-creation and Evaluation

Through data annotation, we have integrated some conceptual knowledge of Chinese landscape painting into the data. Then, the process of downstream task head tuning enables the knowledge to be embedded into the model and transformed into prior knowledge. To evaluate the alignment capability of the fine-tuned model driven by conceptual knowledge, we conducted the human and AI co-creation experiments.

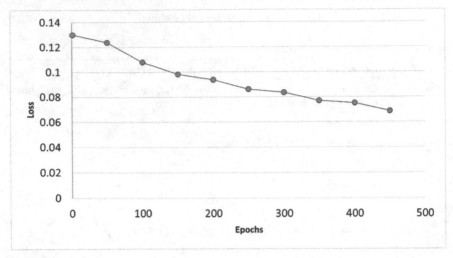

Fig. 4. Changes in the value of loss during model training

6.1 Driven by Basic Concepts

The professional users first prompted AI to create some scenarios by combining the concepts of elements and relationships. As shown in Fig. 5, the input concepts such as numbers, characters, actions, and directional relations can be mapped to the content of the output images. Furthermore, we find that abstract concept embeddings may elicit accurate visual representations. For example, all bodies of water, whether rivers or lakes, were labelled as water during annotation. Now, when the users expressing ideas with sub-concepts such as lake, river, etc., which do not appear in our labels, the type of water produced is mostly as expected.

6.2 Driven by Compositional Schemas

The professional users then instructed the model by the five compositional schemas of Chinese landscape painting. It can be seen from Fig. 6 that the compositional features of the generated images conform to the creative intention.

6.3 Driven by Detailed Creative Intention

The professional users further examined whether these compositional schemas can be matched with more detailed creative expressions. Figure 7 shows some experimental results. It can be seen that the abstract schemas can be stably combined with the details of the painting.

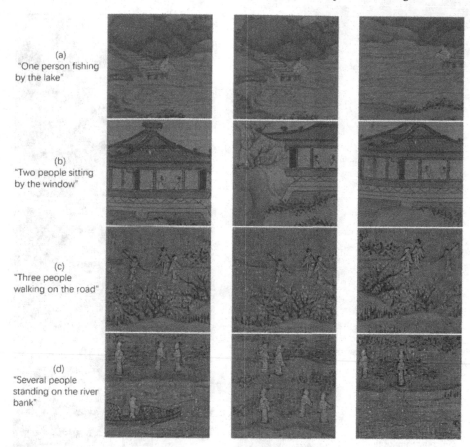

Fig. 5. Capability of aligning to basic concepts. The text description on the left is the compositional element and relationship input by the professional users. The images output by the model are on the right.

6.4 Driven by Conceptual Analogies

The professional users finally performed conceptual analogy-based generation to test whether the abstract concepts embedding is helpful for the large model to apply learned conceptual knowledge to new contexts. As shown in Fig. 8, the model can associate the new scene description with the existing composition elements, and initially complete the conceptual analogy-based generation. For example, if there is a scene of "three men standing at the gate" in the training dataset, the model will transform it and apply it to image generation with the theme of "Neighbors chatting at the gate". Similarly, the concept and visual elements in "A woman walking with a child" are applied to image

458   J. Wang et al.

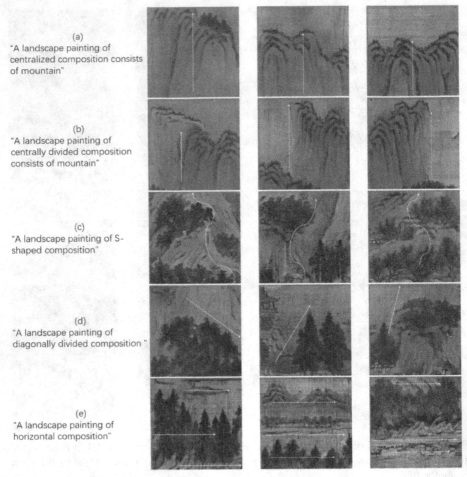

Fig. 6. Capability of aligning to compositional schemas. The text on the left is the compositional schemas input by the professional users. The images on the right are the corresponding output of the model. The white lines in the picture are added by the researcher.

generation with the theme of "Mother taking a child to school". In addition, the model can also reasonably infer the identity of the characters from the scene, so as to extract available elements for regeneration, such as the images generation of "A boatman", "A farmer", and "A scholar". However, this inference-based generation capability is relatively limited, and combinatorial elements are sometimes lost.

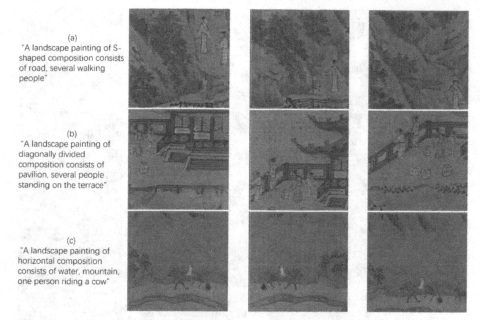

(a)
"A landscape painting of S-shaped composition consists of road, several walking people"

(b)
"A landscape painting of diagonally divided composition consists of pavilion, several people standing on the terrace"

(c)
"A landscape painting of horizontal composition consists of water, mountain, one person riding a cow"

Fig. 7. Results of mapping compositional schemas to detailed creative intention. The text on the left is the composition schema, elements, and relations input by the professional users. The images output by the model are on the right.

6.5 Evaluation

Based on the mapping relationship between abstract concepts and visual representations, we have customized the large model for Chinese landscape painting creation. Subsequently, we tested the capability of human-aligned GAI driven by conceptual knowledge in human-GAI co-creation scenarios. Five invited users scored the alignment ability of the model from the dimensions of consistency, poetry, and vividness based on their own experience. As shown in Table 4, the concept-driven model received the highest evaluation in terms of consistency. All five users agreed that the large model embedded with domain conceptual knowledge is obviously more suitable for the needs of professional creation and may match the users' instructions in most cases. The users recognized the model's representations of the poetry contained in Chinese landscape paintings. They believed that the generated images were in line with the aesthetic taste of professional users. In terms of vividness, the evaluations were relatively low. Some users pointed out that the generated pictures had traces of mechanical superposition, which is not vivid and natural compared with the paintings of human painters. The users were most impressed by the model's generative capabilities based on conceptual analogies. They considered that this best reflects the application potential of large models.

460   J. Wang et al.

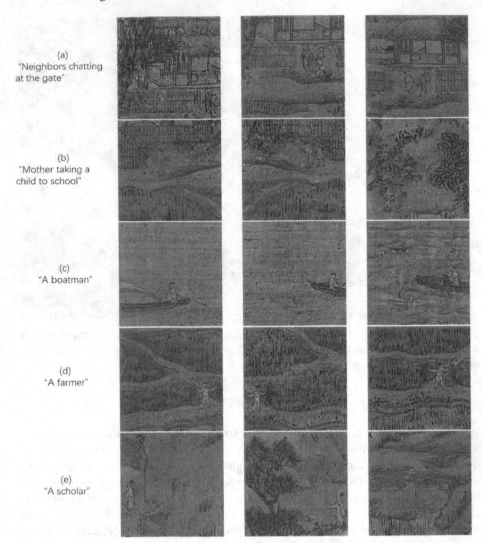

(a)
"Neighbors chatting at the gate"

(b)
"Mother taking a child to school"

(c)
"A boatman"

(d)
"A farmer"

(e)
"A scholar"

Fig. 8. Results of generation driven by conceptual analogies. The text on the left is the new scene and new character identities entered by the professional users. The images output by the model are on the right.

Table 4. Domain User's rating of alignment ability.

	Consistency					Poetry					Vividness				
	U1	U2	U3	U4	U5	U1	U2	U3	U4	U5	U1	U2	U3	U4	U5
Aligned				X	X				X						
Mostly aligned	X	X	X			X	X	X		X			X	X	X
Mostly misaligned											X				
misaligned												X			

7 Conclusions

At present, the discussion about AI cognition is being vigorously developed. Researchers argued that consciousness in AI may be assessed by drawing on neuroscientific theories of consciousness [60]. Inspired by the discussions and practices of interdisciplinary research, this paper theoretically constructs the human-AI alignment system from the perspective of cognition and conducts experimental testing. The co-creation experiments preliminarily confirmed that the integration of abstract concepts into large model could have practical consequences in the construction of human-aligned GAI. However, the experiments in this paper are preliminary. The methods and conclusions of this study need to be verified in more domain scenarios. From a longer-term perspective, building a human-aligned GAI is not only to enable GAI to accurately understand human specific instructions and related domain knowledge, but also to allow GAI's consciousness follow the morality, ethics, and aesthetics of human society, thus becoming a partner in the sustainable development of mankind. Therefore, future research should continue to focus on alignment strategies and build GAIs that can truly benefit the human users.

Acknowledgments. Funding from the Humanities and Social Sciences Research Foundation of the Chinese Ministry of Education (No. 21YJA760005) is gratefully acknowledged.

Disclosure of Interests. All authors in the present study declared that they have no competing interests.

References

1. Ho, J., Jain, A., Abbeel, P.: Denoising diffusion probabilistic models. In: Proceedings of the 34th Neural Information Processing Systems, pp. 6840–6851. Curran Associates Inc., New York (2020). https://doi.org/10.48550/arXiv.2006.11239
2. Nichol, A.Q., Dhariwal, P., Ramesh, A., et al.: Glide: towards photorealistic image generation and editing with text-guided diffusion models. In: Proceedings of the 39th International Conference on Machine Learning, vol. 162, pp. 16784–16804. PMLR, New York (2022). https://doi.org/10.48550/arXiv.2112.10741

3. Rombach, R., Blattmann, A., Lorenz, D., et al.: High-resolution image synthesis with latent diffusion models. In: Proceedings of the 2022 IEEE/CVF Conference on Computer Vision and Pattern Recognition, pp.10674–10685. IEEE, California (2022). https://doi.org/10.48550/arXiv.2112.10752

4. Zhang, J., Miao, Y., Yu, J.: A comprehensive survey on computational aesthetic evaluation of visual art images: metrics and challenges. IEEE Access **9**, 77164–77187 (2021). https://doi.org/10.1109/ACCESS.2021.3083075

5. The TED interview DeepMind's Demis Hassabis on the future of AI. https://www.ted.com/podcasts/ted-interview/deepminds-demis-hassabis-on-the-future-of-ai-transcript. Accessed 9 Jul 2022

6. Corballis, M.C.: From Hand to Mouth: The Origins of Language. Princeton University Press, Princeton (2002)

7. Dunbar, R.: Grooming, Gossip, and the Evolution of Language. Oxford University Press, New York (1996)

8. Fauconnier, G., Turner, M.: The Way We Think. Basic Books, New York (2002)

9. Feist, G.: The Psychology of Science and the Origins of the Scientific Mind. Yale University Press, New Haven (2007)

10. Berry, D.C., Broadbent, D.E.: Interactive tasks and the implicit-explicit distinction. Br. J. Psychol. **79**, 251–272 (1988). https://doi.org/10.1111/j.2044-8295.1988.tb02286.x

11. Cleeremans, A., Jiménez, L.: Implicit learning and consciousness: a graded, dynamic perspective. In: French, R.M., Cleeremans, A. (eds.) Implicit Learning and Consciousness, pp. 1–40. Psychology Press, Hove (2002)

12. Hassin, R.R., Uleman, J.S., Bargh, J.A.: The New Unconscious. Oxford University Press, New York (2005)

13. Lewicki, P., Czyzewska, M., Hoffman, H.: Unconscious acquisition of complex procedural knowledge. J. Exp. Psychol. Learn. Mem. Cogn. **13**, 523–530 (1987). https://psycnet.apa.org/doi/10.1037/0278-7393.13.4.523

14. Kaufman, S.B.: Commentary: investigating the role of domain general mechanisms in the acquisition of domain specific expertise. High Abil. Stud. **18**, 71–73 (2007). https://doi.org/10.1080/13598130701350767

15. Stanovich, K.E.: The Robot's Rebellion: Finding Meaning in the Age of Darwin. University of Chicago Press, Chicago (2005)

16. Lamme, V.A.F.: How neuroscience will change our view on consciousness. Cogn. Neurosci. **1**(3), 204–220 (2010). https://doi.org/10.1080/17588921003731586

17. Lamme, V.A.F.: Visual functions generate conscious seeing. Front. Psychol. **11**, 83 (2020). https://doi.org/10.3389/fpsyg.2020.00083

18. Baars, B.J.: In the theatre of consciousness: global workspace theory, a rigorous scientific theory of consciousness. J. Conscious. Stud. **4**(4), 292–309 (1997)

19. Dehaene, S., Lau, H., Kouider, S.: What is consciousness, and could machines have it? Science **358**, 486–492 (2017). https://doi.org/10.1126/science.aan8871

20. Mashour, G.A., Roelfsema, P., Changeux, J.P., et al.: Conscious processing and the global neuronal workspace hypothesis. Neuron **105**, 776–798 (2020). https://doi.org/10.1016/j.neuron.2020.01.026

21. Brown, R., Lau, H., LeDoux, J.E.: Understanding the higher-order approach to consciousness. Trends Cogn. Sci. **23**, 754–768 (2019). https://doi.org/10.1016/j.tics.2019.06.009

22. Ronneberger, O., Fischer, P., Brox, T.: U-Net: convolutional networks for biomedical image segmentation. In: Navab, N., Hornegger, J., Wells, W.M., Frangi, A.F. (eds.) MICCAI 2015. LNCS, vol. 9351, pp. 234–241. Springer, Cham (2015). https://doi.org/10.1007/978-3-319-24574-4_28

23. He, K., Zhang, X., Ren, S., Sun, J.: Deep residual learning for image recognition. In: Proceedings of the 2016 IEEE Conference on Computer Vision and Pattern Recognition, pp. 770–778. IEEE, California (2016). https://doi.org/10.48550/arXiv.1512.03385

24. Dosovitskiy, A., Beyer, L., Kolesnikov, A., et al.: An image is worth 16×16 words: transformers for image recognition at scale. arXiv preprint arXiv:2010.11929 (2020). https://doi.org/10.48550/arXiv.2010.11929

25. Whitehead, A.N.: Process and Reality. The Free Press, Glencoe (1978)

26. Park, T., Liu, M.Y., Wang, T.C., et al.: Semantic image synthesis with spatially-adaptive normalization. In: Proceedings of the 2019 IEEE/CVF Conference on Computer Vision and Pattern Recognition, pp. 2332–2341. IEEE, California (2019). https://doi.org/10.48550/arXiv.1903.07291

27. Ling, H., Kreis, K., Li, D., et al.: EditGAN: high-precision semantic image editing. In: Proceedings of the 2021 Advances in Neural Information Processing Systems, vol. 34, pp. 16331–16345. Curran Associates, Inc., New York (2021). https://doi.org/10.48550/arXiv.2111.03186

28. Saito, S., Simon, T., Saragih, J., et al.: PIFuHD: multi-level pixel-aligned implicit function for high-resolution 3D human digitization. In: Proceedings of the 2020 IEEE/CVF Conference on Computer Vision and Pattern Recognition, pp. 81–90. IEEE, California (2020). https://doi.org/10.48550/arXiv.2004.00452

29. Radford, A., Kim, J.W., Hallacy, C., et al.: Learning transferable visual models from natural language supervision. In: Proceedings of the 38th International Conference on Machine Learning, vol. 139, pp. 8748–8763. PMLR, New York (2021). https://doi.org/10.48550/arXiv.2103.00020

30. Ramesh, A., Pavlov, M., Goh, G., et al.: Zero-shot text-to-image generation. arXiv preprint arXiv:2102.12092 (2021). https://doi.org/10.48550/arXiv.2102.12092

31. Ramesh, A., Dhariwal, P., Nichol, A., et al.: Hierarchical text-conditional image generation with CLIP latents. arXiv preprint arXiv:2204.06125 (2022). https://doi.org/10.48550/arXiv.2204.06125

32. Gal, R., Alaluf, Y., Atzmon, Y., et al.: An image is worth one word: personalizing text-to-image generation using textual inversion. arXiv preprint arXiv:2208.01618 (2022). https://doi.org/10.48550/arXiv.2208.01618

33. Ruiz, N., Li, Y., Jampani, V., et al.: DreamBooth: fine tuning text-to-image diffusion models for subject-driven generation. arXiv preprint arXiv:2208.12242 (2023). https://doi.org/10.48550/arXiv.2208.12242

34. Kumari, N., Zhang, B., Zhang, R., et al.: Multi-concept customization of text-to-image diffusion. In: Proceedings of the 2023 IEEE/CVF Conference on Computer Vision and Pattern Recognition, pp. 1931–1941. IEEE, California (2023). https://doi.org/10.48550/arXiv.2212.04488

35. Chen, W., Hu, H., Li, Y., et al.: Subject-driven text-to-image generation via apprenticeship learning. arXiv preprint arXiv:2304.00186 (2023). https://doi.org/10.48550/arXiv.2304.00186

36. Reda, F., Kontkanen, J., Tabellion, E., Sun, D., Pantofaru, C., Curless, B.: FILM: frame interpolation for large motion. In: Avidan, S., Brostow, G., Cissé, M., Farinella, G.M., Hassner, T. (eds.) Computer Vision, ECCV 2022. LNCS, vol. 13667, pp. 250–266. Springer, Cham (2022). https://doi.org/10.1007/978-3-031-20071-7_15

37. Esser, P., Chiu, J., Atighehchian, P., Germanidis, A.: Structure and content-guided video synthesis with diffusion models. arXiv preprint arXiv:2302.03011 (2023). https://doi.org/10.48550/arXiv.2302.03011

38. Davidson, D.: The Mind Matters: Consciousness and Choice in a Quantum World. Oxford University Press, Oxford (1993)

39. Stable Diffusion (sd-v1-4). https://github.com/CompVis/stable-diffusion. Accessed 03 Jul 2022
40. Fang, W.: Images of the Mind. Princeton University Press, Princeton (1984)
41. Fang, W.: Beyond Representation: Chinese Painting and Calligraphy, 8th–14th Century. Metropolitan Museum of Art and Yale University Press, New Haven (1992)
42. Port, R.F., Gelder, T.V.: Mind as Motion: Explorations in the Dynamics of Cognition. MIT Press, Cambridge (1995)
43. Rabinovich, M.I., Zaks, M.A., Varona, P.: Sequential dynamics of complex networks in mind: consciousness and creativity. Phys. Rep. **883**, 1–32 (2020). https://doi.org/10.1016/j.physrep.2020.08.003
44. Khona, M., Fiete, I.R.: Attractor and integrator networks in the brain. Nat. Rev. Neurosci. **23**, 744–766 (2022). https://doi.org/10.48550/arXiv.2112.03978
45. Chang, R., Wang, J.: Painting style alignment: restoration of ancient Chinese landscape paintings driven by aesthetic cognition and aesthetic computation. In: Proceedings of the 14th International Conference on Applied Human Factors and Ergonomics, vol. 71, pp. 241–251. AHFE International, New York (2023). https://doi.org/10.54941/ahfe1003264
46. Chang, R., Wang, J.: Color pattern analogy: AI-assisted Chinese blue–green landscape painting restoration. In: Proceedings of the 8th Conference on Information and Network Technologies, pp.1–6. IEEE, California (2023). https://doi.ieeecomputersociety.org/10.1109/ICINT58947.2023.00008
47. Ji, X., Vedaldi, A., Henriques, J.: Invariant information clustering for unsupervised image classification and segmentation. In: Proceedings of the 2019 IEEE/CVF International Conference on Computer Vision, pp. 9864–9873. IEEE, California (2019). https://doi.org/10.48550/arXiv.1807.06653
48. Karimi, D., Dou, H., Warfield, S. K.: Deep learning with noisy labels: exploring techniques and remedies in medical image analysis. Med. Image Anal. **65**,101759 (2020). https://doi.org/10.48550/arXiv.1912.02911
49. Parrish, A., Laszlo, S., Aroyo, L.: "Is a picture of a bird a bird": policy recommendations for dealing with ambiguity in machine vision models. arXiv preprint arXiv:2306.15777 (2023). https://doi.org/10.48550/arXiv.2306.15777
50. Muñoz, J.P., Boger, R., Dexter, S., Low, R.: Mosquitoes and public health: improving data validation of citizen science contributions using computer vision. In: Wickramasinghe, N., Bodendorf, F. (eds.) Delivering Superior Health and Wellness Management with IoT and Analytics. HDIA, pp. 469–493. Springer, Cham (2020). https://doi.org/10.1007/978-3-030-17347-0_23
51. Bansal, A., Chu, H.M., Schwarzschild, A., et al.: Universal guidance for diffusion models. In: Proceedings of the 2023 IEEE/CVF Conference on Computer Vision and Pattern Recognition, pp. 843–852. IEEE, California (2023). https://doi.org/10.48550/arXiv.2302.07121
52. Chefer, H., Alaluf, Y., Vinker, Y., et al.: Attend-and-excite: attention-based semantic guidance for text-to-image diffusion models. ACM Trans. Graph. **42**(4), 1–10 (2023). https://doi.org/10.48550/arXiv.2301.13826
53. CLIP (ViT-L/14). https://github.com/OpenAI/CLIP. Accessed 25 Apr 2022
54. Wang, Y., Kordi, Y., Mishra, S., et al.: Self-instruct: aligning language model with self-generated instructions. arXiv preprint arXiv:2212.10560 (2022). https://doi.org/10.48550/arXiv.2212.10560
55. Dubois, Y., Li, X., Taori, R., et al.: AlpacaFarm: a simulation framework for methods that learn from human feedback. arXiv preprint arXiv:2305.14387 (2023). https://doi.org/10.48550/arXiv.2305.14387
56. Chang, R., Song, X., Liu, H.: Between Shanshui and landscape: an AI aesthetics study connecting Chinese and Western paintings. In: Stephanidis, C., Antona, M., Ntoa, S. (eds.) HCI

International 2022 Posters: 24th International Conference on Human-Computer Interaction, HCII 2022, Virtual Event, June 26–July 1, 2022, Proceedings, Part III, pp. 179–185. Springer, Cham (2022). https://doi.org/10.1007/978-3-031-06391-6_24

57. Li, L.: A study of the composition of Chinese painting. In: Proceedings of the 28th Oriental Scholars Conference (1971)
58. Cahill, J.: The Compelling Image: Nature and Style in Seventeenth-Century Chinese Painting. Harvard University Press, Cambridge (1982)
59. Sullivan, M.: Symbols of Eternity: The Art of Landscape Painting in China. Stanford University Press, Redwood (1979)
60. Chalmers, D.: Could a large language model be conscious? arXiv preprint arXiv:2303.07103 (2023). https://doi.org/10.48550/arXiv.2303.07103

Author Index

Printed in the United States
by Baker & Taylor Publisher Services